The Reasoning of the Court of Justice of the EU

The Reasoning of the Court of Justice of the EU

A Normative Assessment

Edited By

ALEZINI LOXA

2025–2026 Emile Noël Fellow, NYU, USA
Post-doctoral Research Fellow in EU law, Lund University, Sweden

LUIGI LONARDO

Lecturer in EU Law, University College Cork, Ireland

OXFORD
UNIVERSITY PRESS

OXFORD
UNIVERSITY PRESS

Great Clarendon Street, Oxford, OX2 6DP,
United Kingdom

Oxford University Press is a department of the University of Oxford.
It furthers the University's objective of excellence in research, scholarship,
and education by publishing worldwide. Oxford is a registered trade mark of
Oxford University Press in the UK and in certain other countries.

Published in the United States of America by Oxford University Press
198 Madison Avenue, New York, NY 10016, United States of America.

British Library Cataloguing in Publication Data
Data available

Library of Congress Control Number: 2025950213

ISBN 9780198982982

DOI: 10.1093/9780198983002.001.0001

Printed and bound by
CPI Group (UK) Ltd., Croydon, CR0 4YY

MIX
Paper | Supporting responsible forestry
FSC® C013604

The manufacturer's authorised representative in the EU for product safety is
Oxford University Press España S.A. of Parque Empresarial San Fernando de Henares,
Avenida de Castilla, 2 – 28830 Madrid (www.oup.es/en or product.safety@oup.com).
OUP España S.A. also acts as importer into Spain of products made by the manufacturer.

Dedication

To our parents[1]

[1] For the sake of clear, transparent and rational reasoning, we are keen to confirm that the editors are not siblings and that the parents in question are four distinct individuals.

Foreword

It is an honour and privilege to introduce this book edited by Luigi Lonardo and Alezini Loxa, which offers a profound and comprehensive study of the legal reasoning of the Court of Justice of the European Union (the 'Court of Justice' or the 'Court').

As the editors so eloquently explain, the central question this book seeks to answer appears deceptively straightforward: *what makes a ruling of the Court of Justice a good judgment?* Yet the simplicity of this question must be weighed against the complexity of the answers it demands, since it requires a deep understanding of the role of courts—and particularly the Court of Justice—in democratic societies.

Internally, a judgment must set out the reasons underpinning its outcome. Those reasons must be coherent, rational, and sufficiently persuasive that even the losing party can accept an unfavourable result. To that end, the Court of Justice relies on different methods of interpretation, which focus respectively on the text of the law, its context, its purpose, and its legislative history.[2] Moreover, the Court operates in a multilingual environment where all linguistic versions of EU measures of general application (such as Regulations and Directives) enjoy equal legal value.

Externally, the judgment must not transgress the boundary between law and politics and, within a multi-level governance system, must respect the vertical allocation of powers established by the authors of the Treaties. That said, there cannot be a 'disconnect' between the EU legal order and the 27 legal orders of the Member States, as the values on which the EU is founded stem from the constitutional traditions common to the Member States. Those values, as the Court of Justice has stated, define the 'very identity' of the EU as 'a common legal order'.[3] That commonality must therefore pervade the entire body of EU law and, as one contributor argues, guide the Court of Justice in its interpretation of the law.

[2] K. Lenaerts and J.A. Gutiérrez-Fons, *Les méthodes d'interprétation de la Cour de justice de l'Union européenne* (Brussels, Bruylant, 2020).

[3] Judgments of 16 February 2022, *Hungary v Parliament and Council*, C-156/21, EU:C:2022:97, para. 232, and *Poland v Parliament and Council*, C-157/21, EU:C:2022:98, para 264.

Moreover, unlike the US Supreme Court, which enjoys discretion in selecting which cases to hear, the EU Courts must address all legal questions necessary to resolve the case at hand—regardless of how difficult those questions may be, how obscure or ambiguous the legal provisions to be interpreted are, or how politically sensitive the matter is. Otherwise, as the Court itself has held, it risks committing a denial of justice.[4] This means, in essence, that the Court of Justice must always—and I emphasise *always*—provide an answer to the questions raised before it, as it lacks the discretion to cherry-pick which cases to decide. This mission to uphold the rule of law in every case is fundamental to its constitutional role.

Unlike judges of the European Court of Human Rights or the International Court of Justice, those of the Court of Justice do not issue dissenting or concurring opinions. There is one judgment, forged through consensus-building. Collegiality therefore pervades the internal functioning of the Court of Justice, shaping both its deliberative process and its public output.

Furthermore, the preliminary ruling mechanism is the 'keystone' of the EU judicial system.[5] This mechanism establishes a dialogue between the Court of Justice and national courts on questions of EU law. Consequently, when examining the legal reasoning of the Court of Justice, one must bear in mind the specific characteristics of that judicial dialogue and its implications for how judgments are crafted and communicated.

Against this backdrop, the editors of this book have succeeded in bringing together a diverse array of experts in EU law, constitutional law, and political and legal philosophy, who provide different perspectives on how to answer this challenging question.

The book is structured into four parts that guide the reader through a normative assessment of the Court of Justice's legal reasoning.

Part I examines aspects of the Court's reasoning that relate to its internal procedures and organisation, while also considering the broader institutional framework within which the Court operates.

Part II advances various theories of interpretation that the Court of Justice should follow, including the application of the twin principles of *lex specialis* and *lex posterior*, the introduction of a substantive hierarchy within the Treaty provisions themselves, and the role of values in judicial reasoning.

[4] Judgment of 12 July 1957, *Algera and Others v Common Assembly*, 7/56 and 3/57 to 7/57, EU:C:1957:7 (holding that '[u]nless the Court is to deny justice it is therefore obliged to solve the problem [of interpretation brought before it] by reference to the rules acknowledged by the legislation, the learned writing and the case-law of the member countries').

[5] Opinion 2/13 (Accession of the European Union to the ECHR) of 18 December 2014, EU:C:2014:2454, para. 198.

In Part III, the contributors evaluate the Court's formal logic and consistency across different areas of EU law, such as border control, free movement, migration, and Economic and Monetary Union. This part also considers whether interpretation by analogy and the centre of gravity doctrine help strengthen the Court's case law.

Part IV turns to questions of procedural fairness and internal processes, assessing whether the Court's case law on EU citizenship and taxation is coherent and well-reasoned. One chapter examines the so-called 'avoidance techniques' to determine whether the Court's legal reasoning may be employed as a form of strategic decision-making. Finally, another contributor analyses various institutional arrangements to assess whether the legal reasoning of the General Court and that of the Court of Justice converge or diverge in the field of competition law.

Written in a clear and engaging style, this book succeeds in advancing a set of distinct yet complementary criteria by which the Court of Justice may be said to deliver well-reasoned judgments. It is, in every respect, a pleasure to welcome a contribution situated at the crossroads of EU law and legal philosophy. Students, scholars, and judges—particularly those who appreciate the work of towering figures such as Hamilton, Dworkin, Alexy, Habermas, Rawls, and Posner—will find much to value in its insights.

In times when values as profound as democracy, the rule of law, and justice are constantly called into question, this book provides food for thought for those of us who seek to protect and promote those values by entrusting courts—and in particular the Court of Justice—with the noblest of missions: to say, without fear or favour, what the law of the EU is.

Prof. dr. Koen Lenaerts,
President of the Court of Justice of the European Union

Acknowledgements

This book has its origins in a workshop held at Lund University on 17–18 April 2024. The workshop exceeded our own expectations in terms of intellectual engagement and exchange among the participants, and we remain grateful to all those who took part as contributors and commentators. Not all the participants have been able to join this volume, but their insights nonetheless shaped our thinking and enriched the collective discussions from which this project emerged.

We owe a special debt of gratitude to the contributors whose chapters form the core of this book. Their willingness to engage with one another's work and with our feedback, to refine their arguments, and to respect even short deadlines with grace and care made the task of editing a rewarding and inspiring process. We would also like to thank the anonymous reviewers for their constructive comments, which pushed us to sharpen the presentation and contents of the book and situate the volume within a broader comparative framework. Our thanks likewise go to the editorial team at Oxford University Press, particularly Rachel Kavanagh and Cassidy Schumm, for their guidance throughout the process and to Kiruthiga for coordinating the copyediting phase.

This project has benefited from the institutional and collegial environment of Lund University and University College Cork, and we gratefully acknowledge the financial assistance of the Centre for European Studies at Lund University and the Centre for European Integration at University College Cork, without which the workshop that led to the publication of this volume would not have been possible. We would also like to thank Lund University for the funding provided to make this volume available open access. We would finally wish to thank colleagues who contributed indirectly—by offering feedback on draft chapters, sharing ideas, and providing encouragement.

Contents

PART III. FORMAL LOGIC AND CONSISTENCY

PART IV. PROCEDURAL FAIRNESS AND INTERNAL PROCESSES

Contributors

Joxerramon Bengoetxea, PhD (Edinburgh), doctor hc (Helsinki) is Professor of Jurisprudence, Faculty of Law and International Institute for the Sociology of Law, University of the Basque Country/Euskal Herriko Unibertsitatea, Donostia-San Sebastian, Spain. https://orcid.org/0000-0002-4511-4023

Emiliya Bratanova van Harten is PhD researcher, Faculty of Law, Lund University, Sweden. https://orcid.org/0009-0003-5079-0418

Graham Butler is Full Professor of Law, Linnaeus University, Sweden. https://orcid.org/0000-0002-8911-0817

Nathan Cambien is Associate Professor, University of Antwerp, Belgium and Member of the Legal Service, European Commission, Brussels, Belgium. https://orcid.org/0000-0002-8006-7509

Annegret Engel is Associate Professor in EU Law, Faculty of Law, Lund University, Sweden. https://orcid.org/0000-0001-8237-8442

Emily Hancox is Lecturer in Law, School of Law, University of Bristol, United Kingdom. https://orcid.org/0000-0002-1082-3786

Dorota Leczykiewicz is Associate Professor of Law, University of Oxford, United Kingdom. https://orcid.org/0000-0002-0194-9862

Luigi Lonardo is Lecturer in EU Law, University College Cork, Ireland. https://orcid.org/0000-0002-5453-9568

Alezini Loxa, PhD is Emile Noël Fellow, NYU, United States/Lund University, Sweden. https://orcid.org/0000-0002-7345-6266

Menelaos Markakis is Associate Professor of International and European Union Law, Erasmus University Rotterdam, Netherlands, Erasmus Center for Economic and Financial Governance, Netherlands. https://orcid.org/0000-0002-4243-3715

Niamh Nic Shuibhne is Professor of EU Law, School of Law, University of Edinburgh, United Kingdom.

Davor Petrić is Senior Assistant and Postdoctoral Researcher, Department of European Public Law, University of Zagreb Faculty of Law, Croatia. https://orcid.org/0000-0001-7737-2150

Alexandros Politis, PhD is Postdoctoral Researcher, Luxembourg Centre for European Law (LCEL), University of Luxembourg, Luxembourg. https://orcid.org/0009-0006-1325-8758

Luke Dimitrios Spieker is Postdoctoral Researcher, DFG Research Training Group DynamInt, Humboldt University Berlin, Germany, and Senior Research Fellow, Max Planck Institute for Comparative Public Law and International Law, Heidelberg, Germany. https://orcid.org/0009-0007-6242-8642

1

Introduction: Rationale and Criteria for a Normative Assessment of the Reasoning of the Court of Justice of the EU

Alezini Loxa and Luigi Lonardo *

1. Introduction

The Court of Justice of the European Union[1] is an institution of the EU tasked to 'ensure that in the interpretation and application of the Treaties the law is observed'.[2] This Court, whose predecessor delivered its first judgment in 1954,[3] has had the most profound effect on the development of the legal system of the EU—and, more broadly, on the Union's political processes and history. It has contributed to shape the foundational doctrines defining the relationship between the Union and its Member States,[4] as well as to advance important social themes such as equal pay between men and women[5] and, more recently, to define important characteristics of democratic governance.[6] The recognition that this influence exists—positive or negative as it may be—has long been the

* We gratefully acknowledge the suggestions made by Maria Cahill and Patrick O'Callaghan. This introduction is a joint effort, in which Luigi Lonardo is responsible for the first draft of sections 1, 2.1, 2.2, and 3, and Alezini Loxa for the first draft of sections 2.3, 2.4, and 4.

[1] In this introduction, 'the Court' or 'the EU Court' or 'CJEU' is used to refer to the institution as a whole; an explicit distinction between its various components (European Court of Justice, ECJ or General Court, GC) is made when necessary.

[2] Article 19(1) TEU. See also Article 19(3) TEU: 'The Court of Justice of the European Union shall, in accordance with the Treaties:

(a) rule on actions brought by a Member State, an institution or a natural or legal person;
(b) give preliminary rulings, at the request of courts or tribunals of the Member States, on the interpretation of Union law or the validity of acts adopted by the institutions;
(c) rule in other cases provided for in the Treaties'.

[3] Case 1/54, *French Republic v High Authority of the European Coal and Steel Community.*

[4] C-26/62 *Van Gend & Loos*; C-6/64 *Costa v Enel.*

[5] Case C-43/75 *Defrenne II.*

[6] C-64/16 *Associação Sindical dos Juízes Portugueses*; C-896/19 *Repubblika.*

Alezini Loxa and Luigi Lonardo, *Introduction: Rationale and Criteria for a Normative Assessment of the Reasoning of the Court of Justice of the EU* In: *The Reasoning of the Court of Justice of the EU*. Edited by: Alezini Loxa and Luigi Lonardo, Oxford University Press.
DOI: 10.1093/9780198983002.003.0001

consensus among jurists,[7] sociologists,[8] and political scientists.[9] Considering the prestige and the authority it enjoys, as well as the compliance with its rulings,[10] this is a very successful Court by international and national standards alike.

Legal reasoning has very high stakes. Like any legal act of the EU, judgments of the Court must be motivated:[11] this is the key against arbitrariness.[12] When imposed on judges, the duty to motivate decisions serves the separation of powers, as it is a safeguard for people sovereignty.[13] This duty also reflects the belief in the 'uncoerced force of the better argument',[14] in the strength of *persuasion* over that of *coercion*.[15] It is also crucial for the parties to a proceeding, their lawyers, and the relevant epistemic community.[16]

What the Court does is scrutinized closely by practitioners and academics. It was mentioned that the Court is a successful institution, often praised but also, perhaps more often nowadays, criticized. The criticism usually levelled is that the reasoning is unclear, or inconsistent with precedent or the text of a provision,[17] or illogical (or a combination of all of these), and, in sum,

[7] JHH Weiler, 'The Transformation of Europe' (1991) 100 Yale Law Journal 2403; Miguel Poiares Maduro, *We the Court: The European Court of Justice and the European Economic Constitution: A Critical Reading of Article 30 of the EC Treaty* (Hart Publishing; Distributed in the United States by Northwestern University Press 1998).

[8] Antoine Vauchez, *Brokering Europe: Euro-Lawyers and the Making of a Transnational Polity* (1st edn, Cambridge University Press 2015) 1.

[9] Robert O Keohane and Stanley Hoffmann, *The New European Community: Decisionmaking and Institutional Change* (Routledge 1991); Karen J Alter, 'Who Are the "Masters of the Treaty"? European Governments and the European Court of Justice' (1998) 52 International Organization 121; Alec Stone Sweet, *The Judicial Construction of Europe* (Oxford University Press 2004).

[10] Cases of overt defiance are very few, are usually the result of highly exceptional circumstances, and invariably attract very strong criticism.

[11] Article 296 TFEU.

[12] A decision is not arbitrary when it is 'supported by arguments thought to be relevant which are independent from the person of the speaker/author of those arguments': András Jakab, 'Judicial Reasoning in Constitutional Courts: A European Perspective' (2013) 14 German Law Journal 1215, 1218 fn 11. If that author believes the audience holds this belief, it incentivizes misrepresenting true motivations in public: Jon Elster, 'Alchemies of the Mind: Transmutation and Misrepresentation' (1997) 3 Legal Theory 133, 150.

[13] Hamilton believed that 'The courts must declare the sense of the law; and if they should be disposed to exercise WILL instead of JUDGMENT, the consequence would equally be the substitution of their pleasure to that of the legislative body'. Alexander Hamilton and others (eds), *The Federalist* (Cambridge University Press 2003) no 78, 412. Emphasis in the original.

[14] Jürgen Habermas, *The Inclusion of the Other: Studies in Political Theory* (Ciaran P. Cronin and Pablo De Greiff eds, MIT Press 2000) 37.

[15] Plato stressed that laws should persuade rather than coerce (through threat of penalty, brute force, or command), although there is ambiguity as to why. Laws 720a-e4. See also Christopher Bobonich, 'Persuasion, Compulsion and Freedom in Plato's Laws' (1991) 41(ii) Classical Quarterly 365.

[16] Lon L Fuller and Kenneth I Winston, 'The Forms and Limits of Adjudication' (1978) 92 Harvard Law Review 353, 366 defining adjudication as 'a device which gives formal and institutional expression to the influence of reasoned argument in human affairs'.

[17] Hjalte Rasmussen, 'Towards a Normative Theory of Interpretation of Community Law' [1992] University of Chicago Legal Forum 150.

unpersuasive—a criticism often premised on nothing other than that those kinds of things are a problem. But does the Court reason well or poorly (in general, or in a specific judgment)? Who can and who should establish that? And on what grounds can one offer a solid, serious, and constructive criticism of the Court's reasoning? If these questions are not addressed, criticism runs the risk of being immediately dismissed as irrelevant, at least by colleagues in academia and at the Court. Accusations of arbitrariness should not be arbitrary.

The aim of this volume is to provide a systematization and examples of *normative* assessments of the legal reasoning, or more broadly of the decision-making process, of the Court of Justice of the European Union. By *normative*, we refer to an evaluation of judicial reasoning on the basis of certain standards that are not merely descriptive or empirical, but grounded in philosophical, legal, or political theory. These benchmarks are introduced, discussed, and justified in Section 3. Even though the authors in the volume vary widely in their assessment, their approach is not to be understood as *subjective* in the sense of being personal or arbitrary, in so far as it shares with the other chapters, instead, common minimum assumptions about the decision-making process of the Court, it is theoretically anchored, and it adopts clear normative benchmarks.

Ronald Dworkin wrote that *the* question of jurisprudence is 'what, in general, is a good reason for decision by a court of law'.[18] The chapters of this book sketch possible answers to a question that is both more specific and more general: what is a good basis for a decision by the Court of Justice of the EU? It is more specific because it focuses on one Court, and it is more general because it includes more than just reason-giving. Our normative assessments evaluate the quality of the motivation for a judgment.[19] Before we proceed, we need to address an obvious problem of method. From the outside, we cannot know what is the *real* basis or motivation whereby a certain judicial conclusion is reached; that is, we cannot know what has actually happened in the deliberation.[20] Judgments of the Court are signed collectively, and therefore

[18] Ronald Dworkin, 'Review: Wasserstrom: The Judicial Decision' (1976) 75(1) Ethics 47.

[19] Gunnar Beck, *The Legal Reasoning of the Court of Justice of the EU, Volume 36* (Hart Publishing Ltd 2013) 1: 'Descriptive legal reasoning, which may also be referred to as explanatory legal reasoning, does not aim to prescribe judicial behaviour; instead, it seeks to explain how judges do in fact decide cases.'

[20] It is difficult to know it for decisions by individuals, and this is complicated in the case of collective decision-making. It is deliberately made virtually impossible in the case of courts by the secret of deliberation, which is designed to insulate judges from some distortions. Psychologists or historians have tried to penetrate this process. The results are not particularly satisfactory. See the pioneering Theodore Schroeder, 'The Psychologic Study of Judicial Opinion' (1918) 6 Cal L Rev 89, 93, claiming that judicial behaviour can be traced 'by a chain of causation running back to the earliest infancy' of the judge. This reductionist claim seems both implausible and impossible to prove.

presented always as unanimous decisions, and an outsider has no expedient way of verifying if this is actually the case. To address this problem, a useful distinction drawn in the scholarship on judicial decision-making is between the process of discovery and the process of justification.[21] With some simplification, discovery is how judges actually reach their conclusion, and it is an 'internal' process (to the mind of the judge or to the court); justification is the defence they give for the conclusion, and, in the case of the Court, it consists of the motivation contained in the published decisions. This entails that the two processes are not one and the same.[22] Strictly speaking, only in the process of justification is there for sure 'reasoning' in the sense of *giving reasons*, arguing rationally for the motivations behind a judgment.[23] The same cannot be assumed for the process of discovery. Conceivably, in the secret of deliberation, judges might bargain or act irrationally rather than argue rationally.[24] What we all agree on is that reasoning appears in the process of justifying—of defending—the decision, no matter in what way that outcome has been reached. Most of the discussion in this book will therefore necessarily focus on the process of justification (the judicial legal reasoning in the strict sense: the publicly available motivations for a judgment)—but occasionally the process of discovery is also touched upon.

This introduction discusses the rationale for a normative assessment and the current state of the literature (section 2), the possible frameworks that one may adopt when conducting a normative assessment, depending on *object and benchmark* (section 3), and provides an overview of the content of each chapter (section 4). In this introduction we try to keep assumptions to a bare minimum, and operate at a level of abstraction, with little reference to specific judgments: these are the object of in-depth analysis in the remaining chapters.

[21] Richard Wasserstrom, *The Judicial Decision: Toward a Theory of Legal Justification* (Stanford University Press 1961). Terminology varies on related phenomena. A distinction is made between 'internal' and 'external'—Jerzy Wróblewski, 'Legal Syllogism and Rationality of Judicial Decision' (1974) 5 Rechtstheorie 33; Robert Alexy, *A Theory of Legal Argumentation: The Theory of Rational Discourse as Theory of Legal Justification* (Ruth Adler tr, Oxford University Press 2010)—or between 'first-order' and 'second-order' directives (Jerzy Wróblewski, *The Judicial Application of Law* (Zenon Bankowski and Neil MacCormick eds, Kluwer Academic Publishers 1992) 91–93) or justification (Neil MacCormick, *Legal Reasoning and Legal Theory* (Reprinted, 1st edn 1978, Clarendon Press 2003) 19 and 100), and between 'main scheme' and 'secondary schemes' (see Hans-Joachim Koch and Helmut Rüssmann, *Juristische Begründungslehre* (Beck 1982) 48 ff).

[22] This assumption finds support in the account of some judges who describe how they reach decisions: see 2.2 below.

[23] This means that the title of the volume is somewhat misleading. Referring exclusively to 'legal reasoning' carries the assumption that reason is the only kind of possible basis for a judicial decision.

[24] Richard A Posner, 'The Role of the Judge in the Twenty-First Century' (2006) 86 Boston University Law Review 1049, 1051: 'judicial deliberation is overrated by those (mainly professors) who believe that protracted discussion among judges with strongly differing views is productive.'

2. Rationale and State of the Literature

2.1 Reasons for a normative assessment of courts in general, and of the CJEU in particular

An academic assessment of a court's legal reasoning serves as an accountability mechanism by subjecting judicial decisions to independent scrutiny. This academic examination has an advantage compared to other forms of external scrutiny (of the kind that one could imagine could be commissioned by a political actor) because the academic analysis is (meant to be) motivated by the long-term interest of the community, as opposed to a partisan interest. By publicly critiquing judicial reasoning, academics can encourage judges to articulate their reasoning in ways that may enhance whatever benchmark is considered desirable (examples include transparency and soundness of reasoning, and accountability to the parties in a dispute and the broader polity).[25] This, in turn, might be beneficial for the Court as it may result in higher effectiveness.[26]

This is particularly important at times when it is entirely normal—indeed, probably the default position—for legal scholars to be critical of the Court.[27] Quick turnaround times in online outlets increase the temptation to say something (anything?).[28] Even before a judgment is out, commentators speculate on the different lines of reasoning that could be followed by the Court. And who does not like to play Advocate General? The ink on the judgments is not dry and we rush to provide a comment. Once the judgment is out, the reflex of the academic is to explain why the Court was wrong, why the reasoning is unclear, why an undergraduate student would have done it better. If done seriously, criticism is vital, and it is to be welcomed and encouraged. By this we mean not just praising or rejecting the reasoning of the Court but rather a criticism that rigorously engages with the text of a judicial decision based on openly acknowledged normative assumptions, specific criteria, and, possibly, a shared understanding of the constraints under which the Court operates. This

[25] See generally Maurice Adams et al (eds), *Judging Europe's Judges. The Legitimacy of the Case Law of the European Court of Justice* (Hart Publishing 2013) and in particular Koen Lenarts, 'The Court's Outer and Inner Selves: Exploring the External and Internal Legitimacy of the European Court of Justice' ibid, 13-14.

[26] Chiara Giorgetti, 'What Happens after a Judgment Is Given? Judgment Compliance and the Performance of International Courts and Tribunals' in Theresa Squatrito and others (eds), *The Performance of International Courts and Tribunals* (1st edn, Cambridge University Press 2018).

[27] See, already, Joseph HH Weiler, 'The Court of Justice on Trial—A Review of Hjalte Rasmussen: *On Law and Policy in the European Court of Justice*' (1987) 24 Common Market Law Review 555.

[28] A similar point is suggested by Jan Komárek, 'Freedom and Power of European Constitutional Scholarship' (2021) 17 European Constitutional Law Review 422, 434 and 440.

book contributes to the development of such criticism, hoping to ground it in existing theories, to enrich it with analytical tools, and, in a word, to sharpen it.

The volume adds to the growing field of EU legal theory, that is to say, research that engages with the set of principles and concepts that underpin the EU legal system (2.4), and to studies of international courts (2.3). It does so by weaving together two strands of literature, spanning legal and moral philosophy, on these foundational concepts, namely on judicial decision-making and on theories of interpretation (2.2).

2.2 Theoretical background

To introduce theories on judicial decision-making, a useful starting point is an old *querelle* between formalists and realists. The formalist paradigm is associated with the idea that a judge is *la bouche de la loi*[29]—implying no role for the judge but that 'of an umpire, calling balls and strikes',[30] that is, an operator without any meaningful discretion. A legal conclusion is reached through the selection, interpretation, and application of the relevant rules.[31] This is not the entirety of legal reasoning, of course, because in some exceptional, contentious, difficult cases, deduction alone may not be sufficient.[32] By and large, the Court operates as a formalist court. Contrary to the formalist paradigm, realists maintain instead that a judge first reaches a conclusion (in this, the judge has wide discretion), then rationalizes it by trying to justify it with reference to existing law.[33] This is probably best understood as a debate not between *explanations* but between normative commitments. Judges are not *just* mechanically applying anything—at least, not judges in a Court, such as the ECJ, where cases arrive almost always because mechanical application is impossible, indeterminate, or dissatisfactory, and on which reasonable people can reasonably disagree.[34] If they did, we would not need various degrees of jurisdiction, nor this book, as decisions would be mathematically predictable as is the trajectory of a stone that has been tossed.

[29] Charles de Secondat Baron de Montesquieu, *De l'Ésprit des Loix* (1st edn 1758, Gallimard 1995) XI, 6.

[30] Posner (n 24) 1051.

[31] Joxerramon Bengoetxea, *The Legal Reasoning of the European Court of Justice: Towards a European Jurisprudence* (Clarendon Press; Oxford University Press 1993) 127; Beck (n 19) 115.

[32] ibid ix. 'In this area [in this penumbra of uncertainty] men cannot live by deduction alone', as Hart wrote in 'Positivism and the Separation of Law and Morals' (1958) 71(4) Harvard Law Review 593, 608.

[33] Jerome Frank, Law and the Modern Mind (1930).

[34] See chapter by Bengoetxea and Lonardo on the identification of hard and less hard cases.

Perhaps a more relevant question for our purposes is what counts as a good reason. This has something to do with conceptions of 'law' and of the legal system. Here, we can distinguish schematically between two positions, which we can call internal and external: the first posits that all legal reasons can, in one way or another, be reconducted to the text of a provision (by and large, this is the point of view 'internal' to the Court) and the second posits that this is not necessarily the case, either descriptively or normatively (this is a perspective 'external' to the Court). For the first, associated with (exclusive) legal positivism, a judge's discretion is bound by the text of a provision, and departure from that text is to be justified by reference to some other text within the legal system; for the second, closer to the natural law tradition of Dworkin and Fuller, a court's discretion and legitimacy should not be bound exclusively to whether the arguments used by that court can be traced back to a written text. A commitment to either of those paradigms makes a difference for the kind of 'law' one believes judges *should* apply (the text of the Treaties? General principles? Morality?). The question is about the meta-rules (and their public justification) that judges should apply to determine or to guide the application of rules,[35] *and where to find them*—that is, what are the justificatory premises for a judgment: textualism? Coherence? Originalism? Some moral or value-driven conception of the law, *à la* Dworkin?

The strand of literature on theories of interpretation is of interest for both political and legal philosophers.[36] The theory of interpretation—broadly speaking, the inquiry into how to find or to assign meaning to signs—develops from a dogmatic tradition, entailing its own binding canons,[37] namely grammatical (textual), systematic, logical (contextual), and historical interpretation, in the enduring classification of Von Savigny.[38] The theory evolved from around the latter half of the past century, owing important perspectives on the argumentative structure of legal interpretation to studies on legal rhetoric, showing that application of the law is not merely a deductive endeavour but it is problem-oriented and owes much to rhetoric.[39] Later theories of argumentation and legal reasoning have developed these approaches and outlined new ones.[40] The analysis of the language of jurisprudence and the clarification of

[35] Posner (n 24) 1051.

[36] More on this is said in the chapter by Bengoetxea and Lonardo, but a full account on the impact of these theories on EU law is, to the best of our knowledge, missing.

[37] Emilio Betti, *Diritto Metodo Ermeneutica. Scritti Scelti. A Cura Di Giuliano Crifò* (Giuffrè 1991).

[38] Friedrich Carl Von Savigny, *System des heutigen Römischen Rechts*, vol. I, Berlin 1840, 213 and following.

[39] See chapter by Bengoetxea and Lonardo.

[40] Ulfrid Neumann, Juristische Argumentationslehre (Nomos 1986); Manuel Atienza, *Las razones del derecho: teorías de la argumentación jurídica* (UNAM 1991).

the classical rules of legal method,[41] the (meta-)principle of coherence,[42] and theories of rational discourse play a special role.[43] The rationality of law and jurisprudence was also addressed.[44] The theory of legal argumentation thus blends into the philosophy of law, the theory of science, and general practical philosophy. These theories inform our common descriptive and normative assumptions on the methods of interpretation the Court uses to assign meaning to the relevant provisions.

2.3 Normative assessments of international courts

This book is situated in a broader strand of literature offering normative assessments of international courts. Evaluative works of such kind usually have as a starting point the legitimacy or authority of such courts. By adopting a comparative perspective, researchers have tried to identify or theorize the factors that lead to the authority of international courts or, conversely, the factors that undermine their legitimacy.[45] While such work would rarely find a counterpart in relation to the CJEU, whose authority or legitimacy is rarely questioned,[46] there are also works that focus on normative assessments of the kind we are undertaking in this book. For example, literature has offered assessments of the case law of the Inter-American Court of Human Rights either with a critical perspective focused on the effects of the case law for the protection of different groups[47] or with a more descriptive approach analysing the workings of the Court.[48] Moreover, in an edited collection, Føllesdal, Peters,

[41] Koch and Rüssmann (n 21).

[42] Ronald Dworkin, *Law's Empire* (10th edn, Belknap Press of Harvard Univ Press 1997); Aleksander Peczenik, *On Law and Reason* (1st edn 1989, Springer 2009).

[43] Alexy (n 21); Jürgen Habermas, *Between Facts and Norms: Contributions to a Discourse Theory of Law and Democracy* (William Rehg tr, 4th edn, MIT Press 2001); K Günther, *Der Sinn für Angemessenheit* (Frankfurt a.M. 1988).

[44] MacCormick (n 21) 265; Aulis Aarnio, *The Rational as Reasonable: A Treatise on Legal Justification* (Springer 1987) 185.

[45] See for example Nienke Grossman and others (eds), *Legitimacy and International Courts* (Cambridge University Press 2018); Mikael Rask Madsen, Karen J Alter, and Laurence R Helfer (eds), *International Court Authority* (Oxford University Press 2018). See Natalia Torres Zúñiga, *The Inter-American Court of Human Rights: The Legitimacy of International Courts and Tribunals* (Routledge, Taylor & Francis Group 2023) for an ideology critique of the legitimacy discourses. See also Kanstantsin Dzehtsiarou, *European Consensus and the Legitimacy of the European Court of Human Rights* (Cambridge University Press 2015) for an examination of the doctrine of consensus through the lens of legitimacy.

[46] See n 10.

[47] See for example, Gabriela Cristina Braga Navarro, *The Effectiveness of the Inter-American Court of Human Rights: The Case of Indigenous Territorial Rights* (Hart 2024).

[48] Jo M Pasqualucci, *The Practice and Procedure of the Inter-American Court of Human Rights* (2nd edn, Cambridge University Press 2012).

and Ulfstein have offered a specific set of normative criteria as bases which can be used to assess the case law of the European Court of Human Rights.[49] These are the principles of subsidiarity, effectiveness, proportionality, the rule of law, and the principle of implied powers. Closer to this type of work, our book also aims to propose a minimum set of criteria guiding the normative assessment of the Court. However, instead of providing a set of principles that could operate as benchmarks of critique, our edited collection suggests a more abstract systematization of ways in which one can develop a normative assessment.

2.4 Studies of the Court of Justice of the EU

This book contributes to lawyerly studies of the Court. Within this, we can identify three branches.

The first consists of studies dedicated specifically to the legal reasoning of the Court, including the (classic) work by Bengoetxea[50] and the more recent contributions by Sankari,[51] Paunio,[52] and Beck,[53] among others.[54] What these books have in common is that they are descriptive in outlook, albeit they carry (and defend) normative assumptions as well. Conway's is perhaps the only explicitly normative book on the Court's legal reasoning.[55] Normative accounts of the Court's reasoning abound, but they are usually limited to specific policy areas.[56] Most of the book-length works have focused on the internal market and have provided assessments in light of coherence and conferral of competence, while a recent work by Sadl puts forward the concept of a good judgment as a form of context-conscious decision-making as a benchmark by which to

[49] Andreas Føllesdal, Birgit Peters, and Geir Ulfstein (eds), *Constituting Europe: The European Court of Human Rights in a National, European and Global Context* (Cambridge University Press 2013).

[50] Bengoetxea (n 31).

[51] Suvi Sankari, *European Court of Justice Legal Reasoning in Context* (Europa Law Publishing 2013).

[52] Elina Paunio, *Legal Certainty in Multilingual EU Law: Language, Discourse and Reasoning at the European Court of Justice* (First issued in paperback 2020, Routledge 2013).

[53] Beck (n 19).

[54] Koen Lenaerts and José Gutiérrez-Fons, *Les méthodes d'interprétation de la Cour de justice de l'Union européenne* (Bruylant 2020); Adams et al (eds) (n 25).

[55] Gerard Conway, *The Limits of Legal Reasoning and the European Court of Justice* (1st edn, Cambridge University Press 2012).

[56] Some examples in the areas of the common agricultural policy, citizenship, foreign policy, and rule of law backsliding are given in Francis Snyder, 'New Directions in European Community Law' (1987) 14(1) Journal of Law and Society 167; Michelle Everson, 'The Legacy of the Market Citizen' in Shaw and More (eds) *New Legal Dynamics of the European Union* (Clarendon Press 1995); Panos Koutrakos, 'Judicial Review in the EU's Common Foreign and Security Policy' (2018) 67(1) International and Comparative Law Quarterly 1; Laurent Pech and Dimitry Kochenov, 'Respect for the Rule of Law in the Case Law of the European Court of Justice: A Casebook Overview of Key Judgments since the Portuguese Judges Case', SIEPS, 2021.

assess the Court's case law in the area of free movement of goods and persons.[57] Our volume should be seen as complementary to these works.[58] Going beyond justifications or praise for the reasoning, we aim to offer a systematic presentation of different ways in which the case law of the Court can be assessed.

The second branch consists of 'critical studies' (very broadly speaking) of the Court. Pioneering in this regard was Rasmussen,[59] whose work ignited a debate over the Court's judicial activism. The seminal works of Cappeletti and of Stein also paved the way for fruitful research on 'Integration through law' and led to the analysis of the political role of the Court and lawyers. Later, Hartley[60] and Snyder[61] were, from different perspectives, among the most critical voices. It is not only academics but also other judges who criticize the Court, both judicially and extrajudicially.[62] In this branch, we can also find works engaging with the concept of judicial politics or judicial activism.[63] Even though EU legal scholarship has not been associated to a critical tradition, a new critical epistemological trend has emerged in the past years.[64] In this context, certain authors have argued for the adoption of a specific theoretical outlook when studying the Court, suggesting importing the American critical legal studies tradition as a way of examining EU law and case law.[65] This book aligns with this recent trend in EU law studies to adopt a more critical perspective, thereby

[57] Niamh Nic Shuibhne, *The Coherence of EU Free Movement Law: Constitutional Responsibility and the Court of Justice* (1st edn, Oxford University Press 2013); Vilija Velyvyte, *Judicial Authority in EU Internal Market Law: Implications for the Balance of Competences and Powers* (Hart Publishing 2022); Urška Šadl, *Good Judgment: The European Court of Justice as a Context-Conscious Lawmaker* (Hart 2024).

[58] Oreste Pollicino, 'Legal Reasoning of the Court of Justice in the Context of the Principle of Equality Between Judicial Activism and Self-Restraint' (2004) 5(3) German Law Journal 283; Daniel Sarmiento, 'Editorial: A Court that Dare Not Speak Its Name: Human Rights at the Court of Justice' (2018) 29(1) European Journal of International Law 1; Koen Lenaerts, 'EU Citizenship and the European Court of Justice's "Stone-by-Stone" Approach'(2015) 1 International Comparative Jurisprudence 1; Koen Lenaerts and José Gutiérrez-Fons, 'The Constitutional Allocation of Powers and General Principles of EU Law' (2010) 47(6) Common Market Law Review 1629.

[59] Hjalte Rasmussen, *On Law and Policy in the European Court of Justice: A Comparative Study in Judicial Policymaking* (Kluwer Academic Publishers 1986).

[60] Trevor Hartley, 'The European Court, Judicial Objectivity and the Constitution of the European Union' (1996) 122 The Law Quarterly Review 95.

[61] Snyder (n 56).

[62] See the President of Germany Roman Herzog and Lüder Gerken, 'Stoppt den Europäischen Gerichtshof' [*Stop the European Court of Justice*], *Frankfurter Allgemeine Zeitung*, 8 September 2008, in strong criticism of the Grand Chamber judgment in Case C-144/04, *Mangold*, [2005] ECR I-9981.

[63] Bruno de Witte, Elise Muir, and Mark Dawson edited the collection *Judicial Activism at the European Court of Justice* (Edward Elgar 2013) and returned to the topic with their *Revisiting Judicial Politics in the European Union* (Edward Elgar 2024).

[64] See, for first analysis, Päivi Johanna Neuvonen, 'A Way of Critique: What Can EU Law Scholars Learn from Critical Theory?' (2022) 1 European Law Open 60 and the literature there cited.

[65] Tamara Perišin and Siniša Rodin on *The Transformation or Reconstitution of Europe, The Critical Legal Studies Perspective on the Role of the Courts in the European Union* (Hart 2018); Ivana Isailović, 'Introduction: Critical Legal Approaches in EU Law—Reflections on New Research Directions' (2024) 15(4) Transnational Legal Theory 493.

enriching the discourse and analysis in this field.[66] At the same time, it showcases a breadth of ways in which a critical perspective can be adopted, not necessarily following a single or uniform theoretical perspective.

The third branch concerns the relationship between the Court, its reasoning, and European integration more broadly. Following the seminal abovementioned work by Cappelletti and Stein, and incorporating insights from political science, it sees the Court as a political actor.[67] Often, such works are found in interdisciplinary volumes or lie at the outer boundaries of legal scholarship. For example, the edited collection by Madsen, Nicola, and Vauchez takes stock of the recent methodological turn in EU law scholarship and suggests various interdisciplinary approaches and novel methodological ways of analysing the Court's reasoning.[68] Similarly, three volumes by Bailleux, Jacquot, Bernand, and Landenne on EU judicial narratives combine law with political science and philosophy in order to show that the Court's rulings have a discursive and constructivist function for the production of European identity and authority.[69] Our aim is not to step outside the premises of legal discipline or to provide methodological tools for EU law scholarship, even though—inevitably—the edited collection also hints to ways of studying the Court. The core aim of this book is rather to inform the field of EU legal theory by the proposition that the normative assessment of the Court can and should take into account the distinct characteristics of the EU legal order and of its judiciary, before engaging with different analyses.

3. Criteria: A Systematization of Normative Assessments

What is a good basis or motivation for a judgment? Each chapter seems to have a different view on that. And there are many normative theories on this. The plurality of answers suggests that we cannot provide a final answer. It generally

[66] While our book offers the basis for structuring criticisms to the Court, the assessments herein should not necessarily be labelled as *critical* (see by contrast the conceptualization in Päivi Neuvonen and Paul Linden-Retek (eds), *Critical Theory and European Union Law*, Hart forthcoming). While critical approaches typically aim to expose ideological biases or destabilize normative claims and legal authority, this book takes a constructive stance.

[67] Anne-Marie Burley and Walter Mattli, 'Europe before the Court: A Political Theory of Legal Integration' (1993) 47 International Organization 41.

[68] Mikael Mask Madsen, Fernanda Nicola, and Antoine Vauchez, *Researching the European Court of Justice, Methodological Shifts and Law's Embeddedness* (Cambridge University Press 2022).

[69] Antoine Bailleux, Elsa Bernard, and Sophie Jacquot (eds), *Les récits judiciaires de l'Europe: Concepts et typologie* (Bruylant 2019); Antoine Bailleux and others (eds), *Les récits judiciaires de l'Europe: Dynamiques et conflits* (Bruylant 2021); Antoine Bailleux and others (eds), *Les récits judiciaires de l'Europe: Diffusion, réception et coproduction—Tome III* (Bruylant 2023).

depends on who makes the observation, where, and when. Reasoning that is good for a national court which needs to apply a preliminary ruling might be incomprehensible for the parties in the main proceedings. Reasoning that is acceptable in the legal culture of one Member State may be perceived as insufficient or downright deficient in the legal culture of another Member State. A very detailed motivation might sound like a good idea today but might be detrimental in a future case if it spells out in needless detail a thought process that will turn out to be too constraining and to produce an unjust result. Meta-normative (and so on) positions are similarly indeterminate: there is no shared view, for example, on the ultimate goal of the (EU) judiciary, on its 'role-distinct obligations'[70] (such as delivering a judgment that is fair for the parties, in a reasonable time, and justified with reference to the applicable law), as there is not one on the forms of the *telos* of European integration. One shared meta-normative position that emerges, perhaps, and only very implicitly, is that *arbitrariness* in judicial decision-making should be avoided. While we cannot give an absolute answer to what is a 'good motivation' for a judgment, what we can do is offer taxonomies for such assessments, and thereby hopefully give the reader some indications as to what assessments are to be preferred.

Very schematically, an assessment of the motivation for a judgment can focus on the process (how was it reached?), or on the outcome (what consequences does it have?), or on the 'in-between' (what justifications were given for it?), or on a combination of those. Focus on process and focus on outcome are the two ends of the spectrum within which we believe all normative assessments fall. On one end of the spectrum, one can, following a modified version of a Benthamite claim, take the view that a good process is one that, regardless of the consequences of, or the public justification offered for, a decision, ensures that the judgment is reached without distortions (those stemming either from the self-interest or from irrationality of the decision-makers) during that process.[71] For example, as long as there are sufficient guarantees that a judge did not receive a bribe, was not threatened, or was not drunk, anything goes. This is not a serious proposal for a court of law: while creating institutions that respect this thin normative view process might ensure an acceptable outcome, adjudication has 'higher responsibility toward rationality'.[72] On the other hand

[70] Patrick O'Callaghan, 'Internal Coherence and the Possibility of Judicial Integrity' in Richard Mullender and others (eds), *Law and Imagination in Troubled Times: A Legal and Literary Discourse* (Routledge 2020).

[71] A sophisticated version of this institutional design, for juries, assemblies, and electoral systems, is defended by Jon Elster, *Securities against Misrule: Juries, Assemblies, Elections* (Cambridge University Press 2013) 2. Note that, unlike us, he is not primarily concerned with evaluating the public justification of decisions.

[72] Fuller and Winston (n 16) 367.

Table 1.1 Types of normative assessments

Object	Process-related	In-between	Outcome
Benchmarks	Procedural fairness and internal processes	Standards of rational argumentation (logical validity, consistency, coherence across various cases)	Consequences produced by the reasoning (for the parties, the relation to national courts, to the legislator etc)

of the spectrum, there is a very natural temptation to assess a motivation on the basis of the outcome it produces.[73] The problem is that there are many normative views on what constitutes a good outcome, and it is not clear how we can choose between them.

Within these extremes, there are several possible types of a normative assessments (Table 1.1), expounded in sections 3.1 and 3.2.

This matrix is not exhaustive, as it merely captures the contributions in this volume; nor are the categories mutually exclusive, as they overlap to some extent.[74] In the Conclusion, Alezini Loxa suggests more types of normative assessments which were not represented in this book, or which were only implicit in the various chapters. The framework claims nonetheless a strong conceptual unity in the descriptive starting point, namely on what the factors that affect the reasoning of the Court are. In particular, we note that divergence in the description of how the Court operates yields differences in the normative assessment. What all the contributions in this volume have in common is that they share, as a lowest common denominator, some descriptive propositions on how the Court reasons. These can be conceived of as the factors influencing judicial reasoning. They can be categorized as follows, with some factors overlapping:[75] internal procedures of the CJEU, legal reasons (including precedent), individual personalities, dialogue with other actors, and formal logic matter in some way or another. The first concerns the procedure through which it is decided on the formation of the court, on the *juge rapporteur*, and on the involvement of other members of the court in any give case. The second

[73] This is a consequentialist view that may be associated to utilitarianism and pragmatism.

[74] It would, of course, be possible to rationalize the table by establishing some meta-criteria or levels of analysis, but it is not necessary to do so for the purposes of showing what kind of normative assessments are possible, and it is arguably a waste of time in general.

[75] There is no canonical list of these factors, although the realist tradition distinguishes between legal and non-legal factors. This is a distinction that satisfies a positivistic view of the legal system, a view which is not a necessary premise for the purposes of our normative assessment.

relates to issues of interpretation, precedent, selection, and application of relevant rules. The third is about the people, such as the judge, *référendaire*, or Advocate General, who are materially involved in shaping a decision. The fourth is about the relationship of the Court with the parties in a case (and their lawyers), with other institutions (including other courts, such as national courts or international courts), and with the public in general. The fifth concerns the principles of identity and non-contradiction, and rules on validity of logical operations. The factors do not have predictive value and are not meant to be normative, but they do carry minimal normative assumptions.[76] Where the authors differ is on the relative weight of each of the factors in an accurate description of judicial reasoning.

It should also be recalled that every normative assessment will be informed by a scholar's initial (perhaps metaphysical) commitment to what counts as acceptable justification. Normative assessments with an 'internal' point of view intend to take a Court-based perspective which does not seek to challenge the philosophy of EU law or the vision for EU law that the Court has (namely that the EU has equipped itself with a legal order within which the task of the Court is to interpret and apply EU law), but rather accepts it as the starting point of the analysis and assesses the reasoning on the Court's own terms. Most of the chapters move within these premises. This perspective implies that the Court is right in the same way as a native speaker is always right: what could appear, to an external observer, as a 'grammatical' mistake is instead just a natural evolution of the system. What remains to be done, for the academic, is to make explicit what is implicit, to clarify obscure points, to flatten out (apparent?) contradictions in the case law. It is almost Talmudic: perceived inconsistencies are seen as opportunities for deeper learning and understanding, requiring effort to resolve. This perspective also implies that the role of the legal scholar can be that of *justifying* the Court's reasoning. All those within this perspective are assessments of the *context of justification* alone.

The external point of view rejects that interpretation of the text of EU law provisions alone holds (or should hold) the central place that adherence to the internal paradigm suggests. If the text of a provision does not provide a solution to a case at hand, then what should constrain the discretion of the Court? This may entail an analysis of the (intended, or foreseen) consequences of judgments: what are the policy or value considerations that should guide their decision-making? It might also require a different (perhaps broader) conception of law which is relevant for the resolution of a dispute by the Court. This

[76] All these factors are explored in more detail in the chapter by Bengoetxea and Lonardo.

calls for a 'substantive' approach.[77] When it comes to EU law, this perspective is not wedded to a vision of the legal order as it appears from the case law of the Court. Sometimes, even its fundamental premises may be rejected.[78] EU law is not necessarily what the Court says it is.[79] From this perspective, it is difficult to admit that the role of legal scholarship can be that of *justifying* the reasoning of the Court. Normative assessments within this perspective may criticize both the *context of discovery* and the *context of justification*.[80]

The internal and external—and the formalist and realist—paradigms operate as the theoretical background to any assessment. They inform the assessor's idea of both what the role of the judge is (or ought to be) in the process of judicial reasoning and the conception of law. In practice, perhaps, the normative difference between the formalist and realist paradigms is minimal for most cases decided by the CJEU, where text alone does not determine univocally the existence of the applicable norm, or the outcome of the application of the norm to facts (or both),[81] whereas the one between internal and external points of view is significant as they present distinct conceptions of law.

3.1 The object of critique

The first taxonomy of normative assessment is by reference to the object of study, as one may zoom in on any of the 'phases': process, 'in-between', and outcome. Within these phases, one may single out one or more of the factors identified earlier in this introduction as influencing the Court's decision-making (internal procedures, legal reasons, individual personalities, dialogue with other actors, formal logic).

First, as a matter of process, there can be an assessment focusing on the internal procedure. An example in this book is the chapter by Cambien, on how the institutional architecture within the CJEU leads to the General Court and the European Court of Justice having two distinct roles—which justifies, in the author's opinion, a difference in reasoning styles and even outcomes.

Second, there are assessments of the 'in-between'. They discuss the Court's use of legal reasons (how the Court should solve uncertainty or normative indeterminacy, and how it should use precedent), or its formal logic, including

[77] Chapter by Leczykiewicz.
[78] Chapter by Butler.
[79] Chapter by Loxa.
[80] Chapters by Butler and by Nic Shuibhne respectively.
[81] Riccardo Guastini, 'Interpretare, Construire, Argomentare' [2015] Osservatorio sulle fonti 1.

but not limited to internal coherence. Probably owing to the influence of the formalist paradigm, nearly all chapters touch upon this in one way or another. The assessment can also relate to individuals. This is the hardest to find, but scholars closer to the realist tradition will make it clear that by 'the Court' they really mean 'the judges'.[82]

Third, the assessment can relate to the outcome of the case; for example, on the 'good' it promotes, or on its effects on the Court's position vis-à-vis other actors. Implicitly, all the chapters discuss this when they assess whether the Court is persuasive for the public. Explicitly, the chapters by Loxa and by Bratanova do so for the consequences that the judgments have for the parties in the dispute.

3.2 Benchmarks

The second taxonomy of normative assessments is based on the benchmarks one uses to assess judicial reasoning and in this, a variety of standards can be utilized. These include the standards of rational argumentation (logic, including the logic of consequences), procedural fairness, and efficiency.[83]

Let us consider standards of rational argumentation, as espoused by, among others, Wróblewski,[84] Aarnio,[85] Alexy,[86] Peczenik,[87] and Maccormick[88] (some among the many theorists that consider a 'good' justification a rational justification[89]). What they all have in common is that they develop theories to circumscribe the discretion of the decision-maker (their aim is to constrain arbitrariness).

A first standard of rational argumentation is formal logical validity: in this context, a statement is rational if it is justified by its premises.[90] Hence, the Court may be criticized if non-sequiturs appear in the justification. Rationality also presupposes the use of rules of justificatory reasoning which link the justificatory arguments as premises to the justified conclusion.[91] The difficulty is,

[82] Chapter by Butler.
[83] They have also been termed 'process performance criteria': Theresa Squatrito and others (eds), *The Performance of International Courts and Tribunals* (1st edn, Cambridge University Press 2018) 14.
[84] Wróblewski (n 21).
[85] Aarnio (n 44).
[86] Alexy (n 21).
[87] Peczenik (n 42).
[88] MacCormick (n 21).
[89] Markus Ukkola, 'Systemic Interpretation in EU Public Procurement Law' (University of Helsinki 2018) 79 <http://hdl.handle.net/10138/235396>.
[90] Jerzy Wróblewski, 'Justification of Legal Decisions' (1979) 33 Revue Internationale de Philosophie 277, 277, calls this 'internal rationality'.
[91] Wróblewski (n 90) 277 calls this 'external rationality'.

of course, in the identification of those premises. Here, standards vary. The text of a rule, which usually results from some prior agreement between relevant parties, is generally considered an acceptable premise.[92] But, realistically, text (as language) has, often, at least some indeterminacy, allowing for different interpretations. As Bengoetxea and Lonardo write:

> [T]he structure of justification in clear cases can be circumscribed to deductive, syllogistic reasoning, whereas the structure of justification in hard cases will be syllogistic only in appearance, the construction of each of the premises (choice of applicable provisions, conflict of applicable provisions, filling in gaps, interpretation of applicable provisions, qualification of proven facts, choice of consequences) will be the epicentre of the justification. The clearer *that* construction is, the better the quality of argumentation.[93]

Together with[94] or in addition to text, some logic of consequences is also generally, though much more controversially, accepted.[95] This can be in the form of reasoning *ad absurdum*, or from *telos*, routinely used by courts,[96] or from other more explicit 'policy-based' arguments. For Dworkin, the public justification of a judicial decision should be ultimately value-driven, by the (moral) principles of justice, fairness, and procedural due process which represent the community's legal practice. Coherence can therefore be the overarching meta-criterion that should guide the judges' choice.[97] The theory of communicative rationality by Habermas suggests benchmarks such as freedom, truth, normative correctness, and sincerity.[98] Coming to EU law, one may look to Articles 1[99] or 2[100] TEU as the ultimate guiding meta-principle. As mentioned, it is not clear how we can choose between these options.

A second standard of rational argumentation is the principle of identity and non-contradiction. Coherence is one important benchmark: good reasoning

[92] Jakab (n 12).
[93] Chapter by Bengoextea and Lonardo.
[94] Paul Craig, '*Pringle* and the Nature of Legal Reasoning' (2014) 21 Maastricht Journal of European and Comparative Law 205, 210.
[95] Neil MacCormick, 'On Legal Decisions and Their Consequences: From Dewey to Dworkin' (1983) 58 New York University Law Review 239.
[96] Those that Jakab (n 12) 1241 calls 'evaluating arguments', within the logic of consequences.
[97] Dworkin (n 42) 225. Variations on the theme of coherence as meta-principle are in Lonardo's and Hancox's chapters.
[98] Habermas (n 14).
[99] Chapter by Petrić.
[100] Chapter by Spieker.

does not stand in contradiction with itself—both within the same judgment and across judgments. Inconsistency across cases may be on the selection of a source of law, as the difficulties in the identification and application of general principles show, according to Leczykiewicz. There would be inconsistency also if, for example, the Court found that the Charter applies and does not apply in two similar cases, and this is discussed by Bratanova. The question becomes one of justifying the differences in factual or legal circumstances (distinguishing, or overruling precedent). This is also an exercise that requires a rational argumentation (absent which the justification is defective: the chapter by Loxa on EU and non-EU migrants centres on this kind of issue).

There are then other benchmarks: procedural fairness demands that the judicial process itself be equitable and transparent,[101] as well as predictable, entailing that the public justification should also be accessible and clear. Hence, the chapters by Butler, Nic Shuibhne, and Bengoetxea and Lonardo criticize the Court for its (strategic?) use of gaps and silences in the argumentation. Relatedly, Politis uncovers a normative inversion at the Court's case law in taxation and citizenship which seems to give priority to secondary instead of primary law. In such cases, the results of the judicial process can undermine predictability. One may also consider efficiency standards as benchmarks against which to assess the Court's reasoning. The chapter by Butler, for example, when it says that the Court sometimes arrives at an outcome without knowing it, implies that the institution is not in control of its own processes. These benchmarks, together with the objects of critique presented earlier, illustrate the ways in which normative assessments of the Court are constructed in the remainder of this book.

4. The Content

Part one collects chapters exemplifying diverging paradigms while parts two, three and four gather contributions representative of each of various benchmarks of assessment.

[101] Fuller and Winston (n 16) 364: 'the distinguishing characteristic of adjudication lies in the fact that it confers on the affected party a peculiar form of participation in the decision, that of presenting proofs and reasoned arguments for a decision in his favour'; MacCormick (n 95) 240.

Part I A Question of Paradigm?

The first part juxtaposes a chapter operating within the internal point of view with one operating with the external point of view.

Joxerramon Bengoetxea and Luigi Lonardo's chapter discusses the conditions and prerequisites under which the judgments of the ECJ can be critically assessed or appraised.[102] They suggest moving beyond the dichotomy discovery/justification, to consider instead the context of justification, which 'relates to the actual process that leads to the decision, it is about opening the (partially) "black box" of institutional, sociological, perhaps even psychological processes'. This means, descriptively, to identify some essential characteristics of the Court, relating to its internal procedure and organization, as well as to the fact that it is in practice bound by text and precedent in the first place; normatively, they argue that the answer to the question moving the inquiry of this book is relative, and that an appraisal cannot be made exclusively on the publicly available justification nor on the (largely secret) inner mechanics of the decision-making at the Court, but should ideally take both into account.

Dorota Leczykiewicz's chapter challenges the interpretation framework altogether, proposing instead a 'substantive', non-positivistic framework for thinking of the ECJ's reasoning, which places textual interpretation in the broader context of constrained discretion. The purpose of the framework is to better capture the Court's role as both an adjudicating and a law-making court, and to allow a fuller articulation of the criteria that need to be met by the CJEU before its judgments are considered valid statements of EU law's content.

Part II Normative Indeterminacy and Justificatory Premises

The second part contains assessment of legal reasons by focus on how the Court does or ought to address normative indeterminacy and ensure rational argumentation in its decisions.

Emily Hancox's chapter makes the normative case for the principles of *lex specialis* and *lex posterior* to guide the CJEU in situations when the Court has

[102] This chapter builds on, and reproduces in part, Joxerramon Bengoetxea, 'Text and Telos in the European Court of Justice: Four Recent Takes on the Legal Reasoning of the ECJ' (2015) 11(1) European Constitutional Law Review 184, which reviews Beck (n 19) 486; Conway (n 55) 344; Paunio (n 52) 234; and Sankari (n 51) 275.

to interpret norms of similar hierarchical status. While the principles of *lex specialis* and *lex posterior* may now be invoked in a somewhat mechanical fashion, this overlooks their underlying basis, which is to give effect to the intentions of the legislature. Despite the EU's lack of democratic legitimacy when compared with a nation state, she justifies the role for legislative intent in the reasoning of the CJEU by drawing upon the Treaties and the EU's underlying constitutional framework.

Following, the chapter by Luke Dimitrios Spieker makes the case for putting some order in the relationship between the text of the Treaties and the Court's case law: instead of perceiving the myriad of Treaty provisions as norms of *formally* equal rank, Spieker suggests examining the Treaties from a *substantive* perspective. Such a change in perspective reveals that the Treaties in fact form a much more organized, hierarchical system, taking the shape of a pyramid. At the top of this pyramid are the founding values in Article 2 TEU, which have taken central place in the Court's more recent jurisprudence.

Davor Petrić discusses the role of different values—legal, moral, social, and political –in the interpretation of law. To frame his discussion, Petrić relies on the argumentative theory of legal interpretation by MacCormick and Summers in order to identify the distinct ways in which values may appear in the legal reasoning of the Court of Justice. He suggests that the Court's case law could be understood rationally if we were to perceive Article 1 TEU as guiding its argumentation. Similarly, Luigi Lonardo suggests a way to rationalize the case law of the Court in the Common Foreign and Security Policy, opting for a Court-based perspective, praising the case law for its human rights-oriented outcome but criticizing it for the reasoning that, it is suggested, should be spelt out more explicitly by recourse to the (implied) hierarchies that the case law builds.

Part III Formal Logic and Consistency

This third part turns to the rationality of the Court, this time with focus on formal logic and consistency both within specific cases and across its case law more broadly.

Emiliya Bratanova von Harten critically examines the use of the Charter in the area of border control, migration and asylum. She shows how the Court applies variable criteria when it comes to identifying the scope of application of EU law for the purposes of application of the Charter and argues for the more coherent use of the Charter among the different areas of the AFSJ as part of a concrete constitutional architecture.

Continuing along similar lines, Alezini Loxa scrutinizes the differentiation that both case law and EU law scholarship has established between free movement and migration with a focus on the rights of family members. By examining the relevant law and case law on the rights of family members of EU and non-EU migrants, Loxa suggests that the differentiation is based on shaky grounds. She argues that the line of reasoning of the ECJ not only undermines the rights of family members of EU migrants (fracturing the relation of the EU to its insiders) but also is not consistent with the constitutional commitment of the EU to protect family life under both the Charter and the recent accession to the Istanbul Convention.

The chapter that follows focuses on the reasoning of the ECJ in relation to horizontal and vertical division of competences. Specifically, Annegret Engel looks at the centre of gravity theory, identifies the challenges this theory creates for the constitutional set-up of the EU, and proposes alternative methods of interpretation the Court could use when dealing with conflicts of legal basis. Menelaos Markakis then goes on to look at the reasoning of the ECJ in the Economic and Monetary Union and its various stages of evolution. Through an overview of the relevant case law, Markakis assesses how the Court has attempted to bring coherence to this area by connecting strands of case law developed across different generations.

Part IV Procedural Fairness and Internal Processes

In the fourth and final part, contributions assess procedural fairness as well as the importance of internal processes for an assessment of the case law of the Court.

On procedural fairness, the clarity of the reasoning of the Court in the area of EU citizenship is criticized by Niamh Nic Shuibhne. By tracing how the Court refers to its previous case law and identifying different formulas by which the Court does so, Nic Shuibhne identifies silences in relation to case law developments that depart from previous decisions. Alexandros Politis looks at the case law of the ECJ in tax law and EU citizenship. Politis suggests that the Court often fully aligns with the secondary legislator, even in cases where secondary law is not in force, and he maps the different ways in which this has taken place in the case law. The chapter defines the 'secondary legislator approach', distinguishes it from other *prima facie* similar approaches and shows that Court seems to have successively been influenced by a non-applicable *ratione materiae* legislation, then by soft law adopted by the secondary legislator and, subsequently, by a non-applicable *ratione temporis* legislation. Graham Butler highlights methods and techniques whereby a judgment does *not* say something. These 'avoidance techniques'[103] are conceptualized in the following three: dismissing, narrowing, and relinquishment. The chapter argues that 'the Court's practice of deciding not to decide is a deliberate and multifaceted strategy that serves various purposes, including managing its workload, avoiding contentious issues, and maintaining its position within the EU institutional architecture'.

Finally, on process, Nathan Cambien looks at the reasoning of the CJEU in the area of competition law from an institutional perspective. Cambien's contribution examines to what extent institutional constraints influence or even dictate the reasoning and outcome in a given case, both at the level of the General Court and Court of Justice. In this connection, his chapter focuses on issues such as the level of jurisdiction, the 'formation' of the chamber (ie the number of judges sitting in a case), the presence or absence of an Advocate-General (AG) opinion, and the type of procedure (direct action vs preliminary proceedings).

A conclusion by Alezini Loxa draws together the threads of the different assessments. It suggests that while authors have diverse theoretical starting points, common themes emerge across all the contributions in relation to coherence and sincerity. Moreover, the chapter suggests alternative systematizations of normative assessments which were not (explicitly) addressed by the contributions. The chapter concludes with a reflection on the institutional responsibility of the Court to provide the epistemic community with the tools necessary to assess it as a means of a dialectical process that can enhance the quality of decision-making in EU law.

Overall, this book makes a unique contribution to the growing field of EU legal theory by offering a systematization of normative assessments of the Court. Without attempting to offer an exhaustive way of studying the Court, we hope that the two alternative taxonomies put forward in the introduction and conclusion, as well as the variety of departure points of the different contributors, will provide a reference point and inspire similar works. We also hope that future works offering criticisms of the Court will use this book as a starting point both to reflect on the foundational agreements we have shared with the authors in the book and to openly acknowledge the frameworks and criteria that can guide the respective assessments.

[103] Jed Odermatt, 'Patterns of Avoidance: Political Questions before International Courts' (2018) 14 International Journal of Law in Context 221.

References

Aarnio A, *The Rational as Reasonable: A Treatise on Legal Justification* (Springer 1987)
Alexy R, *A Theory of Legal Argumentation: The Theory of Rational Discourse as Theory of Legal Justification* (Ruth Adler tr, Oxford Univ Press 2010)
Alter KJ, 'Who Are the "Masters of the Treaty"?: European Governments and the European Court of Justice' (1998) 52 International Organization 121
Atienza M, *Las razones del derecho: teorías de la argumentación jurídica*, Madrid 1991
Bailleux A, Bernard E, and Jacquot S (eds), *Les récits judiciaires de l'Europe 3 vols* (Bruylant 2019–23)
Beck G, *The Legal Reasoning of the Court of Justice of the EU* (Hart Publishing Ltd 2013)
Bengoetxea J, 'Text and Telos in the European Court of Justice: Four Recent Takes on the Legal Reasoning of the ECJ' (2015) 11(1) European Constitutional Law Review 184
Bengoetxea J, *The Legal Reasoning of the European Court of Justice: Towards a European Jurisprudence* (Clarendon Press; Oxford University Press 1993)
Betti E, *Diritto Metodo Ermeneutica. Scritti Scelti. A Cura Di Giuliano Crifò* (Giuffrè 1991)
Bobonich C, 'Persuasion, Compulsion and Freedom in Plato's Laws' (1991) 41(ii) Classical Quarterly 365
Braga Navarro GC, *The Effectiveness of the Inter-American Court of Human Rights: The Case of Indigenous Territorial Rights* (Hart 2024)
Burley A and Mattli W, 'Europe before the Court: A Political Theory of Legal Integration' (1993) 47 International Organization 41
Conway G, *The Limits of Legal Reasoning and the European Court of Justice* (1st edn, Cambridge University Press 2012)
Craig P, '*Pringle* and the Nature of Legal Reasoning' (2014) 21 Maastricht Journal of European and Comparative Law 205
de Witte B, Muir E, and Dawson M (eds), *Judicial Activism at the European Court of Justice* (Edward Elgar 2013)
Dworkin R, 'Review: Wasserstrom: The Judicial Decision' (1976) 75(1) Ethics 47
Dworkin R, *Law's Empire* (10th edn, Belknap Press of Harvard Univ Press 1997)
Dzehtsiarou K, *European Consensus and the Legitimacy of the European Court of Human Rights* (Cambridge University Press 2015)
Elster J, *Securities against Misrule: Juries, Assemblies, Elections* (Cambridge University Press 2013)
Elster J, 'Alchemies of the Mind: Transmutation and Misrepresentation' (1997) 3 Legal Theory 133
Everson M, 'The Legacy of the Market Citizen' in Shaw and More (eds) *New Legal Dynamics of European Union* (Clarendon Press 1995)
Føllesdal A, Peters B, and Ulfstein G (eds), *Constituting Europe: The European Court of Human Rights in a National, European and Global Context* (Cambridge University Press 2013)
Frank J, Law and the Modern Mind (1930)
Fuller L and Winston K, 'The Forms and Limits of Adjudication' (1978) 92 Harvard Law Review 353
Giorgetti C, 'What Happens after a Judgment Is Given? Judgment Compliance and the Performance of International Courts and Tribunals' in Theresa Squatrito and others (eds), *The Performance of International Courts and Tribunals* (1st edn, Cambridge University Press 2018)
Grossman N and others (eds), *Legitimacy and International Courts* (Cambridge University Press 2018)

Guastini R, 'Interpretare, Construire, Argomentare' [2015] Osservatorio sulle fonti 1
Günther K., *Der Sinn für Angemessenheit* (Frankfurt a.M 1988)
Habermas J, *Between Facts and Norms: Contributions to a Discourse Theory of Law and Democracy* (4th edn, MIT Press 2001)
Habermas J, *The Inclusion of the Other: Studies in Political Theory* (Ciaran P. Cronin and Pablo De Greiff eds, MIT Press 2000)
Hamilton A and others (eds), *The Federalist* (Cambridge University Press 2003)
Hart HLA, 'Positivism and the Separation of Law and Morals' (1958) 71(4) Harvard Law Review 593, 608
Hartley T, 'The European Court, Judicial Objectivity and the Constitution of the European Union' (1996) 122 The Law Quarterly Review 95
Herzog R and Gerken L, 'Stoppt den Europäischen Gerichtshof' [*Stop the European Court of Justice*], *Frankfurter Allgemeine Zeitung*, 8 September 2008
Isailović I, 'Introduction: Critical Legal Approaches in EU Law—Reflections on New Research Directions' (2024) 15(4) Transnational Legal Theory 493
Keohane R and Hoffmann S, *The New European Community: Decisionmaking and Institutional Change* (Routledge 1991)
Koch HJ and Rüssmann H, *Juristische Begründungslehre* (Beck 1982)
Komárek J, 'Freedom and Power of European Constitutional Scholarship' (2021) 17 European Constitutional Law Review 422
Koutrakos P, 'Judicial Review in the EU's Common Foreign and Security Policy' (2018) 67(1) International and Comparative Law Quarterly 1
Lenaerts K, 'EU Citizenship and the European Court of Justice's "Stone-by-Stone" Approach' (2015) 1 International Comparative Jurisprudence 1
Lenaerts K and Gutiérrez-Fons JA, 'The Constitutional Allocation of Powers and General Principles of EU Law' (2010) 47(6) Common Market Law Review 1629
Lenaerts K and Gutiérrez-Fons JA, *Les méthodes d'interprétation de la Cour de justice de l'Union européenne* (Bruylant 2020)
MacCormick N, 'On Legal Decisions and Their Consequences: From Dewey to Dworkin' (1983) 58 New York University Law Review 239
MacCormick N, *Legal Reasoning and Legal Theory* (Reprinted, first edn 1978, Clarendon Press 2003)
Mask Madsen M, Nicola F, and Vauchez A, *Researching the European Court of Justice, Methodological Shifts and Law's Embeddedness* (Cambridge University Press 2022)
Montesquieu C, *De l'Ésprit des Loix* (1st edn 1758, Gallimard 1995), XI
Neumann U, *Juristische Argumentationslehre* (Darmstadt 1986)
Neuvonen PJ, 'A Way of Critique: What Can EU Law Scholars Learn from Critical Theory?' (2022) 1 European Law Open 60
Neuvonen PJ and Linden-Retek P (eds), *Critical Theory and European Union Law*, Hart (forthcoming)
Nic Shuibhne N, *The Coherence of EU Free Movement Law: Constitutional Responsibility and the Court of Justice* (1st edn, Oxford University Press 2013)
O'Callaghan P, 'Internal Coherence and the Possibility of Judicial Integrity' in Richard Mullender and others (eds), *Law and Imagination in Troubled Times: A Legal and Literary Discourse* (Routledge 2020)
Odermatt J, 'Patterns of Avoidance: Political Questions before International Courts' (2018) 14 International Journal of Law in Context 221
Pasqualucci JM, *The Practice and Procedure of the Inter-American Court of Human Rights* (2nd edn, Cambridge University Press 2012)

Paunio E, *Legal Certainty in Multilingual EU Law: Language, Discourse and Reasoning at the European Court of Justice* (Routledge 2013)
Pech L and Kochenov D, 'Respect for the Rule of Law in the Case Law of the European Court of Justice: A Casebook Overview of Key Judgments since the Portuguese Judges Case', SIEPS, 2021
Peczenik A, *On Law and Reason* (1st edn 1989, Springer 2009)
Perišin T and Rodin S, *The Transformation or Reconstitution of Europe: The Critical Legal Studies Perspective on the Role of the Courts in the European Union* (Hart 2018)
Poiares Maduro M, *We the Court: The European Court of Justice and the European Economic Constitution: A Critical Reading of Article 30 of the EC Treaty* (Hart 1998)
Pollicino O, 'Legal Reasoning of the Court of Justice in the Context of the Principle of Equality Between Judicial Activism and Self-Restraint' (2004) 5(3) German Law Journal 283
Posner R, 'The Role of the Judge in the Twenty-First Century' (2006) 86 Boston University Law Review 1049
Rask Madsen M, Alter KJ, and Helfer LR (eds), *International Court Authority* (Oxford University Press 2018)
Rasmussen H, 'Towards a Normative Theory of Interpretation of Community Law' [1992] University of Chicago Legal Forum 150
Rasmussen H, *On Law and Policy in the European Court of Justice: A Comparative Study in Judicial Policymaking* (M Nijhoff 1986)
Šadl U, *Good Judgment: The European Court of Justice as a Context-Conscious Lawmaker* (Hart 2024)
Sankari S, *European Court of Justice Legal Reasoning in Context* (Europa Law Publishing 2013)
Sarmiento D, 'Editorial: A Court that Dare Not Speak Its Name: Human Rights at the Court of Justice' (2018) 29(1) European Journal of International Law 1
Schroeder T, The Psychologic Study of Judicial Opinion (1918) California Law Review 89
Snyder F, 'New Directions in European Community Law' (1987) 14(1) Journal of Law and Society 167
Squatrito T and others (eds), *The Performance of International Courts and Tribunals* (1st edn, Cambridge University Press 2018)
Stone Sweet A, *The Judicial Construction of Europe* (Oxford University Press 2004)
Torres Zúñiga N, *The Inter-American Court of Human Rights: The Legitimacy of International Courts and Tribunals* (Routledge, Taylor & Francis Group 2023)
Vauchez A, *Brokering Europe: Euro-Lawyers and the Making of a Transnational Polity* (1st edn, Cambridge University Press 2015)
Velyvytė V, *Judicial Authority in EU Internal Market Law: Implications for the Balance of Competences and Powers* (Hart Publishing 2022)
Von Savigny F, *System des heutigen Römischen Rechts*, vol. I (Berlin Veit 1840)
Wasserstrom R, *The Judicial Decision: Toward a Theory of Legal Justification* (Stanford University Press 1961)
Weiler JHH, 'The Court of Justice on Trial—A Review of Hjalte Rasmussen: *On Law and Policy in the European Court of Justice*' (1987) 24 Common Market Law Review 555
Weiler JHH, 'The Transformation of Europe' (1991) 100 The Yale Law Journal 2403
Wróblewski J, *The Judicial Application of Law* (Zenon Bankowski and Neil MacCormick eds, Kluwer Academic Publishers 1992)
Wróblewski J, 'Legal Syllogism and Rationality of Judicial Decision' (1974) 5 Rechtstheorie 33
Wróblewski J, 'Justification of Legal Decisions' (1979) 33 Revue Internationale de Philosophie 277

PART I

A QUESTION OF PARADIGM?

2

Quality of the Judgments of the Court of Justice: Coherence, Efficiency, and the Context of Explanation

Joxerramon Bengoetxea and Luigi Lonardo

1. Introduction

This chapter aims at discussing the conditions and prerequisites under which the judgments of the Court of Justice of the EU ('the Court') can be critically assessed or appraised.[1] There are heuristic and methodological conditions related to knowledge of, and access to, the necessary information concerning the case (the identification of the relevant points for discovery and justification),[2] and conditions related to normative standpoints. The latter can be external (ie a normative horizon from which the Court's judgments are evaluated) or internal (ie a rational reconstruction of the Court's own criteria).[3] Discovery and justification are often presented as the two dominant starting points for a normative assessment of the Court's judgments, conflicting rather than conflating: justification is based on the reasoning and the decision-making process, where coherence is the main rationale (rational argumentation within the law), whereas discovery is based on the outcome or result of the decision, where its efficiency, implications, and consequences dominate the assessment

[1] This chapter builds on, and reproduces in part, Joxerramon Bengoetxea, 'Text and Telos in the European Court of Justice: Four Recent Takes on the Legal Reasoning of the ECJ' (2015) 11(1) European Constitutional Law Review 184, which reviews Gunnar Beck, *The Legal Reasoning of the Court of Justice of the EU* (Hart Publishing 2012) 486; Gerard Conway, *The Limits of Legal Reasoning and the European Court of Justice* (Cambridge University Press 2012) 344; Elina Paunio, *Legal Certainty in Multilingual EU Law* (Ashgate 2013) 234; and Suvi Sankari, *European Court of Justice Legal Reasoning in Context* (Europa Law Publishing 2013) 275.

[2] The recent practice of streaming oral hearings, as well as of publishing on the Court's website (a translation of) the request for a preliminary reference and the decision by the national court following such preliminary ruling, are welcome developments because they make the material more accessible to the legal community and the general public. This benefit offsets possible disadvantages.

[3] See Introduction to this volume, Section 3.3.

Joxerramon Bengoetxea and Luigi Lonardo, *Quality of the Judgments of the Court of Justice: Coherence, Efficiency and the Context of Explanation* In: *The Reasoning of the Court of Justice of the EU*. Edited by: Alezini Loxa and Luigi Lonardo, Oxford University Press.
DOI: 10.1093/9780198983002.003.0003

(policy-based evaluations). Each position has its own merits. They are somewhat related to the distinction drawn in the Introduction between the descriptive interpretation framework and the realist framework, with each paradigm assigning diverging relative weight to various factors in the context of discovery and of justification.[4] Under the discovery-vs-justification approach, the classical distinction based on the choice between the two major paradigms of interpretation—literal, based on text, and teleological, based on telos—becomes a secondary question.[5] The new paradigm pits justification, based on coherence, against discovery, based on efficiency and results. However, this chapter claims the relevance of a third context of decision-making, the context of explanation, mediating the discovery-vs-justification dichotomy. The context of explanation relates to the actual process that leads to the decision; it is about opening the (partially) 'black box' of institutional, sociological, perhaps even psychological processes. Normatively, this entails that an assessment of a judgment based exclusively on the reasons made publicly available runs the risk of being naive; and conversely, a criticism based exclusively on the speculation as to what may or may not have happened in the secret of deliberation remains an idle exercise. Moving beyond the dichotomy of discovery and justification also has a descriptive dimension. Neither the interpretation nor the realist paradigm alone can offer a full account of how a court reasons.

This chapter aims to contribute to a general normative appraisal of the legal reasoning of the Court, going beyond, but starting out from, the enquiry into how the Court reaches its conclusion, and appraising how well (or how poorly) it does so. This, in turn, requires identifying indicators—that is, the criteria (and meta-criteria) that academics should use for such assessment—whether they do so from an internal point of view, assessing the choice and use of arguments of interpretation, or from an external assessment of the reasons and motives and the factors that influence the decision and how the Court reacts to such factors. Section 2 considers the scope and possibilities for such an appraisal of the Court's reasoning. It discusses the key factors influencing judicial decision-making identified in the Introduction to this volume as those influencing judicial decision-making: internal procedure, legal reasons (especially interpretation), dialogue with other actors, individual personalities,

[4] See Introduction to this volume, Section 3.1.

[5] A similar distinction is contained in HLA Hart, 'Positivism and the Separation of Law and Morals' (1958) 71(4) Harvard Law Review 593, 610 and following. See also Genaro R Carrió, *Notas Sobre Derecho y Lenguaje* (5th edn, Praxis Jurídica Ediciones 2024) 58–61. Historically, Friedrich Carl von Savigny's classification (see *System des heutigen Römischen Rechts*, vol. I, Berlin 1840, 213 following), which distinguished between grammatical, logical, historical, and systematic interpretation, was very influential.

formal logic. On the strength of that analysis, Section 3 addresses directly some key questions relating to a normative assessment of the legal reasoning of the Court.

2. The Importance of the Context of Explanation

2.1 The factors influencing the Court's decision-making

From the perspective of the context of explanation (somehow complementing and moving beyond the dichotomy between discovery and justification), a few features of the ECJ need to be highlighted.[6]

The first feature is the weight of internal procedures, which also gives the chance to mention the role of single individuals. The Court acts always as a college, sitting either in plenary session, consisting of all the judges, for which the quorum is seventeen; in the Grand Chamber of fifteen judges, with a quorum of eleven; or in chambers of five or three judges. Whether the case goes to a formation of three, five, fifteen, or plenary is decided by the administrative meeting of the Court upon of the proposal of a rapporteur judge appointed by the President for each case. Procedure is written, but there may be an oral hearing. After the oral phase is closed, the AG delivers an opinion, and after the opinion, the judge-rapporteur will announce to the rest of the formation whether the judgment will follow the opinion or not, or whether a *tour de table* meeting is necessary in order to know the views of the formation. A draft report is circulated among the formation and the rest of the judges acting in the case can state deliberation notes to express their (concurring or diverging) views and suggestions for amendments. Oral deliberation in college will follow until a draft judgment is agreed. This is then sent to the *lecteur d'arrêts*, and to translation. Sometimes, translators (lawyer-linguists) raise before the Chambers concerns or doubts as to the meaning or translatability of terms used or of ambiguous phrasing provoked by compromises reached at the deliberation. Judges can, and do, check their own language versions to approve the translations.

No dissenting opinions are expressed or published. Dissent is absorbed in the judgment, and the resulting style is impersonal and highly structured, notwithstanding the important role of the judge-rapporteur. Efforts made to

[6] Some of the features highlighted here are personal opinions, not necessarily accepted facts about the Court. They are subjective and open to debate.

accommodate diverging views may result in ambiguous or vague language, or may lead to some contentious *obiter* to be removed, sometimes compromising the coherence of the judgment.

All judgments must be reasoned and the reasoning is best perceived when both the opinion of the AG and the judgment are contrasted. One can then detect the relevant 'silences' and divergences.

The ECJ is a multilingual court that deliberates and drafts its judgments in French with the help of different sorts of multilinguistically minded jurists. Other jurists (*lecteurs d'arrêts*) help ensure consistency of style and reasoning (including citations). The ECJ is multilingual as regards *input* and *output* (22+ languages), but francophone as regards *throughput*, even though there are signs that his might be changing soon. In spite of the francophone Court, English is by far the largest and dominant semiotic context for the academic discussion of the Court's jurisprudence throughout Europe and the whole world. This 'diglossic' condition of the Luxembourg elite is sometimes overlooked by critics.

The second feature is dialogue with other actors. Dialogue is central to decision-making of the ECJ, especially in references for preliminary rulings, where the ECJ does not decide the case but 'only' interprets EU law. The Court does not pick its own cases, but is seized by national courts or by direct parties, and reacts to their claims or queries.[7] It does obviously have some leeway in the way it frames the preliminary questions put to it, for example by rephrasing them.[8]

Even if the CJEU were to be considered activist, it would still be *reactive*, always reacting to the cases brought before it. However, in some of its judgments the Court has also been proactive, in that its interpretations on the effectiveness and autonomous meaning of EU concepts have generated further references as they are applied to new situations by 'creative' jurists. By framing certain *formulae* or *dictae* in leading cases, the Court might generate a line of cases decided on the ratio of the leading case, in what the incumbent President of the Court has called the 'stone-by-stone approach'.[9]

[7] This is now partly nuanced by the extension of the requirement to obtain leave to appeal to the European Court of Justice to additional categories of cases heard by the General Court at first instance, carried by the recent reform to the Court's statute with Regulation of the European Parliament and of the Council amending Protocol No 3 on the Statute of the Court of Justice of the European Union, 2022/0906 (COD), Brussels, 6 March 2024.

[8] On which see the important contribution of Urška Šadl and Anna Wallerman, '"The Referring Court Asks, in Essence": Is Reformulation of Preliminary Questions by the Court of Justice a Decision Writing Fixture or a Decision-Making Approach?' (2019) 25 European Law Journal 416.

[9] Koen Lenaerts, 'EU Citizenship and the European Court of Justice's "Stone-by-Stone" Approach' (2015) 1 International Comparative Jurisprudence 1.

This practice also enhances the dialogue perspective, and creates a sort of shared social field and an emerging European legal culture based on shared styles and methods of legal reasoning, originally applied for EU law and perhaps also ECHR law, but then spilling over into 'national' constitutional interpretation. The spectrum of legal culture has a definite influence on the positive law.

An overall idea of European law coherence (*ius commune europaeum*[10]) seems to be in the making. This is elaborated in discourses concerning the relevance and purpose of law. Even post-Brexit UK constitutional and HR lawyers are partaking in this new way of thinking about law. Whether this automatically turns the Court into a political actor is another issue, which largely depends on one's concept of the political.

Beyond this dialogue between courts and legal professions, the ECJ also establishes a certain dialogue with itself over time in different cases, or with the General Court on appeal and the AG in the same case, and with other institutions, the parties to the cases, and other repeat players.

The third feature is the role of legal reasons. The law the ECJ chiefly deals with, EU law, is multilingual law, and no linguistic version overrides the rest. It is not possible to know which version conveys the 'intended' meaning, if such a concept makes any sense at all. This is a challenge for theories that postulate the existence of an objective, textual meaning.

Precedents are particularly important, because they can lead to a particular type of case or dispute being considered as 'clear'. The distinction between clear cases and hard cases is therefore related to the existence of precedents, or to the availability of clear provisions dealing with the case situation, but there are also inbuilt procedural norms that point to the importance of the distinction before the Court. To begin with, from the perspective of the referring courts, all references for preliminary rulings on interpretation originate, by definition, in hard cases. This does not mean they will also be hard for the Court. Thus, it is not necessary for the AG to give an opinion if the case raises no new point of law, and in fact about one third of the judgments are delivered without one. Also, the fact that a Chamber of the General Court can delegate the decision to a single judge where the questions of law or fact raised present little difficulty, points to the a priori importance of the clear case/hard case distinction. Finally, the delegation of preliminary references to the General Court in certain subject areas (discussed in the next section) also indicates a structural distinction

[10] See Armin Von Bogdandy, Pedro Cruz Villalón, and Peter Huber, *Handbuch Ius Publicum Europaeum*, vol 2 (Müller 2007).

between clear and hard cases. At any rate the structure of justification in clear cases (direct actions) can be circumscribed to deductive, syllogistic reasoning, whereas the structure of justification in hard cases will be syllogistic only in appearance, the construction of each of the premises (choice of applicable provisions, conflict of applicable provisions, filling in gaps, interpretation of applicable provisions, qualification of proven facts, choice of consequences) will be the epicentre of the justification. The clearer *that* construction is, the better the quality of argumentation.

Finally, the Court ensures the observance and the 'effectiveness' of the 'autonomous' legal 'system' of the EU and this also means that it is not expected to, nor supposed to, approach EU law from any particular national legal mindset—not even a combination of national outlooks—but rather with an *ethos* that could be defined as communautaire (this is most probably the spirit the Court had in mind when deciding *CILFIT*,[11] and confirming it in *Consorzio*[12]).

Ignoring or overlooking these and other relevant features might lead to subjective approaches to the Court's reasoning or critiques of its 'style', modelled upon an assumption that the correct style and theory of interpretation is the one from one's national judicial culture: one favouring literal interpretation or one favouring teleological interpretation.

2.2 Normative disagreements

Disagreements between teleological and literal interpretation are recurrent in national and international legal theory and can be addressed from dogmatic, socio-legal, and cultural or philosophical standpoints. At the risk of sketching an overly simplistic caricature, the disagreements take place at different levels.

One cleavage is 'conservative versus progressive'. In the 'conservative' camp we could pile textualists, literalists, historical-originalists, and perhaps minimalists, while the progressive or 'creative' camp attracts teleologists, meta-teleologists, activists, dynamicists, integrationists, and alternativists. But nothing determines that the cleavage should follow those lines and conservatives may turn to creativity if necessary to pursue a given agenda, or the other way round. The US Supreme Court is a good example. In *Loving v Virginia*, an originalist reading of the Fourteenth Amendment led to the (socially progressive) outcome of invalidating a law banning inter-racial marriage.[13]

[11] C-283/81 *CILFIT* ECLI:EU:C:1982:335.
[12] C-561/19 *Consorzio Italian Management* ECLI:EU:C:2018:264.
[13] 1967 *Loving v Virginia* 388 US at 8, 10.

Another disagreement arises from the fact that criticisms of the Court's interpretation are sometimes elevated from the theory of statutory or treaty interpretation to the loftier domains of constitutional theory. The charge is then that the Court engages in undue decision-making, on the questionable assumption that a text-constrained interpretation respects the rule of law, whereas creative interpretation, departing from the text, would imply overstepping the judicial role to enter the forum of politics, something reserved for the other two branches in the *trias politica* (which presupposes the separation of powers within the system) or to the member states in the federal distribution of competences established by the Treaties. That is why courts, and the ECJ, will justify their decisions by reference to 'the law', meaning the spectrum of formal and official sources of EU law (as mandated by Article 19 TEU); that is, that they are applying the law as they interpret it, not making it. The contest becomes one between judicial activism and judicial self-restraint. With regard to EU law and the ECJ, this tension can be seen as one between a communautaire or integrationist agenda favouring expansive interpretation and conceiving the EU as a *sui generis* constitutional and supranational legal order as opposed to a deference-based, restrained direction that conceives the EU legal order as international, inter-governmental law. If one sticks to a more dynamic and hermeneutic concept of (EU) law and conceives it as a coherent law of integration, the criticism of the Court would be that it was not being activist enough, but rather deferential and compliant.

At the end of the day, different concepts of (EU) law lurk behind the dispute. As Suvi Sankari observes, references to 'unambiguous wording' of certain treaty provisions and reproach for the 'ECJ inventing EU law' are revealing as to the critic's 'general approach to EU law'.[14] They tell us more about the assumptions and preferences of the scholar who defends them than about the quality of the reasoning being assessed. Taking the argument to the extreme, if one dislikes the direction of an 'ever closer union between the peoples of Europe' then only judgments of the Court that slow or reverse that course will be acceptable. But if there is no predetermined, fixed notion of what the Treaty makers meant or intended, or what they would have preferred in the present, then surely no objective control could possibly conclude that a given interpretation furthering this ever closer union was wrong.

Language, discourse and reasoning are important dimensions often overlooked by these debates. In the mid-1990s the charge of activism was linked

[14] Sankari (n 1) 61.

to the court's defective reasoning.[15] The political objection to European integration was presented as a legal fault, as a failure of legal method on the part of the Court. The criticisms coming from political science, from international law, and even from constitutional law spilled over theories of legal reasoning, somehow assuming that literal interpretation should, in principle, prevail—as an end-point, not just as the default option on interpretation, not just as the starting point of any interpretation. Some critics *described* the Court of Justice as an activist court pursuing an integrationist agenda,[16] and others drew the conclusion that its wings had to be trimmed. Presented this way, there is a risk of distorting the legal-reasoning dimension of the Court's jurisprudence: how does the Court actually justify its decisions? How does it operate and deliberate? What type of law does it deal with and what are the main features of the legal field in which it operates and which it shapes?

Does it all boil down to a question of being conservative or progressive or should we also have a normative (but objective, that is, independently verifiable) view as to what makes a judgment and its reasoning acceptable? One could take the view that legal argumentation is not just a function of assuming the institutional role assigned to one institution, but also of engaging in practical reason. When the observer engages in practical reason, is he or she already immersed in the hermeneutic circle, *engagé* within the legal field? We are observing social and institutional practices (judicial reasoning), trying to make sense of them, and perhaps trying to criticize, and thus implicitly also to improve those practices; but we are not objective and neutral observers, even if we attempt, as hopefully we all do, to be impartial and rational, even if we aspire to be 'scientific', striving for inter-subjective agreement. But in this observation we are involved in the critically internal point of view, not in the external, purely logical-analytical point of view. It is not clear how one can choose between the theories proposed by those advancing the external perspective. Does it require adopting the sort of postpositivism, based on the implicit legitimacy of principled law, represented by Dworkin,[17] Habermas,[18] Alexy,[19]

[15] See eg Trevor Hartley, 'The European Court, Judicial Objectivity, and the Constitution of the European Union' (1996) 112 Law Quarterly Review 95.

[16] Gunnar Beck, 'Judicial Activism in the Court of Justice of the EU' (2017) 36(2) University of Queensland Law Journal 333.

[17] Ronald Dworkin, *Law's Empire* (10th edn, Belknap Press of Harvard Univ Press 1997).

[18] Jürgen Habermas, *Between Facts and Norms: Contributions to a Discourse Theory of Law and Democracy* (William Rehg tr, 4th edn, MIT Press 2001) 51.

[19] Robert Alexy, *A Theory of Legal Argumentation: The Theory of Rational Discourse as Theory of Legal Justification* (Ruth Adler tr, Oxford Univ Press 2010).

MacCormick (latter),[20] Atienza,[21] and Matteucci,[22] rather than the Kelsenian positivism?[23]

Practical reasoning involves the socially relevant practice of justifying one's normative stances and critiques by giving reasons and engaging in rational discourse with interlocutors or audiences.[24] When the normative domain is related to the law, this practice can, but need not always, become institutional and institutionalized, and different actors with different functions and powers will engage in legal reasoning: legislators, policy makers, administrators, lawyers, legal scholars acting as experts, among others. In the context of the EU, the duty to give reasons concerns all institutions issuing legal acts and member state authorities when acting within the scope of EU law (Article 296 TFEU). Article 41 of the Charter of Fundamental Rights of the Union relates the duty of the administration to give reasons for its decisions to the right to good administration. The duty of 'motivation' or reasoning concerns all law-making institutions, but also all institutions applying the law and, *a fortiori*, all institutions interpreting or reconstructing the law and all jurists putting forward propositions of law or contentions about the law. The good-reasons approach is the antidote to free-rein discretion. It constraints arbitrariness. But what are good reasons? This may differ with institutions and with legal cultures. Good reasons are not absolute, valid in all situations and all systems. They are system-relative; they depend on each institution and each jurisdiction. A sociological enquiry in, or rational reconstruction of the reasoning 'culture' of, each institution will deliver different accounts of what the good reasons of each system are.

When it comes to the Court, when judges engage in this justificatory practice, giving reasons or arguments for its decisions, deciding on disputes strictly speaking, we obtain judicial reasoning. Taking the part for the whole, this judicial reasoning is most commonly referred to as simply legal reasoning, or sometimes legal argumentation. This applies to the Court including its judges and Advocates General. To what extent and under what conditions the variety of reasons given and the ways these different reasons hang together (coherence)

[20] Joxerramon Bengoetxea, Neil MacCormick, and Leonor Moral Soriano, 'Integration and Integrity in the Legal Reasoning of the European Court of Justice' in Gráinne De Búrca and JHH Weiler, *The European Court of Justice* (Oxford University Press 2001).

[21] Manuel Atienza, *Las Razones Del Derecho. Teorías de La Argumentación Jurídica* (Universidad Nacional Autónoma de México 2005).

[22] Nicola Matteucci, *Organizzazione Del Potere e Libertà* (Il Mulino 2016).

[23] Otto Pfersmann, 'Prolégomènes Pour Une Théorie Normativiste de "L'État de Droit"' (2016) 7 Ius Gentium 72.

[24] The workshop held in Lund in 2024, where we discussed the contributions that eventually morphed into the chapters of this book, is an example of an academically institutionalized practice of legal reasoning, but not institutionalized in view of applying or reconstructing the law, as jurists would do in a court of law in any court procedure.

are considered valid or legitimate or rational or acceptable forms of argumentation, that is, good reasons?

This, the starting question of this volume, is the subject of the different theories of legal reasoning. By and large, these theories can be descriptive and/or prescriptive, analytical and/or critical, postulating how the Court has to decide its cases and imposing from our practical reason standpoint the standards upon which it is to be evaluated, such as sticking to the ordinary meaning, paying heed to the subjective intention of the law-maker, and (thus) respecting the separation of powers and the rule of law. If only it were possible to know what the law-maker intended. This is already a *partie prise*. It is founded on the threefold premise that ordinary meaning is normally a relatively straightforward matter, and that when it is not, the subjective intention of the legislator is discoverable and decisive. If we contend that the Court does not respect the rule of law when it resorts to teleological or dynamic methods we are already postulating a normative understanding of the rule of law as equivalent to an 'objective' meaning of the text, whatever that may be. Situations of doubt, gaps, antinomies, and disagreements on meaning are then minimized or downplayed and judicial methodology becomes like following a manual, simply following the rules, sticking to the (objective, pre-interpretative) meaning of the text.

Between the superficial descriptive approach—'in case X the Court did so and so, resorting to interpretative method so and so'—and the normative approach— 'the Court should avoid dynamic arguments based on consequences'—we find the hermeneutic, rational reconstruction, or interpretative approach. Reconstruction remains descriptive—the Court says that interpretation must proceed according to the following criteria (as it does, for example, in *CILFIT* or *Consorzio)* —but adds an internally critical or *rational* dimension—the Court is not following its own directives of interpretation or is creating new ones. Rational reconstruction, like reflective equilibrium, allows the observer to evaluate the Court's decision-making on its own institutional standards, as analytically reconstructed from a series of sources among which the Court's own doctrine of interpretation as expressed in its own case law features prominently.

The distinction between the context of discovery and the context of justification is sometimes blurry and circular but remains relevant in any analysis of the Court's reasoning. Discovery itself may be pre-determined by the need for justification, and justification often proceeds by taking a distance from discovery (trying to look and sound as formal as possible, and avoiding the impression the Court is following its own preference). The frontier between the two contexts is not always clear when it comes to silences or to the methods of interpretation. As regards silences, almost by definition, they will not feature explicitly in the judgment. Silences are to be identified elsewhere, in a different level of analysis: discovery. How the Court decides to frame a legal question, the classification or qualification of a case as falling within free movement or environmental protection, the level of generality of the *ratio*, the arguments that are put forward by some parties but not addressed by the Court to the extent that we can get to know them, the unstated consequences of the decision: these are all interesting elements that blur the distinction between discovery and justification, or rather that require more sophisticated research into any theory of discovery.

As regards interpretation, criticisms of the Court's activism basically rely on a discovery-related interpretation, that is, that it is pursuing a given agenda and that before it moves on to the analysis of the issues of interpretation raised by the case and by the parties and interveners, it has already made up its mind on how it is to be decided.[25] It could be so, but how to substantiate this hunch? Where are the indicators? Would the *réunion générale* and the *rapport prélable* produced by each *rapporteur* already hint at the *fumus boni iuris* or at the intuitive answer, the right answer, and would it be shared by all the judges?

On the other hand, analysing the context of justification, it is possible to reply that the scope of positive law, the Treaties themselves, taken as a system and the specific articles, as well as most EU legislation, is explicitly and openly pursuing certain objectives, and the Court is resorting to these in its interpretation and doing so transparently. In the citizenship cases, for instance, if the integrationist agenda were straightforward, it would be easy to predict the Court's decisions.[26] Similarly, one would expect to find greater consistency in the cases on asylum, or on the European Arrest Warrant. Perhaps it is futile, after all, to expect predictability from the ECJ, or indeed from any court.[27] Each case is decided on its own merits, and attention to detail and the idiosyncrasy of each factual situation may lead to distinguishing the ratio or classifying the problem matter under a different rubric, leaving aside the contextuality and malleability of meaning.

If one believes that words (terms and concepts used in the legal sources) have a predetermined, objective, or fixed meaning, one would expect a great

[25] See chapter by Butler in this volume.
[26] See, similarly, Sankari (n 1).
[27] See, similarly, Gunnar Beck, *The Legal Reasoning of the Court of Justice of the EU, Volume 36 (Modern Studies in European Law)* (Hart Publishing Ltd 2013).

consistency in the application of the law. There would be little difference in the ways in which a lower, first instance court and an apex court interpret those words and those provisions. What we see, by contrast, is great divergence. The preliminary reference procedure was set up, among other reasons, precisely because of an assumption, both practical and theoretical, that problems of interpretation are endemic to law and would inevitably arise in the application of EU law. Even if there is no pre-given 'natural', objective meaning, communication and shared understandings are pragmatically possible and not all legal statements (provisions) are, in fact, a matter of interpretation. Not all is moot in the law; otherwise everything would be problematized. Having stated this, it seems difficult to picture the Court, a collegiate body working in a multilingual context, representing very different cultures, as having a consensus view of the law and a clear idea of how it would decide the case, ex ante, only to simply window-dress the decision, ex post, by a careful choice of methods of interpretation and an elaborate reasoning. In the process of discovery, the judges, especially the rapporteur, are already focusing on how a given argument can be framed. Judges are, somehow, thinking as a college, as impersonal decision-makers.

Thus, even if we assumed, for the sake of argument, that the decision was already made, the judges would still have to agree on the reasoning, the window-dressing, to see how the ready-made decision would be justified and presented to the public, first according to their own institutional standards of interpretation (rational reconstruction, again) and second by analysing the general acceptability of the decision and the arguments to the public, to the relevant audiences. This second point is not blunt. It may be that in the early years the Court profited, if we can use this optimistic term, from the proverbial 'benign neglect'. Perhaps this was generally the case for all the institutions. But at any rate, this is clearly not the case now. The Court is well aware of reactions to its case law, not least by the national judiciaries and their apex courts, and by analysing the lines of cases and decisions on a given subject such as anti-discrimination, data protection or consumer protection, to mention only three, we can see how the Court refines its interpretation by distinguishing or limiting the ratio.

This is why the neglect was perhaps not benign after all. Courts need to be subjected to criticism. Critical reactions to the Court are an essential input for quality of judicial output, just as in the academic context. Debate and open rational discourse are crucial not only for the quality of legal reasoning, but for any dialogical construction of meaning. A new hermeneutic concept of law develops from this critical dialectical dimension, a concept of law based on following rules, but also on contributing to their recognition and development by citizens who adopt a critical internal point of view.

In this sense, it is worth remembering how studies of legal reasoning took off in the late 1970s and early 1980s. The debate in legal theory was still dominated by the contrast between natural law, legal realism, and legal positivism, and issues of interpretation were secondary. Where the rules did not clearly resolve a case (gaps, penumbra situations), the judge was seen as having strong discretion, in either Hart's or Kelsen's positivism. This meant full-blown practical discretion. Yet, legal realism had shown there were important steadying factors, or limits to discretion, of a socio-cultural, political, or economic nature. Natural law also provided some normative guidance, albeit from an extra-legal dimension.

In Europe the emphasis was on reason in law, that is, 'legal reasoning', and the analysis of theories and arguments of legal interpretation, decision-making, and topoi. The Brussels school of rhetoric (Perelman, Olbrechts-Tyteca),[28] the impact of hermeneutics (Gadamer)[29] and of discourse theory in Germany (Habermas),[30] the study of legal cultures and legal argumentation (Tarello,[31] Guastini and the Genoa school,[32] but also Conte,[33] Jori,[34] Pattaro,[35] Atienza and the Alicante school,[36] the Basque school with Igartua, Barrere, Ezquiaga, Iturralde, and many others) and analytical legal philosophy applied to judicial decision-making (Wróblewski[37]) all paved the way for the first groundbreaking analyses of legal reasoning as a special case of practical reasoning in philosophy with a group of authors that would eventually converge in the so-called Bielefelder Kreis: MacCormick,[38] Summers,[39] Wróblewski,[40]

[28] Chaïm Perelman and Lucie Olbrechts-Tyteca, *Traité de l'argumentation: la nouvelle rhétorique* (6th edn, Éd de l'Université de Bruxelles 2008).

[29] Hans-Georg Gadamer, *Truth and Method* (2nd rev edn, Continuum 2003).

[30] Habermas (n 18); Jürgen Habermas, *Reason and the Rationalization of Society* (Thomas A McCarthy tr, Nachdr, Beacon 2007).

[31] Giovanni Tarello, *Il Realismo Giuridico Americano* (2nd edn, Roma Tre Press 2023); Giovanni Tarello, *Storia Della Cultura Giuridica Moderna. Assolutismo e Codificazione Del Diritto* (Il Mulino 1976).

[32] Giovanni Tarello, Riccardo Guastini and Giorgio Rebuffa (eds), *Cultura giuridica e politica del diritto* (Il Mulino 1988); Riccardo Guastini, *Nuovi studi sull'interpretazione* (Aracne 2009).

[33] Amedeo Giovanni Conte, *Filosofia del linguaggio normativo. I. Studi 1965–1981* (Giappichelli 1989); *Filosofia del linguaggio normativo. II. Studi 1982–1994. Con una lettera di Norberto Bobbio* (Giappichelli 1995); *Filosofia dell'ordinamento normativo. Studi 1957–1968* (Giappichelli 1997).

[34] Jori, *Saggi di metagiurisprudenza* (Giuffrè 1985).

[35] Enrico Pattaro, *Filosofia del diritto, diritto, scienza giuridica* (Clueb 1978).

[36] Manuel Atienza and Juan Ruiz Manero, *Las Piezas Del Derecho. Teoría de Los Enunciados Jurídicos* (4th edn, Editorial Ariel 2007).

[37] Jerzy Wróblewski, *The Judicial Application of Law* (Springer 1992).

[38] Neil MacCormick, *Legal Reasoning and Legal Theory* (Reprinted, 1st edn 1978, Clarendon Press 2003).

[39] Neil MacCormick and R Summers (eds), *Interpreting Statutes: A Comparative Study* (Ashgate 1991).

[40] n 36.

Aarnio,[41] Peczenik,[42] Alexy,[43] Taruffo.[44] The indeterminacy of law was confined to hard cases, where hard discretion was to be avoided, by recourse to systemic coherence. The feel was still formalist.

Then came the cultural or interpretative turn, and the special attention to the scope of legal culture legal history and the philosophy of law. Dworkin's insistence on taking rights seriously and enhancing the forum of principles, understood as cohering and integrating the law, required a different, committed point of view. Jurists seemed to share many of these principled approaches to the law in the modern constitutional culture Dworkin was reconstructing in *Law's Empire* (1986). There was an idea of fit or integrity that went well beyond logical consistency. The judicial decision had to add to the chain novel of the law, respecting and developing its narrative coherence. Perhaps these theories came at a turning point in constitutionalism (or constitutional governance) where the legislature was losing the leading role it had in the codification age and even in the highly regulatory post-war welfare state where the will of the legislator (voluntas) and the technical and bureaucratic know-how of the administration became prominent and the judiciary was confined to a lesser role applying the legal syllogism as *la bouche qui pronnonce les môts de la loi*, on the basis of their traditional authority (auctoritas) and on their knowledge of the law, at least on the Continent.

In fact, this was especially the case on the Continent, where European Community law was emerging as a special case of administrative and international law. The European Community added a further, quasi-federal, dimension to the mediation of judicial authority by institutional and political processes. We can add to this EU layer the importance of fundamental rights, the European Court of Human Rights, and constitutional courts. The European Court of Justice also experienced these developments, especially after the accession of the common law jurisdictions. A new type of coherence had to be found in this new 'pluralist' context, where different legal systems would be articulated according to federal principles.

Legal reasoning has gained ground due to the law's and the courts' central role in contemporary liberal democracy as both enabling and constraining political power and mediating politics with other social systems and with society at large. In this sense the requirement to justify judgments and other

[41] Aulis Aarnio, *The Rational as Reasonable: Treatise on Legal Justification* (Dordrecht 1987).

[42] Robert Alexy and Aleksander Peczenik, *The Concept of Coherence and Its Significance for Discursive Rationality* (1990) 3 Ratio iuris 130-147.

[43] Alexy (n 19); Robert Alexy, *A Theory of Constitutional Rights* (Oxford University Press 2010).

[44] Michele Taruffo, *La prova dei fatti giuridici: Nozioni generali* (Giuffrè 1992).

decisions in law by proving good reasons—acceptable reasons according to the legal culture—is a factor constraining decision-makers' discretion, and limiting the arbitrariness of decision-makers' decisions, and ultimately making them accountable to citizens and to society at large. This includes that the discretion of judges is also limited to what can be acceptably justified through reasons-giving. Courts could no longer rely exclusively on their *auctoritas* (although many judges see themselves as representing a power of the state), and even though courts remained resilient to democratic models of governance, they at least had to display *ratio*, their ultimate source of legitimacy when applying the law.[45] Reliance on the 'uncoerced force of the better argument' (to use Habermas' notion[46]) is, even though optimistic in practice, a significant achievement.

Analytical interest in reasoning was accompanied by an interest in conflict resolution where courts have become a central element in a complex system of dispute resolution, a juridical field. Legal reasoning, providing good reasons, shows the decision-makers' respect for the addressees of their decisions, inducing compliance with the decision while at the same time enabling criticism. This argumentative dimension has contributed to an enhanced recourse to, and trust in, the courts,[47] in a context where other players—parties, repeat players, institutions, the media—are also interacting. Providing reasons in support of a decision, addressing the arguments and points raised by the parties in a case, or by the referring courts, or by the lower courts in appeal cases, or even addressing judgments in similar cases made by courts in the same jurisdiction (*stare decisis* or not) or even by courts in other jurisdictions, in other legal systems (comparative precedents with no *stare decisis*), is already a way of engaging in judicial dialogues—a sort of anticipated or imaginary, virtual dialogue with a vague or undefined interlocutor.

The ECJ has been no stranger to these developments. Indeed, one can say that it has brought along a culture of legal reasoning, argumentation and dialogue; a given dynamic style that has influenced national courts' approach to law, at least when interpreting and applying EU law. Domestic courts engage in a similar imaginary dialogue with the ECJ, not only when referring questions for preliminary rulings to the Court, but also when applying EU law in their

[45] Kaarlo Tuori, *Ratio and Voluntas: The Tension between Reason and Will in Law* (Routledge 2016).

[46] Jürgen Habermas, *The Inclusion of the Other: Studies in Political Theory* (Ciaran P. Cronin and Pablo De Greiff eds, MIT Press 2000) 37.

[47] The statistics of judicial activity, available at the Court's website, suggest as much, with an increasing workload, the lion's share of which is made up by questions referred by other courts.

cases.[48] The process is gradual and convergence through coherence will be a long process, federal tensions being unavoidable. But the destination displays a *multilayered lawscape* where jurisdictions interact and coordinate through judicial dialogue. This is the new European legal culture, an ongoing process of justification and dialogue. How judicial dialogues emerge and evolve depends on the ideal type or model of judge (and on judicial function), on the existence of more than one legal system that the judge needs to consider when settling disputes and adjudicating (multilevel systems with inter-legalities), and on the prevailing institutional practices and judicial culture, including the approaches to legal reasoning and justification of judicial decisions.

In this polycentric multilevel Europe, judges apply law made by legislators at different levels, local, regional (sub-state), national (state), supranational (federal European), transnational, or international. In the European context, domestic judges apply norms originating in all those different levels, belonging to different legal systems, which are, arguably, subsystems of a complex European legal system (perhaps the *ius commune europaeum*), where the apex European courts can give guidance and orientation, but domestic judges applying European law remain 'national', belonging to the 'national' judiciaries, subject to the national (state) institutions of judicial governance and national discipline. In some cases, the ECJ is seen as intrusive and competence-creeping into areas that are considered protected by sovereignty. Domestic judges remain civil servants of a state judicial system; they depend, functionally and organically, on their Member State judiciaries (national Councils or other systems) and their salaries are paid nationally. The principle of judicial independence and self-governance shields them from interference from legislators or executives at any level, subnational, national, supranational, or international. But it does not shield them from the interpretation of European law made by the Court of Justice and intruding or creeping into domestic law. Domestic judges can no longer abstract the application of the law from the fact that there is a permanent context of inter-legalities, an interplay of legal systems, each within its area of competence, but all cohabiting in relative and delicate harmony and requiring mutual trust and faithful cooperation. This is where coherence theories can help rather than primacy, rather than supremacy, finding and

[48] Occasionally, the dialogue is far from imaginary. See eg Gustav Krohn Schaldemose, Rass Holdgaard, and Daniella Elkan, 'From Cooperation to Collision: The ECJ's *Ajos* Ruling and the Danish Supreme Court's Refusal to Comply' (2018) 55 *Common Market Law Review* 17; Luigi Lonardo, 'The Veiled Irreverence of the Italian Constitutional Court and the Contours of the Right to Silence for Natural Persons in Administrative Proceedings: Judgment of the Court (Grand Chamber) 2 February 2021, Case C-481/19, *DB* v *Consob*, ECLI:EU:C:2021:84' (2021) 17 European Constitutional Law Review 707.

constructing common principles that can be shared across systems. All courts involved in these interactions (dialogues) could display deference and comity to each other.

The jurisprudence of the Court of Justice has established the principle of the institutional and procedural autonomy of the Member States to structure their administration, judicial remedies, and procedures, as long as the principles of equivalence and effectiveness are preserved.[49] As Dawson, de Witte, and Muir explain,[50] 'the Court of Justice continues to develop new lines of cases asserting its far-reaching ability to review domestic institutional arrangements such as in relation to judicial independence (or lack thereof) or the banking union. The Court therefore inhabits a "political space" to which it is called upon to respond.' This claim by the Court to review the judicial independence in the Member States is delicate. Apex courts of the Member States are particularly eager to avoid any competence creep in those matters, *a fortiori* in matters that concern them directly and individually, such as the administration of justice and the organization of the judiciary, which they consider an essential part of their national constitutional identity,[51] protected by Article 4(2), TEU, and which they seem determined to protect. In other words, domestic judges have multiple layers of identity and loyalty: they apply law made by different legislators and they need to interpret those laws according to the general principles and practical reason informing them, but also seeking an overall coherence between them through conform or consonant interpretation.

[49] C-33/76 *Rewe-Zentralfinanz eG v Landwirtschaftskammer für das Saarland* [1976] ECLI:EU:C:1976:188; C-199/82 *Amministrazione delle Finanze dello Stato v SpA San Giorgio* [1983] ECLI:EU:C:1983:318.

[50] Mark Dawson, Bruno de Witte, and Elise Muir, 'Introduction: Locating Judicial Politics', in Mark Dawson, Bruno de Witte, and Elise Muir (eds), *Revisiting Judicial Politics in the European Union* (Elgar Publishing 2024) 1.

[51] This rationale of uniformity informs the Court's attempt to balance rule of law requirements and constitutional identity of the Member States: C-157/21, *Poland v Parliament and Council* ECLI:EU:C:2022:98, para 265: 'as is apparent from Article 4(2) TEU, the European Union respects the national identities of the Member States, inherent in their fundamental structures, political and constitutional, such that those States enjoy a certain degree of discretion in implementing the principles of the rule of law'; but in no way does it follow that 'that obligation as to the result to be achieved may vary from one Member State to another'. See also para 266: 'Whilst they have separate national identities, inherent in their fundamental structures, political and constitutional, which the European Union respects, the Member States adhere to a concept of "the rule of law" which they share, as a value common to their own constitutional traditions, and which they have undertaken to respect at all times.' And the EU itself also has an identity to protect, see Case C-204/21 *Commission v Poland* ECLI:EU:C:2023:442, para 67: 'Article 2 TEU is not merely a statement of policy guidelines or intentions, but contains values which are an integral part of the very identity of the European Union as a common legal order, values which are given concrete expression in principles containing legally binding obligations for the Member States (judgment of 16 February 2022, *Hungary* v *Parliament and Council*, C-156/21, EU:C:2022:97, paragraph 232).'

The Court of Justice and the ECHR can help them achieve these aims, and avoid confrontation by seeking coherence. Even when applying or executing reserved competences, domestic judges have to take all care to avoid jeopardizing the rights that individuals may draw from EU law, such as national treatment or non-discrimination, so as not to compromise the principle of uniformity.[52] Such is the reflective equilibrium of the multilayered European lawscape, the new pluralist legal culture of Europe seeking coherence.

3. A Normative Appraisal of the Reasoning of the ECJ

3.1 On legal reasons

Should the Court introduce (or recognize) an explicit hierarchy between literal, systematic, and teleological interpretation? Perhaps the Court does not prioritize between text, context, and *telos* in an explicit, normative sense, but it does follow a pattern, perhaps one could say a method, that always starts from the text of the provision, often checking the language versions, especially when a party refers to any possible discrepancy between them. Text and context (coming short of system-*économie*) are always necessary starting points. *Telos* is not a must-source of interpretation.[53] However, if the case has gone all the way to the Kirchberg plateau in Luxembourg (where the Court of Justice sits) it is probably because questions concerning interpretation are contentious and the parties to the case have argued on the basis of language, system, and

[52] '[A]ccording to settled case-law, while the Member States are free to exercise their competences in all their reserved areas, they are ne'ertheless required do so in compliance with EU law, since they may not disregard their obligations deriving from that law': C-791/19 *Commission v Poland* ECLI:EU:C:2021:596, para 56. See also Case C-204/21 *Commission v Poland* ECLI:EU:C:2023:442, para 63:'. . . it is apparent from the settled case-law of the Court that, although the organisation of justice in the Member States, in particular, the establishment, composition, powers and functioning of the national courts, and the rules governing the process for appointing judges or those applicable to the status of judges and the performance of their duties, falls within the competence of those States, the fact remains that, when exercising that competence, the Member States are required to comply with their obligations deriving from EU law and, in particular, from Articles 2 and 19 TEU (see, to that effect, judgments of 15 July 2021, Commission v Poland (Disciplinary regime for judges), C-791/19, EU:C:2021:596, paragraphs 56, 60 to 62 and 95 and the case-law cited, and of 22 February 2022, RS (Effect of the decisions of a constitutional court), C-430/21, EU:C:2022:99, paragraph 38 and the case-law cited).'

[53] It is settled case law that in interpreting a provision of EU law, it is necessary to consider not only its wording, by considering the latter's usual meaning in everyday language, but also the context in which the provision occurs and the objectives pursued by the rules of which it is part. The source of that sentence is C 292/82 *Merck* ECLI:EU:C:1983:335 para 12, which, however, did not contain a mention of the telos, reading instead 'in interpreting a provision of Community law it is necessary to consider not only its wording but also the context in which it occurs and the objects of the rules of which it is part.'

telos (goals and/or effectiveness and/or consequences). If the Court prioritized between the methods, it would be committing itself to a particular strategy, such as textual priority, in cases where it might regret having done so, where *telos* would have seemed to carry the day. If there were any hierarchy between methods of interpretation, it would be implicit. In the analytical framework one of us developed back in the 1990s, dynamic interpretation relies on three different arguments of interpretation:[54]

a. teleological arguments that reason from the goals or aims the norm aspires to achieve; they are forward looking but rely on the values that support such goals;
b. effectiveness arguments that seek to give operational usefulness to the norm, under a functional logic; and
c. arguments from consequences that evaluate the results of interpreting the norm one way or another; they consider the impact of interpretation.

These dynamic arguments tend to see the law in action, in contrast with systemic arguments that tend to be static, seeking anchors for the norm-interpretations in the rest of the provisions found in the *sedes materiae*, in general principles of law and legal concepts (*topoi*) or in values of the system (axiological arguments) contained in constitutional provisions or international human rights treaties. Whereas teleological reasoning is forward-looking, axiological reasoning, based on values, is an anchor giving stability to legal interpretation.[55]

The next question, *should there be criteria to decide when a method of interpretation ought to be applied?* Is tentatively answered in the classical lawyerly way: it depends! It depends on what arguments have convincingly been put forward by the parties. If the parties rely on *telos*, consequences, or effectiveness, then the Court ought to address and consider the merits of such arguments, and if they seem to contradict the text of the provision, the Court would need to provide a plausible explanation for such clash. If the parties have not relied on any such argument, the Court can, on its own initiative, rely on text, system, and *telos*, without committing itself to so-called second level directives of interpretation (those that dictate which categories of arguments are preferable, for example 'language, system and *telos*, in that order'), to prioritize

[54] Joxerramon Bengoetxea, *The Legal Reasoning of the European Court of Justice* (Oxford University Press 1993).
[55] See chapters by Petric and Spieker in this volume.

between any of them. What is at stake is the quality of argumentation, rather than the quality of reasoning. But if interpretation lays a claim to being correct, and if the fulfilment of this claim must be publicly verifiable, then interpretation *is* argumentation.[56] The quality of the Court's 'argumentation' does depend directly on whether it addresses, convincingly, the arguments of the parties, but not so much as to whether it has favoured system rather than *telos* in a given case. Leaving a relevant argument unaddressed is a flaw in argumentative practice and affects the quality of judicial decision-making. The Court should avoid it, and critical scholars should highlight it.

How should the Court explain and justify that a literal construction of the provision is better left aside for a more principled one based on the ethos of integration? Take, for example, *Foto-Frost*,[57] where the teleological justification—centralizing questions of validity at the CJEU—overrides the literal interpretation of Article 267 TFEU, where the obligation to refer questions of validity is only imposed on courts of last resort. To shed some light on this debate we can ask two subsidiary questions. One is: *how do we know which is the 'correct' or best literal interpretation when the text of the provision contains ambiguous, imprecise, obscure, evaluative terms, or when language versions appear to diverge?* The sources of interpretation overlap with the reasons why doubts arise on the text of the legal provision or of the precedent, and lead to the methods or arguments resorted to in order to solve the problems of interpretation: semiotic, systematic, and dynamic arguments. If the interpretative doubt is due to the obscurity of the language, then the method of interpretation will be, first, textual or language-based. We are back to the first and second questions asked above in this section. And the next related question is *how can a philosophy of European integration deliver any specific argument of interpretation, other than through the legal texts adopted by the institutions, where the necessary consensus is reached for passing such acts?* In other words, the constitutional sources of (primary) EU law, including its principles and aims, instantiate the philosophy of European integration binding all EU institutions, including the Court, when making or applying the law. A simple reading of Articles 1, 2, 3, 4 et seq. of the TEU gives an indication of the constitutional project.[58] Arguably, the values proclaimed in Article 2 make this norm a very fundamental one. For example, the need to stick to the text agreed upon by the

[56] For this reason, judgments must be motivated. Neil MacCormick and Robert S Summers (eds), *Interpreting Statutes: A Comparative Study* (Routledge 2016) 60.

[57] C-314/85 *Foto-Frost* ECLI:EU:C:1987:452.

[58] See, similarly, Bast and von Bogdandy, 'The Constitutional Core of the Union: On the CJEU's New Constitutionalism' (2024) MPIL Research Paper Series 2024-06.

legislator is also an argument based on the need to preserve the democratic character of the Union. It might be that there are some types of cases where recourse to these constitutional considerations is especially called for. Probably, these values can show up in any type of case, even the seemingly straightforward legal situations, even the type of cases that will be delegated to the General Court for preliminary rulings.[59] This point calls for further research; but we are not certain this can be turned into some prognosis *à la* legal realism, whereby judges necessarily decide all cases on the basis of their policy or value preference, rather than on the basis of text.

How can the Court protect the essential characteristics of the EU legal order without compromising the attainment of other constitutional commitments (such as complying with international law, or joining the ECHR)? This question arises because the Court has found that EU law is an autonomous legal order with specific characteristics[60] and this may be on a trajectory of conflict with some rules, especially on the international obligations of the EU, contained in the Treaties. The answer is that an analytical and coherent reconstruction of EU law would try to systematize the multilevel and complex federal and cosmopolitan dynamics of all the laws involved, local, provincial, substate, state, suprastate, international, and transnational. This can be done with the help of the structural principles in the Treaties related to the distribution of competences, conferred powers, primacy, supremacy, direct effect of norms, direct applicability of sources, conform interpretation, federal loyalty, respect for constitutional identity, subsidiarity, proportionality. These structural features of the EU may be as important as the values proclaimed in Article 2 TEU, at least from a constitutional standpoint. In a nutshell, they are about cooperation and coordination. The aim would be to systematize EU, ECHR, and Public International Law into a coherent whole, in permanent tension, just like there is a tension between the ECJ and the Member State apex courts.

3.2 On dialogue with other actors

What should be the relationship between the reasoning of the ECJ and the reasoning of various national courts, and how should they affect each other? The same federal logic of cooperation/coordination between multilayered

[59] On which see *infra*.

[60] Opinions 2/13 Accession to ECHR ECLI:EU:C:2014:2454; C-15/17 *Bosphorous* ECLI:EU:C:2018:557; Opinion 1/17 *CETA* ECLI:EU:C:2019:341.

subsystems of law would apply upwards and downwards, although the *hierarchy* relationship (primacy and uniformity) does not apply upwards or sideways. National courts can only suggest, but not impose, their interpretations or principles of reasoning on the CJEU. Similarly, the decisions of one Member State's national court do not necessarily bind the courts of other Member States. But seeking an overall coherence between the systems makes sense in all directions. This calls for a dialogical rather than hierarchical relationship between all the relevant apex courts in each system.

Judicial dialogues, when sincere and constructive, can provide clues for enhancing coherence. They need not support the same conclusion, nor even the same analysis, but they would share the language, the conceptual framework, the constitutional ethos, the methodological approach and the type of interpretative arguments necessary to collectively reach a decision (any decision, not necessarily the same in any given case where more than one court is involved), because of the different weight given to one or another consideration, or because of the different analysis of the case (eg classification of the problem situation as falling under one legal category rather than another). The same goes for Member State courts who make references to the Court or take its reasoning into account. The Kirchberg judges need not follow the legal analysis of the referring court, but they do need to explain how and why they differ. A 'good' justification for a judgment is a relative concept, depending on the arguments that can be accepted by the relevant community. The challenge to uniformity is arguably increased by the recent reform of the Court's statute, whereby the General Court acquired jurisdiction for certain preliminary references.[61] The reform heightens the difficulty of 'sharing uniformity'[62] not only between national courts and the Luxembourg court, but also within the CJEU itself.

A similar dialogical relationship as between courts applies between the Court and the Advocate General. A question concerning the AG is *does the presence of an opinion by Advocate General affect the clarity of the justification found in judgments?* The answer depends on the extent to which the Court engages with the reasoning of the AG, how transparent and sincere the Court is in addressing the arguments, not only of the AG but of all the parties and *amici curiae*. If the Court does not engage, or resorts to silencing some (relevant) points raised by the AG (or by any of the intervening parties, for that matter), then there will be an incomplete justification. This does not mean that it will

[61] See n 6.
[62] Takis Tridimas, 'Sharing Uniformity: A New Era Beckons' (2024) 1 LCEL Research Paper Series 2.

be a faulty or failed justification, but simply a less thorough and more selective one. If the Court explains why it is leaving some arguments unaddressed, for example because its analysis takes a different route, then the quality of justification need not falter. The quality of justification is enhanced by engaging in a dialogue with the reasoning of the AG, the more there is a debate between the AG and the Court.

Can we know (and therefore assess) when and why the Court opts to silence out or avoid certain arguments? Could it be that the Court has an explicit agenda to enhance the acceptability of its decisions by being most economic and austere, at least in some cases? In many cases, the Court may be brief, it might leave out some relevant *obiter*, but it gives a coherent answer giving a sense of direction. In other cases, exhaustiveness might be the preferred strategy, and the Court may want to give the impression that it has carried out a thorough analysis of each of the points (some appeals give this impression, but the coherence of the reasoning could be compromised by exhaustiveness: the reasoning is *exhausted*). Completeness sometimes, economy other times: does this amount to justification *à la carte*? The Court will not tell much about its justificatory strategy, it prefers to be casuistic and not commit itself to a grand strategy. If this were the case, it would be perfectly within the discretion of the Court.

3.3 On individual personalities

What lessons, if any, should we draw from psychology, cognitive science, or behavioural economics about the process of what is actually going on in the different stages of deliberation, regardless of the justification given in public? Any understanding of the process of judicial decision-making should go beyond the discovery/justification dichotomy and cover the context of explanation. The many considerations discussed between the judges (dialogue internal to the institution) and in each of the judicial chambers, what we could call 'the institutional and sociological *html* of the judgment'. Much research is needed in this area. Perhaps not even the protagonists of the deliberation are aware of all the nuances, motives, and motivations affecting and influencing their peers.

One of the ramifications of this debate is the deontological one regarding sincerity and transparency of judicial strategies in the judgment, or in any other form of communication in which judges may engage, regarding their judicial work and their function. The judgment would have a sort of *motifs* or *considérants* explaining the *feuille de route* (roadmap): what the choices were, what the stakes were, what outcomes and effects certain decisions would have, what problems and misunderstandings would follow if certain reasoning was to be followed . . . We are back in the very essence of judicial justification. Are we reinventing the wheel? Was that the genuine meaning of the *considérants* (*attendu que, vu que*) of the initial *arrêts*? From this perspective, the quality of the judgments have improved over time. Reading the old judgments, one does get the impression of a more encrypted type of justification. The current style has probably profited from the common law influence and from the Nordic accessions; it has become more readable and didactic, even moralistic, and less cryptic or formulaic.

This leads to another question, which we have left to the end: *How explicit should members of the Court be, during their tenure, when they write extra-judicially on the case law?* This is one of the dilemmas of the delicate issue of deontology of judges (or their clerks) acting as judges in the Court formation deciding on the case and acting as opinion makers, writing or lecturing extrajudicially on the issues raised by the case, or by the case law, during or after tenure. Can they use insider knowledge to reveal who said what, should they stick to Chatham House rules, should they refrain from reproducing or reporting about any view defended in the *delibéré* and stick to explain what the Court decided? Sometimes judges simply do not have as much time as the scholars to dissect their own judgment in the light of all relevant cases, and they move on to the next case, which they will eventually also leave behind, unless there is great attention and expectations from the political, financial, media, legal-professional, or academic *milieu*. The one clear deontological rule is that judges should not disclose any details of deliberation while the case is pending. But can these details be revealed years later? How many years later? Why should there be anything to conceal or anything too sensitive to disclose and in the actual motivation and public discussion of the judgments?

References

Aarnio A, *The Rational as Reasonable: Treatise on Legal Justification* (Dordrecht 1987).

Alexy R, *A Theory of Constitutional Rights* (Oxford University Press 2010)

Alexy R, *A Theory of Legal Argumentation: The Theory of Rational Discourse as Theory of Legal Justification* (Ruth Adler tr, Oxford Univ Press 2010).

Alexy R and Peczenik A, 'The Concept of Coherence and Its Significance for Discursive Rationality' (1990) 3 Ratio iuris 130–47

Atienza M, *Las Razones Del Derecho. Teorías de La Argumentación Jurídica* (Universidad Nacional Autónoma de México 2005)

Atienza M and Ruiz Manero J, *Las Piezas Del Derecho. Teoría de Los Enunciados Jurídicos* (4th edn, Editorial Ariel 2007)

Bast and von Bogdandy, 'The Constitutional Core of the Union: On the CJEU's New Constitutionalism' (2024) MPIL Research Paper Series 2024-06

Beck G, *The Legal Reasoning of the Court of Justice of the EU, Volume 36 (Modern Studies in European Law)* (Hart Publishing Ltd 2013)

Beck G, 'Judicial Activism in the Court of Justice of the EU' (2017) 36(2) University of Queensland Law Journal 333

Bengoetxea J, 'Text and Telos in the European Court of Justice: Four Recent Takes on the Legal Reasoning of the ECJ' (2015) 11(1) European Constitutional Law Review 184

Bengoetxea J, *The Legal Reasoning of the European Court of Justice* (Oxford University Press 1993)

Bengoetxea J, Maccormick N, and Moral Soriano L, 'Integration and Integrity in the Legal Reasoning of the European Court of Justice' in Gráinne De BúRca and JHH Weiler, *The European Court of Justice* (Oxford University Press 2001)

Carrió GR, *Notas Sobre Derecho y Lenguaje* (5th edn, Praxis Jurídica Ediciones 2024)

Conte AG, *Filosofia del linguaggio normativo. 3 vols I. Studi 1965–1981* (Giappichelli 1989–97)

Dawson M, de Witte B, and Muir E, 'Introduction: Locating Judicial Politics', in M Dawson, B de Witte, and E Muir (eds), *Revisiting Judicial Politics in the European Union* (Edward Elgar Publishing 2024)

Dworkin R, *Law's Empire* (10th edn, Belknap Press of Harvard University Press 1997)

Gadamer H, *Truth and Method* (2nd rev edn, Continuum 2003)

Guastini R, *Nuovi studi sull'interpretazione* (Aracne 2009)

Habermas J, *The Inclusion of the Other: Studies in Political Theory* (MIT Press 2000)

Habermas J, *Between Facts and Norms: Contributions to a Discourse Theory of Law and Democracy* (4th edn, MIT Press 2001)

Habermas J, *Reason and the Rationalization of Society* (Thomas A McCarthy tr, Nachdr, Beacon 2007)

Hart HLA, 'Positivism and the Separation of Law and Morals' (1958) 71(4) Harvard Law Review 593

Hartley T, 'The European Court, Judicial Objectivity, and the Constitution of the European Union' (1996) 112 Law Quarterly Review 95

Jori, *Saggi di metagiurisprudenza* (Giuffrè 1985).

Krohn Schaldemose G, Holdgaard R, and Elkan D, 'From Cooperation to Collision: The ECJ's *Ajos* Ruling and the Danish Supreme Court's Refusal to Comply' (2018) 55 Common Market Law Review 17

Lenaerts K, 'EU Citizenship and the European Court of Justice's "Stone-by-Stone" Approach' (2015) 1 International Comparative Jurisprudence 1

Lonardo L, 'The Veiled Irreverence of the Italian Constitutional Court and the Contours of the Right to Silence for Natural Persons in Administrative Proceedings: Judgment of the Court (Grand Chamber) 2 February 2021, Case C-481/19, *DB* v *Consob*, ECLI:EU:C:2021:84' (2021) 17 European Constitutional Law Review 707

MacCormick N, *Legal Reasoning and Legal Theory* (Reprinted, 1st edn 1978, Clarendon Press 2003)

MacCormick N and Summers RS (eds), *Interpreting Statutes: A Comparative Study* (Routledge 2016)

Matteucci N, *Organizzazione Del Potere e Libertà* (Il Mulino 2016)

Pattaro E, *Filosofia del diritto, diritto, scienza giuridica* (Clueb 1978)

Perelman C and Olbrechts-Tyteca L, *Traité de l'argumentation: la nouvelle rhétorique* (6e éd, Éd de l'Université de Bruxelles 2008)

Pfersmann O, 'Prolégomènes Pour Une Théorie Normativiste de "L'État de Droit"' (2016) 7 Ius Gentium 72

Šadl U and Wallerman A, '"The Referring Court Asks, in Essence": Is Reformulation of Preliminary Questions by the Court of Justice a Decision Writing Fixture or a Decision-Making Approach?' (2019) 25 European Law Journal 416

Sankari S, *European Court of Justice Legal Reasoning in Context* (Europa Law Publishing 2013)

Tarello G, *Il Realismo Giuridico Americano* (2nd ed, 1st ed 1962, Roma Tre Press 2023)

Tarello G, *Storia Della Cultura Giuridica Moderna. Assolutismo e Codificazione Del Diritto* (Il Mulino 1976)

Tarello G, Guastini R, and Rebuffa G (eds), *Cultura giuridica e politica del diritto* (Il Mulino 1988)

Taruffo M, *La prova dei fatti giuridici. Nozioni generali* (Giuffrè 1992)

Tridimas T, 'Sharing Uniformity: A New Era Beckons' (2024) 1 LCEL Research Paper Series 2

Tuori K, *Ratio and Voluntas: The Tension between Reason and Will in Law* (Routledge 2016).

Von Bogdandy A, Cruz Villalón P, and Huber P, *Handbuch Ius Publicum Europaeum* (Müller 2007)

Von Savigny F, *System des heutigen Römischen Rechts*, vol. I (Berlin Veit 1840)

Wróblewski J, *The Judicial Application of Law* (Springer 1992)

3

Reasoning of the Court of Justice of the EU: Challenging the Interpretation Framework

Dorota Leczykiewicz

1. Introduction

The chapter offers a critical reflection on the theoretical framework dominating the scholarship on the reasoning of the Court of Justice of the EU.[1] This framework is referred to throughout as the 'interpretation framework' to emphasize its central element—the conviction that the Court's adjudicatory activity can be conceptualized as interpretation of text, where traceability to written law (EU Treaties or EU legal acts) is treated as an exhaustive standard of legality. The chapter exposes the flaws of the interpretation-based theory of EU law reasoning and uses as examples two judgments of the CJEU, *Melloni* and *Cussens*,[2] to demonstrate the descriptive mismatch between this theory and the Court's reasoning, as well as its inability to expose those elements of the Court's reasoning that most require normative justification.

The chapter observes that the approach to sources of law and legal justification in the interpretation framework reveals that the framework is not normatively neutral and, instead, presupposes a particular understanding of judicial function, and thus of legitimacy of judicial decision-making. Because of its reductionist assumptions about acceptability of judicial choices, the interpretation framework fails to invite the correct questions of judicial propriety

[1] By 'reasoning of the Court of Justice of the EU' I mean reasoning of the Court's judges, as externalized in judgments. I do not include opinions of Advocates General, which are neither dispositive of cases nor binding on the Court's judges, national courts, or other institutional and non-institutional parties (individuals) in a given or future cases.

[2] Case C-399/11 *Stefano Melloni v Ministerio Fiscal*, Judgment of 26 February 2013, ECLI:EU:C:2013:107; Case C-251/16 *Edward Cussens and Others v T. G. Brosman*, Judgment of 22 November 2017, ECLI:EU:C:2017:881.

Dorota Leczykiewicz, *Reasoning of the Court of Justice of the EU: Challenging the Interpretation Framework*
In: *The Reasoning of the Court of Justice of the EU*. Edited by: Alezini Loxa and Luigi Lonardo, Oxford University Press. © Dorota Leczykiewicz 2026. DOI: 10.1093/9780198983002.003.0004

and supranational legitimacy. In response, the chapter argues that the Court's relationship with law is much more rich, nuanced, and theoretically interesting than the interpretation framework is allowing. The chapter argues that a proper theoretical account of the CJEU's reasoning needs to offer not only a comprehensive and accurate description of what happens in judgments but also, by exposing the critical elements of the Court's reasoning, a useful starting point for its assessment in *legal* terms. Because the interpretation framework does not satisfy these requirements, it should be rejected, and the 'interpretation' label should be abandoned entirely as the terminological framing of the Court's reasoning. Only such rejection will permit unbiased engagement with the Court's law-making activity, as well as its decisional authority. While it is not disputed that 'interpretation' can be a broader concept than the interpretation framework currently allows, retention of the 'interpretation' label misdirects the effort to provide a fuller account of the reasons which make the Court's reasoning *legally* valid.

2. 'Interpretation' as the prevailing intellectual framework

In theoretical accounts of the reasoning of the Court of Justice of the EU, *interpretation* has emerged as the prevailing intellectual framework.[3] In that framework, interpretation is understood as ascription of meaning to a text (linguistic messages) and is seen as conceptually intertwined with the process of applying law to facts.[4] Under the interpretation framework, the theoretical model of application of EU law is said to comprise four stages: '(a) the individuation of the applicable norm . . ., (b) ascertaining a fact as having been proved for legal purposes and with a view to the applicable norm, (c) formulating this fact in the language of the applicable norm, . . . (d) the binding determination of the legal consequences of the proved facts on the basis of the applicable norm'.[5] It

[3] J Bengoetxea, *The Legal Reasoning of the European Court of Justice: Towards a European Jurisprudence* (Clarendon Press 1993) 6 and 79; N Fennelly, 'Legal Interpretation at the Court of Justice' (1996) 20 Fordham International Law Journal 656; A Arnull, *The European Union and its Court of Justice* (1st edn, OUP 1999) 607; J Bengoetxea, N MacCormick, and L Moral Soriano, 'Integration and Integrity in the Legal Reasoning of the European Court of Justice' in G de Búrca and JHH Weiler (eds), *The European Court of Justice* (OUP 2003) 43; G Conway, *The Limits of Legal Reasoning and the European Court of Justice* (CUP 2012) 12 and 19; G Beck, *The Legal Reasoning of the Court of Justice of the EU* (Hart Publishing 2013) 115; J Komárek, 'Legal Reasoning in EU Law' in D Chalmers and A Arnull (eds), *Oxford Handbook of European Union Law* (OUP 2015) 28, 45 extensively relying on Bengoetxea, ibid. See also Introduction to the present volume.

[4] Bengoetxea (n 3) 94–95. 'Legal reasoning . . . deals with interpretation of legal norms and with the choice of norms that will apply to the case at hand'. ibid, 145.

[5] ibid 127. Similarly, Beck (n 3) 115.

is a syllogistic vision of legal reasoning, relying on the distinction between law and fact and positioning interpretation as the logical first step of that process.[6]

In addition to the law-application model summarized above, interpretation scholars display other convictions or assumptions, which are either expressly asserted or flow logically from their overarching position. In this way, we are conditioned to believe not only that 'interpretation' is the correct way to think about the activity of the EU Court, but also that legal positivism is the correct concept of law, that syllogism is the common element of all legal reasoning, that in all judgments the Court is applying law that stems from EU law's formal sources,[7] that written rules are the starting point of all legal reasoning, that substantive reasoning (which here comprises various forms of normative reasoning, such as moral, economic, social) is separate from legal reasoning, and that substantive reasons, if at all relevant in the process of judicial decision-making, are merely 'second-order' reasons.[8] The interpretation framework insists on a narrow conception of *legal* justification as excluding substantive reasons.[9]

The focus on formal sources of EU law (EU Treaties and EU legal acts, as defined by the TFEU) is particularly interesting. It goes hand in hand with the positivistic vision of (EU) law, which presupposes that all law is enacted (posited).[10] Such an approach allows scholars to avoid difficult questions about the EU law's validity standard, presumably because no one will question the status of the Treaties and legal acts adopted on their basis as sources of law. Indeed, in the interpretation framework, EU law is uncritically presented as a system 'based on' the Treaties, and deriving *all* its legitimacy from that source, and only that source, because of the Treaties' reputation as the EU's 'Constitution'.[11] Apart from any politicized assertions about autonomy and sovereignty of the

[6] Bengoetxea (n 3) 127 describes this step as 'the individuation of the applicable norm'. The syllogistic vision of legal reasoning emphasizes its deductive elements. While interpretation scholars do not insist that the entirety of the Court's reasoning is deductive, they nevertheless largely ignore the non-deductive elements.

[7] Formal sources of EU law are the Treaties and EU legal acts, as regulated by Articles 288–291 TFEU. They are also referred to as 'written EU law'.

[8] Bengoetxea (n 3) 126–34; Beck (n 3) 115–17.

[9] Bengoetxea (n 3) 272–73, who contrasts substantive reasons with those that constitute 'legal justification', defined by the author as claims that connect a judicial decision with enacted law. Bengoetxea claims that 'the acceptability approach', rather than truth or validity, is the most appropriate for substantive arguments. At p 262, the author describes substantive arguments as 'not as relevant as the arguments drawn from legal sources'.

[10] L Green and T Adams, 'Legal Positivism', Stanford Encyclopedia of Philosophy, https://plato.stanford.edu/ index.html (visited 30 March 2025).

[11] Bengoetxea, MacCormick, and Moral Soriano (n 3) 61–62; Bengoetxea (n 3) 225: 'all [EU] authority derives from the Treaties', and 41: 'The EEC Treaty is the Constitution of the EEC. This is the source of validity of all other norms in the chain of validity it itself institutes'; Beck (n 3) 236.

EU which the formalistic vision of EU legal sources surreptitiously reinforces, its adoption can also be explained as a necessary consequence of the chosen understanding of the process of interpretation. The material which the interpretation framework is prepared to recognize as 'law' needs to be capable of undergoing a process of ascribing meaning to linguistic messages.[12] EU Treaties and legal acts fit that description because of their textual and unified character,[13] unlike other sources of EU law, such as the principle of legality or national legal traditions. As a consequence, the latter escape the interpretation scholars' attention.

Perhaps surprisingly, the insistence in the interpretation framework that all (EU) law is written law does not translate into a strong preference for literal interpretation of that law. Indeed, a common approach among interpretation scholars is to include as a variety of 'interpretation' teleological reasoning,[14] sometimes expanded to truly unfathomable proportions through the notion of 'effectiveness' or *effet utile*.[15] Legal propositions that have no grounding in the wording of EU provisions are still described as their 'interpretations' merely because they are said to contribute to their effectiveness.[16] To account for such tenuous moves, interpretation scholars tend to mention 'general principles' or 'principles' as the other source of EU law.[17] This addition allows them to account for propositions lacking textual grounding in EU provisions but avoid the difficult question about the status of CJEU judgments as a source of (EU) law.[18] By recognizing 'general principles' as a source of EU law, they choose the easy, although not entirely consistent, way out.

[12] Bengoetxea (n 3) 95. See also A Albors Llorens, 'The European Court of Justice, More than a Teleological Court' (1999) 2 Cambridge Yearbook of European Legal Studies 373, 375.

[13] EU Treaties and legal acts are naturally not monolinguistic. They are published in all official languages of the EU. However, they are assumed to express unitary content across all their language versions.

[14] Fennelly (n 3) 664 ff; Beck (n 3) 207; Komarek (n 3) 45–46; M Poiares Maduro, 'Interpreting European Law—Judicial Adjudication in a Context of Constitutional Pluralism' Working Paper IE Law School WPLS08-02, published 05.02.2008, 3 and 10; K Lenaerts and JA Gutiérrez-Fons, 'To Say What the Law of the EU Is: Methods of Interpretation and the Court of Justice' EUI Working Paper AEL 2013/9, 24.

[15] Lenaerts and Gutiérrez-Fons (n 14) 25; Beck (n 3) 195.

[16] A Somek, 'Is Legality a Principle of EU Law?' in S Vogenauer and S Weatherill (eds), *General Principles of Law: European and Comparative Perspectives* (Hart Publishing 2017) 53, 64, describes this phenomenon as 'a-legality', that is, presenting as interpretations statements 'without explicit and unequivocal anchor in the Treaty'.

[17] Bengoetxea (n 3) 69; Beck (n 3) 194–207. Naturally, within the interpretation framework there is pressure to present general principles and other principles referred to by the Court as also based on the Treaties. Article 19 TEU (imposing a duty on the Court to ensure that 'law' is observed) is routinely cited as the Treaty source of legal propositions whose content cannot be traced, even remotely, to any Treaty provision. A Arnull, 'What Is a General Principle of EU Law?' in R de la Feria and S Vogenauer (eds), *Prohibition of Abuse of Law: A New General Principle of EU Law?* (Hart Publishing 2011) 7, 8.

[18] Bengoetxea (n 3) 69. Beck (n 3), who uses the concept of *topoi* rather than sources of law, oscillates between seeing CJEU judgements, which he calls 'precedents', as 'legal *topoi*' (239) and seeing them

3. What Is Wrong with the Interpretation Framework?

The interpretation framework as a theory of the EU Court's reasoning suffers from a range of weaknesses which disqualify it as a descriptive theory. The most important of them is the inaccuracy of the adopted law-application model and the inconsistency of the legal validity standard implicit in the analysis. On the more normative side, there is the framework's deficiency in accounting for the Court's case law as a source of EU law, inadequate engagement with substantive reasons, and the associated reduction of legal reasoning to purely formalistic moves, as well as a very thin conception of judicial propriety, legitimizing judicial overreach under a guise of formally sound reasoning. Below, I address each of these weaknesses in turn.

3.1 Inaccuracy of the law-application model

I have explained above that the law-application model accompanying the interpretation framework presupposes that the CJEU applies (EU) law to facts and that interpretation is the first step of this process.[19] Naturally, it would be much harder to challenge the accuracy of this model if its main precepts stemmed directly from the Treaties. What may come as a surprise is that we do not actually face this difficulty. First, of all of provisions regulating the Court's jurisdiction, only in the context of one of them, Article 267 TFEU (the preliminary ruling procedure),[20] is the Court said to 'interpret' the Treaties and acts adopted by 'the institutions, bodies, offices or agencies of the Union'. No other Treaty provision uses this term to describe the Court's adjudicatory activity.[21] What this means is that the Treaties are not universally imposing the interpretation framework.

merely as 'the wider legal context of relevant provisions, principles and unwritten rules at any time although . . . not generally included amongst the systemic *topoi*' (290).

[19] As I have noted above (text to n 6), this is generally known as the 'syllogistic' model. Its unsuitability as a complete model of judicial reasoning has been frequently pointed out in the literature. See for example N MacCormick, *Legal Reasoning and Legal Theory* (Clarendon Press 1978, reprinted with a new Foreword in 1994) xiii and 74; A Aarnio and A Peczenik, 'The Foundation of Legal Reasoning' (1981) 12 Rechtstheorie 133, 136; A Marmor, *Interpretation and Legal Theory* (Clarendon Press 1994) 128.

[20] The fundamental distinction between interpreting the Treaty and acts adopted on its basis; review of legality; and adjudicating disputes between states, Community (now Union) institutions, and states or individuals and Community institutions (concerning validity or claims for compensation) was present already in the Treaty of Rome (1957) and has persisted across all Treaty revisions and organisational transformations of what is now the European Union.

[21] Instead, the Court is said to 'review the legality' of various EU acts (Articles 263 and 269 TFEU). On the EU Treaties' authority, the Court has also jurisdiction to adjudicate infringement actions

On the flipside, of all Treaty provisions regulating the Court's jurisdiction, it is Article 267 TFEU which poses the greatest obstacle to the law-application model adopted by interpretation scholars. What this means is the very provision which mentions 'interpretation' distances the CJEU's activity from the law-application model of judicial reasoning. Indeed, as is generally acknowledged, the preliminary ruling procedure operates on the basis of a distinction between (EU) law interpretation and (EU) law application, where the former is shared between the national courts and the CJEU, while the latter is the purview of national courts alone.[22] The interpretive stage of the Court's reasoning under Article 267 TFEU cannot thus be presented as the first stage of the process of *applying law to facts*. Naturally, we could artificially expand the term 'facts' to include also EU norms subjected to the CJEU's review or national rules which are indirectly reviewed as part of the preliminary ruling procedure. But the bending of the 'fact' category should make us pause and question the framework which uses this particular (syllogistic) model of the CJEU's reasoning.

3.2 Inconsistent standard of legal validity

I have observed above that there is a tendency among scholars using the interpretation framework to avoid questions of legal validity in EU law.[23] This avoidance allows them to fluctuate between a positivist approach to sources of law, which 'recognizes political rulers as the only source of valid law and

brought against the Member States (Articles 258 and 259 TFEU), actions for EU institutions' failure to act (Article 265 TFEU), actions for compensation against the EU (Article 268 TFEU), and staff disputes with EU institutions (Article 270 TFEU).

[22] This is a purely procedural point, not a legitimacy one. Under the preliminary ruling procedure, the Court does not have the capacity to order investigative measures through which additional facts can be established, nor does it deal with or evaluate evidence. Facts of the case before the national court in which a preliminary ruling is sought are described in the reference sent by that national court. The Court sometimes applies the law it announces to these facts by stating, seemingly abstractly, what consequences follow for a case characterized by such facts, given the Court's adopted meaning of the relevant provision, but the CJEU is not procedurally equipped to pronounce a judgment on the facts that is binding on the parties before the national court. Indeed, national courts sometimes 'depart' from the preliminary ruling rendered because of their different appreciation of the case's facts. This pattern is generally encapsulated by reference to a distinction under the preliminary ruling procedure between 'law interpretation' (in which the Court is involved) and 'law application' (in which the Court is not). M Broberg and N Fenger, *Broberg and Fenger on Preliminary References to the European Court of Justice* (3rd edn, Oxford University Press 2021) Ch 12.

[23] Text to n 18. Raz defines legal validity as 'legal bindingness' or the fact of creating normative effects in law. J Raz, 'Legal Validity' in *The Authority of Law* (2nd edn, Oxford University Press 2009) 146, 149.

adopts the will of the political ruler as its validity standard',[24] and a softer, less restrictive approach, which accepts that not all law is derived from written law. This is particularly visible in the context of 'general principles' or 'principles', which on the one hand are considered in some instances to 'refer to "natural law" rules based on the binding acceptance of criteria of justice, equity, etc.', but on the other are described as 'troublesome'.[25]

As a category, EU Treaties mention 'general principles' in Article 6(3) TEU, and only with respect to fundamental rights. However, in judgments and in scholarly accounts, other propositions, not relating to fundamental rights, are also described as 'general principles'. The standard claim that the EU Court's reliance on self-devised 'general principles' is legitimized by Article 19 TEU is unconvincing because it is based on the circular argument that it is appropriate to define the Court's duty expressed in this provision (to 'ensure that . . . the law is observed') by reference to a category (general principles) over which the Court has total control. A much more convincing account is that 'general principles' are judicial creations,[26] and thus their appearance in judgments constitutes the Court's assertion of law-making authority. In this regard, 'general principles' are not different from other legal propositions unilaterally introduced by the Court, such as the national courts' duty to disapply conflicting national law or the duty of consistent interpretation, or the more concrete substantive ideas (such as the prohibition on national rules restricting access to that state's market) which are not referred to by the Court as 'general principles' but, similarly to them, lack substantive grounding in the Treaties.[27]

The fact that the inclusion of 'general principles' and other 'principles' among EU law sources cannot be accounted for under a single theory of legal

[24] John O Tyler, Jr, 'Legal Validity', Internet Encyclopedia of Philosophy, https://iep.utm.edu/legal-va/ (accessed 30 March 2025).

[25] Bengoetxea (n 3) 72–73. Tridimas describes 'general principles' as gap fillers, which suggests that they do not derive their legal validity from the Treaties. T Tridimas, *The General Principles of EU Law* (2nd edn, Oxford University Press 2006) 17.

[26] TC Hartley, *The Foundations of European Union Law* (7th edn, Oxford University Press 2010) 141.

[27] In the absence of an express provision in the Treaties, the duty to give effect to EU law is justified in the Court's case law by reference to 'the spirit of the Treaty' or 'the system of the Treaties', where a particular proposition is presented as 'inherent' in that system. For example, in *Van Gend* (Case 26-62 *NV Algemene Transport- en Expeditie Onderneming van Gend & Loos v Netherlands Inland Revenue Administration*, ECLI:EU:C:1963:1), the judgment that introduced the doctrine of direct effect, the Court stated that the question needed to be considered in the light of '*the spirit*, the general scheme and the wording of those provisions' (emphasis added; note that the spirit is listed first). In the *Da Costa* judgment (Joined cases 28 to 30-62 *Da Costa en Schaake NV, Jacob Meijer NV, Hoechst-Holland NV v Netherlands Inland Revenue Administration*, ECLI:EU:C:1963:6), the CJEU held: 'When [the Court] gives an interpretation of the Treaty in a specific action pending before a national court, the Court *limits itself* to deducing the meaning of the Community rules from the wording and *spirit of the Treaty*' (emphasis added). Duplicitously, drawing content from the 'spirit of the Treaty' is presented by the Court as 'limited' deduction.

validity is nowhere addressed in the interpretation framework. Interpretation scholars are torn here by two mutually exclusive commitments—one towards a formal theory of sources, and the other towards a denial of the law-making effect of CJEU judgments.

3.3 The missing account of the Court's case law

Naturally, the denial of a law-making effect of CJEU judgments is descriptively and normatively very problematic. Descriptively, it is in stark contrast with the Court's own approach, according to which its judgments have binding effect that is broader than that which can be associated with the principle of *res judicata*. The Court's past case law is a component of many doctrines, such as that of state liability for judicial breach of EU law,[28] the national court's duty to reopen a closed administrative case,[29] and the exceptions to the otherwise strict duty to refer a case to the CJEU by a court from whose judgment there is no further judicial remedy.[30] In addition, Article 99 of the Court's Rules of Procedure allows the Court to decide by a 'reasoned order' and not a judgment, inter alia, '[w]here a question referred to the Court for a preliminary ruling is identical to a question on which the Court has already ruled' or 'where the reply to such a question may be clearly deduced from existing case-law'.[31]

But there is also a normative dimension to the insistence that the Court's judgments do not have a law-making effect. If standard accusations of judicial activism levelled against the Court are any indication, EU law scholars have a strong expectation that the Court's previous case law will be followed in subsequent judgments.[32] Continuity with past judgments is thus understood as a legal requirement, or at least as a condition of the Court's decisions' legitimacy. The interpretation framework, which rejects legal validity of judicial

[28] Joined cases C-46/93 and C-48/93 *Brasserie du Pêcheur SA v Bundesrepublik Deutschland and The Queen v Secretary of State for Transport, ex parte: Factortame Ltd* [1996] ECR I-1029, ECLI:EU:C:1996:79, para 57.

[29] Joined cases C-392/04 and C-422/04 *i-21 Germany GmbH and Arcor AG & Co. KG v Bundesrepublik Deutschland* [2006] ECR I-8559; ECLI:EU:C:2006:586, para 52.

[30] Case 283/81 *Srl CILFIT and Lanificio di Gavardo SpA v Ministry of Health* [1982] ECR 3415; ECLI:EU:C:1982:335; Case C-561/19 *Consorzio Italian Management and Catania Multiservizi SpA v Rete Ferroviaria Italiana SpA*, ECLI:EU:C:2021:799, para 66.

[31] Rules of Procedure of the Court of Justice, OJ L 265, 29.9.2012, p. 1. For more on the normative effects of CJEU judgments, see M Jacob, *Precedents and Case-based Reasoning in the European Court of Justice* (Cambridge University Press 2014) 262–69.

[32] A Arnull, 'Judicial Activism and the European Court of Justice: How Should Academics Respond?' in M Dawson, B de Witte, and E Muir (eds), *Judicial Activism at the European Court of Justice* (Edward Elgar 2013) 211, 216, and 231.

law, participates in a fiction that the CJEU is not a law-making institution. This fiction is convenient for the Court because it shields it from the *problem of authority*, that is, questions about the source of its law-making powers.[33] That problem arises both in the context of the Court's untethered case law (legal propositions whose content obviously does not stem from written EU law) and of those judgments which could reasonably be described as interpretations of EU Treaties and legal acts but make law by settling their meaning for the future.

The failure to account for the CJEU's case law makes the interpretation framework ineffective in explaining the Court's law-making power. Here, legal theory reminds us that judicial authority to make law does not have to be formal (derived from an express act of legal empowerment) but can be 'historical', as in common law jurisdictions, where the judicial power to make law is recognized and renewed with its each individual use, but on the condition that that use is properly justified and continuity with the past is adequately demonstrated.[34] But such a conception of judicial law's authority requires a different approach to judicial justification. In a framework where authority of judicial law rests on its continuity with the past and the quality of reasons provided in support of a particular proposition, notional references to Treaty or secondary law would quickly be exposed as insufficient in legitimizing the Court's adjudicatory activity. More would be expected of the Court in order *legally* to justify its judgments.

3.4 No place for substantive reasons

It could be maintained that the problem of EU judicial law's authority could be accommodated by a 'small' modification in the interpretation framework, according to which the concept of 'interpretation' would be expanded to include engagement with past decisions and the underlying political morality of EU law. In other words, the way to save the interpretation framework would be to use Dworkin's concept of 'interpretation' as including not only written sources but also the Court's own case law and values and standards of the

[33] Interpretation-based accounts which unusually recognize the law-making effect of the Court's judgments avoid answering the question from where the authority of the CJEU could come. The absence of a theoretical justification for treating the Court's judgments as a source of law is described as a 'pragmatic' approach. See Komárek (n 3) 44. The recognition of the law-making effect of the Court's judgments is, however, only superficial because it is not mirrored by a corresponding adaptation of the described 'methods of interpretation', as illustrated, for example, by ibid, 45.

[34] GJ Postema, *Bentham and the Common Law Tradition* (Clarendon Press 1986) 13 and 33–38; AWB Simpson, 'The Common Law and Legal Theory' in W Twining (ed), *Legal Theory and Common Law* (Basil Blackwell 1986); RHS Tur, 'Time and Law' (2002) 22 Oxford Journal of Legal Studies 463.

community's political morality.[35] The problem for interpretation scholars is, however, that such a quick fix of their theory cannot be administered without removing one its central precepts, namely the proposition that *legal* correctness is independent from moral, social, and economic concerns, that is, substantive reasons.[36] Under the interpretation framework, with its limited understanding of legal justification, questions of coherence, formal justice, and legal certainty, so central in Dworkin's theory, cannot effectively arise.[37] While it is undisputable that the written layer of EU law, whose meaning is expounded in an interpretative process, serves as an important legality standard, excluding the whole category of substantive reasons from *legal* reasoning amounts to excluding exactly these elements which are necessary for engaging with questions of coherence and formal justice. This state of affairs is particularly inappropriate in relation to a judicial institution which operates in the interspace between public international law and national law and is part of a legal system which is highly dependent on national law.[38]

[35] R Dworkin, *Law's Empire* (Hart Publishing 1998) 225, 239, and 243, and 'Law as Interpretation' (1982) 9 Critical Inquiry 179.

[36] As we remember (text to n 7 to 9), the interpretation framework reduces the account of the Court's legal reasoning to purely formalistic steps. Substantive reasons are either left out of the judgments' legal analysis or are relegated to the inferior role of 'extra-legal' reasons. According to PS Atiyah and RS Summers, *Form and Substance in Anglo-American Law: A Comparative Study in Legal Reasoning, Legal Theory, and Legal Institutions* (Clarendon Press 1987) 5, substantive reasons include 'goal' reasons and 'rightness' reasons. 'A good rightness reason [derives its justificatory force] from the way in which the decision (or rule) adopted accords with a socio-moral norm of rightness'. ibid 6.

[37] Dworkin (n 35) ch 6. For an example of a chapter that finds this narrow approach to the legality question in EU law challenging, see S Weatherill, 'The Court's Case Law on the Internal Market: A Circumloquacious Statement of the Result, Rather than a Reason for Arriving at It?' in M Adams, H de Waele, J Meeusen, and G Straetmans (eds), *Judging Europe's Judges: The Legitimacy of the Case Law of the European Court of Justice* (Hart Publishing 2015) 87, 88.

[38] The EU legal system, despite its apparent claims to autonomy (understood as detachedness and self-sufficiency: see the judgments of Case 26-62 *NV Algemene Transport- en Expeditie Onderneming van Gend & Loos v Netherlands Inland Revenue Administration* [1963] ECR 1, ECLI:EU:C:1963:1, Joined cases C-402/05 P and C-415/05 P *Yassin Abdullah Kadi and Al Barakaat International Foundation v Council of the European Union and Commission of the European Communities* [2008] ECR I-06351, ECLI:EU:C:2008:461, para 282; Opinion 2/13 *Compatibility of the draft agreement with the EU and FEU Treaties*, ECLI:EU:C:2014:2454, para 170), is not actually autonomous from either public international law or Member State laws. The initial binding effect of the Treaties can be explained only by reference to public international law standards. The Treaties' domestic applicability is dependent on states either choosing a monist approach to international law or the Treaties specifically (in which case they apply them without additional transposition) or transposing the Treaties into domestic law. In terms of the EU law's regulatory space, it occupies a terrain previously regulated by either international and/or national law. Structurally and operationally, EU law is highly reliant on national law (for making it regulatorily complete and for enforcement) and on national authorities, whose existence and conduct is regulated by national law. For a chapter that unequivocally debunks the idea that the EU legal order is completely 'new', ie not reliant for its authority on national legal orders, see JHH Weiler and UR Haltern, 'Constitutional or International? The Foundations of the Community Legal Order and the Question of Judicial *Kompetenz-Kompetenz*' in A-M Slaughter, A Stone Sweet, and JHH Weiler (eds), *The European Court and National Courts: Doctrine and Jurisprudence* (Hart Publishing 1998) 331, 340.

3.5 Thin conception of judicial propriety

The most serious weakness of the interpretation framework is its insistence that traceability of a legal proposition to a written text is an exhaustive proof of authority (a conclusive legitimacy trait). This insistence reveals a commitment to a view mentioned already above, according to which all EU law is 'based on' the Treaties, and deriving *all* its legitimacy from the Treaties[39] and, by extension, from acts adopted by EU institutions on their basis (EU secondary law), even though the Treaties are not equivalent to state constitutions and EU secondary law is not equivalent to state parliamentary legislation.[40] What this means is that the interpretation framework makes unjustified assumptions about the position of EU texts in the EU legal order without appreciating the normative consequences of such assumptions for what is required from the Court to fulfil its duty as a judicial institution.[41] This goes hand in hand with the already mentioned inconsistent and unduly narrow account of EU sources of law. In consequence, the interpretation framework hides rather than emphasizes questions of judicial propriety and supranational legitimacy. This is particularly problematic in the case of a court whose law-making function is more dominant than the dispute resolution function.

What emerges from these observations is that through a reductionist definition of law as only enacted law, the interpretation framework impoverishes our understanding of the EU judges' relationship with (EU) law.[42] Even though this account in no way fits EU law, interpretation scholars cultivate a vision of the judicial role which reduces it to application of law created by other actors (a form of 'legal formalism').[43] This account is acceptable, if at all, only if it is indeed the case that in a given legal system the process of enacting law exhausts all normative choices involved, meaning that references to substantive

[39] Text to n 11. For this view, see for example Bengoetxea, MacCormick, and Moral Soriano (n 3) 61–62.

[40] On the incorrectness of seeing the Treaties as constitutional documents and the ratification of the Treaties as a constitutional moment, see C Möllers, 'Pouvoir Constituant-Constitution-Constitutionalisation' in A von Bogdandy and J Bast (eds), *Principles of European Constitutional Law* (Hart Publishing 2009) 169.

[41] On the content of judicial duty, and the fact that it is not exhausted merely by displaying fidelity to 'the whole set of legal rules', see MacCormick (above n 19) 33 and 242. See also, J Bell, *Policy Arguments in Judicial Decisions* (Clarendon Press 1983) 24.

[42] Bell maintains that a legal community arrives at an understanding of the judicial function as part of their construction the concept of 'law': J Bell, *Judiciaries within Europe: A Comparative Review* (Cambridge University Press 2009) 7–8. The interpretation framework's understanding of 'law' is thus intertwined with how the role of the CJEU is conceived. See also, D Leczykiewicz, 'Why Do the European Court of Justice Judges Need Legal Concepts?' (2008)14 European Law Journal 773, 778.

[43] M Stone, 'Formalism' in JL Coleman, KE Himma, and SJ Shapiro, *Oxford Handbook of Jurisprudence and Philosophy of Law* (Oxford University Press 2004) 166, 171.

arguments in the process of applying the enacted law (whether by judges or other actors) are unnecessary.[44] But these conditions do not obtain in EU law. Neither the treaty-making nor the legislative process exhaust all normative choices, nor does the Court restrict its reasoning to drawing inferences only from objectives, concerns, and values already expressed in enacted law. Indeed, the Court is known to expand the range of objectives which a given EU legislative act was pursuing, and has famously chosen a certain conception of the Internal Market and Free Movement before any pronouncement to that effect was made by the EU legislator.[45] EU law academics have been describing this phenomenon since its inception, although the struggle is patent to differentiate between legitimate (lawful) and illegitimate (unlawful) uses of judicial authority in that regard.[46]

4. Accounting For and Assessing the Court's Judgments

The purpose of this section is to illustrate the descriptive and evaluative deficiencies of the interpretation framework. The unsuitability of the interpretation framework and the need for a more sophisticated approach to judicial reasoning can be shown by reference to any CJEU judgment, but the two judgments examined below demonstrate two specific challenges to which the interpretation framework is unable to provide an answer. The first challenge, illustrated by reference to the *Melloni* judgment, relates to the interpretation framework's failure to account for the centrality of the consequentialist argument in the Court's reasoning. The *Melloni* judgment demonstrates that the interpretation framework fails descriptively. A different challenge is illustrated by the *Cussens* judgment. The discussion of that judgment exposes the danger of alleging that the Court is 'interpreting' existing law when it is in fact introducing completely new prohibitions and granting new administrative and judicial powers, in this case for national tax authorities and courts. The interpretation framework, which the Court is itself using in the *Cussens* judgment, is hiding from view the elements which are problematic from the rule of law perspective, making it harder for observers and commentators to subject

[44] ibid.

[45] See N Nic Shuibhne, 'How Does the Court of Justice Deal with Its Own Previous Case Law in the Field of Union Citizenship? Assessing and Refining Methods of Communicative Reasoning' in this volume. S Weatherill, *The Internal Market as a Legal Concept* (Oxford University Press 2017) 31; J Zglinski, 'Governing the Internal Market: From Judicial Politics to Ordinary Politics' in M Dawson, B de Witte, and E Muir (eds), *Revisiting Judicial Politics in the European Union* (Edward Elgar 2024) 171.

[46] Arnull (n 32).

the Court's reasoning to adequate normative evaluation. It is only when the interpretation framework is set aside that we are able to assess the judgment by reference to EU law's past, as a source of its correctly understood legal validity, and the values of legal certainty, non-retroactivity, protection from arbitrariness, and administrative legality.[47]

4.1 *Melloni*: consequentialist through and through

Melloni[48] raised the question of whether a Spanish court had to surrender Mr Melloni to Italian authorities, and in this way allow the incarceration of an individual who had been tried *in absentia*, despite the fact that in doing so it would have to violate Article 24(2) of the Spanish Constitution (the right to a fair trial). The Spanish Constitutional Court was of the opinion that Article 53 of the EU Charter of Fundamental Rights permitted national courts to apply a higher standard of fundamental rights protection than the one guaranteed by EU law (the European Arrest Warrant (EAW) Framework Decision).[49] It follows that formalistically the case could be presented as concerning 'interpretation' of Article 53 of the Charter, or more specifically what this provision authorized in terms of the national courts' entitlement not to fulfil their obligations under EU secondary law.[50]

Article 53 states that '[n]othing in this Charter shall be interpreted as restricting or adversely affecting human rights and fundamental freedoms as recognised, in their respective fields of application, by Union law and . . . and by the Member States' constitutions'. In *Melloni*, the Court concludes that 'Article 53 of the Charter *must be interpreted* as not allowing a Member State to make the surrender of a person convicted in absentia conditional upon the conviction being open to review in the issuing Member State, in order to avoid

[47] Please note that my previous discussion of these two cases did not focus specifically on the unsuitability of the interpretation framework. Instead, I have used a more directly evaluative approach. D Leczykiewicz, '"Constitutional Justice" and Judicial Review of EU Legislative Acts' in G de Búrca, D Kochenov, and A Williams (eds), *Europe's Justice Deficit? Beyond Good Governance* (Hart Publishing 2014) 97; D Leczykiewicz, 'Prohibition of Abusive Practices as a "General Principle" of EU Law' (2019) 56 *Common Market Law Review* 703.

[48] Case C-399/11 *Stefano Melloni v Ministerio Fiscal*, ECLI:EU:C:2013:107.

[49] Council Framework Decision 2002/584/JHA of 13 June 2002 on the European arrest warrant and the surrender procedures between Member States, OJ L 190, 18.7.2002, p. 1, as amended by Council Framework Decision 2009/299/JHA of 26 February 2009 OJ L 81, 27.3.2009, p. 24.

[50] The Court formulated the question it was answering in the preliminary ruling as concerning the issue of 'whether Article 53 of the Charter *must be interpreted* as allowing the executing Member State to make the surrender of a person convicted in absentia conditional upon the conviction being open to review in the issuing Member State, in order to avoid an adverse effect on the right to a fair trial and the rights of the defence guaranteed by its constitution'. *Melloni* (n 48) para 55 (emphasis added).

an adverse effect on the right to a fair trial and the rights of the defence guaranteed by its constitution.'[51] Naturally, following MacCormick, the 'must' that the Court invokes to justify the conclusion is the 'must' of duty, not of logical or causal necessity.[52] Thus, the question remains—on what ground was the CJEU duty-bound to hold that a Member State (inclusive of its courts) cannot protect the right to a fair trial more generously when executing the arrest warrant?

The review of the Court's reasoning confirms that 'interpretation' is not the right framing for the steps which the Court took in the judgment between paragraph 55 and 64. Crucially, in these paragraphs, the Court is not at all looking at the wording of Article 53 of the Charter. Could it perhaps be said that the Court is engaging in teleological rather than literal interpretation? Unfortunately for the proponents of the interpretation framework, that too would be inaccurate because the Court is not at all interested in the purpose of Article 53 or the Charter as a whole. Instead, the Court instantly jumps to a consequentialist argument which undermines, rather than gives effect to the text of Article 53, nowhere properly considered by the CJEU.[53]

The consequentialist argument used by the Court concerns the effectiveness of the EAW mechanism, which is threatened by the national court's interpretation of Article 53. If the Spanish court's understanding of Article 53 was followed, the execution of a European arrest warrant would be subjected to conditions not allowed by the EAW Framework Decision, that is, an act of EU secondary law. The Court concludes immediately, in the subsequent paragraph, that '[s]uch an interpretation of Article 53 of the Charter cannot be accepted.'[54] The paragraphs that follow do not add any further consequentialist points but make it explicit that what dictates the purported 'interpretation' of Article 53 is the desire to safeguard the primacy of EAW Framework Decision; national courts are expected to breach their domestic constitutional standards in order to give full effect to that EU act. Ultimately, the 'interpretation' which the Court gives to Article 53 is the following:[55]

> where an EU legal act calls for national implementing measures, national authorities and courts remain free to apply national standards of protection of

[51] ibid para 64 (emphasis added).

[52] MacCormick (n 19) 33.

[53] Article 53 of the Charter is never expressly interpreted, whether in terms of literal meaning, purpose, systemic links or historically. The Court, however, recalls the Spanish Constitutional Court's proposed interpretation of Article 53 and the Court's reasoning in the judgment can be read as a response to that court's arguments.

[54] *Melloni* (n 48) para 57.

[55] *Melloni* (n 48) para 60 (emphasis added).

fundamental rights, *provided that* the level of protection provided for by the Charter, as interpreted by the Court, and *the primacy, unity and effectiveness of EU law are not thereby compromised.*

Note that Article 53 of the Charter does not mention primacy, unity or effectiveness of EU law. In fact, it does not subject the prohibition contained therein, on using the Charter to affect adversely the protection of fundamental rights, including the protection offered by national constitutions, to any conditions. What this means is that the outcome in *Melloni* is determined exclusively by non-textual considerations; considerations which are not only absent from the 'interpreted' text but go against its natural meaning and purpose. Yes, the Court could be said to be interpreting EU law more broadly, including its 'spirit', but we do not learn from the judgment why the spirit of EU law excludes a concern for fundamental rights protection, national constitutional traditions, and, on a more practical level, the benefits of displaying engagement with concerns raised by a national constitutional court.[56] This is not to say that the EU judges should be denied the competence to construct the EU's constitutional system or to define 'the essential characteristics of EU law',[57] but merely to point out that, by insisting that the Court's reasoning should be viewed only from the perspective of ascribing meaning to linguistic messages constituting the officials sources of EU law, the interpretation framework fails as a descriptive account.

4.2 *Cussens*: an untraceable 'general principle'

The second judgment I would like to look at is *Cussens*,[58] a chamber judgment whose main import has been confirmed by the Grand Chamber of the CJEU.[59]

[56] Poignantly, the CJEU did engage with these concerns in a subsequent judgment, Case C-42/17 *Criminal proceedings against M.A.S. and M.B.*, Judgment of 5 December 2017, ECLI:EU:C:2017:936, relating to the proper conduct of criminal proceedings for VAT infringements, going so far as to review its previous judgment of 8 September 2015, in *Taricco and Others* (C-105/14, EU:C:2015:555). *M.A.S.* has a similar pattern to *Melloni* in that in it effectiveness of an EU act is in conflict with certain fundamental protections offered by national (constitutional) law.

[57] Opinion 2/13 *Compatibility of the draft agreement with the EU and FEU Treaties*, ECLI:EU:C:2014:2454, para 167.

[58] Case C-251/16 *Edward Cussens and Others v T. G. Brosman*, ECLI:EU:C:2017:881. For a fuller account of the Court's reasoning in the case, see Leczykiewicz, 'Prohibition of Abusive Practices as a "General Principle" of EU Law' (n 47).

[59] See Case C-359/16 *Criminal proceedings against Ömer Altun and Others*, EU:C:2018:63; Joined cases C-115, 118, 119 & 299/16 *N Luxembourg 1 et al.*, ECLI:EU:C:2018:143-147 and the parallel Cases C-116 & 117/16 *Skatteministeriet v T Danmark and Y Denmark Aps*, ECLI:EU:C:2018:144, all decided by the Court on 26 February 2019.

The case concerned the question of whether a national tax authority was permitted and required to treat transactions, concluded in 2002, aimed at reducing the applicant's VAT liability as having no commercial reality and therefore an 'abusive practice', prohibited by an EU law 'general principle', with the effect that the applicant's VAT liability could be retrospectively increased by virtue of unwritten EU law.

In the operative part, the Court held that '[t]he principle that abusive practices are prohibited must be interpreted as being capable, regardless of a national measure giving effect to it in the domestic legal order, of being applied directly in order to refuse to exempt from value added tax sales of immovable goods'.[60] If that ruling were to be explainable under the interpretation framework, all three of its components: (1) that EU law prohibits abusive practices as a general category (and not only in specific contexts), (2) that the prohibition is of a kind that does not require domestic transposition before it authorizes a national tax authority to take action against the applicant, and (3) that the prohibition has been imposed in a way which permits its application to the transactions at hand and does not raise concerns of retroactivity, would have to constitute interpretations of written EU law. To conform to the interpretation framework, each legal proposition relied on by the Court would have to be traceable to either a Treaty provision or a text of an EU legal act. This would seem not to be a difficult requirement given the fact that the Court itself maintains in paragraph 41 of the judgment that it is engaging in the process of 'interpretation', a claim which carries the weight of justifying the review of transactions that had been concluded before the Court first mentioned the prohibition of abusive practices in the sphere of VAT (the *Halifax* judgment).[61] Also, when dealing with the accusation of retroactivity, the CJEU maintains

[60] *Cussens* (n 58).

[61] Case C-255/02 *Halifax plc, Leeds Permanent Development Services Ltd and County Wide Property Investments Ltd v Commissioners of Customs & Excise*, [2006] ECR I-1609, ECLI:EU:C:2006:121. As will be explained later, the *Halifax* judgment can be seen as the source of the prohibition only in the material sense. It states that an EU Directive contains a prohibition of abusive practices in the sphere of VAT. So, in purely material terms, EU law can be described as regulating abuse of tax (VAT) law. However, the *Halifax* judgment is not addressing the constitutional question of whether the prohibition of abuse is binding on individuals without any legislative implementation, or the temporal question of whether it can be applied to transactions which predate the *Halifax* ruling. Moreover, the *Halifax* case does not match the facts of *Cussens*. *Halifax* concerned an abuse of right expressly created by Article 17(2)(a) of the VAT Directive (the right to deduct input VAT from the tax due), while *Cussens* concerned a tax advantage created by Irish law. In addition, the activity carried out by the appellants in *Cussens* was not subjected to tax due to EU law. Thus, *Cussens* is the first case before the CJEU where abuse of national tax law is at stake. For these reasons, it is actually *Cussens*, not *Halifax*, which is the first judgment in which the Court stipulated that the prohibition on abusive practices did not require prior implementation and extended the EU concept of abuse to entitlements created by national law as long as they arose in a sphere otherwise already regulated by EU law.

that its competence under Article 267 TFEU is merely interpretative; the Court's ruling merely 'clarifies and defines . . . the meaning and scope of [EU] law as it must be, or ought to have been, understood and applied from the date of its entry into force'.[62]

A simple question exposes the interpretation framework's dissonance with the legal reality of the case: the entry into force of what? Which is the EU law that entered into force before the reviewed transactions, to which the Court has now given meaning through interpretation, the meaning that law supposedly has always had? The operative part of the judgment suggests that the Court is interpreting 'the principle that abusive practices are prohibited', but where is this principle expressed? And does its source predate the reviewed transactions?

The only formal EU source that substantively covered the area in question and predated the reviewed transactions was the Sixth VAT Directive,[63] which, however, nowhere in its text, whether the provisions or the preamble, refers to the prohibition of abuse.[64] It only mentions abuse as a concern which Member States have to have in mind when introducing various exemptions. Thus, it simply cannot be maintained that in *Cussens* the Court is 'interpreting' the Sixth VAT Directive. Moreover, even if it was so maintained through some indirect reference to its Articles 13 to 15,[65] which contain the word 'abuse', a prohibition on abusive practices so inferred could not apply directly to the applicant because as a prohibition derived from a Directive it would have to be subjected to the same restrictions that a Directive is subjected to in EU law when it is being relied on against a private party.[66] According to the Court's own case law, referred to in *Cussens*,[67] Directives cannot of themselves create obligations for private parties (the so-called *Marshall* prohibition). To use a

[62] *Cussens* (n 58), para 41.

[63] Sixth Council Directive 77/388/EEC of 17 May 1977 on the harmonisation of the laws of the Member States relating to turnover taxes—Common system of value added tax: uniform basis of assessment, OJ L 145, 13.6.1977, p 1. The Directive was repealed and replaced by Council Directive 2006/112/EC of 28 November 2006 on the common system of value added tax, OJ L 347, 11.12.2006, p 1.

[64] *Halifax*, the judgment that mentioned the principle prohibiting abusive practices as stemming from the Sixth VAT Directive but post-dated the relevant transactions and presented a different factual pattern (see n 61), referred to an earlier case: Joined cases C-487/01 and C-7/02 *Gemeente Leusden and Holin Groep BV cs v Staatssecretaris van Financiën*, ECLI:EU:C:2004:26, in which the Court, relying on Article 13(B) of the Directive, described prevention of abuse as an 'objective recognized and encouraged by the Directive' (para 76). There is a difference between a concern being an objective of a particular EU act, even its principle, and the same concern constituting a self-executing 'general principle'.

[65] See above n 64.

[66] See D Leczykiewicz, 'Effectiveness of EU Law Before National Courts: Direct Effect, Effective Judicial Protection, and State Liability' in A Arnull and D Chalmers (eds), *Oxford Handbook of European Union Law* (Oxford University Press 2015) 212, 221.

[67] *Cussens* (n 58) para 26.

Directive's principle against a private party to increase their VAT liability is to allow exactly what the Court's case law precludes.

As mentioned above, the Court is fully aware of this constraint, which is why it explicitly rejects in the *Cussens* judgment the view that the principle it is relying on is 'a rule established by a directive'.[68] But if not the Sixth VAT Directive, then what? The only text that the CJEU can be considered to interpret is the Court's own judgment in the *Halifax* case.[69] In *Cussens*, the Court's tactic is to mention *Halifax* alongside its other judgments employing the concept of abuse (for example, abuse of free movement rights) to say that the wide-spread use of the concept of abuse points to the principle's 'general, comprehensive character'.[70] This conclusion, on the other hand, allows the Court to elevate the prohibition of abusive practices to the status of 'general principle of EU law' and exploit its case law on 'general principles' to hold that, given the prohibition's status as a 'general principle', it can apply directly to the transactions also without its national implementation. All of this clearly shows that the only 'text' or 'source' the Court is interpreting is its own case law.

I have discussed elsewhere why the Court was incorrect to maintain that the prohibition of abusive practices displays the character of a 'general principle of EU law'.[71] The point we need to acknowledge here is that it is only and exclusively the Court's own judgments that could provide the material for the 'interpretive' conclusion reached in the case. An EU provision to which the principle could be traced is simply not there, or, to the extent that we could maintain that it is there, it could not be used because it is included in a Directive. If this is the case, the interpretation framework needs to be rejected as providing a universal theory of the CJEU's reasoning. It needs to be replaced with a framework which exposes the Court's judgments as law-making events and facilitates direct interrogation of the foundations on which CJEU rulings are based. Instead of hiding the problematic elements, such as reliance on cases that have arisen in a different context or do not actually contain the propositions which the Court needs to arrive at a particular conclusion, the theory of the Court's reasoning should identify and expose them. It should facilitate the commentators' task of assessing if the Court is staying true to the full range of its own

[68] ibid para 27.

[69] However, the operative part of the *Halifax* judgment states: 'The Sixth Directive must be interpreted as precluding any right of a taxable person to deduct input VAT where the transactions from which that right derives constitute an abusive practice.'

[70] *Cussens* (n 58) para 31.

[71] Leczykiewicz, 'Prohibition of Abusive Practices as a "General Principle" of EU Law' (n 47).

rulings and to the national legal traditions, and in this way preserving the true coherence of EU law.

5. Exposing CJEU Judgments as Law-Making Events

Cases such as *Cussens*, as well those laying down obligations stemming for national courts from Article 267 TFEU and Article 19(1) TEU[72]—which I do not have space to discuss in the present chapter—are undeniable evidence that the legal reasoning of the CJEU cannot be accounted for without recognizing the law-making effect of the Court's judgments. One way of recognizing that effect would be to insist that CJEU judgments themselves are a source of (EU) law. In section 2.3, I observed that such a modification of the interpretation framework would necessitate a discussion about the source of that authority. I suggested that such questions did have answers but a theory that could provide them would be radically different from the interpretation framework. The expansion of the category of sources of law cannot be carried out without a more fundamental reformulation of the theory of the Court's reasoning.[73]

The alternative approach is to expose CJEU judgments as law-making events without necessarily ascribing them the status of 'sources of law'. This approach has the benefit of giving judge-made law a start date. In this way it allows us to question any judgment which maintains that its retroactivity does not have to be accounted for because the Court is merely interpreting pre-existing law, a tactic we saw in *Cussens*, and previously in *Mangold*.[74] The goal

[72] These obligations concern the removal of any national rules that make the preliminary ruling procedure (Article 267 TFEU) less effective or those that infringe the principle of judicial independence enshrined, in the Court's view, in Article 19(1) TEU. Joined cases C-188/10 and C-189/10, *Aziz Melki and Sélim Abdeli*, ECLI:EU:C:2010:363, para 38; Case C-157/21, *Republic of Poland v European Parliament and Council of the European Union*, ECLI identifier: ECLI:EU:C:2022:98, para 198.

[73] The interpretation framework can only account for CJEU judgments as applications of law and not as its source. Beyond traceablity to written law, it does not lay down any criteria of a legitimate exercise of this law-making authority. Traditionally, common law jurisdictions have a much more developed theory of judge-made law, especially given the fact that they are committed to retrospectivity of judge-made law. In the common law theory, judgments are regarded as legitimate exercises of law-making authority if they display continuity with the past and conformity to legal reason. The requirement of continuity with the past is considered to be complied with when judges make law in reliance of and with respect for the principles already present in law. See A Beever, 'The Declaratory Theory of Law' (2013) 33 Oxford Journal of Legal Studies 421.

[74] Case C-144/04 *Werner Mangold v Rüdiger Helm* [2005] ECR I-9981, ECLI:EU:C:2005:709. We remember that in *Cussens*, the Court dealt with this problem by relying on *Halifax* as a judgment 'interpreting' the VAT Directive and insisting that both *Halifax* and the present judgment were interpretations of EU law since 'it entered into force'. The judgment does not specify what 'law' entered into force before the reviewed transactions. Given the operative part of the judgment, it would seem that that law was the general principle prohibiting abusive practices. However, its existence as a self-executing 'general principle' is for the first time proclaimed only in *Cussens*.

is not to stifle judicial development of the law, but to demand adequate normative justification.

The challenge for a theory of legal reasoning of the CJEU is to deliver the normative standards against which the Court's law-making and its in-judgment justification could be assessed. Some of these normative standards originate in the Court's own case law: the principle of limited scope of Union law;[75] the principle of legal certainty;[76] the principle of national procedural autonomy,[77] to mention just the ones that would be relevant in a case such as *Cussens*. National legal traditions too should be the source of normative standards for CJEU judgments because continuity with them needs also to be ensured. The interpretation framework, with its attachment to textual and exclusively EU-derived sources of law, and excluding substantive reasons from legal reasoning, is unable to accommodate this deeper engagement with the normative standards stemming from community's past at all relevant levels: international, European, and national.

6. Conclusion

The purpose of the chapter was to interrogate a theoretical framework which uses the concept of 'interpretation' as its descriptive and evaluative tool. I have shown that, despite assertions to the contrary, this framework is not normatively neutral and in fact presupposes a particular understanding of the judicial function, and thus of the legitimacy of judicial decision-making. Because the interpretation framework hides under the carpet of 'interpretation' questionable moves, it implicitly legitimizes them, to the detriment of the EU legal tradition. By treating judicial choices as interpretation of textual law, it fails to invite the necessary questions of judicial propriety and supranational legitimacy.

The example of the *Melloni* judgment has shown how traceability to a written text as a source of a judgment's legitimacy can be abused. The *Cussens* judgment, on the other hand, has demonstrated that in some contexts traceability

[75] M Dougan, 'Judicial Review of Member State Action under the General Principles and the Charter: Defining the "Scope of Union Law"' (2015) 52 Common Market Law Review 1201.

[76] According to the Court's case law, the principle of legal certainty prevents retroactive imposition of measures with punitive effects. Legal certainty prevented the prohibition of abusive practices generating independent disadvantageous effects in *Kofoed*. Case C-321/05 *Hans Markus Kofoed v Skatteministeriet* [2007] ECR I-5795; ECLI:EU:C:2007:408.

[77] According to this judicial principle, there is separation between matters of substance and procedure, the latter of which continue to be regulated by the Member States unless the EU has adopted a harmonizing (legislative) measure. Case 45-76 *Comet BV v Produktschap voor Siergewassen* [1976] ECR 2043, ECLI:EU:C:1976:191.

to a written text is not at all the relevant standard, even in the eyes of the Court, although the Court is still claiming to be 'interpreting' EU law. Any framework which invites marginalization of the most relevant and constitutionally significant standards of judicial law's validity needs to be rejected by legal theorists intending to say something useful and meaningful about the reasoning of the EU Court. As publications by those who intimately know the case law of the Court and the ins and outs of the EU legal order abundantly demonstrate,[78] those knowledgeable in EU law intuitively gravitate away from the interpretation scholars' misguided approach.

It is undisputable that my criticism of the interpretation framework is based on a view of the judges' relationship with law which is challenging to accept by those influenced by the ideas of legal positivism. The criticism is rooted in the view that law is ultimately customary; historical evidence (domestic and European legislative enactments, Treaty ratifications, European and domestic judicial decisions) constitute evidence for the law but not the law itself.[79] It is their continued reception and reconfirmation by legal officials that renews them as sources of current law and elucidates their content. The role of the judge is to fully appreciate the wide variety of considerations used in the institutionalized discourse of legal reasoning across the legal tradition it represents, which in the case of the CJEU comprises not only the EU legal tradition *sensu stricto*, but also customary international law, and, perhaps most significantly, the national legal traditions. Any account that does not reflect the plurality, the complexity, and the political morality of EU law needs to be rejected.

References

Aarnio A and Peczenik A, 'The Foundation of Legal Reasoning' (1981) 12 Rechtstheorie 133

Albors Llorens A, 'The European Court of Justice, More than a Teleological Court' (1999) 2 Cambridge Yearbook of European Legal Studies 373

Arnull A, *The European Union and its Court of Justice* (OUP, 1st edn, 1999)

Arnull A, 'What Is a General Principle of EU Law?' in R de la Feria and S Vogenauer (eds), *Prohibition of Abuse of Law: A New General Principle of EU Law?* (Hart Publishing 2011)

[78] See for example, Weatherill (n 37) or C Barnard, *The Substantive Law of the EU: The Four Freedoms* (7th edn, Oxford University Press 2022), which offers extensive discussion of rules, tests, and definitions introduced by the CJEU in relation to free movement and EU citizenship, and makes no attempt to present these case law rules, tests, or definitions as logical inferences from Treaty provisions.

[79] See M Krygier, 'Law as Tradition' (1986) 5 Law and Philosophy 237, 255; N MacCormick, *Institutions of Law: An Essay in Legal Theory* (OUP 2007) 67. See also S Besson, 'General Principles and Customary Law in the EU Legal Order' in S Vogenauer and S Weatherill (eds), *General Principles of Law: European and Comparative Perspectives* (Hart Publishing 2017) 106, 116–17, who argues that part of EU law is customary law, whose validity is acquired through practice, independently from its recognition in the Treaties or by the CJEU.

Arnull A, 'Judicial Activism and the European Court of Justice: How Should Academics Respond?' in M Dawson, B de Witte, and E Muir (eds), *Judicial Activism at the European Court of Justice* (Edward Elgar 2013)

Barnard C, *The Substantive Law of the EU: The Four Freedoms* (7th edn, Oxford University Press 2022)

Beck G, *The Legal Reasoning of the Court of Justice of the EU* (Hart Publishing 2013)

Beever A, 'The Declaratory Theory of Law' (2013) 33 Oxford Journal of Legal Studies 421

Bell J, *Judiciaries within Europe: A Comparative Review* (Cambridge University Press 2009)

Bell J, *Policy Arguments in Judicial Decisions* (Clarendon Press 1983) 24

Bengoetxea J, *The Legal Reasoning of the European Court of Justice: Towards a European Jurisprudence* (Clarendon Press 1993)

Bengoetxea J, MacCormick N, and Moral Soriano L, 'Integration and Integrity in the Legal Reasoning of the European Court of Justice' in G de Búrca and JHH Weiler (eds), *The European Court of Justice* (OUP 2003)

Conway G, *The Limits of Legal Reasoning and the European Court of Justice* (CUP 2012)

Besson S, 'General Principles and Customary Law in the EU Legal Order' in S Vogenauer and S Weatherill (eds), *General Principles of Law: European and Comparative Perspectives* (Hart Publishing 2017)

Broberg M and Fenger N, *Broberg and Fenger on Preliminary References to the European Court of Justice* (3rd edn, Oxford University Press 2021)

Dougan M, 'Judicial Review of Member State Action under the General Principles and the Charter: Defining the Scope of Union Law' (2015) 52 Common Market Law Review 1201

Dworkin R, 'Law as Interpretation' (1982) 9 Critical Inquiry 179

Dworkin R, *Law's Empire* (Hart Publishing 1998)

Fennelly N, 'Legal Interpretation at the Court of Justice' (1996) 20 Fordham International Law Journal 656

Green L and Adams T, 'Legal Positivism', Stanford Encyclopedia of Philosophy, https://plato.stanford.edu/ index.html (visited 30 March 2025)

Hartley TC, *The Foundations of European Union Law* (7th edn, Oxford University Press 2010)

Jacob M, *Precedents and Case-based Reasoning in the European Court of Justice* (Cambridge University Press 2014)

Komarek J, 'Legal Reasoning in EU Law' in D Chalmers and A Arnull (eds), *Oxford Handbook of European Union Law* (OUP 2015)

Krygier M, 'Law as Tradition' (1986) 5 Law and Philosophy 237

Leczykiewicz D, 'Why Do the European Court of Justice Judges Need Legal Concepts?' (2008) 14 European Law Journal 773

Leczykiewicz D, '"Constitutional Justice" and Judicial Review of EU Legislative Acts' in G de Búrca, D Kochenov, and A Williams (eds), *Europe's Justice Deficit? Beyond Good Governance* (Hart Publishing Oxford 2014)

Leczykiewicz D, 'Effectiveness of EU Law before National Courts: Direct Effect, Effective Judicial Protection, and State Liability' in A Arnull and D Chalmers (eds), *Oxford Handbook of European Union Law* (Oxford University Press 2015)

Leczykiewicz D, 'Prohibition of Abusive Practices as a "General Principle" of EU Law' (2019) 56 Common Market Law Review 703

Lenaerts K and Gutiérrez-Fons JA, 'To Say What the Law of the EU Is: Methods of Interpretation and the Court of Justice' EUI Working Paper AEL 2013/9, 25

MacCormick N, *Legal Reasoning and Legal Theory* (Clarendon Press Oxford 1978, reprinted with a new Foreword in 1994)

MacCormick N, *Institutions of Law. An Essay in Legal Theory* (OUP 2007)
Marmor A, *Interpretation and Legal Theory* (Clarendon Press 1994)
Möllers C, 'Pouvoir Constituant-Constitution-Constitutionalisation' in A von Bogdandy and J Bast (eds), *Principles of European Constitutional Law* (Hart Publishing 2009)
Poiares Maduro M, 'Interpreting European Law—Judicial Adjudication in a Context of Constitutional Pluralism' Working Paper IE Law School WPLS08-02, published 05.02.2008
Postema GJ, *Bentham and the Common Law Tradition* (Clarendon Press 1986)
Raz J, 'Legal Validity' in *The Authority of Law* (2nd edn, Oxford University Press 2009)
Simpson AWB, 'The Common Law and Legal Theory' in W Twining (ed), *Legal Theory and Common Law* (Basil Blackwell 1986)
Somek A, 'Is Legality a Principle of EU Law?' in S Vogenauer and S Weatherill (eds), *General Principles of Law: European and Comparative Perspectives* (Hart Publishing2017)
Stone M, 'Formalism' in JL Coleman, KE Himma, and SJ Shapiro, *Oxford Handbook of Jurisprudence and Philosophy of Law* (Oxford University Press 2004)
Summers RS, *Form and Substance in Anglo-American Law: A Comparative Study in Legal Reasoning, Legal Theory, and Legal Institutions* (Clarendon Press 1987)
Tridimas T, *The General Principles of EU Law* (2nd edn, Oxford University Press 2006)
Tur RHS, 'Time and Law' (2002) 22 Oxford Journal of Legal Studies 463
Tyler Jr JO, 'Legal Validity', Internet Encyclopedia of Philosophy, https://iep.utm.edu/legal-va/ (accessed 30 March 2025)
Weatherill S, 'The Court's Case Law on the Internal Market: "A Circumloquacious Statement of the Result, Rather than a Reason for Arriving at It?"' in M Adams, H de Waele, J Meeusen and G Straetmans (eds), *Judging Europe's Judges: The Legitimacy of the Case Law of the European Court of Justice* (Hart Publishing 2015)
Weatherill S, *The Internal Market as a Legal Concept* (Oxford University Press 2017)
Weiler JHH and Haltern UR, 'Constitutional or International? The Foundations of the Community Legal Order and the Question of Judicial *Kompetenz-Kompetenz*' in A-M Slaughter, A Stone Sweet, and JHH Weiler (eds), *The European Court and National Courts—Doctrine and Jurisprudence* (Hart Publishing 1998)
Zglinski J, 'Governing the Internal Market: From Judicial Politics to Ordinary Politics' in M Dawson, B de Witte, and E Muir (eds), *Revisiting Judicial Politics in the European Union* (Edward Elgar 2024)

PART II

NORMATIVE INDETERMINACY AND JUSTIFICATORY PREMISES

4

A Normative Case for the Principle of *Lex Specialis* in EU Law

*Emily Hancox**

1. Introduction

Identifying the available norm(s) is one of the first stages of any judicial decision.[1] No provision may govern the case at hand, or there may be more than one applicable norm.[2] Those provisions may conflict—meaning one norm 'constitutes, has led to, or may lead to, a breach of the other'[3]—or they may accumulate.[4] A judge must either select one, or consider whether to give effect to each provision to some extent. What remains under-appreciated is the extent to which the CJEU is confronted with more than one applicable norm. Despite several general studies of EU legal reasoning,[5] there is minimal discussion—descriptive or normative—regarding how the CJEU prioritizes norms. The only notable exception is the relationship between primary and secondary Union law.[6] Most scholarship on the CJEU's legal reasoning only touches

* I am extremely grateful to Alezini Loxa and Luigi Lonardo for their comments on an earlier draft, and to the workshop participants for broader debates and discussions.

[1] R Dworkin, *Taking Rights Seriously* (Duckworth 1978) 65.

[2] J Bengoetxea, N MacCormick, and L Moral Soriano, 'Integration and Integrity in the Legal Reasoning of the European Court of Justice' in G de Búrca and J Weiler (eds), *The European Court of Justice* (OUP 2001) 53.

[3] J Pauwelyn, *Conflict of Norms in Public International Law: How WTO Law Relates to Other Rules of International Law* (CUP 2003) 176. For other definitions of norm conflict see eg W Jenks, 'The Conflict of Law-Making Treaties' (1953) 30 British Yearbook of International Law 401, 451; H Hamner Hill, 'A Functional Taxonomy of Normative Conflict' (1987) 6 Law and Philosophy 227; W Czapliński and G Danilenko, 'Conflicts of Norms in International Law' (1990) 21 Netherlands Yearbook of International Law 3, 12; E Vranes, 'The Definition of Norm Conflict in International Law and Legal Theory' (2006) 17 European Journal of International Law 395.

[4] Pauwelyn (n 3) 161.

[5] See, eg, J Bengoetxea, *The Legal Reasoning of the European Court of Justice: Towards a European Jurisprudence* (OUP 1993); G Beck, *The Legal Reasoning of the Court of Justice of the EU* (Hart 2012); G Conway, *The Limits of Legal Reasoning and the European Court of Justice* (CUP 2012); A Jakab, *European Constitutional Language* (CUP 2016).

[6] See, eg, P Syrpis (ed), *The Judiciary, the Legislature and the EU Internal Market* (CUP 2012); G Davies, 'Legislative Control of the European Court of Justice' (2014) 51 Common Market Law Review 1579; P Syrpis, 'The Relationship between Primary and Secondary Law in the EU′ (2015) 52 Common

Emily Hancox, *A Normative Case for the Principle of* Lex Specialis *in EU Law* In: *The Reasoning of the Court of Justice of the EU*. Edited by: Alezini Loxa and Luigi Lonardo, Oxford University Press. © Emily Hancox 2026.
DOI: 10.1093/9780198983002.003.0006

briefly upon the interpretative techniques for selecting between norms, such as the principles of *lex specialis* and *lex posterior* prioritizing either the more specific or the later norm.[7]

Normative assessments of CJEU reasoning often focus on the CJEU's perceived 'activism', suggesting that the CJEU relies on more purposive—as opposed to literal—interpretative techniques.[8] What underlies such accusations is often the idea that CJEU decisions are 'the product of subjective preferences as regards deeply contested economic and/or social questions'.[9] How the CJEU construes the interaction between provisions could also be perceived as 'activist'. *Commission v UK (Right to Reside)*[10] offers an illustration here. The decision concerned the UK's decision to restrict entitlement to social security benefits in the UK only to those EU nationals fulfilling the criteria for 'lawful residence' under Directive 2004/38 (essentially only EU nationals with private wealth or exercising some form of economic activity).[11] Before assessing the compatibility of the UK rule with EU law, the CJEU had to select between applicable provisions. For economically inactive Union citizens, the UK's eligibility criteria appeared to comply with Article 24(1) of Directive 2004/

Market Law Review 461; E Muir, *EU Equality Law: The First Fundamental Rights Policy of the EU* (OUP 2018); E Ni Chaoimh, *The Legislative Priority Rule and the EU Internal Market for Goods: A Constitutional Approach* (OUP 2022); M van den Brink, *Legislative Authority and Interpretation in the European Union* (OUP 2024).There is also some discussion of the problem in the context of the interaction between the Charter and general principles. See, eg, C Semmelmann, 'General Principles in EU Law between a Compensatory Role and an Intrinsic Value' (2013) 19 European Law Journal 458; HHC Hofmann and BC Mihaescu, 'The Relation between the Charter's Fundamental Rights and the Unwritten General Principles: Good Administration as the Test Case' (2013) 9 European Constitutional Law Review 73; E Gualco, *General Principles of EU Law as a Passe-Partout Key within the Constitutional Edifice of the European Union: Are the Benefits Worth the Side Effects?* (2016) Birmingham Law School Institute of European Law Working Paper 05/2016.

[7] An exception here is R de Graaff, *Concurrence in European Private Law* (Eleven International Publishing 2020). For more brief discussion see, eg, Bengoetxea (n 5) 246; Beck (n 5) 222–23; J Komárek, 'Legal Reasoning in EU Law' in D Chalmers and A Arnull (eds), *The Oxford Handbook of European Union Law* (OUP 2015) 46.

[8] See, eg, H Rasmussen, *On Law and Policy in the European Court of Justice: A Comparative Study in Judicial Policymaking* (Nijhoff 1986); P Neill, 'The European Court of Justice: a Case Study in Judicial Activism' (European Policy Forum 1995); T Hartley, 'The European Court, Judicial Objectivity and the Constitution of the European Union' (1996) 112 Law Quarterly Review 95; G Beck, 'Judicial Activism in the Court of Justice of the EU' (2017) 36(2) University of Queensland Law Journal 333.

[9] M Dougan, 'Judicial Activism or Constitutional Interaction? Policy Making by the ECJ in the Field of Union Citizenship' in HW Micklitz and B de Witte (eds), *The European Court of Justice and the Autonomy of the Member States* (Intersentia 2011) 116.

[10] Case C-308/14 *Commission v UK (Right to Reside)* EU:C:2016:436.

[11] Directive 2004/38/EC of the European Parliament and of the Council of 29 April 2004 on the Right of Citizens of the Union and Their Family Members to Move and Reside Freely within the Territory of the Member States [2004] OJ L 158/77. Lawful residence typically refers to Union citizens who are working or are self-employed in a host Member State, or are otherwise self-sufficient: Directive 2004/38, Article 7. The UK treated an application for social benefits as evidence that an EU national is not self-sufficient, see C O'Brien, 'The ECJ Sacrifices EU Citizenship in Vain: *Commission v United Kingdom*' (2016) 54(1) Common Market Law Review 209, 212.

38 granting equal treatment to 'Union citizens residing on the basis of [that] Directive'. But the UK position seemed in tension with Regulation 883/2004 prohibiting discrimination against 'habitually resident' Union citizens when claiming social security benefits.[12]

The CJEU did not address the apparent conflict between the measures and concluded that the UK rule complied with both.[13] To reach this conclusion, the CJEU merged the provisions to replace the personal scope of the Regulation with that of the Directive.[14] The CJEU stressed that the Regulation aimed to coordinate rather than harmonize 'the conditions creating the right to social security benefits'.[15] Usually, for Union citizens not in employment, the Regulation would cover all 'nationals of a Member State . . . who are or have been subject to the legislation of one or more Member States'[16] wherever they are habitually resident.[17] However, in *Commission v UK*, for Union citizens not in employment, by overlooking the habitual residence test and constructing a gap in its place, the CJEU allowed the distinct conditions for accessing benefits under Directive 2004/38 to act as a filler.[18] The CJEU has been accused of reading the provisions together so as to achieve a desired result, and thus acting in a politically motivated manner.[19]

In this chapter, I set out a normative argument as to why the CJEU ought to rely instead on the principle of *lex specialis* in cases such as *Commission v UK*. My focus is thus on the relationship between provisions with the same formal rank. This includes the relationship between provisions of the Treaties that have the 'same legal value'.[20] Also included is the relationship between provisions of secondary law. Article 289(3) TFEU does not distinguish between 'legislative acts' on the basis of the decision-making procedure utilized (ie whether the ordinary legislative procedure is used), nor is there a hierarchy between regulations, directives, and decisions.[21] Section 2 sets out the problem

[12] Regulation 883/2004 on the coordination of social security systems [2004] OJ L 166/1, Article 2(1).
[13] *Commission v UK* (n 10) para 67.
[14] O'Brien (n 11) 233.
[15] *Commission v UK* (n 10) para 65.
[16] Article 2(1).
[17] Articles 11(3)(e) and 70(4). Habitual residence is defined further in Regulation 987/2009 laying down the procedure for implementing Regulation 883/2004, [2009] OJ L 284/1, Article 11.
[18] *Commission v UK* (n 10) paras 65–68.
[19] O'Brien (n 11) 209l.
[20] Articles 1(3) TEU and 1(2) TFEU. See also, Article 6(1) TEU.
[21] Case C-259/95 *Parliament v Council* EU:C:1997:454; [1997] ECR I-05303, paras 23. No hierarchy exists between binding legislative regulations and directives despite the order of Article 289 TFEU. Directives can amend and repeal regulations and vice versa, eg, Article 38(1) of Directive 2004/38. Cf Article 290 TFEU, which establishes a hierarchy between legislative and non-legislative acts according to procedure. Despite procedural differences in the adoption of Regulation 883/2004 (assent procedure) and Directive 2004/48 (co-decision), this difference does not feature in the CJEU's reasoning. See further, J Bast, *On the Grammar of EU Law: Legal Instruments* (Jean Monnet Working Paper

of norm overlap and the generally accepted interpretative techniques for prioritizing between norms. A normative framework for evaluating different techniques is then developed in Section 3, and it is argued that there are good reasons for relying upon the principle of *lex specialis* over other interpretative principles. Not only does the principle cohere with the EU's constitutional values, but it offers greater legal certainty. Section 4 then sketches how this might work in practice, and the limits of the *lex specialis* principle. Section 5 concludes.

2. Overlapping Norms

2.1 The problem of norm overlap

We are all subject to multiple legal rules. In our daily lives we may interact (often unthinkingly) with legal regimes relating to, for example, employment, data protection, child welfare, taxation, road safety—and the list could go on. Generally, such situations are unproblematic. Normative accumulation in this way can 'add rights or obligations to already existing rights or obligations (without contradicting any of these rights or obligations)'.[22] Interactions become more important the more similar provisions are: one may be an explicit exception to the other, or a specific application of the other.[23] Matters become more complex where those legal rules conflict, that is, when one rule '*constitutes, has led to, or may lead to, a breach of the other*'.[24]

'Norm overlaps',[25] where a factual scenario falls within the scope of several legal rules, are not uncommon. A drafter may not foresee the interaction with another rule. Or parties may enter into a contract against the background of more general rules. For example, in English law, as in many other jurisdictions, a claim may arise in both tort and in contract.[26] In *Henderson v Merrett Syndicates*, the (then) House of Lords accepted claimants could bring a claim

9/03, 2003); J Bast, 'Legal Instruments' in A von Bogdandy and J Bast (eds), *Principles of European Constitutional Law* (Hart 2006).

[22] Pauwelyn (n 3).
[23] ibid 163.
[24] ibid 176 (emphasis in original).
[25] See further, E Hancox, 'Judicial Approaches to Norm Overlaps in EU Law: A Case Study on the Free Movement of Workers' (2021) 58 Common Market Law Review 1057.
[26] See, A Taylor, 'Concurrent Duties' (2019) 82 Modern Law Review 17.

in negligence against defendants with whom they were also in a contractual relationship.[27] Likewise, claims can arise under a statutory scheme and in negligence,[28] and in both criminal and tort law.[29]

EU law is no different. At the level of primary law, the direct effect of some Treaty provisions can result in multiple provisions being applicable. Well-known illustrations can be found in the fields of free movement and competition law. A set of facts may fall within the scope of Article 18 TFEU, prohibiting discrimination on grounds of nationality, as well as one of the more specific free movement rules (Articles 34, 45, 49, 56, and 63 TFEU).[30] Conduct may also infringe both Articles 101 TFEU (prohibiting agreements that restrict competition) and 102 TFEU (prohibiting abuse of a dominant position).[31] As was made clear in the *Superleague* case, 'the same conduct may give rise to an infringement of both [Articles 101 and 102], even though they pursue different objectives and have distinct scopes. Those articles may thus apply simultaneously where their respective conditions of application are met.'[32] At the level of secondary law, the increased volume of secondary legislation brings with it overlapping regimes.[33] However, this is not new. Cases regarding maternity pay may fall under both the Gender Recast Directive[34] and the Pregnant Workers Directive.[35] Likewise, cases on social benefits can fall under the Citizens' Rights Directive, Regulation 883/2004, and Regulation 492/2011.[36]

[27] [1995] 2 AC 145 (HL).

[28] *Rowley & Ors v Secretary of State for Department of Work and Pensions* [2007] EWCA Civ 598; [2007] WLR 2861, [73] per Dyson LJ.

[29] D Nolan and K Oliphant, *Lunney & Oliphant's Tort Law: Text and Materials* (7th edn, OUP 2023) 52.

[30] See, eg, Case C-213/90 *ASTI* EU:C:1991:291; Case C-251/98 *Baars* EU:C:2000:205; Case C-384/08 *Attanasio Group* EU:C:2010:133; Case C-566/15 *Erzberger* EU:C:2017:562.

[31] Case 66/86 *Ahmed Saeed* EU:C:1989:140; [1989] ECR 803, para 37; Case T-712/14 *CEAHR v Commission* EU:T:2017:748, para 94; Case C-307/18 *Generics (UK) and Others* EU:C:2020:52, para 146.

[32] Case C-333/21 *European Superleague Company* EU:C:2023:1011, para 119.

[33] EUR-Lex, 'Legal acts—statistics' <https://eur-lex.europa.eu/statistics/legislative-acts-statistics.html> accessed 10 May 2025.

[34] Directive 2006/54/EC of the European Parliament and of the Council of 5 July 2006 on the implementation of the principle of equal opportunities and equal treatment of men and women in matters of employment and occupation (recast) [2006] OJ L 204/23.

[35] Council Directive 92/85/EEC of 19 October 1992 on the introduction of measures to encourage improvements in the safety and health at work of pregnant workers who have recently given birth or are breastfeeding [1992] OJ L 348/1.

[36] Regulation 492/2011 of the European Parliament and of the Council of 5 April 2011 on freedom of movement for workers within the Union [2011] OJ L 141/1. See, eg, Case C-111/91 *Commission v Luxembourg (childbirth and maternity allowances)* EU:C:1993:92, paras 22, 32; Case C-85/96 *Martínez Sala* EU:C:1998:217, paras 24, 26–27; Case C-140/12 *Brey* EU:C:2013:565, para 61; Case C-238/15 *Bragança Linares Verruga* EU:C:2016:949.

2.2 Methodologies for resolving norm overlaps

2.2.1 The task of the judge

Cases in which there is more than one available norm are categorized as 'hard cases' requiring resort to second order justification.[37] When more than one norm applies, positive law may set out how to determine the relationship between provisions. Otherwise, the court (or other decision-maker) is tasked with determining their inter-relationship when interpreting the law. The court may select one; both may apply; or some form of 'fusion' approach may be adopted in which one provision alters the scope of application of the other. To guide the court, there are several generally accepted principles of legal reasoning.

Directions for resolving overlaps can be set out in positive law. To offer an illustration, under the Vienna Convention on the Law of Treaties, Article 30(3) provides that for treaties with identical parties 'the earlier treaty applies only to the extent that its provisions are compatible with those of the later treaty'.[38] In the Italian Codice Civile, incompatibility between laws is resolved in favour of the more recent.[39] In the EU legal order, there is some general guidance on the interaction between the EU Treaties and external Treaties[40] and that between the Charter and other sources of fundamental rights.[41] Otherwise, there are specific priority clauses as discussed below.[42] For the most part, however, the EU Treaties do not set out the general interpretative principles for the CJEU to follow, nor are they found elsewhere in the EU legal order.

Courts can also develop a general approach to resolving overlaps. In the UK, for example, it is trite law that a later statute repeals an earlier statute to the extent that they are inconsistent.[43] The CJEU has set out its general approach to interpretation, that is, it will look to the 'wording and the objectives [of a provision], but also ... its context and the provisions of European Union law as a whole'.[44] What the CJEU has not clarified is how it prioritizes between norms. There are, however, generally accepted legal arguments that the CJEU might

[37] Bengoetxea (n 5) 168.

[38] Vienna Convention on the Law of Treaties (Adopted 23 May 1969, entered into force 27 January 1980) 1155 UNTS 331 (VCLT). See also Article 59 VCLT on the termination of incompatible treaties.

[39] Article 15.

[40] Article 351 TFEU.

[41] Articles 52(2)–(4) CFR.

[42] Section 2.2.2.

[43] This is known as the doctrine of implied repeal and was developed in *Ellen Street Estates v Minister of Health* [1934] 1 KB 590, 595.

[44] See, Case C-583/11 P *Inuit Tapiriit Kanatami and Others v Parliament and Council* EU:C:2013:625, para 50; Case C-621/18 *Wightman* EU:C:2018:999, para 47.

be expected to apply,[45] such as the principles of *lex specialis* and *lex posterior*, according priority between norms on the basis of specificity and date respectively. Other legal arguments may also guide the CJEU, including concurrent application, substantive hierarchies, and more teleological approaches.

A hierarchy between interpretative methods can also be set out in law. For instance, the Vienna Convention sets out that treaties shall, first, 'be interpreted in good faith in accordance with the ordinary meaning to be given to the terms of the treaty in their context and in the light of its object and purpose',[46] before listing 'supplementary means of interpretation'.[47] In EU law, meanwhile, the Treaties provide no guidance regarding the hierarchy of interpretative techniques and the CJEU has not set out any order of priority between them.

2.2.2 Priority Clauses

Priority clauses offer an *ex ante* solution to the inter-relationship between norms by setting out the relationship between provisions or entire instruments.[48] The existence of such clauses depends on the foresight of those involved in Treaty-drafting or in the legislative process. A basic categorization includes: (1) clauses providing for the priority of the containing norm; (2) clauses assigning priority to another norm (and setting out the subsidiary nature of the containing norm); and (3) clauses granting priority on a case-by-case basis to the norm offering greater advantages, such as more extensive protection of human rights.[49]

In EU law, the CJEU is required to respect any such clauses as a corollary of its responsibility to 'ensure that in the interpretation and application of the Treaties the law is observed'[50] and to rule 'on the interpretation of Union law

[45] See eg Jenks (n 3) 436; M Hirsch, 'Interactions between Investment and Non-Investment Obligations' in P Muchlinski, F Ortino, and C Schreuer (eds), *The Oxford Handbook of International Investment Law* (OUP 2008) 160; R Michaels and J Pauwelyn, 'Conflict of Norms or Conflict of Laws: Different Techniques in the Fragmentation of Public International Law' (2011–12) 22 Duke Journal of Comparative & International Law 349, 354.

[46] Article 31(1) VCLT.

[47] Article 32 VCLT.

[48] I use the term 'priority clause' to reflect the utility of such clauses outside of conflicts between norms. Other labels include 'compatibility clauses' (Czapliński and Danilenko (n 3) 13) and 'conflict clauses' (JB Mus, 'Conflicts between Treaties in International Law' (1998) 45 Netherlands International Law Review 208, 214; D Pulkowski, *The Law and Politics of International Regime Conflict* (OUP 2014) 319).

[49] Compiled on the basis of H Blix and JH Emerson, *The Treaty Maker's Handbook* (Oceana Publications 1973) 210; Czapliński and Danilenko (n 3) 13; Mus (n 48) 214; International Law Commission, *Fragmentation of International Law: Difficulties Arising from the Diversification and Expansion of International Law* (13 April 2006) UN Doc A/CN4/L682, para 268; CJ Borgen, 'Treaty Conflicts and Normative Fragmentation' in D Hollis (ed), *The Oxford Guide to Treaties* (OUP 2012) 457; Pulkowski (n 48) 319.

[50] Article 19(1) TEU.

or the validity of acts adopted by the institutions'.[51] There are several illustrations of priority clauses in EU law.[52] For instance, Article 18 TFEU states that '[w]ithin the scope of application of the Treaties, and without prejudice to any special provisions contained therein, any discrimination on grounds of nationality shall be prohibited'. Where a situation falls within the scope of one of the more specific rights to non-discrimination in the Treaties,[53] Article 18 TFEU will not apply. The CJEU repeatedly clarifies that it 'applies independently only to situations governed by [EU] law in regard to which the Treaty lays down no specific prohibition of discrimination'.[54] *Weigel* provides a good illustration here. After finding that a national measure did not contravene Article 45 TFEU on the free movement of workers, the CJEU held that '[t]here is therefore no need to express a view on Article [18 TFEU] in so far as the facts at issue in the main proceedings fall within the scope of Article [45 TFEU]'.[55]

2.2.3 *Principle of* lex specialis

The principle of *lex specialis* offers a way of selecting between applicable provisions by granting priority to whichever is more specific.[56] The logic behind the principle is to secure the intentions of the (constitutional) legislature. Supposedly, a lawmaker, 'in regulating a specific area, wants to create special rules that trump the general rules in the field'.[57] The foundation of the principle is thus in legislative intent and, as a result, the principle only makes sense within a unified legal system. As Michaels and Pauwelyn note, the principle operates to the extent that '(i) all legal rules in play coexist within a single overarching system and (ii) the decision which rule to apply can be imputed, albeit by fiction, to a unitary lawmaker with a coherent legislative intent'.[58]

The CJEU explicitly recognizes and applies the principle of *lex specialis*.[59] For instance, in some conflicts the CJEU has found one provision to be 'a *lex*

[51] Article 19(3) TEU.

[52] Eg Article 38 TEU; Articles 16, 18, 22(2), 25, 55, 57, and 218 TFEU. Regulation 492/2011, Article 36(2).

[53] Articles 34, 35, 45, 49, 56, and 63 TFEU.

[54] Case C-10/90 *Masgio* EU:C:1991:107, para 12.

[55] Case C-387/01 *Weigel* EU:C:2004:256, paras 58.

[56] See generally, H Grotius, *The Rights of War and Peace* (Liberty Fund 2005) bk 2; E de Vattel, *The Law of Nations or Principles of the Law of Nature*, vol 2 (Sweet, Stevens and Maxwell 1834) ch XVII; Jenks (n 3) 446; G Fitzmaurice, 'Treaty Interpretation and Other Treaty Points' (1957) 33 British Yearbook of International Law 203, 236; Czapliński and Danilenko (n 3) 20; Michaels and Pauwelyn (n 45) 354; Beck (n 5) 222; B Simma and D Pulkowski, 'Of Planets and the Universe: Self-Contained Regimes in International Law' (2006) 17 European Journal of International Law 483, 287.

[57] Michaels and Pauwelyn (n 45) 354.

[58] ibid 354–55.

[59] See eg Case 91/78 *Hansen* EU:C:1979:65, para 10; Case C-444/00 *Mayer Parry Recycling* EU:C:2003:356, para 51; Case C-252/05 *Thames Water Utilities* EU:C:2007:276, para 39; Case C-582/08 *Commission v UK* EU:C:2010:429, para 35; Case C-128/11 *Usedsoft* EU:C:2012:407, para 51.

specialis that prevails'[60] over the other. Recourse is not always had to the principle of *lex specialis*, however, without this being explained. When the principle applies thus remains unclear. There is relatively little CJEU case law on the operation of the principle of *lex specialis*, as returned to below in Section 4.

2.2.4 *Principle of* lex posterior

The principle of *lex posterior* determines priority between norms according to whichever is adopted later in time.[61] As with the principle of *lex specialis*, the principle aims at ensuring respect for the intentions of the legislature and has similar pre-requisites.[62] By prioritizing the more recent norm, the assumption is that the legislature is aware of the earlier law and intends to overrule it.[63] Applying the more recent norm also ensures that the views of the current legislature (or framer of the constitution) prevails over those of previous legislatures. Again, given the focus on legislative intent, a unified legal system is a prerequisite. In EU law there is no explicit reference by the CJEU to the principle of *lex posterior*, but there is implicit evidence of its use.[64]

2.2.5 Concurrent Application

Selecting between norms—as results from the principles of *lex posterior* and *lex specialis*—may not always be appropriate. An alternative approach is to apply both norms. Following a comparative study of national legal orders, de Graaff argues that respect for legislative intent may require that each provision 'should be realised to the greatest possible extent' unless 'cumulative application would lead to inconsistent outcomes which cannot exist concurrently'.[65] Courts may adjust or combine provisions from each rule, in particular the level of compensation, so that the resulting provision contains aspects of both.[66]

The CJEU sometimes finds that a national measure must comply with more than more provision.[67] *Travel Vac*, for instance, concerned a consumer

[60] Case C-439/01 *Cipra* EU:C:2003:31, para. 40. See *Mayer Parry Recycling* (n 59), para 57; Case C-272/03 *Siig* EU:C:2004:805, para 16; Case C-110/03 *Belgium v Commission* EU:C:2005:223, para 39; Case C-441/02 *Commission v Germany* EU:C:2006:253, para. 40; *Thames Water Utilities* (n 59), para 39.

[61] See generally, Jenks (n 3) 445; Czapliński and Danilenko (n 3) 19; Mus (n 48) 219.

[62] Michaels and Pauwelyn (n 45) 354–55.

[63] International Law Commission (n 49) para 226. In the UK, the principle of implied repeal is also a consequence of Parliamentary sovereignty.

[64] See, eg, Case C-133/22 *LACD* EU:C:2023:710 in which the adoption of a harmonized standard in Directive 2011/83 regarding a commercial guarantee in distance sales contracts takes priority over the rules in Directive 1999/44.

[65] De Graaff (n 7) 4.

[66] ibid 33.

[67] Case 45/75 *Rewe-Zentrale* EU:C:1976:22, para 21 on Articles 37 and 95 EEC; *Hansen* (n 59) para 9 on Articles 37, 92, and 93 EEC; Case C-481/99 *Heininger* EU:C:2001:684 on Council Directive 85/

contract for a time-share in a holiday complex. Given that the contract was concluded away from business premises, the question was asked whether it could fall within the scope of Directive 85/577 on contracts negotiated away from business premises as well as Directive 94/47 on timeshares.[68] According to the CJEU, 'whilst it is true that time-share contracts are covered by Directive 94/47, this does not preclude a contract having a time-share element from being covered by Directive 85/577 if the conditions for the application of that directive are otherwise fulfilled'.[69] The rationale is both to respect legislative intent, as '[n]either directive contains provisions ruling out the application of the other', and to ensure consumer protection.[70]

2.2.6 Substantive hierarchies

Despite the focus here on overlaps between norms of the same formal rank, there is the possibility of a substantive hierarchy. International law recognizes norms norm of *jus cogens*,[71] that is, a norm 'that admit[s] no derogation and that can be amended only by a new general norm of international law of the same value'.[72] Similarly, in the UK, judges recognize a hierarchy between statutes that grant precedence to so-called constitutional statutes[73]

577/EEC of 20 December 1985 to protect the consumer in respect of contracts negotiated away from business premises [1985] OJ L 372/31 and Council Directive 87/102/EEC of 22 December 1986 for the approximation of the laws, regulations and administrative provisions of the Member States concerning consumer credit [1986] OJ 1987 L 42/48.

[68] Directive 94/47/EC of the European Parliament and the Council of 26 October 1994 on the protection of purchasers in respect of certain aspects of contracts relating to the purchase of the right to use immovable properties on a timeshare basis [1994] OJ L 280/83.

[69] Case C-423/97 *Travel-Vac* EU:C:1999:197; [1999] ECR I-02195, para 22.

[70] ibid.

[71] On which see, eg, JA Carrillo Salcedo, 'Reflections on the Existence of a Hierarchy of Norms in International Law' (1997) 8 European Journal of International Law 583; Pauwelyn (n 3) 21; D Shelton, 'Normative Hierarchy in International Law' (2006) 100 American Journal of International Law 291; Hirsch 157; J Vidmar, 'Norm Conflicts and Hierarchy in International Law: Towards a Vertical International Legal System?' in E de Wet and J Vidmar (eds), *Hierarchy in International Law: The Place of Human Rights* (OUP 2012); D Shelton, 'International Law and "Relative Normativity"' in M Evans (ed), *International Law* (4th edn, OUP 2014). VCLT Article 53 confirms the superiority of norms of *jus cogens* over other norms of international law.

[72] Shelton, 'Normative Hierarchy in International Law' (n 71) 297.

[73] According to Laws LJ (who first developed the notion of 'constitutional statutes'): 'a constitutional statute is one which (a) conditions the legal relationship between citizen and State in some general, overarching manner, or (b) enlarges or diminishes the scope of what we would now regard as fundamental constitutional rights. (a) and (b) are of necessity closely related: it is difficult to think of an instance of (a) that is not also an instance of (b) . . . Ordinary statutes may be impliedly repealed. Constitutional statutes may not' (*Thoburn v Sunderland City Council* [2002] EWHC 195, [2003] QB 151, [62]). The concept of constitutional statutes was later confirmed by the Supreme Court in *R (HS2 Action Alliance Ltd) v Secretary of State for Transport* [2014] UKSC 3, [2014] 1 WLR 324.

on the grounds of their normative importance to the UK constitutional settlement.[74]

Until recently it would have been difficult to argue for a normative hierarchy in EU law. The closest the CJEU had come to endorsing the idea of a 'higher law' was the ruling in *Kadi* that 'no circumstances permit any challenge to the principles that form part of the very foundations of the Community legal order'.[75] Lately, the CJEU has begun to imbue Article 2 TEU with increased constitutional significance. Article 2 TEU is referred to as an 'integral part of the very identity of the European Union as a common legal order'[76] and scholars are increasingly arguing that a substantive hierarchy exists in EU law.[77]

2.2.7 Contextual, dynamic, or teleological approaches

There are other approaches that are perhaps more difficult to place within existing categories. Approaches to norm inter-relationship are classified by Bengoetxea under 'systemic and contextual criteria'.[78] Similarly, Beck notes the possibility of 'systemic arguments which focus on the systemic coherence of the rule in question with the following categories of norms and purposive proclamations . . . relevant other secondary legislation'.[79] This might mean construing overlapping provisions in light of the Treaties or of other secondary law. *Travel Vac*, discussed above, could be understood as construing provisions in a manner to enhance consumer protection. Likewise, *Commission v UK (Right to Reside)* could be understood as a case in which one provision of secondary law is read in light of the other.

[74] On the normative importance of constitutional statutes, see eg P Craig, 'Constitutionalising Constitutional Law: *HS2*' [2014] Public Law 373, 389; F Ahmed and A Perry, 'Constitutional Statutes' (2016) 37 Oxford Journal of Legal Studies 461, 467.

[75] Joined Cases C-402/05 P and C-415/05 P *Kadi v Council and Commission* EU:C:2008:461, para 304.

[76] Case C-204/21 *Commission v Poland (Indépendance et vie privée des juges)* EU:C:2023:442, para 67. See also Case C-156/21 *Hungary v Parliament and Council* EU:C:2022:97, para 127; Case C-448/23 *Commission v Poland (Contrôle ultra vires de la jurisprudence de la Cour—Primauté du droit de l'Union)* EU:C:2025:165, Opinion of AG Spielmann, paras 66–69.

[77] See, eg, J Bast and A von Bogdandy, 'The Constitutional Core of the Union: On the CJEU's New, Principled Constitutionalism' (2024) 61 Common Market Law Review 1471, 1496; M Bonelli and M Claes, 'Judicial Politics in the EU Rule of Law Crisis' in M Dawson, B de Witte, and E Muir (eds), *Revisiting Judicial Politics in the European Union* (Edward Elgar Publishing 2024) 117; Spieker in this volume.

[78] Bengoetxea (n 5) 240.

[79] Beck (n 5) 191.

3. Developing a Normative Standard

3.1 Difficulties in developing a normative framework

Given that the EU Treaties provide no guidance as to the hierarchy between interpretative techniques, and the CJEU has not set out its own hierarchy, there exists judicial discretion regarding the appropriate method. What is more, theories of legal reasoning often fail to set out the meta-principles that guide the choice of interpretative principle.[80] How then to select between the different possible methodologies? Scholars have struggled in general to develop a yardstick against which to evaluate the legal reasoning of the CJEU.[81] Several debates in the literature highlight the struggle to develop a shared framework.

The first concerns the appropriate standards for judging the CJEU. Do we assess the CJEU against national constitutional courts or supreme courts, or against other international courts or tribunals? A well-known line of critique suggests that the CJEU is an 'activist' court.[82] While somewhat hard to pin down, the critique appears to centre on how the CJEU does not pay sufficient attention to the wording of provisions. Rasmussen when discussing *Van Gend en Loos*[83] considers that the Court 'went beyond the textual stipulations of [Article 189(3) EEC,] leaving behind it a variety of well-merited, legal interpretative principles'.[84] Hartley likewise refers to key constitutional cases such as *Van Gend en Loos*, *Van Duyn*,[85] and *Chernobyl*[86] as 'judgments outside, or contrary to, the text', that is, a judgment 'which contradicts the text on the basis of any reasonable interpretation of it'.[87] Such claims, however, often appear to boil down to political disagreement or to an importation of national standards of interpretation that may not be appropriate for the CJEU.[88]

A second debate concerns the need for output-legitimacy. Given the EU's so-called democratic deficit, it is often assumed that EU legitimacy must be derived from the results achieved.[89] When applied to legal reasoning, 'an

[80] Beck (n 5) 133; Jakab (n 5) 45.
[81] See Conway (n 5) 84; Introduction to this volume.
[82] Eg Rasmussen (n 8); Hartley (n 8); Neill (n 8).
[83] Case 26/62 *Van Gend en Loos* EU:C:1963:1; [1963] ECR 1.
[84] Rasmussen (n 8) 12.
[85] Case 41/74 *Van Duyn v Home Office* EU:C:1974:133.
[86] Case C-70/88 *Parliament v Council (Chernobyl)* EU:C:1990:217.
[87] Hartley (n 8) 96.
[88] M Poiares Maduro, 'Interpreting European Law: Judicial Adjudication in a Context of Constitutional Pluralism' (2008) 1 European Journal of Legal Studies 137; T Horsley, 'Reflections on the Role of the Court of Justice as the "Motor" of European Integration: Legal Limits to Judicial Lawmaking' (2013) 50 Common Market Law Review 931, 937.
[89] A Menon and S Weatherill, 'Democratic Politics in a Globalising World: Supranationalism and Legitimacy in the European Union' (2007) LSE, Law, Society and Economy Working Papers 13/2007.

output-oriented concept of legitimacy would point toward consequentialist and potentially innovative interpretation.'[90] Such critiques have been called 'instrumentalist' by van den Brink.[91] He draws attention to criticism of the CJEU's case law on citizens' rights and how support for the CJEU's reasoning is dependent on whether the outcome of the case coheres with the commentator's idea of justice.[92] Such an approach can lead to inconsistent approaches to norm interaction. The alternative would be to adopt a more formalistic approach, 'marked by an impersonal external standard that is beyond manipulation or subjection decision.'[93] This argument is revisited in Section 3.3 below in relation to the *lex specialis* principle.

A third distinction drawn by Beck is between 'scientific' and 'heuristic' accounts of legal reasoning.[94] Scientific accounts posit there to be only one correct way to reach a legal decision in a case: one must simply discover the answer. As Bobek notes, this approach to legal reasoning 'fuels the belief that there is a "proper" method for the Court to solve cases.'[95] Heuristic accounts on the other hand do not dispute that there are justifiable forms of legal argumentation. However, such methods cannot fully resolve cases and the emphasis is instead on 'reckonability' or predictability. Rather than propose a solution to all overlaps, my aim here is more limited in developing a normative justification for the use of the *lex specialis* principle.

Given the difficulties in developing a shared framework for evaluating CJEU reasoning, one might question whether any normative standard might simply collapse. Bengoetxea suggests it comes down to 'the ideology of judicial decision-making and . . . legal culture of the legal audience.'[96] Similarly, Bobek notes that 'what the proper method is, may often be heavily determined by inadvertent projections of own national approaches and conventions, however they might be couched in terms of an "European" legal tradition.'[97] The suggestion is that any normative standard will potentially, even inadvertently, betray one's own national preconceived notions regarding the judicial role. On this view, an attempt at developing a normative standard is futile. However, it is argued that we can find a normative standard from within the Treaties themselves.

[90] Conway (n 5) 96.
[91] M van den Brink, 'Justice, Legitimacy and the Authority of Legislation within the European Union' (2019) 82 Modern Law Review 293.
[92] ibid.
[93] Conway (n 5) 96.
[94] Beck (n 5).
[95] M Bobek, 'Legal Reasoning of the Court of Justice of the EU' (2014) 39 European Law Review 419.
[96] Bengoetxea (n 5) 132.
[97] Bobek (n 95) 418, 419.

3.2 Democracy and the principle of *lex specialis*

Given the CJEU's role in ensuring that the law is observed, we can look to the EU Treaties for guidance as to the appropriate methods of interpretation,[98] since they form a 'basic constitutional charter'[99] for the EU. Not only that—the Treaties have an 'uncharacteristic degree of normative power on the basis of the frequency, nature and scope of . . . repeated amendments'.[100] The Treaties can thus provide an external justification for prioritizing between interpretative methods and for the use of a particular methodology.

Looking to the EU's 'constitutional core' seems appropriate here.[101] According to Article 2 TEU, the EU is '*founded* upon human dignity, freedom, democracy, equality, the rule of law and respect for human rights' (my emphasis). Among Treaty provisions, Article 2 TEU is increasingly being given constitutional significance in the case law of the CJEU.[102] According to the CJEU, '[t]he values contained in Article 2 TEU have been identified and are shared by the Member States. They define the very identity of the European Union as a common legal order' and the EU 'must be able to defend those values'.[103] The methodology for resolving norm overlaps ought thus to be justified on the grounds of its coherence with the EU's founding values.

Democracy and the rule of law feature frequently in arguments over the correct principle of interpretation. A representative democracy requires in part that a legislature (or the Member States in drafting the Treaties) can 'translate its collective decisions into law' and that this translation 'does not break down between the promulgation and application or adjudication of the law'.[104] Democracy is thus often relied upon to support a more literal or originalist approach to interpretation.[105] Such approaches cannot assist in determining the relationship between norms but the commitment in EU law to democracy can be understood as mirroring the concerns of the *lex specialis* principle.

Underlying the principle of *lex specialis* is a concern to ensure respect for the intentions of the (constitutional) legislature. The *lex specialis* principle

[98] For arguments to this effect see T Horsley, *The Court of Justice of the European Union as an Institutional Actor: Judicial Lawmaking and Its Limits* (CUP 2018); V Velyvyte, *Judicial Authority in EU Internal Market Law: Implications for the Balance of Competences and Powers* (Hart 2022).

[99] *Kadi* (n 75) para 281. See also, Opinion 1/91 *Re the EEA Agreement* EU:C:1991:490, para 21.

[100] Horsley (n 98) 30.

[101] Bast and von Bogdandy (n 77).

[102] See Section 2.2.6 above.

[103] *Hungary v Parliament and Council* (n 76) para 127.

[104] Conway (n 5) 92.

[105] Conway (n 5) Chapter 3; Jakab (n 5) 27–28; Horsley (n 98), Chapter 4; van den Brink, *Legistlative Authority and Interpretation in the European Union* (n 6).

assumes that the legislature is aware of the earlier law and intends to overrule it.[106] The assumption is that a lawmaker, 'in regulating a specific area, wants to create special rules that trump the general rules in the field'.[107] In aiming to respect legislative intent, the principle builds upon more literal and originalist methods of interpretation, looking to both wording and context.

One possible objection is that respecting legislative intent does not necessarily justify the conclusion that either the more specific or the more recent norm should apply. For de Graaff 'it cannot be taken for granted that the legislature intended the specific rule to trump the general rule'.[108] Similarly, Milanovic considers it is a 'fiction' that the legislature 'could not possibly have intended to legislate two hierarchically equal norms that are ultimately contradictory'.[109] De Graaff highlights alternative readings of legislative intent such as for the more advantageous rule to apply.[110] He argues instead that we should examine whether the legislature intended for a particular rule to be exhaustive:[111] the question should always be one of interpretation, starting from the position that the legislature intended both rules to apply.[112] In many ways the objection contains the seeds of the response. A contextual assessment will often indicate the appropriateness of the principles, as discussed in Section 4 below.

3.3 The rule of law and the principle of *lex specialis*

A potential objection to the democratic justification for the principle of *lex specialis* is that this argument prioritizes democracy over other values in the Treaties. Why not, for instance, construe norms in a manner that protects fundamental rights or promotes substantive equality to the greatest possible extent? The vague[113] and multi-lingual[114] wording of the Treaties and the compromises inherent in secondary Union law[115] have been relied upon to justify a

[106] International Law Commission (n 49) point 226.
[107] Michaels and Pauwelyn (n 45) 354.
[108] De Graaff (n 7) 28.
[109] M Milanovic, 'The Lost Origins of *Lex Specialis*: Rethinking the Relationship between Human Rights and International Humanitarian Law' in JD Ohlin (ed), *Theoretical Boundaries of Armed Conflict and Human Rights* (CUP 2016) 78–117, 109.
[110] ibid.
[111] ibid.
[112] ibid.
[113] A Stone Sweet, *Judicial Construction of Europe* (OUP 2004) 24.
[114] E Paunio, *Legal Certainty in Multilingual EU Law: Language, Discourse and Reasoning at the European Court of Justice* (Routledge 2013).
[115] O Pollicino, 'Legal Reasoning of the Court of Justice in the Context of the Principle of Equality Between Judicial Activism and Self-Restraint' (2004) 5 GLJ 282, 288.

more purposive or teleological method of interpretation.[116] Presumably, such interpretative methods would subsume questions of norm inter-relationship. Overlapping norms would instead be construed so as to achieve the stated goal. Such approaches are evident in the case law of the CJEU and there are cases reconciling norms in a manner that enhances, for example, freedom of movement,[117] or consumer protection.[118]

The rule of law, also found in Article 2 TEU, provides a further justification for the principle of *lex specialis*. An approach to norm inter-relationship focused on the *outcome* would mean determining the inter-relationship of provisions in a manner that best achieves a stated goal.[119] Such an approach suffers from two core problems. First, there is a difficulty of selecting the appropriate standard. Second, and related, an approach based on outcome is far less predictable and thus presents problems from a rule of law perspective.

First, the problem with an approach based on the outcome is what value the CJEU should employ when construing overlapping norms. Several values appear in the EU Treaties with seemingly equal status yet with the potential for conflict.[120] Respect for human rights and democracy can, for instance, be potentially viewed as in tension.[121] How should the CJEU select between these values in the case at hand? There is also a question of the level of generality at which the dispute is viewed. The CJEU is often criticized for prioritizing the objective of 'ever closer Union'.[122] Such teleological interpretation works at a very high level of generality.[123] Secondary legislation is also replete with values and goals that could also act a yardstick for evaluation. To return to *Commission v UK (Right to Reside)*,[124] introduced in Section 1, one could look at the case from the perspective of free movement. The legal bases of Directive 2004/38 and Regulation 883/2004 include Articles 21 and 48 TFEU, both of which are related to the free movement of EU nationals. This legal basis could be authority for interpreting overlapping provisions in a manner that promotes free movement. Lower-level goals can, however, also be found in the secondary laws themselves. For instance, Directive 2004/38 sets out both that

[116] ibid 288; J Basedow, 'The Judge's Role in European Integration: The Court of Justice and its Critics' in H Micklitz and B de Witte (eds), The European Court of Justice and the Autonomy of the Member States (Intersentia 2011) 65–79.

[117] Case C-287/05 *Hendrix* EU:C:2007:494.

[118] *Travel-Vac* (n 69).

[119] See Section 2.2.7 above.

[120] Beck (n 5) 175.

[121] J Waldron, 'The Core of the Case against Judicial Review' (2006) 115 Yale Law Journal 1346.

[122] Beck (n 5) 1219.

[123] See G Conway, 'Conflicts of Competence Norms in EU Law and the Legal Reasoning of the ECJ' (2010) 11 German Law Journal 966.

[124] *Commission v UK* (n 10).

'Union citizenship should be the fundamental status of nationals'[125] and that '[p]ersons exercising their right of residence should not, however, become an unreasonable burden'.[126] Again, the CJEU might select one of these goals as the guiding principle. Indeed, this was a critique of *Commission v UK*, that the decision evidenced 'a new teleological principle—the need to accommodate Member States' desires to discriminate, in order to avoid offending national welfare sensitivities'.[127]

Second, an approach based on outcome will be far less consistent and it will be far more difficult to predict the outcome. Conway notes the rule of law problems with such forms of interpretation. In his view, an instrumental approach to interpretation threatens the rule of law.[128] He notes the risk of subjectivity 'since abstract and general provisions can always be interpreted at a sufficiently high level of generality to in effect give judges great leeway and a de facto discretion'.[129] Indeed, this leeway is evident if we compare *Commission v UK (Right to Reside)* with earlier cases on access to social benefits that appear to prioritize the goals of free movement and equal treatment.[130] Applying the principle of *lex specialis* removes the risk of selectivity between goals and ensures greater predictability in decision-making.

4. Operationalizing the Principle of *Lex Specialis*

4.1 General considerations

It is not possible within the scope of this chapter to set out all circumstances in which the CJEU ought to adopt the *lex specialis* principle. What the following discussion does is to set out the basic parameters of when the principle would be expected to apply and its interaction with other possible approaches to overlaps. Given that the *lex specialis* principle is not found in the Treaties, identifying the specific contours of the rule is difficult. However, the *lex specialis* principle is already found—explicitly and implicitly—in the case law of the CJEU and existing practice will form the starting point of the analysis.

125 Recital 3.
126 Recital 10.
127 O'Brien (n 11) 240.
128 Conway (n 5) 115.
129 ibid.
130 See, eg, Case C-85/96 *Martínez Sala* EU:C:1998:217; *Hendrix* (n 117).

In general terms, the principle of *lex specialis* will either be 'an application of a general standard in a given circumstance'[131] or 'a *modification, overruling* or *setting aside*'[132] of the *lex generalis*. The *lex specialis* must also 'contain all the elements of the *lex generalis* and at least one additional element'.[133] Greater detail or specificity is thus not. For one norm to be a modification on another, those provisions must also have the per se sufficient 'same subject matter'.[134] The problem is that the principle of *lex specialis* does not, in and of itself, provide any criteria for identifying when two or more norms have the same subject matter.[135] Without an articulated system for identifying when the principle of *lex specialis* applies, there is a danger that the principle may become a guise for highly political decisions.[136] There is also a question of what role the *lex generalis* ought to play, especially in cases in which no conflict exists between provisions. The prioritization of the more specific norm does not invalidate the *lex generalis*.[137]

4.2 Establishing a relationship of specificity

Legal scholarship proposes several different factors that ought to be taken into account when determining if the principle of *lex specialis* applies. The first is whether the relevant norms pursue the same goal;[138] Pulkowski argues that where 'several treaties have been made in pursuit of different societal goals, it should not be presumed that states intended to privilege one policy goal over another one simply by virtue of opting for a more specific formulation under one of the treaties'.[139] A second factor looks to the context of the overlapping norms and their place within a wider system.[140] CJEU case law demonstrates a similar methodology for establishing a relationship of specificity.

[131] International Law Commission (n 49) para 88.
[132] ibid.
[133] De Graaff (n 7) 27.
[134] Fitzmaurice (n 51) 236; Pauwelyn (n 3) 389; A Lindroos, 'Addressing Norm Conflicts in a Fragmented Legal System: The Doctrine of *Lex Specialis*' (2005) 74 Nordic Journal of International Law 27, 44; International Law Commission (n 49) para 116; Pulkowski (n 48) 327.
[135] Lindroos (n 118) 42; N Prud'homme, 'Lex Specialis: Oversimplifying a More Complex and Multifaceted Relationship?' (2007) 40 Israel Law Review 356, 380; Simma and Pulkowski (n 56) 489.
[136] Lindroos (n 118) 42.
[137] International Law Commission, *Fragmentation of International Law: Difficulties Arising from the Diversification and Expansion of International Law: Conclusions* ((18 July 2006) UN Doc A/CN4/L702, 9.
[138] Pulkowski (n 48) 328.
[139] ibid.
[140] International Law Commission (n 49) para 119.

The need for measures to pursue a similar objective was made clear in *Hansen*.[141] The CJEU found a *lex specialis* relationship between Article 37 EEC (now Article 37 TFEU) on state monopolies and Articles 92 and 93 EEC (now Articles 92 and 93 TFEU) on state aids. Key to establishing this relationship was 'that those provisions pursue the same objective, which is to ensure that the two categories of intervention on the part of a Member State, namely action by a State monopoly and the granting of aid, do not distort the conditions of competition within the common market or create discrimination against the products or trade of other Member States'.[142] Conversely, in *Otis*, the CJEU held that where rules concern 'distinct questions' the principle of *lex specialis* does not apply.'[143] However, in that case the difference was an obvious one and concerned Treaty provisions relating to very different issues. The applicants argued that a relationship of specialty existed between Articles 317 and 322 TFEU; the former concerns the powers of the EU institutions to establish and implement the EU's budget, while Article 335 TFEU confers legal capacity on the EU and governs the way it is represented.[144]

4.3 Role of the *lex generalis*

Where there is a conflict between norms (including between overlapping norms), the principle of *lex specialis* requires that the more specific norm prevails at the expense of the more general norm. The CJEU in *Cipra* adopted a similar understanding of the principle of *lex specialis*. A conflict arose between two different provisions of a regulation relating to road transport.[145] The first provision required drivers transporting goods by road to have at least eleven consecutive hours of daily rest in a twenty-four-hour period. The second provision set out a different minimum rest period for those situations when a vehicle has two drivers. In that instance there is a minimum rest period of eight consecutive hours every thirty hours. The dispute in *Cipra* concerned a vehicle with two drivers who had each complied with the rest periods of eight hours;

[141] *Hansen* (n 59).
[142] ibid.
[143] Case C-199/11 *Otis and Others* EU:C:2012:684, para 32. See also Case C-2/56 *Geitling v High Authority* EU:C:1957:4, [1957] ECR 3, 20.
[144] *Otis and Others* (n 143) para 32.
[145] Council Regulation 3820/85 of 20 December 1985 on the harmonization of certain social legislation relating to road transport [1985] OJ L 370/1.

rest during a period of thirty hours but not with the requirement of eleven hours of rest in twenty-four hours. The CJEU held that the drivers did not also need to comply with the requirement of eleven consecutive hours of rest since, given the context,[146] the provision on rest periods for vehicles with two drivers was 'a *lex specialis* that prevails'[147] over the other norm.

Where there is a conflict between norms and the more general rule sets out guiding principles that are implemented by the *lex specialis*, the *lex generalis* may still play a role in determining the outcome of a case. In this context, 'the specific rule should be read and understood within the confines or against the background of the general standard, typically as an elaboration, updating or a technical specification of the latter.'[148] In *Mayer Parry Recycling*, the CJEU recognized the continuing role of the *lex generalis* as an aid to the interpretation of the *lex specialis*. In that case, a framework directive on waste management set out several general principles, which were later implemented by a specific directive on packaging waste. When discussing the operation of the principle of *lex specialis* in that case, the CJEU held that the more specific rules 'prevail . . . in situations which [they] specifically seek . . . to regulate.'[149] However, the *lex generalis* 'remain[ed] very important for the interpretation and application' of the *lex specialis*.[150] The same is true where the *lex specialis* derogates from the *lex generalis*. In *KS and KD*, the CJEU noted that Article 24(1) TEU and Article 275 TFEU amount to 'a derogation from the rule of the general jurisdiction which Article 19 TEU confers on the [CJEU] to ensure that in the interpretation and application of the Treaties the law is observed' as a result, they must 'be interpreted narrowly'.[151]

In the absence of a conflict, Pauwelyn argues that, outside of norm conflicts, the principle of *lex specialis* still offers some guidance to judges. The principle operates as a reason for courts to start by examining the more specific rule.[152] In many ways this reflects the underlying logic of the *lex specialis* principle as aiming to identify the more efficacious norm. However,

[146] *Cipra* (n 60) para 35.
[147] ibid para 40. See also, *Mayer Parry Recycling* (n 59) para 57; *Siig* (n 60) para 16; *Belgium v Commission* (n 60) para 39; *Commission v Germany* (n 60) para 40; *Thames Water Utilities* (n 59) para 39.
[148] International Law Commission (n 49) para 56.
[149] *Mayer Parry Recycling* (n 59) para 57.
[150] ibid.
[151] Case C-29/22 P *KS and KD* EU:C:2024:725, para 62.
[152] Pauwelyn (n 3) 411.

> to say that the *lex specialis* must be examined first does not amount to saying that the *lex generalis* no longer applies. Both norms apply and it makes logical sense to examine first the *lex specialis*. But nothing precludes that the *lex generalis* is still relevant and adds certain rights or obligations.[153]

Where overlapping norms accumulate, then, the expectation is that the CJEU will begin by analysing the more specific norm. Should that norm not apply, however, there is nothing to prevent the more general norm applying.

5. Conclusion

This chapter draws attention to norm overlaps in EU law and the methodologies for resolving such overlaps. The method of prioritizing between or combining norms is of fundamental importance. Should a judge choose to prioritize just one norm then '[f]rom a hermeneutic point of view, the choice of the applicable provisions is crucial because the rest of the reasoning process will depend on the selected provision'.[154] This is especially so should the relevant provisions have a differing scope of application. If norms are somehow combined, then again this may alter the outcome of the case.[155]

Despite the importance of norm inter-relationship, normative assessments of CJEU reasoning have often focused upon textual interpretation, and generally the interpretation of Treaties.[156] This chapter has sought to set out how democracy and the rule of law, as part of the EU's constitutional core, can provide external justification for the principle of *lex specialis* in EU law. While not all cases involving overlaps between norms of the same formal rank can be resolved utilizing the *lex specialis* principle,[157] where provisions have the same subject matter it offers a more objective standard.

[153] ibid. Similarly, the International Law Commission notes how '[t]he application of the special law does not normally extinguish the relevant general law' citing *Military and Paramilitary Activities in and against Nicaragua (Nicaragua v United States of America) (Merits)* ICJ Reports 1986, para 179 in support (International Law (n 49), para 82).

[154] Bengoetxea, MacCormick, and Moral Soriano (n 3) 53.

[155] De Graaff (n 7).

[156] For a notable exception, see van den Brink, *Legislative Authority and Interpretation in the European Union* (n 6).

[157] Hancox (n 25) 1092.

References

Ahmed F and Perry A, 'Constitutional Statutes' (2016) 37 Oxford Journal of Legal Studies 461

Basedow J, 'The Judge's Role in European Integration: The Court of Justice and Its Critics' in H Micklitz and B de Witte (eds), *The European Court of Justice and the Autonomy of the Member States* (Intersentia 2011)

Bast J, *On the Grammar of EU Law: Legal Instruments* (Jean Monnet Working Paper 9/03, 2003)

Bast J, 'Legal Instruments' in A von Bogdandy and J Bast (eds), *Principles of European Constitutional Law* (Hart 2006)

Bast J and von Bogdandy A, 'The Constitutional Core of the Union: On the CJEU's New, Principled Constitutionalism' (2024) 61 Common Market Law Review 1471

Beck G, *The Legal Reasoning of the Court of Justice of the EU* (Hart 2012)

Beck G, 'Judicial Activism in the Court of Justice of the EU' (2017) 36(2) University of Queensland Law Journal 333

Bengoetxea J, *The Legal Reasoning of the European Court of Justice: Towards a European Jurisprudence* (OUP 1993)

Bengoetxea J, MacCormick N, and Moral Soriano L, 'Integration and Integrity in the Legal Reasoning of the European Court of Justice' in G de Búrca and J Weiler (eds), *The European Court of Justice* (OUP 2001)

Blix H and Emerson JH, *The Treaty Maker's Handbook* (Oceana Publications 1973)

Bobek M, 'Legal Reasoning of the Court of Justice of the EU' (2014) 39 European Law Review 418

Bonelli M and Claes M, 'Judicial Politics in the EU Rule of Law Crisis' in M Dawson, B de Witte, and E Muir (eds), *Revisiting Judicial Politics in the European Union* (Edward Elgar Publishing 2024)

Borgen CJ, 'Treaty Conflicts and Normative Fragmentation' in D Hollis (ed), *The Oxford Guide to Treaties* (OUP 2012)

Carrillo Salcedo JA, 'Reflections on the Existence of a Hierarchy of Norms in International Law' (1997) 8 European Journal of International Law 583

Conway G, 'Conflicts of Competence Norms in EU Law and the Legal Reasoning of the ECJ' (2010) 11 German Law Journal 966

Conway G, *The Limits of Legal Reasoning and the European Court of Justice* (CUP 2012)

Craig P, 'Constitutionalising Constitutional Law: *HS2*' [2014] Public Law 373

Czapliński W and Danilenko G, 'Conflicts of Norms in International Law' (1990) 21 Netherlands Yearbook of International Law 3

Davies G, 'Legislative Control of the European Court of Justice' (2014) 51 Common Market Law Review 1579

de Graaff R, *Concurrence in European Private Law* (Eleven International Publishing 2020)

de Vattel E, *The Law of Nations or Principles of the Law of Nature*, vol 2 (Sweet, Stevens and Maxwell 1834)

Dougan M, 'Judicial Activism or Constitutional Interaction? Policy Making by the ECJ in the Field of Union Citizenship' in HW Micklitz and B de Witte (eds), *The European Court of Justice and the Autonomy of the Member States* (Intersentia 2011)

Dworkin R, *Taking Rights Seriously* (Duckworth 1978)

Fitzmaurice G, 'Treaty Interpretation and Other Treaty Points' (1957) 33 British Yearbook of International Law 203

Grotius H, *The Rights of War and Peace* (Liberty Fund 2005)

Gualco E, *General Principles of EU Law as a Passe-Partout Key within the Constitutional Edifice of the European Union: Are the Benefits Worth the Side Effects?* (2016) Birmingham Law School Institute of European Law Working Paper 05/2016

Hamner Hill H, 'A Functional Taxonomy of Normative Conflict' (1987) 6 Law and Philosophy 227

Hancox E, 'Judicial Approaches to Norm Overlaps in EU Law: A Case Study on the Free Movement of Workers' (2021) 58 Common Market Law Review 1057

Hartley T, 'The European Court, Judicial Objectivity and the Constitution of the European Union' (1996) 112 Law Quarterly Review 95

Hirsch M, 'Interactions between Investment and Non-Investment Obligations' in P Muchlinski, F Ortino, and C Schreuer (eds), *The Oxford Handbook of International Investment Law* (OUP 2008)

Hofmann HCC and Mihaescu BC, 'The Relation between the Charter's Fundamental Rights and the Unwritten General Principles: Good Administration as the Test Case' (2013) 9 European Constitutional Law Review 73

Horsley T, 'Reflections on the Role of the Court of Justice as the "Motor" of European Integration: Legal Limits to Judicial Lawmaking' (2013) 50 Common Market Law Review 931

Horsley T, *The Court of Justice of the European Union as an Institutional Actor: Judicial Lawmaking and Its Limits* (CUP 2018)

International Law Commission, *Fragmentation of International Law: Difficulties Arising from the Diversification and Expansion of International Law* (13 April 2006) UN Doc A/CN4/L682

International Law Commission, *Fragmentation of International Law: Difficulties Arising from the Diversification and Expansion of International Law: Conclusions* (18 July 2006) UN Doc A/CN4/L702

Jakab A, *European Constitutional Language* (CUP 2016)

Jenks W, 'The Conflict of Law-Making Treaties' (1953) 30 British Yearbook of International Law 401

Komárek J, 'Legal Reasoning in EU Law' in D Chalmers and A Arnull (eds), *The Oxford Handbook of European Union Law* (OUP 2015)

Lindroos A, 'Addressing Norm Conflicts in a Fragmented Legal System: The Doctrine of *Lex Specialis*' (2005) 74 Nordic Journal of International Law 27

Menon A and Weatherill S, 'Democratic Politics in a Globalising World: Supranationalism and Legitimacy in the European Union' (2007) LSE, Law, Society and Economy Working Papers 13/2007.

Michaels R and Pauwelyn J, 'Conflict of Norms or Conflict of Laws: Different Techniques in the Fragmentation of Public International Law' (2011–12) 22 Duke Journal of Comparative & International Law 349

Milanovic M, 'The Lost Origins of *Lex Specialis*: Rethinking the Relationship between Human Rights and International Humanitarian Law' in JD Ohlin (ed), *Theoretical Boundaries of Armed Conflict and Human Rights* (CUP 2016)

Muir E, *EU Equality Law: The First Fundamental Rights Policy of the EU* (OUP 2018)

Mus JB, 'Conflicts between Treaties in International Law' (1998) 45 Netherlands International Law Review 208

Neill P, 'The European Court of Justice: a Case Study in Judicial Activism' (European Policy Forum 1995)

Ni Chaoimh E, *The Legislative Priority Rule and the EU Internal Market for Goods: A Constitutional Approach* (OUP 2022)

Nolan D and Oliphant K, *Lunney & Oliphant's Tort Law: Text and Materials* (7th edn, OUP 2023)
O'Brien C, 'The ECJ Sacrifices EU Citizenship in Vain: *Commission v United Kingdom*' (2016) 54(1) Common Market Law Review 209
Paunio E, *Legal Certainty in Multilingual EU Law: Language, Discourse and Reasoning at the European Court of Justice* (Routledge 2013)
Pauwelyn J, *Conflict of Norms in Public International Law: How WTO Law Relates to Other Rules of International Law* (CUP 2003)
Poiares Maduro M, 'Interpreting European Law: Judicial Adjudication in a Context of Constitutional Pluralism' (2008) 1 European Journal of Legal Studies 137
Pollicino O, 'Legal Reasoning of the Court of Justice in the Context of the Principle of Equality Between Judicial Activism and Self-Restraint' (2004) 5 GLJ 282
Prud'homme N, 'Lex Specialis: Oversimplifying a More Complex and Multifaceted Relationship?' (2007) 40 Israel Law Review 356
Pulkowski D, *The Law and Politics of International Regime Conflict* (OUP 2014)
Rasmussen H, *On Law and Policy in the European Court of Justice: A Comparative Study in Judicial Policymaking* (Nijhoff 1986)
Semmelmann C, 'General Principles in EU Law between a Compensatory Role and an Intrinsic Value' (2013) 19 European Law Journal 458
Shelton D, 'International Law and "Relative Normativity"' in M Evans (ed), *International Law* (4th edn, OUP 2014)
Shelton D, 'Normative Hierarchy in International Law' (2006) 100 American Journal of International Law 291
Simma B and D Pulkowski, 'Of Planets and the Universe: Self-Contained Regimes in International Law' (2006) 17 European Journal of International Law 483
Stone Sweet A, *Judicial Construction of Europe* (OUP 2004)
Syrpis P (ed), *The Judiciary, the Legislature and the EU Internal Market* (CUP 2012)
Syrpis P , 'The Relationship between Primary and Secondary Law in the EU' (2015) 52 Common Market Law Review 461
Taylor A, 'Concurrent Duties' (2019) 82 Modern Law Review 17
van den Brink M, 'Justice, Legitimacy and the Authority of Legislation within the European Union' (2019) 82 Modern Law Review 293
van den Brink M, *Legislative Authority and Interpretation in the European Union* (OUP 2024)
Velyvyte V, *Judicial Authority in EU Internal Market Law: Implications for the Balance of Competences and Powers* (Hart 2022)
Vidmar J, 'Norm Conflicts and Hierarchy in International Law: Towards a Vertical International Legal System?' in E de Wet and J Vidmar (eds), *Hierarchy in International Law: The Place of Human Rights* (OUP 2012)
Vranes E, 'The Definition of Norm Conflict in International Law and Legal Theory' (2006) 17 European Journal of International Law 395

5

Primary Law as Pyramid: The Case for Substantive Hierarchies in EU Primary Law

Luke Dimitrios Spieker[*]

1. Introduction

Any law student across Europe will be well familiar with a particular geometrical shape: the *pyramid*. Today, the idea that a legal system consists of several, hierarchical levels—thus taking the shape of a pyramid—has a solid grip on our legal imagination. Once we embrace this idea, it appears difficult to go back and understand a legal system in any other way. Nevertheless, a growing trend suggests moving beyond the pyramid. Globalization and differentiation have fostered interactions among different legal systems that are hard to perceive in hierarchical terms. This is visible in the European Union as well, where many struggle to perceive the Union's own law and its interaction with the Member States' legal systems as hierarchical system (Section 2). My argument, however, goes into a different direction: embracing hierarchies within *primary law* may help reduce much of its complexity and eventually foster the Union's development into a more mature constitutional system.

To substantiate my hypothesis, this chapter proceeds in three steps. First, it will explain *why* there is a need to restructure the Treaties (Section 3). Today's primary law is complex, fragmented, and detailed. Importantly, there is no distinction between provisions of genuinely constitutional content and those that lack constitutional character. This creates challenges for its interpretation and application. Conventional methodological tools, such as systematic interpretation or balancing, reach their limits when all provisions of primary law are

* This chapter builds on Luke Dimitrios Spieker, *EU Values Before the Court of Justice* (OUP 2023) 87 ff, 107 ff.

Luke Dimitrios Spieker, *Primary Law as Pyramid: The Case for Substantive Hierarchies in EU Primary Law* In: *The Reasoning of the Court of Justice of the EU*. Edited by: Alezini Loxa and Luigi Lonardo,
Oxford University Press. © Luke Dimitrios Spieker 2026. DOI: 10.1093/9780198983002.003.0007

treated as being of equal rank. Further, such an approach may produce outcomes that are hardly compatible with the achieved stage of integration.

In a second step, this chapter will develop a proposal for *how* the Court could respond to these challenges by reorganizing the Treaties in hierarchical terms (Section 4). Instead of perceiving the myriad of Treaty provisions as norms of *formally* equal rank, this contribution suggests approaching the Treaties from a *substantive* perspective. Such a shift reveals that the Treaties form a nuanced, hierarchical system. At the heart of this proposal are the founding values in Article 2 TEU, which have taken a central place in the Court's jurisprudence. During the past decade, the Luxembourg judges have begun to operationalize these values.[1] Even if their justiciability remains controversial,[2] the Court has acknowledged that 'Article 2 TEU is not merely a statement of policy guidelines or intentions, but contains values which . . . are given concrete expression in principles containing legally binding obligations for the Member States'.[3] Their function as interpretative tool is therefore beyond doubt.[4]

This turn to values should go hand in hand with a turn to hierarchies. The Court has emphasized that Article 2 TEU enshrines the Union's 'constitutional identity'.[5] Accordingly, these values seem to stand at the summit of the EU legal order and outline the basic features of the Union's constitutional framework. At the same time, these values are given more specific expression by other Treaty provisions. This allows the Court to introduce substantive hierarchies between those Treaty provisions that concretize an Article 2 TEU value and those that do not. This could lead to a threefold, hierarchical division of primary law: Article 2 TEU at its summit (the EU's constitutional core), provisions giving expression to a value on the second level (the EU's constitutional law), and the rest of primary law on a third one.

In a third step, this chapter will examine the implications of this scheme for legal interpretation and resolution of conflicts among Treaty provisions (Section 5). Hierarchies imply precedence, constitutions imply supremacy. Based on these insights, the Court can interpret Treaty provisions in light of higher-ranking ones and resolve conflicts not by balancing, but by precedence. As this chapter shows, Luxembourg's case law already features some of these suggestions. After tracing the Court's judicial practice in this respect,

[1] For an overview, see Luke Dimitrios Spieker, *EU Values before the Court of Justice* (OUP 2023).
[2] See only Case C-769/22 *Commission v Hungary (Valeurs de l'Union).*
[3] Case C-156/21 *Hungary v Parliament and Council* EU:C:2022:97, para 232.
[4] See the chapter by Petric in this volume.
[5] Case C-156/21 *Hungary v Parliament and Council* EU:C:2022:97, para 127.

the chapter will explore trajectories for a future application of my proposal (Section 6).

Before diving into these issues, it should be stressed that this proposal is limited in three ways. First, it concerns only the *internal* relationship of provisions of *primary* law, not their interplay with *secondary* law or the *external* relationship with the legal orders of the Member States or international law. Second, it is less addressed to the Union's *political* institutions, but rather aims at providing an avenue for a *judicial* reorganization of primary law. Third, and flowing from this focus, the proposal suggests the introduction of *substantive*, not *formal*, hierarchies, which would require Treaty amendments.

2. Theory

2.1 Thinking in hierarchies

The idea of understanding a legal order as a hierarchical structure goes back to the Vienna school of legal thought and was advanced in particular by Adolf Merkl and Hans Kelsen.[6] Leaving aside the contentious issue of a 'basic norm', the crucial insight was that provisions of a legal order can be rearranged in a hierarchical setting. This hierarchy has a direct impact on the validity of legal provisions: higher-ranking law conditions the adoption of lower-ranking law (creation) and takes priority in case of conflict (derogation).[7] Such a reasoning can fulfil several functions in a legal system.

First, it is intimately connected to the rise of constitutional democracy. Initially, many European constitutions were documents of subordinate legal significance. The second half of the twentieth century heralded a change in this respect. The 'Stufenbau' provided a theoretical basis for the primacy of the constitution.[8] And indeed, today most European constitutions unfold some

[6] See eg Hans Kelsen, *Pure Theory of Law* (University of California Press 1967) and Adolf Merkl, 'Prolegomena einer Theorie des rechtlichen Stufenbaues' in Alfred Verdross (ed), *Gesellschaft, Recht und Staat. Festschrift Hans Kelsen zum 50. Geburtstage gewidmet* (Springer 1931) 252.

[7] In detail, see András Jakab, *European Constitutional Language* (CUP 2016) 329 ff. Today, this idea can be found in almost every European jurisdiction, see eg Thomas Vesting, *Legal Theory* (Hart 2018) 39 ff; Eric Millard, *Théorie générale du droit*, 2nd edn (LGDJ 2022) 78 ff; Norberto Bobbio, *Studi per una teoria generale del diritto* (Giappichelli 2012). Of course, every legal order comes with its specificities, see eg Denys de Béchillon, 'Sur la conception française de la hiérarchie des normes' (1994) 32 Revue interdisciplinaire d'études juridiques 81.

[8] Véronique Champeil-Desplats, 'Hiérarchie des normes, principe justificatif de la suprematie de la constitution' in Michel Troper and Dominique Chagnollaud (eds), *Traité international de droit constitutionnel*, vol 1 (Dalloz 2012) 733; Christoph Grabenwarter, 'Die Verfassung in der Hierarchie der Rechtsordnung' in ibid and Otto Depenheuer (eds), *Verfassungstheorie* (Mohr Siebeck 2010) 391, para 32.

kind of 'primacy', 'Vorrang', 'primauté', 'supremacía', or 'supremazia'.[9] This had important implications for modern constitutional thought, such as the subordination of ordinary law to the constitution, the rise of constitutional courts, and eventually a reinforcement of constitutional rights. Overall, this primacy led—in varying degrees—to a constitutionalization of the legal order.[10]

Second, hierarchies can foster a legal system's consistency and coherence. Coherence goes beyond the mere absence of contradiction and amounts to something more: provisions of a legal order should 'make sense' as a whole. As Neil MacCormick argued, legal texts can only be coherent in relation to something.[11] Hierarchical relationships can provide this 'something', namely points of reference that reduce complexity in a legal system.

Ultimately, the concept of hierarchies is not restricted to formal understandings, but remains open to more nuanced, substantive approaches. In this sense, every legal order will know some kind of *substantive hierarchies* among provisions at the same formal level. Even if certain provisions might be of equal *formal* rank, this does not mean that they are also of equal *substantive* significance. This significance is established according to the content of legal provisions.[12] Some speak of 'material', 'normative', or 'axiological' hierarchies.[13] In international law, the International Law Commission refers to 'informal' hierarchies that do not follow from legislative enactment but emerge as a '"natural" aspect of legal reasoning'.[14]

The effect of substantive hierarchies is softer and unfolds especially in constitutional adjudication. If two constitutional provisions of equal formal, but diverging substantive, rank collide, this does not affect the validity of the inferior one. Yet, it may lead to an interpretation of substantively inferior provisions in light of substantively superior ones. Such an approach can be observed in many jurisdictions, where constitutional courts identified—sometimes without any textual support—hierarchical structures within the constitution.

[9] Elena Bindi and Mario Perini, 'Legal Effect of Constitutions' (paras 69 ff) and Maria Elvira Méndez-Pinedo, 'Supremacy/Primacy' (paras 34 ff) both in Rainer Grote and others (eds), *Max Planck Encyclopedia of Comparative Constitutional Law* (OUP 2017).

[10] See eg Mattias Kumm, 'Who Is Afraid of the Total Constitution?' (2006) 7 GLJ 341.

[11] Neil MacCormick, *Rhetoric and the Rule of Law: A Theory of Legal Reasoning* (OUP 2010) 189, 193. See also András Jakab, 'The Reasoning of Constitutional Courts in Europe' in Armin von Bogdandy and others (eds), *The Max Planck Handbooks in European Public Law*, vol IV (OUP 2023) 169, 182 ff.

[12] On such 'content-based hierarchies', see Cesare Pinelli, 'Theories Concerning the Hierarchy of Norms' in Grote and others (n 9) paras 32 ff.

[13] See eg Uwe Volkmann, *Grundzüge einer Verfassungslehre* (Mohr Siebeck 2013) 93 ff; Orlando Scarcello, 'On the Role of Normative Hierarchies in Constitutional Reasoning' (2018) 31 Ratio Juris 346, 349 ff; Riccardo Guastini, 'Gerarchie normative' (2013) 21 revus 57, 61.

[14] International Law Commission, Fragmentation of International Law, A/CN.4/L.682 (13 April 2006) para 85.

Overarching conceptions such as those of a constitutional core or identity,[15] 'Verfassungsidentität' in Germany,[16] 'principi supremi' in Italy,[17] an 'invisible constitution' in Hungary,[18] or the 'basic structure' in India[19] provide vivid illustrations of these attempts.

2.2 Demise of hierarchies?

Despite its success, the hierarchical understanding of a legal system has become subject to growing criticism. For one, the concept is often considered out of touch with today's realities. Globalization and differentiation of societies generate more complex legal orders that can no longer be grasped using the straightforward concept of hierarchies.[20] As such, many have started to broaden their imagination and develop alternative ideas. Some have moved towards 'legal networks'; others suggest thinking in 'legal spaces' or 'organized clouds'.[21] These approaches aim at providing more flexible and inclusive understandings for transnational or hybrid legal phenomena.

This critique becomes even stronger in the EU context. Many reject hierarchical thinking as too state-centred and simplistic to adequately grasp the Union's complex and polycentric character. Along these lines, scholars often invoke the 'problem of translation' from state-based underpinnings to spheres beyond the state.[22] These objections centre on the relationship of EU and

[15] For a comparative assessment of European jurisdictions, see Christian Calliess and Gerhard van der Schyff (eds), *Constitutional Identity in a Europe of Multilevel Constitutionalism* (CUP 2019).

[16] See eg BVerfG, Judgment of 30 June 2009, 2 BvE 2/08—*Lisbon*, paras 208 ff. In detail, Monika Polzin, 'Constitutional Identity, Unconstitutional Amendments and the Idea of Constituent Power: The Development of the Doctrine of Constitutional Identity in German Constitutional Law' (2016) 14 I-CON 411.

[17] See eg Corte Costituzionale, 1146/1988 (IT:COST:1988:1146) para 2.1. In detail, Pietro Faraguna, *Ai confini della Costituzione. Principi supremi e identità costituzionale* (Franco Angeli 2015).

[18] See eg the concurring opinion of Judge Sólyom in Hungarian Constitutional Court, Decision 23/1990 (X. 31.) AB. In detail, Gábor Halmai, 'Silence of Transitional Constitutions: The "Invisible Constitution" Concept of the Hungarian Constitutional Court' (2018) 16 I-CON 969.

[19] See eg *Kesavananda Bharati v State of Kerala* [1973] Supp SCR 1. In detail, Sudhir Krishnaswamy, *Democracy and Constitutionalism in India: A Study of the Basic Structure Doctrine* (OUP 2011).

[20] Through time, see eg René David, 'Sources of Law' in Kötz Zweigert and Ulrich Drobnig (eds), *International Encyclopedia of Comparative Law*, vol 2 (Mohr Siebeck 1981) para 403; Andreas Fischer-Lescano and Gunther Teubner, 'Regime-Collisions: The Vain Search for Legal Unity in the Fragmentation of Global Law' (2004) 25 Michigan Journal of International Law 999; Guillaume Tusseau, 'Debating Legal Pluralism and Constitutionalism: New Trajectories for Legal Theory in the Global Age' in Katharina Boele-Woelki and others (eds), *General Reports of the XXth General Congress of the International Academy of Comparative Law* (Springer 2021) 507.

[21] See eg François Ost and Michel Van de Kerchove, *De la pyramide au réseau?* (Presses univ. Saint-Louis Bruxelles 2002) 539, Dana Burchardt, 'The Concept of Legal Space' (2022) 11 Global Constitutionalism 518, or Mireille Delmas-Marty, *Ordering Pluralism* (Hart 2009) 149 ff.

[22] See only Kaarlo Tuori, 'European Constitutionalism' in Roger Masterman and Robert Schütze (eds), *The Cambridge Companion to Comparative Constitutional Law* (CUP 2019) 521, 528.

national law, where pluralist approaches have gained much ground.[23] Such approaches reject the idea of clear hierarchies and favour more flexible conceptualizations. Some use the picture of a 'mobile' to emphasize that the relationship among the different legal orders and their institutions remains in constant motion.[24] Others speak of 'heterarchy' instead of hierarchy.[25]

At the same time, the concept of hierarchies seems only partially implemented within the EU legal order itself. The Treaties are formally superior to secondary legislation, which is adopted following legal bases, procedures, and limitations stipulated in primary law.[26] Things become less clear, though, when looking at the internal relations among provisions of primary law. While many proposed revising the Treaties so as to distinguish between provisions of constitutional and ordinary character,[27] such a revision never materialized. Formally, the two Treaties, TEU and TFEU, have 'the same legal value' (Article 1(3) TEU). This applies also to the protocols and annexes that form 'an integral part' of primary law (Article 51 TEU). In this sense, the Court of Justice refers to the Treaties not in terms of vertical hierarchies but rather in a more horizontal manner as a 'network of principles, rules and mutually interdependent legal relations'.[28]

Against this backdrop, rethinking primary law in terms of substantive hierarchies might seem outdated, naïve, or outright *contra legem*. Yet, my argument goes in the opposite direction. First, the objections outlined before do not unfold the same force in the context of primary law. Much of the critique focuses on hierarchies among *different* legal orders, not interactions within *one* legal system. Second, it cannot be denied that all provisions of primary law have the same formal rank. Introducing a formal hierarchy among them would require Treaty change. Still, that does not exclude a relation of substantive precedence among them. As Armin von Bogdandy and Jürgen Bast have noted, the 'formal *equality* of norms does not imply their substantive *equivalence*'.[29]

[23] For an overview, see Hugo Canihac, 'From Constitutional Pyramid to Constitutional Pluralism' in Jan Komárek (ed), *European Constitutional Imaginaries* (OUP 2023) 160.

[24] Andreas Voßkuhle, 'Pyramid or Mobile?' in *Dialogue between Judges* (Council of Europe 2014) 36.

[25] Daniel Halberstam, 'Constitutional Heterarchy' in Jeffrey L Dunoff and Joel P Trachtman (eds), *Ruling the World?* (CUP 2009) 326.

[26] For exceptions and possible reversals, see eg Politis in this volume.

[27] See eg European Parliament, Resolution on the constitutionalisation of the Treaties (25 October 2000), O.J. C 197/186, I. 4; EUI, *A Basic Treaty for the European Union: A Study of the Reorganisation of the Treaties* (15 May 2000) 1; Jean-Luc Dehaene, Richard von Weizsäcker, and David Simon, *The Institutional Implications of Enlargement* (18 October 1999) 12 ff.

[28] See eg Case C-284/16 *Achmea* EU:C:2018:158, para 33; Case C-621/18 *Wightman and Others* EU:C:2018:999, para 45; Opinion 1/17 *CETA* EU:C:2019:341, para 109.

[29] Armin von Bogdandy and Jürgen Bast, 'The Constitutional Core of the Union' (2024) 61 CML Rev 1471, 1492.

In this vein, my proposal concerns more subtle, judicial forms to reorganize a legal text—namely by introducing substantive hierarchies. In the following sections, this chapter will demonstrate *why* the Court should, and *how* it could, embrace such an approach.

3. *Why* the Court Should Embrace Substantive Hierarchies in Primary Law

As noted before, relations of substantive precedence are part and parcel of constitutional interpretation and an essential judicial tool to render a legal text manageable. In this sense, thinking in hierarchies remains a useful approach to reduce a legal system's complexity and foster its coherence. This need for coherence becomes particularly apparent in the EU context. Today's primary law is complex, fragmented, and detailed. As noted before, it consists of not only two Treaties of overlapping contents but also a myriad of protocols, reservations, and annexes that regulate in considerable detail a vast array of matters without differentiating between genuinely constitutional provisions and issues that would usually be regulated through legislation.[30] In judicial practice, this framework poses both a methodological and a substantive challenge that underline the need for substantive hierarchies.

3.1 Methodological challenge

Usually, there are three ways to establish coherence between provisions of equal formal rank and resolve conflicts among them. First, courts can employ a systematic, systemic, or contextual interpretation.[31] While textual, historical, or teleological interpretations identify the meaning of a provision, a systematic interpretation seeks to harmonize it with its legal context. This tool is of special relevance at the level of EU primary law.[32] Textual interpretations

[30] Some even argue that EU law is 'over-constitutionalized', see Dieter Grimm, 'The Democratic Costs of Constitutionalisation: The European Case' (2015) 21 ELJ 460. For a critique, see Luke Dimitrios Spieker, 'Was Grimm Wrong? Putting the Over-Constitutionalization of EU law to the Test' (2025) 26 GLJ 416.

[31] In detail Koen Lenaerts and José A Gutiérrez-Fons, *Les méthodes d'interprétation de la Cour de justice de l'Union européenne* (Bruylant 2020) 27 ff.

[32] Jan Komárek, 'Legal Reasoning in EU Law' in Damien Chalmers and Anthony Arnull (eds), *The Oxford Handbook of European Union Law* (OUP 2015) 29, 37 ff. See also Sebastian AE Martens, *Methodenlehre des Unionsrechts* (Mohr Siebeck 2013) 431 ff; Hans Kutscher, 'Methods of Interpretation as Seen by the European Court of Justice' Judicial and Academic Conference (27–28 September 1976), I-16, I-36 f, I-40.

are rendered difficult due to the indeterminacy of many Treaty provisions and by the fact that they are equally authentic in each of the twenty-four official language versions (Article 55 TEU). Further, the lack of openly accessible *travaux* for Lisbon often prevents the use of originalist interpretations. As such, the Court has emphasized time and again that a Treaty provision 'must be placed in its context'.[33] But how do we select the provisions that should serve as context? Despite judicial pronouncements to the contrary, this context can hardly cover 'provisions of Community law as a whole'.[34] The reason is simple: the more (potentially contradictory) provisions a court must take into account, the less guidance this method provides and the more we must rely on the judges' intuition in a particular case. This demonstrates the need to distinguish certain provisions that can serve as points of reference for a systematic interpretation.

Second, courts can revert to the methods of *lex posterior* or *lex specialis*.[35] Whereas *lex posterior* does not apply if all provisions have been adopted by the same author in a single stroke, *lex specialis* proves to be of limited value for the interpretation of primary law as well. On one hand, it heavily relies on the lawmakers' intentions by assuming that they wanted to create special rules that trump the general ones in the respective field.[36] In primary law, such an intention is difficult to determine. As noted before, the *travaux* to the Lisbon Treaty are not accessible and the preparatory documents to the European Convention will usually not contain any indications concerning specific norm conflicts. For that reason, scholars such as Emily Hancox have assumed the applicability of *lex specialis* only if explicitly stipulated.[37] On the other hand, the principle has a very limited field of application. It only applies when rules treat the 'same substantive matter',[38] not when they concern 'distinct' questions.[39] Moreover, one important situation, in which *lex specialis* is supposed to apply, concerns situations where a more specific rule gives concrete expression to a more general one.[40] In that case, however, the general rule continues to 'give

[33] See already Case 283/81 *CILFIT* EU:C:1982:335, para 20.
[34] ibid.
[35] See Hancox in this volume.
[36] Ralf Michaels and Joost Pauwelyn, 'Conflict of Norms or Conflict of Laws: Different Techniques in the Fragmentation of Public International Law' (2012) 22 Duke Journal of Comparative & International Law 349, 353.
[37] On Arts 18(1) TFEU and 21(1) TFEU or Art 52(2) of the Charter, see Emily Hancox, 'Judicial Approaches to Norm Overlaps in EU Law' (2021) 58 CML Rev 1057, 1074–78.
[38] ILC (n 14) paras 89, 116 ff. See also Dirk Pulkowski, *The Law and Politics of International Regime Conflict* (OUP 2014) 327.
[39] Case C-199/11 *Otis* EU:C:2012:684, para 32.
[40] ILC (n 14) paras 98 ff.

direction for the interpretation and application of the relevant special law' and may even prevail, especially if the specific rule would 'frustrate the purpose' of the general one.[41]

And third, a usual way of reconciling conflicting provisions of equal rank is balancing. This method can be traced in different variations in nearly all European jurisdictions, including the Court of Justice. In this spirit, the Luxembourg judges have balanced conflicting fundamental rights[42] and other interests protected by primary law, such as animal welfare, security, transparency, or fundamental freedoms.[43] Nevertheless, balancing is not only highly contested with regard to its rationality;[44] it also becomes increasingly problematic with the extent of provisions that have to be taken into account. Again, the logic is relatively simple: the more interests, guarantees, and policy choices gain constitutional status, the more trade-offs through balancing are required. This is likely to weaken the status of each constitutional provision and impedes the predictability and clarity of judicial outcomes. For that reason, many courts accord, from the outset, a greater weight to certain constitutionally protected interests. This is common practice both at the national[45] and the EU level.[46] At the same time, this shifts the balancing process into a relation of substantive precedence—in other words: one of substantive hierarchy.

3.2 Substantive challenge

Perceiving all Treaty provisions as being of equal rank thus impedes the workability of the Treaties. Moreover, it can produce outcomes that are hardly compatible with the achieved stage of integration. To recall, today's corpus of primary law consists of more than 400 articles and no less than 38 Protocols

[41] International Law Commission, Fragmentation of International Law, Report of the Study Group, A/CN.4/L.702 (18 July 2006) para 14(9) and (10).

[42] See eg Case C-13/23 *cdVet Naturprodukte* EU:C:2024:175, para 40; Case C-752/18 *Deutsche Umwelthilfe* EU:C:2019:1114, para 50; Case C-275/06 *Promusicae* EU:C:2008:54, paras 68, 70.

[43] See eg Case C-336/19 *Centraal Israëlitisch Consistorie van België* EU:C:2020:1031, para 65; Case C-584/10 P *Commission v Kadi* EU:C:2013:518, paras 128 ff; Cases C-92 and 93/09 *Volker and Schecke* EU:C:2010:662, para 77; Case C-112/00 *Schmidberger* EU:C:2003:333, paras 77, 81.

[44] See only Matthias Jestaedt, 'The Doctrine of Balancing—Strengths and Weaknesses' in Matthias Klatt (ed), *Institutionalized Reason* (OUP 2011) 152, 159 ff.

[45] The Bundesverfassungsgericht, for instance, accords—abstractly—a greater weight to freedom of expression vis-à-vis other interests, see eg BVerfG, Order of 10 October 1995, 1 BvR 1476/91, *Soldiers are murderers*, para 119. See also Christian Bumke and Andreas Voßkuhle, *German Constitutional Law* (OUP 2019) 159 ff.

[46] See eg Takis Tridimas, 'Wreaking the Wrongs: Balancing Rights and the Public Interest the EU Way' (2023) 29 CJEL 185, 195.

with a plethora of detailed provisions. All these provisions have the same formal value, which may lead to rather odd results: formally, the Union's founding values or the Charter of fundamental rights (Article 6(2) TEU) have the same legal value as Protocol No 31 concerning imports of petroleum products refined in the Netherlands Antilles or Protocol No 32 regarding the acquisition of holiday homes in Denmark. As noted before, this does not mean that the Court *actually* accords the same weight to these texts. Yet, it demonstrates the need for mechanisms that allow for differentiation or precedence.

Such a relationship of substantive order is only weakly developed at the level of primary law. Even today, many areas of primary law, especially the Union's sectoral policies, do not sufficiently reflect genuinely constitutional requirements, such as fundamental rights or judicial review. Three examples may serve as illustration. In the context of the AFSJ, there was—and in part still is—a longstanding tension between fundamental rights and surrenders under the European Arrest Warrant and transfers under the Dublin system. In the context of the financial crisis, very similar tensions arose concerning EU instruments of macro-economic policy. Without going into detail, many lament that the Union's responses reveal considerable deficiencies in terms of democracy, fundamental rights, and effective judicial protection.[47] Similar observations can be made in the context of the internal market. As early as the 1990s, an influential article highlighted that there is no hierarchical relationship between fundamental rights and market freedoms. By implication, fundamental rights 'cease to be a "trump card" . . . Instead, two norms of equal qualitative significance are balanced one against the other'.[48] In a Union increasingly emancipated from its common market purpose, we should rather assume an inverse hierarchy.

[47] On these conflicts, see eg among many others Evangelos Venizelos, 'Democratic Legitimacy at National Level and Solidarity between Financially Unequal Member States' [2017] European Politeia 282; Anastasia Poulou, 'Human Rights Accountability in European Financial Assistance' in Mark Dawson (ed), *Substantive Accountability in Europe's New Economic Governance* (CUP 2023) 267; Ana Bobić, *The Individual in the Economic and Monetary Union: A Study of Legal Accountability* (CUP 2024) 48 ff.

[48] Jason Coppel and Aidan O'Neill, 'The European Court of Justice: Taking Rights Seriously?' (1992) 29 CML Rev 669, 689 ff. See—among many others—Stephanie Reynolds, 'Explaining the Constitutional Drivers behind a Perceived Judicial Preference for Free Movement over Fundamental Rights' (2016) 53 CML Rev 643, 664 ff. Some even consider this a central 'constitutional problem' of the Union, see Sacha Garben, 'The European Union and its Three Constitutional Problems' in Matej Avbelj (ed), *The Future of EU Constitutionalism* (Hart 2023) 87, 95 ff.

4. *How* the Court Could Introduce Substantive Hierarchies in Primary Law

In sum, the usual methodological tools, such as systematic interpretation, *lex specialis*, or balancing, are of limited value if we perceive all provisions of primary law as being of equal rank. Further, such an understanding may lead to results that are difficult to square with the Union's development into a more mature constitutional order. In response to these challenges, the following section will revisit the idea of introducing *substantive hierarchies* in EU primary law. This discussion is certainly not new.[49] As early as the 1980s Pierre Pescatore noted that 'a clear hierarchy of values emerges in the Court's case law, insofar as certain Treaty provisions are singled out as "essential"'.[50] In this spirit, the Court started early on to employ the Community's objectives and general principles as structuring devices. However, recourse to these instruments has become increasingly problematic. Since the 1980s, our understanding of EU law has radically changed. The Court has deepened its constitutional approach, developed the Union's 'constitutional framework', and placed the values in Article 2 TEU at the very heart of its constitutional jurisprudence. Based on these developments, this chapter argues that Article 2 TEU could become the starting point for conceptualizing primary law in terms of substantive hierarchies.

4.1 Previous attempts

Early on, the Court started to interpret the Treaty provisions in light of (or even 'in conformity with'[51]) the Community's objectives formerly enshrined in Articles 2 and 3 EEC (today Article 3 TEU).[52] This blend of teleological (objectives . . .) and systematic (. . . codified in the Treaties) considerations was the guiding approach in the interpretation of primary law.[53] Lisbon, however,

[49] See Alan Rosas and Lorna Armati, *EU Constitutional Law*, 3rd edn (Hart 2018) 53 ff and especially in German scholarship Martin Nettesheim, 'Normenhierarchien im EU-Recht' (2006) 41 Europarecht 737; Andreas von Arnauld, 'Normenhierarchien innerhalb des primären Gemeinschaftsrechts' (2003) 38 Europarecht 191; Markus Heintzen, 'Hierarchisierungsprozesse innerhalb des Primärrechts der Europäischen Gemeinschaft' (1994) 29 Europarecht 35.

[50] Pierre Pescatore, 'Die Gemeinschaftsverträge als Verfassungsrecht' in Wilhelm G Grewe and others (eds), *Festschrift zum 70. Geburtstag von Hans Kutscher* (Nomos 1981) 319, 331 (author's translation).

[51] See eg Case 53/81 *Levin* EU:C:1982:105, para 15.

[52] See eg Case 85/76 *Hoffmann-La Roche* EU:C:1979:36, para 125; Cases 6 and 7/73 *Commercial Solvents* EU:C:1974:18, para 32; Case 6/72 *Continental Can* EU:C:1973:22, paras 22–26.

[53] See only Pierre Pescatore, 'Les objectifs de la Communauté européenne comme principes d'interprétation dans la jurisprudence de la Cour de justice (1972)' in Fabrice Picod (ed), *Études de droit communautaire européen 1962–2007* (Bruylant 2008) 383.

led to a highly disparate and vaguely outlined set of objectives. This weakens their ability to provide guidelines for interpretation.[54] Further, Lisbon placed these objectives in a new context, namely behind the Union's common values. The Union thus moves 'from a legal entity that, in the first place, exists to strive for certain goals to one which, above all, expounds what it stands for'.[55] This shift should find its expression in Luxembourg's methodology. Thus, it does not seem far-fetched to add a new device to the Court's toolbox: interpreting primary law in light of Article 2 TEU.

In parallel to the rise of objectives, the Court made ample use of freestanding principles. Principles can structure and systematize the law. They make it manageable and provide guidelines for its coherent interpretation and application.[56] At the EU level, principles are either of a functional (eg primacy, direct effect, effectiveness, equivalence, sincere cooperation, subsidiarity, mutual trust . . .) or substantive (eg fundamental rights, the rule of law, democracy . . .) nature. In both capacities they exert an 'enhanced interpretational authority'.[57] For instance, the *Titanium Dioxide* ruling can be read as commanding the Community legislature to choose from among several available legal bases the procedure which provides for the strongest participation of the European Parliament. This interpretation is justified by relying on the 'fundamental democratic principle'.[58]

Yet, the identification of freestanding principles is subject to increasing challenges. Many argue that there are no reliable criteria for the development of general principles.[59] The Court has often been accused of fabricating general principles in some kind of 'platonic heaven'.[60] Some even suspect the

[54] Armin von Bogdandy, 'Founding Principles' in ibid and Jürgen Bast (eds), *Principles of European Constitutional Law*, 2nd edn (Hart 2009) 11, 15 f.

[55] Joris Larik, 'From Speciality to a Constitutional Sense of Purpose: On the Changing Role of the Objectives of the European Union' (2014) 63 ICLQ 935, 951. In similar terms Giuliano Amato and Nicola Verola, 'Freedom, Democracy, the Rule of Law' in Giuliano Amato and others (eds), *The History of the European Union* (Hart 2019) 57, 60.

[56] Jakab (n 7) 39; von Bogdandy (n 54) 17; Urška Šadl and Joxerramon Bengoetxea, 'Theorising General Principles of EU Law in Perspective' in Stefan Vogenauer and Stephen Weatherill (eds), *General Principles of Law* (Hart 2017) 41. See already Pierre Pescatore, *Introduction à la science du droit* (Centre universitaire de l'État luxembourgeois 1978) 120.

[57] Takis Tridimas, 'The General Principles of EU Law and the Europeanisation of National Laws' (2020) 13 REAL 5, 8.

[58] Case C-300/89 *Titanium Dioxide* EU:C:1991:244, paras 18–20. Later on, however, the Court stressed that democratic concerns 'cannot . . . determine the choice of legal basis', see Case C-130/10 *Council v Parliament* EU:C:2012:472, para 79. On this 'democracy maximising rationale', see Annegret Engel, *The Choice of Legal Basis for Acts of the European Union* (Springer 2018) 87.

[59] See eg Joana Mendes, 'Taking on the Structural Weakness of EU Law's General Principles' (2023) 2 ELO 693. In detail, see Franz C Mayer, 'Constitutional Comparativism in Action' (2013) 11 I-CON 1003, 1007.

[60] Fiercely AG Mazák, Opinion in Case C-411/05 *Palacios de la Villa* EU:C:2007:106 para 86.

establishment of a European 'Freirechtsschule', in which legal methods do not play any role at all.[61] Despite these challenges, the need for principles has not lessened—it has just changed. The increasing breadth and complexity of EU law diminishes the need to cover gaps in the written law but reinforces the structuring and systematizing function of principles. Further, EU law's codification and consolidation lead to a presumption of completeness, which leaves less room for freestanding principles. Hence, general principles should be derived in much closer interaction with the Treaty text—which leads us to Article 2 TEU.

4.2 Suggested approach: Turning to Article 2 TEU

The proposal advanced in this chapter proceeds in three steps. First, I begin from the premise that Article 2 TEU contains the constitutional core of the EU legal order. In consequence, the provision not only stands at the summit of this legal order but outlines its basic constitutional features. Article 2 TEU could thus serve, second, as a starting point for a hierarchical restructuring of the entire Treaty framework. I suggest that all Treaty provisions that give specific expression to a founding value feature a genuinely constitutional content. They form the Union's substantive constitutional law. Third, this would give rise to a threefold, substantive hierarchy: Article 2 TEU at the top, the Union's substantive constitutional law at a second level, and the rest of primary law—featuring no link to Article 2 TEU—at a third one.

Starting with the first step, it is generally acknowledged that Article 2 TEU is special. Already before Lisbon, scholars agreed that the provision's predecessors—Article 6(1) TEU-Amsterdam and Article I-2 of the Constitutional Treaty—feature 'un rang essentiel dans la hiérarchie des normes du droit de l'Union'.[62] Its *wording* evokes a constitutive function. The Union is 'founded' on certain values—and only on them. In terms of *location*, Article 2 TEU has been moved to the very top of the provisions governing the Treaties and could thus be perceived as an overarching point of reference.

[61] Lüder Gerken and others, *'Mangold' als ausbrechender Rechtsakt* (Sellier 2009) 18.

[62] With regard to Art I-2 of the failed Constitutional Treaty, see eg Marianne Dony, 'Les valeurs, objectifs et principes de l'Union' in ibid and Emmanuelle Bribosia (eds), *Commentaire de la Constitution de l'Union européenne* (Editions de l'Université de Bruxelles 2005) 33, 37; Takis Tridimas, *The General Principles of EU Law*, 2nd edn (OUP 2007) 16. With regard to Art 6(1) TEU-Amsterdam/Nice, see eg Hélène Gaudin, 'Amsterdam: l'échec de la hiérarchie des normes?' (1999) 35 Revue trimestrielle de droit européen 1; Anne Peters Peters, *Elemente einer Theorie der Verfassung Europas* (Duncker&Humblot 2001) 341 f.

In terms of *protection*, the special procedure in Article 7 TEU strongly supports the thesis that Article 2 TEU transcends the other Treaty provisions. The Court's decision in *Kadi* followed this approach by stating that no Treaty provision can authorize a derogation from these principles.[63] Some have read this as establishing a new level of untouchable primary law.[64] Along these lines, many perceive Article 2 TEU as the Union's untouchable core,[65] some even as an absolute limitation for future Treaty revisions.[66] Finally, in terms of *content*, Article 2 TEU contains a set of constitutional principles on which the EU legal order is founded. These principles define, outline, and circumscribe the Union's constitutional features.

Even a short comparison reveals that many Member State constitutions feature a more or less detailed provision outlining the central and guiding principles of the respective legal order. Article 20 of the German Basic Law, for instance, is understood as a 'Verfassung der Verfassung', while Article 1 of the Spanish Constitution contains the 'constitución de la constitución' and Austrian constitutional law draws on the 'Baugesetze der Verfassung'.[67] The Court of Justice seems to have embraced a similar reading of Article 2 TEU. When outlining the features of the Union's 'constitutional framework' in Opinion 1/17, the Court mentioned—at its very top—'the founding values set out in Article 2 TEU . . .'.[68] Its decisions on the rule of law conditionality regulation are even more explicit: 'The values contained in Article 2 TEU . . . define the very identity of the European Union as a common legal order.'[69]

[63] Cases C-402 and 415/05 P, *Kadi* EU:C:2008:461, para 303.

[64] See, among many others, Christina Eckes, 'Protecting Supremacy from External Influences: A Precondition for a European Constitutional Legal Order?' (2012) 18 ELJ 230, 241.

[65] Marcus Klamert and Dimitry Kochenov, 'Article 2 TEU' in Manuel Kellerbauer and others (eds), *The Treaties and the Charter of Fundamental Rights—A Commentary*, 2nd edn (OUP 2024) para 1; Andreas Voßkuhle, *The Idea of the European Community of Values* (Bittner 2017) 116; Daniel Sarmiento, 'The EU's Constitutional Core' in Alejandro Saiz Arnaiz and Carina Alcoberro Llivina (eds), *National Constitutional Identity and European Integration* (Intersentia 2013) 177, 184 ff.

[66] Koen Lenaerts and Piet Van Nuffel, *EU Constitutional Law* (OUP 2021) para 3.010; Frank Schorkopf, 'Value Constitutionalism in the European Union' (2020) 21 GLJ 956, 963; Reijer Passchier and Maarten Stremler, 'Unconstitutional Constitutional Amendments in European Union Law' (2016) 5 CJICL 337, 356 ff. On this debate, see also Pablo Cruz Mantilla de los Ríos, 'European Constitutional Identity as the Unamendable Core of the EU Treaties' (2024) 20 EuConst 545.

[67] See eg Markus Kotzur, 'Art. 20 GG' in Ingo von Münch and Philipp Kunig (eds), *Grundgesetz-Kommentar*, vol 1, 8th edn (Beck 2025) para 195, Angel Garrorena Morales, *El Estado español como Estado social y democrático de derecho* (Tecnos 1984) 13 ff and Ludwig K Adamovich and others, *Österreichisches Staatsrecht*, vol 1, 3rd edn (Verlag Österreich 2020) 120 ff.

[68] See eg Opinion 1/17 *CETA* EU:C:2019:341, para 110.

[69] Case C-156/21 *Hungary v Parliament and Council* EU:C:2022:97, para 127. See also Hélène Gaudin, 'Ce que l'Union européenne signifie: l'identité de l'Union et de ses États membres' (2023) (133) Revue trimestrielle de droits de l'homme 17, 22 ff; Gerhard van der Schyff, 'Parameters of EU and Member State Constitutional Identity: A Topic in Development' (2022) 4 European Yearbook of Constitutional Law 89, 101 ff; Pablo Cruz Mantilla de los Ríos, 'La identidad constitucional de la Unión europea: una categoría jurídica en construcción' (2022) 70 Estudios de Deusto 153.

This leads to the second step. Based on these insights, Article 2 TEU can become a tool to identify manifestations of the 'constitutional' in EU law. As early as 1994, Fernand Herman noted that the Union's constitution 'is dispersed throughout texts which also contain legal norms which are in no way "constitutional". There is a need to . . . distinguish between those which have a genuine constitutional character and the others.'[70] Despite many proposals,[71] such a division was never realized. And indeed, the Court often refers to the Treaties in their *entirety* as a 'constitutional charter'.[72] During the past decade, however, the Court has started to distinguish certain elements from the plethora of Treaty provisions that form the Union's 'constitutional framework'.[73] Opinion 1/17 in particular establishes a 'constitutional blueprint' of contemporary EU law:[74]

> [T]he Union possesses a constitutional framework . . . That framework encompasses the founding values set out in Article 2 TEU . . . the general principles of EU law, the provisions of the Charter, and the provisions of the EU and FEU Treaties, which include, inter alia, rules on the conferral and division of powers, rules governing how the EU institutions and its judicial system are to operate, and fundamental rules in specific areas, structured in such a way as to contribute to the implementation of the process of integration.[75]

For Takis Tridimas, this provides a 'sense of prioritization' or 'heightened importance', which may increase the interpretative authority of these provisions.[76] Still, the Court's approach remains a tentative, heterogeneous sketch. The Court explains neither why certain elements are part of the 'constitutional framework' while others are not, nor what the implications of such a determination are.

This chapter seeks to provide a more coherent method for identifying constitutional provisions in EU primary law: *the Union's substantive constitutional law comprises those provisions that give expression to the values in Article 2 TEU.* To distinguish the building blocks of the Union's substantive constitution from the vast array of Treaty provisions, the Court needs to assess whether an

[70] Fernand Herman, Second Report of the Committee on Institutional Affairs on the Constitution of the European Union (9 February 1994), European Parliament, Session Doc. A3-0064/94.
[71] See n 19.
[72] See eg Cases C-357/19 and others *Euro Box Promotion* EU:C:2021:1034, para 247; Cases C-402 and 415/05 P *Kadi* EU:C:2008:461, para 281; Case 294/83 *Les Verts* EU:C:1986:166, para 23.
[73] See Opinion 2/13 *ECHR Accession II* EU:C:2014:2454, paras 165-177.
[74] Borrowing from Tridimas (n 46) 12.
[75] Opinion 1/17 *CETA* EU:C:2019:341, para 110.
[76] Tridimas (n 46) 195 f.

individual provision gives specific expression to a value enshrined in Article 2 TEU. Such links can be found across the Court's more recent jurisprudence. In the Portuguese judges case, for instance, it emphasized that Article 19(1)(2) TEU 'gives concrete expression to the value of the rule of law stated in Article 2'.[77] The same applies to Charter rights. Several rulings established a continuum between the freedom of expression in Article 11 of the Charter and the value of democracy.[78] Moreover, Article 10(1) TEU 'gives concrete form to the value of democracy referred to in Article 2 TEU'.[79] In its rule of law conditionality judgments, the Court pushed this approach even further: a vast array of Charter rights 'define the scope' of the values of human dignity, freedom, equality, and respect for human rights, whereas Articles 8, 10, 19(1), 153(1), and 157(1) TFEU substantiate the values of equality or non-discrimination.[80]

Certainly, these bits and pieces do not form a complete constitutional picture yet. However, the nascent jurisprudence is still at its very beginning. While a comprehensive assessment of possible links to Article 2 TEU must be left to further research,[81] this chapter can provide some illustrations. As seen before, the Union's constitutional law would include Charter rights as a concretization of the value of 'respect for human rights'. Further, it would cover provisions on the Union's institutional framework and the legislative process, which give expression to the value of democracy. Further still, the Union's competences and their limitations, such as the principle of conferral, could be understood as specific manifestations of the rule of law. This could apply to the principles of direct effect and primacy as well, which are the basis for the effectiveness of EU law on the ground and therefore an 'essential component of the rule of law, a value enshrined in Article 2 TEU'.[82] This would submit primacy to the values in Article 2 TEU, which corresponds to the growing case law limiting the 'ousting effect' of primacy in the interests of legal certainty or legitimate expectations, all components of the rule of law.[83]

[77] Case C-64/16 *Associação Sindical dos Juízes Portugueses* EU:C:2018:117, para 29.

[78] See eg Case C-163/10 *Patriciello* EU:C:2011:543, para 31; Case C-140/20 *Commissioner of An Garda Síochána* EU:C:2022:258, para 43; Case C-470/21 *La Quadrature du Net and Others* EU:C:2024:370, para 68.

[79] See eg Case C-502/19 *Junqueras Vies* EU:C:2019:1115, para 63; Case C-207/21 P *Commission v Poland (Protocole no 36)* EU:C:2022:560, para 81; Case C-814/21 *Commission v Poland (Éligibilité et qualité de membre d'un parti politique)* EU:C:2024:963, para 158.

[80] Case C-156/21 *Hungary v Parliament and Council* EU:C:2022:97, para 157 f.

[81] In detail Spieker (n 1) 95 ff. On further possible connections, see Tom L Boekestein, 'Making Do With What We Have: On the Interpretation and Enforcement of the EU's Founding Values' (2022) 23 GLJ 431, 451.

[82] Case C-441/17 R *Commission v Poland (Białowieza Forest)* EU:C:2017:877, para 102.

[83] Case C-409/06 *Winner Wetten* EU:C:2010:503, para 67. In detail, see Mathieu Leloup and Luke Dimitrios Spieker, 'Rethinking Primacy's Effects: On Creating, Avoiding and Filling Legal Vacuums in the National Legal System' (2024) 61 CML Rev 913.

At the same time, these examples indicate what is not part of the Union's substantive constitution. The Union policies contained in Part Three of the TFEU do not give immediate expression to a value enshrined in Article 2 TEU. This concerns not only policy areas, such as agriculture, transport, health, consumer, or environmental protection, but also the AFSJ and the so-called economic constitution, including fundamental freedoms, competition, and state aid. Even if the latter provisions guarantee individual autonomy and could thus be understood as giving specific expression to the value of 'freedom',[84] their central objective is the realization of a common market.[85] This corresponds to their respective titles in the TFEU. Their facet as guarantees for individual freedom is then better expressed through the corresponding guarantees in Article 15 to 17 of the Charter.

Finally, as a *third step*, this differentiation can be translated into a threefold, hierarchical structure (see Figure 5.1). At the top stands Article 2 TEU—the Union's constitutional core. The second tier features those provisions that give expression to a value in Article 2 TEU. They constitute primary law's genuinely constitutional provisions. The rest of primary law forms a third level. These three levels can be distinguished in at least two respects. On one hand, each level presents a different degree of concretization. On the other hand, each level features a different scope and protection. To provide a simple example: at the third level, fundamental freedoms protect a certain conduct (eg the freedom to provide services). While the scope of protection afforded at this level is broad (including eg measures of equivalent effect), its degree of protection is comparatively weak (eg restrictions can be justified by relying on a broad range of grounds). At the second level, there are provisions corresponding to fundamental freedoms, such as Articles 15 to 17 of the Charter. Their scope of protection should be narrower.[86] At the same time, such infringements would be subject to stricter judicial scrutiny. Finally, the values in Article 2 TEU, such as 'respect for human rights', protect only the very essence

[84] On this link, see Elias Deutscher, 'The Competition–Democracy Nexus Unpacked' (2022) 41 YEL 197; Carsten König, 'Zum Verfassungsrang der Grundfreiheiten und des europäischen Wettbewerbsrechts' (2022) 57 Europarecht 48, 52 ff.

[85] For an overview, see Rufat Babayev, *Private Autonomy in EU Internal Market Law* (Hart 2024) 50 ff; Thorsten Kingreen, 'Fundamental Freedoms' in von Bogdandy and Bast (n 54) 515, 530.

[86] This is *not* the status quo! Pointing rather towards equivalence, see eg Art 52(2) CFR and the Explanations to the Charter, O.J. 2007 C 303/17, Art 15. Similarly, the Court noted that Art 15 of the Charter 'reiterates' inter alia the free movement of workers, see Case C-166/20 *Lietuvos Respublikos sveikatos apsaugos ministerija* EU:C:2021:554, para 32; Case C-284/15 *ONEm and M* EU:C:2016:220, para 33. In detail, see Spieker (n 30) 445 f.

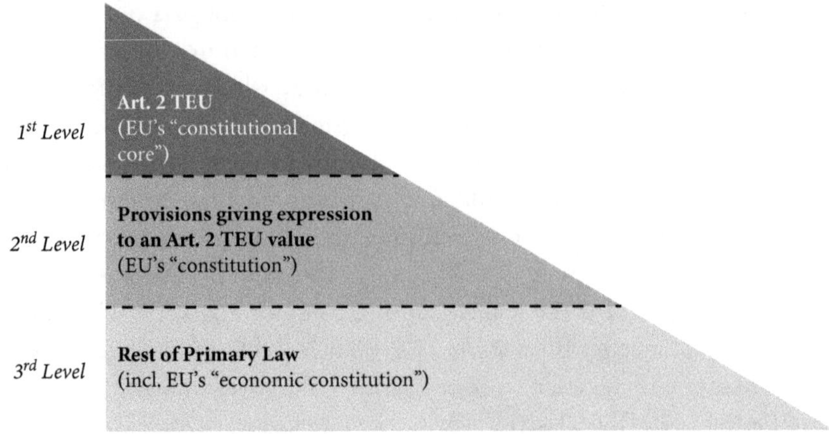

Figure 5.1 Substantive hierarchy of Treaty provisions

of second-level Treaty provisions, ie the essence of fundamental rights mentioned in Article 52(2) of the Charter.[87]

5. Impact

5.1 Effects on judicial reasoning

Against this backdrop, the hierarchical stratification of primary law can have two effects. First, Article 2 TEU can become a focal point for the *interpretation* of primary law. Provisions of the second level, the Union's substantive constitution, must be interpreted in its light. At the same time, these provisions exert an effect on the third level. As noted earlier (see Section 2), the notion of 'constitution' comes with certain effects in constitutional adjudication. Constitutions have primacy. This means that constitutional provisions serve not only as formal yardsticks for the validity of ordinary law, but also as substantive guidelines for its interpretation. Based on these insights, provisions at the third level should be interpreted in light of the Union's constitutional law at the second level. This could give rise to an interpretation cascade.

[87] On the link of essence and Art 2 TEU, see Armin von Bogdandy and others, 'Reverse Solange—Protecting the Essence of Fundamental Rights against EU Member States' (2012) 49 CML Rev 489, 509 ff; Koen Lenaerts, 'Limits on Limitations: The Essence of Fundamental Rights in the EU' (2019) 20 GLJ 779.

Second, the system of substantive hierarchies may become a tool of *conflict resolution* among provisions of primary law. The stronger the connection to Article 2 TEU, the stronger a provision's normative force. In consequence, a provision of the second level will have a greater weight when measured against conflicting provisions of the third one. They take substantive precedence. Take, for instance, a conflict between the free movement of goods and the freedom of assembly.[88] Giving specific expression to the value of 'democracy', the freedom of assembly under Article 12 of the Charter is allocated at the second level. Hence, there is a relation of precedence between the Charter right and Article 34 TFEU, which entails interpreting the latter in conformity with the former. A similar reasoning can apply also to conflicts between the second and the first level. When provisions of the same level collide, such conflicts can be resolved by precedence if one of them is affected in its essence protected under Article 2 TEU.

5.2 Traces in judicial practice

The Court's case law already reflects such an interpretation in light of Article 2 TEU. Three examples can serve as illustrating examples in this respect. To start with, the Court has increasingly sought to close gaps in judicial protection by recourse to Article 2 TEU. This concerns especially judicial review in the Common Foreign and Security Policy (CFSP).[89] By exception to the Court's general jurisdiction, Articles 24(1)(2) TEU and 275(1) TFEU exclude judicial review of acts adopted in this policy area. This 'carve out', in turn, is subject to a so-called claw back in Article 275(2) TFEU, which established the Court's jurisdiction regarding actions for annulment against restrictive measures. During the past decade, the Court combined a narrow reading of the 'carve out' with a broad one of the 'claw back'. While the 'claw back' now includes the Court's jurisdiction to hear preliminary rulings[90] and actions for damages regarding restrictive measures,[91] the 'carve out' does not exclude reviewing CFSP acts related to staff matters, public procurement, or the conclusion of international

[88] This conflict was at the heart of Case C-112/00 *Schmidberger* EU:C:2003:333. For a more recent example, see the 'clash' of the freedom of establishment and Art 11 of the Charter in Case C-719/18 *Vivendi* EU:C:2020:627, paras 57 ff.

[89] In detail on this trend and its limits, see Luigi Lonardo's contribution in this volume.

[90] On references for validity, see Case C-72/15 *Rosneft* EU:C:2017:236, paras 59 ff. On references for interpretation, see Case C-351/22 *Neves 77 Solutions* EU:C:2024:723.

[91] Case C-134/19 P *Bank Refah Kargaran* EU:C:2020:793, paras 23 ff.

treaties.[92] This case law culminated in *KS and KD v Council*, according to which the 'carve out' excludes the Court's jurisdiction only regarding measures directly related to 'political or strategic choices' in the CFSP.[93] As such, fundamental rights violations occurring in the 'day-to-day management' of CFSP measures, such as missions, can be brought before the Court.

This extension was largely justified by interpreting the respective Treaty provisions in light of Article 2 TEU.[94] In *KS and KD v Council*, for instance, the Court stressed that the 'basic principles of the EU legal order', including 'respect for the rule of law and fundamental rights, values expressed in Article 2 TEU', form the 'context' in which to interpret the Court's jurisdiction.[95] This reasoning is expressed even more strongly in Advocate General Capeta's opinion. According to her, the 'rule of law not only empowers the EU Courts to ensure that other EU institutions and bodies abide by the law, but also *binds* the EU Courts themselves to follow the law'.[96] The question is therefore whether to 'strictly abide by the wording of the Treaties', which limits the Court's jurisdiction, or whether to 'give preference to EU constitutional principles'.[97] She chose the latter path. Even if the principle of the rule of law cannot 'lead to the modification of the Treaties by the EU Courts', it nonetheless obliges the Court to interpret primary law in its light.[98] Against this backdrop, the Union's constitutional principles, such as the rule of law, take precedence. Finally, it should be noted that Article 47 of the Charter would not have justified the Court's extensive interpretation. Article 51(2) specifically states that the Charter cannot 'modify powers and tasks as defined in the Treaties'.[99] This is different with Article 2 TEU.

[92] See eg Case C-455/14 P *H v Council and Others* EU:C:2016:569, paras 39 ff; C-439/13 P *Elitaliana* EU:C:2015:753, paras 41 ff; Case C-658/11 *Parliament v Council (Mauritius)* EU:C:2014:2025, paras 69 ff.

[93] Cases C-29 and 44/22 P *KS and KD v Council* EU:C:2024:725, paras 116-118. For examples where this is the case, see paras 126–31. On such a 'political question doctrine' see already Graham Butler, 'In Search of the Political Question Doctrine in EU Law' (2018) 45 LIEI 329.

[94] See eg Case C-455/14 P *H v Council and Others* EU:C:2016:569, para 41; Case C-72/15 *Rosneft* EU:C:2017:236, para 72; Case C-14/19 P *CSUE v KF* EU:C:2020:492, paras 59, 66; Case C-134/19 P *Bank Refah Kargaran* EU:C:2020:793, para 35; Case C-351/22 *Neves 77 Solutions* EU:C:2024:723, paras 51–53.

[95] Cases C-29 and 44/22 P *KS and KD v Council* EU:C:2024:725, paras 68, 119. See also Editorial, 'From Opinion 2/13 to KS and KD: Confronting a Legacy of Constitutional Tensions' (2024) 61 CML Rev 1455, 1460.

[96] AG Capeta, Opinion in Cases C-29 and 44/22 P *KS and KD v Council*, para 94.

[97] ibid para 95.

[98] ibid paras 99–100. See the very similar reasoning by AG Bobek in Case C-14/19 P *CSUE v KF*, para 69.

[99] See Cases C-29 and 44/22 P *KS and KD v Council* EU:C:2024:725, para 71 and Case C-72/15 *Rosneft* EU:C:2017:236, para 74.

The second example relates to the interpretation of the TEU's final provisions. In *Wightman*, the Court had to determine whether Article 50 TEU permits a Member State to unilaterally revoke its notification to exit the Union. After finding that the provision's wording and objectives are inconclusive in this respect, the Court moved to interpret Article 50 TEU 'in the light of the Treaties taken as a whole'.[100] When outlining this interpretative 'context', the Court referred to the 'importance of the values of liberty and democracy . . . which are among the common values referred to in Article 2 of that Treaty . . . and which thus form part of the very foundations of the European Union legal order'.[101] Flowing form Article 49 TEU, all Member States 'have freely and voluntarily committed themselves to those values'. Forcing a state to withdraw against its will would be 'inconsistent' with these values.[102] In consequence, a Member State can, in a democratic process, decide to revoke the notification of its intention to exit.

Finally, the third example concerns the relationship of Article 2 TEU and the protection of national identity under Article 4(2) TEU. Several judgments established a clear substantive precedence of the Union's common values over national identity concerns.[103] The reasoning was articulated with much clarity in the fourth infringement procedure concerning the overhaul of the Polish judiciary. The Court stressed that Article 4(2) TEU 'must be read taking into account the provisions, of the same rank, enshrined in Article 2 and the second subparagraph of Article 19(1) TEU'.[104] The Court refers to provisions of the same *formal*, not *substantive* rank. This becomes clear in the following passages, which state that Article 4(2) TEU 'cannot exempt Member States from the obligation to comply with the requirements arising from those provisions.' Even if the Member States 'enjoy a certain degree of discretion in implementing the principles of the rule of law, it in no way follows that that obligation as to the result to be achieved may vary from one Member State to another'.[105] The

[100] Case C-621/18 *Wightman and Others* EU:C:2018:999, para 46.
[101] ibid para 62. In detail on the Court's reasoning, see Armin Cuyvers, 'Wightman, Brexit, And the Sovereign Right to Remain' (2019) 56 CML Rev 1303, 1311 ff.
[102] Case C-621/18 *Wightman and Others* EU:C:2018:999, paras 65, 67.
[103] Case C-156/21 *Hungary v Parliament and Council* EU:C:2022:97, paras 233 f. See also Opinion of AG Kokott in Case C-490/20 *Pancharevo* EU:C:2021:296, paras 73, 116 ff; AG Collins in Case C-430/21 *RS (Effet des arrêts d'une cour constitutionnelle)* EU:C:2022:44, para 64; AG Emiliou in Case C-391/20 *Cilevičs and Others* EU:C:2022:166, para 87 and AG Cruz Villalón in Case C-62/14 *Gauweiler* EU:C:2015:7, para 61. See also Spieker (n 1) 230 ff; Pedro Cruz Mantilla de los Ríos, 'Identidad nacional y valores de la Unión Europea: límites a una interpretación extensiva del artículo 4.2 TUE' (2022) (114) Revista de Derecho Político 245, 269 ff; Lucia S Rossi, '2, 4, 6 (TUE) . . . l'interpretazione dell'"Identity Clause" alla luce dei valori fondamentali dell'Unione' in *Liber Amicorum Antonio Tizzano* (Giappichelli 2018) 858, 866.
[104] Case C-204/21 *Commission v Poland (Independence and private life of judges)* EU:C:2023:442, para 71.
[105] ibid para 73.

same reasoning was applied in the Commission's infringement proceedings against the Czech Republic and Poland concerning the right of Union citizens to join political parties. This time, the Court stressed that 'Article 4(2) TEU . . . cannot exempt Member States from the obligation to comply' with the principle of democracy enshrined in Articles 2 and 10 TEU.[106]

6. Potential

This chapter made the case for conceptualizing primary law in terms of substantive hierarchies. From a substantive perspective, primary law should be understood as a pyramid. This reasoning not only explains recent developments in the case law, but can help the Court to remedy deficiencies in many areas of EU law. This chapter concludes with a tentative outlook sketching possible trajectories of future development. The multifaceted potential of substantive hierarchies in primary law can be illustrated in three areas.

To start with, the approach suggested in this chapter could be employed at the Court's 'own doorstep' by affording more effective judicial protection against EU acts in Luxembourg. Pursuant to Article 263(4) TFEU, individuals can only challenge EU measures in case they are of direct and individual concern to them. Since *Plauman*, the Court interpreted this provision in very narrow terms.[107] Even if individuals can challenge EU acts in national courts, the parties have no general 'right' to a reference beyond Article 267(3) TFEU. As such, this system is difficult to reconcile with effective judicial protection. *Unión de Pequeños Agricultores* was a missed opportunity in this respect. Despite fierce critique from within the Court,[108] the Luxembourg judges left it to the Member States to reform the system of legal remedies.[109] The substantive hierarchies developed in this chapter provide the Court with a toolbox to revisit *UPA* and live up to the promise of a 'complete system of legal remedies and procedures'.[110]

More recent case law sends mixed signals in this respect. On one hand, *Venezuela v Council* can be seen as a cautious sign of change. After recalling

[106] Case C-808/21 *Commission v Czech Republic* EU:C:2024:962 paras 158–61; Case C-814/21 *Commission v Poland* EU:C:2024:963, paras 155–58.

[107] Case 25/62 *Plaumann* EU:C:1963:17, p 107. On the state of the art, Koen Lenaerts, Ignace Maselis, and Kathleen Gutman, *EU Procedural Law*, 2nd edn (OUP 2023) paras 7.112 ff.

[108] AG Jacobs, Opinion in Case C-50/00 P *UPA* EU:C:2002:197, paras 102 ff.

[109] Case C-50/00 P *UPA* EU:C:2002:462, para 41; Case C-263/02 P *Jégo-Quéré* EU:C:2004:210, para 36.

[110] Case 294/83 *Les Verts v Parliament* EU:C:1986:166, para 23.

that it 'follows from Article 2 TEU that the European Union is founded on values, such as the rule of law', the Court interpreted Article 263(4) TFEU extensively as including actions brought by a third state against a regulation imposing restrictive measures.[111] In the slipstream of this decision, Advocate General Emiliou called upon the Court to reconsider *Plauman*. He stressed that the 'constitutional changes' since when this case was decided, especially the principle of the rule of law in Article 2 TEU, 'cannot be overlooked when issues concerning individuals' access to justice arise'.[112] Further, he emphasized that 'the rules concerning its jurisdiction and, more generally, access of private parties to justice must be interpreted, as far as possible, in the light of the principles of effective judicial protection and of the rule of law'.[113]

On the other hand, the General Court dismissed an action brought by several judges' associations against a Council decision that approved Poland's recovery and resilience plan under NextGenerationEU. This decision contained several milestones relating to guaranteeing judicial independence, which—according to the applicants—did not meet the standards set out by the Court. The General Court ascertained a lack of 'direct concern' under Article 263(4) TFEU and rejected a broader reading of Article 263(4) TFEU in light the Union's constitutional principles.[114] It remains to be seen whether the Court of Justice will confirm this view.[115]

Second, Article 2 TEU could lead to an interpretation of primary law that strengthens the Union's democratic character. Many proposals for improvement, such as general parliamentary participation in law-making, transnational lists, or overcoming the unanimity requirement in the Council, require legislation or Treaty amendments. Nevertheless, there remains also room for interpretation both by the Court and the other Union institutions. As noted before, the Court has often resorted to the principle of representative democracy when interpreting primary law.[116] Article 2 TEU can serve as a new point of reference. Such an interpretation could command the consolidation of the 'Spitzenkandidatenprinzip'. Pursuant to Article 17(7) TEU, the European Council shall 'take into account' the result of the elections to the European Parliament when proposing a candidate for Commission President.

[111] Case C-872/19 P *Venezuela v Council (Affectation d'un État tiers)* EU:C:2021:507, paras 48 f.
[112] AG Emiliou, Opinion in Case C-731/23 P *Nicoventures Trading and Others v Commission* EU:C:2025:435, para 135.
[113] ibid para 137.
[114] Cases T-530 to 533/22 *Medel and others v Council* EU:T:2024:363, paras 113-115. For a similarly brief rejection of extending the standing of MEPs under Article 263 TFEU, see Case T-628/22 *Repasi v Commission* EU:T:2023:353, paras 30-38.
[115] See Case C-555/24 P.
[116] See n 43.

Read in light of the principle of democracy, this provision could be understood as binding.[117]

Finally, the principles enshrined in Article 2 TEU can radiate into the sectoral policy areas and thus realign them with the Union's constitutional core. As noted before (see Section 3), many Treaty areas do not sufficiently reflect the principles in Article 2 TEU. This applies especially to the 'sectoral constitutions' of the various Union policies,[118] such as the Union's economic constitution or the Area of Freedom, Security and Justice. With regard to the Union's economic constitution, this chapter has already indicated some possible trajectories for further development. Article 2 TEU could help overcome deficiencies with respect to democracy, fundamental rights, and judicial review in the Union's monetary policy, especially in cases of financial assistance. Further, the approach suggested in this chapter could rebalance the problematic relationship of fundamental freedoms and fundamental rights.[119]

In this context, solidarity has the potential to become a central notion. In recent case law, the Court has characterized the solidarity mentioned in Article 2 TEU as a 'fundamental principle' of EU law.[120] With regard to the solidarity *among Member States*, the conflicts during the financial crisis and pandemic have put this kind of solidarity to the test.[121] Even though many EU responses ended up before the Court, it refrained from approaching the respective legal bases from the perspective of solidarity. Neither *Gauweiler* nor *Weiss* embraced the notion.[122] Nevertheless, solidarity could have supported the Court's reasoning in upholding the adopted crisis measures—also vis-à-vis contestation from Karlsruhe.[123]

[117] See eg Daniel Calleja and Clemens Ladenburger, 'The Future of European Union Law' in *70 Years of EU Law* (2023) 377, 387.

[118] Borrowing from Kaarlo Tuori, 'The Many Constitutions of Europe' in Kaarlo Tuori and Suvi Sankari (eds), *The Many Constitutions of Europe* (Routledge 2016) 3.

[119] Agustín Menéndez, 'The Guardianship of European Constitutionality' in Mads Andenas and others (eds), *The Reach of Free Movement* (Asser 2017) 173, 183 ff. On the different options, see concisely Niamh Nic Shuibhne, 'The Social Market Economy and Restriction of Free Movement Rights: *plus c'est la même chose*?' (2019) 57 JCMS 111, 119 f.

[120] Case C-156/21 *Hungary v Parliament and Council* EU:C:2022:97, para 129. See already Case C-848/19 P *Germany v Poland* EU:C:2021:598, para 38. Critically with regard to solidarity as a 'general principle', see Marcus Klamert, 'Loyalty and Solidarity as General Principles' in Katja S Ziegler and others (eds), *Research Handbook on General Principles in EU Law* (Elgar 2022) 118, 132–34; Koen Lenaerts and Stanislas Adam, 'La solidarité, valeur commune aux états membres et principe fédératif de l'Union européenne' (2021) 57 Cahiers de droit européen 307, 314 f.

[121] See eg Vestert Borger, *The Currency of Solidarity* (CUP 2020) 23 ff and Michael Ioannidis, 'Between Responsibility and Solidarity. COVID-19 and the Future of the European Economic Order' (2020) 4 ZaöRV 773.

[122] But see in the context of Art 122(1) TFEU Case C-370/12 *Pringle* EU:C:2012:756, para 115 ('spirit of solidarity').

[123] In this sense, Ana Bobić, '(Re)Turning to Solidarity in EU Economic Governance: A Normative Proposal' in Anuscheh Farahat and Xabier Arzoz Santisteban (eds), *Contesting Austerity* (Hart 2021) 115.

At the same time, *external* solidarity with migrants or refugees from third countries is in desperate need of improvement.[124] The Court has stressed in this context that a Member State's failure in the duty of solidarity, by not implementing the Union's common policy on asylum, subsidiary protection and temporary protection, 'strikes at the very root of the EU legal order'. Referring not only to Article 80 TFEU, but also to Article 2 TEU, it made such failures an extremely costly endeavour.[125] Also the *internal* solidarity among Union citizens has witnessed a deterioration. Until the U-turn in *Dano*, the Court required 'a certain degree of financial solidarity' between Union citizens.[126] An interpretation of the relevant provisions, such as Article 20 and 21 TFEU and the Citizens' Rights Directive, in light of the principle of solidarity can justify a return to a more substantial Union citizenship.

The Commission's infringement procedure against the Maltese 'golden passport' scheme could be a first step in this direction. While the judgment has been subject to many different readings, the Court seems to interpret Union citizenship in Article 20 TFEU in light of solidarity as prohibiting Member States from commercializing their nationality and thus Union citizenship.[127] Due to the plethora of rights associated with that status, Union citizenship is 'one of the principal concrete expressions of the solidarity which forms the very basis of the process of integration'.[128] Accordingly, 'Union citizenship is based on the common values contained in Article 2 TEU'. As solidarity requires a certain belonging to the society in question, Member States are prevented from conferring their nationality in the absence of a 'special relationship of solidarity and good faith' to the individual in question. This demonstrates the potential of interpreting Treaty provisions in light of the solidarity in Article 2 TEU.

[124] Alina Carrozzini and Luigi Lonardo, 'The Many Faces of Solidarity and Its Role in the Jurisprudence of the Area of Freedom, Security and Justice' in Eva Kassoti and Narin Idriz (eds) *The Principle of Solidarity* (Asser 2023) 261.

[125] Case C-123/22 *Commission v Hungary* EU:C:2024:493, paras 115–17.

[126] Case C-184/99 *Grzelczyk* EU:C:2001:458, para 44.

[127] In detail, see Luke Dimitrios Spieker and Ferdinand Weber, '*Commission v Malta* (C-181/23): A "Miracle" of Union Citizenship?' (2025) 50 EL Rev 487, 494–96. See also Peter Hilpold, 'Unionsbürgerschaft in der EU-Werteunion: Malta wird Staatsbürgerschaftshandel untersagt' (2025) 36 Europäische Zeitschrift für Wirtschaftsrecht 757, 761.

[128] Case C-181/233 *Commission v Malta (Citoyenneté par investissement)* EU:C:2025:283, paras 93 and 95.

References

Adamovich LK and others, *Österreichisches Staatsrecht*, vol 1, 3rd edn (Verlag Österreich 2020)

Amato G and Verola N, 'Freedom, Democracy, the Rule of Law' in Giuliano Amato and others (eds), *The History of the European Union* (Hart 2019)

Babayev R, *Private Autonomy in EU Internal Market Law* (Hart 2024)

Bindi E and Perini M, 'Legal Effect of Constitutions' in Rainer Grote and others (eds), *Max Planck Encyclopedia of Comparative Constitutional Law* (OUP 2017)

Bobbio N, *Studi per una teoria generale del diritto* (Giappichelli 2012)

Bobić A, *The Individual in the Economic and Monetary Union: A Study of Legal Accountability* (CUP 2024)

Bobić A, '(Re)Turning to Solidarity in EU Economic Governance: A Normative Proposal' in Anuscheh Farahat and Xabier Arzoz Santisteban (eds), *Contesting Austerity* (Hart 2021)

Boekestein T, 'Making Do With What We Have: On the Interpretation and Enforcement of the EU's Founding Values' (2022) 23 German Law Journal 431

Borger V, *The Currency of Solidarity* (CUP 2020)

Bumke C and Voßkuhle A, *German Constitutional Law* (OUP 2019)

Burchardt D, 'The Concept of Legal Space' (2022) 11 Global Constitutionalism 518

Calleja Crespo D and Ladenburger C, 'The Future of European Union Law' in *70 Years of EU Law* (2023)

Calliess C and van der Schyff G (eds), *Constitutional Identity in a Europe of Multilevel Constitutionalism* (CUP 2019)

Canihac H, 'From Constitutional Pyramid to Constitutional Pluralism' in Jan Komárek (ed), *European Constitutional Imaginaries* (OUP 2023)

Carrozzini A and Lonardo L, 'The Many Faces of Solidarity and Its Role in the Jurisprudence of the Area of Freedom, Security and Justice' in Eva Kassoti and Narin Idriz (eds), *The Principle of Solidarity* (Asser 2023)

Champeil-Desplats V, 'Hiérarchie des normes, principe justificatif de la suprematie de la constitution' in Michel Troper and Dominique Chagnollaud (eds), *Traité international de droit constitutionnel*, vol 1 (Dalloz 2012)

Coppel J and O'Neill A, 'The European Court of Justice: Taking Rights Seriously?' (1992) 29 Common Market Law Review 669

Cruz Mantilla de los Ríos P, 'European Constitutional Identity as the Unamendable Core of the EU Treaties' (2024) 20 European Constitutional Law Review 545

Cruz Mantilla de los Ríos P, 'Identidad nacional y valores de la Unión Europea: límites a una interpretación extensiva del artículo 4.2 TUE' (2022) (114) Revista de Derecho Político 245

Cruz Mantilla de los Ríos P, 'La identidad constitucional de la Unión europea: una categoría jurídica en construcción' (2022) 70 Estudios de Deusto 153

Cuyvers A, 'Wightman, Brexit, and the Sovereign Right to Remain' (2019) 56 Common Market Law Review 1303

David R, 'Sources of Law' in Kötz Zweigert and Ulrich Drobnig (eds), *International Encyclopedia of Comparative Law*, vol 2 (Mohr Siebeck 1981)

de Béchillon D, 'Sur la conception française de la hiérarchie des normes' (1994) 32 Revue interdisciplinaire d'études juridiques 81

Dehaene JL, von Weizsäcker R, and Simon D, *The Institutional Implications of Enlargement* (18 October 1999)

Delmas-Marty M, *Ordering Pluralism* (Hart 2009)

Deutscher E, 'The Competition–Democracy Nexus Unpacked' (2022) 41 Yearbook of European Law 197
Dony M, 'Les valeurs, objectifs et principes de l'Union' in Marianne Dony and Emmanuelle Bribosia (eds), *Commentaire de la Constitution de l'Union européenne* (Editions de l'Université de Bruxelles 2005)
Eckes C, 'Protecting Supremacy from External Influences: A Precondition for a European Constitutional Legal Order?' (2012) 18 European Law Journal 230
Editorial, 'From Opinion 2/13 to KS and KD: Confronting a Legacy of Constitutional Tensions' (2024) 61 Common Market Law Review 1455
Elvira Méndez-Pinedo M, 'Supremacy/Primacy' in Rainer Grote and others (eds), *Max Planck Encyclopedia of Comparative Constitutional Law* (OUP 2017)
Engel A, *The Choice of Legal Basis for Acts of the European Union* (Springer 2018)
EUI, *A Basic Treaty for the European Union: A Study of the Reorganisation of the Treaties* (15 May 2000)
Faraguna P, *Ai confini della Costituzione. Principi supremi e identità costituzionale* (Franco Angeli 2015)
Fischer-Lescano A and Teubner G, 'Regime-Collisions: The Vain Search for Legal Unity in the Fragmentation of Global Law' (2004) 25 Michigan Journal of International Law 999
Garben S, 'The European Union and Its Three Constitutional Problems' in Matej Avbelj (ed), *The Future of EU Constitutionalism* (Hart 2023)
Garrorena Morales A, *El Estado español como Estado social y democrático de derecho* (Tecnos 1984)
Gaudin H, 'Ce que l'Union européenne signifie: l'identité de l'Union et de ses États membres' (2023) (133) Revue trimestrielle de droits de l'homme 17
Gaudin H, 'Amsterdam: l'échec de la hiérarchie des normes?' (1999) 35 Revue trimestrielle de droit européen 1
Gerken L and others, *'Mangold' als ausbrechender Rechtsakt* (Sellier 2009)
Grabenwarter C, 'Die Verfassung in der Hierarchie der Rechtsordnung' in Christoph Grabenwarter and Otto Depenheuer (eds), *Verfassungstheorie* (Mohr Siebeck 2010)
Grimm D, 'The Democratic Costs of Constitutionalisation: The European Case' (2015) 21 European Law Journal 460
Guastini R, 'Gerarchie normative' (2013) 21 Revus 57
Halberstam D, 'Constitutional Heterarchy' in Jeffrey L Dunoff and Joel P Trachtman (eds), *Ruling the World?* (CUP 2009)
Halmai G, 'Silence of Transitional Constitutions: The "Invisible Constitution" Concept of the Hungarian Constitutional Court' (2018) 16 Internation Journal of Constitutional Law 969.
Hancox E, 'Judicial Approaches to Norm Overlaps in EU Law' (2021) 58 Common Market Law Review 1057
Heintzen M, 'Hierarchisierungsprozesse innerhalb des Primärrechts der Europäischen Gemeinschaft' (1994) 29 Europarecht 35
Herman F, Second Report of the Committee on Institutional Affairs on the Constitution of the European Union (9 February 1994), European Parliament, Session Doc. A3-0064/94
Hilpold P, 'Unionsbürgerschaft in der EU-Werteunion: Malta wird Staatsbürgerschaftshandel untersagt' (2025) 36 Europäische Zeitschrift für Wirtschaftsrecht 757
International Law Commission, Fragmentation of International Law, A/CN.4/L.682 (13 April 2006)
Ioannidis M, 'Between Responsibility and Solidarity: COVID-19 and the Future of the European Economic Order' (2020) 4 Zeitschrift für ausländisches öffentliches Recht und Völkerrecht 773

Jakab A, 'The Reasoning of Constitutional Courts in Europe' in Armin von Bogdandy and others (eds), *The Max Planck Handbooks in European Public Law*, vol IV (OUP 2023)
Jakab A, *European Constitutional Language* (CUP 2016)
Jestaedt M, 'The Doctrine of Balancing—Strengths and Weaknesses' in Matthias Klatt (ed), *Institutionalized Reason* (OUP 2011)
Kelsen H, *Pure Theory of Law* (University of California Press 1967)
Kingreen T, 'Fundamental Freedoms' in Armin von Bogdandy and Jürgen Bast (eds), *Principles of European Constitutional Law*, 2nd edn (Hart 2009)
Klamert M and Kochenov D, 'Article 2 TEU' in Manuel Kellerbauer and others (eds), *The Treaties and the Charter of Fundamental Rights—A Commentary*, 2nd edn (OUP 2024)
Klamert M, 'Loyalty and Solidarity as General Principles' in Katja S Ziegler and others (eds), *Research Handbook on General Principles in EU Law* (Edward Elgar 2022)
Komárek J, 'Legal Reasoning in EU Law' in Damien Chalmers and Anthony Arnull (eds), *The Oxford Handbook of European Union Law* (OUP 2015)
König C, 'Zum Verfassungsrang der Grundfreiheiten und des europäischen Wettbewerbsrechts' (2022) 57 Europarecht 48
Kotzur M, 'Art. 20 GG' in Ingo von Münch and Philipp Kunig (eds), *Grundgesetz-Kommentar*, vol 1, 8th edn (Beck 2025)
Krishnaswamy S, *Democracy and Constitutionalism in India: A Study of the Basic Structure Doctrine* (OUP 2011)
Kumm M, 'Who Is Afraid of the Total Constitution?' 7 (2006) 7 German Law Journal 341
Kutscher H, 'Methods of Interpretation as seen by the European Court of Justice' Judicial and Academic Conference (27–28 September 1976)
Larik J, 'From Speciality to a Constitutional Sense of Purpose: On the Changing Role of the Objectives of the European Union' (2014) 63 International and Comparative Law Quarterly 935
Leloup M and Spieker LD, 'Rethinking Primacy's Effects: On Creating, Avoiding and Filling Legal Vacuums in the National Legal System' (2024) 61 Common Market Law Review 913
Lenaerts K, 'Limits on Limitations: The Essence of Fundamental Rights in the EU' (2019) 20 German Law Journal 779
Lenaerts K and Adam S, 'La solidarité, valeur commune aux états membres et principe fédératif de l'Union européenne' (2021) 57 Cahiers de droit européen 307
Lenaerts K and Gutiérrez-Fons JA, *Les méthodes d'interprétation de la Cour de justice de l'Union européenne* (Bruylant 2020)
Lenaerts K, Maselis I, and Gutman K, *EU Procedural Law*, 2nd edn (OUP 2023)
Lenaerts K and Van Nuffel P, *EU Constitutional Law* (OUP 2021)
MacCormick N, *Rethoric and the Rule of Law: A Theory of Legal Reasoning* (OUP 2010)
Martens SAE, *Methodenlehre des Unionsrechts* (Mohr Siebeck 2013)
Mayer FC, 'Constitutional Comparativism in Action' (2013) 11 International Journal of Constitutional Law 1003
Mendes J, 'Taking on the Structural Weakness of EU Law's General Principles' (2023) 2 European Law Open 693
Menéndez A, 'The Guardianship of European Constitutionality' in Mads Andenas and others (eds), *The Reach of Free Movement* (Asser 2017)
Merkl A, 'Prolegomena einer Theorie des rechtlichen Stufenbaues' in Alfred Verdross (ed), *Gesellschaft, Recht und Staat. Festschrift Hans Kelsen zum 50. Geburtstage gewidmet* (Springer 1931)

Michaels R and Pauwelyn J, 'Conflict of Norms or Conflict of Laws: Different Techniques in the Fragmentation of Public International Law' (2012) 22 Duke Journal of Comparative & International Law 349
Millard E, *Théorie générale du droit*, 2nd edn (LGDJ 2022)
Nettesheim M, 'Normenhierarchien im EU-Recht' (2006) 41 Europarecht 737
Nic Shuibhne N, 'The Social Market Economy and Restriction of Free Movement Rights: *plus c'est la même chose*?' (2019) 57 Journal of Common Market Studies 111
Ost F and Van de Kerchove M, *De la pyramide au réseau?* (Presses universitaires Saint-Louis Bruxelles 2002) 539
Passchier R and Stremler M, 'Unconstitutional constitutional amendments in European Union law' (2016) 5 Cambridge Journal of International and Comparative Law 337
Pescatore O, *Introduction à la science du droit* (Centre universitaire de l'État luxembourgeois 1978)
Pescatore O, 'Die Gemeinschaftsverträge als Verfassungsrecht' in Wilhelm G Grewe and others (eds), *Festschrift zum 70. Geburtstag von Hans Kutscher* (Nomos 1981)
Pescatore O, 'Les objectifs de la Communauté européenne comme principes d'interprétation dans la jurisprudence de la Cour de justice (1972)' in Fabrice Picod (ed), *Études de droit communautaire européen 1962–2007* (Bruylant 2008)
Peters A, *Elemente einer Theorie der Verfassung Europas* (Duncker&Humblot 2001)
Pinelli C, 'Theories Concerning the Hierarchy of Norms' in Rainer Grote and others (eds), *Max Planck Encyclopedia of Comparative Constitutional Law* (OUP 2017)
Polzin M, 'Constitutional Identity, Unconstitutional Amendments and the Idea of Constituent Power: The Development of the Doctrine of Constitutional Identity in German Constitutional Law' (2016) 14 Internation Journal of Constitutional Law 411
Poulou A, 'Human Rights Accountability in European Financial Assistance' in Mark Dawson (ed), *Substantive Accountability in Europe's New Economic Governance* (CUP 2023)
Pulkowski D, *The Law and Politics of International Regime Conflict* (OUP 2014)
Reynolds A, 'Explaining the Constitutional Drivers behind a Perceived Judicial Preference for Free Movement over Fundamental Rights' (2016) 53 Common Market Law Review 643
Rosas A and Armati L, *EU Constitutional Law*, 3rd edn (Hart 2018)
Rossi LS, '2, 4, 6 (TUE) . . . l'interpretazione dell'"Identity Clause" alla luce dei valori fondamentali dell'Unione' in *Liber Amicorum Antonio Tizzano* (Giappichelli 2018)
Šadl U and Bengoetxea J, 'Theorising General Principles of EU Law in Perspective' in Stefan Vogenauer and Stephen Weatherill (eds), *General Principles of Law* (Hart 2017)
Sarmiento D, 'The EU's Constitutional Core' in Alejandro Saiz Arnaiz and Carina Alcoberro Llivina (eds), *National Constitutional Identity and European Integration* (Intersentia 2013)
Scarcello O, 'On the Role of Normative Hierarchies in Constitutional Reasoning' (2018) 31 Ratio Juris 346
Schorkopf F, 'Value Constitutionalism in the European Union' (2020) 21 German Law Journal 956
Spieker LD, *EU Values before the Court of Justice* (OUP 2023)
Spieker LD, 'Was Grimm Wrong? Putting the Over-constitutionalization of EU Law to the Test' (2025) 26 German Law Journal 416
Spieker LD and Weber F, '*Commission v Malta* (C-181/23): A "Miracle" of Union Citizenship?' (2025) 50 European Law Review 487
Tridimas T, 'Wreaking the Wrongs: Balancing Rights and the Public Interest the EU Way' (2023) 29 Columbia Journal of European Law 185

Tridimas T, 'The General Principles of EU Law and the Europeanisation of National Laws' (2020) 13 Review of European Administrative Law 5

Tridimas T, *The General Principles of EU Law*, 2nd edn (OUP 2007)

Tuori K, 'European Constitutionalism' in Roger Masterman and Robert Schütze (eds), *The Cambridge Companion to Comparative Constitutional Law* (CUP 2019)

Tuori K, 'The Many Constitutions of Europe' in Kaarlo Tuori and Suvi Sankari (eds), *The Many Constitutions of Europe* (Routledge 2016)

Tusseau G, 'Debating Legal Pluralism and Constitutionalism: New Trajectories for Legal Theory in the Global Age' in Katharina Boele-Woelki and others (eds), *General Reports of the XXth General Congress of the International Academy of Comparative Law* (Springer 2021)

van der Schyff G, 'Parameters of EU and Member State Constitutional Identity: A Topic in Development' (2022) 4 European Yearbook of Constitutional Law 89

Venizelos E, 'Democratic Legitimacy at National Level and Solidarity between Financially Unequal Member States' (2017) European Politeia 282

Vesting T, *Legal Theory* (Hart 2018)

Volkmann U, *Grundzüge einer Verfassunsglehre* (Mohr Siebeck 2013)

von Arnauld A, 'Normenhierarchien innerhalb des primären Gemeinschaftsrechts' (2003) 38 Europarecht 191

von Bogdandy A, 'Founding Principles' in Armin von Bogdandy and Jürgen Bast (eds), *Principles of European Constitutional Law*, 2nd edn (Hart 2009)

von Bogdandy A and Bast J, 'The Constitutional Core of the Union' (2024) 61 Common Market Law Review 1471

von Bogdandy A and others, 'Reverse Solange—Protecting the Essence of Fundamental Rights against EU Member States' (2012) 49 Common Market Law Review 489

Voßkuhle A, *The Idea of the European Community of Values* (Bittner 2017)

Voßkuhle A, 'Pyramid or Mobile?' in *Dialogue between Judges* (Council of Europe 2014)

6

Between Values and Self-Preservation in the Interpretation of EU Law

Davor Petrić[*]

1. Introduction

Article 2 of the Treaty on the European Union (TEU) lists a number of values, such as human dignity, fundamental rights, freedom, justice, democracy, equality, and the rule of law. The same provision states that the Union is *founded* on these values and that they are *common* to all Member States. As a declaratory and solemn provision, it says nothing more about those values, such as what are their origin or nature or essence, or their possible uses or functions or legal effects, or other such details.

A traditional, legal positivist view would be that values have no place in judicial decision-making in general or the interpretation of law in particular.[1] This view is premised on a separation between law and morality.[2] The same view was espoused in several landmark rulings in which the Court of Justice of the EU noted that it is not 'called upon to broach' (non-legal) value questions, but instead 'must restrict itself to a legal interpretation'.[3]

* I am grateful to the editors, Luigi Lonardo and Alezini Loxa, for their questions and suggestions, which have helped to shape this chapter into something quite different (and, I hope, better) than its first draft. I also thank all participants at the workshop 'The Legal Reasoning of the Court of Justice of the European Union: A Normative Assessment' held at Lund University in April 2024 and at the conference 'Central and Eastern European Network of Jurisprudence' held at the University of Padova in September 2023, in particular Joxerramon Bengoetxea, Graham Butler, Xavier Groussot, Niamh Nic Shuibhne, Luke Dimitrios Spieker, Takis Tridimas, Ivan Padjen, and Claudio Sarra, for helping me to clarify my ideas, although many gaps and weaknesses certainly remain and are, of course, my own responsibility.

[1] Giulio Itzcovich, 'The European Court of Justice' in András Jakab, Arthur Dyevre and Giulio Itzcovich (eds), *Comparative Constitutional Reasoning* (Cambridge University Press 2017) 277, 302–03.

[2] HLA Hart, 'Positivism and the Separation of Law and Morals' (1958) 71 Harvard Law Review 593.

[3] Case C-34/10 *Brüstle* EU:C:2011:669, para 30; see also Case C-159/90 *Grogan* EU:C:1991:378, paras 19–20.

Davor Petrić, *Between Values and Self-Preservation in the Interpretation of EU Law* In: *The Reasoning of the Court of Justice of the EU*. Edited by: Alezini Loxa and Luigi Lonardo, Oxford University Press.
 DOI: 10.1093/9780198983002.003.0008

At the same time, some authors have argued that, even though they may not be visible in the judgments of the Court of Justice, values are essential in the interpretation of EU law, just like in every other legal order. These values would hence represent what was in different contexts referred to as the 'constitutional *télos*' or 'end'[4] and 'constitutional *óntos*' or 'essence'[5] of EU law. Similar points were echoed in the recent jurisprudence of the Court of Justice. It was thus held that '[t]he values contained in Article 2 TEU . . . define the very identity of the European Union as a common legal order'.[6] And moreover, 'Article 2 TEU is not a mere statement of policy guidelines or intentions, but contains values which . . . are given concrete expression in principles comprising legally binding obligations for the Member States'.[7] In that sense, Article 2 TEU may be seen as 'a provision of EU primary law that figures on top of the EU's constitution—in other words, a *Grundnorm* for European integration'.[8] From this *Grundnorm* all other provisions of EU law would draw their validity, and ultimately should be interpreted in conformity with it.

A turning point that brought Article 2 TEU into the spotlight came following interference with judicial independence in several Member States.[9] The question raised in legal scholarship—which started to receive answers in the case law—was what the rule of law as a founding value requires in terms of shielding national judges from different kinds of pressures, internal and external, especially pressures coming from other branches of the government. Scholars also explored, more generally, how values from Article 2 TEU relate to different provisions found in other parts of the Treaties, as well as how those values can be enforced and protected through procedures established by the Treaties.[10] Given its ever-increasing engagement with the value-related issues, the jurisprudence of the Court of Justice was said to be moving towards the stage of 'value constitutionalism'.[11] Nevertheless, it seems that there still remains a

[4] Miguel Poiares Maduro, 'Interpreting European Law: Judicial Adjudication in a Context of Constitutional Pluralism' (2007) 1 European Journal of Legal Studies 137.

[5] Siniša Rodin, 'Liberal Constitutionalism, Rule of Law and Revolution by Other Means' [2021] Il Diritto dell'Unione Europea 203.

[6] Case C-156/21 *Hungary v Parliament and Council (Conditionality Regulation)* EU:C:2022:97, para 127.

[7] Case C-157/21 *Poland v Parliament and Council (Conditionality Regulation)* EU:C:2022:98, para 264.

[8] Jan Wouters, 'Revisiting Art. 2 TEU: A True Union of Values?' (2020) 5 European Papers 255, 258; see also Spieker's chapter in this book.

[9] Matteo Bonelli and Monica Claes, 'Judicial Serendipity: How Portuguese Judges Came to the Rescue of the Polish Judiciary' (2018) 14 European Constitutional Law Review 622.

[10] cf contributions in András Jakab and Dimitry Kochenov (eds), *The Enforcement of EU Law and Values: Ensuring Member States' Compliance* (Oxford University Press 2017).

[11] Frank Schorkopf, 'Value Constitutionalism in the European Union' (2020) 21 German Law Journal 956.

lot to be said about values, their substance, and their functions, in the legal reasoning of the Court of Justice more specifically. Although the literature on the reasoning of the Court is abundant,[12] only recent developments in its case law have managed to bring the question of values to the forefront.[13]

In this contribution, I will discuss the content of different values—legal, moral, social, and political, and not only those mentioned in Article 2 TEU—that can be found in the reasoning of the Court of Justice. To get there, I will first briefly cover specific forms in which values may appear as arguments that justify particular outcomes of interpretation of EU law (Section 2), and then focus on the content with which the Court substantiates these values (Section 3). Following that, I will consider the merits of the Court's 'value jurisprudence' and of the process in which these values are expounded (Section 4), before I conclude (Section 5). The main point I will be making is that, not least given the uncertainty, indeterminacy, and malleability of the content of EU values, the Union's structural and institutional interests (existential, if you wish)—reflected in Article 1 TEU and its integrationist outlook ('ever closer union')—might be the ultimate consideration in the interpretation of EU law, which overrides all other considerations, including Article 2 TEU and fundamental values. If that is the case, what becomes more important than the substance of values is the institutional framework and processes within which these values can be contested, negotiated, and (temporarily) settled, in the shadow of the aforementioned existential interests. In particular, my suggestion is to look for (more) open judicial decision-making, (more) transparent judicial reasoning, and exceptional and minimalist judicial reliance on value-based arguments.

2. Shapes of Values

In the interpretation of EU law, values may come in different shapes and forms.[14] For one, the Court of Justice may rely on them as self-standing, distinct arguments of interpretation.[15] In the same way as the Court of Justice uses other arguments—textual or linguistic, contextual or systemic, or teleological

[12] See Introduction to this book, and many classic titles cited therein.

[13] Luke Dimitrios Spieker, *EU Values Before the Court of Justice* (Oxford University Press 2023).

[14] For further discussion, see Davor Petrić, 'The Court of Justice of the EU: A Contextualist Court' (2023) 8 University of Bologna Law Review 11, 31–32.

[15] In what follows, I describe the reasoning of the Court of Justice in the context of justification. For more on legal interpretation as argumentation, and distinction between 'discovery' and 'justification' in judicial interpretation of the law, see the Introduction to this book, as well as the chapter written by Joxerramon Bengoetxea and Luigi Lonardo.

or purposive arguments[16]—it may cite the argument from values to directly justify the outcome it reaches when interpreting provisions of EU law. Since values are typically linked to objectives and purposes that certain provisions or legal acts aim to achieve, they may *prima facie* be regarded as teleological arguments. (Although values may also be regarded as systemic arguments, or wear a label of some other kind, since these conceptual categories do not have sharp edges and can overlap—and it is, of course, a matter of one's interpretation how to understand, describe, or classify a given argument of interpretation.) What is important is that the argument from values opens the Court's reasoning to moral considerations. It is thus unsurprising that values in this form are rarely found in the Court's rulings.[17]

Values can also be expressed in the form of other types of arguments of interpretation. This is a typical and common situation. Here, values appear implicitly in the reasoning of the Court of Justice. So, values would be traced back to some source of positive law and presented as distinct legal arguments. Their non-legal origin would thus be dressed in legal attire. For instance, values could be expressed via the systemic argument which aims for a consistent and harmonious interpretation of provisions of EU law.[18] To give some examples: values of dignity or equality can be linked to respective provisions of the Charter of Fundamental Rights of the EU,[19] or secondary law instruments that are giving concrete expression to those values such as directives on equal treatment in employment matters or race equality.[20] There are also provisions of the Treaties and secondary law which are permeated by values from Article 2 TEU,[21] and have to be interpreted in conformity with values enlisted (or implied) therein.[22]

[16] Case 26/62 *Van Gend & Loos* EU:C:1963:1, 12–13 ('the spirit, the general scheme and the wording'); Case C-129/19 *Presidenza del Consiglio dei Ministri v BV* EU:C:2020:566, para 38 ('the wording, the context and the objectives').

[17] Itzcovich (n 1) 303. For an example where values were cited as self-standing arguments, see Joined Cases C-322/19 and C-385/19 *KS and Others* EU:C:2021:11, paras 69–73; and Joined Cases C-322/19 and C-385/19 *KS and Others* EU:C:2020:642, Opinion of Advocate General de la Tour, paras 85–87.

[18] cf Luke Dimitrios Spieker, 'Breathing Life into the Union's Common Values: On the Judicial Application of Article 2 TEU in the EU Value Crisis' (2019) 20 German Law Journal 1182, 1201; and Tom Boekestein, 'Making Do With What We Have: On the Interpretation and Enforcement of the EU's Founding Values' (2022) 23 German Law Journal 431, 437–38.

[19] Title I ('Dignity'), Article 1 and Title III ('Equality'), Articles 20–23.

[20] Council Directive 2000/78/EC establishing a general framework for equal treatment in employment and occupation, OJ L 303, 2 December 2000 (see recitals 3, 9, and 11, in particular); Council Directive 2000/43/EC implementing the principle of equal treatment between persons irrespective of racial or ethnic origin, OJ L 180, 19 July 2000 (see recitals 6–9 and 12, in particular).

[21] For instance, solidarity finds expression in Articles 67, 80, 194, and 222 TFEU. As argued in Koen Lenaerts and José A Gutiérrez-Fons, 'High Hopes: Autonomy and the Identity of the EU' (2023) 8 European Papers 1495, 1500, values from Article 2 TEU 'pervade the entire body of EU law'.

[22] Case C-64/16 *Associação Sindical dos Juízes Portugueses* EU:C:2018:117; Case C-140/20 *G. D.* EU:C:2022:258, para 43.

Moreover, values can be expressed through general principles of law,[23] which sit at the borderline between systemic and teleological arguments.[24] When the Court of Justice introduces general principles of EU law, it relies on sources like common constitutional traditions and international treaties. Yet from those sources it crafts principles that 'fit' best within the scheme of the Treaties and ultimate objectives and fundamental values of the EU integration, and thus capture the Union's 'political morality', to use Dworkin's vocabulary.[25] And obviously, values can be expressed through purposes of legal provisions ('The objective of this provision is achieving *equality*')[26] and consequences associated with those purposes ('Interpretation that *would result in* restrictions of the freedom of individuals, which is the aim of this provision, must be rejected'). In all these cases, although it formally cites legal arguments, the Court of Justice has to engage with matters of morality that require value judgments. Which interpretations are the most consistent with the system established by the Treaties? What kind of a system is established by the Treaties? Which principles fit best within it? Which purposes does EU law pursue, and are some more important than others? Which consequences are good or bad? And what do we consider as good and bad in the first place? The answers to these questions, captured by different systemic and teleological arguments, inevitably introduce non-legal considerations into the Court's reasoning.

[23] There seems to be a great deal of overlap between the concepts of (general) principles and values, which are sometimes conflated; see eg Takis Tridimas, *General Principles of EU Law* (Oxford University Press 199) 349; Dimitry Kochenov, 'The *Aquis* and Its Principles: The Enforcement of the "Law" versus the Enforcement of "Values" in the EU' in Jakab and Kochenov (n 10) 9. However, there are some differences between the two, which are useful for distinguishing between the argument from general principles and the argument from values, at least as a broad and general matter. For instance, principles are usually constructed by the Court of Justice from several sources of positive law, like national constitutional traditions or international law. Unlike values, which are merely declared or 'discovered', and as such 'pre-positive', so we would not talk about values as being established by the Court of Justice. Moreover, principles may be characterized as *deontological* and values as *teleological* in nature; see Jürgen Habermas, *Between Facts and Norms: Contributions to a Discourse Theory of Law and Democracy* (translated by William Rehg, MIT Press 1996) 253–57. Put differently, principles require or command a specific course of action, which is why they are legally binding in a stricter sense (although not in the same manner as legal rules, which typically bind in an 'all or nothing' fashion), whereas values merely recommend or suggest something as a desirable or good course of action among many possible courses of action, yet they are not legally binding in a strict sense. Rather, their bindingness is more in the moral or practical domain. Hence, values would be aspirational, goal-oriented, dynamic, forward-looking, similar to purposes/goals/aims/objectives of EU law, which is why legal theorists tend to put them in the same category of teleological arguments. Principles, meanwhile, are somewhat more static, backward-looking (or at best present-looking), intended to systematize the law and make it more coherent (in conceptual but also value terms), and for that reason often placed in the category of systemic arguments.

[24] cf Joxerramon Bengoetxea's term 'teleo-systemic criteria' of interpretation, in *The Legal Reasoning of the European Court of Justice: Towards a European Jurisprudence* (Clarendon Press 1993) 250–51.

[25] Ronald Dworkin, 'Law as Interpretation' (1982) 60 Texas Law Review 527.

[26] Case 43/75 *Defrenne* EU:C:1976:56.

Finally, values can appear in the Court's reasoning as meta-arguments that justify the choice of other arguments of interpretation. As explained by Neil MacCormick and Robert Summers, arguments in interpretation 'have genuine justificatory force to the extent that they are grounded in values, particularly the underpinning values of legal and constitutional order'.[27] These values, therefore, 'form the ultimate level of justification of interpretative arguments and of their underlying directives of interpretation'.[28] For example, the Court of Justice will typically justify the textual arguments (ie argument from ordinary meaning) by referring to the values associated with separation of powers such as democracy and the rule of law,[29] or those associated with legal certainty like notice and predictability;[30] it will justify the systemic arguments by referring to coherence and completeness of law,[31] which are generic values of great importance for every legal order; and so on.

Similarly, values as meta-arguments can be used to determine how conflicts between rival arguments of interpretation, which point to equally plausible outcomes, should be resolved.[32] As such, values appear as 'constitutional interpretive tiebreakers' in the Court's reasoning.[33] In those situations, values as 'tiebreakers' might suggest, for instance, that an interpretation that ensures maximum conformity with the Charter should be prioritized over the competing interpretations that are also aligned with the Charter but to a somewhat lesser degree; or that an interpretation which ensures that more situations are treated equally in law or in fact should be prioritized over the competing interpretations that leave more differences in treatment.[34] Used in this way, values can be essential for mitigating fundamental tensions inherent in judicial interpretation of (EU) law, such as the tension between 'particular' and 'general', that is between justice for individuals involved in a particular case and wider interests of the society,[35] or between liberalism (with a focus on fundamental

[27] Neil MacCormick and Robert Summers, 'Interpretation and Justification' in Neil MacCormick and Robert Summers (eds), *Interpreting Statutes: A Comparative Study* (Ashgate Publishing 1991) 511, 532.

[28] ibid.

[29] Joined Cases C-310/98 and C-406/98 *Met-Trans and Sagpol* EU:C:2000:154, para 32; Case C-906/19 *Criminal proceedings against FO* EU:C:2021:715, paras 41–45.

[30] Case C-361/06 *Feinchemie Schwebda and Bayer CropScience* EU:C:2008:296, para 50.

[31] Case 314/85 *Foto-Frost* EU:C:1987:452, paras 16–17.

[32] cf Boekestein (n 18) 437–438.

[33] Case C-129/19 *Presidenza del Consiglio dei Ministri v BV* EU:C:2020:375, Opinion of Advocate General Bobek, paras 100 ff; see also *Presidenza del Consiglio dei Ministri v BV* (n 16) paras 39–55.

[34] For instance, differences between cross-border and internal situations, or movement and non-movement situations, etc.

[35] cf Jan Komárek, 'Judicial Legitimacy in the European Union' in Claire Kilpatrick and Joanne Scott (eds), *New Legal Approaches to Studying the Court of Justice: Revisiting Law in Context* (Oxford University Press 2020) 125.

rights protection) and democracy (with a focus on majoritarianism) more broadly.

3. Content of Values

Irrespective of the form in which a specific value may appear in the reasoning of the Court of Justice, the key question would concern its substance and meaning. So, it may be asked, as a general matter, what kind of content does the Court of Justice give to different values when interpreting EU law?

Broadly speaking, it could be said that EU values, in particular those founding values of Article 2 TEU, are characteristics of liberal democracy as a political order and liberal constitutionalism as a legal order.[36] Some have suggested that perhaps the only thing about the EU on which everyone would likely agree is 'the liberal credentials of the integration project'.[37] So, values in EU law are not ideology-neutral or randomly engraved in the system of the Treaties that Member States have established. Rather, these values represent 'fundamental constitutional choice[s]' intentionally made by the Member States,[38] which thereby defined the kind of community they want to take part in and jointly build.

Nevertheless, it seems difficult to pin down what exactly would be the defining characteristics of liberalism, if we can agree that it underpins EU values. Would it be individualism? Protection of the weak(er)? Restriction of the majority factions? Being suspicious of those who possess power? Or perhaps tolerance? Or the harm principle?[39] It is hard to put this as a general matter, given that liberalism is a dense notion in itself, and in any event seems dependent on the context. And moreover, liberalism is relativist with its dogmas, given that it does not endorse absolute meanings of values that are associated with it.

What makes everything even more complicated is the often-mentioned value pluralism in the EU, that is, the cultural and historical diversity of its Member States (from which the 'united in diversity' motto comes), which is itself protected by the Treaties. As Armin von Bogdandy and Luke Dimitrios

[36] Rodin (n 5) 226–231.

[37] Tomasz Tadeusz Koncewicz, 'Values' in Sacha Garben and Laurence Gormley (eds), *Oxford Encyclopedia of EU Law* (Oxford University Press 2023) para 32.

[38] Rodin (n 5); cf *Hungary v Parliament and Council (Conditionality Regulation)* (n 6) para 127.

[39] The view of John Stuart Mill that the liberty of an individual should be limited only when necessary to prevent harm to others.

Spieker elaborate, the diversity of Member States and their constitutional traditions is extraordinary; we have

> the republics and monarchies, parliamentary and semi-presidential systems, strong and weak parliaments, competitive and consensual democracies, strong and weak political party systems, strong and weak social institutions, unitary and federal systems, strong, weak or absent constitutional courts, diverse and perhaps even incompatible systems of judicial independence, significant divergences in the content and level of protection of fundamental rights, not least Ottoman, Catholic, Protestant, secular, socialist, anarcho-syndicalist, postcolonial and statist constitutional traditions.[40]

So, even when we say that the EU founding values are *common to* and *shared by* the Member States, we can at best say that every Member State knows some version or conception of nominally the same concept, which in large part depends on its legal and political culture.[41] Hence, in each of them we may get different answers to questions such as: What exactly is understood as a *democratic* society? What is a proper degree of *separation of powers* between the branches of government? What are the specific requirements of the *rule of law* (*Rechtsstaat, état de droit, stato di diritto*)? Because as Neil MacCormick and Robert Summers rightly noted, 'in different systems and at different times' all these concepts 'have been subject to competing and even conflicting interpretations and degrees of acceptance'.[42] In the EU, it is therefore possible that EU institutions and national institutions may have different understanding of the content of founding values (some or all of them). And when it comes to the interpretation of EU law, the Court of Justice and national courts may likewise have different working definitions of specific values. This could lead them to interpret the same law in a different manner, arrive at contradictory outcomes

[40] Armin von Bogdandy and Luke Dimitrios Spieker, 'Countering the Judicial Silencing of Critics: Article 2 TEU Values, Reverse *Solange*, and the Responsibilities of National Judges' (2019) 15 European Constitutional Law Review 391, 422.

[41] cf Monica Claes, 'Editorial Note: How Common are the Values of the European Union?' (2019) 15 Croatian Yearbook of European Law and Policy vii. One good example would be neutrality, *neutralité* in French and *Neutralität* in German. In the 1958 French Constitution, it is enshrined in the principle of *laïcité* (Article 1) and requires a strict separation of the state from all religious matters. In the 1949 German Basic Law, the same concept is enshrined in various provisions (eg Articles 3, 4, and 140) but leads to a cooperative separation, meaning that the state can cooperate with religious communities, without discriminating between them. So, in these two countries, the value of neutrality has a completely different meaning; yet in both, it arguably forms a part of their constitutional identity.

[42] MacCormick and Summers (n 27) 534–35.

of interpretation, and eventually settle the same kinds of disputes in a different manner.[43]

Still, given that EU law appears to be sufficiently functional and viable, perhaps it could be that 'the legal orders forming part of it share a similar enough understanding of fundamental principles, *the deep culture of the law*'.[44] So, different understandings of the EU founding values in different Member States may be minimal and compatible enough to keep the EU constitutional edifice in place and running. Or it could be that differences between the Member States in how they understand these values may be more pronounced—which is perhaps not a stretch of imagination in an era of illiberal democracies and rule of law 'backsliding'—but there is something else that makes the Union persevere. What then could be this 'something else'?

3.1 Beyond values . . .

Some have argued that EU values are underspecified or largely devoid of substance.[45] They merely provide a nominal frame, an empty shell, which gets substantiated from case to case with fragments of particular interests, which then shape the outcomes of interpretation of EU law. Given the origins and nature of the EU integration process, those would primarily be market capitalist or economic interests.

Elaborating this view, Andrew Williams suggested that the Treaties and the case law of the Court of Justice were from the beginning defined more by the 'technical' rather than the 'ethical', which made values relatively unimportant.[46]

[43] cf Boekestein (n 18) 449–50; see also Davor Petrić, 'A Reflection on the Methods of Interpretation of EU Law' (2023) 17 Vienna Journal on International Constitutional Law 83, 99–104 (discussing Case C-493/17 *Weiss* EU:C:2018:1000 and BVerfG, 2 BvR 859/15, Judgment of the Second Senate of 5 May 2020 (*PSPP*) DE:BVerfG:2020:rs20200505.2bvr085915, as an example of two courts working with different conceptions of values of democracy and the rule of law, which informed their reasoning and assessment of validity of the European Central Bank's decision on the public sector asset purchase programme).

[44] Suvi Sankari, 'Constitutional Pluralism and Judicial Adjudication: On Legal Reasoning, Minimalism and Silence by the Court of Justice' in Gareth Davies and Matej Avbelj (eds), *Research Handbook on Legal Pluralism and EU Law* (Edward Elgar 2018) 309, 311 (italics added).

[45] cf Dimitry Kochenov and Andrew Williams, 'Europe's Justice Deficit Introduced' in Dimitry Kochenov, Gráinne de Búrca, and Andrew Williams (eds), *Europe's Justice Deficit?* (Hart Publishing 2015) 1. The alternative view would be to say that EU values are not vacant or lacking substance but that their substance is of a different kind, ie they embody a rationale that is different from what we are used to seeing in nation-states' constitutional orders; see discussion that follows.

[46] Andrew Williams, 'Taking Values Seriously: Towards a Philosophy of EU Law' (2009) 29 Oxford Journal of Legal Studies 549. Tomasz Koncewicz similarly remarked that 'the uneasy blend of the functional (pragmatism) [ie market integration through law] and the idealist (values) strands were the defining features of the integration' from the very beginning; see Koncewicz (n 37) para 6.

The integration was centred on the establishment of the common market and was meant to be achieved 'through law'. The primary concern for the Union and its Court thus became the effectiveness of the Treaties and the effective functioning of the market. This served 'as a means of ensuring the EU's continuing existence',[47] and 'provided and continues to provide the parameters for value definition'.[48] If at some point certain values came into play, or conflicted with other interests or with each other, the Court approached those situations 'in accordance with the overall aim of the legal order's continuing integrity and existence'.[49]

What we were left with was 'functional constitutionalism', which permeates the Union's legal and institutional structure, and which is qualitatively different from traditional state constitutional practices in the sense that it places the market and the 'legal' at its core and squeezes out the 'political' and other related notions such as democracy, social justice, rights, and so on.[50] Put differently, traditional constitutionalism, characterized by liberal socio-political values, deontological reasoning (per Kant), and rationalism (as it came out from the Age of Enlightenment), with reason as the source of knowledge and experience, is replaced by functional constitutionalism characterized by economic values, utilitarian reasoning (per Bentham), and market rationalism, with efficiency as the measure of everything.

From this, the conclusion would be that values, such as those listed in Article 2 TEU, cannot be what makes the EU's *Grundnorm*. Rather, its *Grundnorm* is what Williams referred to as 'survival through economic integration', which ensures peace among the EU's nation-states.[51] This was the foundation on top of which the EU legal order developed, and which determined how EU law was interpreted. As he explained further,

[47] Williams (n 46) 569.

[48] ibid 562.

[49] ibid 563. See also Jacob van de Beeten, 'On Metaphor and Meaning: The Autonomy of EU Legal Order Through the Lens of Project and System' (2023) 8 European Papers 1441, 1459–60, who similarly argued that the case law reveals a structural bias in the sense that the Court of Justice shows strong commitment to preservation of the systemic integrity and functioning of the EU legal order, which is hence treated as an end in itself and has to be given priority over values. A reply to that was that there cannot be a clash between the EU's structure and its values, 'since the EU constitutional structure is instrumental in protecting and promoting those values', so the Court naturally must protect that structure in order to protect EU values; see Lenaerts and Gutiérrez-Fons (n 21) 1496.

[50] Turkuler Isiksel, *Europe's Functional Constitution* (Oxford University Press 2016). Joseph Weiler sees the legitimacy of such constitutional order in 'political messianism', where 'the justification for action and its mobilizing force derive not from process, as in classical democracy, or from result and success, but from the ideal pursued, the destiny to be achieved, the promised land waiting at the end of the road. Indeed, in messianic visions the end always trumps the means'; see JHH Weiler, 'The Political and Legal Culture of European Integration: An Exploratory Essay' (2011) 9 International Journal of Constitutional Law 678, 683.

[51] Williams (n 46) 570.

> [t]hat basic norm was a presupposed original constitution that saw the survival of Europe . . . through one lens: the preservation of a capitalist economic system. This did not require, indeed it positively ignored, any sophisticated sense of justice. Any other interpretation would have moved the EU away from survival to the adoption of a contradictory theory of society, something which might have jeopardized that survival provoking, as it no doubt would have done, the very ideological conflict it was in part designed to resist. The EC Treaty, validated by this necessity *in extremis* of survival, through the mechanism of a common market, was thus a product of the perceived basic norm.[52]

Under this view, in cases that saw a question of values in EU law being raised before the Court of Justice, those values were instrumentalized for the sake of the 'survival through economic integration'. In other words, they were re-interpreted in a limited and minimalist manner in order not to 'challenge or undermine the *grundnorm*'.[53] Putting together economic integration and the effectiveness of law as the key to the survival of the Union led to case law in which market, business interests, and primacy of EU law got the upper hand whenever they clashed with other social interests, such as protection of fundamental rights, which threatened the integrity of the market or the EU's regulatory efforts. As a consequence, many domains of public policy have been subordinated to the imperatives of EU economic integration and the crude effectiveness of its law, which has arguably destabilized democracy and social justice.[54] This was the basis of the classic criticism of the Court having a market-oriented, pro-business bias.[55] Likewise, the Court was criticized for using the rule of law value as a justification for the supremacy and effectiveness of EU law.[56] And the same criticism could apply to its fundamental rights jurisprudence as it was developed since the 1970s: first defensively, to fend off national challenges against its absolute claim of supremacy, and then offensively, which expanded the Court's jurisdiction into the matters of national competences.[57]

52 ibid.
53 ibid.
54 Isiksel (n 50).
55 cf Fritz W Scharpf, 'The Asymmetry of European Integration, Or Why the EU Cannot be a "Social Market Economy"' (2010) 8 Socio-Economic Review 211.
56 cf Dimitry Kochenov, 'Rule of Law as a Tool to Claim Supremacy' (2020) RECONNECT Working Paper No 9; see also Case C-441/17 R *Commission v Poland* EU:C:2017:877, para 102: '[T]he effective application of EU law . . . [is] an essential component of the rule of law, a value enshrined in Article 2 TEU and on which the European Union is founded'.
57 Jason Coppel and Aidan O'Neill, 'The European Court of Justice: Taking Rights Seriously' (1992) 29 Common Market Law Review 669.

3.2 . . . and towards self-preservation

If values are not the *Grundnorm* in EU law, that is, if Article 2 TEU is not a provision that sits at the very top of the EU constitutional order but economy and effectiveness are the *Grundnorm*, could then Article 1 TEU be the highest-ranking provision? This provision puts forward 'the process of creating an ever closer union among the peoples of Europe' as the ultimate purpose of the integration project. And the 'ever closer union' is to be achieved through the effective market and the effective application of EU law, which seems to be taken almost axiomatically. Hence, every provision, every objective, and every value in EU law would be instrumental 'to the implementation of the process of integration that is the raison d'être of the EU itself'.[58]

'Ever closer union' as the EU's grand objective and its *Grundnorm* could be considered as the driver of the so-called integrationist jurisprudence of the Court of Justice. The claim –not infrequently made—would be that whenever in doubt about the interpretation of EU law, the Court will (almost) always opt for the 'federal' or 'centralizing' solution that enhances integration, favours the Union and its institutions, and promotes its interests.[59] So, there may exist an in-built '*communautaire* tendency' in the Court's approach to the interpretation of EU law, which would lead it to consistently adopt 'pro-integration' outcomes.[60] Also referred to as 'the preference for Europe', it is purportedly

> determined by the genetic code transmitted to the Court by the founding fathers, who entrusted to it the task of ensuring that the law is observed in the application of a Treaty whose primary objective is an 'ever closer union among the peoples of Europe'.[61]

[58] Opinion 2/13 *EU Accession to the ECHR* EU:C:2014:2454, para 172. This ruling of the Court was criticized for showing greater concern for the realization of the EU's objectives from Article 3 TEU at the expense of the EU's values from Article 2 TEU, thereby 'invers[ing] the constitutional hierarchy of norms, placing the objectives of EU integration above (and beyond) the values that motivate it'; see Violeta Moreno-Lax and Katja S Ziegler, 'Autonomy of the EU Legal Order—A General Principle? On the Risks of Normative Functionalism and Selective Constitutionalisation' in Katja S Ziegler, Päivi J Neuvonen, and Violeta Moreno-Lax (eds), *Research Handbook on General Principles in EU Law* (Edward Elgar 2022) 227, 246.

[59] cf Hjalte Rasmussen, *On Law and Policy in the European Court of Justice: A Comparative Study in Judicial Policymaking* (Martinus Nijhoff 1986); Trevor Hartley, 'The European Court, Judicial Objectivity, and the Constitution of the European Union' (1996) 112 Law Quarterly Review 95.

[60] Gunnar Beck, *The Legal Reasoning of the Court of Justice of the EU* (Hart Publishing 2012) 318–331. Sacha Garben referred to this as the 'in dubio, pro integratione' interpretive maxim; see 'Editorial: Of Ends and Means' (2025) 50 European Law Review 381.

[61] Giuseppe Federico Mancini and David Keeling, 'Democracy and the European Court of Justice' (1994) 57 Modern Law Review 175, 186.

Yet effectiveness-cum-integrationism does not take us far either. It rather leaves us with the same question that was raised initially, and that is the question of essence of such a *Grundnorm*. What would be its defining characteristics? Put differently, what makes EU law more effective, or the internal market more functional, or integration more solid, or union among the peoples of Europe ever closer?

The answer to this question seems elusive. It can be anything, basically. As Advocate General Tamara Ćapeta wrote, '[i]ntegration as a term does not mean anything in itself'.[62] European integration is underpinned by so many diverse objectives, interests, and policies at the macro level, some of which in some situations may be contradictory. But what would make them integrationist or more integrationist than others? Is market more functional if the regulators follow some degree of economic interventionism or full-on laissez-faire? Or is integration stronger if it gives preference to market and competition or to social justice and equity? Or is the union among the peoples of Europe closer when it is built around socially liberal or conservative policies? Any of these alternatives could arguably qualify as integrationist.[63] But if 'integration' can mean anything, then 'integration' means nothing. Absent a relatively intelligible measure, we cannot know when exactly something would be 'in the interest of integration'. Even Robert Schuman, in his address when the idea of the European Coal and Steel Community was launched, said that 'Europe will not be made all at once, or according to a master plan'. So, in such a diverse and dynamic political community as the EU, there is arguably nothing that could help us with measuring integration.

Of course, when talking about the case law of the Court of Justice, those who are sure about its '*communautaire* tendency' may think that whatever the Court says is 'in the interest of integration', is surely in the interest of integration. So, when the Court gives preference to one value or objective at the expense of some other, we could assume that the outcome thereby reached must be integrationist. But that would leave us with a very inconsistent, even random, picture of what makes something integrationist.[64] Because in the Court's jurisprudence, we can find cases that would suggest that, say, restrictions of market freedoms for the sake of fundamental rights protection are

[62] Tamara Ćapeta, 'Ideology and Legal Reasoning at the European Court of Justice' in Tamara Perišin and Siniša Rodin (eds), *The Transformation or Reconstitution of Europe* (Hart Publishing 2018) 89, 105.
[63] ibid 104–07.
[64] cf Siniša Rodin, 'A Metacritique of the Court of Justice of the European Union' [2016] Il Diritto dell'Unione Europea 193 (noting that despite the solid record of 'Europeanizing' judgments there are many examples in which the Court sided with 'de-centralizing values', like Case C-333/13 *Dano* EU:C:2014:2358).

both okay and not okay from the perspective of market integration or effectiveness of EU law.[65] This is inevitable, given that the Treaties themselves do not state anything as absolute and untouchable. For every market freedom that is in principle guaranteed and considered to be essential for the functioning of the internal market, there exist public policy exceptions that may justify its restriction.[66] So, when allowing restrictions of market freedoms for the sake of public policy objectives, although the market is likely made less effective, the integration is perhaps made more solid.

Some have attempted to offer a measure of integration that is more structural, institutional, or functional and less substantive, and, as such, more useful when trying to describe effectiveness-cum-integrationism as the *Grundnorm* in EU law. For an outcome to be considered in the interest of European integration, it would have to strengthen the Union and its federal elements, broaden the scope of EU law and increase its effectiveness, or enlarge the powers of EU institutions.[67] Such outcomes would, for example, confirm the direct effect of provisions of EU law, or preserve their autonomy (by, for example, excluding interferences of international law) or primacy over 'external' (national, international) law; or narrow exceptions from application of provisions of EU law as well as discretion of national authorities to derogate from EU law; or enlarge the EU courts' power of judicial review, the European Parliament's legislative powers, the European Commission's powers in international representation, the EU agencies' regulatory powers; and so on.

These considerations will probably be at play only very exceptionally, because not every case before the Court of Justice raises obvious value-related questions, which the Court finds relevant to reflect on in its reasoning. And cases that concern the 'ever closer union' or the 'survival through economic integration', even implicitly, should be even rarer. Perhaps only in some landmark cases, a few in the thousands that the Court hears every year, might these considerations be decisive.[68]

[65] Examples typically cited are Case C-36/02 *Omega* EU:C:2004:614 and Case C-438/05 *Viking* EU:C:2007:772.

[66] Although one could also say that by designating something as a rule or principle (which ought to be interpreted extensively, per argument from effectiveness) and something else as an exception to that rule or principle (which ought to be interpreted restrictively), a certain value or ideological hierarchy has been imposed, which will consistently prefer certain types of outcomes; cf Aristel Skrbic, 'Ideology in the Adjudication of the ECJ' (2023) 42 Law and Philosophy 561.

[67] Trevor Hartley, *The Foundations of European Community Law* (4th edn, Oxford University Press 1998) 78; see also Case C-621/18 *Wightman* EU:C:2018:978, Opinion of Advocate General Campos Sánchez-Bordona, para 133: 'The objective of achieving "an ever closer union among the peoples of Europe"... favours an interpretation of the rules of EU law which tends to strengthen, and not dissolve, the European Union.'

[68] cf Gerard Conway, 'The Quality of Decision-Making at the Court of Justice of the European Union' in Mátyás Bencze and Gar Yein Ng (eds), *How to Measure the Quality of Judicial Reasoning* (Springer

Still, it is important to have some idea about what might be going on in those hard cases. As already mentioned, values that may appear in the reasoning of the Court of Justice do not have a settled content, which makes them highly indeterminate and malleable. And the reason is both open-endedness of political ideologies (liberalism) and fickleness of the integration and its dynamic (and whatever would be in the interest of integration), which thus cannot provide reliable input to substantiate those values. Moreover, at times we might have several values involved whose content would be somewhat determinate, yet they may contradict each other, and the Court would need something to break the tie.[69] Either way, we would need something to justify which value (or which conception of the same value) prevails, even when that something is not fully explicated in the Court's judgment. As I suggested, that would be the functionalist reading of Article 1 TEU's 'ever closer union', which favours values (or conceptions of values) that further structural interests of the Union and its institutions. So, founding values and their specific conceptions are validated through the interpretation of EU law in hard cases only insofar as they fit into this broader, unrevealed functionalist narrative.[70] Read in this way, Article 1 TEU would be the ultimate justification in the interpretation of EU law, the meta-meta-argument and the highest constitutional tiebreaker that can settle the conflict of values as meta-arguments of interpretation.

Although this last point certainly requires a more careful elaboration, which exceeds the limits of this contribution and my current capabilities, some judgments may serve as indicative examples, I hope. For instance, when the Court of Justice interpreted Treaty provisions on its jurisdiction in the field of common foreign and security policy, alternative interpretations were both underpinned by contradictory conceptions of the rule of law.[71] One

2018) 225 (noting similarly that only in important cases does the Court's 'pro-integration policy' dominate over 'a more conventional hermeneutic discipline' in the interpretation of EU law).

[69] cf Lenaerts and Gutiérrez-Fons (n 21) 1501, who admit that 'one cannot rule out the fact that the values contained in art. 2 TEU may occasionally conflict with one another', so that, for example, 'upholding the rule of law may sometimes oppose an unfettered protection of fundamental rights'.

[70] cf Siniša Rodin's reference to the temptation of Christ in the desert by Satan, as it is narrated in the Gospel of Matthew. In their exchange both Satan and Jesus refer to particular verses from the Psalms, which are all in principle equally authoritative. But what makes one reading of those verses better and valid and disregards the reading of other verses is found in 'a broader and pre-arranged scheme, a narrative according to which the life and death of Christ is instrumental to the fulfillment of the God's plan, and accordingly, written authority is validated only insofar as it fits into that plan which, itself, remains tacit'; in Siniša Rodin, 'Interpretation in the Court of Justice of the European Union, Originalism, Purposivism and *l'économie générale*' (2019) 34 American University International Law Review 601, 631–32.

[71] Case C-72/15 *Rosneft* EU:C:2017:236, paras 58–81. For a discussion, see Luigi Lonardo's contribution to this book.

(restrictive) interpretation was justified with the rule of law as defined by separation of powers (institutional balance) and federal principle (conferral). The other (broad) interpretation was justified with the rule of law as defined by effective protection of individual rights, legal certainty and justice, coherence of the system of judicial protection, uniformity of law, and unity of the legal order. But the latter conception of the rule of law and the values related to it was strongly in favour of structural interests of the Union, since it implied enlargement of the power of judicial review of the Court of Justice in an area dominated by national interests and intergovernmental decision-making, which ultimately might have been the decisive consideration.[72]

The same would go for cases in which national courts suggest alternative interpretations of EU values. When the Court of Justice and national courts adopt contradictory understandings of the content of the same values, it has been argued that 'the functioning of the EU legal order can only be upheld by asserting the primacy of EU law as the *ultima ratio*'.[73] In other words, if the alternatives supported by the Court and national courts are valid (applicable/effective) versus invalid (inapplicable/ineffective) EU law, the functionalist reading of Article 1 TEU as the unspoken *Grundnorm* would be the ultimate consideration that breaks the tie in favour of the former.

4. The Value of Values and the Value of Process

So far, we have heard about exceptional circumstances in which values are invoked in the interpretation of EU law; about many question marks when it comes to their content, either in theory or as we can read it out from the reasoning of the Court of Justice; and about Article 1 TEU and the Union's structural and institutional interests that seem to override Article 2 TEU values when all is said and done. Where does all that leave us?

The functionalist reading of the 'ever closer union' clause from Article 1 TEU, as was shown, can give us some measurable notions that could be considered 'integrationist' and conducive to the effectiveness of the EU market and legal order. But any attempt to read out more substantive notions from this provision

[72] For another example discussed in the literature, see Case C-105/03 *Pupino* EU:C:2005:386, para 36, in which the Court of Justice explicitly relied on Article 1 TEU 'in the name of ensuring an effective application of the EU's objectives', and as a result 'extended by itself its jurisdiction to protect individual rights'; in Xavier Groussot and Anna Zemskova, 'The Resilience of Rights and European Integration' in Antonina Bakardjieva Engelbrekt and Xavier Groussot (eds), *The Future of Europe: Political and Legal Integration Beyond Brexit* (Hart Publishing 2019) 97, 101.

[73] Boekestein (n 18) 449. In my reading, this is what happened in the *Weiss/PSPP* saga (n 43).

would likely bring more uncertainty than clarity, as suggested earlier. And the reason is that the core of Article 1 TEU as the *Grundnorm* in EU law would not be some fixed predetermined destination or a final 'union' which awaits Europe and its peoples, because nobody knows (or can know) where that destination is or what that union should look like. So, there is no one or one correct answer to these questions. If that is indeed the case, the core of Article 1 TEU might instead be 'the process of creating'. The union is arguably meant to be dynamic and permanently in the making—as the Schuman's Declaration proclaimed, it 'will not be made all at once, or according to a master plan'—to keep bringing the peoples of Europe closer and closer together but never to make them 'one people', thus resembling Zeno's dichotomy paradox (or paradox of motion), or an asymptote that infinitely grows smaller between the curve and the line but never gets to zero.[74] And through partaking in the common market—trading, working, and receiving services abroad, and living through economic highs and lows—and witnessing the effects of the same law, the peoples of Europe are starting to make joint concrete lived experiences. To paraphrase again the Schuman Declaration, the 'ever closer union' 'will be built through concrete achievements', based on the common market and the common law, 'which first [need to] create a de facto solidarity'. So, one small, slow step at a time, moving together, without knowing what comes next.

In such a setting, what becomes of central importance, in my view, is the *process* through which the 'ever closer union' and related integration interests of Article 1 TEU, together with the founding values of Article 2 TEU, are interpreted and reinterpreted. The value can be found, then, in the process and not in the end result. And this process-oriented approach, when used to observe the value jurisprudence of the Court of Justice, introduces certain expectations and requirements.

First, there is the organization of procedures before the Court of Justice. As things currently stand, the main procedures, in particular the preliminary ruling procedure from Article 267 TFEU, are organized to bring forward as many voices as possible—from Member States and EU institutions to national courts and private parties in the proceedings before them, and so on. This legitimizes the Court's final say in the interpretation of EU values and interests, as is often said. There is still room for improvement, however. The Court could be even more open to its main interlocutors in the preliminary ruling

[74] cf Kalypso Nicolaïdis, 'The Idea of European Demoicracy' in Julie Dickson and Pavlos Eleftheriadis (eds), *Philosophical Foundations of European Union Law* (Oxford University Press 2012) 247, 252 (writing about the way the EU's political *demoi* are gradually opening to each other, which is 'sharing, pooling, enmeshing, but not unifying').

procedure, and those are national courts, whose involvement does not need to stop at the moment of mailing a reference.[75] Also, the Court could do well to begin formally admitting *amicus curiae* briefs, which would enable the general public to weigh in on important cases and controversies that raise existential and value-related questions.[76] Recently the Court indeed started investing in the openness and transparency of its procedures, when it decided to livestream hearings in some important cases, publish references for preliminary rulings and the parties' submissions, open its historical archives, become active on social media, and others. These efforts are in line with the often overlooked part of Article 1 TEU which is about 'an ever closer union among the peoples of Europe', but such union 'in which decisions are taken as openly as possible . . . to the citizen'.

Besides judicial procedures, the Court's reasoning could also become more open and transparent. It could engage more with the value-based arguments and concerns raised by referring courts, EU institutions, national governments, even its Advocates General,[77] and not only when it agrees with them. It is true that there are institutional factors, such as collegial decision-making, appearance of unanimity in judgments, and informal practice of searching for compromise and consensus whenever possible, that limit the Court's 'argumentative discourse [. . .] to the very essential'.[78] Nevertheless, there should be ways for the Court to continue making its rulings less terse and cryptic and more discursive and dialectical, given that the style of reasoning adopted decades ago in a different historical and socio-political context does not sit well with the contemporary value jurisprudence.[79]

Then there is the question of how much 'value talk' in the reasoning of the Court of Justice is enough (or too much), and how precise should it be. On the one hand, overreliance on values and their overspecification risks causing

[75] cf Rob van Gestel and Jurgen de Poorter, 'Supreme Administrative Courts' Preliminary Questions to the CJEU: Start of a Dialogue or Talking to Deaf Ears?' (2017) 6 Cambridge International Law Journal 122.

[76] cf Alberto Alemanno, 'Public Participation Before the Court of Justice of the EU: Enhancing Outside Party Judicial Participation via Amicus Curiae Briefs' (2025) 17 Erasmus Law Review (forthcoming).

[77] Whose opinions are more open to these kinds of non-legal arguments; for a general discussion, see Mitchel de S-O-l'E Lasser, *Judicial Deliberations: A Comparative Analysis of Judicial Transparency and Legitimacy* (Oxford University Press 2009).

[78] Koen Lenaerts, 'The Court's Outer and Inner Selves: Exploring the External and Internal Legitimacy of the European Court of Justice' in Maurice Adams, Henri de Waele, Johan Meeusen, and Gert Straetmans (eds), *Judging Europe's Judges: The Legitimacy of the Case Law of the European Court of Justice* (Hart Publishing 2013) 13, 46.

[79] cf Nika Bačić Selanec and Tamara Ćapeta, 'The Rule of Law and Adjudication of the Court of Justice of the EU' in Tamara Ćapeta, Iris Goldner Lang, and Tamara Perišin (eds), *The Changing European Union: A Critical View on the Role of Law and the Courts* (Hart Publishing 2022) 35.

a surge in litigation rates and consequently their 'inflation' and loss of justificatory weight. And clearly one should always bear in mind the lack of the Court's democratic credentials and the counter-majoritarian dilemma. On the other hand, complete avoidance of value-based arguments takes away from the transparency and accountability of judicial decision-making in the EU. Engagement with values may shed light on the normative choices the Court inevitably makes when interpreting EU law. This invites the Court's audience, most importantly the EU legislator, to respond to and challenge those choices, their desirability, and their normative implications, through political process. Moreover, a good degree of clarity in the Court's value-informed reasoning also gives a proper explanation and guidance about the normative background of EU law to national courts, which raises the prospects of effective and consistent decentralized enforcement of EU law at the national level.[80]

To thread a fine line between the two extremes of overuse/underuse, many have endorsed judicial minimalism and value exceptionalism. The Court of Justice is used to not saying more than it needs to in order to dispose of a specific dispute.[81] So far, its value jurisprudence has been developed in an incremental and piecemeal manner, step by step.[82] The main example concerns the rule of law, and how it was concretized through the requirement of effective judicial protection under Article 19(1) TEU and the right to a fair trial under Article 47 of the Charter, to cover concepts of judicial independence, impartiality, autonomy, legality, and so on.[83] In the process, the Court threw in metaphysical and poetic phrases (such as 'essence' or 'identity'), often in *obiter dicta*, which served as conversation-starters, to nudge other actors to express themselves on the content of this value. Now, the Court is expected to do the same with other fundamental values—to interpret and specify them in a minimalist fashion and by defining negative obligations ('what cannot be done'), without imposing detailed positive obligations ('what must be done').[84]

[80] cf Maduro (n 4) 142–44.

[81] In Case C-673/16 *Coman* EU:C:2018:385, for instance, the Court decided the question of recognition of same sex marriages between the EU Member States on grounds of free movement, which are limited and appear more 'technical', and not on grounds of values and rights (human dignity, equality, etc), thereby evading moralization and imposition of one-size-fits-all social solutions.

[82] cf Marcus Klamert and Dimitry V Kochenov, 'Article 2 TEU' in Manuel Kellerbauer, Marcus Klamert, and Jonathan Tomkin (eds), *The Treaties and the Charter of Fundamental Rights—A Commentary* (2nd edn, Oxford University Press 2023) 26; and Koncewicz (n 37) para 28: 'While the commitment to the core is intact, the working out of the consequences, trimming down, or expanding the content never ends.'

[83] cf *Hungary v Parliament and Council (Conditionality Regulation)* (n 6) paras 236–37.

[84] Spieker (n 18) 1210–11. In a similar vein, it was argued that the Court of Justice is only asking for 'value alignment', which should 'not be confused with constitutional modelling'; see Lenaerts and Gutiérrez-Fons (n 21) 1505. See also Joined Cases C-357/19, C-379/19, C-547/19, C-811/19, and C-840/19 *Euro Box Promotion* and Others EU:C:2021:1034, para 229 (emphasizing that neither Article

Put differently, the Court should keep drawing 'red lines' around each value, one line after another, without 'colouring' the space between them.[85] And it should keep 'red lines' as a last resort, for exceptional cases only.

This minimalistic approach promises not to 'overload[] the founding values with content' and thus over-constitutionalize them,[86] which leaves room for politics in the process.[87] It is perhaps the only viable approach in pragmatic terms, given that the case law cannot move the needle on its own, absent support from other political and institutional actors.[88] Likewise, it seems to be optimally tailored for preserving national and constitutional pluralism and safeguarding the 'federal balance' in the EU.[89]

Given the unknown and uncertain *finalité* of the 'ever closer union', I think that judicial minimalism may fit the 'process of creating' clause from Article 1 TEU. It can keep the substance of the EU's identity, values, and interests sufficiently fluid and permanently contestable. In this way the Court of Justice cannot frustrate changes that will inevitably happen and does not have its hands tied if, at some point, it decides to change course. But it has to live with the tension between having values open for democratic contestation and constant (re)negotiation on one hand, and preservation of the Union, its constitutional order, and values as its anchor on the other. This tension is built into the fabric of Article 1 TEU. It professes an 'ever closer union' 'among the peoples of Europe', where the former notion is about unity and the latter about diversity.[90] To add a temporal dimension to these notions, we have 'unity' as dynamic, progressive, forward-looking, and dream-like and 'diversity' as static, conservative, backward-looking, and reality-checking. So, the Court gets to say what

2 TEU nor any other provision of EU law require Member States to adopt 'a particular constitutional model', which must be the same in all of them); and *Hungary v Parliament and Council (Conditionality Regulation)* (n 6) para 233 (holding that, in line with Article 4(2) TEU, Member States 'enjoy a certain degree of discretion in implementing the principles of the rule of law', yet 'the result to be achieved [through implementation of those principles] may [not] vary from one Member State to another').

[85] cf Lenaerts and Gutiérrez-Fons (n 21) 1505–06: 'EU law provides for a framework of reference within which the Member States may make their own constitutional choices . . . [T]hose choices must, first, be sufficient in themselves to guarantee compliance with [Article 2 TEU] values . . . [W]ithout that framework, the EU cannot operate'.

[86] Boekestein (n 18) 439–40.

[87] cf Ferdinand Weber, The Pluralism of Values in an Identity-Framed Verbund: Federal Belonging in the European Union After the Rule of Law Conditionality Judgments' (2022) 47 European Law Review 514, 533 (suggesting that decisions like these 'should belong to the democratic, not the judicial realm').

[88] Koncewicz (n 37) para 18: 'Only with the engagement of all three stakeholders [the EU, the Member States, and the citizens] will the European values command their own content and work out its own parameters'.

[89] von Bogdandy and Spieker (n 40) 422.

[90] Groussot and Zemskova (n 72) 106.

the law is and what values are for '[a] community that springs from the dream of coming together and the reality of (still) living apart'.[91]

Finally, bearing in mind this tension between unity and diversity that is reflected in its value jurisprudence, it is important for the Court to be as open as possible for interaction and exchange with legal orders and communities with which the EU is structurally entangled.[92] Those are, in particular, national laws, that is, common constitutional traditions of the Member States, and international treaties to which they have acceded, the most important being the European Convention on Human Rights, which was adopted within the auspices of the Council of Europe (whose advisory body is Venice Commission, another important transnational actor in this regard).[93] The EU's 'union of values' is therefore an indispensable piece of a multi-layered and multi-level puzzle.[94] Ideally, this engagement should go beyond the reasoning in judicial decisions. Hence, all involved actors—the Court of Justice, the European Court of Human Rights, and national high courts—should support supranational judicial associations and professional networks as well as informal avenues for dialogue, not only with each other but also with academic community, civil society, and the media. The union of values is something that needs to be cultivated. It depends on cooperation that is voluntary and in good faith, and on building trust and social capital between everyone involved.[95]

5. A Concluding Remark

That a thriving Union and effective EU law is the ultimate concern for its Court, as I have suggested here, does not mean that the Union's 'lower instance' courts entrusted with a general jurisdiction will share the same sentiment (certainly not all of them). No EU, no Court of Justice. But national judges would still keep their jobs and have a law to take care of. So, the 'ever closer union' clause of Article 1 TEU would not always be the knockout argument for them. Rather, it would be the 'diversity' clause of the same provision. That is what they bring to the table. And for national courts to voice their concerns, the 'process of

[91] Koncewicz (n 37) para 51.
[92] cf Opinion 2/13 (n 58) para 170.
[93] Boekestein (n 18) 441.
[94] Wouters (n 8) 262–63.
[95] cf Monica Claes, 'Safeguarding a Rule of Law Culture in the Member States: Engaging National Actors' (2023) 29 Columbia Journal of European Law 214.

creating' clause of Article 1 TEU is equally essential, the 'process' being the judicial one.

With that in mind, I want to close with a word about the place of national judges in my account. As members of the previously described community who are (supposed to be) socialized in the environment inhabited by authoritative and reputable supranational courts, they would carry responsibilities of their own. Most importantly, when they propose alternative interpretations of EU values or different visions of the future of integration, they should make their argument through reference to what is common to all constitutional orders, through reference to a shared interpretive framework, instead of making closed, inward-looking, parochial argument based solely on national concerns. To borrow words from one landmark ruling, national courts should be 'convinced' that their understanding of EU law 'is equally obvious to the courts of the other Member States and to the Court of Justice'.[96] And even when they disagree with the Court of Justice and contest its views, they should do it in an honest, reasonable, and constructive manner.[97] This is the only way to have a meaningful judicial conversation about the EU's values and identity, which can make the Court of Justice accept compromises about the effectiveness of EU law and functioning of its market.[98] There are examples that show how national concerns can be framed as common and shared matters, which place certain limits on unfettered application of market freedoms,[99] or on the absolutist claim of effectiveness and primacy of EU law,[100] or on automatic compliance with the principle of mutual trust.[101] This is already contained not only in the 'diversity' clause of Article 1 TEU, but in other provisions of the primary law such as Article 2 TEU (emphasizing 'commonality' of values), Article 4(2) TEU and Article 6(3) TEU, and Articles 52(4) and 53 of the Charter.[102] National courts have always contributed to the shaping of EU values and pushed the Court of Justice to rise to the occasion. They will likely do the same

[96] Case 283/81 *CILFIT* EU:C:1982:335, para 16.

[97] cf Ana Bobić and Mark Dawson, 'Making Sense of the "Incomprehensible": The *PSPP* Judgment of the German Federal Constitutional Court' (2020) 57 Common Market Law Review 1953, 1985: 'Constructive instances of contestation of primacy of EU law are those that remain within a reasonable interpretation of the values contained in Article 2 TEU.'

[98] cf Groussot and Zemskova (n 72) 108: 'The telos of European integration is not only about unity but also about diversity. In practice, this means that the effectiveness of EU law is not absolute and that there are situations in which it is accepted that EU law should yield and where the national interests should prevail . . . we can call [this] the "diversity of effectiveness".'

[99] See *Omega* (n 65).

[100] Case C-42/17 *M. A. S. and M. B. (Taricco II)* EU:C:2017:936.

[101] Joined Cases C-404/15 and C-659/15 PPU *Aranyosi and Căldăraru* EU:C:2016:198; for a discussion, see Groussot and Zemskova (n 72) 108 ff.

[102] Groussot and Zemskova (n 72) 114.

as long as there is the Union as we know it.[103] It is, for better or for worse, the EU's way.

References

Alemanno A, 'Public Participation Before the Court of Justice of the EU: Enhancing Outside Party Judicial Participation via Amicus Curiae Briefs' (2025) 17 Erasmus Law Review (forthcoming)

Bačić Selanec N and Ćapeta T, 'The Rule of Law and Adjudication of the Court of Justice of the EU' in Tamara Ćapeta, Iris Goldner Lang, and Tamara Perišin (eds), *The Changing European Union: A Critical View on the Role of Law and the Courts* (Hart Publishing 2022)

Beck G, *The Legal Reasoning of the Court of Justice of the EU* (Hart Publishing 2012)

Bengoetxea J, *The Legal Reasoning of the European Court of Justice: Towards a European Jurisprudence* (Clarendon Press 1993)

Bobić A and Dawson M, 'Making Sense of the "Incomprehensible": The *PSPP* Judgment of the German Federal Constitutional Court' (2020) 57 Common Market Law Review 1953

Boekestein T, 'Making Do with What We Have: On the Interpretation and Enforcement of the EU's Founding Values' (2022) 23 German Law Journal 431

Bonelli M and Claes M, 'Judicial Serendipity: How Portuguese Judges Came to the Rescue of the Polish Judiciary' (2018) 14 European Constitutional Law Review 622

Ćapeta T, 'Ideology and Legal Reasoning at the European Court of Justice' in Tamara Perišin and Siniša Rodin (eds), *The Transformation or Reconstitution of Europe* (Hart Publishing 2018)

Claes M, 'Editorial Note: How Common Are the Values of the European Union?' (2019) 15 Croatian Yearbook of European Law and Policy vii

Claes M, 'Safeguarding a Rule of Law Culture in the Member States: Engaging National Actors' (2023) 29 Columbia Journal of European Law 214

Conway G, 'The Quality of Decision-Making at the Court of Justice of the European Union' in Mátyás Bencze and Gar Yein Ng (eds), *How to Measure the Quality of Judicial Reasoning* (Springer 2018)

Coppel J and O'Neill A, 'The European Court of Justice: Taking Rights Seriously' (1992) 29 Common Market Law Review 669

de S-O-l'E Lasser M, *Judicial Deliberations: A Comparative Analysis of Judicial Transparency and Legitimacy* (Oxford University Press 2009)

Dworkin R, 'Law as Interpretation' (1982) 60 Texas Law Review 527

Garben S, 'Editorial: Of Ends and Means' (2025) 50 European Law Review 381

Groussot X and Zemskova A, 'The Resilience of Rights and European Integration' in Antonina Bakardjieva Engelbrekt and Xavier Groussot (eds), *The Future of Europe: Political and Legal Integration Beyond Brexit* (Hart Publishing 2019)

[103] Even the German constitutional court's (infamous) *PSPP* ruling (n 43) might be celebrated in the future as a leading cause for reinterpretation of EU values, if the Court of Justice at some point replaces its current deferential attitude with strict(er) scrutiny of the ECB's exercise of powers—similarly to what happened earlier with the famous *Solange I* and *Solange II* doctrines on human rights protection, which led the Court to increase the standard of protection of fundamental rights in the EU constitutional order.

Habermas J, *Between Facts and Norms: Contributions to a Discourse Theory of Law and Democracy* (tr William Rehg, MIT Press 1996)

Hart HLA, 'Positivism and the Separation of Law and Morals' (1958) 71 Harvard Law Review 593

Hartley T, *The Foundations of European Community Law* (4th edn, Oxford University Press 1998)

Hartley T, 'The European Court, Judicial Objectivity, and the Constitution of the European Union' (1996) 112 Law Quarterly Review 95

Isiksel T, *Europe's Functional Constitution* (Oxford University Press 2016)

Itzcovich G, 'The European Court of Justice' in András Jakab, Arthur Dyevre, and Giulio Itzcovich (eds), *Comparative Constitutional Reasoning* (Cambridge University Press 2017)

Jakab A and Kochenov D (eds), *The Enforcement of EU Law and Values: Ensuring Member States' Compliance* (Oxford University Press 2017)

Klamert M and Kochenov D, 'Article 2 TEU' in Manuel Kellerbauer, Marcus Klamert, and Jonathan Tomkin (eds), *The Treaties and the Charter of Fundamental Rights – A Commentary* (2nd edn, Oxford University Press 2023)

Kochenov D, 'Rule of Law as a Tool to Claim Supremacy' (2020) RECONNECT Working Paper No 9

Kochenov D, 'The *Aquis* and Its Principles: The Enforcement of the "Law" versus the Enforcement of "Values" in the EU' in András Jakab and Dimitry Kochenov (eds), *The Enforcement of EU Law and Values: Ensuring Member States' Compliance* (Oxford University Press 2017)

Kochenov D and Williams A, 'Europe's Justice Deficit Introduced' in Dimitry Kochenov, Gráinne de Búrca, and Andrew Williams (eds), *Europe's Justice Deficit?* (Hart Publishing 2015)

Komárek J, 'Judicial Legitimacy in the European Union' in Claire Kilpatrick and Joanne Scott (eds), *New Legal Approaches to Studying the Court of Justice: Revisiting Law in Context* (Oxford University Press 2020)

Koncewicz TT, 'Values' in Sacha Garben and Laurence Gormley (eds), *Oxford Encyclopedia of EU Law* (Oxford University Press 2023)

Lenaerts K, 'The Court's Outer and Inner Selves: Exploring the External and Internal Legitimacy of the European Court of Justice' in Maurice Adams, Henri de Waele, Johan Meeusen, and Gert Straetmans (eds), *Judging Europe's Judges: The Legitimacy of the Case Law of the European Court of Justice* (Hart Publishing 2013)

Lenaerts K and Gutiérrez-Fons JA, 'High Hopes: Autonomy and the Identity of the EU' (2023) 8 European Papers 1495

MacCormick N and Summers R, 'Interpretation and Justification' in Neil MacCormick and Robert Summers (eds), *Interpreting Statutes: A Comparative Study* (Ashgate Publishing 1991)

Mancini GF and Keeling D, 'Democracy and the European Court of Justice' (1994) 57 Modern Law Review 175

Moreno-Lax V and Ziegler K, 'Autonomy of the EU Legal Order—A General Principle? On the Risks of Normative Functionalism and Selective Constitutionalisation' in Katja S Ziegler, Päivi J Neuvonen, and Violeta Moreno-Lax (eds), *Research Handbook on General Principles in EU Law* (Edward Elgar 2022)

Nicolaïdis K, 'The Idea of European Demoicracy' in Julie Dickson and Pavlos Eleftheriadis (eds), *Philosophical Foundations of European Union Law* (Oxford University Press 2012)

Petrić D, 'A Reflection on the Methods of Interpretation of EU Law' (2023) 17 Vienna Journal on International Constitutional Law 83

Petrić D, 'The Court of Justice of the EU: A Contextualist Court' (2023) 8 University of Bologna Law Review 11
Poiares Maduro M, 'Interpreting European Law: Judicial Adjudication in a Context of Constitutional Pluralism' (2007) 1 European Journal of Legal Studies 137
Rasmussen H, *On Law and Policy in the European Court of Justice: A Comparative Study in Judicial Policymaking* (Martinus Nijhoff 1986)
Rodin S, 'A Metacritique of the Court of Justice of the European Union' [2016] Il Diritto dell'Unione Europea 193
Rodin S, 'Interpretation in the Court of Justice of the European Union, Originalism, Purposivism and *l'économie générale*' (2019) 34 American University International Law Review 601
Rodin S, 'Liberal Constitutionalism, Rule of Law and Revolution by Other Means' [2021] Il Diritto dell'Unione Europea 203
Sankari S, 'Constitutional Pluralism and Judicial Adjudication: On Legal Reasoning, Minimalism and Silence by the Court of Justice' in Gareth Davies and Matej Avbelj (eds), *Research Handbook on Legal Pluralism and EU Law* (Edward Elgar 2018)
Scharpf FW, 'The Asymmetry of European Integration, Or Why the EU Cannot be a "Social Market Economy"' (2010) 8 Socio-Economic Review 211
Schorkopf F, 'Value Constitutionalism in the European Union' (2020) 21 German Law Journal 956
Skrbic A, 'Ideology in the Adjudication of the ECJ' (2023) 42 Law and Philosophy 561
Spieker LD, 'Breathing Life into the Union's Common Values: On the Judicial Application of Article 2 TEU in the EU Value Crisis' (2019) 20 German Law Journal 1182
Spieker LD, *EU Values Before the Court of Justice* (Oxford University Press 2023)
Tridimas T, *General Principles of EU Law* (Oxford University Press 2006)
van de Beeten J, 'On Metaphor and Meaning: The Autonomy of EU Legal Order Through the Lens of Project and System' (2023) 8 European Papers 1441
van Gestel R and Jurgen de Poorter, 'Supreme Administrative Courts' Preliminary Questions to the CJEU: Start of a Dialogue or Talking to Deaf Ears?' (2017) 6 Cambridge International Law Journal 122
von Bogdandy A and Spieker LD, 'Countering the Judicial Silencing of Critics: Article 2 TEU Values, Reverse *Solange*, and the Responsibilities of National Judges' (2019) 15 European Constitutional Law Review 391
Weber F, 'The Pluralism of Values in an Identity-Framed Verbund: Federal Belonging in the European Union After the Rule of Law Conditionality Judgments' (2022) 47 European Law Review 514
Weiler JHH, 'The Political and Legal Culture of European Integration: An Exploratory Essay' (2011) 9 International Journal of Constitutional Law 678
Williams A, 'Taking Values Seriously: Towards a Philosophy of EU Law' (2009) 29 Oxford Journal of Legal Studies 549
Wouters J, 'Revisiting Art. 2 TEU: A True Union of Values?' (2020) 5 European Papers 255

7

An Assessment of the Reasoning by Implied Hierarchy in the Case Law of the Court of Justice in Common Foreign and Security Policy

Luigi Lonardo

1. Introduction

This chapter is dedicated to an important aspect of the EU legal order: while, as a general rule, all acts of EU institutions are subject to judicial review,[1] this is not the rule in the field of Common Foreign and Security Policy, where the EU Treaties limit the involvement of the judiciary in the ways detailed in section 2 of this chapter.[2] Conceptually, this aspect is perceived by some authors as somewhat uncomfortable, because it is considered an awkward exception in a system based on the rule of law;[3] and increased litigation in the area has

[1] This follows from Article 263 first paragraph TFEU. It is settled case law that the 'European Union is a union based on the rule of law in which all acts of its institutions are subject to review of their compatibility with, in particular, the Treaties, general principles of law and fundamental rights': C-362/14 *Schrems* para 60.

[2] Something similar happens in some states where foreign policy decisions are not subject to judicial review. See for a historical perspective on France Virginie Martin, 'Les Relations Extbrieures, "Domaine Réservé" Du Pouvoir Executif?' (2014) 28 Giornale di Storia Costituzionale 77; and for a comparative perspective, Joris Larik, *Foreign Policy Objectives in European Constitutional Law* (Oxford University Press 2016).

[3] Some clear statements of the (puzzling) constitutional ambiguity of the limited jurisdiction of the CJEU, and of CFSP more broadly, are in Ramses A Wessel, 'Lex Imperfecta: Law and Integration in European Foreign and Security Policy' (2016) 1 European Papers 439–68; Graham Butler, 'The Coming of Age of the Court's Jurisdiction in the Common Foreign and Security Policy' (2017) 13 European Constitutional Law Review 673; Panos Koutrakos, 'Judicial Review in the EU's Common Foreign and Security Policy' (2018) 67 International and Comparative Law Quarterly 1; Marise Cremona, '"Effective Judicial Review Is of the Essence of the Rule of Law": Challenging Common Foreign and Security Policy Measures Before the Court of Justice' (2017) 2017 2 European Papers 671, 673; Marise Cremona, 'The Position of CFSP/CSDP in the EU's Constitutional Architecture' in Steven Blockmans and Panos Koutrakos (eds), *Research Handbook on the EU's Common Foreign and Security*

Luigi Lonardo, *An Assessment of the Reasoning by Implied Hierarchy in the Case Law of the Court of Justice in Common Foreign and Security Policy* In: *The Reasoning of the Court of Justice of the EU*. Edited by: Alezini Loxa and Luigi Lonardo, Oxford University Press. © Luigi Lonardo 2026. DOI: 10.1093/9780198983002.003.0009

highlighted that the precise boundaries of the Court's jurisdiction are unclear.[4] It is important to identify these contours not only for litigants, but also for a more general reason, namely that the EU has a constitutional commitment to accede to the European Convention for the Protection of Human Rights and Fundamental Freedoms (ECHR): the ECJ, however, previously halted this accession because, *inter alia*, it held that the European Court of Human Rights (ECtHR) could not have jurisdiction on acts by the EU on which the ECJ itself cannot rule.[5] It is thus necessary to clarify what, if any, the latter acts are.

Despite the uncertainty, the Court has done its best to deliver justice in CFSP, but the case law is still partly inconsistent, developing, and difficult to rationalize. This is perhaps what the contracting parties wanted. The Member States, when negotiating the Lisbon Treaty, found a compromise that was politically viable, but which is a headache for lawyers. The Member States left the hot potato to someone else: and here we are. The political reasons that led to the Member States' compromise are recalled in section 3 of this chapter.[6]

The Court has tried to manage the uncertainty through a reasoning by *implied hierarchy*, which is characteristic of its case law at least since *Mangold*,[7] whereby a provision is interpreted in the light of (higher-ranking) principles of Union law (this is the 'hierarchy'), and whereby a lower-ranking norm gives expression to a higher-ranking norm (this link between norms is the 'implied' part, because it is not stated in the Treaties). In *Rosneft*, the Court held that Article 47 Charter—the right to an effective judicial protection—is 'a reaffirmation of the principle of effective judicial protection'.[8] This, as mentioned, clashes with the Treaty articles limiting the Court's jurisdiction (Article 24 TEU and 275 TFEU). In *Rosneft*, those Treaty articles are interpreted in the light of the hierarchically superior principle of effective judicial protection: it is in fact *that principle* that implies that 'the exclusion of the Court's jurisdiction in the field of the CFSP should be interpreted strictly'.[9] The reasoning by implied hierarchy is also visible in the other direction. In *KS and KD*, the ECJ stated that that Articles 24 TEU and 275 TFEU give expression to principle of

Policy (Edward Elgar Publishing 2018); Peter Van Elsuwege, 'Judicial Review and the Common Foreign and Security Policy: Limits to the Gap-Filling Role of the Court of Justice' [2021] Common Market Law Review 1731.

4 As witnessed by the litigation discussed in this chapter.
5 Article 6 TEU; see also Opinion 2/13, *Accession to the ECHR* paras 249–57.
6 The more remote ones are discussed, among others, in Luigi Lonardo, *EU Common Foreign and Security Policy after Lisbon: Between Law and Geopolitics* (Springer 2022) Chapter 3.
7 C-144/04 *Mangold* paras 74–76.
8 C-72/15 *Rosneft* para 73.
9 ibid para 74.

conferral and of institutional balance.[10] This jurisprudence is recalled in section 4 of this chapter.

In terms of normative assessment, the chapter proposes two lines of argument in section 5. The first is that the outcome of the case law is commendable, because, as a result of the CJEU's judgments, fundamental rights are more protected—at least procedurally—than they were before.[11] The second is one suggestion for partly clarifying the case law, and thus reducing the ambiguity over the boundaries of the Court's jurisdiction, by making explicit that the reasoning of the Court is based on the implied hierarchy as I have just described.[12] To reach its conclusions the court employs various techniques, whereby systematic and teleological interpretation are preferred to literal interpretations. But such preference ought to be justified.[13] Discarding a literal interpretation when the result it produces is not absurd may run the risk of disregarding the (so to say, 'objective') rationale of the provision and the (so to say, 'subjective') intention of the drafters.[14] It was argued for example that 'the Court has extended its jurisdiction contrary to the wording of the Treaties and the *ratio* of Article 24(1) paragraph 2 TEU and Article 275 TFEU'.[15] I argue instead that it is the role of the Court to ensure that, within the autonomous, self-sufficient, and complete legal order of the EU,[16] general principles of law are recognized and respected,[17] if necessary by interpreting the applicable primary law in conformity with those—hierarchically superior—principles.[18] Those principles are applied, in turn, because they find expression in the relevant applicable provisions of primary law. But conflicting rules of one rank often give

[10] C-29/22 P *KS and KD* para 73.

[11] Inextricably linked to the (procedural) issue of the jurisdiction—the acts and the actions over which the Court can decide—is the (substantive) issue of the level of scrutiny of the judiciary over the acts of the Council. For reasons of space, in this chapter I focus on the former, mentioning the latter only in Section 5.2.

[12] Koen Lenaerts and José A Gutiérrez-Fons, 'A Constitutional Perspective' in Robert Schütze and Takis Tridimas, *Oxford Principles of European Union Law: The European Union Legal Order: Volume I* (Oxford University Press 2018) 107–08: 'internally, the principle of hierarchy of norms permeates the EU legal order.' On hierarchical reasoning in EU law, see chapters by Hancoz and Spieker in this volume and bibliography there cited.

[13] See also chapter by Bengoetxea and Lonardo on the need to justify the premises of reasoning and the setting aside of text for telos and system.

[14] For the distinction see András Jakab, 'Judicial Reasoning in Constitutional Courts: A European Perspective' (2013) 14 German Law Journal 1215.

[15] Koutrakos (n 3) 23.

[16] Lenaerts and Gutiérrez-Fons (n 12); Koen Lenaerts, José A Gutiérrez-Fons, and Stanislas Adam, 'Exploring the Autonomy of the European Union Legal Order' (2021) 81 Zeitschrift für ausländisches öffentliches Recht und Völkerrecht/Heidelberg Journal of International Law 47.

[17] This statement is of course a 'philosophy' or 'vision' of EU law that not everyone shares, but which, I feel, is an accurate representation of the case law.

[18] See instead the equation between Treaty provisions and general principles in Koen Lenaerts and Piet Van Nuffel, *EU Constitutional Law* (Tim Corthaut ed, Oxford University Press 2022) 630.

expression to conflicting principles. What appear to be clashes between rules of formally equal ranking can thus be reduced (or elevated) to conflict between higher-ranking rules (to complicate the implied hierarchy further, sometimes the initial conflict is not even between rules of formal equal ranking[19]). If the clash is between principles, the case law does not provide one overarching criterion for solving the conflict. This is not to mean that the Court balances principles incorrectly,[20] but rather that it should argue more clearly *how* it does so: perhaps those general principles are in turn giving expression to some (even higher) essential characteristics of EU law.[21] Additionally, and relatedly, it should explain why the *consequence* of effective judicial protection is the existence of the Court's jurisdiction. The current case law on CFSP achieves a laudable outcome for not-so-convincing reasons.

2. The Relevant Provisions

Article 24 TEU, in the relevant part, reads: 'The Court of Justice of the European Union shall not have jurisdiction with respect to provisions [of Common Foreign and Security Policy], with the exception of its jurisdiction to monitor compliance with Article 40 of this Treaty and to review the legality of certain decisions as provided for by the second paragraph of Article 275 of the Treaty on the Functioning of the European Union.' Article 275 TFEU second paragraph reads as follows: 'the Court shall have jurisdiction to monitor compliance with Article 40 of the Treaty on European Union and to rule on proceedings, brought in accordance with the conditions laid down in the fourth paragraph of Article 263 of this Treaty, reviewing the legality of decisions providing for restrictive measures against natural or legal persons adopted by the Council on the basis of Chapter 2 of Title V of the Treaty on European Union.' Article 40 TEU, in turn, confirms that the principle of conferral does apply to CFSP: if an act falls under the CFSP, then it cannot be adopted pursuant to other competences, and vice-versa.

[19] This form of implied hierarchy appears for example in cases concerning the identification of provisions of *secondary* legislation providing limits to *Charter* rights. See for example for a derogation (which 'constitutes an expression' of the principle of mutual trust) to Charter rights in Case C-483/20 *Commissaire général aux réfugiés et aux apatrides* para 37.

[20] Contra, Thomas Verellen, 'KS and KD, on the Jurisdiction of the CJEU within the CFSP: Taking Conferral Seriously?' (*Thomasverellen.com*, 12 September 2024) <https://www.thomasverellen.com/blog/ks-and-kd-on-the-jurisdiction-of-the-cjeu-within-the-cfsp-taking-conferral-seriously> accessed 30 September 2024.

[21] See *Rosneft* para 73 for the statement that effective judicial protection is 'of the essence of the rule of law'. For the notion of essential characteristics of EU law, see Opinion 2/13 para 167.

The combination of Article 24 TEU and Article 275 TFEU appears to severely limit the role of the judiciary in monitoring the powers of the Member States or of the Council (and of any other Union's body, agency, or institution) whenever they act pursuant to CFSP. On a literal interpretation, in fact, Article 275 TFEU second paragraph foresees the Court's jurisdiction in only three cases. First, a specific type of CFSP act, restrictive measures, can be challenged through the procedure set out in the fourth paragraph of Article 263 TFEU (the action for annulment).[22] Second, when restrictive measures are challenged, the ground of review is their legality. Third, Article 40 TEU as a ground of review is independent from the procedure or the content of the act. Compliance with Article 40 TEU can be reviewed by the Court in direct actions, preliminary rulings on the validity of acts, infringement proceedings, and so on.

In my view, a literal interpretation of Article 275 second paragraph TFEU would entail that the action for the review of the legality of restrictive measures could not stem from a preliminary ruling (because that procedure is Article 267, not 263 TFEU), unless, that is, the applicant challenges the decision on the grounds of Article 40 TEU. Further, the only CFSP acts whose legality can be challenged are restrictive measures—not, for example, budgetary decisions or those relating to staff management. A literal reading of that provision also suggests that the Court does not have jurisdiction to rule on actions for non-contractual liability brought for damages allegedly arising out of CFSP acts.

The case law of EU courts paints a different picture. This is because, the Court says, Articles 24 TEU and 275 TFEU give expression to the principles of conferral and of institutional balance,[23] whereas Article 19 TEU,[24] the Court says, gives expression to the principle of the rule of law,[25] of which effective judicial protection is the essence.[26] It is in the context provided by that rule of general application (Article 19 TEU) that the limitation imposed by Article 24 TEU is to be read. The restriction of the Court's jurisdiction is an exception and, as such, it is to be interpreted narrowly. The judgments can be read as a constant balancing act between the principle of the rule of law on one hand, and the principles of conferral and of institutional balance on the other hand.

[22] But see Takis Tridimas, 'The European Court of Justice and the Draft Constitution: A Supreme Court for the Union?' in T Tridimas and P Nebbia (eds), *European Union Law for the Twenty-First Century: Rethinking the New Legal Order, Vol. 1* (Hart Publishing, 2004) 128 for the proposition that 'review of legality' encompasses both annulment actions and preliminary ruling procedure.

[23] *KS and KD* paras 72 and 73.

[24] The role of the Court of Justice is to 'ensure that in the interpretation and application of the Treaties the law is observed' (Art 19 TEU), and Article 47 Charter mandates that everyone has a right to an effective legal remedy.

[25] C-64/16 *Portuguese judges* para 32.

[26] *Rosneft* para 73.

Primary law gives expression to those, respectively, in Articles 19 TEU/47 Charter and in Articles 24 TEU/275 TFEU.

The post-Lisbon case law in this area is characterized by a systematic and teleological reasoning by *implied hierarchy*. To be sure, the Court justifies its conclusions also on literal grounds, but in my view its systematic and teleological interpretation is in contrast with a literal one,[27] to the point that they could be considered implicit Treaty amendments.[28] The Court has in fact established an overall broad jurisdiction over CFSP acts (including acts which do not provide for restrictive measures) in direct and indirect actions, as well as in actions for damages, as detailed in Section 4.

3. Drafting the Lisbon Treaty: A Compromise between Two Main Positions

The Member States' choice to draft the current—legally complex, ambiguous, if not downright incoherent with the rest of the system—rules on the jurisdiction of the Court in CFSP at the moment of negotiating the Lisbon Treaty may explained as a compromise between two positions expressed at the time.

3.1 First main position: Member States must retain competence in foreign policy

The UK spearheaded the first position—which, however, seemed to be a widespread belief among Member States—that foreign security and defence matters are of utmost importance and that they define the nature of the European Union.[29] Security was inextricably linked, in the UK's vision, to the nature of the EU. Gordon Brown made it clear, in the UK Government's white paper of 23 July 2007, that the new Treaty 'will set out clearly where the EU does and

[27] See, similarly, Thomas Verellen, 'H v. Council: Strengthening the Rule of Law in the Sphere of the CFSP, One Step at a Time' (2016) 2016 1 European Papers—A Journal on Law and Integration 1041, 1047; Koutrakos (n 3). Not everyone agrees. See eg Sara Poli, 'The Common Foreign Security Policy after Rosneft: Still Imperfect but Gradually Subject to the Rule of Law' (2017) 54 Common Market Law Review 1799, 1823 stating that in *Rosneft* 'the Court has simply clarified the wording of the Treaties'.

[28] Lonardo, *EU Common Foreign and Security Policy after Lisbon: Between Law and Geopolitics* (n 6) 148.

[29] The link, sometimes explicit, sometimes implicit, between EU integration and defence integration is also discussed in Jolyon Howorth, 'European Defence Policy between Dependence and Autonomy: A Challenge of Sisyphean Dimensions' (2017) 19 The British Journal of Politics and International Relations 13.

does not have power to act'. The United Kingdom had presented four red lines at the IGC mandate of June 2007, one of which was the preservation of an independent foreign and defence policy.[30] It was the UK's firm intention to 'establish that national security is a matter for Member States'.[31] In the autumn of 2007, Gordon Brown maintained that the Lisbon Treaty had 'secured the defence of the national interest in such a way that no fundamental change is taking place in the relationship between the European Union and Britain . . . which is shown in the protocols as well as in the opt-ins that we have achieved'.[32] The white paper in fact contained a statement (in bold): 'The IGC Mandate contains a declaration confirming that the provisions on CFSP will not affect the responsibilities of the Member States, as they currently exist, for the formation and conduct of their foreign policy, or of their national representations in third countries and international organisations';[33] the objective, in particular, was to preserve the relationship with NATO: 'The text will explicitly make it clear that, for its members, NATO remains the foundation of their collective defence and the forum for implementing such a commitment.'[34] As the Prime Minister reported, these concerns were indeed respected in the Lisbon Treaty.[35]

The choice to retain competence in CFSP may derive from the belief that foreign policy decisions tend to be overriding concerns, which justify the relinquishment of the normal rules—because all *energy and resources* must be put in the achievement of the foreign policy objective. A classic definition by IR theorists is telling: security is a 'move that takes politics beyond the established rules of the game and frames the issue either as a special kind of politics or as above politics'.[36] This is perhaps also an explanation for the fact that military security in the EU is one of the few areas which is not, in principle, subject to the market. Security and defence is the area in which, if it is taken to the extreme, 'might prevails over right'.[37] Foreign policy deals with the 'other'. It is often the case that collective bodies adopt different rules when acting in relation to other entities than when acting 'internally'. The duty of sincere

[30] The others were labour and social legislation, common law system (including police and judicial process), and tax and social security system.

[31] UK Government, 'The Reform Treaty. The British Approach to the European Union Intergovernmental Conference' (July 2007) 7 (herein, 'White paper').

[32] House of Commons Debate of 22 October 2007 c.

[33] White paper 8.

[34] ibid 9.

[35] Reference shall be had, for example, to protocols 10 and 11 on Permanent Structured Cooperation and Article 42 TEU.

[36] Barry Buzan, Ole Waever, and Jaap de Wilde, *Security: A New Framework for Analysis* (Lynne Rienner 1998) 3.

[37] La Fontaine says 'la raison du plus fort est toujours la meilleur'; also Menander Monost 409: βιας παρουσης ουδεν ισχυει νομος.

cooperation is deemed not to apply to 'political exceptions' in *internal* deliberations of institutions: within the Council, each Member State is in principle free to propose and foster its own interests—but this freedom is halted when the Council acts externally, that is, when it relates to other institutions.[38]

Also due to this salience of the policy, mistakes in foreign policy are perceived as being harder to correct than in domestic politics, and Member States might therefore want to do everything possible to retain flexibility in decision-making (thus loosening the binding effects of EU law and subtracting CFSP acts to judicial review):[39] in addition to the repeated mention of this objective in the White Paper, Gordon Brown declared it was 'absolutely clear that the basis of foreign and security policy will remain intergovernmental—a matter for Governments to decide'.

Foreign policy is, therefore, definitional. It is deeply associated with the history and the legacy of a community. The Foreign Secretary explained to Parliament the UK's choice to insist on foreign policy red lines by stating that 'the site of legitimacy for citizens is the nation . . . It is . . . to the nation state that people owe and commit a significant part of their sense of identity. I think that any attempt to produce foreign policy that negates that sense of identity would be quite dangerous because it would corrode the sense of legitimacy'.[40] As Madison wrote about the colonies in North America, 'if we are to be one nation in any respect, it clearly ought to be in respect to other nations'.[41] Foreign policy is heavily influenced by national identity, more than domestic policies are: several studies, mostly from a constructivist perspective, account for this.[42]

3.2 Second main position: Member States' foreign policy should be integrated

One the other side, some Member States stressed their commitment to effectiveness and common values. In the words of French foreign minister Kouchner,

[38] A Woodhouse, 'With Great Power, Comes No Responsibility? The "Political Exception" to Duties of Sincere Cooperation for National Parliaments' (2017) 54(2) Common Market Law Review 443.

[39] Montaigne: *malum consilium est, quod mutari non potest* (a bad decision is one that cannot be changed).

[40] House of Commons Select Committee of Foreign Affairs Third Report (2009) para 61.

[41] A Hamilton, J Madison, and J Jay, *The Federalist* (Cambridge University Press 2012) 212. He also considers trade among the 'obvious and essential' tasks of a federal administration of foreign affairs, in addition to other competences that under EU law would fall squarely under CFSP/CSDP.

[42] V Kononenko, 'Review of National Identities and Foreign Policy in the European Union: The Russia Policy of Germany, Poland, and Finland, by Siddi, M.' (2019) 57(2) Journal of Common Market Studies 426–7; S Vucetic, 'Identity and Foreign Policy' (*ad vocem*) Oxford Research Encyclopaedia of Politics.

the new Treaty would have to make 'Europe more effective, more democratic, more protective'.[43] Where did these desires come from? In French public political discourse, it was often linked to a powerful belief in the existence of an inevitable, if tormented, progress toward an ideal of Europe. It is also conceivable that the real motivation lied elsewhere. The influence of identity in shaping political beliefs over the EU is very relevant in the account of a more recent theory of EU integration, post-functionalism. Hooghe and Marks, for example, stress how the tension between Member States' identity and the legal construction of the EU has been 'mobilized' by 'political entrepreneurs': 'it is not unusual for an individual to have a strong national attachment and yet be positively oriented to European integration. What matters is whether a person conceives of her national identity as exclusive or inclusive of other territorial identities. Individuals with exclusive national identities are predisposed to Euroscepticism if they are cued to believe that love of their country and its institutions is incompatible with European integration.'[44] Moreover, it cannot be excluded that it is precisely the importance of security and defence what makes the desire of integration stronger. If it is true that 'effective integration in defence . . . would be more constraining than integration in other sectors',[45] this may be precisely the reason to pursue further integration also to signal desire for closer cooperation in other areas.

A desire for effectiveness was the basis for the need to cooperate through a CFSP fully integrated within the EU legal order. This desire was especially professed by France and Germany. Already in 2003, a Franco–German statement on the institutional structure of the EU was pivoting on a reform 'answering three exigences: clarity, legitimacy, and effectiveness.'[46] That statement was already proposing to bring defence under EU law 'proper', and to introduce Qualified Majority Voting in CFSP. This is an instance in which the realist assumption that states act to preserve national security may also account for cooperation: as the UK's white paper states, '[i]n many situations, 27 voices are louder than one, and when we speak in concert with our EU partners, our demands have a greater chance of being heard'. The need for an independent

[43] Speech to the National Assembly, 4 July 2007, session of 3pm.

[44] Liesbet Hooghe and Gary Marks, 'A Postfunctionalist Theory of European Integration: From Permissive Consensus to Constraining Dissensus' (2009) 39 British Journal of Political Science 1, 13.

[45] Anand Menon, 'Defence Policy and the Logic of "High Politics"' in Philipp Genschel and Markus Jachtenfuchs (eds), *Beyond the Regulatory Polity?* (Oxford University Press 2013) 78 <http://www.oxfordscholarship.com/view/10.1093/acprof:oso/9780199662821.001.0001/acprof-9780199662821-chapter-4> accessed 25 September 2019.

[46] Contribution franco-allemande à la Convention européenne sur l'architecture institutionnelle de l'Union du 15 janvier 2003, faite à Paris et à Berlin; Contribution de M. Dominique de Villepin et M. Joschka Fischer).

European defence decoupled from NATO was also expressed by Spain, in opposition to the UK, and justified on functional terms: no single EU state could face the investment necessary for an EU defence academy and crisis management operations.[47]

Other professed beliefs (whether genuine or not), such as shared values and the protection of fundamental rights, may lead to cooperation and marginalization of action that cannot affect the rights of individuals. The language in French public discourse during the intergovernmental conference is a case in point, as it is heavily reliant on the notions of shared values. These included, for example, the protection of citizens (a goal achieved through making the Charter a legally binding instrument).[48] Examples from the government's declarations abound.[49] Even more recently, with regard to CFSP as well, the narrative, shared by Germany, is still deeply embedded in the language of common values, notably 'pluralism, solidarity and justice, upholding the rule of law everywhere in the EU and promoting it abroad'.[50]

4. Implied Hierarchy in the Case Law on Common Foreign and Security Policy

To make explicit the implied hierarchy: the reasoning of the Court is deeply rooted, on the one hand, in the principles of the rule of law,[51] which is higher in the hierarchy than primary law provisions are, and in democratic principles.[52] On the other hand, the case law also needs to respect the principles of conferral and of institutional balance, which are also one step higher in the hierarchy than primary law provisions.

[47] Rapport d'information Déposé par la Délégation de l'Assemblée Nationale pour l'Union Européenne, sur les Comptes Rendus ses Missions ses *Missi Dominici* sur le suivi de la Conférence Intergouvernementale, et présente par M. Pierre Lequiller—3 October 2007.

[48] Minister Kouchner, Speech to the National Assembly, 4 July 2007, session of 3pm: 'Le nouveau traité assurera également une meilleure protection des citoyens. La Charte des droits fondamentaux, qui n'avait qu'une portée déclaratoire dans le traité de Nice, deviendra juridiquement contraignante dans tous les États membres, à l'exception du Royaume-Uni.'

[49] Again Kouchner: 'Nous, les Français, sommes de retour en Europe. Saisissons cette chance pour agir et pour porter haut nos valeurs.'

[50] Franco-German Meseberg Declaration of 2018.

[51] See already C-402/05 P, *Kadi and Al Barakaat International Foundation v Council and Commission*, EU:C:2008:461 para 316: 'the review by the Court of the validity of any Community measure in the light of fundamental rights must be considered to be the expression, in a [Union] *based on the rule of law*, of a constitutional guarantee stemming from the EC Treaty as an autonomous legal system which is not to be prejudiced by an international agreement.'

[52] C-658/11 *European Parliament v Council (Mauritius)* EU:C:2014:2025 para 81.

The Court first found jurisdiction to decide on the validity of acts adopted under the CFSP in cases involving international agreements concluded by the EU. In *Mauritius*[53] and *Tanzania*,[54] the Court found that it had jurisdiction because it was asked to interpret a provision of general application (Article 218 TFEU for the conclusion of international agreements); it also referred to the need to ensure the respect for the prerogatives of the European Parliament. Both arguments show a reasoning by implied hierarchy. In *Mauritius*, the Court held that a provision, especially one of general application as Article 218 TFEU, must 'must take account of the specific features which the Treaties lay down in respect of each field of EU activity, particularly as regards the powers of the institutions'.[55] I read this as a statement to the effect that the general principle of institutional balance is hierarchically superior to Article 218 TFEU and the latter must comply with—and be interpreted in the light of—the former. In *Mauritius*, the Court also held that Article 218(10) TFEU, which confers a right to the European Parliament to be informed 'immediately and fully informed at all stages of the procedure' for the conclusion of an international agreement, 'is an expression of the democratic principles on which the European Union is founded',[56] with the same statement being repeated in *Tanzania*.[57] These cases introduced an important aspect that would later morph into reasoning by implied hierarchy: 'the final sentence of the second subparagraph of Article 24(1) TEU and the first paragraph of Article 275 TFEU introduce a derogation from the rule of the general jurisdiction which Article 19 TEU confers on the Court to ensure that in the interpretation and application of the Treaties the law is observed, and they must, therefore, be interpreted narrowly.'[58] There is no *explicit* hierarchy between Article 24 and Article 19 TEU, but simply a relationship of rule and exception within provisions of formally equal rank.

The Court also found that it has jurisdiction to rule on the validity of acts adopted under CFSP—not just to rule on the application of procedures of general application to those acts. In particular, it held that it has jurisdiction to interpret a CFSP act, even when it is not a restrictive measure. This happened in cases involving public procurement or staff management cases. In *Elitaliana*, the Court reviewed a decision relating to public procurement, adopted under the Common Security and Defence Policy (CSDP) in the context of the EU

[53] ibid.
[54] C-263/14 *European Parliament v Council (Tanzania)* EU:C:2016:435. Later cases on CFSP international agreements include Case C-244/17 *Commission v Council (Kazakhstan)* EU:C:2018:662.
[55] *Mauritius* para 53.
[56] ibid para 81.
[57] ibid para 70.
[58] ibid para 70.

mission EULEX Kosovo. The contested decision allegedly infringed EU public procurement rules. The Court found that it had jurisdiction to interpret and apply the Financial Regulation (which applies to the award of a public contract giving rise to expenditure charged to the Union budget), regardless of the CFSP origin of the contested decision. In *H*, the Court found that a decision, adopted under the CSDP, determining where to deploy a member of staff seconded by a Member State to an EU mission was reviewable because it constituted a measure of 'staff management'.[59] The Court reasoned that since it has jurisdiction to rule on issues relating to members of staff seconded by EU institutions, it could also rule on this specific decision concerning a member of staff seconded by a Member State.[60] That jurisdiction, the Court added, 'stems, respectively, as regards the review of the legality of those acts, from Article 263 TFEU and, as regards actions for non-contractual liability, from Article 268 TFEU, read in conjunction with the second paragraph of Article 340 TFEU, taking into account Article 19(1) TEU and Article 47 of the Charter'.[61] Both *H* and *Elitaliana* repeated the *Mauritius* formula that Articles 24 TEU and 275 TFEU are exceptions to Article 19 TEU, and must be interpreted narrowly. *H*, however, goes one step further.[62] It explains, 'in that regard', that this is *also* due to the fact that Article 19 TEU gives expression to the value of the rule of law.[63] This introduces the element of implied hierarchy—it does so very implicitly, of course, but in my view undeniably so.

In *CO and others*,[64] the ECJ gave its first preliminary ruling on staff management in the context of CSDP missions. In the *Jenkinson* saga, the applicant sought to qualify his successive temporary contracts (in CSDP missions, including EULEX Kosovo) as one permanent one, and requested as well that the EU be held extra-contractually liable for the damages caused by the illegality of the Joint Action (a pre-Lisbon CFSP act) establishing EULEX Kosovo. Initially, in *Jenkinson I*, the General Court found it did not have jurisdiction to rule on such claims.[65] The ECJ disagreed and referred the case back to the General Court,[66] which once again found against the applicant.[67] In its judgment in *Jenkinson II*, the ECJ confirmed the General Court's decision.[68] Several other

[59] C-455/14 P *H v Council* para 55.
[60] ibid.
[61] ibid para 58.
[62] ibid para 41, referring to *Segi and Others v Council*, C-355/04 P, EU:C:2007:116, paragraph 51 and to Opinion 2/13 paras 168 and 169.
[63] C-455/14 P *H v Council* paras 40–41.
[64] Case C-283/20 *Eulex Kosovo*.
[65] T-602/15, *Jenkinson I* EU:T:2016:660.
[66] C-43/17 P, *Jenkinson I* EU:C:2018:531.
[67] T-602/15 RENV *Jenkinson II* EU:T:2021:764.
[68] C-46/22 P *Jenkinson II*.

staff cases arising from the EULEX Kosovo are currently pending[69]—they had been suspended awaiting the judgment in *Jenkinson*.[70] That judgment confirmed what the General Court had held, namely that the applicant's case should be dismissed, and that the extra-contractual liability of the Union could not be engaged, without there being any need to examine the validity of the CFSP act establishing EULEX Kosovo.

In *Rosneft*, the Court was invested for the first time, in the context of a preliminary ruling procedure, with a request to adjudicate on the validity of a CFSP decision containing restrictive measures. The Grand Chamber justified this conclusion based on systematic and teleological grounds. First, the court considered that Article 275 TFEU does not expressly prohibit the review of restrictive measures through a preliminary ruling procedure.[71] This is a systematic argument because it implies the (systemic) rule that what is not explicitly prohibited is allowed, which is in turn predicated on a philosophy of the EU legal order as being complete.[72] Second, there was the reasoning by implied hierarchy: the (higher-ranking) principle of effective judicial protection, enshrined in Article 47 Charter, is 'the essence of the rule of law',[73] so the exception to the Court's jurisdiction (contained in the lower-ranking primary law) must be interpreted narrowly.[74] Third, since national courts could not annul a CFSP Decision—following the *Foto Frost*[75] rationale—then the CJEU should have this power.[76]

In *Venezuela*, the Grand Chamber held that the country of Venezuela had locus standi to challenge restrictive measures adopted by the European Union. This conclusion was based on the finding that a third country is a 'legal person' for the purposes of the fourth paragraph of Article 263 TFEU. The case did not turn on an interpretation of a CFSP provision, but the reasoning is worth mentioning as it also interprets primary law (Article 263 TFEU) in the light of the (higher-ranking) principle of the rule of law. The decision was in fact based partly on grounds of 'reasonableness' ('if an entity has an existence sufficient for it to be subject to restrictive measures . . . that entity also has an existence sufficient to contest those measures'[77]) and partly on a teleological reasoning that shows the interpretative force of the higher ranking principle over primary

[69] Cases T-204/19 *BL and BM v Council*; T-183/21 *QP v Council*; T-190/21 *RI v Council*.
[70] Case C-46/22 P *Jenkinson II* ECLI:EU:C:2023:419 Opinion of AG De La Tour fn 9.
[71] *Rosneft* para 70.
[72] Lenaerts and Gutiérrez-Fons (n 16).
[73] *Rosneft* para 73.
[74] ibid paras 74–75.
[75] Case C-314/85 *Foto Frost*.
[76] *Rosneft* paras 76–78.
[77] C-872/19 P *Venezuela* para 47.

law: 'an interpretation of the fourth paragraph of Article 263 TFEU *in the light of* the principles of effective judicial review and the rule of law militates in favour of finding that a third State should have standing to bring proceedings.'[78]

In *Bank Refah*, the Court held that it can hear an action for damages allegedly suffered by a natural or legal person due to the wrongful inclusion in restrictive measures adopted under CFSP. This is because, first, Articles 24 TEU and 275 TFEU introduce a derogation from the rule of Article 19 TEU, and such derogation must be interpreted restrictively. Second, the action for damages is autonomous and subject to specific conditions. Third, the principle of the rule of law and Article 47 Charter entail that an action for damages must be available to ensure the effectiveness of EU law.

In *KS and KD*, the ECJ found it has jurisdiction to hear actions for damages caused by the EU's civilian missions or military operations.[79] In essence, the Court reinterpreted its previous case law recalled earlier (*Elitaliana*, *H*, etc), to find the effect that those judgments meant that the Court has jurisdiction on CFSP decisions, except for those 'directly relating to a political or strategic choice of the Union'.[80] In my view, that finding of *KS and KD*, which makes no mention of procedure, also stands for the proposition that the Court has jurisdiction also to hear infringements actions for failure by a Member State to observe a duty stemming from the provisions of CFSP,[81] unless these directly relate to a political or strategic choice. The implied hierarchy in *KS and KD* is that Articles 24 TEU and 275 TFEU also give expression to hierarchically superior principles: those of institutional balance and of conferral.[82] To be sure: the Court does not say explicitly that Article 24 TEU and 275 TFEU give expression to those principles, but I think this is what is implicit in paragraph 73 of the judgment.

From *Mauritius*, though *H and Rosneft*, to *KS and KD*, the picture of implied hierarchy is getting clearer: we are getting closer to the systemic vision articulated in Opinion 2/13. In particular, paragraphs 165–169 of that Opinion outline that the EU is based on certain essential characteristics, which are the principles of conferral and of institutional balance, the protection of fundamental rights as condition for validity of EU law, and the values (including the rule of law). *These characteristics are those guiding the case law on CFSP, since*

[78] ibid para 50 (emphasis added).

[79] In its first instance judgment, the General Court had reached the opposite conclusion. See also Case C-488/22 P *KQ* ECLI:EU:C:2023:284.

[80] *KS and KD* para 116.

[81] See, similarly, already AG Tanchev in C-619/18 *Commission v Republic of Poland (Age of retirement)* para 48.

[82] *KS and KD* para 73.

they are given concrete expression in the relevant provisions of primary law, as outlined in the judgments above.

5. The Normative Assessment

5.1 Normative assessment on the outcome: better to have this case law than not to

One could take the view that individuals are better off with this case law than they were 'before *Rosneft*'. This is because the case law affords, at least procedurally—through preliminary rulings, with *Rosneft*, and actions for damages, with *KS and KD*—guarantees to individuals whose rights are affected by EU law. There are, therefore, more (opportunities for) protection for fundamental rights than what a literal interpretation of the Treaties would allow, not only in national but also in EU courts.

Tridimas argues that rights are better served by competition between courts.[83] It seems indeed convincing to maintain that the presence of national courts, EU courts, and the ECtHR orchestrates a rich legal composition that fortifies the protection of fundamental rights. Central to this composition is the notion of competition—a dynamic force propelling judicial bodies to excel in the protection of rights. This leads to a virtuous cycle of improvement, compelling each court to refine its jurisprudence, adapt to societal evolution, and remain vigilant against encroachments on fundamental rights. This collective endeavour also ensures that no single judicial body monopolizes the guardianship of rights, fostering instead a healthy ecosystem of checks and balances. Moreover, competition between courts serves as a bulwark against complacency. Judicial bodies are held to account, if indirectly, to (better) justify their decisions in the face of public and technical scrutiny (ie by other courts). This transparent exchange engenders public trust in the judiciary, reinforcing its legitimacy as a guardian of fundamental rights.

The case law could also be commended in so far as it contributes to honouring the constitutional commitment to joining the ECHR (with the limitations discussed in the next paragraph). Article 6(2) TEU establishes in fact a legal duty for the EU to accede to the ECHR. This provision states in no

[83] Takis Tridimas, 'The ECJ and the National Courts: Dialogue, Cooperation, and Instability' in Damian Chalmers and Anthony Arnull (eds), *The Oxford Handbook of European Union Law* (Oxford University Press 2015).

uncertain terms that the EU 'shall accede' to the ECHR. It is being debated whether the case law of the Court has removed all (self-imposed[84]) obstacles to accession,[85] but it takes a step in that direction.

5.2 Normative assessment on the reasoning by implied hierarchy, or the *Mangoldization* of everything

I suggest that this is how the Court's reasoning might be made clearer, while still remaining within the Court's constitutional logic of the EU's legal order as autonomous, complete, and self-sufficient. First, its inner logic of implied hierarchy could be made explicit. Second, the Court should justify how the conclusion that it has jurisdiction follows from the inner logics of implied hierarchy. Third, on the substance, the Court should ensure that the judicial protection is indeed effective, and not only procedurally so.

First, the hierarchical reasoning should be spelt out and justified better. The court appears to establish an implied hierarchy between the general principles and the Treaties (without saying it and without justifying it), as the latter are *de facto* interpreted in light of, and in order to ensure conformity with, general principles. This hierarchy is perhaps what justifies recurring to a systematic and teleological interpretation. Since the Treaties cannot breach a general principle, there is a duty of conform interpretation.

The Court should recognize that it is the respect for the general principle of the rule of law which entails that Article 275 TFEU or Article 263 fourth paragraph TFEU must be interpreted in the way that they have been interpreted in *Rosneft*, *H*, *Bank Refah*, or *Venezuela*.[86] A literal interpretation of Article 275 TFEU, in particular, is not tenable because it is contrary to the (hierarchically superior) general principle of effective judicial protection. Article 47 Charter is not in itself overriding (read: 'hierarchically superior to') the letter of Article 275 TFEU, so there is no issue of hierarchy between primary law

[84] See Opinion 2/94 and Opinion 2/13, in which the Court considered that the draft accession agreement of the EU to the ECHR was not compatible with EU law.

[85] See Daniel Sarmiento and Sara Iglesias Sánchez, 'Insight: "KS and Neves 77: Paving the Way to the EU's Accession to the ECHR"' (*EU Law Live*, 12 September 2024) <https://eulawlive.com/insight-ks-and-neves-77-paving-the-way-to-the-eus-accession-to-the-echr/> accessed 30 September 2024; Jasper Krommendijk, 'One Step Closer after KS and KD: EU Accession to the ECHR' (*Realaw Blog*, 1 October 2024) <https://realaw.blog/2024/10/01/one-step-closer-after-ks-and-kd-eu-accession-to-the-echr-by-jasper-krommendijk/> accessed 4 November 2024.

[86] The systematic–teleological interpretation of Article 275 TFEU in *Rosneft*, for example, is not merely due to the rule that 'everything that is not explicitly prohibited is allowed' (a rule which could hardly exist in the Union's legal order, due to the principle of conferral), but is justified only in light of *effective judicial protection* as essence of the *rule of law*.

provisions: it is not Article 47 Charter but the principle of effective judicial protection, to which Article 47 gives expression, which determines the outcome.[87] Conversely, *KS and KD* suggests that Articles 24 and 275 TFEU give expression to the principle of conferral and institutional balance.[88] There are many other examples of this reasoning by implied hierarchy in the case law, outside CFSP. Article 47 Charter is to *Rosneft*[89]—and Article 24 TEU and 275 TFEU are to *KS and KD*—what Article 19 TEU is to *Portuguese judges*, namely, the provision of primary law giving expression to the applicable general principle. In *Portuguese judges*, the Court held precisely that 'Article 19 TEU ... gives concrete expression to the value of the rule of law stated in Article 2 TEU'.[90] The same link exists between the principle of non-discrimination and Article 21 Charter in *Egenberger*[91] and *Cresco Investigation*.[92] Article 17(1) Charter, the Court held in *Neves 77*, 'gives concrete expression to the principle of respect for property'.[93] In *Puppinck*, the Court found that the power of legislative initiative conferred to the Commission by virtue of 17(2) TEU 'is one of the expressions of the principle of institutional balance'.[94] The Court also found that 'the spirit of solidarity between Member States, mentioned in [Article 194 TFEU], constitutes a specific expression, in the field of energy, of the principle of solidarity', as it held in its judgment in *Opal*.[95] These are just some examples of the relationship between principles and rules of primary law, but there are implied links between rules of all ranks.[96] A particularly consequential one is that sometimes a provision of secondary law 'gives expression' to a hierarchically superior norm.[97] In *Slovakia and Hungary v Council*,

[87] *Rosneft* para 74.
[88] *KS and KD* para 73.
[89] And to *H* paras 39–41; C-134/19 P *Bank Refah*, paras 35–36; to *Venezuela* paras 48–50.
[90] *Portuguese judges* para 32.
[91] C-414/16 *Egenberger* para 76.
[92] Case C-193/17 *Cresco Investigation* para 76.
[93] Case C-351/22 *Neves 77* para 81.
[94] Case C-418/18 P *Puppinck* para 60.
[95] Case C-848/19 P *Germany v Poland [Opal]* para 38.
[96] Sometimes, rules of primary law give expression to a value contained in Article 2 TEU, which might suggest that there is a hierarchy between provisions of formal equal ranks (eg Case C-418/18 P *Puppinck* para 64, for the statement that. Article 10(1) TEU 'gives concrete expression to democracy as a value'; similarly, Case C-502/19 Junqueras Vies para 63 and C-181/23 *Commission v Malta (citizenship by investment)* para 89). See chapter by Petric and Speaker in this volume. Confusingly, however, provisions of primary law can also give expression to another provision of primary law, showing all the limits of reasoning by formal hierarchy: in Joined Cases C-200/07 and C-201/07 *Marra* para 41, the Court appears to say that Article 18 of the Protocol on the privileges and immunities of the European Union gives expression to the principle of sincere cooperation under Article 4(3) TEU; in *Commission v Malta (citizenship by investment)* para 93, the Court finds that 'Union citizenship is thus one of the principal concrete expressions of the solidarity which forms the very basis of the process of integration'.
[97] And sometimes a provision of secondary law gives expression to another provision of secondary law, such as in Case C-105/03 *Pupino* para 46.

relocation decisions adopted by the Council in the context of the so-called migrant crisis were considered valid because they contained mechanisms that gave full expression to Article 72 TFEU.[98] In the *Ritual Slaughtering* case, the Court held that the derogation for religious rites contained in a Regulation on animal slaughtering 'gives expression, in accordance with Article 10(1) of the Charter, to the positive commitment of the EU legislature to ensure effective observance of freedom of religion'.[99] In *Anagnostakis*, the Court found that the provision of the Regulation on the European Citizens Initiative mandating that the Commission must motivate refusals to register the initiative 'constitutes a specific expression . . . of the obligation to state reasons for legal acts enshrined in Article 296 TFEU'.[100] And so on. We are yet to see this kind of argument in CFSP—as far as secondary law is concerned. But its seeds are there: provisions of a Council Decision cannot be scrutinized if they are 'directly relating to a political or strategic choice' of the Union because those provisions give concrete expression to the principle of conferral.

There are difficulties, however. So far, the Court has not provided a non-arbitrary criterion to determine what gives expression to what. Arguably, if a norm constitutes a (general, structural) principle of a system, nearly everything in that system should be an expression of that norm. For example, much like Article 47 Charter, Article 275 TFEU also gives expression to a (hierarchically superior) principle: the maintenance of the distinctive EU institutional machinery,[101] that is, the principles of conferral and of institutional balance, in so far as the Court monitors that EU institutions act within the limits of the powers conferred upon by the Treaties.[102] In Opinion 2/13, the Court stated that the essential characteristics of the EU legal order 'include those relating to the constitutional structure of the EU, which is seen in the principle of conferral of powers referred to in Articles 4(1) TEU and 5(1) and (2) TEU, and in the institutional framework established in Articles 13 TEU to 19 TEU'. If

[98] *Slovakia and Hungary v Council* para 308, scrutinizing Article 5(7) of Council Decision (EU) 2015/1601 of 22 September 2015, providing that 'Member States retain the right to refuse to relocate an applicant only where there are reasonable grounds for regarding him or her as a danger to their national security or public order.' For a narrative of the cases on Article 72 TFEU and its expressions in secondary law, see my 'Law and order and internal security of Member States: The nature and operation of Article 72 TFEU' (forthcoming in a special issue).

[99] Case C-336/19 *Centraal Israëlitisch Consistorie van België and Others* para 44.

[100] Case C-589/15 P *Anagnostakis* para 28.

[101] Opinion 2/13 para 158: 'a particularly sophisticated institutional structure'.

[102] KS and KD para 73. See also AG Capeta with reference to Article 275 TFEU: 'in the light of the principle of the separation of powers (referred to as the principle of institutional balance in the European Union), which is an important part of the rule of law and the principle of democracy, it is not the prerogative of courts to replace policy choices made by competent political institutions.' Joined Cases C-29/22 P and C-44/22 P *KS and KD* AG Opinion para 114.

virtually any clash between provisions of primary or secondary law can be expressed in terms of a clash between general principles, how to balance those? Is the general principle of the rule of law superior to conferral and institutional balance? Granted, as far as CFSP is concerned, this question is premised on the wrong assumption that rule of law and institutional machinery are two separate things. Instead, the latter in instrumental to the former and it should be interpreted according to this function. This is because

> the CJEU must *in so far as possible* avoid the existence of lacunae which would contravene the normative foundations of the Union. The avoidance of normative gaps may even be regarded as a prerequisite for the autonomy of the EU legal order. From this perspective, 'the very nature of EU law requires the Court of Justice to "find" the law ("Rechtsfindung") by fashioning general principles of law where necessary'.[103]

It seems to me that the solution one should draw from the case law is that the principle of institutional balance is merely an aspect of the principle of the rule of law itself. The principle of institutional balance is an aspect of the rule of law as stated by the Court in the above-mentioned case on the validity of the relocation decisions, *Slovakia and Hungary v Council*, with reference to the democratic participation. In that case, the court found the Council's decision to be valid, due to the decision-making procedure foreseen by the Treaties. It stated that

> due consultation of the Parliament in the cases provided for by the Treaty constitutes an essential procedural requirement disregard of which renders the measure concerned void. Effective participation of the Parliament in the decision-making process, in accordance with the procedures laid down by the Treaty, represents an essential element of the institutional balance intended by the Treaty. This function reflects the fundamental democratic principle that the people should take part in the exercise of power through the intermediary of a representative assembly.[104]

While this reasoning is applicable (and was indeed applied) for the scrutiny of the procedural aspects of agreements relating exclusively to CFSP[105] it is hard

[103] Van Elsuwege (n 3) 1733; Lenaerts, Gutiérrez-Fons, and Adam (n 16) 78.
[104] Cases C-643/15 and C-647/15 *Slovakia and Hungary v Council* para 160.
[105] C-658/11, *Parliament v Council*, 2014, paras 69–74.

to accept with reference to CFSP decisions, for which there is no such role of the Parliament.[106] Although it was not always applied in those cases,[107] Article 40 TEU serves precisely to monitor the respect for conferral and institutional balance.[108]

How, then, should the Court justify the balancing between the general principle of the rule of law and the general principle of conferral and institutional balance in favour of the rule of law?

A possible answer is purely quantitative: more than one general principle militates in favour of that position. If there is a general principle of effectiveness and coherence of EU law[109]—separated from the principle of effective judicial protection—that is, an '*effet utile*' of EU law, then this also 'adds weight' to the plate on which the rule of law sits.

Another possible answer is to consider that the lack of the Court's jurisdiction is an exception even within the institutional machinery set up by the Treaty of Lisbon, and this is why—assuming that the EU is an autonomous, coherent, and complete legal order—as it is an exception, it should be interpreted narrowly. This reasoning also shows how institutional balance is a component of the general principle of the rule of law, since Articles 24 TEU and 275 TFEU are read as exceptions to the general rule contained in Article 19 TEU, which, in turn,

> gives concrete expression to the value of the rule of law, entrusting the responsibility for ensuring the full application of Union law in all Member States and judicial protection of individuals under Union law to national courts and tribunals and the Court of Justice of the European Union.[110]

Yet another possible answer is to suggest, as Spieker does, that the Court should introduce a 'substantive hierarchy', that is, one related to the content

[106] See, to that effect, case C-130/10 para 82 acknowledging 'the choice made by the framers of the Treaty of Lisbon conferring a more limited role on the Parliament with regard to the Union's action under the CFSP'. See also Marise Cremona, 'External Competences and the Principle of Conferral' in Robert Schütze and Takis Tridimas (eds), *Oxford Principles of European Union Law: The European Union Legal Order: Volume I* (Oxford University Press 2018) <https://oxford.universitypressscholarship.com/view/10.1093/oso/9780199533770.001.0001/isbn-9780199533770> accessed 21 April 2022, 1120 discussing the different involvement of the Parliament in the adoption of 'sanctions' under Article 75 and 215 TFEU.

[107] See eg Case C-244/17 *Commissionv.Council (Kazakhstan)* EU:C:2018:662.

[108] Lenaerts and Van Nuffel (n 18) 806.

[109] C-138/19 P *Bank Refah Kargaran* AG Opinion para 67 finding that action for damages must be admissible even against CFSP acts on the grounds that other readings of Article 275 TFEU would generate indefensible anomalies which would run counter to the effectiveness and coherence of the judicial remedies established by the Treaties.

[110] Lenaerts and Van Nuffel (n 18) 79.

of the values of Article 2 TEU also as far as the general principles are concerned: the general principle of the rule law should be explicitly considered more important than the principle of conferral. It is hard to see how this could work in practice, as it would be a very decisive step toward federalization, explicitly subordinating the boundaries of Union action drawn by the Member States to some other principle. In addition, the confusing terminology in the Treaties, coupled with the uses of implied hierarchies with the Court, shows the limits of formal hierarchical thinking.[111] What this discussion shows is that the reasoning might be made more explicit, but the inconsistency in the system remains and it is hard to rationalize. It is simply reflective of a political compromise. The parties intended that this ambiguity should be tolerated—and perhaps only reduced, rather than completely removed, by judgments of the Court.

Second, admitting that the Treaties must be interpreted in conformity with general principles, the Court should justify that its solutions are necessary: why does effective judicial protection necessitate the Court's jurisdiction? For example, as Poli writes:

> while extending the Court's jurisdiction in the field of the CFSP beyond the black letter of the Treaty is to be welcomed, as is the protection provided to individuals in the name of the right to effective judicial protection, in contrast, extending standing to challenge restrictive measures to third countries is not required by respect for the rule of law. Compliance with this value is ensured by the EU institutions in granting standing to nationals of a third country who are the object of individual sanctions, to challenge them before the EU judiciary.[112]

As Van Elsuwege recalls, in *UPA* and *Jégo Quéré* the Court did state that the principle of effective judicial protection does not allow the Court to go beyond its jurisdiction, and that Treaty amendments are needed to modify the system of judicial review. But the precise contours of the Court's jurisdiction are, here, *precisely quod erat demonstrandum*. And the dictum in *UPA* and *Jégo Quéré* appears overturned by decisions such as *Rosneft* and *Bank Refah*, which, *de facto*, amend the system of judicial remedies in the EU.

[111] See text accompanying fn 98.

[112] Sara Poli, 'The Right to Effective Judicial Protection with Respect to Acts Imposing Restrictive Measures and Its Transformative Force for the Common Foreign and Security Policy' (2022) 59 Common Market Law Review 1045, 1078.

There are, in fact other ways to construe the case law of the Court. For example, the Court could conceivably make recourse to Article 40 TEU as it would lead to the same result of protecting the fundamental rights of individuals. It would be a question of drawing the boundaries of CFSP in a way to decide what may or may not validly constitute a CFSP act on pain of breaching Article 40 TEU: the Court could find that, as a rule, CFSP decisions cannot affect the rights of individuals (restrictive measures must be implemented by a TFEU Regulation if they are to affect rights) and if they do so, they could not lawfully be CFSP acts. For example, the case law does not explain what is a 'restrictive measure' for the purposes of Article 275 TFEU. The case law focuses instead on when a restrictive measure is *against natural or legal persons.*[113] In the case law on restrictive measures, instead, a procedural rule (*locus standi*) serves as a jurisdictional tool to safeguard the general principle—but the same could be done by a literal and systematic interpretation of Article 40 TEU.[114]

The 'gap-filling role [of the Court] is not unlimited',[115] writes Van Elsuwege, but what are the limits of the duty of consistent interpretation of primary law with general principles (are they the same as those encountered by national courts in the interpretation of secondary law with primary law)? If my earlier analogy between *Egenberger* and *Rosneft* stands, it would seem that there are similarities in the way the Court does statutory and constitutional interpretation.

The Court should not advocate for an interpretation *contra legem*, but the current interpretation of Article 275 TFEU does depart significantly from its literal interpretation. One wonders: what should the drafters of the Treaties have written to exclude the Court's jurisdiction—or is that simply impossible?

Third, as a matter of substance, the Court should do more to achieve its stated outcomes of ensuring a judicial protection which is *effective*. In fact, despite the Court's case law, EU law does not provide full access to justice in the area of CFSP. As AG Kokott held in her view on Opinion 2/13, 'the uniform interpretation and application of EU law in the context of the CFSP cannot be ensured'.[116] The case law has evolved essentially only in regard to 'cases of a

[113] See in detail Joni Heliskoski, 'Made in Luxembourg: The Fabrication of the Law on Jurisdiction of the Court of Justice of the European Union in the Field of the Common Foreign and Security Policy' [2018] Europe and the World: A Law Review <https://scienceopen.com/document?vid=134d81a1-1ada-4f15-b8a7-3f6a9e856a23> accessed 29 July 2022.

[114] As I argued in Luigi Lonardo, 'Commission v Council (Kazakhstan): The Subject-Matter Question in EU External Relations Law, or the Asymmetry of Art. 40 TEU' (2020) 45 European Law Review 427.

[115] Van Elsuwege (n 3) 1733.

[116] View of AG Kokott in Opinion procedure 2/13, paras 100–01. Case C-351/22 *Neves 77 solutions* ECLI:EU:C:2023:907 AG Capeta Opinion para 77.

cross-policy nature and procedures pertaining to restrictive measures',[117] and work remains to be done to ensure accountability of EU missions, or access to justice in case of other acts with defence implications (for example, authorization for financing the transfer or the production of weapons, or other decisions otherwise relating to the financing of war).

To insist on the procedural point of jurisdiction, consider for example the case law on restrictive measures, which, as mentioned, does not define what a restrictive measure is, but limits itself to 'a review of the legality of decisions of an individual nature'.[118] It is settled case law that measures of general applications are considered not to be restrictive measures. From a perspective of effective judicial protection, this conclusion is lamentable.[119] It leaves without protection—that is, without legal remedy—a large chunk of humanity that is affected, both *formally* and *materially*, by the measures.

A similar criticism may be moved when one considers the Court's scrutiny of the legality of the measures of individual nature: such review is very 'light', offering only a veneer of protection that, in practice, strikes down measures when the Council made factual mistakes (and even to achieve this, an applicant must wait at least several months and commit a great amount of resources before the Court delivers its final judgment), and in few other instances. The judgments are imbued with the language of effectiveness, but 'avoid the imposition of substantive constraints on the Council'. Limitations or derogations from fundamental rights are justified by the invocation of an exceptional context (in *RT France*)[120] or of 'the need to ensure that the freezing measures are effective and, in short by overriding considerations to do with safety or the conduct of the international relations of the Union and of its Member States' (*OMPI*)'[121].[122]

6. Conclusion

The fragmentation of the case law is not accidental. It is perhaps the inevitable reflection of the ambiguity left by the political compromise reached by the

[117] Van Elsuwege (n 3) 1752.
[118] Lenaerts and Van Nuffel (n 18) 797. C-72/15 *Rosneft* paras 98–103.
[119] Van Elsuwege (n 3) 1753.
[120] T-125/22 *RT France* para 92.
[121] C-27/09 P *France v People's Mojahedin Organization of Iran* EU:C:2011:853, para 67.
[122] Luigi Lonardo, 'Challenging EU Sanctions against Russia: The Role of the Court, Judicial Protection, and Common Foreign and Security Policy' [2023] Cambridge Yearbook of European Legal Studies 1, 23.

Member States themselves when they negotiated the Lisbon Treaty. They have agreed just enough to allow the system to function—nothing more. Political consensus has not meant conceptual clarity. This is not a design flaw—it is a design choice.

It could be argued that resolving the perceived ambiguity is not the Court's task. But in practice, the Court has assumed responsibility for shaping the framework itself. It does not wait for the political branches or for the Member States to settle these tensions. It interprets them into balance, and in doing so, it preserves the viability—and, to a fair extent, the justice—of the legal order.

My interpretative proposal merely makes explicit what the Court leaves implicit. It names the underlying rationale that guides the case law, that is, it points out the links and the relationships between rules of unequal formal rank. The Court does not need to spell it out. It can afford a degree of implicitness. The flexibility enables it to adjust the case law to deliver a fair outcome depending on the circumstances of each case. But this implicitness has costs. They are, however, mostly intellectual. They show the difficulty, for the academic interpreter, to see clearly in the case law, to systematize the judgments. In sum, the ambiguity is not resolved by recourse to a comparative exercise,[123] or by a *Rechtsdogmatik*[124] providing for constitutional theory.[125] It seems to me that these are costs we can bear. One should credit the Court for its pragmatic approach. It delivered justice—maybe not through some immaculate doctrinal construction, but by striking a workable and fair balance case by case.

Would the result change if the Court adopted the more explicit reasoning proposed in this chapter? No, the outcome would remain the same. The jurisdictional line would still be drawn where it is, that is, quite mutably. But, respectfully, the quality of the reasoning would improve because it would be more transparent.

[123] While the national practices (of Member States, see *supra* n 1) provide useful intellectual reference for comparison, it shall be recalled that the interpretation of autonomous concepts of EU law is, for the Court, independent from the meaning of equivalent concepts under national law.

[124] Of the kind proposed by Jakab (n 14); Armin Von Bogdandy and Jürgen Bast, 'Die Systematik des Verfassungsrechts der europäischen Gesellschaft' in Jürgen Bast and Armin von Bogdandy (eds), *Unionsverfassungsrecht: Eine Neubestimmung anhand der Grundlagen im EU-Vertrag* (1. Auflage, Nomos Verlagsgesellschaft mbH & Co KG 2025); or Spieker in this volume.

[125] Richard A Posner, 'Against Constitutional Theory' (1998) 73 New York University Law Review 1–23, defining constitutional theory as 'the effort to develop a generally accepted theory to guide the interpretation of the Constitution of the United States'.

References

Buzan B, Waever O, and de Wilde J, *Security: A New Framework for Analysis* (Lynne Rienner 1998)

Cremona M, '"Effective Judicial Review Is of the Essence of the Rule of Law": Challenging Common Foreign and Security Policy Measures Before the Court of Justice' (2017) 2017 2 European Papers 671

Cremona M, 'External Competences and the Principle of Conferral' in Robert Schütze and Takis Tridimas (eds), *Oxford Principles of European Union Law: The European Union Legal Order: Volume I* (Oxford University Press 2018)

Cremona M, 'The Position of CFSP/CSDP in the EU's Constitutional Architecture' in Steven Blockmans and Panos Koutrakos (eds), *Research Handbook on the EU's Common Foreign and Security Policy* (Edward Elgar Publishing 2018)

Hamilton A, Madison J, and Jay J, *The Federalist* (Cambridge University Press 2012)

Heliskoski J, 'Made in Luxembourg: The Fabrication of the Law on Jurisdiction of the Court of Justice of the European Union in the Field of the Common Foreign and Security Policy' (2018) 2(1) Europe and the World: A Law Review 1–20

Hooghe L and Marks G, 'A Postfunctionalist Theory of European Integration: From Permissive Consensus to Constraining Dissensus' (2009) 39 British Journal of Political Science 1

House of Commons Select Committee of Foreign Affairs Third Report (2009) para 61.

Howorth J, 'European Defence Policy between Dependence and Autonomy: A Challenge of Sisyphean Dimensions' (2017) 19 The British Journal of Politics and International Relations 13

Jakab A, 'Judicial Reasoning in Constitutional Courts: A European Perspective' (2013) 14 German Law Journal 1215

Kononenko V, 'Review of "National Identities and Foreign Policy in the European Union: The Russia Policy of Germany, Poland, and Finland, by Siddi, M." (2019) 57(2) Journal of Common Market Studies 426–427

Koutrakos P, 'Judicial Review in the EU's Common Foreign and Security Policy' (2018) 67 International and Comparative Law Quarterly 1

Krommendijk J, 'One Step Closer after KS and KD: EU Accession to the ECHR' (*Realaw Blog*, 1 October 2024) <https://realaw.blog/2024/10/01/one-step-closer-after-ks-and-kd-eu-accession-to-the-echr-by-jasper-krommendijk/> accessed 4 November 2024

Larik J, *Foreign Policy Objectives in European Constitutional Law* (Oxford University Press 2016)

Lenaerts K and Gutiérrez-Fons JA, 'A Constitutional Perspective' in Robert Schütze and Takis Tridimas, *Oxford Principles Of European Union Law: The European Union Legal Order: Volume I* (Oxford University Press 2018)

Lenaerts K and Van Nuffel P, *EU Constitutional Law* (Tim Corthaut ed, First published in paperback, Oxford University Press 2022)

Lenaerts K, Gutiérrez-Fons JA, and Adam S, 'Exploring the Autonomy of the European Union Legal Order' (2021) 81 Zeitschrift für ausländisches öffentliches Recht und Völkerrecht / Heidelberg Journal of International Law 47

Lonardo L, 'Commission v Council (Kazakhstan): The Subject-Matter Question in EU External Relations Law, or the Asymmetry of Art.40 TEU' (2020) 45 European Law Review 427

Lonardo L, *EU Common Foreign and Security Policy after Lisbon: Between Law and Geopolitics* (Springer 2022)

Lonardo L, 'Challenging EU Sanctions against Russia: The Role of the Court, Judicial Protection, and Common Foreign and Security Policy' [2023] Cambridge Yearbook of European Legal Studies 1, 23

Martin V, 'Les Relations Exterieures, "Domaine Réservé" Du Pouvoir Executif?' (2014) 28 Giornale di Storia Costituzionale 77

Menon A, 'Defence Policy and the Logic of "High Politics"' in Philipp Genschel and Markus Jachtenfuchs (eds), *Beyond the Regulatory Polity?* (Oxford University Press 2013)

Poli S, 'The Common Foreign Security Policy after Rosneft: Still Imperfect but Gradually Subject to the Rule of Law' (2017) 54 Common Market Law Review 1799

Poli S, 'The Right to Effective Judicial Protection with Respect to Acts Imposing Restrictive Measures and Its Transformative Force for the Common Foreign and Security Policy' (2022) 59 Common Market Law Review 1045

Posner R, 'Against Constitutional Theory' (1998) 73 New York University Law Review 1–23

Sarmiento D and Iglesias Sánchez A, 'Insight: "KS and Neves 77: Paving the Way to the EU's Accession to the ECHR"' (*EU Law Live*, 12 September 2024) <https://eulawlive.com/insight-ks-and-neves-77-paving-the-way-to-the-eus-accession-to-the-echr/> accessed 30 September 2024

Tridimas T, 'The European Court of Justice and the Draft Constitution: A Supreme Court for the Union?' in T Tridimas and P Nebbia (eds), *European Union Law for the Twenty-First Century: Rethinking the New Legal Order, Vol. 1* (Hart Publishing 2004)

Tridimas T, 'The ECJ and the National Courts. Dialogue, Cooperation, and Instability' in Damian Chalmers and Anthony Arnull (eds), *The Oxford Handbook of European Union Law* (Oxford University Press 2015)

UK Government, 'The Reform Treaty. The British Approach to the European Union Intergovernmental Conference' (July 2007) 7 (herein, 'White paper')

Van Elsuwege P, 'Judicial Review and the Common Foreign and Security Policy: Limits to the Gap-Filling Role of the Court of Justice' [2021] Common Market Law Review 1731

Verellen T, 'H v. Council: Strengthening the Rule of Law in the Sphere of the CFSP, One Step at a Time' (2016) 2016 1 European Papers—A Journal on Law and Integration 1041

Verellen T, 'KS and KD, on the Jurisdiction of the CJEU within the CFSP: Taking Conferral Seriously?' (*Thomasverellen.com*, 12 September 2024) <https://www.thomasverellen.com/blog/ks-and-kd-on-the-jurisdiction-of-the-cjeu-within-the-cfsp-taking-conferral-seriously> accessed 30 September 2024

von Bogdandy A and Bast J, 'Die Systematik des Verfassungsrechts der europäischen Gesellschaft' in Jürgen Bast and Armin von Bogdandy (eds), *Unionsverfassungsrecht: Eine Neubestimmung anhand der Grundlagen im EU-Vertrag* (1. Auflage, Nomos Verlagsgesellschaft mbH & Co KG 2025)

Vucetic S, 'Identity and Foreign Policy' (*ad vocem*) Oxford Research Encyclopaedia of Politics (2017)

Wessel RA, 'Lex Imperfecta: Law and Integration in European Foreign and Security Policy' (2016) 1 European Papers - A Journal on Law and Integration 439

Woodhouse A, 'With Great Power, Comes No Responsibility? The "Political Exception" to Duties of Sincere Cooperation for National Parliaments' (2017) 54(2) Common Market Law Review 443

PART III

FORMAL LOGIC AND CONSISTENCY

8

The Road Not Taken: Applying the EU Charter of Fundamental Rights to Migration and Asylum Cases

Emiliya Bratanova van Harten

1. Introduction

The scope of application of the Charter of Fundamental Rights of the European Union has been found to be a notoriously elusive subject.[1] Different criteria for the scope of application of the Charter have already been identified in existing literature, but these seem to be inconsistently applied throughout the different thematic fields of European Union (EU) law, usually to the effect of excluding refugees and migrants from the remit of EU law.[2] Therefore, understanding the reasoning of the Court of Justice of the European Union[3] when delimiting the scope of application of the Charter, especially in migration and asylum cases where human rights and often lives are at stake, requires a detailed appraisal of the considerations and elements the judges take into consideration. Are there any set criteria that the Court is bound to apply? If so, how do the judges decide which criteria to apply in each particular case pertaining to migrants and refugees? Finally, are there criteria which are specific to the migration and asylum thematic area?

A comprehensive analysis of the application of the CFREU would be too ambitious to fit within the scope of this chapter. This is why in section 2 I will first outline the current state of affairs in the scholarship on the general applicability of the CFREU, answering the first question. I will answer the second

[1] Charter of Fundamental Rights of the European Union [2000] OJ C/364 (43) (CFREU, the Charter).

[2] Emily Hancox, 'The Meaning of "Implementing" EU Law under Article 51(1) of the Charter: Åkerberg Fransson' (2013) 50 CMLR 1411, 1431; Petr Mádr, 'Article 51 of the EU Charter of Fundamental Rights from the Perspective of the National Judge' (2020) 13(4) RevEurAdminL 53, 69.

[3] The CJEU or the Court.

Emiliya Bratanova van Harten, *The Road Not Taken: Applying the EU Charter of Fundamental Rights to Migration and Asylum Cases* In: *The Reasoning of the Court of Justice of the EU*. Edited by: Alezini Loxa and Luigi Lonardo, Oxford University Press. © Emiliya Bratanova van Harten 2026. DOI: 10.1093/9780198983002.003.0011

question in section 3 and the third one in section 4. Section 3 will zoom in on an analysis of the applicability of CFREU in several cases which concern refugees and migrants exemplifying how the judges decide not to apply any of the established criteria for assessing the relation between EU law and the national measures implementing it (nexus criteria), and section 4 will focus on the infamous humanitarian visas case of *X and X v État belge*.[4] The case is highly contentious and has been criticized by several scholars for incorrect reasoning on points of law and fact.[5] However, so far no analysis from the perspective of the application criteria of the CFREU has been done and this chapter aims to fill this gap, claiming that the case sheds new light on the interpretation of the application of the CFREU, especially in migration and asylum cases.

In brief, the analysis shows that there is a certain consistency in the inconsistency of the construction of the scope of EU law as the necessary precondition for the application of the Charter. This (in)consistency allows significant leeway for the judges to apply or disapply EU law, depending on the thematic area of law the respective cases concern. This is observed specifically in the area of migration and asylum, where human rights principles give way to other principles and values which prioritize the unity of EU law and policy.

2. Nexus Criteria for the Application of the Charter of Fundamental Rights

The applicability of the Charter of Fundamental Rights of the EU is regulated in its Article 51(1), according to which '[t]he provisions of this Charter are addressed to the institutions and bodies of the Union with due regard for the principle of subsidiarity and to the Member States only when they are implementing Union law'.[6] The interpretation of this provision is far from an easy task and needs to be understood in light of the case law of the CJEU. A fundamental source on this matter is the case of *Åkerberg Fransson*, where the CJEU held:

> Since the fundamental rights guaranteed by the Charter must therefore be complied with *where national legislation falls within the scope of European Union law*, situations cannot exist which are covered in that way by European

[4] Case C-638/16 PPU, *X and X v État belge* [2017] ECLI:EU:C:2017:173 [GC].
[5] (n 59).
[6] CFREU, art 51(1).

> Union law without those fundamental rights being applicable. The applicability of European Union law entails applicability of the fundamental rights guaranteed by the Charter.[7]

On the basis of the wording of Article 51(1) CFREU, two situations need to be distinguished: the first deals with disputes claiming that EU institutions and EU bodies apply EU law in a way that violates one or more provisions of the Charter, and the second concerns disputes claiming that Member States violate one or more provisions of the Charter when 'they are implementing Union law'. Both scenarios are relevant to the protection of the fundamental rights of migrants and refugees under the Charter, as the two EU agencies specialized in the areas of border management and asylum—the European Border and Coast Guard Agency (Frontex) and the European Union Asylum Agency (EUAA)—are generally bound by the CFREU in their actions (and omissions).[8] However, in the few cases where individuals pursued disputes against Frontex, the issue of the potential violation of the Charter was not addressed on the merits, as strict admissibility criteria foreclosed such an analysis.[9] Therefore, in order to analyse how the CJEU interprets the applicability of the CFREU in cases concerning migrants and refugees, it seems more pertinent to focus on the interpretation of whether Member States implement EU law in cases where a violation of the Charter is alleged, that is, the second mentioned scenario.

[7] C-617/10, *Åklagaren v Hans Åkerberg Fransson* [2013] ECLI:EU:C:2013:105 [GC], para 21, emphasis mine.

[8] EU agencies presumably implement EU law in the same way as EU institutions and EU bodies, unless certain conditions apply (see Case C-370/12, *Thomas Pringle v Government of Ireland* [2012] ECLI:EU:C:2012:756, para 179; Joined Cases C-8/15 P to C-10/15 P, *Ledra Advertising Ltd And Others v the European Commission and the European Central Bank* [2016] ECLI:EU:C:2016:701 [GC], para 67; see also Articles 263, 265, 267, 277, Consolidated version of the Treaty of the Functioning of the European Union [2012] OJ C 326/47 (TFEU). Natural and legal persons have a limited number of legal remedies before the CJEU when they wish to challenge the human rights compliance of actions and omissions by EU institutions and bodies, namely, actions for annulment under Article 263 TFEU; actions for failure to act under Article 265 TFEU; and actions for damages under Article 268 in conjunction with Article 340 TFEU.

[9] So far there have not been cases against the EUAA. All of the cases brought by individuals against Frontex have been dismissed on admissibility grounds at first instance. See Case T-282/21, *SS and ST v European Border and Coast Guard Agency* [2022]; Case T-600/22, *ST v European Border and Coast Guard Agency* [2023]; Case T-136/22, *Alaa Hamoudi v European Border and Coast Guard Agency* [2023]; Case T-600/21, *WS and others v European Border and Coast Guard Agency* [2023] ECLI:EU:T:2023:492. However, on appeal of the latter two cases, the CJEU accepted that Frontex may be held accountable for human rights violations. Both cases were referred back to the first instance for reassessment of the facts. See Case C-136/24 P, *Alaa Hamoudi v European Border and Coast Guard* Agency [2025] ECLI:EU:C:2025:977 [GC]; Case C-679/23 P, *WS and others v European Border and Coast Guard Agency* [2025] ECLI:EU:C:2025:976 [GC]. Another 'failure to act' case was brought against Frontex in October 2024, see Case T-511/24, *FM v European Border and Coast Guard Agency* [2024]. In the partly admissible 'access to information' case brought against Frontex, the application of the CFREU has not been material to the case. See Case T-205/22, *Marie Naass and Sea-Watch v European Border and Coast Guard* [2024] ECLI:EU:T:2024:266.

It has proven difficult to define precisely when Member States are bound by the CFREU.[10] However, the overview of the available case law shows that such decisions are to be made based on an assessment of whether a nexus exists between the subject matter of the EU provision(s) and the respective Member State measure in question. A crucial factor in this assessment is whether EU law imposes a specific obligation on the national level.[11] While the CJEU interprets the situations of 'implementing Union law' broadly,[12] this raises further questions as to the strength and type of nexus between the EU law and the national measure required to trigger the application of the Charter under Article 51(1). More concrete guidance on the assessment criteria the Court applies to this matter can be found in its settled case law:

> [t]he concept of 'implementation of Union law', within the meaning of Article 51(1) of the Charter, presupposes a *degree of connection* between an act of EU law and the national measure at issue above and beyond the matters covered being closely related or one of those matters having an indirect impact on the other . . . [I]n order to determine whether a national measure involves 'implementing Union law' within the meaning of Article 51(1) of the Charter, it is necessary to determine, inter alia, whether that national legislation is *intended to implement a provision of EU law*; the nature of the legislation at issue and whether it *pursues objectives other than those covered by EU law*, even if it is capable of indirectly *affecting EU law*; and also whether there are *specific rules of EU law* on the matter or rules which are capable of affecting it.[13]

[10] Angela Ward, 'Article 51—Field of Application' in Steve Peers and others (eds), *The EU Charter of Fundamental Rights: A Commentary* (2nd edn, Hart Publishing 2021), 1610.

[11] ibid.

[12] *Åklagaren v Hans Åkerberg Fransson* (n 7), paras 24, 27.

[13] Case C-185/23, *protectus s. r. o. v Výbor Národnej rady Slovenskej republiky na preskúmavanie rozhodnutí Národného bezpečnostného úradu* [2024] ECLI:EU:C:2024:657, paras 42–43 (references omitted, emphasis mine). These criteria have been spelled out in earlier case law, among others Case C-83/20, *BPC Lux 2 Sàrl and Others v Banco de Portugal and Others* [2022] ECLI:EU:C:2022:346; Case C-262/20, *VB v. Glavna direktsia 'Pozharna bezopasnost i zashtita na naselenieto'* [2022] ECLI:EU:C:2022:117, para 60; Case C-485/19, *LH v Profi Credit Slovakia s. r. o.* [2021] ECLI:EU:C:2021:313, para 37; Case C-686/18, *Adusbef and Others v Banca d'Italia and Others* [2020] ECLI:EU:C:2020:567, paras 51–52; para 27; Case C-177/18, *Almudena Baldonedo Martín v Ayuntamiento de Madrid* [2020] ECLI:EU:C:2020:26, paras 58–59; Case C-218/15, *Gianpaolo Paoletti and others* [2016] ECLI:EU:C:2016:748, para 14; Case C-206/13, *Cruciano Siragusa v Regione Sicilia—Soprintendenza Beni Culturali e Ambientali di Palermo* [2014] ECLI:EU:C:2014:126, paras 24–25; Case C-87/12, *Kreshnik Ymeraga et al. v Ministre du Travail, de l'Emploi et de l'Immigration* [2013] ECLI:EU:C:2013:291, para 41; Case C-40/11, *Yoshikazu Iida v Stadt Ulm* [2012] ECLI:EU:C:2012:691, para 79; Case C-309/96, *Daniele Annibaldi v Sindaco del Comune di Guidonia and Presidente Regione Lazio* [1997] ECR 1997 Page I-07493, paras 21–23.

The above quote points to the need for an analysis of a number of criteria in order to establish if a nexus between a national measure and the relevant EU law exists: a first factor to be considered is whether the national measure is intended to implement EU law, regardless of whether this is explicitly stated in the national legislation (what Pirker calls the 'criterion of the character of the rule of national law'); a second factor which comes into play is whether the national measure pursues objectives other than those of EU law (the 'criterion of the convergence of objectives'); a third factor is an assessment of the degree of affectation of the national measure on the implementation of EU law (the 'criterion of the impact on EU law'); and a fourth factor is whether EU law has specific regulations on the matter at issue or whether such specific regulations are capable of affecting the national measure in place (the 'criterion of the density of EU regulation' or 'specificity', according to Tecqmenne).[14]

The CJEU does not specify the relation between these elements of the assessment of the nexus, whether they are cumulative, or whether fulfilling or failing one of the requirements is sufficient to meet the threshold or, respectively, rule out the implementation of EU law straightforwardly. For example, does the finding that a certain EU measure does not impose an obligation on a Member State suffice to rule out that the national measure implements EU law, without the need to assess the presence or absence of the other elements? Or is a finding that the national measure pursues objectives different from those of the corresponding EU measure sufficient to decide that the Charter does not apply? It seems from the cited paragraph, namely '*inter alia*', that the factors elaborated therein are not comprehensive. Other factors could also be considered in future case law.

Some light can be shed on the above questions by previous analysis on the matter. Pirker has established that most of the case law on the applicability of the Charter focuses on an analysis of the fourth criterion, namely the availability of specific EU regulations and their capability to affect the respective national measures, or the criterion on the density of EU regulation.[15] This criterion allows for establishing a spectrum characterizing situations of 'higher' or 'lower' density of EU regulation of national matters.[16] This approach is reminiscent of a competence analysis, an observation confirmed by the CJEU in

[14] Benedikt Pirker, 'Mapping the Scope of Application of EU Fundamental Rights: A Typology' (2018) 3(1) EurPapers 133, 137; Maxime Tecqmenne, 'Minimum Harmonisation and Fundamental Rights: A Test-Case for the Identification of the Scope of EU Law in Situations Involving National Discretion? ECJ (Grand Chamber) 19 November 2019, Joined Cases C-609/17 and C-610/17, *TSN*' (2020) 16 EurConstLRev 493, at 498ff.

[15] Pirker (n 14) 138.

[16] ibid 139.

some cases.[17] According to this rationale, in the cases where the EU has exclusive or shared competence to act and *has exercised* this competence, the CFREU shall be found to apply. Regarding the other three criteria, Pirker has found that the first criterion is not sufficient to establish the applicability of the CFREU on its own. Rather, it serves not to exclude situations whereby certain national measures do not specifically implement EU law from the ambit of Article 51(1) CFREU.[18] Finally, he has convincingly shown that the CJEU seems to resort to the second and third factors as a 'safety valve' in cases where the analysis under the fourth criterion 'does not yield a satisfactory result'.[19] According to him, 'the case law of the Court can be fitted within the corners of the mentioned criteria, [and therefore] [t]he Court has thus indeed achieved a certain degree of coherence'—a coherence not without its problems.[20]

The problem with this neat categorization pertains to the fact that when interpreting the application of the Charter, the CJEU makes certain choices, which have often been implicit.[21] These implicit choices leave the impression of inconsistencies, with which researchers continue to grapple. Looking for additional criteria for assessment, Lazzerini has identified another categorization of cases of narrow, broad, and intermediate reading of the scope of application of the Charter.[22] For example, even though 'neither the original interest of or the objectives pursued by the Union, nor the intent of the Member State in adopting the national provision in question, seem to be determinant', there is nothing to rule out that these may still be of certain weight when the CJEU needs to make a choice between a narrow or a broad reading of Article 51(1) CFREU.[23]

Hancox and Mádr suggest that the thematic field of application of EU law may serve as another factor for the predictability of the scope of application of the Charter.[24] For example, the abovementioned four assessment criteria

[17] ibid 146: 'In a number of cases, the Court clarified that the scope of application of EU fundamental rights corresponds to the actual exercise of EU competences, not their potential future exercise or mere existence'.

[18] Pirker (n 14) 138.

[19] ibid 138 and 153ff. However, given the limited CJEU case law which focuses on this criterion, Priker is of the opinion that the delimitation of the content of the criterion is still pretty vague.

[20] ibid 138.

[21] See Hancox (n 2) 1422. With regard to the cases *Karner* and *Kücükdeveci*, C-71/02, *Herbert Karner Industrie-Auktionen GmbH v Troostwijk GmbH* [2004] ECLI:EU:C:2004:181 and C-555/07, *Seda Kücükdeveci v. Swedex GmbH & Co. KG* [2010] ECLI:EU:C:2010:21 [GC].

[22] Nicole Lazzerini, 'The Scope and Effects of the Charter of Fundamental Rights in the Case Law of the European Court of Justice' in Giuseppe Palmisano (ed), *Making the Charter of Fundamental Rights a Living Instrument* (Brill/Nijhoff 2014) 40.

[23] C-298/16, *Teodor Ispas, Anduța Ispas v. Direcția Generală a Finanțelor Publice Cluj* [2017] ECLI:EU:C:2017:650, Opinion of AG Bobek, para 42.

[24] Hancox (n 2) 1431. See also Mádr (n 2) 69.

for establishing the nexus are not relevant when the dispute at hand concerns an allegation that a certain national measure obstructs one of the fundamental freedoms, that is, the freedom of movement of goods, persons (workers), services, and capital, as enshrined in Article 26(2) TFEU.[25] In those cases the CFREU is automatically found to apply,[26] without necessarily resorting to an explicit assessment of the four criteria, despite or because of the fact that it could be said that a situation concerning the fundamental freedoms fulfills by default the fourth qualifying criterion (density of EU regulation/specificity).

To summarize this section, in order for a national measure to implement EU law, and therefore trigger the application of the Charter, a certain degree of connection between the national and the EU levels needs to be in place. To establish such a connection, the Court assesses the character of the national measure and its connection to EU law with its specific provisions by analysing the two-way affectation of EU law on the national level and vice versa, including the existence and degree of obligation imposed by EU law on the domestic level. While the criteria are clearly spelled out in a significant number of cases, the Court does not find it necessary to undertake an explicit analysis of the four factors in each case where the application of the Charter is at stake. This lack of transparency further complicates the legitimacy of some of its reasoning, especially when the application of these criteria could lead to contradictory findings, such as in cases pertaining to migrants and refugees, as the next sections demonstrate.

3. Applying the CFREU to Asylum and Migration Cases

After having outlined the general nexus criteria for the application of the CFREU, this section dives into two migration and asylum-related cases, whereby the Charter was found applicable to one of them but not to the other. There are just a few cases in this thematic area of EU law which discuss the application of the Charter, and in sections 3 and 4 I have specifically selected the cases which raise key questions pertaining to the reasoning of the Court when assessing the application of the Charter, regardless of the different outcomes.[27]

[25] See more recently Case C-544/19, *'ECOTEX BULGARIA' EOOD v Teritorialna direktsia na Natsionalnata agentsia za prihodite—Sofia* [2021] ECLI:EU:C:2021:803, para 89.

[26] C-390/12, *Robert Pfleger and Others* [2014] ECLI:EU:C:2014:281, para 36. See also C-260/89, *Elliniki Radiophonia Tiléorassi AE and Panellinia Omospondia Syllogon Prossopikou v. Dimotiki Etairia Pliroforissis and Sotirios Kouvelas and Nicolaos Avdellas and others (ERT)* [1991] ECLI:EU:C:1991:254, para 43.

[27] A more recent, but less contentious, case is Case C-352/23, *LF v Zamestnik-predsedatel na Darzhavna agentsia za bezhantsite* [2024] ECLI:EU:C:2024:748.

In analysing these cases, I use the four assessment criteria presented earlier as a framework of reference in order to test the consistency of the Court's reasoning. It should be stated that there are migration-related cases where the Court refers to the above criteria, but these concern third country nationals claiming to derive rights from the EU citizenship of their family members.[28] While a purposive selection does not allow for generalizations, the cases analysed in this chapter provide fertile ground for unravelling the implicit considerations behind the Court's reasoning on the application of the Charter to migration and asylum cases and elucidate the need for more clarity in the name of legal certainty and the rule of law.

3.1 *NS, ME and Others*—the Charter applies

The case of *NS, ME and Others*[29] is notorious regarding the application of the distribution criteria concerning asylum seekers across the EU Member States, pursuant to the Dublin II Regulation, in force at the time.[30] According to the facts of the case, NS was an Afghan national who sought asylum in the UK after having been intercepted in Greece. The applicant had not sought asylum in Greece and alleged that a return to Greece would result in breaching his fundamental rights. The cases of ME and four other applicants from Afghanistan, Iran and Algeria were similar to the case of NS in that they all had passed through Greece without seeking asylum before applying for international protection in Ireland. They claimed that the asylum procedures and reception conditions in Greece were inadequate. Because of that, they requested the United Kingdom and Ireland, as the responsible national authorities, to exercise their discretionary powers under Article 3(2) of the Dublin II Regulation and to examine their asylum applications, instead of returning them to Greece. Ireland and the United Kingdom, as the responding states, claimed that the

[28] See Joined Cases C-420/22 and C-528/22, *NW and PQ v. Országos Idegenrendészeti Főigazgatóság, Miniszterelnöki Kabinetirodát vezető minister* [2024] ECLI:EU:C:2024:344; *Kreshnik Ymeraga* (n 13), para 41; C-40/11, *Yoshikazu Iida* (n 13), para 79. On the incomparable situation of third country nationals and EU citizens (and those deriving rights from EU citizenship), see Daniel Thym, 'Between "Administrative Mindset" and "Constitutional Imagination": The Role of the Court of Justice in Immigration, Asylum and Border Control Policy' (2019) 2 EurLawRev 139.

[29] Joined Cases C-411/10 and C-493/10, *NS v Secretary of State for the Home Department and ME and Others v Refugee Applications Commissioner and Minister for Justice, Equality and Law Reform* [2011] ECLI:EU:C:2011:865 [GC].

[30] Council Regulation 343/2003 of 18 February 2003 establishing the criteria and mechanisms for determining the Member State responsible for examining an asylum application lodged in one of the Member States by a third-country national [2003] OJ L 50/1 (Dublin II Regulation).

derogations permitted under the said Article 3(2) fell outside the scope of EU law.[31] On this point, the CJEU disagreed with the following arguments.

In reaching the conclusion that national measures implemented by way of derogations permitted under the Dublin II Regulation still amounted to implementing EU law, the CJEU did not perform anything similar to an analysis of the four assessment criteria outlined in section 2. In a brief reasoning, the main factor was that 'the discretionary power [granted under Article 3(2) of the Dublin II Regulation] . . . forms an integral part of the Common European Asylum System provided for by the FEU Treaty and developed by the European Union legislature'.[32] Moreover, the derogation 'gives rise to the specific consequences provided for by that regulation. Thus, a Member State which decides to examine an asylum application itself becomes the Member State responsible within the meaning of [the] Regulation.'[33] In its assessment, the CJEU followed the analysis of AG Trstenjak:

> the crucial factor is that Regulation No 343/2003 lays down *exhaustive rules* for determining the Member State responsible for examining an asylum application. The option afforded to the Member States to examine asylum applications pursuant to Article 3(2) of Regulation No 343/2003 is *an integral part* of those rules, which is, inter alia, reflected in the fact that the regulation lays down *comprehensive rules* governing the legal consequences of such a decision.[34]

It can be said that the CJEU implicitly applied the fourth assessment criterion, namely whether EU law imposes any obligations on Member States. It transpires from the above quotes that the density of EU law as regards the discretionary measure in question, as per Pirker's typology, is high. This decision has been a welcome development in the CJEU case law on the application of the CFREU, as it has made it unnecessary to question the relevance of fundamental rights in situations where derogations from EU law and the

[31] Which would be the case in situations where Member States have availed themselves of implementing measures stemming from EU law which does not require harmonization among Member States and only introduces minimum standards, provided that these measures 'do not undermine the coherence of that action'. Joined Cases C-609/17 and C-610/17, *Terveys- ja sosiaalialan neuvottelujärjestö (TSN) ry v Hyvinvointialan liitto ry and Auto- ja Kuljetusalan Työntekijäliitto AKT ry v Satamaoperaattorit ry (TSN v. AKT)* [2019] ECLI:EU:C:2019:981 [GC], para 48. See also Tecqmenne (n 14).

[32] *NS and ME and Others* (n 29), para 65.

[33] ibid para 67.

[34] Case C-411/10 and C-493/10, *NS v Secretary of State for the Home Department* [2011] ECLI:EU:C:2011:611, Opinion of AG Trstenjak, para 80, emphasis mine.

implications therefrom are regulated by EU law to a high degree.[35] However, in terms of clarity on the interpretation of the scope of EU law, much is left wanting due to lack of consistency in the reference to and the application of the abovementioned assessment criteria. The same inconsistency is also manifested in the case of *Zakaria*, analysed below.

3.2 *Zakaria*—the Charter does not apply

Despite the high level of regulation of the protection of external borders and the corresponding *exclusive implied* competences of the EU to act in that area,[36] the case of *Zakaria* presents a more nuanced picture of the application of fundamental rights in the context of border procedures.[37] The case concerns the application of operative border measures under the Schengen Borders Code in effect at the material time.[38] Mr Mohamad Zakaria was a Palestinian refugee with a travel document issued by Lebanon. He was travelling from Lebanon to Copenhagen, Denmark, via Riga, Latvia, as he was a permanent resident in Lund, Sweden, which is easy to reach from Copenhagen Airport. The border guards at Riga Airport allegedly inspected his travel documents in 'an offensive and provocative manner, which violated human dignity'.[39] As a result of the lengthy procedure, Mr Zakaria missed his connecting flight to Denmark. Mr Zakaria lodged a complaint against the unlawful conduct of the border guards for non-material damages. In part of the judgment the CJEU had to assess whether unlawful conduct during border procedures fell within the scope of EU law. The analysis was rather brief. The CJEU stated that

> the decision to refer does not provide sufficient information regarding the main proceedings, in particular regarding the relevant facts, *for the Court to determine the relevance of Article* 6 of Regulation No 562/2006 for the

[35] See Ward (n 10), 1576, text to n 149; 1590, text to n 267.

[36] Even though border management is a shared competence, 'the Union enjoys ERTA-exclusive competences on the facilitation and exemption of short-term visas, as well as on the management of external border controls [. . . as these areas are] already covered to a large extent by (Union) rules'. Paula García Andrade, 'EU External Competences in the Field of Migration: How to Act Externally when Thinking Internally' (2018) 55 CMLR 157, 166, references omitted.

[37] C-23/12, *Mohamad Zakaria* [2013] ECLI:EU:C:2013:24.

[38] Regulation 562/2006 establishing a Community Code on the rules governing the movement of persons across borders, OJ 2006 L 105/1.

[39] *Mohamad Zakaria* (n 37), para 11.

> purposes of examination of that action. Consequently, the Court is *not in a position to determine* whether the situation of the claimant in the main proceedings is governed by European Union law within the meaning of Article 51(1) of the Charter.[40]

Article 6 of the Schengen Borders Code of 2006 states that in the conduct of border checks '[b]order guards shall, in the performance of their duties, fully respect human dignity'. Despite this explicit provision, the CJEU refused to analyse the applicability of the CFREU to operational border checks in cases where entry is not refused. Unlike other cases where the Court had to decide on the scope of implementation of EU law, in this case it did not apply a presumption of relevance of the Charter to the question posed for a preliminary ruling at the admissibility stage.[41] Instead, it refused to deal with the matter as a whole. This judgment has attracted criticism due to its vagueness and inconsistency in relation to previous case law.[42]

One way to understand the Court's reasoning is that it reconfirms the requirement for a national provision to have to relate not only to fundamental rights protection, but also to a specific EU competence which is exercised.[43] However, this suggestion remains informed conjecture in light of the silence of the Court on the matter, despite strong indications for the applicability of the second (convergence of objectives) and/or fourth (density of EU regulation) criteria specifically.[44]

[40] ibid para 39, emphasis mine.

[41] Joined Cases C-257/21 and C-258/21, *Coca-Cola European Partners Deutschland GmbH v L.B. and R.G.* [2022] ECLI:EU:C:2022:529, para 35: 'questions relating to EU law enjoy a presumption of relevance. The Court may refuse to rule on a question referred by a national court for a preliminary ruling only where it is quite obvious that the interpretation of EU law that is sought bears no relation to the actual facts of the main action or its purpose, where the problem is hypothetical, or where the Court does not have before it the factual or legal material necessary to give a useful answer to the questions submitted to it' (references omitted). See also *NW and PQ* (n 28), para 54.

[42] Hancox (n 2) 1424, citing C-101/01, *Bodil Lindqvist* [2003] ECLI:EU:C:2003:596, para 82; and C-28/05, *G. J. Dokter, Maatschap Van den Top and W. Boekhout v. Minister van Landbouw, Natuur en Voedselkwaliteit* [2006] ECLI:EU:C:2006:408, para 71.

[43] Hancox (n 2) 1424. See also Case C-244/20, *F.C.I. v Instituto Nacional de la Seguridad Social (INSS)* [2021] ECLI:EU:C:2021:854, para 61.

[44] On the relevance of the second criterion, see Case C-682/15, *Berlioz Investment Fund SA v. Directeur de l'administration des contributions directes* [2017] ECLI:EU:C:2017:373, para 40: 'it is irrelevant that the national provision serving as the basis for a penalty . . . is included in a law that was not adopted in order to transpose Directive 2011/16, since the application of that national provision is intended to ensure that of the directive' (references omitted). On the fourth criterion, it is doubtful that the protection of external borders, as per art 77, TFEU, cannot be considered 'a specific EU competence', since it does not address Member States, as Hancox suggests, because this field is a shared competence and EU law strongly affects national laws in this area, as border protection is an exclusive implied competence of the EU. See Hancox (n 2) 1424 and text to note 96 therein.

The two cases analysed in this section exemplify the decision of the Court not to apply the identified nexus criteria developed in its settled case law[45] when analysing the scope of application of the CFREU to migration and asylum-related cases, regardless of whether the conclusion is that the respective national measure implements EU law (*NS, ME and Others*) or not (*Zakaria*). The leeway that the judges enjoy in this area of EU law seems to be made possible by the refusal to apply the explicit nexus criteria, instead opting for lack of transparency and consistency of the judicial reasoning. However, this choice can be appraised by virtue of the specificities of the area of EU law that the Court interprets.

The final section delves into the possible reasons why the Court seems to repeatedly not apply the nexus criteria specifically to cases pertaining to EU migration and asylum law. A first glimpse is provided by the substantive parts of the *NS, ME and Others* case, but the answer to the question is best manifested in *X and X v État belge*, analysed in section 4.[46] While *NS, ME and Others* was welcome in that it included situations of permitted discretionary measures on the national level in the remit of EU law, thus strengthening the fundamental rights of asylum seekers in the EU, it is reproachable from a legal certainty point of view because of the omission to apply a consistent reasoning approach. However, substantively speaking, the *NS, ME and Others* case is also reproachable for another reason. Namely, because it shows the significant weight the Court attaches to the Dublin system as an integral part of the Common European Asylum System,[47] which can be to the detriment of the protection of human rights of asylum seekers and migrants, as the case of *X and X v État belge* also indicates.[48] This deprioritization of human rights principles in this context may very well explain the reticence of the Court to interpret broadly the criterion of 'implementing European Union law', and respectively the scope of application of the Charter, in cases concerning migrants and refugees.

[45] *protectus s. r. o.* (n 13), para 41.
[46] (n 4).
[47] *NS and ME and Others* (n 29), para 65.
[48] On the prioritization of the mutual trust principle as a manifestation of the 'integration paradigm' in the Area of Freedom, Security and Justice over fundamental rights protection, see Takis Tridimas, 'Competence, Human Rights, and Asylum: What Price Mutual Recognition?' in Sacha Garben and Inge Govaere (eds), *The Division of Competences between the EU and the Member States: Reflections on the Past, the Present and the Future* (Hart Publishing 2017); and Henry Labayle and Jean Sylvestre Bergé, 'Les Principes de l'Espace de Liberté, de Sécurité et de Justice' (2016) juillet-septembre Rev trimestrielle de droit eur 589.

4. Deciphering the Court's Interpretation of 'Implementing European Union Law' in *X and X v État belge*

4.1 The Court's narrow interpretation

X and X v État belge is illustrative of the cases where the CFREU is found not to apply, to the detriment of migrants' and refugees' fundamental rights.[49] It introduces further requirements to the four nexus criteria outlined in the CJEU's earlier case law, without being explicit about them and the need therefor. This vagueness does not contribute to the clarity of the applied criteria but alternatively reaffirms the abovementioned leeway of the judges in applying the Charter, providing them with the possibility to follow diametrically diverging lines of reasoning. In the politically highly sensitive area of migration and asylum this 'freedom' may result in interpretation aligning with (more or less) exclusionary political positions. This somewhat broad leeway gives a clue as to why the Court seems to interpret narrowly the application of the Charter in migration and asylum-related cases.

The case of *X and X v État belge* arose as a result of an application for a visa with limited territorial validity as per Article 25 of the Visa Code[50] by a Syrian family of five at the Belgian Embassy in Beirut, Lebanon. The family resided in Aleppo, Syria, an area known for its high level of destruction and risk to life due to the ongoing civil war in Syria at the material time. At the time of their visa application, the family openly expressed their wish to apply for asylum once they reached Belgium. The CJEU found that the CFREU did not apply to the situation at hand, as a visa with Limited Territorial Validity (LTV) as per Article 25 of the Visa Code, which is to be issued on the basis of 'humanitarian grounds' or 'international obligations', fell outside the scope of EU law.[51]

Nonetheless, the Visa Code does not define either 'humanitarian grounds' or 'international obligations'. This was exactly the main question referred to the CJEU for a preliminary ruling in the said case: whether 'international obligations' include all the rights guaranteed by the CFREU, including, in particular, those guaranteed by Articles 4 (prohibition of torture and inhuman or

[49] (n 4).

[50] Regulation 810/2009 establishing a Community Code on Visas [2009] OJ L 243/1, art 25(1) (Visa Code).

[51] Article 25(1)a of the Visa Code: 'A visa with limited territorial validity shall be issued *exceptionally*, in the following cases: (a) when the Member State concerned considers it necessary on *humanitarian grounds*, for reasons of national interest or *because of international obligations*, (i) to derogate from the principle that the entry conditions laid down in Article 5(1)(a), (c), (d) and (e) of the Schengen Borders Code must be fulfilled' (emphasis mine).

degrading treatment or punishment) and 18 (right to asylum), and whether they also cover obligations stemming from the ECHR and Article 33 (*non-refoulement* principle) of the Geneva Convention.[52] In its preamble, the Visa Code provides that it 'respects fundamental rights and observes the principles recognised in particular by the Council of Europe's Convention for the Protection of Human Rights and Fundamental Freedoms and by the Charter of Fundamental Rights of the European Union'.[53] In order for fundamental rights to apply, though, Member States should implement EU law.

As mentioned, in the case of *X and X v État belge*, the CJEU held that Belgium was not implementing EU law, despite the fact that the applicants applied for LTV visas in accordance with Article 25(1)a of the Visa Code. In its analysis, the CJEU did not find it necessary to reiterate any of the four nexus criteria. Without much clarity, it briefly mentioned a few relevant factors which led it to conclude that EU law did not apply. These factors are listed below.

First, the CJEU reiterated that the Visa Code was adopted on the basis of Article 62(2)a and b(ii) of the Treaty of Nice, according to which the Code regulated the issuance of visas 'for intended stays of *no more than three months*'.[54] This was the main reason for the CJEU to rule that the intention of the applicant family to apply for asylum in Belgium would exceed ninety days by default, as asylum precludes return to the third country of origin throughout its duration, which usually lasts for years.[55] It further clarified that it was not exactly the intention of the applicant that counted for the CJEU to come to the conclusion that the Visa Code did not apply, but the fact that the objective of the Visa Code seems to be incompatible with asylum.[56] Second, if the situation at hand was not deemed to fall within the scope of the Visa Code, the CJEU assessed if the EU had adopted any legal measures in accordance with its competence under Article 79(2)a, TFEU, namely to govern the issuance of long-term and residence permits to third country nationals on humanitarian grounds, within which scope the situation of the Syrian family would fall.[57] As this had not been the case, it concluded that the matter was governed by national law only.

[52] *X and X* (n 4), para 28(1).
[53] Visa Code, rec 29.
[54] *X and X* (n 4), para 40. UN Convention Relating to the Status of Refugees, 189 UNTS 150, 28 Jul. 1951 (entry into force: 22 Apr 1954).
[55] ibid para 42.
[56] ibid para 47: 'the purpose of the application (for an LTV visa with view to an asylum application) differs from that of a short-term visa.'
[57] ibid para 44; TFEU, art 79(2)a.

In the rest of the judgment, the CJEU established two additional factors which corroborated its finding above. The first one had to do with the need to uphold the general structure of the Dublin Regulation, which precluded the free choice of a Member State where people in need of international protection would like to apply for asylum; the second was related to the territorial scope of the Common European Asylum System, which excludes from its scope situations whereby people in need of international protection would like to apply for asylum at a diplomatic representation of a Member State in a third country.[58] As a result, the CJEU did not provide clarity as to the scope of 'international obligations' in the provision regulating the issuance of an LTV visa. The prioritization by the CJEU of the protection of the principles enshrined in the Dublin Regulation (mutual trust, inter-Member State solidarity) over the human rights protection of individuals as part of EU law has drawn serious criticism.[59] It points, once again, to a strict interpretation by the CJEU of national measures 'implementing EU law' in situations whereby individual human rights are at stake in the otherwise highly harmonized contexts of the Schengen Borders Code, as in *Zakaria*, and the Visa Code, as in the case of *X and X v État belge*.

An alternative path, not followed by the CJEU, has been offered by Advocate General Mengozzi in his Opinion to the *X and X v État belge* case. The first factor of essence for him was that the visa applications of the applicants were admitted, processed, and rejected in accordance with the Visa Code by the Belgian authorities.[60] This assessment corresponds to the first assessment criterion, namely, whether the national measure is intended to implement EU law. However, we saw that this first factor can exclude certain measures from the purview of EU law, but is not sufficient in itself to bring the measure within the scope of EU law.

The second element the Advocate General considered was whether the intention of the applicants to apply for asylum once they were on Belgian territory could be deemed to bring their application outside the scope of the Visa Code.

[58] ibid paras 48–49.

[59] Evelien Brouwer, 'The European Court of Justice on Humanitarian Visas: Legal Integrity v. Political Opportunism?' (2017) CEPS Commentary 1, 4. See also Stephanie Law, 'Humanitarian Admission and the Charter of Fundamental Rights' in Marie-Claire Foblets and Luc Leboeuf (eds), *Humanitarian Admission to Europe: The Law between Promises and Constraints* (Nomos 2020) 112; Caoimhe Sheridan and Amanda Taylor, 'Looking Like a Cat, Walking Like a Cat, Sounding Like a Cat but Actually Being a Dog: What the X and X Judgment Means for the Scope of the EU Charter?' (EDAL, 5 April 2017), <https://www.asylumlawdatabase.eu/en/journal/looking-cat-walking-cat-sounding-cat-actually-being-dog-what-x-and-x-judgment-means-scope-eu> accessed 25 January 2025.

[60] Case C-638/16 PPU, *X and X v. État belge* [2017] ECLI:EU:C:2017:93, Opinion of AG Mengozzi, para 49.

In essence, this test corresponds to the second assessment criterion, which is an assessment of the objectives of the national measure and their correspondence to the objectives of the applicable EU law. However, this test is modified in the sense that it is not contested by the parties that the national measure in place does not pursue objectives other than those of EU law, as the Belgian government directly referred to provisions of the Visa Code in the national proceedings. The claim put forward by the European Commission was that the applicants pursued objectives other than those of EU law[61]—namely, that their wish to apply for asylum in Belgium was to be understood as a requirement for them to apply for a long-term visa (under national law), instead of for a short-term one under the Visa Code. However, as stated by the Advocate General, the intention of the applicants was a potential substantive ground for a rejection of their applications in accordance with Article 32 of the Visa Code, and '*cannot alter the nature or purpose of their applications*'.[62] Unlike the second assessment criterion (criterion of the convergence of objectives), the assessment of the objectives of EU law is replaced by an assessment of the *applicants' intentions/ objectives*, which is problematic.

An assessment of the third (criterion of the impact on EU law) nexus criterion is absent from the Advocate General's analysis. And while it could be said that the judgment implicitly contains an assessment of the third criterion, namely, that the national measure could be deemed to be to the detriment of the primacy, unity, and effectiveness of EU law,[63] an analysis of the crucial fourth criterion, performed in section 4.2, would have been the game changer in this case.

4.2 The road not taken—application of the density criteria

In what follows, I illustrate how an analysis of the fourth nexus criterion—an analysis of whether EU law has specific regulations on the matter at issue could contribute to more clarity and consistency in the CJEU case law. I focus specifically on the fourth criterion for two reasons. The first is that, as Pirker has

[61] ibid para 46.
[62] ibid para 50, emphasis in the original.
[63] *X and X* (n 4), para 48; text to n 58. If a national measure, including fundamental rights as protected under the relevant MS constitutional order, is found to be inconsistent with the primacy, unity and effectiveness of EU law, that national measure will have to be disapplied, even if it offers a higher level of protection than the CFREU. Ward (n 10), 1563; Case C-399/11, *Stefano Melloni v Ministerio Fiscal* [2013] ECLI:EU:C:2013:107 [GC], para 60.

illustrated, the fourth criterion has been considered as having the most weight in the assessment of the CJEU on the application of Article 51(1) CFREU, as compared to the first, second, and third criteria. The second is that, as I have shown above, it seems that neither the CJEU nor Advocate General Mengozzi performed an analysis of the fourth nexus criterion.[64] Its application shows that the crux of the matter lies in the assessment of the link between Article 25 (on the issuance of LTV visas) and Article 32 (on the rejection of visas) of the Visa Code, an analysis of which would provide an answer to the questions posed for a preliminary ruling.[65]

An analysis of the fourth assessment criterion in essence requires an assessment of whether EU law imposes specific obligations on Member States. This assessment hinges on a competence analysis, but also, as shown above, requires a very contextual exploration of the concrete situation at hand. It is not enough to establish that the Visa Code requires 'further harmonisation of national legislation and handling practices at local consular missions'.[66] A few questions need to be specified. The first one is whether the provision in question, namely Article 25 of the Visa Code, obstructs one of the fundamental freedoms. In those cases, the CFREU automatically applies. The second question is whether Article 25 imposes a specific obligation on Member States; and if this is the case, whether it imposes a minimum standard of protection or whether, in case it allows for a derogation, the discretionary power granted to Member States forms an integral part of the Schengen system, following the CJEU judgment of *NS, ME and Others*.[67]

In answering the first question, it is clear that the case of *X and X v État belge* does not involve a situation which has the potential to obstruct any of the fundamental freedoms underpinning the EU project. On the contrary, the case falls within the scope of the Area of Freedom, Security and Justice, which has the primary objective to protect the freedom of movement of EU citizens.[68] In cases where the protection of fundamental freedoms of migrants and refugees is concerned, the CJEU seems to be prone to taking a more restrictive (narrower) position in the interpretation of human rights principles.[69]

[64] However, there are some elements of an analysis of the fourth criterion in the AG's opinion, as will be demonstrated.

[65] A possible line of reasoning which was brushed aside unsubstantiated by the judges. *X and X* (n 4), para 46.

[66] Visa Code, rec 3, citing the Hague Programme, Item 1.7.3. [2005] OJ C 53/7.

[67] *NS and ME and Others* (n 29).

[68] Treaty of the European Union [2012] OJ C 326/13, art 3(2).

[69] To the same effect, see Labayle and Bergé (n 48) 605.

Having answered the first question in the negative, I move on to the second question, whether Article 25 imposes a specific obligation on Member States. As shown above, Article 25, regulating the issuance of visas with limited territorial validity, states that such visas 'shall be issued exceptionally' in a number of cases which are stated in an exhaustive list. On the one hand, Member States seem not to have discretion to refuse the issuance of such a visa, provided that the applicants' situation is based on humanitarian grounds or is protected by certain international obligations.[70] On the other hand, the provision stipulates explicitly that the LTV visa *shall* be issued 'when the Member State concerned *considers it necessary* . . . to derogate from the principle that the [required] entry conditions laid out in [Article 6] of the Schengen Border Code must be fulfilled'.[71] This formulation leaves sufficient ground for discretion to Member States when assessing the necessity to derogate from the entry conditions in place.[72] The question becomes, then, if the derogation allowed forms 'an integral part' of the system of rules established by the regulation in question, as was found to be the case in *NS, ME and Others*.[73] For Advocate General Mengozzi, this question should be answered in the affirmative.[74] He brought forward two arguments to support this claim. The first is that the expression 'humanitarian grounds' is a concept of EU law and cannot be left to the national law of Member States.[75] The second pertains to the relationship between Article 25 and Article 32 of the Visa Code. Article 32 on the refusal of visas states that it applies without prejudice to Article 25(1). However, it does not become clear from this wording whether the issuance of an LTV visa is left to the assessment of the Member States as a stand-alone provision, or whether it is an integral part of the Visa Code Regulation. The answer to this question can be found in the provision of Article 23(4) on the decisions of the visa applications. It stipulates:

> Unless the application has been withdrawn, a decision shall be taken to: (a) issue a uniform visa in accordance with Article 24; (b) issue a visa with limited territorial validity in accordance with Article 25; (c) refuse a visa in accordance with Article 32;

[70] By analogy with Case C-84/12, *Rahmanian Koushkaki v Bundesrepublik Deutschland* [2013] ECLI:EU:C:2013:862 [GC], para 47.
[71] Visa Code, art 25(1)a(i), emphasis mine.
[72] By analogy with *Rahmanian Koushkaki* (n 70), para 60. See also *X and X v État belge* (n 4), paras 128ff.
[73] *NS and ME and Others* (n 29), para 65.
[74] *X and X v État belge* (n 60), para 83.
[75] ibid para 130.

or transfer the application to the competent diplomatic representation, in case it was different from the one applied to. The list of possible decisions is exhaustive. It means in essence that if neither a uniform nor an LTV visa is issued by the competent representation, the visa application is to be refused as per Article 32.[76] Therefore, if Member States decide to apply Article 25, this decision automatically precludes the application of Article 32, the application of which also implements EU law. Moreover, the Visa Code regulates many aspects of the issuance of LTV visas: for example, the issuing Member State is obliged to inform other Member States 'without delay',[77] or to collect and share statistics on the issuance of different types of visas, including on LTV visas[78] or the way the visa sticker should be filled in, including in the case of LTV visas.[79] Therefore, the claim that the issuance of LTV visas falls within the discretion of Member States and, consequently, EU law does not apply would be difficult to maintain, if an assessment of the fourth nexus criterion had been undertaken.

The issuance of LTV visas falls within the scope of a highly harmonized matter, namely the establishment of the procedures and conditions for the issuance of certain types of visas. The case could instead be categorized as a derogation case, whereby the national measure in place should be tested in accordance with the criteria in the *NS, ME and Others* judgment in order to establish whether the discretion enjoyed by Member States forms an integral part of the Schengen system. Had the CJEU chosen this path, it could have possibly claimed that LTV visas, being an exceptional measure, could not be held to form an integral part of the Schengen system. However, such an outcome could probably be undesirable, as it would excise all LTV visas from the purview of EU law, for example visas for medical treatment, and not only those applied for by people in need of international protection. In order to distinguish those cases from cases related to asylum, the CJEU relied predominantly on an assessment of the objectives of the national measure and the respective EU law measure, the second nexus criterion. This choice confirms Pirker's finding that the CJEU seems to resort to the second factor as a 'safety valve' in cases when the analysis under the fourth criterion 'does not yield a *satisfactory* result'.[80]

It seems that the 'satisfactory result' in the *X and X v État belge* was to rely on an analysis of the objectives of EU law and of the national measure which in the end amounted to the finding that the Belgian authorities were wrong to

[76] To the same effect, see ibid para 131.
[77] Visa Code, art 25(4).
[78] Visa Code, art 48(3)a.
[79] Visa Code, Annex VII. Filling in the Visa Sticker.
[80] Pirker (n 14) 138 and 153ff, emphasis mine.

apply EU law in the cases of asylum seekers applying for LTV visas in diplomatic representations of EU Member States in third countries. It pointed to the lack of EU measures with regard to humanitarian visas, despite the existing EU competence under Article 79(2)a TFEU, thus reaffirming the existing case law according to which national measures which fall within the scope of EU competences where the EU has not exercised those competences yet, do not implement EU law.[81]

As has been demonstrated, the choice to apply, explicitly or implicitly, any or a combination of an assessment of different nexus criteria may yield totally different outcomes. Therefore, indeed, there is a sufficient margin of discretion for the judges in their choice of criteria, as well as in the possibility to steer the judgment in diverging directions, without sacrificing the consistency of the judicial reasoning. In this respect, Spijkerboer aptly points out with regard to the case of *X and X v État belge* that '[t]he court had several alternatives, and had to make a choice [. . . and that] the options preferred by the court as well as the alternatives are the outcome of a combination of legal analysis and political choice'.[82]

5. Conclusion

This chapter has illustrated, on the one hand, the lack of consistency in the CJEU's reasoning on the application of the Charter of Fundamental Rights in migration and asylum cases, but also, on the other hand, the strong potential for such consistency based on the four nexus criteria which have already appeared in its case law: the criterion of the character of the rule of national law; the criterion of the convergence of objectives; the criterion of the impact on EU law; and the criterion of the density of EU regulation. For reasons related to the deprioritization of human rights principles as compared to other principles in the Area of Freedom, Security and Justice, the Court does not seem to explicitly apply these criteria in cases pertaining to migration and asylum which results in inconsistency, as the analysis showed. Therefore, it seems that by choosing inconsistency, the Court manages to introduce political considerations in its legal reasoning. However, the four nexus criteria, and more specifically the

[81] Case C-361/07, *Olivier Polier v Najar EURL* [2008] ECLI:EU:C:2008:16, para 13.

[82] Thomas Spijkerboer, 'Bifurcation of People, Bifurcation of Law: Externalization of Migration Policy before the EU Court of Justice' (2018) 31(2) JRS 216, 232.

lack of a specific hierarchy between them, obviously allow for a degree of discretion regarding the choice of which criteria to apply in each particular case. This chapter's main claim is that the leeway in the reasoning of the Court does not need to come at the expense of consistency and that the latter ought to be applied to cases pertaining to EU migration and asylum law, too.

Moreover, the finding—that the lack of inconsistency is the only consistency—is problematic specifically in the Area of Freedom, Security and Justice, as the human rights and often the lives of migrants and refugees are concerned. The Court has a heightened responsibility in these cases to ensure more clarity and legal certainty not only for the sake of migrants and refugees, but also of EU law as a whole, as the application of the Charter is closely connected to the accountability and the legitimacy of the EU. Clarifying certain judicial choices made by the judges could instead do much more good than harm, and this chapter should be read as an invitation for the CJEU to do just that.

References

Brouwer E, 'The European Court of Justice on Humanitarian Visas: Legal Integrity v. Political Opportunism?' (2017) CEPS Commentary 1, <https://cdn.ceps.eu/wp-content/uploads/2017/03/Visa%20Code%20CJEU%20E%20Brouwer%20CEPS%20Commentary_0.pdf>

García Andrade P, 'EU External Competences in the Field of Migration: How to Act Externally When Thinking Internally' (2018) 55 Common Market Law Review 157

Hancox E, 'The Meaning of "Implementing" EU Law under Article 51(1) of the Charter: Åkerberg Fransson' (2013) 50 Common Market Law Review 1411

Labayle H and Sylvestre Bergé J, 'Les Principes de l'Espace de Liberté, de Sécurité et de Justice' (2016) juillet-septembre Rev trimestrielle de droit européen 589

Law S, 'Chapter 2: Humanitarian Admission and the Charter of Fundamental Rights' in Marie-Claire Foblets and Luc Leboeuf (eds), *Humanitarian Admission to Europe: The Law between Promises and Constraints* (Nomos 2020)

Lazzerini N, 'The Scope and Effects of the Charter of Fundamental Rights in the Case Law of the European Court of Justice' in Giuseppe Palmisano (ed), *Making the Charter of Fundamental Rights a Living Instrument* (Brill/Nijhoff 2014)

Mádr P, 'Article 51 of the EU Charter of Fundamental Rights from the Perspective of the National Judge' (2020) 13(4) RevEurAdminL 53

Pirker B, 'Mapping the Scope of Application of EU Fundamental Rights: A Typology' (2018) 3(1) European Papers 133

Sheridan C and Taylor A, 'Looking Like a Cat, Walking Like a Cat, Sounding Like a Cat but Actually Being a Dog: What the X and X Judgment Means for the Scope of the EU Charter?' (EDAL, 5 April 2017), <https://www.asylumlawdatabase.eu/en/journal/looking-cat-walking-cat-sounding-cat-actually-being-dog-what-x-and-x-judgment-means-scope-eu> accessed 25 January 2025.

Spijkerboer T, 'Bifurcation of People, Bifurcation of Law: Externalization of migration policy before the EU Court of Justice' (2018) 31(2) JRS 216

Tecqmenne M, 'Minimum Harmonisation and Fundamental Rights: A Test-Case for the Identification of the Scope of EU Law in Situations Involving National Discretion? ECJ (Grand Chamber) 19 November 2019, Joined Cases C-609/17 and C-610/17, *TSN*' (2020) 16 European Constitutional Law Review 493

Thym D, 'Between "Administrative Mindset" and "Constitutional Imagination": The Role of the Court of Justice in Immigration, Asylum and Border Control Policy' (2019) 2 European Law Review 139

Tridimas T, 'Competence, Human Rights, and Asylum: What Price Mutual Recognition?' in Sacha Garben and Inge Govaere (eds), *The Division of Competences between the EU and the Member States: Reflections on the Past, the Present and the Future* (Hart Publishing 2017)

Ward A, 'Article 51—Field of Application' in Steve Peers and others (eds), *The EU Charter of Fundamental Rights: A Commentary* (2nd edn, Hart Publishing 2021)

9

Insiders, Outsiders, and the Limits of Analogous Interpretation in the ECJ Case Law

Alezini Loxa

1. Introduction

Among the many EU law doctrines, none remains as largely uncontroversial as the fundamental normative division between us, the EU citizens at the centre of the legal order, and the others, non-EU migrants. Next to the Treaty framework and the different legal bases for free movement of persons and migration, the case law of the Court of Justice of the EU has been central in sustaining the dividing line between the insiders and outsiders of EU law.

The status of EU citizenship as the normative foundation of the rights of EU migrants has been at the centre of the relevant case law, with an emphasis on an unbridgeable normative differentiation between EU and non-EU migrant.[1] Such a clear boundary has been confirmed also in relation to the non-discrimination principle under Article 18 TFEU which, according to the case law, is only meant to protect EU nationals.[2] In addition, the Court has avoided

[1] Judgment of 20 September 2001, *Grzelczyk*, C-184/99, ECLI:EU:C:2001:458; Judgment of 8 March 2011, *Ruiz Zambrano*, C-34/09, ECLI:EU:C:2011:124; Judgment of 29 April 2025, *Commission/Malta*, ECLI:EU:C:2025:283 on EU citizenship as a fundamental status; see also Opinion of Advocate General Szpunar delivered on 29 November 2016 in *Fahimian*, C-544/15, ECLI:EU:C:2017:255; Opinion of Advocate General Szpunar delivered on 28 January 2015, in *P and S*, C-579/13, ECLI:EU:C:2015:39; Opinion of Advocate General Mengozzi delivered on 27 June 2018 in *C and A*, C-257/17, ECLI:EU:C:2018:503; Opinion of Advocate General Mengozzi delivered on 30 April 2014 in *Dogan*, C-138/13, ECLI:EU:C:2014:287 on the differentiation with non-EU migrants.

[2] Judgment of 4 June 2009, *Vatsouras and Koupatantze*, C-22/08 and C-23/08, ECLI:EU:C:2009:344; Gareth Davies, 'When Do Union Citizens and Their Families Have the Right to Equal Treatment on Grounds of Nationality in EU Law?' (2024) European Journal of Migration and Law 281–83; Daire McCormack-George, 'Equal Treatment of Third-Country Nationals in the European Union: Why Not' (2019) 21 European Journal of Migration and Law 53.

Alezini Loxa, *Insiders, Outsiders, and the Limits of Analogous Interpretation in the ECJ Case Law* In: *The Reasoning of the Court of Justice of the EU*. Edited by: Alezini Loxa and Luigi Lonardo, Oxford University Press. © Alezini Loxa 2026. DOI: 10.1093/9780198983002.003.0012

a generalized analogous application of EU free movement case law to the area of migration.[3]

Legal scholarship has investigated this differentiation in two ways. First, there are scholarly accounts which have investigated the difference and have provided normative justifications behind the structure of the Treaty framework and the case law.[4] Second, there is a significant amount of critical legal scholarship which, rather than justifying the differentiation, investigates the various injustices produced thereby and identifies different structural reasons behind this.[5] This chapter makes a contribution to the latter stream of scholarship by exposing some fundamental points of incoherence in the way in which the Court sustains the normative differentiation between EU and non-EU migrants, with a focus on family reunification rights.

Specifically, in this chapter I suggest that while the overall framework regulating the rights of EU and non-EU migrants is different, there are specific areas where the rights attributed to both serve the same purpose and function. Exemplary in this regard is the case of family reunification. A closer examination of the historical background and the purpose of the relevant framework shows that family reunification is regulated in EU law as a means to promote integration and the right to family life for both EU and non-EU migrants (Section 2). In such cases, resolving the dispute by repeating the mantra of 'a different status and rights of a different kind' between EU and non-EU migrants amounts to a fictitious construction, rather than a justification based on the interpretation of EU law.

[3] Most recently in Judgment of 29 July 2024, *CU and ND*, Joined Cases C-112/22 and C-223/22, ECLI:EU:C:2024:636; Virginia Passalaqua, Op-Ed: 'Another Blow to Discriminatory Conditions of Access to Social Benefits: Joined Cases ND and CU (C-112 and 223/22)', EU Law Live, September 2024; Jonas Bornemann and Maria Haag, 'Testing the Inspirational Link between EU Citizenship and Migration Law: C-112/22 and C-223/22 CU and ND on Indirect Discrimination of Long-Term Residents', European Law Blog, September 2024.

[4] See Daniel Thym, '"Citizens" and "Foreigners" in EU Law: Migration Law and Its Cosmopolitan Outlook' (2016) 22 European Law Journal 296; Daniel Thym, 'EU Migration Policy and Its Constitutional Rationale: A Cosmopolitan Outlook' (2013) 50 CLM Rev 709.

[5] Thomas Spijkerboer, 'Coloniality and Recent European Migration Case Law' in Stijn Smet and Vladislava Stoyanova (eds), *Migrants' Rights, Populism and Legal Resilience in Europe* (Cambridge University Press 2022); Hanna Eklund, 'Peoples, Inhabitants and Workers: Colonialism in the Treaty of Rome' (2023) 34 European Journal of International Law 831; Sergio Carrera and Anja Wiesbrock, 'Civic Integration of Immigrants: A Challenge to Proportionality and Non-Discrimination in the Common European Immigration Policy?' in Dagmar Schiek, Hildegard Schneider, and Ulrike Liebert (eds), *European Economic and Social Constitutionalism after the Treaty of Lisbon* (Cambridge University Press 2011); Kees Groenendijk, 'The Long-Term Residents Directive, Denizenship and Integration' in Anneliese Baldaccini, Elspeth Guild, and Helen Toner (eds), *Whose Freedom, Security and Justice? EU Immigration and Asylum Law and Policy* (1st edn, Hart Publishing Ltd 2007); Sarah Ganty, 'Integration Duties in the European Union: Four Models' (2021) 28 Maastricht Journal of European and Comparative Law 784.

To show this, the analysis maps how the Court has interpreted the relation between the Family Reunification Directive and the Citizens' Rights Directive in the case law. By an assessment of the *context of justification* alone,[6] I point to what is missed in the Courts' interpretation and to the inconsistencies it creates both in relation to incorrect application of the law and in relation to misapplication of previous case law (Section 3). Without challenging the vision of EU law that the Court has on the special status of EU citizenship—rather, accepting it as the starting point of the analysis—I argue for a different interpretation on textual, systematic, and teleological grounds. In brief, I argue that the line of reasoning of the Court, while occasionally promoting the rights of non-EU migrants, undermines the rights of family members of EU migrants (Section 4) and is not consistent with the constitutional commitment of the EU to protect family life under both the Charter and the recent accession to the Istanbul Convention (Section 5).[7] I then conclude the chapter (Section 6).

2. Family Reunification and EU Law

Before providing a normative assessment of the Court's justification, it is important to map the relevant legal framework and to understand the history and purpose of the instruments regulating the rights of family reunification for EU and non-EU migrants. This section will provide an overview of the relevant instruments and discuss residence rights for family members under Directive 2004/38 and Directive 2003/86.[8] It will further tease out the purpose of autonomous residence rights for family members and the different conditions under which such rights are regulated in the two instruments.

As regards EU migrants, family reunification is regulated under Directive 2004/38 (Citizens' Rights Directive) adopted on the basis of the Treaty provisions on EU citizenship, free movement, and non-discrimination.[9] The Directive provides for an extensive scope of family members that are entitled to

[6] See Introduction in this volume.

[7] Charter of Fundamental Rights of the European Union [2016] OJ C 202/389; Council of Europe Convention on preventing and combating violence against women and domestic violence, CETS No 210, 11 May 2011.

[8] Directive 2004/38/EC of the European Parliament and of the Council of 29 April 2004 on the right of citizens of the Union and their family members to move and reside freely within the territory of the Member States amending Regulation (EEC) No 1612/68 and repealing Directives 64/221/EEC, 68/360/EEC, 72/194/EEC, 73/148/EEC, 75/34/EEC, 75/35/EEC, 90/364/EEC, 90/365/EEC, and 93/96/EEC [2004] OJ L 158/77; Council Directive 2003/86/EC of 22 September 2003 on the right to family reunification [2003] OJ L 251/12.

[9] See Articles 12, 18, 40, 44, and 52 EC Treaty, Consolidated versions of the Treaty on European Union and of the Treaty establishing the European Community (2002) [2002] OJ C 325/01.

accompany or join EU migrants in the host state, as well as for their rights when residing there.[10] The rights of family members of EU migrants were already protected by the Court in the interpretation of the free movement of workers framework.[11] In the relevant case law, the Court safeguarded the rights of EU migrants to be joined or accompanied by their family members in light of the need to guarantee that workers moved in liberty and dignity, and could thus be integrated in the host state.[12] This approach had been subject to criticism in scholarship for not respecting the right to family life as such, but rather only protecting it in so far as it served an economic end that could further promote free movement in the internal market.[13] The adoption of the Citizens' Rights Directive marked a shift in the purpose behind the attribution of family rights to EU migrants. With a Treaty framework that established general free movement rights for EU citizens and not just those who are economically active, and with the Charter of Fundamental Rights adopted (even in non-binding form), the aspiration of the Commission was human rights-oriented. The purpose of adopting a new Directive for the free movement of persons was to disconnect the rights of family members from the pre-existing functionalist narrative, and to connect them to the preservation of family unity.[14]

Regarding non-EU migrants, the attribution of family reunification rights was for the first time regulated in 2003 through a horizontal instrument that applies to all regularly resident migrants across the Member States. The adoption of Directive 2003/86 (Family Reunification Directive) as part of the EU migration policy was the outcome of a much more ambitious plan on the part of the Commission.[15] In the late 1990s, the Commission put forward a proposal for an instrument that would regulate family reunification for all those who did not fall under the free movement rules, that is, economically inactive EU migrants, non-EU migrants, and also nationals of Member States who

[10] Articles 2, 3, and 23 Directive 2004/38.

[11] See Regulation (EEC) No 1612/68 of the Council of 15 October 1968 on freedom of movement for workers within the Community [1968] OJ L 257/2. In the free movement of workers framework, the protection of family members appeared under more utilitarian terms; see Judgment of 13 February 1985, *Diatta v Land Berlin*, 267/83, ECLI:EU:C:1985:67; Judgment of 11 July 2002, *Carpenter*, C-60/00, ECLI:EU:C:2002:434 for self-employed.

[12] See Judgments of 17 September 2002, *Baumbast and R*, C-413/99, EU:C:2002:493, para 50, Judgment of 13 November 1990, *Di Leo/Land Berlin*, C-308/89, ECLI:EU:C:1990:400 para 13.

[13] See Tamara Hervey, 'Migrant Workers and Their Families in the European Union: The Pervasive Market Ideology of Community Law' in Jo Shaw and Gillian More (eds), *New Legal Dynamics of European Union* (Clarendon Press 1995); Clare McGlynn, *Families and the European Union Law, Politics and Pluralism* (Cambridge University Press 2006).

[14] Proposal for a European Parliament and Council Directive on the right of citizens of the Union and their family members to move and reside freely within the territory of the Member States COM(2001)0257 final [2001] OJ C 270E/150, section 2.4.

[15] Article 63.3.a. EC Treaty Nice version.

had never left their home state.[16] By way of this proposal, and with a strong human rights orientation, the Commission sought to consolidate the protection of family life in the EU, as a means to promote the living conditions of everyone in the territory of the Member States. According to the Commission, 'The presence of family members makes for greater stability and deepens the roots of these people since they are enabled to lead a normal family life'.[17] By analogy to family reunification rights for EU nationals falling under the free movement framework, the Commission suggested that fair treatment of non-EU migrants was 'indispensable' if they were to lead a normal life in the host states and would help them to integrate in local societies.[18] However, this horizontal regulation of family life was not accepted by the Council.[19] The scope of the instrument was limited to non-EU migrants and the Family Reunification Directive was finally adopted in 2003.

The Directive applies to all non-EU migrants who reside in the Member States, with the exclusion of those whose status is considered uncertain or temporary.[20] The purpose of granting family reunification rights to non-EU migrants under this framework is to promote economic and social cohesion under Article 3 TEU, as acknowledged in recital 4 of the Directive. Even though Article 3 TEU is not explicitly referred to, the recital mentions the central role of family reunification in the creation of sociocultural stability and integration for migrants and explains that such outcome serves to promote economic and social cohesion as fundamental objectives stated in the Treaty. Unlike the extensive circle of family members covered under the Citizens' Rights Directive, the Family Reunification Directive attributes this right to the nuclear family of non-EU migrants and allows discretion for the rest.[21]

Comparing the two Directives as regards family reunification rights, it is clear that the Citizens' Rights Directive allows for reunification of a more extensive circle of family members; the conditions set for family reunification are also less stringent in relation to those of the Family Reunification Directive.

[16] Proposal for a Council Directive on the right to family reunification, COM(99)0638 final, Article 1, Article 3(c).

[17] ibid Section 2.2.

[18] ibid Section 7.2.

[19] Amended proposal for a Council directive on the right to family reunification COM(2002)0225 final, Section 2.4.

[20] Article 3 Family Reunification Directive, see also Amended proposal COM(2002)0225 final.

[21] The 1999 proposal for the Directive provided for a larger scope of family members entitled to reunification, see Proposal COM(99)0638 final, Article 5 with obligation for spouse and unmarried partner in line with Judgment of 17 April 1986, *Netherlands v Reed*, 59/85, ECLI:EU:C:1986:157, ascendants and children of full age. This was rejected by the Council, Council of the European Union, Press Release, 2370th Council meeting—Justice, Home Affairs and Civil Protection, Brussels, 27 and 28 September 2001, 12204/01 (Presse 334). See Article 4 of the Family Reunification Directive.

While both instruments condition the right to family reunification on economic considerations, the extent of these conditions is stricter for non-EU migrants. In detail, the Citizens' Rights Directive requires economic activity in the form of employment, self-employment, or self-sufficiency of the EU migrant and comprehensive insurance cover as a prerequisite for family reunification under Article 7(2). The Family Reunification Directive provides that the non-EU migrants have to show 'stable and sufficient resources', unlike the 'sufficient resources' demanded for EU migrants, while on top of insurance cover, non-EU migrants also need to show adequate accommodation under Article 7(1).[22]

In addition, both instruments provide for the possibility that family members establish an autonomous right of residence. This means a right of residence that is no longer tied to their relation to the migrant-sponsor of the family reunification. In the case of family members of EU migrants such rights are regulated under Articles 12 and 13 of the Citizens' Rights Directive. These articles refer to various situations related to the death of the EU migrant, their departure from the host state, or the breakdown of the family relationship, and set various conditions in order to ensure that the family members will not be exposed to vulnerability in the case that the family relationship is terminated or will not stay in an abusive relationship to avoid losing their permit. For the purposes of the analysis that will follow, Article 13(2)(c) provides that an autonomous right to reside might be granted to family members if this is demanded by particularly difficult circumstances. The provision mentions as an example the case of having been the victim of domestic violence during a marriage to or partnership with an EU migrant. It is important to note that in all cases where an autonomous residence right is provided under the Citizens' Rights Directive, such right is tied to economic conditions. Specifically, in all the relevant cases, and regardless of the reason why a family member claims an autonomous residence right, they need to have economic activity (work, self-employment, or sufficient resources) and comprehensive sickness insurance. The relevant residence rights become disconnected from economic considerations only after the migrants acquire a right to permanent residence in accordance with Article 16 Citizens' Rights Directive after a five-year residence period.

In the Family Reunification Directive, family members are entitled to an autonomous right to reside after five years of legal residence under Article

[22] Judgment of 21 April 2016, *Khachab*, C-558/14, ECLI:EU:C:2016:285 on the meaning of stable and sufficient recourses.

15(2). Member States are allowed to limit the autonomous rights of the spouse or unmarried children in the case of breakdown of the family relationship. Specifically, they have the discretion of granting such a right to adult children and dependent relatives under Article 4(2) of the Family Reunification Directive and the possibility to provide it in cases of widowhood, divorce, separation, or death of first-degree relatives in the direct ascending or descending line, as well as in cases of particularly difficult circumstances. Article 15(3) of the Directive, which refers to widowhood, divorce, separation, or death, suggests that an autonomous residence permit may be issued to family members. According to this article, Member States shall also lay down provisions on granting an autonomous residence permit in the event of particularly difficult circumstances.

Before examining how the Court has related the autonomous residence rights attributed to family members by each of these Directives, it is important to explain why these provisions were included in the instruments. After the much-criticized *Diatta* judgement, where the Court found that rights of residence for migrant spouses end when their marriage to an EU migrant resolves, it became clear that the rights of family members are always attached to the rights of the EU migrant-sponsor.[23] This meant that victims of domestic violence would potentially have to choose between leaving their abusive partners and losing their residence rights or staying in an abusive relationship to maintain their residence status. To avoid having to make such a choice, and to make up for the vulnerability of the migration status of family members, the Commission suggested the creation of an autonomous permit in the case of breakdown of the family situation, which was introduced for the first time in the Family Reunification Directive.[24] This right went a lot further than the provisions for EU migrants at the time.[25] The vulnerability of migrant family member victims of domestic violence is of the same kind regardless of whether the abusive relationship is with an EU or a non-EU migrant. Naturally then, in the proposal for the Citizens' Rights Directive, the Commission included the same right. The same reason appeared behind the provision, which was that

[23] C-267/83, *Diatta v Land Berlin*; Tamara Hervey, 'A Gendered Perspective on the Right to Family Life in European Community Law' in Nanette A Neuwahl and Allan Rosas (eds), *The European Union and Human Rights* (Brill 1995); Louise Ackers, 'Citizenship, Gender, and Dependence in the European Union: Women and Internal Migration' (1996) 3 Social Politics: International Studies in Gender, State & Society 316.

[24] Proposal for a Council Directive on the right to family reunification, COM(99)0638 final, Explanatory Memorandum Article 13 para 1: 'Access to an autonomous status enables family members to cease depending on the applicant's residence permit and to enjoy certainty as to their own legal position.'

[25] ibid Explanatory Memorandum, Article 13(3).

no migrant should have to stay in an abusive relationship for fear that leaving the relationship would mean having to leave the host state.[26]

Eventually the provision of 13(2)(c) was adopted in the Citizens' Rights Directive with a view to protect migrant women and end their dependency on the EU migrant-sponsor in case of abuse.[27] This is exactly the purpose served by the provision of Article 15(3) of the Family Reunification Directive. Looking at these provisions and the preparatory texts to their adoption, it becomes clear that the retention of residence rights by migrants victims of domestic violence serves a single purpose. It is based on a recognition of vulnerability of migrant women whose residence status in the host state is very much dependent on the residence status of their sponsor. In order to do away with such vulnerability in cases where migrant women are exposed to domestic violence, both instruments created the possibility of retention of the residence right. At the same time, only one of the two provisions explicitly refers to the need of economic activity or self-sufficiency and sickness insurance in order to secure such a right.

3. The Limits of Comparison

This section compares two cases in which the Court engaged with the relation between the provision of Article 13(2)(c) of the Citizens' Rights Directive and under Article 15(3) of the Family Reunification Directive. First, in *X v État belge* the Court was called to compare these to provisions for the purpose of assessing the validity of 13(2)(c) of the Citizens' Rights Directive in light of the Charter.[28] In that case the Court emphasized the systematic and teleological differences of the Citizens' Rights Directive and the Family Reunification Directive and it ruled against the comparability of the situtations covered by these two provisions. On the contrary, in *Sagrario*, which concerned the meaning of 'particularly difficult circumstances' as a ground for an autonomous residence permit under Article 15(3) of the Family Reunification Directive, the Court focused on the common purpose of this provision to Article 13(2)(c) of the Citizens' Rights Directive in order to use the latter as an interpretative aid.[29]

[26] Proposal on citizen's rights Directive COM(2001)0257 final, Explanation to Article 13(2).

[27] Amended Proposal COM/2003/0199 final, Explanation to Article 13(2), point (c) (amendment 52).

[28] Judgment of 2 September 2021, *X v État belge* (Droit de séjour en cas de violence domestique), C-930/19, ECLI:EU:C:2021:657.

[29] Judgment of 12 September 2024, *Sagrario*, C-63/23, ECLI:EU:C:2024:739.

3.1 The fiction of differentiation

The Grand Chamber judgement in *X v État belge* stands out for the 'unnecessary' emphasis of the CJEU on differentiating the purpose, effects, and degree of the rights granted to migrants experiencing domestic abuse depending on whether their spouse is an EU or a non-EU migrant.[30] The case concerned an Algerian migrant, a victim of domestic violence in their marriage to a French national, who sought an autonomous right to reside in Belgium under the Citizens' Rights Directive. The Belgian law transposing the Citizens' Rights Directive and the Family Reunification Directive, respectively, provided the following.[31] In case of family members of EU migrants, the retention of residence rights for victims of domestic violence was dependent on sufficiency of resources and sickness insurance. In case of family members of non-EU migrants, the retention of the right to reside was subject only to proof of the existence of domestic violence in the relationship. This meant that family members of EU migrants needed to abide by stricter conditions to be able to establish a residence right in the case that they had suffered from domestic violence. They thus found themselves in a less favourable situation in relation to migrants whose family members were non-EU migrants. Noting that the differentiation of treatment of migrant victims of domestic violence was based on whether the victim drew residence rights from an EU migrant or a non-EU migrant, the Belgian Court asked whether Article 13 of the Citizens' Rights Directive is incompatible with Articles 20 or 21 of the Charter.

Since Article 21(2) of the Charter which refers to discrimination on the basis of nationality is a specific expression of Article 18 TFEU and the Court has held that the latter only applies to discrimination between nationals of EU Member States, the provision was irrelevant to the resolution of the dispute.[32] Instead, the Court examined the case through the lens of Article 20 of the Charter, which requires that comparable situations should not be treated differently.[33] This is not taken to mean just a factual comparison, as would be

[30] Francesca Strumia, 'Speaking Too Little, Yet Saying Too Much: The Wrong Signals about EU Values: X. v. Belgian State' (2022) 59 CML Rev 1202.

[31] Loi sur l'accès au territoire, le séjour, l'établissement et l'éloignement des étrangers (Moniteur belge of 31 December 1980, p. 1458). Article 42c(1) and (4) transposed Article 13(2) of Directive 2004/38 into Belgian law and Article 11(2) of the same law transposed Article 15(3) of Directive 2003/86 into Belgian law.

[32] C-930/19, *X v État belge*, paras 50–51; C-22/08 and C-23/08, *Vatsouras and Koupatantze*, para 52; Explanations relating to the Charter of Fundamental Rights [2007] OJ 2007 C-303/17; Bjarney Friðriksdóttir, *What Happened to Equality? The Construction of the Right to Equal Treatment of Third-Country Nationals in European Union Law on Labour Migration* (Brill Nijhoff 2017); McCormack-George (n 2).

[33] C-930/19, *X v État belge*, paras 54–57.

the case in national courts examining non-discrimination cases. After all, it would be hard to establish a hypothetical scenario where two migrant victims of domestic violence, one married to an EU migrant and the other married to a non-EU migrant, find themselves in non-comparable situations. Indeed, the Belgian Court had as a starting point the identical nature of the two situations.[34] In contrast, disregarding the potential factual comparability, the Court resolved the case by examining the comparability of the Citizens' Rights Directive and the Family Reunification Directive.[35]

After providing an overview of Article 13(2) of the Citizen's Rights Directive and Article 15(3) of the Family Reunification Directive, and acknowledging that the two provisions establish very different conditions, the Court went on to examine the objective of the two provisions. It held that indeed their objective is the same, that is, protecting family members who are victims of violence.[36] However, this was not enough of itself, as 'the comparability of the situations must be assessed in the light of all the elements which characterise them'.[37] To do so the Court went on to examine the fields covered by the two Directives, their subject-matter, their objectives, and the discretion allowed by the two instruments. In sum, the Court proceeded in a systematic, contextual, and teleological comparison of the two instruments before looking at the element of discretion allowed by the provisions.

First, the Court suggested that the fields covered by the two Directives are different. Specifically, the Citizens' Rights Directive falls within the Union's objective under Article 3 TEU to establish an internal market.[38] Free movement is a primary law right, and the Directive was adopted to give effect to such right. The rights granted to family members of EU migrants were attributed in order to facilitate the free movement of the latter. In contrast to that, the Family Reunification Directive fell under the objective of the EU to create a common migration policy under Article 79 TFEU and created common rules which were to be transposed into domestic law. The different legal basis was not the end of the Court's analysis on this point. Rather, it was important to explain why the field of common migration policy, where the Family Reunification Directive belongs, does not come with the same intensity of harmonization demands. Specifically, the Court drew on the AG Opinion and suggested that EU competence in migration is a power to undertake harmonization without

[34] ibid para 59.
[35] ibid para 58.
[36] ibid para 70.
[37] ibid.
[38] ibid para 71.

any normative demand as to what such harmonization might look like.[39] This proposition defies the normative underpinning that the Treaties embed in migration policy in Article 79(1) TFEU and Article 80 TFEU. Harmonization in migration is not based on the power to create any common policy whatsoever. Rather, the Treaty demands that such common policy needs to ensure, among others, the fair treatment of non-EU migrants and to be governed by the principle of solidarity. Moreover, by highlighting that the power to harmonize in the area of migration is something entirely different from the competence in free movement, the Court added a mythical quality to EU citizenship, while concealing that in this legal area competence is also shared. The extent and intensity of harmonization that has already taken place is indeed different in the areas of free movement and migration, but the conferral of powers is exactly the same, and so is the application of the principle of pre-emption.[40]

Second, the Court proceeded to examine the subject-matter of the two Directives, and it found that it was different. The Citizens' Rights Directive concerns free movement and residence by EU citizens and family members, and most importantly, it sets the limitations to a right provided under primary law.[41] The Family Reunification Directive has the purpose of determining common criteria for the rights of lawfully resident migrants. In the Family Reunification Directive, the EU legislator intended to ensure the approximation of national laws relating to the conditions of admission and residence of non-EU migrants.[42] The Court suggested that instead, '[as] is apparent from the very wording of Articles 20 and 21 TFEU, the right of Union citizens and their family members to move and reside freely within the territory of the Member States is not unconditional' and the Citizens' Rights Directive was adopted to set the relevant conditions.[43] Contrary to this suggestion, neither Article 20 nor Article 21 TFEU refer to the rights of family members in their text. Even though the Court has acknowledged that rights for family members might arise from these provisions in exceptional circumstances to ensure the genuine enjoyment of the rights of EU citizenship, secondary law has historically been adopted with a view to creating family reunification rights for EU migrants.[44] In this regard, the approximation of laws for the entry and residence

[39] ibid para 76; Opinion of Advocate General Szpunar delivered on 22 March 2021 in *X v État belge*, C-930/19, paras 122–23.

[40] ibid para 22; Protocol No 25 on the exercise of shared competence, [2012] OJ C 326/307.

[41] C-930/19, *X v État belge*, paras 77–78.

[42] ibid paras 79–80.

[43] ibid para 78.

[44] See Judgment of 8 March 2011, *Ruiz Zambrano*, C-34/09, ECLI:EU:C:2011:124; Judgment of 10 May 2017, *Chavez-Vilchez and others*, C-133/15, ECLI:EU:C:2017:354.

of family members of EU migrants under the Citizens' Rights Directive is much like the approximation sought by the Family Reunification Directive for non-EU migrants.

Third, the objectives of the instruments were found to be different. The Citizens' Rights Directive aims to facilitate the exercise of a primary law right, that of free movement of EU citizens.[45] As a secondary objective, the Directive also protects family life and integration.[46] In contrast, in the Family Reunification Directive the integration and protection of family are the primary objectives.[47] Finally, the Court held that there was a difference in the discretion available to Member States, and that the Family Reunification Directive allowed for broader discretion in its transposition. It has already been suggested that both instruments are Directives and, as EU law stands today, there are no first-class and second-class Directives with different legal effects.[48] However, what is important to unpack are the following crucial points raised by the Court. The Court suggested that the discretion of Member States is limited in the application of the Citizens' Rights Directive, whereas by contrast the discretion conferred under the Family Reunification Directive 'is broad as regards, specifically, the conditions for granting, on the basis of Article 15(3) of that directive, an autonomous residence permit'.[49] The Court based the fact on the reference made by Article 15(4) to national law for the conditions of the granting of such a permit.[50] In *passim* the Court also referred to the possibility of Member States to adopt more favourable provisions in the case of the Citizens Rights Directive under Article 37, but it failed to mention the exact same possibility under Article 3(5) of the Family Reunification Directive. On this specific point of difference in discretion allowed by the two provisions, it is not necessarily the finding of the Court that confuses. Indeed, the reference to national law in the provision of the Family Reunification Directive, even if circumscribed by the demands of respecting the effectiveness EU law and the principle of proportionality, does suggest the existence of discretion on this matter.[51] Rather, what the Court misses is the comparator. It should have compared the discretion available under the two provisions at stake in the situation and it is not convincing enough to compare the discretion available under a

[45] C-930/19, *X v État belge*, para 81.

[46] ibid para 82 with reference to the case law of the Court already in judgments of 17 April 1986, *Reed*, 59/85, EU:C:1986:157, para 28.

[47] ibid para 82.

[48] See however the difference between exhaustive and non-exhaustive harmonization, Judgment of 1 July 2014, *Ålands Vindkraft*, C-573/12, ECLI:EU:C:2014:2037, which was not relevant in this case.

[49] C-930/19, *X v État belge*, paras 84–85.

[50] ibid para 86.

[51] ibid para 88.

specific provision of the Family Reunification Directive and the Citizens' Rights Directive *in toto*.

Overall, the Court found that despite the fact that the two provisions share the same objective of protecting migrant victims of domestic violence, they have their origin in Directives that relate to different fields, principles, subject-matters, and objectives.[52] In addition, the Court repeated the phrase that is very often met in case law on the rights of EU migrants, which is that those who fall within the scope of the Citizens' Rights Directive 'enjoy a different status and rights of a different kind'.[53] For these reasons, the Court considered that the situations of migrant victims of domestic violence who find themselves covered by two different instruments depending on whether they were married to an EU or a non-EU migrant are not comparable.[54]

3.2 The possibility of analogy

Three years later the Court had the opportunity to clarify the meaning of Article 15(3) of the Family Reunification Directive, this time without having to relate the situation of a family member of a non-EU migrant to that of an EU one. *Sagrario* concerned autonomous residence permits for family members under the Family Reunification Directive, and more specifically the meaning of the concept of 'particularly difficult circumstances'. The case, which originated in a preliminary reference by a Spanish Administrative Court, concerned the autonomous residence rights of a mother and her two children. They applied for a long-term residence permit together with the father-sponsor. The latter had his application rejected due to the existence of a criminal record, which then led to the rejection of the permit of the mother and children. Following this rejection, the mother and the children applied for an autonomous residence permit under Article 15(3) of the Family Reunification Directive. They claimed that they would be exposed to particularly difficult circumstances by losing their permit for reasons beyond their control.

In that case, the Court proceeded in a classic exercise of interpretation of EU law. That is, it tried to identify the appropriate interpretation of the concept of 'particularly difficult circumstances' under Article 15(3) of the Family Reunification Directive by having recourse to the text of the provision,

52 ibid para 89.
53 ibid para 89.
54 ibid para 91.

its context, the objectives of the provision, and the Family Reunification Directive, as well as its legislative history.[55] On a textual interpretation, the Court followed the AG, and suggested that the concept of 'particularly difficult circumstances' requires the existence of particularly serious or arduous circumstances which expose the family member to 'significant insecurity or vulnerability going beyond the usual hazards of a normal family life'.[56] On the objectives of the provision, the Court drew a distinction between the objectives of the Family Reunification Directive as a whole, the objective of the provision of Article 15, and the specific objectives of the second sentence of Article 15(3).[57]

According to the Court, while the Directive and Article 15 seek to protect family life through reunification, the purpose of the second sentence of Article 15(3) is to create an independent status which can facilitate the estrangement of family members from their sponsor.[58] Drawing on the findings of *X v État belge* presented in the previous section, the Court suggested that the objective of this provision is to protect victims of domestic violence committed by the sponsor during the marriage.[59] Understanding the concept of particularly difficult circumstances as meaning situations of domestic violence was further supported by the legislative history of the provision presented in Section 2.[60] The Court further invoked the guidelines of the Commission on the application of the Directive which list examples of particularly difficult circumstances, among which is the situation of domestic violence.[61]

Where things get interesting for the purposes of this contribution is in the final step of the Court's justification, that is, the examination of context of the relevant provision. When the Court turned to that step to support that particularly difficult circumstances should be understood as circumstances that result from the family situation even if they have not occurred as a result of the marital breakdown, it suggested that such interpretation is supported by the similar provision of Article 13(2)(c) of the Citizens' Rights Directive.[62] Arguably, the Court could have avoided this particular mention, as after all in

[55] C-63/23, *Sagrario*, para 37.
[56] ibid para 38; Opinion of Advocate General Richard de la Tour delivered on delivered on 7 March 2024 in C-63/23, *Sagrario*, para 49.
[57] C-63/23, *Sagrario*, paras 42–44.
[58] ibid para 45.
[59] ibid para 46.
[60] ibid para 47 and reference to the Commission Proposal, COM(1999) 0638.
[61] ibid para 48; Communication from the Commission to the European Parliament and the Council of 3 April 2014 on guidance for application of Directive 2003/86/EC on the right to family reunification, COM(2014) 210 final.
[62] C-63/23, *Sagrario*, para 56.

X v État belge the main finding was that of incomparability of the two instruments regulating family reunification for EU and non-EU migrants despite the similarities of the specific provisions. What is more, there was no mention of the Citizens' Rights Directive in the parties' written submissions, whereas the AG also drew a differentiation between the two provisions.[63] Despite this, the Court pointed out that the objective of that provision is the same as the objective of Article 15(3), which is to ensure the protection of family member victims of domestic violence, referring once again to *X v État belge* for this finding.[64] Eventually the Court held that the meaning of particularly difficult circumstances should be taken as circumstances stemming from the family situation which are particularly serious or arduous and expose them to significant insecurity or vulnerability, causing them to have a need for the protection afforded by an autonomous permit, regardless of whether the marital relationship has broken down.[65] The Court's interpretation of the concept of 'particularly difficult circumstances' does not lie far from the one provided by the AG, but in adopting this interpretation the Court used the Citizens' Rights Directive as an interpretative aid.

In *Sagrario*, it becomes clear that the Court's notion of differentiation between EU and non-EU migrants does not operate both ways. By this I mean that the Court avoids addressing the comparability of the two situations when it has to rule on the question of the Citizens' Rights Directive and its compliance with the Charter, but is very eagerly suggesting an analogy when it comes to using the same Directive as an aid for interpretation of secondary law regarding the rights of non-EU citizens.

4. The Inconsistent Fiction of Differentiation in the Court's Case Law

Reading *Sagrario* together with *X v État belge* attests to the inconsistency in the Court's case law. Admittedly, the circumstances of these cases were different both in relation to the vulnerability of the migrant family members involved and the need for comparison between the two frameworks regulating family reunification. However, *Sagrario* would not be the first case in which the Court

[63] Opinion of AG Richard de la Tour in C-63/23, *Sagrario*, para 39.
[64] C-63/23, *Sagrario*, para 56 with reference to C-930/19, *X v État belge*, paras 70 and 89.
[65] C-63/23, *Sagrario*, para 58.

has drawn an analogy to the Citizens' Rights Directive to interpret concepts of migration law.

Specifically, in cases concerning family reunification for refugees, the Court has invoked case law from the Citizen's Rights Directive to interpret the concept of 'dependent' family members, while acknowledging that a broader interpretation should apply by virtue of the special vulnerability of refugees.[66] What is more, *in Landeshauptmann von Wien* the Court proceeded in a comparative analysis between the Long-term Residence Directive and the Citizens' Rights Directive in order to define the concept of 'absence' from the territory of a host Member State for the purposes of losing the long-term residence status.[67] Such cases point to inconsistencies in how the Court has structured the notion of differentiation between EU and non-EU migrants.

I would argue that the key reason for such differentiation and for the connection drawn to the Citizens' Rights Directive in this latter set of cases is in fact the absence of any need for direct comparison between EU and non-EU migrants. The case law has consistently emphasized not only the centrality of EU citizens for the project of EU integration, but also the paradox of interpreting EU law in any way that might privilege non-EU migrants. Already in *Metock*, where the Court had to clarify whether family reunification for EU migrants required that the family members had previously established lawful residence in another Member State, it was pointed out that such a scenario would be 'paradoxical' in so far as it would lead to better treatment for non-EU migrants by comparison to EU citizens.[68]

While in principle the Court wants to uphold the better treatment of EU migrants, its judgment in *X v État belge* has the effect of creating higher standards for their most vulnerable family members and this could have been avoided. By stating that the rights of EU migrants are of a different kind, the Court does not explain why the rights of their family members should be subject to more conditions for the acquisition of an autonomous residence. According to the Court, this paradoxical outcome is not the result of EU law. Rather, this is the result of Belgian law that did not apply more conditions for migrant victims of domestic violence in the transposition of the Family Reunification Directive,

[66] Judgment of 12 December 2019, *Bevándorlási és Menekültügyi Hivatal (Regroupement familial—sœur de réfugié)*, C-519/18, ECLI:EU:C:2019:1070, 45–52.

[67] Judgment of 20 January 2022, *Landeshauptmann von Wien (Perte du statut de résident de longue durée)*, C-432/20, ECLI:EU:C:2022:39, para 43. This is also in light of the purpose of the Directive to bring the status of long-term residents as close as possible to that of EU citizens, see Recital 2, Council Directive 2003/109/EC of 25 November 2003 concerning the status of third-country nationals who are long-term residents [2004] OJ L 16/44.

[68] Judgment of 25 July 2008, *Metock and others*, C-127/08, ECLI:EU:C:2008:449, para 77.

even though it had the discretion to.[69] According to Strumia, the Court could have reached the same conclusion by suggesting that the Belgian legislature had to enact more favourable conditions and waive the financial condition for granting a permit under an application of the Citizens' Rights Directive in light of the Charter.[70]

I argue that instead, by focusing on national law as the reason behind this unequal treatment, the Court conceals the fact that the paradox lies with the EU legislation. The Citizens' Rights Directive does not go as far as to create an autonomous right of residence for victims of domestic violence who are not at least self-sufficient, aligning thereby with the residence rights of economically inactive EU migrants. At the same time, the legislature adopts measures on non-EU migrants with no reference to economic self-sufficiency, as after all residence rights for all non-EU migrants are closely tied to economic activity. That is the case as regards both entry to the EU territory and renewal of family reunification permits and access to long-term residence status. When the Court is faced with the limitations in cases such as *X v État belge,* it should instead review the Citizens' Rights Directive in light of the broader constitutional characteristics of EU law, or even the external commitments of the EU to protect the rights of victim of domestic violence, as I will explain in the section below.

By confirming the limitations found in secondary law as regards EU migrants the Court is lowering the standards for everyone, representing a 'defeat for the vulnerable'.[71] Such an approach sits in contrast with cases such as *Sagrario*, where what is at stake is rather the interpretation of secondary law applicable to non-EU migrants. In such cases, the Court invokes the Citizens' Rights Directive as an interpretative aid in order to ensure the coherent understanding of certain concepts across all areas of EU law.[72] Arguably the Court is in favour of analogies in the interpretation of secondary law on migration to restore some coherence in an otherwise fragmented legal area. At the same time, the Court rejects any comparison when the internal inconsistencies of EU legislation can challenge the validity of secondary law. In such cases, and aligning with established praxis in the field of EU citizenship, the Court sidelines the opportunity to discuss the limitations of the Citizens' Rights Directive

[69] C-930/19, *X v État belge*, para 88.
[70] Strumia (n 30) 1207.
[71] ibid 1216.
[72] Such an approach is not without limitations. See the inconsistent case law on the concept of public policy for EU and non-EU migrants: Koen Lenaerts, 'The Concept of Public Policy in the Area of Freedom, Security and Justice' in Koen Lenaerts and others (eds), *Shaping a Genuine Area of Freedom, Security and Justice* (Hart 2024).

in relation to the protection of fundamental rights and attributes constitutional priority to EU secondary law.[73]

5. Arguing for Equally Extensive Rights as Part of the EU Commitment to Protect Fundamental Rights

In this section I will draw on internal and external commitments to protect fundamental rights in order to discuss how the Court has missed the opportunity to ensure the protection of human rights—particularly for family members of EU migrants—beyond the limitations inherent in the Citizens' Rights Directive.

First, as regards the EU constitutional architecture, the following should be noted. The case *X v État belge* presented above is exemplary of the complicated relation of the Court with the application of the Charter as a means of judicial review. While the Court is extensively using the Charter as a basis for review in cases relating to non-EU migrants and their rights, the same is not true as regards EU migrants. As Nic Shuibhne suggested in a different context, the Court's case law in the field of free movement of persons is characterized by a 'hegemonic attribution of supremacy to secondary law, which fails to engage the constitutional protocols epitomising the Union legal order more generally'.[74] In *X v État belge*, the Court accepted as legitimate the standards of the Citizens' Rights Directive without further examination of the relevance or appropriateness of the economic conditioning of residence rights for victims of domestic violence, thereby dictating the minimum standards of protection.[75] The full absence of the Charter as a mechanism for review in the case of EU migrants creates incoherence in an EU fundamental rights protection system, as highlighted by Iglesias Sánchez.[76] As she mentions, 'in a rather paradoxical fashion, the progressive development of EU law has led to a situation

[73] Elise Muir, 'EU Citizenship, Access to "Social Benefits" and Third-Country National Family Members: Reflecting on the Relationship Between Primary and Secondary Rights in Times of Brexit' (2019) 2018 European Papers—A Journal on Law and Integration 1353. See also chapter by Politis in this volume.

[74] Niamh Nic Shuibhne, 'Limits Rising, Duties Ascending: The Changing Legal Shape of Union Citizenship' (2015) 52 CML Rev 889, 891.

[75] See also Vladislava Stoyanova, 'On the Bride's Side? Victims of Domestic Violence and Their Residence Rights under EU and Council of Europe Law' (2019) 37 Netherlands Quarterly of Human Rights 311.

[76] Sara Iglesias Sánchez, 'The Constitutional Status of Foreigners and European Union Citizens: Loopholes and Interactions in the Scope of Application of Fundamental Rights' in Daniel Thym (ed), *Questioning EU Citizenship: Judges and the Limits of Free Movement and Solidarity in the EU* (Hart Publishing 2017).

in which EU law on free movement of persons is still reminiscent of an internationalist approach, whereas the EU migration policy seems to have adopted a constitutional approach'.[77] Developing these criticisms, it is argued that in an EU legal system with a complete constitutional structure, it would make sense for the Charter to be used both as a guide for interpretation and also, and most importantly, as a means of human rights review for secondary legislation. This would allow the Court to protect EU migrants and their family members from unjust effects of EU secondary law, and it would resemble the way human rights function in constitutional and federal systems.[78]

Next to the position of the Charter, it is important to reflect on the external commitments of the EU to fundamental rights protection, particularly in relation to victims of domestic violence. In finding that the provisions of the Citizens' Rights Directive are in compliance with Article 20 of the Charter in *X v État belge*, and that the more relaxed provisions of the Family Reunification Directive can become stricter upon state discretion, the Court made no reference to international human rights obligations regarding victims of domestic violence. The absence of any reference to the Istanbul Convention is striking.[79] Articles 59–61 of the Istanbul Convention provide obligations relating to the grant of autonomous residence permits to victims of domestic violence as well as the grant of subsidiary protection and the application of a gender-sensitive interpretation to the Geneva Convention. The demands of the Istanbul Convention attracted attention for having the potential to generate change as regards migrant victims of domestic violence and their claims to residence rights.[80] After a first conservative ruling in *NA*, the Court was called to decide on the compatibility of the Citizens' Rights Directive with the Charter in case *X v État belge*.[81] While the case limited some of the effects of *NA*, by no means did it provide a gender-sensitive reading of EU law in line with the Convention. Admittedly, the Istanbul Convention was not binding the EU at the time and

[77] ibid 262.

[78] Xavier Groussot and Gunnar Thor Petursson, 'The EU Charter of Fundamental Rights Five Years On: The Emergence of a New Constitutional Framework?' in Ulf Bernitz, Sybe de Vries, and Stephen Weatherill (eds), *The EU Charter of Fundamental Rights as a Binding Instrument: Five Years Old and Growing* (Hart Publishing 2015); Xavier Groussot, Gunnar Thor Petursson, and Alezini Loxa, 'The Fundament of the Fundaments? Family Rights and the EU Charter of Fundamental Rights' in Alina Tryfonidou and Marja-Liisa Öberg (eds), *The Family in EU Law* (Cambridge University Press 2024).

[79] See Opinion 1/19 (Istanbul Convention), EU:C:2021:832. The Convention was signed by the EU in 2017 and ratified in October 2023.

[80] See Vladislava Stoyanova, 'A Stark Choice: Domestic Violence or Deportation? The Immigration Status of Victims of Domestic Violence under the Istanbul Convention' [2018] European Journal of Migration and Law 53; Catherine Briddick, 'Combatting or Enabling Domestic Violence? Evaluating The Residence Rights of Migrant Victims of Domestic Violence in Europe' [2020] International and Comparative Law Quarterly 1471.

[81] Case C-115/15 *Secretary of State for the Home Department v NA*, ECLI:EU:C:2016:487.

the case was decided in September 2021, a bit over a month before the publication of *Opinion 1/19* on the accession of the EU to the Istanbul Convention.[82] Still, the Court was aware of its relevance for the purpose of safeguarding the rights of migrant victims of domestic violence, while the Convention had already been ratified by Belgium.[83]

This gender-insensitive reading of EU free movement law is contrasted with the outcome of *Intervyuirasht organ na DAB pri MS*.[84] While the Court has produced ground-breaking rulings in the area of asylum and migration which promote respect for the internal and external human rights obligations of the EU and the Member States, neither internal nor external commitments to human rights protection have guided the Court in the area of EU citizenship.[85] This crucial omission should be addressed not only in order to avoid fragmentation in the application of the Istanbul Convention and to promote the rights of victims of domestic violence in the future, but also in order to extend the constitutional commitment of the EU to fundamental rights protection under Article 2 TEU to all those who fall within the scope of EU law.

Overall, a serious commitment to the protection of fundamental rights as part of the EU constitutional architecture and of the external commitments undertaken by the EU by the accession to the Istanbul Convention would demand the more consistent review of secondary law by reference to the Charter as well as equally extensive protection for migrant family members victims of domestic violence regardless of whether they draw rights from an EU or non-EU migrant-sponsor.

6. Conclusion: The Road to Hell Is Paved with Good Intentions

The Court's case law has been central to our understanding of EU citizenship and EU migration law as based on different normative grounds and with

[82] Opinion 1/19 of 6 October 2021, ECLI:EU:C:2021:832.

[83] See Opinion of AG Szpunar in Case C-930/19 *X v État belge*, mentioning the Istanbul Convention as relevant international law in order to revisit the restrictive finding in C-115/15 *Secretary of State for the Home Department v NA*.

[84] Judgment of 16 January 2024, C-621/21 *Intervyuirasht organ na DAB pri MS (Women victims of domestic violence)*, ECLI:EU:C:2024:47.

[85] Judgment of 11 June 2024, C-646/21 *Staatssecretaris van Justitie en Veiligheid (Persons identifying with the values of the Union)*, EU:C:2024:487 on Iraqi women; Judgment of 4 October 2024, *Bundesamt für Fremdenwesen und Asyl and Others (Femmes afghanes)* Joined Cases C-608/22 and C-609/22, ECLI:EU:C:2024:828 on women fleeing the Taliban regime.

different implications for the EU integration project. While indeed EU nationals are meant to be the central subjects of EU law, this does not mean that secondary law always privileges them and their families in the exercise of their rights. Neither does it mean that their circumstances, or the circumstances of their migrant family members, are so fundamentally different from the circumstances of non-EU migrants.

In this chapter the case of family reunification was in focus as an area which shows the shared features of EU free movement and migration. Family reunification is regulated as a means to promote the right to family life under Article 7 and 24 of the Charter under both the Citizens' Rights Directive for EU migrants and the Family Reunification Directive for non-EU migrants. At the same time, due to the separate legislative histories and contexts of the regulation of family reunification for EU and non-EU migrants, the framework on EU migrants appears still to be guided by considerations that attempt to limit the negative effects of generalized free movement for the internal market.

By avoiding engagement with the compliance of such conditionality with the protection of fundamental rights under both the Charter and the external commitments of the EU to protect fundamental rights, the Court has effectively wounded both the most vulnerable and EU values.[86] Insisting on a fundamental differentiation between EU and non-EU citizens in an inconsistent way has effectively lowered the bar of protection for all migrant victims of domestic violence, and has lowered the standards of protection stemming from EU citizenship. While it is understandable that the Court wants to protect the fundamental status of EU citizenship, it is questionable to what extent avoiding a review of the Citizens' Rights Directive under the Charter or dismissing any comparability to the Family Reunification Directive is necessary to guarantee 'a different status and rights of a different kind'.

References

Ackers L, 'Citizenship, Gender, and Dependence in the European Union: Women and Internal Migration' (1996) 3 Social Politics: International Studies in Gender, State & Society 316

Bornemann J and Haag M, 'Testing the Inspirational Link between EU Citizenship and Migration Law: C-112/22 and C-223/22 CU and ND on Indirect Discrimination of Long-Term Residents', European Law Blog, September 2024

[86] Strumia (n 30) 1216.

Briddick C, 'Combatting or Enabling Domestic Violence? Evaluating The Residence Rights of Migrant Victims of Domestic Violence in Europe' [2020] International and Comparative Law Quarterly 1471

Carrera S and Wiesbrock A, 'Civic Integration of Immigrants: A Challenge to Proportionality and Non-Discrimination in the Common European Immigration Policy?' in Dagmar Schiek, Hildegard Schneider, and Ulrike Liebert (eds), *European Economic and Social Constitutionalism after the Treaty of Lisbon* (Cambridge University Press 2011)

Davies G, 'When Do Union Citizens and Their Families Have the Right to Equal Treatment on Grounds of Nationality in EU Law?'(2024) 26(3) European Journal of Migration and Law 281

Eklund H, 'Peoples, Inhabitants and Workers: Colonialism in the Treaty of Rome' (2023) 34 European Journal of International Law 831

Friðriksdóttir B, *What Happened to Equality? The Construction of the Right to Equal Treatment of Third-Country Nationals in European Union Law on Labour Migration* (Brill Nijhoff 2017)

Ganty S, 'Integration Duties in the European Union: Four Models' (2021) 28 Maastricht Journal of European and Comparative Law 784

Groenendijk K, 'The Long-Term Residents Directive, Denizenship and Integration' in Anneliese Baldaccini, Elspeth Guild, and Helen Toner (eds), *Whose Freedom, Security and Justice? EU Immigration and Asylum Law and Policy* (1st edn, Hart Publishing 2007)

Groussot X and Petursson GT, 'The EU Charter of Fundamental Rights Five Years on: The Emergence of a New Constitutional Framework?' in Ulf Bernitz, Sybe de Vries, and Stephen Weatherill (eds), *The EU Charter of Fundamental Rights as a Binding Instrument: Five Years Old and Growing* (Hart Publishing 2015)

Groussot X, Petursson GT, and Loxa A, 'The Fundament of the Fundaments?: Family Rights and the EU Charter of Fundamental Rights' in Alina Tryfonidou and Marja-Liisa Öberg (eds), *The Family in EU Law* (Cambridge University Press 2024)

Hervey T, 'A Gendered Perspective on the Right to Family Life in European Community Law' in Nanette A Neuwahl and Allan Rosas (eds), *The European Union and Human Rights* (Brill 1995)

Hervey T, 'Migrant Workers and Their Families in the European Union: The Pervasive Market Ideology of Community Law' in Jo Shaw and Gillian More (eds), *New Legal Dynamics of European Union* (Clarendon Press 1995)

Iglesias Sánchez S, 'The Constitutional Status of Foreigners and European Union Citizens: Loopholes and Interactions in the Scope of Application of Fundamental Rights' in Daniel Thym (ed), *Questioning EU Citizenship: Judges and the Limits of Free Movement and Solidarity in the EU* (Hart Publishing 2017)

Lenaerts K, 'The Concept of Public Policy in the Area of Freedom, Security and Justice' in Koen Lenaerts et al (eds), *Shaping a Genuine Area of Freedom, Security and Justice* (Hart 2024)

McCormack-George D, 'Equal Treatment of Third-Country Nationals in the European Union: Why Not' (2019) 21 European Journal of Migration and Law 53

McGlynn C, *Families and the European Union Law, Politics and Pluralism* (Cambridge University Press 2006)

Muir E, 'EU Citizenship, Access to "Social Benefits" and Third-Country National Family Members: Reflecting on the Relationship Between Primary and Secondary Rights in Times of Brexit' (2019) 2018 European Papers—A Journal on Law and Integration 1353

Nic Shuibhne N, 'Limits Rising, Duties Ascending: The Changing Legal Shape of Union Citizenship' (2015) 52 CML Rev 889

Passalaqua V, Op-Ed: 'Another Blow to Discriminatory Conditions of Access to Social Benefits: Joined Cases ND and CU, (C-112 and 223/22)', EU Law Live, September 2024

Spijkerboer T, 'Coloniality and Recent European Migration Case Law' in Stijn Smet and Vladislava Stoyanova (eds), *Migrants' Rights, Populism and Legal Resilience in Europe* (Cambridge University Press 2022)

Stoyanova V, 'A Stark Choice: Domestic Violence or Deportation? The Immigration Status of Victims of Domestic Violence under the Istanbul Convention' [2018] European Journal of Migration and Law 53

Stoyanova V, 'On the Bride's Side? Victims of Domestic Violence and Their Residence Rights under EU and Council of Europe Law' (2019) 37 Netherlands Quarterly of Human Rights 311

Strumia F, 'Speaking Too Little, Yet Saying Too Much: The Wrong Signals about EU Values: X. v. Belgian State' (2022) 59 CML Rev 1202

Thym D, 'EU Migration Policy and Its Constitutional Rationale: A Cosmopolitan Outlook' (2013) 50 CML Rev 709

Thym D, '"Citizens" and "Foreigners" in EU Law. Migration Law and Its Cosmopolitan Outlook' (2016) 22 European Law Journal 296

10

The CJEU's Centre of Gravity Theory in Legal Basis Litigation: A Flawed Concept

Annegret Engel

1. Introduction

This chapter will provide a normative analysis of the most prominent general principle of legal basis litigation: the centre of gravity theory. In order to understand the CJEU's reasoning for establishing and applying the principle, one has to go back to the very beginnings of legal basis litigation in the EU.

In a nutshell, legal basis litigation has evolved as a necessity from the principle of conferral[1] on the one hand, requiring every measure to specify the legal basis it is adopted upon, and from the structural and procedural differences inherent in legal bases on the other.[2] As such, the quest for the correct choice of legal basis has—in the CJEU's own words—'constitutional significance', rendering any measure adopted on an incorrect choice of legal basis invalid.[3] For this reason, the CJEU has developed a range of general principles for the determination of the correct choice of legal basis. Most remarkable here is the shift from a double or multiple legal bases, which was common practice resulting from the 1966 'Luxembourg Compromise',[4] towards the explicit preference for a single legal basis later on,[5] due to the introduction of decision-making procedures in which voting rules differ. Such differences in the decision-making procedures started to occur with the introduction of the Single European

[1] Article 5 TEU, according to which 'the Union shall act only within the limits of the competences conferred upon it by the Member States'.

[2] Most notably, these include the scope and nature of the competence, as well as differences in the legal instruments to be used and the decision-making procedures required.

[3] Case C-370/07, Commission of the European Communities v Council of the European Union, EU:C:2009:590, para 52.

[4] Final Communiqué of the extraordinary session of the Council, Bulletin of the European Communities, March 1966, 5–11.

[5] As Takis Tridimas famously stated in 2009, '[i]ncreasing the quantity of legal bases cannot improve their quality': in 'Terrorism and the ECJ: Empowerment and Democracy in the EC Legal Order' (2009) 34(1) European Law Review 103–26, at p 110.

Annegret Engel, *The CJEU's Centre of Gravity Theory in Legal Basis Litigation: A Flawed Concept* In: *The Reasoning of the Court of Justice of the EU*. Edited by: Alezini Loxa and Luigi Lonardo, Oxford University Press.
 DOI: 10.1093/9780198983002.003.0013

Act (SEA), leading to procedural incompatibilities between the various legal bases. This, in turn, led the way for the development of the centre of gravity theory, which seeks to ensure that only the most central focus, that is, the predominant aim and content, of a measure is taken into account in the quest for the correct—and preferably single—legal basis. Any further incidental effects and their corresponding legal bases are to be disregarded by the legislator as well as the judiciary, thus avoiding any conflicts between differing procedural requirements.[6]

Nowadays, the centre of gravity theory constitutes a cornerstone of legal basis litigation as it is widely used by the EU institutions—in particular the CJEU for judicial review, but also other institutions for their considerations in the legislative process—and across all policy areas in order, where possible, to avoid measures being adopted on multiple legal bases. Nevertheless, as will be shown, the application of the centre of gravity theory does not come without its own problems. First, the current constitutional setup does not provide clear-cut delimitation between the different policy areas, resulting in frequent competence overlaps and the possibility of more than one potential legal basis. Second, the CJEU has not been consistent in applying the criteria of aim and content for the centre of gravity theory, leading to inconsistencies in its judgments and an over-focus on procedure rather than substance. Third, from the early ruling in *Tobacco Advertising*, the CJEU's application of the centre of gravity theory has contributed to and exacerbated pre-emption and competence creep within the EU to the detriment of some (special) legal bases/ competences, which are being undermined, while other generic or horizontal competences serve as default options, such as Article 114 TFEU.

In general, the main argument made here is that the application of the centre of gravity theory has fostered procedural formalism in legal basis litigation to the detriment of more substantive aspects thereof, especially with regard to the principle of conferral. This chapter will thus proceed to analyse the CJEU's responsibility in the application of the centre of gravity theory in legal basis litigation and take the liberty to present a number of suggestions for mitigating the risks discussed on a long-term basis. First and foremost, it is argued that a more holistic approach, including procedural as well as substantive matters in the quest for the correct choice of legal basis, would be better suited under the current or any future constitutional setup. Further, it is suggested that allowing

[6] A more detailed account on the development of general principles in legal basis litigation can be found in Annegret Engel, *The Choice of Legal Basis for Acts of the European Union: Competence Overlaps, Institutional Preferences, and Legal Basis Litigation* (Springer International Publishing 2018).

all relevant legal bases to be used for a measure—predominant or incidental—even with conflicting procedural requirements out of which the most stringent could be applied would contribute to legal certainty in legal basis litigation. A final option put forward in this chapter is to apply the *lex specialis derogat legi generali* principle[7] more broadly instead of the centre of gravity theory, thus avoiding the above-mentioned overuse of Article 114 TFEU and the pre-emption of other more special policy areas and competences in the treaties.

2. Discovering the Flaws: Legal Basis Litigation and the Application of the Centre of Gravity Theory

The centre of gravity theory—as developed by the Court of Justice as a general principle of legal basis litigation—aims to identify the correct choice of a single legal basis by determining the predominant aim and content of a measure. From the outset, this seems to be a straightforward endeavour. However, several problems complicate the task for the judiciary. The following will highlight some of the most obvious flaws in the constitutional setup and in the application of the centre of gravity theory by the CJEU, including the problematic constitutional setup of competence categories, the CJEU's zig-zag approach in applying the criteria of aim and content, and the (over)-use of certain legal bases—such as Article 114 TFEU—as default options. These will be discussed in turn.

2.1 Delimitation impossible: the constitutional setup of competence categories

The quest for the correct choice of legal basis requires the existence of clear-cut delimitation between different areas of competences and their respective legal bases. Unfortunately, however, this is far from being reality under the current constitutional setup of the EU, scattered as it is with conflicts between the different policy areas. While it could be argued that the codification of competence categories[8] under the Treaty of Lisbon has indeed contributed to a diminishing of possible overlaps, the situation remains unsatisfactory, with a

[7] See chapter by Hancox in this volume.

[8] The law distinguishes between exclusive competences (Article 3 TFEU), shared competences (Article 4 TFEU), coordinating competences (Article 5 TFEU) and competences to support, coordinate, or supplement (Article 6 TFEU).

number of double classifications of competences as well as overlaps between them. Admittedly, a certain amount of overlapping competences is inevitable in multilevel governance; however, the drafters of the treaties could have avoided the double classification of competence areas, aggravating the delimitation of competence categories.

Some prominent examples of double classification include the areas of social policy, health, and fisheries. Social policy falls under the Union's coordinating powers according to Article 5(3) TFEU, while some aspects of it are considered shared between the Union and the Member States according to Article 4(2)(b) TFEU. The same can also be said for the area of health, which is artificially divided into public and human health, the former falling within the shared competences according to Article 4(2)(k) TFEU[9] and the latter within the competence to support, coordinate, or supplement according to Article 6(a) TFEU.[10] Another example of double classification is the Union's fisheries policy, which falls within both exclusive and shared competences according to Articles 3(1)(d) TFEU[11] and 4(2)(d) TFEU[12] respectively.

Aside from these rather obvious instances of double classification, further material overlaps are inevitable. For example, a distinction between the customs union,[13] the establishment of the competition rules necessary for the functioning of the internal market,[14] and the internal market itself[15] is far from being self-evident. In particular, competition policies and the internal market have been subject to a constant shift, especially with regard to the most recent developments under the Digital Single Market.[16] Another example can be drawn from the overlap between the Union's economic,[17] monetary,[18] and common commercial policies.[19] These have caused particular judicial uproar in a culminating constitutional battle between the German Federal Constitutional Court and the CJEU in the *PSPP/Weiss* saga.[20] Here, the ECB's

[9] Common safety concerns in public health matters, for the aspects defined in the Treaty.
[10] The protection and improvement of human health.
[11] The conservation of marine biological resources under the common fisheries policy.
[12] Agriculture and fisheries, excluding the conservation of marine biological resources.
[13] Exclusive competence according to Article 3(1)(a) TFEU.
[14] Exclusive competence according to Article 3(1)(b) TFEU.
[15] Shared competence according to Article 4(2)(a) TFEU.
[16] See eg discussion in Annegret Engel, 'The Choice of Legal Basis in EU Competition Law: Shifting the Competence in the Digital Era' (2023) 4 Europarättslig Tidskrift 669–83.
[17] Coordinating competence according to Article 5(1) TFEU. Special provisions shall apply to those Member States whose currency is the euro.
[18] Exclusive competence according to Article 3(1)(c) TFEU. Only applies to Member States whose currency is the euro.
[19] Exclusive competence according to Article 3(1)(e) TFEU.
[20] Case C-493/17, *Weiss and Others*, EU:C:2018:1000 and BVerfG, Judgment of the Second Senate of 05 May 2020, 2 BvR 859/15, 2 BvR 1651/15, 2 BvR 2006/15, 2 BvR980/16. See also discussion in case note by Annegret Engel, Julian Nowag, and Xavier Groussot, 'Is This Completely M.A.D.? Three

Public Sector Purchase Programme (PSPP) was challenged as it was based on the EU's exclusive monetary competence, thus allegedly encroaching on Member States' coordinating competences under the economic policies. While the CJEU upheld the contested PSPP decisions,[21] the German Court rejected this interpretation as *ultra vires* in its judgment, which threatened to undermine the principle of supremacy of EU law and resulted in an infringement procedure against Germany.[22]

Without going further into detail for now, these examples provide clear evidence of the sheer impossible task the judiciary is facing when trying to delimit these policy areas from one another for the purpose of determining the centre of gravity of a measure. This, then, poses the question of what exactly the determining factors for the CJEU's decisions are. Can those considerations be of a substantive nature only—that is, the scope of the competence in question, which ultimately traces back to the principle of conferral—or does this not provide a sufficient answer in the determination of the correct choice of legal basis? And to what extent can the centre of gravity theory be a useful tool for legal basis litigation in this constellation?

2.2 Aim and content—or procedure over substance?

With the development of the centre of gravity theory, the CJEU has made an attempt to establish certain criteria for better determination of the correct choice of legal basis. In the early ruling of *Titanium Dioxide*, the aim and content of the measure were defined as the objective factors to be taken into account in

Views on the Ruling of the German FCC on 5th May 2020' (2020) 3(1) Nordic Journal of European Law 128–50.

[21] Decision of the Governing Council of the European Central Bank of 22 January 2015 and Decision (EU) 2015/774 of the European Central Bank of 4 March 2015 on a secondary markets public sector asset purchase programme (ECB/2015/10) [2015] OJ L 121/20, in conjunction with Decision (EU) 2015/2101 of the European Central Bank of 5 November 2015 amending Decision (EU) 2015/774 on a secondary markets public sector asset purchase programme (ECB/2015/33) [2015] OJ L 303/106, Decision (EU) 2015/2464 of the European Central Bank of 16 December 2015 amending Decision (EU) 2015/774 on a secondary markets public sector asset purchase programme (ECB/2015/48) [2015] OJ L 344/1, Decision (EU) 2016/702 of the European Central Bank of 18 April 2016 amending Decision (EU) 2015/774 on a secondary markets public sector asset purchase programme (ECB/2016/8) [2016] OJ L 121/24, and Decision (EU) 2017/100 of the European Central Bank of 8 December 2016/11 January 2017 (ECB/2017/1) amending Decision (EU) 2015/744 (ECB/2015/10) on a secondary markets public sector asset purchase programme [2017] OJ L 16/51.

[22] EU Commission, Letter of Formal Notice on 9 June 2021, https://ec.europa.eu/commission/presscorner/detail/en/inf_21_2743 (Accessed 18 September 2025).

legal basis litigation.[23] In addition, a distinction was made in *Parliament v Council* between main purpose and mere incidental effects,[24] with the latter not destined to be decisive in the choice of legal basis. This distinction was later refined in cases, such as *Spain v Council*, which rejected a dual legal basis if the contested measure 'reveals that it pursues a twofold purpose or that it has a twofold component and if one of these is identifiable as the main or predominant purpose or component, whereas the other is merely incidental'.[25]

However, the CJEU has not always been consistent in applying its self-imposed criteria. For example, in *Ireland v European Parliament and Council*,[26] on the retention of data generated or processed in connection with the provision of electronic communications services, the Court merely took into account the content of the contested measure for the determination of the correct legal basis. The CJEU's reasoning for this content-only approach remained inconclusive; equally so its reversion back to the full aim-and-content approach shortly after.[27] While it could be argued that less importance is attributed to the aim component anyhow as it only expresses intent rather than actual substance of the measure,[28] the CJEU's zig-zag course contributes little to increasing clarity and legal certainty in legal basis litigation. In addition, the Court has, on occasion, also taken into account the effects of a measure,[29] essentially adding to the confusion. While some have argued in favour of taking into account the effects of a measure more regularly,[30] this does not remedy the legal uncertainty created by such fluctuations in the application of criteria for the centre of gravity theory.

In addition, the more intertwined the contesting policy areas with regard to their material overlap, the more obscure the factors that actually play a role in their delimitation become and they may, at times, resemble what Craig called 'legal formalism',[31] referring to the artificial distinction made by the CJEU

[23] Case C-300/89, Commission of the European Communities v Council of the European Communities (Titanium Dioxide), EU:C:1991:244, para 10.

[24] Case C-70/88, European Parliament v Council of the European Communities, EU:C:1991:373, para 12.

[25] Case C-36/98, Kingdom of Spain v Council of the European Union, EU:C:2001:64, para 59.

[26] Case C-301/06, Ireland v European Parliament and Council of the European Union, EU:C:2009:68.

[27] See eg Case C-130/10, European Parliament v Council of the European Union, EU:C:2012:472.

[28] See eg Bart van Vooren, *EU External Relations Law and the European Neighbourhood Policy: A Paradigm for Coherence* (Routledge 2012) 136.

[29] See eg Case C-88/14, Commission v Parliament and Council (Visa reciprocity), EU:C:2015:499, paras 35 and 42.

[30] This was criticized by Cremona in relation to the contested PNR Agreement, Marise Cremona 'External Relations of the EU and the Member States: Competence, Mixed Agreements, International Responsibility, and Effects of International Law', EUI Working Paper LAW No. 2006/22.

[31] Paul Craig, 'Pringle: Legal Reasoning, Text, Purpose and Teleology'(2013) 20(1) Maastricht Journal of European Comparative Law 3–11, 5.

between economic and monetary objectives in the *Pringle* case.[32] In another case at the crossroads between the common foreign and security policy and the area of freedom, security and justice, the Court reasoned that even if after the application of the centre of gravity theory a contested measure is revealed to 'pursue several objectives at the same time or have several components indissociably linked, without one's being secondary to the other', a dual legal basis would nevertheless be prohibited if the procedural requirements are incompatible, such as with Articles 75 and 215(2) TFEU.[33]

Indeed, more often than not the CJEU places significant emphasis on procedural compatibility rather than on the actual scope of the measure in question and the competence under the respective legal basis. This practice dates back to the CJEU's early case law when procedural differences between the legal bases were introduced. One such example is the introduction of qualified majority voting under the Single European Act (SEA), which affected a variety of legal bases, however not all. Those unaffected, for example what is now Article 352 TFEU, continued to require unanimity voting in the Council, which in turn rendered them less desirable as legal bases.[34] This is also reflected in the CJEU's interpretation. At the time of *Massey-Ferguson*—a case decided well before the introduction of the SEA—a dual legal base consisting of Articles 207 and 352 TFEU was justified in the interest of legal certainty.[35] The same dual legal basis was, however, considered inappropriate just a few years later after the introduction of procedural differences under the SEA in the *Generalised Tariff* case.[36] This essentially relegates Article 352 TFEU from a frequently used horizontal competence to a mere gap-filler, as explicitly stated by the Court in *Opinion 2/94*.[37]

More recently, the CJEU's focus on procedure as opposed to substance is ever more evident. In *RL*,[38] a preliminary reference made by the

[32] Case C-370/12, Thomas Pringle v Government of Ireland, EU:C:2012:756. See further chapter by Markakis in this volume. See also Annegret Engel, 'EU Competences in Crisis: Disentangling the Conflict between Monetary and Economic Legal Bases' (2022) 2 Europarättslig Tidskrift 191–201.

[33] Case C-130/10, *European Parliament v Council of the European Union*, EU:C:2012:472, para 49.

[34] See also Robert Schütze, 'Organized Change towards an "Ever Closer Union": Article 308 EC and the Limits to the Community's Legislative Competence'(2003) 22(1) Yearbook of European Law 79–115.

[35] Case 8-73, *Hauptzollamt Bremerhaven v Massey-Ferguson*, EU:C:1973:90.

[36] Case 45/86, *Commission of the European Communities v Council of the European Communities (Generalised Tariff)*, EU:C:1987:163.

[37] Opinion 2/94, on the Accession by the Community to the European Convention for the Protection of Human Rights and Fundamental Freedoms, EU:C:1996:140, para 29. See also discussion in Graham Butler, 'The EU Flexibility Clause is Dead, Long Live the EU Flexibility Clause' in Antonina Bakardjieva Engelbrekt and Xavier Groussot, *The Future of Europe—Political and Legal Integration Beyond Brexit* (Hart Publishing 2019) 63–95.

[38] Case C-61/22, *RL v Landeshauptstadt Wiesbaden*, EU:C:2024:251.

Verwaltungsgericht Wiesbaden, the Court declared Regulation 2019/1157[39] invalid as it was based on an incorrect legal basis—Article 21(2) TFEU, rather than Article 77(3) TFEU. While the Court's analysis of aim and content of the contested measure as well as the respective scopes of the conflicting legal bases follows the expected standards of review established by previous case law, the Court's emphasis on the procedural differences is striking. In fact, the Court seems to suggest it would have not invalidated the regulation in question had the legal basis it was adopted on not entailed a different decision-making procedure.[40] The Court reasoned that 'by adopting Regulation 2019/1157 on the basis of Article 21(2) TFEU, the EU legislature infringed Article 77(3) TFEU and had recourse to an inappropriate decision-making procedure'.[41] The Court's annulment of the contested measure was thus based not only on an incorrect choice of legal basis but also on its resulting incorrect choice of decision-making procedure.[42]

By contrast, in *UK v Council*,[43] regarding the EEC–Turkey Association Agreement,[44] a Council decision on the coordination of social security systems was challenged for having been adopted on an incorrect legal basis.[45] Here, the Court found that, after the application of the centre of gravity theory, Article 217 TFEU should have been added to the actual legal base used—Article 48 in conjunction with Article 218(9) TFEU. The Court nevertheless concluded that the omission of an otherwise correct legal basis was a 'purely formal defect' which would not merit annulment of the contested measure.[46] The Court explained this rather hands-off approach with the fact that the omission of Article 217 TFEU from the legal base would not have had any effect on the procedure under which the contested decision was adopted, that is, the ordinary

[39] Regulation (EU) 2019/1157 of the European Parliament and of the Council of 20 June 2019 on strengthening the security of identity cards of Union citizens and of residence documents issued to Union citizens and their family members exercising their right of free movement, OJ L 188/67.

[40] Article 21(2) TFEU requires the ordinary legislative procedure, while Article 77(3) TFEU requires the special legislative procedure (unanimity voting in the Council and consultation procedure for the European Parliament).

[41] Case C-61/22, RL v Landeshauptstadt Wiesbaden, EU:C:2024:251, para 62.

[42] ibid, para 63.

[43] Case C-81/13, *United Kingdom of Great Britain and Northern Ireland v Council of the European Union*, EU:C:2014:2449.

[44] Agreement establishing an Association between the European Economic Community and Turkey of 12 September 1963, OJ L 361/29.

[45] Council Decision of 6 December 2012 on the position to be taken on behalf of the European Union within the Association Council set up by the Agreement establishing an association between the European Economic Community and Turkey, with regard to the adoption of provisions on the coordination of social security systems, OJ L 340/19.

[46] Case C-81/13, *United Kingdom of Great Britain and Northern Ireland v Council of the European Union*, EU:C:2014:2449, para 67. See also Case C-210/03, Swedish Match AB and Swedish Match UK Ltd v Secretary of State for Health, EU:C:2004:802, para 44.

legislative procedure. As such, it can be argued that the substantive considerations under which the correct choice of legal basis is to be determined become secondary to the procedural considerations as required under those legal bases.

It is thus evident from the aforementioned cases that the centre of gravity theory is unfit to solve the constitutional conundrum of overlapping competences and the resulting legal basis litigation. This insufficiency has led to procedural aspects becoming the determining factor in the quest for the correct choice of legal basis to the detriment of more substantive issues, such as the scope of competence and the principle of conferral, as important constitutional safeguards in the relationship between Member States and the EU.

2.3 Incidental effect: strengthening Article 114 TFEU

The situation is exacerbated in the light of horizontal competences, in particular Article 114 TFEU, which have continuously been encroaching upon other areas of competence, without a clear indication of which judicial principles are at stake. One of the main problems with Article 114 TFEU is that it serves a double function. First, it is aimed at the approximation of laws 'which have as their object the establishment and functioning of the internal market',[47] which in itself can be construed rather broadly. Second, it also pursues a more specific objective, such as health, safety, or environmental or consumer protection.[48] As such, this provision has served as a legal base for the adoption of a wide range of measures, irrespective of the opening statement of 'save where otherwise provided in the Treaties', which would otherwise assume the application of the *lex specialis derogat legi generali* principle.

While the CJEU has indeed made an attempt to delimit the application of Article 114 TFEU in favour of more special legal bases, most prominently in the famous *Tobacco Advertising* ruling,[49] this has not had a lasting impact on restraining the success story of Article 114 TFEU.[50] Quite the contrary. The Court's ruling in *Tobacco Advertising* was criticized for providing the

[47] Paragraph 1.

[48] Paragraph 3.

[49] Case C-376/98, Federal Republic of Germany v European Parliament and Council of the European Union (Tobacco Advertising), EU:C:2000:544.

[50] See more recent cases on the sale of tobacco products, where Article 114 TFEU was upheld: Case C-358/14 Republic of Poland v European Parliament, EU:C:2016:323; Case C-477/14, Pillbox 38 (UK) Ltd. v Secretary of State for Health, EU:C:2016:324; Case C-547/14, Philip Morris Brands SARL and Others v Secretary of State for Health, EU:C:2016:325.

Commission with a 'drafting guide' to design the proposed measure within the ambit of a desired legal base,[51] thus leading to a continuous 'competence creep'[52] in favour of Article 114 TFEU and to the detriment of other areas of competence, essentially reversing the *lex specialis derogat legi generali* principle into a *lex generalis derogat legibus specialibus* as was already claimed by Trüe.[53]

This certainly holds true and may even be aggravated with the advent of the digital era and the EU's more recent regulatory approach in the Digital Single Market by means of harmonization of EU laws and increasing reliance on Article 114 TFEU as a legal base in digitalization.[54] As could be argued, the application of the centre of gravity theory and the CJEU's broad interpretation of Article 114 TFEU have inadvertently led the way for this quasi-monopoly of one legal base over other treaty provisions. Thus, the centre of gravity theory may have initially seemed a fair and objective approach to legal basis litigation but over time has severely undermined and eroded most other competence areas, which are, as a result, being exposed to a deeply flawed judicial review unsuitable to determine the correct choice of legal basis in a truly objective manner.

3. Mitigating the Risks: Alternative Approaches

Where remedies are sought to mitigate these risks with the current approach to legal basis litigation, most commentators—including myself—have previously pointed to the need for reform of the constitutional setup by means of treaty change.[55] This would seek to abolish the artificial and oftentimes non-existent delimitation between the different competence categories described above, potentially by streamlining the current setup into more simplified distinctions

[51] Stephen Weatherill, 'The Limits of Legislative Harmonisation Ten Years after Tobacco Advertising: How the Court's Case Law has become a "Drafting Guide"'(2012) 12(3) German Law Journal 827–64.

[52] Stephen Weatherill, 'Competence Creep and Competence Control' in Piet Eeckhout and Takis Tridimas (eds), *Yearbook of European Law, Vol. 23, 2004* (OUP 2005) 1–55.

[53] Christiane Trüe, *Das System der Rechtsetzungskompetenzen der Europäischen Gemeinschaft und der Europäischen Union* (Nomos Verlagsgesellschaft 2002).

[54] Annegret Engel, 'Licence to Regulate: Article 114 TFEU as Choice of Legal Basis in the Digital Single Market' in Annegret Engel, Xavier Groussot, and Gunnar Thor Petursson (eds), *New Directions in Digitalisation: Perspectives from EU Competition Law and the Charter of Fundamental Rights* (Springer Nature International 2024) 13–28.

[55] Eg in relation to the conflict between monetary and economic policy areas, see A Engel, J Nowag, and X Groussot (2020) 'Is This Completely M.A.D.? Three Views on the Ruling of the German FCC on 5th May 2020', Nordic Journal of European Law 3(1) 128–50.

without procedural incompatibilities—that is, through supranationalization—or a clustering of competences into much broader policy areas with fewer legal bases to choose from. However, formal amendments of the treaties appear increasingly difficult considering other more pressing crises the EU is currently facing (war in Ukraine, climate change, and the like) and the need for unity in an EU-27 for such an endeavour.[56]

In addition, mere focus on the legislator's responsibility is short-sighted in that it ignores the fact that the judiciary and its use of the centre of gravity theory in legal basis litigation is indeed part of the problem. In particular, this concerns the inconsistencies in applying the criteria of aim and content and the focus on procedure over substance as well as the wide-ranging competence creep as a direct consequence of the CJEU's judgments discussed above. Therefore, it is argued here that the judiciary *can* and *should* also be part of the solution.

The following will provide suggestions for improvement of the current approach, thus aiming to mitigate some of the flaws the application of the centre of gravity theory has brought along. The proposed remedies are neither mutually exclusive nor hierarchically interdependent; they can be used independently or in combination with each other depending on the specific case at hand and at the Court's discretion.

3.1 A more holistic approach

The self-imposed criteria of aim and content have unnecessarily narrowed down the application of the centre of gravity theory and have led to a focus on procedural compatibility over substance to the extent that the determination of the scope of competence has become secondary to the actual choice of legal basis. However, this is contrary to the principle of conferral, which in fact should be the starting point for all legal basis litigation. At its core, the quest for the correct choice of legal basis is a substantive one and not merely procedural. Reducing legal basis litigation to procedural matters—as illustrated above in the *RL* and *UK v Council* case—might be the logical consequence considering the procedural differences inherent in the structure of legal bases; however, it

[56] Cf the failed Constitutional Treaty. See also discussion in Michael Dougan, 'EU Competences in an Age of Complexity and Crisis: Challenges and Tensions in the System of Attributed Powers'(2024) 61(1) CML Rev 93–138.

essentially narrows down the intensity of judicial review and prevents a future-proof application of the centre of gravity theory.

In fact, even though there is no treaty change envisaged for the immediate future, there will eventually be another round of amendments at some point. It is to be expected that this would also entail some redesign of the competence categories with an alignment of procedural requirements, potentially including the removal of the unanimity requirement from any decision-making procedure. However, the abolishment of procedural differences does not render legal basis litigation nugatory. Quite the contrary. Unless we see a complete supranationalization with no other form than plain exclusive competences, legal basis litigation is here to stay. Indeed, this would resemble the situation pre-SEA before procedural differences were introduced. A more sustainable application of the centre of gravity theory or any other general principle of legal basis litigation would ensure a certain level of transferability—a red thread—of the established case law under any kind of constitutional setup. This red thread can only be found in the substance of legal bases, with the principle of conferral at its very core.

Be it as it may, a more holistic approach—including both procedural and substantive issues—would be beneficial under the current as well as any future constitutional setup. Greater focus on substantive matters, such as the overall subject matter of the proposed measure and the scope of the respective competences, might help reduce the negative effects of legal uncertainty created by the application of the centre of gravity. Particularly cases like *RL* and *UK v Council* would benefit from such an approach. That is not to say that procedural matters should not play a role in legal basis litigation; they should, however, not be the determining factor. In addition, a more holistic approach would also prevent the Commission being able to use the CJEU's criteria as a drafting guide for future measures.

3.2 Multiple legal bases

As already mentioned above, the 1966 'Luxembourg Compromise' previously allowed for—if not required—the use of multiple legal bases for the adoption of a single measure, if the latter touched upon a variety of different policy areas. Permitting and including all relevant legal bases for the adoption of a measure would render the application of the centre of gravity theory obsolete and thus escape the complications it entails. Admittedly, the range of policy areas has significantly expanded since the early beginnings of the EU, and with it the potential number of legal bases that can be used—which may lead to an entirely different set of problems, including the compatibility of decision-making procedures. However, it is argued throughout this chapter that procedural aspects should be considered secondary to the actual substantive aspects in the quest for the correct choice of legal basis. In addition, the use of multiple legal bases is nothing unusual and has previously been addressed by the CJEU in applying the most stringent procedural requirements for the voting requirements in the Council and the democracy-maximizing rationale with regard to parliamentary involvement.

This can be seen, for example, in *Parliament v Council*.[57] Here, the Court held that the contested measure,[58] which was adopted on Article 352 TFEU as a single legal base, should have additionally been based on Article 175(3) TFEU. The procedural discrepancies between the two legal bases did not seem to constitute a problem.[59] The Court found that under such circumstances, the legislature would be in compliance with the procedural requirements if co-decision for the Parliament's involvement and the unanimity requirement were to be followed.[60] The democracy-maximizing rationale was first established in Titanium Dioxide, where the Court held that the safeguarding of a high degree of parliamentary participation 'reflects a fundamental democratic principle'.[61] While parliamentary involvement has continuously increased through various treaty amendments, the unanimity requirement represents a remnant of the pre-SEA era in a few policy areas. Nevertheless, applying unanimity instead of qualified majority voting could arguably also add legitimacy to the legislative measure since all Member States have to approve of it.

Therefore, with the application of the most stringent procedure and the democracy-maximizing rationale, procedural incompatibilities would cease to be the focus of legal basis litigation and thus ensure a greater degree of legal certainty in judicial review. Permitting all relevant legal bases to be used for the adoption of a measure would also be in line with the above-mentioned holistic approach. Needless to say, the determining factors for the choice of legal basis/ -es should be of substantive nature; procedural considerations should play a subordinate role in those considerations, if any at all.

[57] Case C-166/07, European Parliament v Council of the European Union, EU:C:2009:499.

[58] Council Regulation (EC) No 1968/2006 of 21 December 2006 concerning Community financial contributions to the International Fund for Ireland (2007 to 2010), OJ L 409/86.

[59] Article 352 TFEU requires unanimity voting in the Council and consent by the European Parliament, while the ordinary legislative procedure applies for Article 175(3) TFEU.

[60] Case C-166/07, European Parliament v Council of the European Union, EU:C:2009:499, para 69.

[61] Case C-300/89, Commission of the European Communities v Council of the European Communities (Titanium Dioxide), EU:C:1991:244, para 20.

3.3 *Lex specialis derogat legi generali*

Another alternative to the centre of gravity theory would be the application of the *lex specialis derogat legi generali* principle, which essentially is a rule of priority.[62] For this principle to be applied, the two competing provisions have to fulfil the same objective or subject matter, while being at different hierarchical levels, that is *lex specialis* or *lex generalis*. Examples of the latter include Articles 114 and 352 TFEU. Currently, the CJEU is using the *lex specialis derogat legi generali* principle scarcely and only in supplementing other principles if those fail to produce a concrete result for a single legal basis, such as the centre of gravity theory,[63] while oftentimes it is unclear whether the *lex specialis derogat legi generali* principle was even applied.[64]

However, rather than using the *lex specialis derogat legi generali* principle as a subordinate or second-class principle of legal basis litigation, it can be argued that a wider application prior to the centre of gravity theory would allow for the proper use of a broader range of policy areas and their legal bases to be used and avoid the excessive adoption of measures on the basis of Article 114 TFEU. As such, Article 114 TFEU should only be applied if no other more special legal base can be found in the treaties, thus functioning as a last resort for the internal market.[65] In addition, a more consistent application of the *lex specialis derogat legi generali* principle would contribute to a firmer hierarchy between generic and special legal bases and thus provide greater legal certainty.

4. Concluding Remarks

The centre of gravity theory has shaped the quest for the correct choice of legal basis as no other general principle of legal basis litigation. In particular, its focus on procedural aspects over substance has defined the case law since the

[62] See chapter by Emily Hancox in this volume.

[63] See eg a line of case law on tobacco products, where the Court nevertheless confirmed a broad interpretation of the Union's competence under Article 114 TFEU, Case C-358/14, *Republic of Poland v European Parliament*, EU:C:2016:323; Case C-477/14, *Pillbox 38 (UK) Ltd. v Secretary of State for Health*, EU:C:2016:324; Case C-547/14, *Philip Morris Brands SARL and Others v Secretary of State for Health*, EU:C:2016:325.

[64] Eg Joined Cases C-317/04 and C-318/04, *European Parliament v Council of the European Union (C-317/04) and Commission of the European Communities (C-318/04) (PNR)*, EU:C:2006:346; and Opinion 1/15, *Draft agreement between Canada and the European Union on the transfer and processing of Passenger Name Record data*, EU:C:2017:592.

[65] Similar to Article 352 TFEU, which also functions as a legal base of last resort; however, without the association to the internal market.

introduction of the Single European Act, essentially relegating the choice of legal basis from a constitutional matter linked to the principle of conferral to a mere procedural issue. This has led to a number of problems with the application of the centre of gravity theory in the present and a concerning outlook for any future developments—judicial or political—affecting legal basis litigation.

This chapter has discussed the difficulties in applying the centre of gravity theory and has analysed the resulting flaws of the principle as it stands. First, the constitutional setup with overlapping competence categories predestines conflicts to occur where no per se delimitation is possible. Second, the CJEU's inconsistencies in applying its own established criteria of aim and content have contributed little to ensuring legal certainty in legal basis litigation and have ultimately led the way for a greater focus on procedure rather than substance. Third, if applied without any restrictions, the centre of gravity theory contributes to a strengthening of generic legal bases, such as Article 114 TFEU, thus enhancing a continuous competence creep and pre-emption of more special legal bases.

In light of these problems, a number of alternative approaches have been put forward, which could help mitigate the risks in applying the centre of gravity theory in legal basis litigation and rendering it more sustainable in the long term. First, a more holistic approach was suggested, advocating for a more conscious review of the substantive requirements for legal bases under the principle of conferral in order to avoid the narrow focus on procedure only. Second, all relevant legal bases should be used for the adoption of a measure, solving the problem of procedural incompatibilities by applying the most stringent procedure and the democracy-maximizing rationale. Third, the application of the *lex specialis derogat legi generali* principle as a step before rather than after the application of the centre of gravity theory would support greater legal certainty in the hierarchical setup of competences.

Overall, this chapter has put forward the argument that the application of the centre of gravity theory has fostered procedural formalism where substance should indeed be the determining factor. While the introduction of procedural differences has acted as an incubator for this development, it can just as easily be reversed in the event of a future treaty change. However, even if such treaty change entailed significant supranationalization across all policy areas, legal basis litigation would continue to exist for the purpose of delimitation from those policy areas where Member States have retained some of their competences. Thus, in the interest of consistency, legal certainty, and sustainable application of the centre of gravity theory, future legal basis litigation should orient itself towards substance rather than procedure.

References

Butler G, 'The EU Flexibility Clause is Dead, Lond Live the EU Flexibility Clause' in Antonina Bakardjieva Engelbrekt and Xavier Groussot, *The Future of Europe—Political and Legal Integration Beyond Brexit* (Hart Publishing 2019)

Craig P, 'Pringle: Legal Reasoning, Text, Purpose and Teleology' (2013) 20(1) Maastricht Journal of European Comparative Law 3

Cremona M, 'External Relations of the EU and the Member States: Competence, Mixed Agreements, International Responsibility, and Effects of International Law', EUI Working Paper LAW No. 2006/22

Dougan M, 'EU Competences in an Age of Complexity and Crisis: Challenges and Tensions in the System of Attributed Powers' (2024) 61(1) CML Rev 93

Engel A, *The Choice of Legal Basis for Acts of the European Union: Competence Overlaps, Institutional Preferences, and Legal Basis Litigation* (Springer International Publishing 2018)

Engel A, 'EU Competences in Crisis: Disentangling the Conflict between Monetary and Economic Legal Bases' (2022) 2 Europarättslig Tidskrift 191

Engel A, 'The Choice of Legal Basis in EU Competition Law: Shifting the Competence in the Digital Era' (2023) 4 Europarättslig Tidskrift 669

Engel A, 'Licence to Regulate: Article 114 TFEU as Choice of Legal Basis in the Digital Single Market', in Annegret Engel, Xavier Groussot, and Gunnar Thor Petursson (eds.) *New Directions in Digitalisation: Perspectives from EU Competition Law and the Charter of Fundamental Rights* (Springer Nature International 2024)

Engel A, Nowag N, and Groussot X, 'Is This Completely M.A.D.? Three Views on the Ruling of the German FCC on 5th May 2020' (2020) 3(1) Nordic Journal of European Law 128

Schütze R, 'Organized Change towards an "Ever Closer Union": Article 308 EC and the Limits to the Community's Legislative Competence' (2003) 22(1) Yearbook of European Law 79

Tridimas T, 'Terrorism and the ECJ: Empowerment and Democracy in the EC Legal Order' (2009) 34(1) European Law Review 103

Trüe C, *Das System der Rechtsetzungskompetenzen der Europäischen Gemeinschaft und der Europäischen Union*'(Nomos Verlagsgesellschaft 2002)

van Vooren B, *EU External Relations Law and the European Neighbourhood Policy: A Paradigm for Coherence* (Routledge 2012)

Weatherill S, 'Competence Creep and Competence Control' in Piet Eeckhout and Takis Tridimas (eds) *Yearbook of European Law, Vol. 23* (OUP 2005)

Weatherill S, 'The Limits of Legislative Harmonisation Ten Years after Tobacco Advertising: How the Court's Case Law Has Become a "Drafting Guide"'(2012) 12(3) German Law Journal 827

11

The Legal Reasoning of the Court of Justice of the European Union in the Area of Economic and Monetary Union: A Normative Assessment

*Menelaos Markakis**

1. Introduction

The Economic and Monetary Union (EMU) is an interesting area, in that its Treaty-based framework has remained largely intact since the Treaty of Maastricht. The Court of Justice of the European Union (CJEU) has laid down and complemented, block by block, the constitutional fundamentals in this area.[1] This chapter provides a normative assessment of CJEU's reasoning in the area of EMU. It principally focuses on landmark rulings of the European Court of Justice (ECJ) in this area that have profoundly shaped the law of EMU as well as EU law more generally. It sheds light on the interpretative methods employed by the CJEU and subjects its EMU case law to critical scrutiny in

* I am very grateful to Alezini Loxa, Luigi Lonardo, Graham Butler and the participants of the conference held at Lund University on 17–18 April 2024 for their helpful comments. The usual disclaimer applies.

[1] See, among others, Kaarlo Tuori and Klaus Tuori, *The Eurozone Crisis: A Constitutional Analysis* (CUP 2014); Alicia Hinarejos, *The Euro Area Crisis in Constitutional Perspective* (OUP 2015); Menelaos Markakis, *Accountability in the Economic and Monetary Union: Foundations, Policy, and Governance* (OUP 2020) esp. chs 6 and 8; Daniel Sarmiento and Moritz Hartmann, 'European Monetary Union and the Courts' in Fabian Amtenbrink and Christoph Herrmann (eds), assisted by René Repasi, *The EU Law of Economic and Monetary Union* (OUP 2020) ch 19; Alicia Hinarejos, 'The Legality of Responses to the Crisis' in ibid, ch 41; Takis Tridimas, 'The ECB and the Court of Justice: Old Toolbox, New Problems' in Thomas Beukers, Diane Fromage, and Giorgio Monti (eds), *The New European Central Bank: Taking Stock and Looking Ahead* (OUP 2022) ch 12; Ana Bobić, *The Individual in the Economic and Monetary Union: A Study of Legal Accountability* (CUP 2024).

Menelaos Markakis, *The Legal Reasoning of the Court of Justice of the European Union in the Area of Economic and Monetary Union: A Normative Assessment* In: *The Reasoning of the Court of Justice of the EU*. Edited by: Alezini Loxa and Luigi Lonardo, Oxford University Press.
DOI: 10.1093/9780198983002.003.0014

order to assess whether the legal reasoning withstands normative evaluation in the various dimensions examined in this chapter.

It should be stressed from the outset that this chapter does not intend to exhaustively examine all EMU cases,[2] and also that there are different ways of categorizing these cases, depending for example on the type of action brought before the CJEU, their subject matter (economic or monetary policy), the chronological order in which the judgments were delivered, and so on.[3] With those points in mind, the chapter is structured as follows. The discussion begins with the very few ECJ rulings that predate the euro crisis (*OLAF case*, *Commission v Council*). It will be shown that these foundational judgments laid the foreground for the euro-crisis judgments. It is then argued that we can distinguish three main stages or categories of cases in EMU since the onset of the euro crisis (see Figure 11.1). The first wave of judgments coincides with the most acute phase of the euro crisis (in chronological order: *Pringle*, *Gauweiler*, *Mallis*, *Ledra Advertising*, *Weiss*). These rulings were immensely important in clarifying the constitutional fundamentals in the area of EMU, in the manner explained below. The second wave of, perhaps lesser known but also fundamental, cases (*Florescu*, *Chrysostomides*, *BPC Lux 2 Sàrl*) plugged important gaps in the earlier judgments and elaborated on the constitutional fundamentals of EMU. The third wave or stage of EMU cases concerns the European Banking Union, which is nowadays a key component of the EMU. A fourth, future wave could concern climate cases brought against the EU institutions for their actions in the EMU (see Figure 11.1). It will be argued that the choice of interpretative methods depends on the particular circumstances of each case, and that the way these methods are applied by the CJEU has sometimes been problematic. Overall, the CJEU is making a concerted effort to bring together the different strands of its jurisprudence in the EMU and the Banking Union, as well as to plug gaps in judicial protection. However, the Cypriot cases (*Mallis*, *Ledra Advertising*, *Chrysostomides*) remain an outlier in this respect.

[2] Other, somewhat 'less significant' EMU cases—at the very least as regards the subject matter of this chapter—are examined in more detail in Menelaos Markakis (n 1) ch 6. Moreover, the somewhat niche line of ECJ case law concerning national central banks is examined in Paul Dermine and Menelaos Markakis, 'Hybrid Governance Structures and Monetary Policy: The Legal and Institutional Position of National Central Banks in the Eurosystem' (2025) 13 Politics and Governance, Article 8943, esp 8–13.

[3] See Menelaos Markakis (n 1) chs 6 and 8. The euro-crisis case law by *national* courts is examined in ibid, ch 7, with further references.

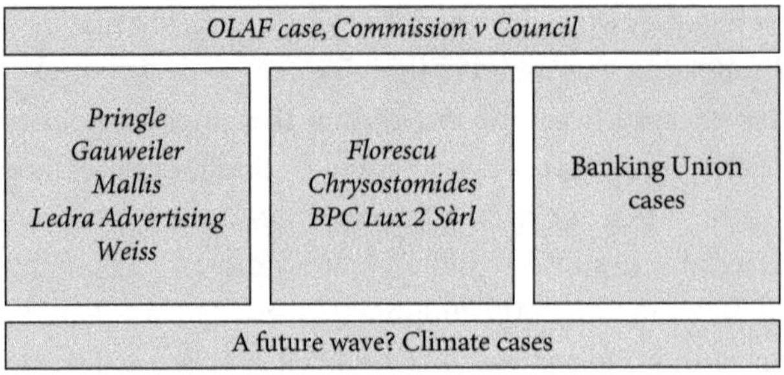

Figure 11.1 The different waves of EMU cases

2. The Pre-crisis Foundational Judgments: *The OLAF Case* and *Commission v Council*

In the first 10+ years after its establishment, there were very few cases concerning the EMU. This was to change in the most dramatic fashion with the onset of the euro crisis, to the point that it led to allegations of overjudicialization in the domain of EMU.[4] Nevertheless, the limited case law of the pre-crisis era served to highlight fundamental points about the legal and institutional framework of EMU. In *Commission v ECB* (also known as *the OLAF case*),[5] the ECJ established that, 'regardless of the distinctive features of its status within the Community legal order',[6] the ECB was subject to the rule of law. Or, as the Court put it, 'recognition that the ECB has such independence does not have the consequence of separating it entirely from the European Community and exempting it from every rule of Community law'.[7] *Commission v Council* (Full Court) highlighted the degree of discretion enjoyed by the EU institutions in the EMU, *in casu* by the Council of the EU in the Excessive Deficit Procedure.[8] The Council could not be forced to take further steps in the Excessive Deficit Procedure with respect to Germany and France, but it still had to act within the confines of the existing framework, such that 'the Council [could not] break free from the rules laid down by Article 104 EC [nowadays Article 126 TFEU] and those which it set for itself in Regulation No 1467/97'.[9] Another important

[4] See further Federico Fabbrini, *Economic Governance in Europe: Comparative Paradoxes and Constitutional Challenges* (OUP 2015) 64.
[5] Case C-11/00 *Commission of the European Communities v European Central Bank* EU:C:2003:395.
[6] ibid, para 64.
[7] ibid, para 135.
[8] Case C-27/04 (Full Court) *Commission of the European Communities v Council of the European Union* EU:C:2004:436.
[9] ibid, para 81; Council Regulation (EC) 1467/97 of 7 July 1997 on speeding up and clarifying the implementation of the excessive deficit procedure [1997] OJ L209/6, as currently in force.

point is that the Court held that, given the importance that the framers of the Treaty attached to observance of budgetary discipline and the aim of the rules laid down for applying budgetary discipline, those rules were to be given an interpretation which ensured that they were fully effective.[10]

2.1 First-wave judgments

2.1.1 The *Pringle* case

The modern era of EMU case law truly begins with *Pringle* (Full Court), and practically every core EMU judgment delivered thereafter builds one way or another on this judgment.[11] The reference to the Court for a preliminary ruling was made in an appeal against a judgment of the High Court (Ireland) in proceedings brought by Mr Pringle, seeking a declaration that the amendment of Article 136 TFEU by European Council Decision 2011/199[12] constituted an unlawful amendment of the TFEU and that by ratifying, approving, or accepting the Treaty establishing the European Stability Mechanism (ESM Treaty) Ireland would undertake obligations incompatible with the EU Treaties. In a nutshell, the ECJ in *Pringle* gave the green light to the establishment of the European Stability Mechanism (ESM). The Court ruled that Member States were free to establish a stability mechanism such as the ESM, provided that the mechanism complied with EU law in its operation, notably with the measures adopted by the EU in the area of coordination of the Member States' economic policies.

The *Pringle* judgment is not important just for EMU law but for EU constitutional law more generally. First and foremost, the Court of Justice established that it had jurisdiction to review the validity of the impugned European Council decision by means of which Article 136 TFEU was amended through a simplified revision procedure (Article 48(6) TEU). It ruled that it was for the Court to verify that the procedural rules laid down in Article 48(6) TEU were followed and that the amendments decided upon concerned only Part Three of the TFEU, which implied that they did not entail any amendment of provisions of another part of the EU Treaties and that they did not increase the

[10] *Commission v Council*, para 74. This constitutes a functional argument: Joxerramon Bengoetxea, *The Legal Reasoning of the European Court of Justice: Towards a European Jurisprudence* (OUP 1993) 251–52.

[11] Case C-370/12 (Full Court) *Thomas Pringle v Government of Ireland and Others* EU:C:2012:756.

[12] European Council Decision 2011/199/EU of 25 March 2011 amending Article 136 of the Treaty on the Functioning of the European Union with regard to a stability mechanism for Member States whose currency is the euro [2011] OJ L91/1.

competences of the Union.[13] Although the impugned Decision formally satisfied the condition that the simplified revision procedure may concern solely provisions of Part Three of the TFEU (of which Article 136 is a part), it was necessary to examine whether the impugned Treaty amendment encroached on the Union's competences in the areas of monetary policy and the coordination of the economic policies of the Member States, the provisions for which are to be found in Part One of the TFEU. In doing so, the Court of Justice had to delineate the EU's competences in the aforementioned areas. This part of the Court's judgment later became the basis for its rulings in *Gauweiler* and *Weiss*, which will be examined below.

More specifically, the Court observed that the TFEU contained no definition of monetary policy and that it referred, in its provisions relating to that policy, to the objectives rather than to the instruments of monetary policy.[14] It went on to examine whether the objectives to be attained by the ESM and the instruments provided to that end fell within monetary policy for the purposes of Articles 3(1)(c) and 127 TFEU. The objective pursued by the ESM, which is to safeguard the stability of the euro area as a whole, was clearly distinct from the objective of maintaining price stability. Even though the stability of the euro area may have repercussions on the stability of the currency used in that area, an economic policy measure could not be treated as equivalent to a monetary policy measure for the sole reason that it could have indirect effects on the stability of the euro.[15] As regards the instruments envisaged in order to attain the objective concerned, the Court succinctly observed that the grant of financial assistance to a Member State clearly did not fall within monetary policy.[16] In light of the objectives to be attained by the ESM, the instruments provided in order to achieve those objectives,[17] and the close link between the ESM, the TFEU provisions relating to economic policy, and the EU economic governance framework, the Court concluded that the establishment of the ESM fell within the area of economic policy.[18]

As regards the Union's competence in the area of the coordination of the Member States' economic policies (Articles 2(3) and 5(1) TFEU), the Court ruled that the EU Treaties did not confer any specific power on the Union to establish a stability mechanism of the kind envisaged by the impugned

[13] *Pringle*, paras 29–37.
[14] ibid, para 53.
[15] ibid, para 56.
[16] ibid, para 57.
[17] These were not analysed by the Court in detail, as they were not included in the impugned Decision.
[18] *Pringle*, para 60.

Decision.[19] Article 122(2) TFEU did not constitute an appropriate legal basis for the establishment of a stability mechanism of the kind envisaged by that decision. The fact that the mechanism envisaged was to be permanent and that its objective was to safeguard the financial stability of the euro area as a whole meant that such action could not be taken by the Union on the basis of that Treaty provision.[20] This clearly has consequences also for the establishment of a future fiscal shock absorption capacity, should the EU institutions wish to draw on Article 122 TFEU again as a legal basis.[21] Moreover, Article 143(2) TFEU enables the Union to grant mutual assistance only to a *non*-euro area Member State, and the Union had no obligation to act under Article 352 TFEU.[22] Having regard to Articles 4(1) and 5(2) TEU, the euro area Member States were entitled to conclude an agreement between themselves for the establishment of the ESM.[23] However, those Member States should not disregard their duty to comply with EU law when exercising their competences in that area. The Court went on to add that the reason why the grant of financial assistance was subject to strict conditionality under Article 136(3) TFEU was to ensure that that mechanism would operate in a way that would comply with EU law, including the measures adopted by the Union in the context of the coordination of the Member States' economic policies,[24] which in effect, together with the Court's interpretation of Article 125 TFEU,[25] constitutionalizes the requirement of (strict) conditionality. The precise form that this conditionality should take depends on the particular circumstances of each case, and the same is true for the Union's measures for the coordination of the Member States' economic policies. In the current author's view, conditionality should be appropriate to the form of assistance provided and the financial instrument(s) chosen.

The Court further ruled that Article 136(3) TFEU merely confirmed that the Member States had the power to establish a stability mechanism and that

[19] ibid, para 64.
[20] ibid, para 65.
[21] See generally, among others, Fabian Amtenbrink and Menelaos Markakis, 'Never Waste a Good Crisis: On the Emergence of an EU Fiscal Capacity' in Alicia Hinarejos and Robert Schütze (eds), *EU Fiscal Federalism: Past, Present, Future* (OUP 2023) 171–204; Fabian Amtenbrink, 'Covid-19 and Fiscal Union' in Federico Fabbrini and Christy Ann Petit (eds), *Research Handbook on Post-Pandemic EU Economic Governance and NGEU Law* (Elgar Publishing 2024) ch 3; Maria Antonia Panascì, 'Unravelling Next Generation EU as a Transformative Moment: From Market Integration to Redistribution' (2024) 61 CMLR 13; Merijn Chamon, 'The Non-Emergency Economic Policy Competence in Article 122(1) TFEU' (2024) 61 CMLR 1501.
[22] *Pringle*, paras 66–67.
[23] ibid, para 68.
[24] ibid, para 69, see also para 72.
[25] See ibid, paras 135–37.

it did not confer any new competence on the Union.[26] Furthermore, even though the ESM Treaty made use of the Union's institutions, that fact was not, in any event, capable of affecting the validity of the impugned European Council decision, which provided only for the establishment of a stability mechanism by the Member States and was silent on any possible role for the Union's institutions.[27]

The Court went on to examine whether the Treaty provisions and general principles of EU law precluded a Member State from concluding and ratifying an agreement such as the ESM Treaty. In doing so, it provided an authoritative interpretation of various Treaty provisions on economic and monetary policy. The Court began by establishing that the activities of the ESM did not fall within monetary policy.[28] It went on to examine whether the commitments that would be undertaken by the euro area Member States in the ESM Treaty were consistent with the EU Treaty provisions relating to economic policy (viz., Articles 2(3), 119–121, and 126 TFEU). It ruled that the ESM was not concerned with the coordination of the economic policies of the Member States, but that it constituted a financing mechanism.[29] The conditionality to which ESM financial assistance would be subject did not constitute an instrument for the coordination of the economic policies of the Member States, but was intended to ensure that the activities of the ESM were compatible with, *inter alia*, Article 125 TFEU and the coordinating measures adopted by the Union.[30] In the current author's view, it is of course undeniable that such conditions make further inroads into the Member States' economic policies.[31]

Perhaps the most important part of the judgment concerns the interpretation of Article 125 TFEU (the so-called no-bailout clause), which provides that neither the Union nor a Member State shall be liable for or assume the commitments of another Member State. This was previously understood to prohibit financial assistance to another Member State, hence the moniker 'no-bailout clause'.[32] According to the Court, it was apparent from the wording used in Article 125 TFEU that it was not intended to prohibit either the Union or the Member States from granting any form of financial assistance whatsoever to a Member State.[33] That reading of Article 125 TFEU was supported,

[26] ibid, paras 72–73.
[27] ibid, para 74.
[28] ibid, paras 93–98. This part of the judgment essentially repeats what was earlier established with respect to the impugned European Council Decision.
[29] *Pringle*, para 110.
[30] ibid, para 111.
[31] See Menelaos Markakis (n 1) ch 3, with further references.
[32] See notably the analysis by Kaarlo Tuori and Klaus Tuori (n 1) 120–36.
[33] *Pringle*, para 130.

according to the Court, by other provisions relating to economic policy and, in particular, Articles 122 and 123 TFEU. First, Article 122(2) TFEU provides that the Union may grant ad hoc financial assistance to a Member State which is in difficulties or is seriously threatened with severe difficulties caused by natural disasters or exceptional occurrences beyond its control. If Article 125 TFEU prohibited any financial assistance whatsoever by the Union or the Member States to another Member State, Article 122 TFEU would have had to state, according to the Court, that it derogated from Article 125 TFEU. Second, the Court noted that Article 123 TFEU, which prohibits the ECB and national central banks from granting overdraft facilities or any other type of credit facility, employed wording which was stricter than that used in Article 125 TFEU. The difference in wording supported, according to the Court, the view that Article 125 TFEU was not intended to prohibit any financial assistance whatsoever to a Member State.[34]

The Court went beyond a textual and systematic interpretation of the no-bailout clause and also had recourse to a historical and teleological interpretation. According to the Court, it was necessary to have regard to the objective pursued by Article 125 TFEU in order to determine which forms of financial assistance were compatible with it.[35] It was apparent from the *travaux préparatoires* relating to the Treaty of Maastricht that the aim of Article 125 TFEU was to ensure that Member States would follow a sound budgetary policy. The prohibition laid down in Article 125 TFEU ensured that Member States remained subject to the logic of the market when they entered into debt, since that should prompt them to maintain budgetary discipline. Compliance with such discipline contributed to maintaining the financial stability of the monetary union. It was therefore held that Article 125 TFEU prohibited the Union and Member States from granting financial assistance as a result of which the incentive of the recipient Member State to conduct a sound budgetary policy would be diminished. However, Article 125 TFEU did not prohibit the granting of financial assistance by one or more Member States to a Member State which remained responsible for its commitments to its creditors provided that the conditions attached to such assistance were such as to prompt that Member State to implement a sound budgetary policy.[36] The Court ruled that a mechanism such as the ESM and the Member States which participate in it were not liable for the commitments of a Member State which

[34] ibid, paras 131–32.
[35] ibid, para 133.
[36] ibid, paras 134–37.

receives stability support and that they did not assume those commitments within the meaning of Article 125 TFEU.[37]

The referring court also asked the Court of Justice whether the allocation by the ESM Treaty of new tasks to the Commission, the ECB, and the CJEU was compatible with their powers as defined in the Treaties. This aspect of the Court's judgment concerning the use of the EU institutions outside the framework of EU law has been subjected to criticism in the relevant specialist literature, the essence of the argument being that the legal statements in *Pringle* concerning the power of the EU institutions to act outside the EU Treaties are problematic for a host of procedural, substantive, and normative reasons.[38] The Court ruled that it was apparent from its earlier case law[39] that the Member States were entitled, in areas which did not fall under the exclusive competence of the Union, to entrust tasks to the institutions outside the framework of the Union, such as the task of coordinating a collective action undertaken by the Member States or managing financial assistance, provided that those tasks did not alter the essential character of the powers conferred on those institutions by the EU Treaties.[40] The duties allocated to the Commission and the ECB in the ESM Treaty constituted tasks of this kind.[41] The activities of the ESM fell under economic policy and the Union did not have exclusive competence in that area.[42] The duties conferred on the Commission and the ECB within the ESM Treaty, important as they were, did not entail any power to make decisions of their own and the activities pursued by those two institutions within the ESM Treaty solely committed the ESM.[43] Nor did the tasks conferred on the two institutions alter the essential character of the powers conferred on them by the EU Treaties.[44] Notably, the Court held that, by its involvement in the ESM Treaty, the Commission promoted the general interest of the Union. The tasks allocated to it enabled it to ensure that the memoranda of understanding concluded by the ESM with recipient Member States were consistent with EU law.[45] This part of the Court's reasoning would later become

[37] ibid, paras 138–47.

[38] Paul Craig, '*Pringle* and Use of EU Institutions outside the EU Legal Framework: Foundations, Procedure and Substance' (2013) 9 EuConst 263.

[39] Joined Cases C-181/91 and C-248/91 *European Parliament v Council of the European Communities and Commission of the European Communities* EU:C:1993:271; Case C-316/91 *European Parliament v Council of the European Union* EU:C:1994:76.

[40] *Pringle*, para 158.

[41] ibid, para 159.

[42] ibid, para 160.

[43] ibid, para 161.

[44] ibid, para 162.

[45] ibid, para 164.

important in *Ledra Advertising* when deciding whether the EU could be held liable for damages caused by its institutions in the framework of the ESM.

The referring national court also observed that the establishment of the ESM outside the EU legal order could have the consequence that the ESM was removed from the scope of the EU Charter of Fundamental Rights. In a finding that would become incredibly important for legal accountability in the EMU, notably as regards bailouts by the ESM, the Court ruled that the Member States were not implementing Union law, within the meaning of Article 51(1) of the Charter, when they established a stability mechanism such as the ESM where the EU Treaties did not confer any specific competence on the Union to establish such a mechanism.[46] It followed that the general principle of effective judicial protection did not preclude the conclusion of the ESM Treaty or its ratification.[47]

2.2 The 'classics' of monetary policy: *Gauweiler* and *Weiss*

The reference by the *Bundesverfassungsgericht* to the Court of Justice for a preliminary ruling in *Gauweiler* (Grand Chamber) concerned the legality of the Outright Monetary Transactions (OMT) by the ECB.[48] The referring court asked whether a programme for the purchase of government bonds on secondary markets, such as the OMT, could be covered by the powers of the European System of Central Banks (ESCB), as defined by primary EU law. The Court relied heavily on *Pringle* and *Commission v ECB* in its judgment. It reiterated that 'the FEU Treaty contains no precise definition of monetary policy but defines both the objectives of monetary policy and the instruments which are available to the ESCB for the purpose of implementing that policy',[49] and that 'in order to determine whether a measure falls within the area of monetary policy it is appropriate to refer principally to the objectives of that measure. The instruments which the measure employs in order to attain those objectives are also relevant.'[50] The impugned monetary policy instrument aimed to safeguard an appropriate monetary policy transmission and the singleness of monetary policy. The latter objective contributed to achieving the objectives

[46] ibid, para 180.
[47] ibid, para 181.
[48] Case C-62/14 (Grand Chamber) *Peter Gauweiler and Others v Deutscher Bundestag* EU:C:2015:400. See further Paul Craig and Menelaos Markakis, '*Gauweiler* and the Legality of Outright Monetary Transactions' (2016) 41 ELRev 4.
[49] *Gauweiler*, para 42.
[50] ibid, para 46.

of that policy, inasmuch as, under Article 119(2) TFEU, monetary policy must be 'single'.[51] Moreover, the objective of safeguarding an appropriate transmission of monetary policy was likely both to preserve the singleness of monetary policy and to contribute to maintaining price stability.[52] The fact that such a programme could also be capable of contributing to the stability of the euro area, which was a matter of economic policy according to *Pringle*, did not call that assessment into question.[53] Reasoning by analogy from *Pringle*, the Court held that a monetary policy measure could not be treated as equivalent to an economic policy measure merely because it could have indirect effects on the stability of the euro area.[54]

As regards the means to be used for achieving the objectives sought by such a programme, the transactions which the ECB's Governing Council had in mind used one of the monetary policy instruments provided for in primary law.[55] The programme announced was intended to rectify the disruption to the monetary policy transmission mechanism caused by the specific situation of government bonds issued by certain Member States. In those circumstances, the mere fact that the programme was specifically limited to those government bonds was not of a nature to imply, of itself, that the instruments used by the ESCB fell outside the realm of monetary policy. No TFEU provision required the ESCB to operate in the financial markets by means of general measures that would necessarily be applicable to all euro area Member States.[56]

It follows from the Court's analysis that a purchase of government bonds undertaken by the ESM in order to safeguard the stability of the euro area falls within *economic* policy, whereas when that instrument is used (or announced, as the case may be) by the ESCB to maintain price stability it constitutes *monetary* policy.[57] The fact that the implementation of the OMT programme was made conditional upon full compliance with a macroeconomic adjustment programme with the European Financial Stability Facility or the ESM did not alter the Court's conclusion that a programme such as that announced by the ECB fell within monetary policy. Although it was possible that a government bond-buying programme could, indirectly, increase the impetus to comply with the adjustment programme and thus, to some extent, further

[51] ibid, para 48.
[52] ibid, paras 49–50.
[53] ibid, para 51.
[54] ibid, para 52.
[55] ibid, paras 53–54. See Article 18.1 of Protocol (No 4) on the Statute of the ESCB and of the ECB.
[56] *Gauweiler*, para 55.
[57] ibid, paras 63–64.

the economic policy objectives of that programme, such indirect effects did not mean that OMT could be treated as equivalent to an economic policy measure.[58]

However, a bond-buying programme could be validly adopted and implemented only insofar as it complied with the principle of proportionality.[59] Since the ESCB was required to make choices of a technical nature and to undertake forecasts and complex assessments, it should be allowed a broad discretion.[60] The Court held:

> Nevertheless, where an EU institution enjoys broad discretion, a review of compliance with certain procedural guarantees is of fundamental importance. Those guarantees include the obligation for the ESCB to examine carefully and impartially all the relevant elements of the situation in question and to give an adequate statement of the reasons for its decisions.[61]

As regards the appropriateness of the impugned measure, the ECB's analysis of the economic situation of the euro area was not vitiated by a manifest error of assessment.[62] The fact that that reasoned analysis had been subject to challenge did not, in itself, call that conclusion into question, since, given that questions of monetary policy were usually of a controversial nature and in view of the ESCB's broad discretion, nothing more could be required of the ESCB apart from that it use its economic expertise and the necessary technical means at its disposal to carry out that analysis with all care and accuracy.[63] The purchase of government bonds on the secondary markets was likely to contribute to reducing those interest rates considered by the ECB to be excessive by dispelling unjustified fears about the break-up of the euro area and therefore to facilitate the ESCB's monetary policy transmission and to safeguard the singleness of monetary policy.[64] Nor did the programme go manifestly beyond what was necessary to achieve those objectives. Notably, the purchase of government bonds was permitted only insofar as it was necessary to achieve the objectives of the programme and such purchases would cease as soon as those objectives had been achieved. Moreover, the potential scale of the programme was limited in a number of ways.[65] Last, in a fairly rare appearance of

[58] ibid, paras 57–59.
[59] ibid, para 66.
[60] ibid, para 68.
[61] ibid, para 69.
[62] ibid, para 74.
[63] ibid, para 75.
[64] ibid, paras 76–77.
[65] ibid, paras 81–90.

what seems to be *stricto sensu* proportionality, the Court held that the ESCB weighed up the various interests in play so as to actually prevent disadvantages from arising when the programme in question was implemented which would be manifestly disproportionate to its objectives, but without elaborating any further on this point.[66]

The last part of the judgment concerns the question whether the programme complies with the prohibition of monetary financing (Article 123(1) TFEU). Relying, again, heavily on *Pringle*, the Court held that that provision prohibited all financial assistance from the ESCB to a Member State, but that it did not preclude, generally, the possibility of the ESCB purchasing bonds previously issued by that State from its creditors.[67] It was clear from the wording of Article 123(1) TFEU that the ESCB was only prohibited from purchasing *directly* from the Member States (namely, on the *primary* market) their debt instruments.[68] Nevertheless, the ESCB did not have the authority to purchase government bonds on *secondary* markets under conditions which would, in practice, mean that its action had an effect equivalent to that of a direct purchase of government bonds from the public authorities and bodies of the Member States, thereby undermining the effectiveness of the prohibition laid down in Article 123(1) TFEU.[69] What ensued in the Court's reasoning was a mix of historical, teleological, and systematic interpretation. The Court held that, in order to determine which forms of purchases were compatible with Article 123(1) TFEU, it was necessary to take account of the objective pursued by that provision.[70] It was apparent from the *travaux préparatoires* relating to the Treaty of Maastricht that the aim of Article 123 TFEU was to encourage the Member States to follow a sound budgetary policy, not allowing monetary financing of public deficits or privileged access by public authorities to the financial markets (Article 124 TFEU) to lead to excessively high levels of debt or excessive deficits.[71] Council Regulation 3603/93 also stated in its preamble that purchases made on the secondary market could not be used to circumvent the objective of Article 123 TFEU.[72] It followed that, when the ECB purchased government bonds on secondary markets, *sufficient safeguards* should be built into its intervention to ensure that the latter did not fall foul of the prohibition

[66] ibid, para 91.
[67] ibid, para 95.
[68] ibid, para 96.
[69] ibid, para 97.
[70] ibid, para 98.
[71] ibid, para 100.
[72] ibid, para 101; Council Regulation (EC) 3603/93 of 13 December 1993 specifying definitions for the application of the prohibitions referred to in Articles 104 and 104b (1) of the Treaty [1993] OJ L332/1.

of monetary financing in Article 123(1) TFEU.[73] The ESCB's intervention could, in practice, have an effect equivalent to that of a direct purchase of government bonds from public authorities and bodies of the Member States if the potential purchasers of those bonds on the primary market knew for certain that the ESCB was going to purchase those bonds on the secondary market within a certain period and under conditions allowing those market operators to act, *de facto*, as intermediaries for the ESCB.[74] However, the implementation of the impugned programme would be subject to conditions intended to avoid precisely that.[75] Nor did the impugned programme lessen the impetus of the Member States to follow a sound budgetary policy.[76] The Member States could not, in determining their budgetary policy, rely on the certainty that the ESCB would at a future point purchase their government bonds and the programme in question could not be implemented in a way which would bring about a harmonisation of interest rates applied to government bonds regardless of the differences arising from the Member States' macroeconomic or budgetary situation. Member States would, in the event of a deficit, be compelled to seek financing on the markets and would not be protected against the consequences which a change in their macroeconomic or budgetary situation could have in that regard.[77] The OMT programme was accompanied by guarantees intended to limit its impact on the impetus to follow a sound budgetary policy.[78]

Once such requirements and safeguards were established, it was only a matter of time before they would be put to the test in a future case concerning a different monetary policy instrument. The reference by the *Bundesverfassungsgericht* to the Court of Justice for a preliminary ruling in *Weiss* (Grand Chamber) concerned the legality of the Public Sector Purchase Programme (PSPP), which was part of the ECB's Asset Purchase Programme.[79] The referring court again asked whether the impugned bond-buying programme fell within the ambit of the ESCB's powers, as well as whether it complied with the prohibition of monetary financing (Article 123 TFEU). It should not be lost on the reader that *Weiss* has the distinct honour of being one of the few cases that led to an open challenge to the supremacy of EU law by, *in casu*, the referring national court.[80]

[73] *Gauweiler*, para 102.
[74] ibid, para 104.
[75] ibid, para 105.
[76] ibid, para 111.
[77] ibid, paras 113–14.
[78] ibid, paras 115–20.
[79] Case C-493/17 (Grand Chamber) *Proceedings brought by Heinrich Weiss and Others* EU:C:2018:1000.
[80] BVerfG, 2 BvR 859/15, 2 BvR 1651/15, 2 BvR 2006/15, 2 BvR 980/16 of 5 May 2020. See further, just in terms of books, Ana Bobić, *The Jurisprudence of Constitutional Conflict in the European Union* (OUP

It was particularly the Court's analysis of the proportionality of the PSPP programme, presented below, that drew the ire of the *Bundesverfassungsgericht*.[81]

In delimiting the Union's monetary policy, the ECJ in *Weiss* drew heavily on *Pringle* and *Gauweiler*. It held that the purpose of the impugned ECB decision was to contribute to a return of inflation rates to levels below, but close to, 2 per cent over the medium term, as the inflation target then was.[82] It pointed out that the Treaty authors chose to define the primary objective of monetary policy—namely the maintenance of price stability—in a general and abstract manner.[83] It did not appear that the specification of that objective as the maintenance of inflation rates at levels below, but close to, 2 per cent over the medium term was vitiated by a manifest error of assessment, nor that it went beyond the framework established by the TFEU.[84]

Shifting the focus to the economic effects of the impugned programme, the Court noted that the PSPP was capable of having an impact both on the balance sheets of commercial banks and on the financing of the Member States covered by the programme, and that such effects could possibly (also) be sought through economic policy measures.[85] Nevertheless, drawing on the ESCB's primary and secondary objectives under Article 127(1) TFEU, it ruled that 'within the institutional balance established by the provisions of Title VIII of the FEU Treaty . . . , the authors of the Treaties did not intend to make an absolute separation between economic and monetary policies'.[86] This was somewhat surprising from a legal perspective, at the very least to EMU lawyers, given that the EU has *exclusive* competence in the area of monetary policy for euro area Member States (Article 3(1)(c) TFEU), whereas it may only *coordinate* the economic policies of the Member States (Articles 2(3) and 5(1) TFEU). The Court was on more defensible ground in recalling, on the basis of its earlier case law, that a monetary policy measure could not be treated as equivalent to an economic policy measure for the sole reason that it could have

2022); Nik de Boer, *Judging European Democracy: The Role and Legitimacy of National Constitutional Courts in the EU* (OUP 2023).

[81] See also Mark Dawson, 'Revisiting Europe's "Law-Politics Imbalance"' in Mark Dawson, Bruno de Witte, and Elise Muir (eds), *Revisiting Judicial Politics in the European Union* (Elgar Publishing 2024) ch 2, who argues that 'the German Constitutional Court's later finding of "incomprehensibility" seems a critique not of the poor reasoning of the CJEU as such but rather the position of the Court towards the ECB (particularly the lowered standard of review it used to *apply* the *Gauweiler* criteria)' (p 27).

[82] *Weiss*, para 54.

[83] ibid, para 55.

[84] ibid, para 56.

[85] ibid, para 59.

[86] ibid, para 60.

indirect effects that could also be sought in the context of economic policy.[87] Notably, the Court held that it could not concur with the referring court's view that any effects of the programme that were knowingly accepted and definitely foreseeable by the ESCB when it was set up should not be regarded as 'indirect effects' of that programme, since that would, in practice, prevent the ESCB from using the means made available to it by the Treaties for the purpose of achieving monetary policy objectives and could—in particular in the context of an economic crisis—represent an insurmountable obstacle to its accomplishing the task assigned to it by primary law.[88]

As regards the proportionality of the PSPP programme, the Court's analysis also followed a similar course to the one in *Gauweiler*. It did not appear that the ESCB's economic analysis—according to which the PSPP was appropriate, in the monetary and financial conditions of the euro area, for contributing to achieving the objective of maintaining price stability—was vitiated by a manifest error of assessment.[89] In view of the foreseeable effects of the PSPP and given that it did not appear that the ESCB's objective could had been achieved by any other type of monetary policy measure entailing more limited action on its part, it was held that, in its underlying principle, the PSPP did not manifestly go beyond what was necessary to achieve that objective.[90] Moreover, the way the programme was set up also helped to guarantee that its effects were limited to what was necessary to achieve the objective concerned.[91] Furthermore, the ESCB had weighed up the various interests involved so as effectively to prevent disadvantages which were manifestly disproportionate to the PSPP's objective from arising on implementation of the programme.[92]

Last but definitely not least, as regards the prohibition of monetary financing (Article 123(1) TFEU), the Court took the opportunity to elaborate on its *dicta* in *Gauweiler*. It held that 'the ESCB cannot validly purchase bonds on the secondary markets under conditions which would, in practice, mean that its intervention has an effect equivalent to that of a direct purchase of bonds from the public authorities and bodies of the Member States'.[93] Moreover, 'the ESCB must build sufficient safeguards into its intervention to ensure that the latter does not fall foul of the prohibition of monetary financing in Article 123 TFEU, by satisfying itself that the programme is not such as to reduce the impetus

[87] ibid, para 61.
[88] ibid, para 67.
[89] ibid, para 78.
[90] ibid, para 81.
[91] ibid, paras 82–92.
[92] ibid, paras 93–99.
[93] ibid, para 106.

which that provision is intended to give the Member States to follow a sound budgetary policy'.[94] 'The safeguards which the ESCB must provide so that those two restrictions are observed will depend both on the particular features of the programme under consideration and on the economic context in which that programme is adopted and implemented'.[95] On the facts of the case, the Court found no violation of the prohibition of monetary financing. Similarly to *Gauweiler*, the focus was again on the various safeguards put in place by the ESCB, as well as on whether it was legally relevant that (some of) the features of the PSPP diverged from those of the OMT programme that the Court had greenlighted in *Gauweiler*.[96]

2.3 The Cypriot cases: *Mallis* and *Ledra Advertising*

Both *Mallis* and *Ledra Advertising* concern the financial assistance programme for Cyprus and were delivered by the Grand Chamber on the same day, on 20 September 2016.[97] The appellants in *Mallis* asked the Court to set aside the orders of the General Court by which it dismissed their actions for annulment of the Eurogroup statement of 25 March 2013 concerning, in particular, the restructuring of the banking sector in Cyprus.[98] By the statement at issue, the Eurogroup indicated that it had reached an agreement with the Cypriot authorities on the key elements of a macroeconomic adjustment programme, which was supported by all the euro area Member States, as well as by the Commission, the ECB, and the International Monetary Fund. In addition, the Eurogroup welcomed the plans for the restructuring of the financial sector that were mentioned in the annex to that statement. The appellants sought to argue that the impugned Eurogroup statement should be imputed to the Commission and the ECB, but the Court held that the Commission's and the ECB's participation in the meetings of the Eurogroup did not alter the nature of the latter's statements and that it could not result in the statement

[94] ibid, para 107.

[95] ibid, para 108.

[96] ibid, paras 109–58. For the application of those safeguards to the Pandemic Emergency Purchase Programme, see Paul Dermine and Menelaos Markakis, 'EU Economic Governance and the COVID-19 Crisis: Between Path-Dependency and Paradigmatic Shift' (2020) 6 International Journal of Public Law and Policy 326, 329.

[97] Joined Cases C-105/15 P to C-109/15 P (Grand Chamber) *Konstantinos Mallis and Others v European Commission and European Central Bank* EU:C:2016:702; Joined Cases C-8/15 P to C-10/15 P (Grand Chamber) *Ledra Advertising Ltd and Others v European Commission and European Central Bank* EU:C:2016:701.

[98] Case T-327/13 *Konstantinos Mallis and Elli Konstantinou Mali v European Commission and European Central Bank* EU:T:2014:909.

at issue being considered to be the expression of a decision-making power of those two institutions.[99] Nor was there anything in the statement at issue reflecting a decision of the Commission and the ECB to create a legal obligation on Cyprus to implement the measures which it contained.[100] Accordingly, the adoption of the Cypriot measures for the restructuring of the banks concerned could not be regarded as having been imposed by a supposed joint decision of the Commission and the ECB that had been given concrete expression in the Eurogroup statement at issue.[101] Last but definitely not least, insofar as the appellants sought the annulment of the Eurogroup statement itself, the Court noted 'not only that the term "informally" is used in the wording of Protocol No 14 on the Eurogroup, annexed to the FEU Treaty, but also that the Eurogroup is not among the different configurations of the Council of the European Union enumerated in Annex I to its Rules of Procedure adopted by Council Decision 2009/937/EU . . . Accordingly, . . . the Eurogroup cannot be equated with a configuration of the Council or be classified as a body, office or agency of the European Union within the meaning of Article 263 TFEU'.[102]

The reasoning in *Mallis* was terse and unsatisfactory. It is rightly argued by Craig that '[t]he rejection of [the appellants'] argument was predicated on a formalistic view of the Eurogroup and its place within the EU institutional architecture, which bears little relation to reality'.[103] 'The "contested statement" was not purely informative; it was determinative of the terms on which assistance would be granted. This was more especially so, given the institutional linkage between the Eurogroup and the decision-making regime under the [ESM], which was to provide the funding.'[104] Craig has criticized these 'twin legal realities', namely the view that the ESM Board of Governors' powers under the ESM Treaty and those of the Eurogroup under the EU Treaties could be 'treated as hermetically sealed insofar as legal accountability is concerned'.[105]

The appellants in *Ledra Advertising* called into question the General Court's assessment concerning the role of the Commission and the ECB in the adoption of the Memorandum of Understanding (MoU) for Cyprus.[106] They

[99] ECJ in *Mallis*, para 57.
[100] ibid, para 58.
[101] ibid, para 60.
[102] ibid, para 61.
[103] Paul Craig, 'The Eurogroup, Power and Accountability' (2017) 23 ELJ 234, 244.
[104] ibid, 245.
[105] ibid, 245–46.
[106] Case T-289/13 *Ledra Advertising Ltd v European Commission and European Central Bank* EU:T:2014:981; Case T-291/13 *Andreas Eleftheriou, Eleni Eleftheriou and Lilia Papachristofi v European Commission and European Central Bank* EU:T:2014:978; Case T-293/13 *Christos Theophilou and Eleni Theofilou v European Commission and European Central Bank* EU:T:2014:979.

submitted that those institutions were the true authors of the bail-in implemented in Cyprus and that the General Court erred in law when examining their argument that the Commission failed to ensure that that MoU was in conformity with EU law. The Court ruled, however, on appeal that the participation of the Commission and the ECB in the procedure resulting in the signature of the MoU did not enable the latter to be classified as an act that could be imputed to them.[107] It recalled that the duties conferred on those two institutions within the ESM Treaty, important as they were, did not entail any power to make decisions of their own, and that the activities pursued by them within the ESM Treaty committed the ESM alone.[108] The fact that one or more EU institutions could play a certain role within the ESM framework did not alter the nature of the ESM acts, which fell outside the EU legal order.[109] However, while such a finding could render an action for annulment against such acts inadmissible, 'it cannot prevent unlawful conduct linked, as the case may be, to the adoption of a memorandum of understanding on behalf of the ESM from being raised against the Commission and the ECB in an action for compensation under Article 268 TFEU and the second and third paragraphs of Article 340 TFEU'.[110] This is the truly innovative part of *Ledra Advertising*. Focusing sharply on the Commission in the remainder of the judgment and relying heavily on *Pringle*, the Court held that 'the Commission . . . retains, within the framework of the ESM Treaty, its role of guardian of the Treaties as resulting from Article 17(1) TEU, so that it should refrain from signing a memorandum of understanding whose consistency with EU law it doubts'.[111] It followed that the General Court had erred in law by holding that it did not have jurisdiction to consider an action for compensation based on the illegality of a number of paragraphs in the MoU concluded with Cyprus.[112]

The Court went on to give itself final judgment on the matter. Importantly, it ruled that, while the Member States did not implement EU law in the context of the ESM Treaty, such that the Charter was not addressed to them in that context,[113] the Charter was addressed to the EU institutions, including when they acted *outside* the EU legal framework.[114] However, the Court dismissed the applicants' claims for compensation, because the Commission could not

[107] ECJ in *Ledra Advertising*, para 52.
[108] ibid, para 53.
[109] ibid, para 54.
[110] ibid, para 55.
[111] ibid, para 59.
[112] ibid, para 60.
[113] See *Pringle*, paras 178–81.
[114] ECJ in *Ledra Advertising*, para 67.

be considered, by dint of having permitted the adoption of the disputed paragraphs in the MoU, to have contributed to a breach of the appellants' right to property guaranteed by Article 17(1) of the Charter.[115] In view of the objective of ensuring the stability of the banking system in the euro area and having regard to the imminent risk of financial losses to which depositors with the two Cypriot banks concerned would have been exposed if the latter had failed, such measures did not constitute a disproportionate and intolerable interference impairing the very substance of the appellants' right to property.[116]

3. Second-wave Judgments on Financial Assistance Programmes

The third and final piece to the Cypriot cases was added in *Chrysostomides* (also decided by the Grand Chamber).[117] Effectively, the applicants at first instance challenged all actions related to the Cypriot financial assistance programme by all the institutions and bodies involved in it. Their central thesis was that the harmful measures should be attributed to the EU authorities concerned, which obliged by means of their acts and conduct the Cypriot authorities to adopt the harmful decrees regarding the banking sector in Cyprus. The case gave the ECJ the opportunity to clarify whether the Eurogroup is an 'institution' within the meaning of Article 340(2) TFEU whose actions may trigger the Union's non-contractual liability.

The Court agreed with the General Court that the term 'institution' within the meaning of that provision encompasses not only the EU institutions listed in Article 13(1) TEU but also all the EU bodies, offices, and agencies that have been established by or under the Treaties and are intended to contribute to the achievement of the EU's objectives.[118] However, it disagreed with the General Court that the Eurogroup was an EU body established by the Treaties and that an action to establish the non-contractual liability of the EU could be brought against it on the basis of Article 340(2) TFEU.[119] The ECJ relied on three arguments in finding that the Eurogroup is not an EU entity established by the Treaties: that the Eurogroup was created outside the Treaties; that it is an

[115] ibid, paras 62–76.
[116] ibid, para 74.
[117] Joined Cases C-597/18 P, C-598/18 P, C-603/18 P, and C-604/18 P (Grand Chamber) *Council of the European Union v Dr. K. Chrysostomides & Co. and Others* EU:C:2020:1028.
[118] ibid, para 80.
[119] ibid, para 90.

informal body; and that it lacks EU competence to act.[120] This reasoning is problematic, for the reasons stated below.

First, the Court held that:

> the Euro Group was created as an intergovernmental body—outside the institutional framework of the European Union—intended to enable the ministers of the [Member States whose currency is the euro] to exchange and coordinate their views on issues relating to their common responsibilities concerning the single currency. It thus provides a bridge between the national level and the EU level for the purpose of coordinating the economic policies of the [Member States whose currency is the euro].[121]

Although Article 137 TFEU and Protocol (No 14) on the Euro Group formalized the existence of the Eurogroup and the participation of the Commission and the ECB at its meetings, they did not alter, according to the Court, its intergovernmental nature in the slightest.[122] As argued extensively elsewhere, the Court did not truly provide an explanation as to why Article 137 TFEU and Protocol (No 14) did not alter the Eurogroup's intergovernmental nature in the slightest. Instead, it cited various paragraphs from the Advocate General's Opinion where he explained why, in his opinion, the Treaty of Lisbon merely recognized the Eurogroup but did not seek to alter its legal nature. The key message flowing from those paragraphs cited in the judgment is that the Lisbon Treaty provisions acknowledged the existence of the Eurogroup as an intergovernmental discussion forum, rather than establishing it as a stand-alone body of the EU, in order to preserve undiminished the Council's fundamental role in the field of economic coordination, as well as the independence of the ECB. It seems that the Court drew specifically—though not necessarily exclusively—on the *literal* and *teleological* interpretation provided by the Advocate General in his Opinion,[123] both of which we have criticized extensively elsewhere.[124]

The second argument used by the Court was that:

[120] ibid, paras 84–89.
[121] ibid, para 84.
[122] ibid, paras 85–87.
[123] Joined Cases C-597/18 P, C-598/18 P, C-603/18 P and C-604/18 P *Council of the European Union v Dr. K. Chrysostomides & Co. and Others*, Opinion of AG Pitruzzella EU:C:2020:390.
[124] Anastasia Karatzia and Menelaos Markakis, 'Financial Assistance Conditionality and Effective Judicial Protection: *Chrysostomides*' (2022) 59 CMLR 501, 521–23; Menelaos Markakis, 'The Non-Contractual Liability of the EU for Actions of the Eurogroup: Cases C-597/18 P, C-598/18 P, C-603/18 P and C-604/18 P *Chrysostomides*' in Daniel Sarmiento, Hélène Ruiz Fabri, and Burkhard Hess (eds), *Yearbook on Procedural Law of the Court of Justice of the European Union—2021* (3rd edn, 2022) Max Planck Institute Luxembourg Research Paper 5/2022, 91, 97–102.

> as both the resolution of the European Council of 13 December 1997 and Article 1 of Protocol No 14 expressly state, and as the Court held in ... Mallis ..., the Euro Group is characterised by its informality, which, as the Advocate General has stated in . . . his Opinion, can be explained by the purpose pursued by its creation of endowing economic and monetary union with an instrument of intergovernmental coordination but without affecting the role of the Council—which is the fulcrum of the European Union's decision-making process in economic matters—or the independence of the ECB.[125]

It is not clear from the judgment why the informal nature of the Eurogroup means that the latter is not an EU entity established by the Treaties for the purposes of the EU's non-contractual liability. Contrary to what the Advocate General had opined, which is nevertheless not explicitly cited in the judgment, it could be questioned whether externality from the EU legal order is a necessary precondition for informality. In reality, formally recognizing the Eurogroup by means of primary EU law provisions would not affect the role of the Council, insofar as those Treaty provisions which confer powers on the Council in this area and render it the fulcrum of the EU's decision-making process in economic matters remained unchanged. It is possible to recognize the existence of an entity *within* the EU institutional framework which would not encroach on the powers of the Council.[126]

It is equally unclear why the informal nature of the Eurogroup is necessary to preserve the ECB's independence. The Eurogroup would, as any other Union institution, body, office or agency, undertake to respect the ECB's independence and not to seek to influence the members of its decision-making bodies in the performance of their tasks (Article 130 TFEU). It is not explained in the judgment why the ECB's interaction with formal EU institutions, such as the Council or the European Parliament, does not affect its independence. If anything, according to the relevant specialist literature, the lack of a counterpart in economic policy at the EU level (often termed as the 'institutional loneliness' of the ECB) is regarded as a danger to the ECB's independence.[127]

The third argument used by the Court was that

[125] ECJ in *Chrysostomides*, para 88; Resolution of the European Council of 13 December 1997 on economic policy coordination in stage 3 of EMU and on Treaty Articles 109 and 109b of the EC Treaty [1998] OJ C35/1.

[126] Anastasia Karatzia and Menelaos Markakis (n 124) 523–24; Menelaos Markakis (n 124) 104–05.

[127] Anastasia Karatzia and Menelaos Markakis (n 124) 524–25; Menelaos Markakis (n 124) 105.

> the Euro Group does not have any competence of its own in the EU legal order, as Article 1 of Protocol No 14 merely states that its meetings are to take place, when necessary, to discuss questions related to the specific responsibilities that the ministers . . . share with regard to the single currency—responsibilities which they owe solely on account of their competence at national level.[128]

However, as explained in more detail elsewhere, it is undeniable that various secondary EU law provisions confer powers on the Eurogroup. This also bears the question of whether secondary EU law may confer powers or tasks to informal, non-EU bodies, especially to the point of involving those bodies in the accountability mechanisms for a formal EU institution (the ECB in banking supervision).[129]

The Court further held that its conclusion regarding the inadmissibility of the actions brought against the Eurogroup was not called into question by the applicants' argument regarding infringement of Article 47 of the EU Charter (Right to an effective remedy and to a fair trial).[130] It ruled that, given that the Eurogroup had no competences of its own in the EU legal order and that it did not have the power to punish a failure to comply with the political agreements concluded within it, those agreements were given concrete expression and were implemented by means, in particular, of acts and action of the EU institutions. Individuals could thus bring before the EU judicature an action to establish the non-contractual liability of the EU against the Council, the Commission, and the ECB in respect of the acts or conduct that those EU institutions adopt following such political agreements.[131] Moreover, the *Ledra* principle applied, meaning that the actions for damages were admissible insofar as they were directed against the Commission and the ECB on account of their alleged unlawful conduct at the time of the negotiation and signing of the MoU with the ESM.[132] In fact, the Court *extended* the *Ledra* principle to the participation of the Commission in the activities of the Eurogroup. More specifically, it held that the Commission retained, in the context of its participation in the activities of the Eurogroup, its role of guardian of the Treaties. It followed that any failure on its part to check that the political agreements concluded within the Eurogroup were in conformity with EU law was liable to

[128] ECJ in *Chrysostomides*, para 89.
[129] Anastasia Karatzia and Menelaos Markakis (n 124) 525–27; Menelaos Markakis (n 124) 105–07.
[130] ECJ in *Chrysostomides*, para 91.
[131] ibid, paras 93–94.
[132] ibid, para 95.

result in non-contractual liability of the EU being invoked under Article 340(2) TFEU.[133] In our view, although this widens the avenues available to litigants in this area, it does not solve all issues regarding legal accountability.[134]

Prior to *Chrysostomides*, the Court (Grand Chamber) decided *Florescu*, which concerned pension entitlements.[135] The impugned provisions of Romanian law, which prohibited combining a retirement pension with a public sector salary, were adopted in order to comply with the MoU that was concluded between the European Community, represented by the Commission, and Romania for the purposes of balance-of-payments assistance.[136] The Court held:

> the Memorandum of Understanding gives concrete form to an agreement between the EU and a Member State on an economic programme, negotiated by those parties, whereby that Member State undertakes to comply with predefined economic objectives in order to be able, subject to fulfilling that agreement, to benefit from financial assistance from the EU. As an act whose legal basis lies in the provisions of EU law . . . and concluded, in particular, by the European Union, represented by the Commission, the Memorandum of Understanding constitutes an act of an EU institution within the meaning of Article 267(b) TFEU.[137]

It was therefore concluded that 'the Memorandum of Understanding must be regarded as an act of an EU institution, within the meaning of Article 267 TFEU, which may be subject to interpretation by the Court'.[138] Following the Court's judgments in *FBF* and *BT*,[139] it is not unreasonable to assume that the provisions of such an MoU may also be declared invalid by the Court following a request for a preliminary ruling, regardless of whether such a MoU produces binding legal effects or not.

[133] ibid, para 96.

[134] For further analysis, see Anastasia Karatzia and Menelaos Markakis (n 124) 531–39; Menelaos Markakis (n 124) 107–10.

[135] Case C-258/14 (Grand Chamber) *Eugenia Florescu and Others v Casa Județeană de Pensii Sibiu and Others* EU:C:2017:448.

[136] See Article 143 TFEU and Council Regulation (EC) 332/2002 of 18 February 2002 establishing a facility providing medium-term financial assistance for Member States' balances of payments [2002] OJ L53/1.

[137] *Florescu*, paras 34–35.

[138] ibid, para 36. See further Menelaos Markakis and Paul Dermine, 'Bailouts, the Legal Status of Memoranda of Understanding, and the Scope of Application of the EU Charter: *Florescu*' (2018) 55 CMLR 643.

[139] Case C-911/19 (Grand Chamber) *Fédération bancaire française (FBF) v Autorité de contrôle prudentiel et de résolution (ACPR)* EU:C:2021:599; Case C-501/18 *BT v Balgarska Narodna Banka* EU:C:2021:249.

Although the impugned MoU did not specifically require the adoption of national legislation such as that at issue in the main proceedings,[140] the Court in *Florescu* held that the purpose of the contested national measure was to implement the undertakings given by Romania in the MoU, which was part of EU law.[141] Although the MoU left Romania some discretion in deciding what measures were most likely to lead to performance of those undertakings, the Court concluded that the impugned measure aimed to implement both the MoU and the Council Decision granting mutual assistance for Romania pursuant to Article 143 TFEU,[142] hence it fell within the scope of the EU Charter of Fundamental Rights.[143] On the facts of the case, the Court found no violation of Article 17(1) of the EU Charter (Right to property).[144]

Last but definitely not least, the Court held in *BPC Lux 2 Sàrl*, which was decided after both *Florescu* and *Chrysostomides*, that the bailout conditions formed part of EU law and that the Member State concerned (Portugal) was implementing Union law within the meaning of Article 51(1) of the EU Charter, at least when financial assistance was granted by the European Financial Stabilisation Mechanism.[145] Following these rulings, it is now only the MoU with the ESM that remains outside the scope of EU law.

4. Third-wave Judgments: the European Banking Union

The third wave or stage of EMU cases concerns the European Banking Union, with plenty of judgments as well as pending cases concerning the Single Supervisory Mechanism (SSM) and the Single Resolution Mechanism (SRM). A detailed exegesis of Banking Union case law merits a chapter (or book) on its own.[146] Suffice it to say for present purposes that these judgments provide

[140] *Florescu*, para 42.

[141] ibid, para 47.

[142] Council Decision 2009/459/EC of 6 May 2009 providing Community medium-term financial assistance for Romania [2009] OJ L150/8.

[143] *Florescu*, para 48.

[144] ibid, paras 49–60.

[145] Case C-83/20 *BPC Lux 2 Sàrl and Others v Banco de Portugal and Others* EU:C:2022:346, paras 28–30. See Council Regulation (EU) 407/2010 of 11 May 2010 establishing a European financial stabilisation mechanism [2010] OJ L118/1, which was adopted on the basis of Article 122(2) TFEU.

[146] See René Smits and Thomaz Braga de Arruda, 'The Banking Union and Union Courts: Overview of Cases as of 30 April 2025' (2025) <https://ebi-europa.eu/publications/eu-cases-or-jurisprudence/> accessed 30 May 2025. See further, among others, Chiara Zilioli and Karl-Philipp Wojcik (eds), *Judicial Review in the European Banking Union* (Elgar Publishing 2021); Laura Wissink, *Effective Legal Protection in Banking Supervision* (Europa Law Publishing 2021); Jouke Tegelaar, *Single Supervision, Single Judicial Protection? Towards Effective Judicial Protection in Single Supervisory Mechanism Composite Procedures* (PhD thesis, Leiden University 2023); Menelaos Markakis, 'Judicial Review of Acts by EU Financial Agencies: European Supervisory Authorities, Single Resolution Board' in

clarity as to which acts are amenable to review before the EU courts, the standard of review employed by the CJEU in the area of the SSM and the SRM, the duty to state reasons, other procedural guarantees, and so on. What is particularly interesting about these judgments, for the purposes of this chapter, is that the CJEU is making a concerted effort to bring together the different strands of its jurisprudence in EMU. No doubt this effort is inspired by Judges, Advocates General, and Référendaires who can stand back from the detail and see the broader picture. These SSM and SRM judgments not only cross-refer to one another but also seek to cross-refer to, or make links with, the earlier EMU judgments (such as *Weiss* or *Ledra Advertising*), where appropriate. We see this for example as regards the standard of review of decisions by the Single Resolution Board (SRB), where the General Court drew a connection with the standard of review for acts by the ECB in the SSM.[147] These findings were confirmed by the Court of Justice in its latest two *Banco Popular* judgments, which were delivered in October 2024.[148] In her Opinion on the two cases, Advocate General Ćapeta had argued that the standard of review established in *ECB v Crédit lyonnais* regarding the SSM should also apply to the SRB and the Commission in the SRM.[149] The Court agreed on this point, referring by analogy to the *ECB v Crédit lyonnais* judgment and the case law cited therein, which included *Weiss*.[150] It is further interesting to note that one of these latest two *Banco Popular* judgments extensively cites *BPC Lux 2 and Others*, as well as *Ledra Advertising*, with regard to the appellants' plea of illegality against the SRM Regulation, alleging a disproportionate interference with the right to property and a lack of adequate compensation for shareholders.[151] Another pertinent example of such cross-references may be drawn from the case law on the judicial review of composite decision-making procedures in the Banking

Annalisa Volpato, Mariolina Eliantonio, Andreas Orator, and Herwig Hofmann (eds), *EU Agencies before the Court of Justice* (Elgar Publishing, forthcoming); Menelaos Markakis, 'Judicial Review of Acts by the Single Resolution Board' in Jonathan Bauerschmidt, Raffaele d'Ambrosio, Diane Fromage, and Andreas Schirk (eds), *AMLA and EU Financial Agencies* (OUP, forthcoming).

[147] Case T-732/19 *PNB Banka and Others v Single Resolution Board* EU:T:2023:721, paras 99–100 (Appeal Case before the Court of Justice C-74/24 P), citing Case C-389/21 P *European Central Bank v Crédit lyonnais* EU:C:2023:368, see esp paras 55–57, which in turn cited *Weiss*.

[148] Case C-541/22 P *Araceli García Fernández and Others v European Commission and Single Resolution Board* EU:C:2024:820; Case C-535/22 P *Aeris Invest Sàrl v European Commission and Single Resolution Board* EU:C:2024:819.

[149] Case C-541/22 P *Araceli García Fernández and Others v European Commission and Single Resolution Board* EU:C:2024:236, Opinion of AG Ćapeta, para 6; Case C-535/22 P *Aeris Invest Sàrl v European Commission and Single Resolution Board* ECLI:EU:C:2024:233, Opinion of AG Ćapeta, para 5.

[150] Case C-541/22 P, para 275. See also Case C-535/22 P, para 266.

[151] See Case C-535/22 P, paras 208ff.

Union, where the Court in *Iccrea Banca*, which concerns composite decision-making procedures in the SRM, drew heavily on *Berlusconi and Fininvest*, which concerns such procedures in the SSM.[152] This is a dynamic area of the CJEU's case law, and future judgments are expected to cast further light on the 'fundamentals' in this area. Much like the case law discussed in the previous waves, SSM/SRM judgments are 'also likely to have ramifications of principled nature in European Union law more generally',[153] for example as regards the annulment of an EU act for misapplying *national* law[154] or other matters of EU constitutional and administrative law.

5. Normative Analysis and Conclusions: *Quo vadis* the ECJ in EMU?

There will be no attempt to summarize the preceding arguments in their entirety. Instead, we will highlight certain features that are of particular importance and draw broader conclusions on the choice and application of interpretative methods by the CJEU in this area.

It was argued above that it is possible to distinguish three main stages or categories of cases in EMU since the onset of the euro crisis. The foundational judgments that preceded the euro crisis (*OLAF case*, *Commission v Council*) laid the foreground for the euro-crisis judgments. The first wave of judgments (*Pringle*, *Mallis*, *Ledra Advertising*, *Gauweiler*, and *Weiss*) shed light on

[152] Case C-414/18 *Iccrea Banca SpA Istituto Centrale del Credito Cooperativo v Banca d'Italia* EU:C:2019:1036; Case C-219/17 *Silvio Berlusconi and Finanziaria d'investimento Fininvest SpA (Fininvest) v Banca d'Italia and Istituto per la Vigilanza Sulle Assicurazioni (IVASS)* EU:C:2018:1023. See further Menelaos Markakis, 'Composite Procedures and Judicial Review in the Single Resolution Mechanism: *Iccrea Banca*' (2020) 13 Review of European Administrative Law 109. See generally Filipe Brito Bastos, *Judging Composite Decision-Making: The Transformation of European Administrative Law* (Hart Publishing 2024).

[153] Daniel Sarmiento and Moritz Hartmann (n 1) 564.

[154] Case T-502/19 *Francesca Corneli v European Central* Bank EU:T:2022:627; Joined Cases C-777/22 P and C-789/22 P *European Central Bank and European Commission v Francesca Corneli* EU:C:2025:580. See further Daniel Sarmiento, 'Setting the Limits of Implementation of National Law by EU Institutions: The *Corneli v ECB* Case (T-502/19)' (EU Law Live, 24 October 2022) <https://eulawlive.com/op-ed-setting-the-limits-of-implementation-of-national-law-by-eu-institutions-the-corneli-v-ecb-case-t-502-19-by-daniel-sarmiento/> accessed 7 January 2026; Menelaos Markakis, 'The General Court Annuls an ECB Decision for Misapplying National Law: Case T-502/19 *Francesca Corneli v ECB*' (REALaw Blog, 8 November 2022) <https://realaw.blog/2022/11/08/the-general-court-annuls-an-ecb-decision-for-misapplying-national-law-case-t-502-19-francesca-corneli-v-ecb-by-m-markakis/> accessed 5 March 2025; Filippo Annunziata and Thomaz Braga de Arruda, 'The *Corneli* Case and the Application of National Law by the European Central Bank: Developments on Article 4(3) SSMR in Case T-502/19 (*Francesca Corneli v ECB*)' in Filippo Annunziata and Michele Siri (eds), *EU Banking and Capital Markets Regulation: Open Issues of Vertical Interplay with National Law* (Springer 2025) 139–66.

the constitutional fundamentals in this area, notably in terms of the division between economic and monetary policy, the meaning to be accorded to key Treaty provisions such as the no-bailout clause (Article 125 TFEU) and the prohibition of monetary financing (Article 123 TFEU), and the judicial avenues available to litigants in this area. The second wave of, in some cases lesser known but also fundamental, cases (*Chrysostomides, Florescu, BPC Lux 2 Sàrl*) plugged important gaps in the earlier judgments and elaborated on the constitutional fundamentals of EMU, *in casu* with respect to bailout programmes. Those rulings also widened, in some cases, the avenues for judicial protection available to litigants, although the earlier judgments continue to cast a long shadow over the EU's system of remedies and procedures in this area. In this connection, it is rightly argued by Hinarejos with regards to these (first- and second-wave) landmark ECJ rulings that:

> It is . . . quite clear that there is a common thread running through all these various challenges, namely an underlying broader concern regarding the consequences of the post-crisis reforms for democratic legitimacy and accountability, as well as for the constitutional structure of EMU and for the future of the EU and its Member States, in general.[155]

The third wave of EMU cases concerns, as we have seen, the Banking Union. It was noted above that these judgments not only refer to one another but also seek to draw links with earlier EMU judgments, where appropriate. As such, they are indicative of the CJEU's efforts to bring together the various strands of its jurisprudence in this area. They continue to raise important issues, not only with regard to EU financial law but also with respect to EU constitutional and administrative law more broadly. A fourth, future wave of cases could comprise climate cases brought against the EU institutions for their actions in the EMU, so as to force them to stick to their legal commitments with respect to climate change and the protection of the environment.[156] Private persons or other EU authorities could have recourse to litigation to make sure that EU institutions (eg the ECB), or national authorities that form part of networks or systems (eg a national central bank forming part of the ESCB and the Eurosystem), go far enough in meeting their objectives and legal obligations.[157] This would

[155] Alicia Hinarejos, 'The Legality of Responses to the Crisis' (n 1) 1398.

[156] See also the expert analysis by Sacha Garben, 'The CJEU and Climate (In)activism?' in Mark Dawson, Bruno de Witte, and Elise Muir (eds), *Revisiting Judicial Politics in the European Union* (Elgar Publishing 2024) ch 12.

[157] See 'ClientEarth v Belgian National Bank' <https://climatecasechart.com/non-us-case/clientearth-v-belgian-national-bank/> accessed 12 April 2024.

also be in line with the recent developments in the case law of the European Court of Human Rights (notably, the *KlimaSeniorinnen* and *Greenpeace Nordic* cases),[158] as well as in the national legal systems concerning the obligations of the government or private entities.[159] It can be reasonably foreseen that such judgments would also draw on the *dicta* in cases such as *Gauweiler* and *Weiss*, as well as, perhaps, on other landmark EMU rulings.[160] It can also be reasonably foreseen that private litigants may soon be challenging before the EU courts acts adopted by the EU institutions effectively penalizing them for not meeting their climate-related obligations.[161] Whatever a future wave of EMU cases may hold, there is little doubt that '[n]ew challenges will no doubt continue to be brought every time the boundaries of integration are pushed forward in this area',[162] whether because it is believed that the relevant authorities are *going too far* in the pursuit of their objectives, or because they are *not going far enough* in the desired direction of travel.

The choice of interpretative methods (literal, systematic, historical, teleological) in the judgments examined above depends on the particular circumstances of each case. The following, enduring observation by Bengoetxea also applies with respect to the CJEU's reasoning in EMU cases:

[158] *Verein KlimaSeniorinnen Schweiz and Others v Switzerland* App no 53600/20 (ECtHR, 9 April 2024); *Greenpeace Nordic and Others v Norway* App no 34068/21 (ECtHR, 28 October 2025). See also Registry of the European Court of Human Rights and European Union Agency for Fundamental Rights, 'Joint Factsheet: Climate Change ECtHR and CJEU Case-Law' (15 December 2025) <https://fra.europa.eu/sites/default/files/fra_uploads/ecthr-fra-2025-climate-change_en.pdf> accessed 7 January 2026. For further analysis, see Stefan Theil, *Towards the Environmental Minimum: Environmental Protection through Human Rights* (CUP 2021).

[159] See, among many others, Esther Engelhard, Tomas Arons, Stijn van Deursen, Elbert de Jong, Anneloes Kuiper-Slendebroek and Daan van Maurik, '*Urgenda, Milieudefensie/Shell and beyond*: Over de invloed van klimaatzaken' [2024] Nederlands Tijdschrift voor Burgerlijk Recht 28. English-speaking readers may also consult Elbert de Jong (ed), *Corporate Accountability and Liability for Climate Change* (Elgar Publishing 2024). On the latest developments in Swedish law, see Linnéa Nordlander, 'Sweden's First Systemic Climate Mitigation Case and the Application of KlimaSeniorinnen: Unpacking the Supreme Court's Judgment in the Aurora Case' (Sabin Center for Climate Change Law Blog, 24 April 2025) <https://blogs.law.columbia.edu/climatechange/2025/04/24/swedens-first-systemic-climate-mitigation-case-and-the-application-of-klimaseniorinnen-unpacking-the-supreme-courts-judgment-in-the-aurora-case/> accessed 28 June 2025; Alexander Hardenberger, Xavier Groussot and Sanja Bogojević, 'Auroramålet och vikten av att ta processuella rättigheter på allvar' (2025) Svensk Juristtidning <https://svjt.se/preprint/auroramalet-och-vikten-av-att-ta-processuella-rattigheter-pa-allvar> accessed 28 June 2025 (an English version will soon follow). See generally Margaretha Wewerinke-Singh and Sarah Mead (eds), assisted by Joe Udell, *The Cambridge Handbook of Climate Litigation* (CUP 2025).

[160] See, eg, the argument by Menelaos Markakis and Diane Fromage, 'The Accountability of the European Central Bank: New Frontiers, New Challenges' (2023) 30 MJ 359, 365.

[161] See René Smits and Thomaz Braga de Arruda (n 146) 3 with respect to periodic penalty payments by the ECB should the banks concerned fail to comply with prudential requirements regarding climate change and nature-related risks.

[162] Alicia Hinarejos, 'The Legality of Responses to the Crisis' (n 1) 1399.

> Justificatory arguments do not appear in isolation; they mutually support each other, and the final, law-applying or law-interpreting decision is justified not by this or that particular argument or reason to be found in the judgment, but rather by the cumulative weight of all the arguments brought together in the Court's opinion as a coherent, mutually supporting structure. There will be (i) arguments drawn from the 'clear' text of legal provisions drawn from certain ought-, should-, or may-sources, (ii) arguments drawn from the semiotic, systemic and dynamic interpretation of the 'problematized' text of provisions drawn from legal ought-, should-, or may-sources, and (iii) arguments drawn from other elements which can be grouped under the heading 'substantive reasonings', e.g. common sense or reasonableness, common knowledge, and general economic, social, or political topoi.[163]

The current author does not take issue so much with that choice of methods in the judgments discussed above so much as with *the way these methods have been applied*, such as in cases such as *Chrysostomides* (by both the Advocate General and the Court of Justice), for the detailed reasons mentioned above. Moreover, the Court has often had recourse to the underlying purpose or objective of the relevant provisions in the Treaties, in order to interpret them or to determine their scope. Textual argumentation as to the scope of particular Treaty provisions which are drafted in vague terms is shaped by background teleological assumptions or objectives. The latter can be either apparent on the face of the judgment or implicit in the Court's reasoning.[164] What often tends to be implicit in the CJEU judgments or Advocate General opinions is the consequences that a ruling to the contrary would entail for the impugned acts or programmes or even for the EU or Eurozone as a whole.[165] Furthermore, these premises or objectives can be contested, and so can the conclusions drawn from them. Another feature of the ECJ's reasoning in EMU case law is that, as the Court incrementally lays down or sheds light on the foundations for this area, it relies heavily on *dicta* in earlier judgments, no matter how thinly or strongly reasoned these were and no matter how few judgments (in some cases, just one) can be lent from its earlier case law to support these findings.

Revisiting those seminal judgments after a little while almost invariably provides the reader with new insights into those rulings. Tridimas observes: 'The study of the case law reveals a dialectic interaction where the judiciary both

[163] Joxerramon Bengoetxea (n 10) 262.
[164] See also Paul Craig, '*Pringle*: Legal Reasoning, Text, Purpose and Teleology' (2013) 20 MJ 3, 9.
[165] See, however, Case C-370/12 (Full Court) *Thomas Pringle v Government of Ireland and Others*, Opinion of AG Kokott EU:C:2012:675, paras 139–40.

generates, and reacts to, constitutional reform.'[166] In the current author's view, there are aspects of these foundational judgments that have aged well; others perhaps not quite. The latter is particularly the case, in the current author's opinion, with respect to the Cypriot cases (*Mallis*, *Ledra Advertising*, *Chrysostomides*), which were analysed in more detail above. This does not of course mean that other EMU judgments, or parts thereof, have not attracted critical commentary. Notably, it is said that the distinction between economic and monetary policy, which was the focal point in *Gauweiler* and *Weiss*, is built on quicksand. However, it may be more appropriate to lay the blame at the feet of the Treaty authors instead.[167]

Overall, in the present author's opinion, the CJEU is making a concerted effort to bring together the different strands of its jurisprudence in EMU, as well as to plug gaps in judicial protection. However, the Cypriot cases remain an outlier and they certainly stand on an isle in this respect. Short of Treaty revision, it is hard to see how the Court could change course in this respect.[168] It should be further noted that, with the exception of certain types of Banking Union cases (eg concerning ECB acts successfully challenged in the SSM or the SRM case law regarding the calculation of *ex ante* contributions by entities to the Single Resolution Fund),[169] it remains very difficult for litigants to win in this area. In this connection, it is rightly observed by Sarmiento and Hartmann that '[t]he technical and political contours of EMU cannot act as a shield that safeguards this area of policy from judicial review'.[170] What is more, we should not be too quick, in the current author's view, to conclude that there is now a 'complete system of legal remedies and procedures' in the area of EMU.[171] Much as the EMU itself remains imperfect or incomplete, so does judicial protection in this area.

[166] Takis Tridimas (n 1) 293.

[167] Fabian Amtenbrink, 'The European Central Bank's Intricate Independence versus Accountability Conundrum in the Post-Crisis Governance Framework' (2019) 26 MJ 165, 168; Fabian Amtenbrink and René Repasi, 'The German Federal Constitutional Court's Decision in Weiss: A Contextual Analysis' (2020) 45 ELRev 757, 760ff. See also Alicia Hinarejos, 'The Legality of Responses to the Crisis' (n 1) 1375.

[168] See also Menelaos Markakis (n 124) 112–13.

[169] See in more detail Menelaos Markakis, 'Judicial Review of Acts by the Single Resolution Board' (n 146).

[170] Daniel Sarmiento and Moritz Hartmann (n 1) 527.

[171] See also Menelaos Markakis (n 1) 242.

References

Amtenbrink F, 'The European Central Bank's Intricate Independence versus Accountability Conundrum in the Post-Crisis Governance Framework' (2019) 26 MJ 165

Amtenbrink F, 'Covid-19 and Fiscal Union' in Federico Fabbrini and Christy Ann Petit (eds), *Research Handbook on Post-Pandemic EU Economic Governance and NGEU Law* (Elgar Publishing 2024)

Amtenbrink F and Markakis M, 'Never Waste a Good Crisis: On the Emergence of an EU Fiscal Capacity' in Alicia Hinarejos and Robert Schütze (eds), *EU Fiscal Federalism: Past, Present, Future* (OUP 2023)

Amtenbrink F and Repasi R, 'The German Federal Constitutional Court's Decision in Weiss: A Contextual Analysis' (2020) 45 ELRev 757

Annunziata F and Braga de Arruda T, 'The *Corneli* Case and the Application of National Law by the European Central Bank: Developments on Article 4(3) SSMR in Case T-502/19 (*Francesca Corneli v ECB*)' in Filippo Annunziata and Michele Siri (eds), *EU Banking and Capital Markets Regulation: Open Issues of Vertical Interplay with National Law* (Springer 2025)

Bengoetxea J, *The Legal Reasoning of the European Court of Justice: Towards a European Jurisprudence* (OUP 1993)

Bobić A, *The Jurisprudence of Constitutional Conflict in the European Union* (OUP 2022)

Bobić A, *The Individual in the Economic and Monetary Union: A Study of Legal Accountability* (CUP 2024)

Brito Bastos F, *Judging Composite Decision-Making: The Transformation of European Administrative Law* (Hart Publishing 2024)

Chamon M, 'The Non-Emergency Economic Policy Competence in Article 122(1) TFEU' (2024) 61 CMLR 1501

Craig P, '*Pringle* and Use of EU Institutions Outside the EU Legal Framework: Foundations, Procedure and Substance' (2013) 9 EuConst 263

Craig P, '*Pringle*: Legal Reasoning, Text, Purpose and Teleology' (2013) 20 MJ 3

Craig P, 'The Eurogroup, Power and Accountability' (2017) 23 ELJ 234

Craig P and Markakis M, '*Gauweiler* and the Legality of Outright Monetary Transactions' (2016) 41 ELRev 4

Dawson M, 'Revisiting Europe's "Law-Politics Imbalance"' in Mark Dawson, Bruno de Witte, and Elise Muir (eds), *Revisiting Judicial Politics in the European Union* (Elgar Publishing 2024)

De Boer N, *Judging European Democracy: The Role and Legitimacy of National Constitutional Courts in the EU* (OUP 2023)

De Jong E (ed), *Corporate Accountability and Liability for Climate Change* (Elgar Publishing 2024)

Dermine P and Markakis M, 'EU Economic Governance and the COVID-19 Crisis: Between Path-Dependency and Paradigmatic Shift' (2020) 6 International Journal of Public Law and Policy 326

Dermine P and Markakis M, 'Hybrid Governance Structures and Monetary Policy: The Legal and Institutional Position of National Central Banks in the Eurosystem' (2025) 13 Politics and Governance, Article 8943

Engelhard E, Arons T, Van Deursen S, De Jong E, Kuiper-Slendebroek A, and Van Maurik D, '*Urgenda, Milieudefensie/Shell and beyond*: Over de invloed van klimaatzaken' [2024] Nederlands Tijdschrift voor Burgerlijk Recht 28

Fabbrini F, *Economic Governance in Europe: Comparative Paradoxes and Constitutional Challenges* (OUP 2015)

Garben S, 'The CJEU and Climate (In)activism?' in Mark Dawson, Bruno de Witte, and Elise Muir (eds), *Revisiting Judicial Politics in the European Union* (Elgar Publishing 2024)

Hardenberger A, Groussot X, and Bogojević S, 'Auroramålet och vikten av att ta processuella rättigheter på allvar' (2025) Svensk Juristtidning <https://svjt.se/preprint/auroramalet-och-vikten-av-att-ta-processuella-rattigheter-pa-allvar> accessed 28 June 2025

Hinarejos A, 'The Legality of Responses to the Crisis' in Fabian Amtenbrink and Christoph Herrmann (eds), assisted by René Repasi, *The EU Law of Economic and Monetary Union* (OUP 2020)

Hinarejos A, *The Euro Area Crisis in Constitutional Perspective* (OUP 2015)

Karatzia A and Markakis M, 'Financial Assistance Conditionality and Effective Judicial Protection: *Chrysostomides*' (2022) 59 CMLR 501

Markakis M, *Accountability in the Economic and Monetary Union: Foundations, Policy, and Governance* (OUP 2020)

Markakis M, 'Composite Procedures and Judicial Review in the Single Resolution Mechanism: *Iccrea Banca*' (2020) 13 Review of European Administrative Law 109

Markakis M, 'The General Court Annuls an ECB Decision for Misapplying National Law: Case T-502/19 *Francesca Corneli v ECB*' (REALaw Blog, 8 November 2022) <https://realaw.blog/2022/11/08/the-general-court-annuls-an-ecb-decision-for-misapplying-national-law-case-t-502-19-francesca-corneli-v-ecb-by-m-markakis/> accessed 5 March 2025

Markakis M, 'The Non-Contractual Liability of the EU for Actions of the Eurogroup: Cases C-597/18 P, C-598/18 P, C-603/18 P and C-604/18 P *Chrysostomides*' in Daniel Sarmiento, Hélène Ruiz Fabri, and Burkhard Hess (eds), *Yearbook on Procedural Law of the Court of Justice of the European Union—2021* (3rd edn, 2022) Max Planck Institute Luxembourg Research Paper 5/2022

Markakis M, 'Judicial Review of Acts by EU Financial Agencies: European Supervisory Authorities, Single Resolution Board' in Annalisa Volpato, Mariolina Eliantonio, Andreas Orator, and Herwig Hofmann (eds), *EU Agencies before the Court of Justice* (Elgar Publishing, forthcoming)

Markakis M, 'Judicial Review of Acts by the Single Resolution Board' in Jonathan Bauerschmidt, Raffaele d'Ambrosio, Diane Fromage, and Andreas Schirk (eds), *AMLA and EU Financial Agencies* (OUP, forthcoming)

Markakis M and Dermine P, 'Bailouts, the Legal Status of Memoranda of Understanding, and the Scope of Application of the EU Charter: *Florescu*' (2018) 55 CMLR 643

Markakis M and Fromage D, 'The Accountability of the European Central Bank: New Frontiers, New Challenges' (2023) 30 MJ 359

Nordlander L, 'Sweden's First Systemic Climate Mitigation Case and the Application of KlimaSeniorinnen: Unpacking the Supreme Court's Judgment in the Aurora Case', Sabin Center for Climate Change Law Blog, 24 April 2025, <https://blogs.law.columbia.edu/climatechange/2025/04/24/swedens-first-systemic-climate-mitigation-case-and-the-application-of-klimaseniorinnen-unpacking-the-supreme-courts-judgment-in-the-aurora-case/> accessed 28 June 2025

Panascì MA, 'Unravelling Next Generation EU as a Transformative Moment: From Market Integration to Redistribution' (2024) 61 CMLR 13

Registry of the European Court of Human Rights and European Union Agency for Fundamental Rights, 'Joint Factsheet: Climate Change ECtHR and CJEU Case-Law' (15 December 2025) <https://fra.europa.eu/sites/default/files/fra_uploads/ecthr-fra-2025-climate-change_en.pdf> accessed 7 January 2026

Sarmiento D, 'Setting the Limits of Implementation of National Law by EU Institutions: The *Corneli v ECB* Case (T-502/19)' (EU Law Live, 24 October 2022) <https://eulawlive.com/op-ed-setting-the-limits-of-implementation-of-national-law-by-eu-institutions-the-corneli-v-ecb-case-t-502-19-by-daniel-sarmiento/> accessed 7 January 2026

Sarmiento D and Hartmann M, 'European Monetary Union and the Courts' in Fabian Amtenbrink and Christoph Herrmann (eds), assisted by René Repasi, *The EU Law of Economic and Monetary Union* (OUP 2020)

Smits R and Braga de Arruda T, 'The Banking Union and Union Courts: Overview of Cases as of 30 April 2025' (2025) <https://ebi-europa.eu/publications/eu-cases-or-jurisprudence/> accessed 30 May 2025

Tegelaar J, *Single Supervision, Single Judicial Protection? Towards Effective Judicial Protection in Single Supervisory Mechanism Composite Procedures* (PhD thesis, Leiden University 2023)

Theil S, *Towards the Environmental Minimum: Environmental Protection through Human Rights* (CUP 2021)

Tridimas T, 'The ECB and the Court of Justice: Old Toolbox, New Problems' in Thomas Beukers, Diane Fromage, and Giorgio Monti (eds), *The New European Central Bank: Taking Stock and Looking Ahead* (OUP 2022)

Tuori K and Tuori K, *The Eurozone Crisis: A Constitutional Analysis* (CUP 2014)

Wewerinke-Singh M and Mead S (eds), assisted by Udell J, *The Cambridge Handbook of Climate Litigation* (CUP 2025)

Wissink L, *Effective Legal Protection in Banking Supervision* (Europa Law Publishing 2021)

Zilioli C and Wojcik KP (eds), *Judicial Review in the European Banking Union* (Elgar Publishing 2021)

PART IV

PROCEDURAL FAIRNESS AND INTERNAL PROCESSES

12

How Does the Court of Justice Deal with its Previous Case Law in the Field of Union Citizenship? Assessing and Refining Methods of Communicative Reasoning

Niamh Nic Shuibhne

1. Introduction

In the case law-rich field of European Union citizenship, the decisions of the Court of Justice are subject to extensive commentary from a range of perspectives. Complementing work that considers the normative and substantive dimensions of this significant body of case law, this contribution considers the Court's reasoning in methodological terms—specifically, as regards how the Court communicates about its own previous case law in later judgments.

Two questions are therefore addressed in this chapter. First, in EU citizenship law, what *are* the methods that the Court applies when it refers to its own previous case law? This question is introduced in Section 2, which presents the main referencing techniques applied by the Court and organizes them into categories described here as *direct* and *indicative* in terms of their communicative reasoning. In Section 3, further investigation of two common indicative formulations—'see, by analogy' and 'see, to this effect'—is undertaken, with the aim of understanding better what these words actually signify. As will be seen, that picture is messy.

Second, in legal reasoning terms, are these the methods that the Court *should* apply? Consideration of this question, in Section 4 of the chapter, draws out themes relating to the *sincerity* of the referencing formulations used in the Court's case law and the significance of *silence*, that is, when relevant though

Niamh Nic Shuibhne, *How Does the Court of Justice Deal with its Previous Case Law in the Field of Union Citizenship? Assessing and Refining Methods of Communicative Reasoning* In: *The Reasoning of the Court of Justice of the EU*. Edited by: Alezini Loxa and Luigi Lonardo, Oxford University Press.
 DOI: 10.1093/9780198983002.003.0016

perhaps inconvenient previous case law is not referred to in subsequent judgments at all.

Overall, the chapter shows that the Court does indeed tend to follow its own previous case law in the field of Union citizenship. However, the analysis does expose certain problems. The Court does not often conceal evolutions of the legal story of Union citizenship. Best practice wanes, though, when relevant previous case law is significantly advanced without clear communicative reasoning: in particular, when it is not engaged with—and in some instances, not even mentioned—in later decisions at all. Even though case law exhibiting these communicative reasoning weaknesses represents a small proportion of citizenship case law in quantitative terms, it produces considerably higher critical volume as regards the Court's methods of legal reasoning. The risk in such circumstances is that judicial intention cannot be understood without clearly communicated reasoning. Thus, even if arbitrary decision-making was never the intention, it can be difficult to refute arguments in that line in situations of judicial silence. The chapter makes a wider plea too about the vital importance of process since the authority of law itself is now increasingly challenged.

2. EU Citizenship Case Law: How Does the Court Reference Previous Case Law?

It is hardly controversial to assert that the reasoning of the Court of Justice can be difficult to understand or that certain pockets of its case law on Union citizenship demonstrate that claim. An example is provided by how different objectives expressed in the preamble to Directive 2004/38[1] are drawn from to support very different outcomes from the perspective of the citizen concerned. In case law that *advances* the rights of the citizen, the Court tends to refer mainly to recital 3.[2] It drew from that text in *Metock*, for example, to proclaim that the Directive 'aims *in particular to "strengthen* the right of free movement and residence of all Union citizens"'.[3] This elevation of the strengthening aim is not indicated by the wording of the recital itself and it does not take account

[1] Directive 2004/38/EC on the right of citizens of the Union and their family members to move and reside freely within the territory of the Member States, 2004 OJ L158/77.

[2] ie 'Union citizenship should be the fundamental status of nationals of the Member States when they exercise their right of free movement and residence. It is therefore necessary to codify and review the existing Community instruments dealing separately with workers, self-employed persons, as well as students and other inactive persons in order to simplify and strengthen the right of free movement and residence of all Union citizens.'

[3] E.g. Case C-127/08 *Metock and Others*, EU:C:2008:449, para 59 (emphasis added).

of other aims expressed elsewhere in the preamble (returned to below). Nevertheless, it was repeated frequently in subsequent, rights-enhancing case law.[4] It is then reasonable to argue that it might be relied upon, that it acquired precedential authority.

In contrast, however, in *McCarthy*, the Court first recalled the *Metock* statement but continued: 'whilst it is true that . . . Directive 2004/38 aims to facilitate and strengthen the exercise of the primary and individual right to move and reside freely within the territory of the Member States that is conferred directly on each citizen of the Union, the fact remains that *the subject of the directive concerns*, as is apparent from Article 1(a), *the conditions governing the exercise of that right*'.[5] Thus, even though *Metock* was referred to, the *particular* emphasis in that ruling on 'strengthening' rights was quietly set aside and a decision *curbing* the rights of the citizen was reached. The *McCarthy* version was restated in later cases too.[6]

In each of these lines of citizenship case law, the Court frames the purpose of the Directive very differently. It seems to do this to set up the outcome that reveals itself later in the judgment in question—to cushion it with legislative language. It is fair to say that the Directive itself enables different outcomes since it does articulate differing objectives in its preamble and across its provisions. Nevertheless, the fact that the Court altered the direction of its own reasoning between the two sets of cases above cannot be overlooked. And how it references its own previous case law to do so is, at best, selective: the system builds two stories, using case law building blocks in each line but failing to intersect them.[7] This is the kind of methodological concern that prompts us to look in more detail at how the Court refers to its own previous case law—and, crucially, from the perspective of communicative reasoning as much as normative and substantive outcomes. If we do take that perspective, we can see that both *direct* and *indicative* language is used. However, we also find instances of

[4] Case C-710/19 *GMA (Demandeur d'emploi)*, EU:C:2020:1037, para 41; Case C-93/18 *Bajratari*, EU:C:2019:809, para 47; Case C-202/13 *McCarthy II*, EU:C:2014:2450, para 28.

[5] Case C-434/09 *McCarthy*, EU:C:2011:277, para 33 (emphasis added); having cited (para 59 of) *Metock* (n 3) in para 31.

[6] E.g. Case C-456/12 *O and B*, EU:C:2014:135, paras 35 (the *Metock* statement) and 41 (the *McCarthy* qualifier); and Case C-233/14 *Commission v Netherlands*, EU:C:2016:396, para 81, mentioning only *McCarthy*. The reverse can be found in Case C-140/12 *Brey*, EU:C:2013:237 ie the Court first cites the more limiting idea (para 53) but then refers to the Directive's 'strengthening' aim later in its judgment (para 71).

[7] Urska Šadl has worked extensively on these questions, often using quantitative research methods, both generally and for EU citizenship law specifically; see eg Urska Šadl and Ioannis Panagis, 'The Force of EU Case Law: An Empirical Study of Precedential Constraint', iCourts Working Paper Series, No. 68, 2016, available at https://papers.ssrn.com/sol3/papers.cfm?abstract_id=2787119.

silence, that is, where relevant previous case law is basically ignored in the text of a later judgment. Examples of each of these findings will now be outlined.

First, *direct language* means that the Court refers to relevant previous case law and then either (a) *straightforwardly follows* the previous case(s); or (b) *develops* a finding from the previous case(s) in a reasonably expected or reasonably logical way; or (c) *expressly distinguishes* the case at hand from the previous case(s) cited.

An example of (a)—straightforwardly following previous case law—is provided by one of the fundamental building blocks of EU citizenship law. In paragraph 63 of *Martínez Sala*, the Court held that 'a citizen of the European Union [...]... lawfully resident in the territory of the host Member State, can rely on Article [18 TFEU] in all situations which fall within the scope *ratione materiae* of [Union] law'.[8] In paragraph 32 of *Grzelczyk*, a ruling delivered three years later, it was affirmed that '[a]s the Court held in paragraph 63 of its judgment in *Martínez Sala*, [...]... a citizen of the European Union, lawfully resident in the territory of a host Member State, can rely on Article 6 [TFEU] in all situations which fall within the scope *ratione materiae* of [Union] law'.[9]

Grzelczyk also provides an example of (b)—developing findings but in reasonably expected or reasonably logical ways—because the Court progressed its findings in *Martínez Sala* to make it clear *also* (in paragraph 33 of *Grzelczyk*) that '[t]hose situations include those involving the exercise of the fundamental freedoms guaranteed by the Treaty *and those involving the exercise of the right to move and reside freely in another Member State, as conferred by [21 TFEU]*' (emphasis added). Not only does that statement represent an expected and logical expansion of *Martínez Sala* in an objective sense, but it was underpinned by a reference to paragraphs 15 and 16 of *Bickel and Franz*, where the Court had stated that 'pursuant to Article [21 TFEU], "[e]very citizen of the Union shall have the right to move and reside freely within the territory of the Member States, subject to the limitations and conditions laid down in this Treaty and by the measures adopted to give it effect'".[10]

Finally, for (c)—where previous case law is expressly distinguished—the example here concerns the Court's assertion that Union citizenship expanded not only the personal but also the material scope of EU law. In paragraph 63 of *Collins*, it held that '[i]n view of the establishment of citizenship of the Union and the interpretation in the case-law of the right to equal treatment enjoyed

[8] Case C-85/96 *Martínez Sala*, EU:C:1998:217.
[9] Case C-184/99 *Grzelczyk*, EU:C:2001:458.
[10] Case C-274/96 *Bickel and Franz*, EU:C:1988:563.

by citizens of the Union, it is no longer possible to exclude from the scope of Article 45(2) TFEU—which expresses the fundamental principle of equal treatment, guaranteed by Article [18 TFEU]—a benefit of a financial nature intended to facilitate access to employment in the labour market of a Member State'.[11] It therefore found, in paragraph 64, that '[t]he interpretation of the scope of the principle of equal treatment in relation to access to employment must reflect this development, as compared with the interpretation followed in [previous case law]'.[12]

Similarly, in *Bidar*, the Court used the same reasoning to bring student maintenance grants within the scope of EU law for the first time, departing from its pre-citizenship approach. The Court acknowledged the previous rulings,[13] then highlighted the legal impact of introducing Union citizenship to the Treaties (as well as the expansion of Treaty provisions on education and vocational training),[14] and therefore concluded that '[i]n view of those developments since the judgments in *Lair* and *Brown*, it must be considered that the situation of a citizen of the Union who is lawfully resident in another Member State falls within the scope of application of the Treaty within the meaning of the first paragraph of Article [18 TFEU] for the purposes of obtaining assistance for students, whether in the form of a subsidised loan or a grant, intended to cover his maintenance costs'.[15]

[11] Case C-138/02 *Collins*, EU:C:2004:172.

[12] Case 316/85 *Lebon*, EU:C:1987:302 (para 26 of which ruled out equal treatment for jobseekers as regards entitlement to social and tax advantages in the host State); Case C-278/94 *Commission v Belgium*, EU:C:1996:321 (para 40 of which excluded entitlement to equal treatment as regards access to certain employment programmes for those 'seeking their first employment' in the host State).

[13] Case C-209/03 *Bidar*, EU:C:2005:169, para 38: 'It is true that the Court held in *Lair* and *Brown* (paragraphs 15 and 18 respectively) that "at the present stage of development of Community law assistance given to students for maintenance and for training falls in principle outside the scope of the EEC Treaty for the purposes of Article [18 TFEU]". In those judgments the Court considered that such assistance was, on the one hand, a matter of education policy, which was not as such included in the spheres entrusted to the Community institutions, and, on the other, a matter of social policy, which fell within the competence of the Member States in so far as it was not covered by specific provisions of the EEC Treaty' (Case 39/86 *Lair*, EU:C:1988:322; Case 197/86 *Brown*, EU:C:198:323).

[14] *Bidar* (n 13), para 39: '[h]owever, since judgment was given in *Lair* and *Brown*, the Treaty on European Union has introduced citizenship of the Union into the EC Treaty and added [a Chapter] devoted inter alia to education and vocational training.'

[15] *Bidar* (n 13), para 42. Directive 2004/38 was adopted but not yet in force at the material time having regard to the facts of the case: thus, in paragraph 43, the Court glossed over the exclusion from equal treatment in Article 24(2) of the Directive for a claimant in Mr Bidar's circumstances ('[t]hat development of Community law is confirmed by Article 24 of Directive 2004/38, which states in paragraph 1 that all Union citizens residing in the territory of another Member State on the basis of that directive are to enjoy equal treatment "within the scope of the Treaty". In that the Community legislature, in paragraph 2 of that article, defined the content of paragraph 1 in more detail, by providing that a Member State may in the case of persons other than workers, self-employed persons, persons who retain such status and members of their families restrict the grant of maintenance aid in the form of grants or loans in respect of students who have not acquired a right of permanent residence, it took the view that the grant of such aid is a matter which, in accordance with Article 24(1), now falls within the scope of the Treaty').

Next, with respect to *silence*, there are well-discussed instances where findings in relevant previous case law were departed from yet not mentioned at all. Examples include case law shifts on the relevance of the Charter of Fundamental Rights, both when national authorities must decide whether a residence right based on Article 20 TEU should be extended to a family member on whom a Union citizen is dependent in the latter's home State[16] and when the right to move and reside conferred by Article 21 TFEU has been exercised but the Union citizen's residence in the host State does not come within the scope of Directive 2004/38.[17] Another example relates to the significance of lawful residence in the host State when it is granted as a matter of national rather than EU law.[18] In the (widely discussed) case law on whether or not a proportionality assessment still requires an examination of each Union citizen's individual circumstances when the EU legislative conditions for lawful residence in a host State are not met, the Court did *mention* its own previous case law in partially departing from it,[19] though only after some interim glossing over of the fundamental question at issue.[20]

[16] Compare Case C-256/11 *Dereci and Others*, EU:C:2011:734, paras 70–73, Case C-40/11 *Iida*, EU:C:2012:691, paras 78–81, and Case C-87/12 *Ymeraga*, EU:C:2013:291, paras 40–43, on the one hand, with Case C-165/14 *Rendón Marín*, EU:C:2016:675, para 81 and Case C-133/15 *Chavez-Vilchez*, EU:C:2017:354, para 70, on the other. The necessary discussion around this case law shift can be found instead in the Opinions of Advocates General: see AG Sharpston in Case C-34/09 *Ruiz Zambrano*, EU:C:2010:560 at point 62 of the Opinion and in Case C-456/12 *O and B* and Case C-457/12 *S and G*, EU:C:2013:837, points 62–63 of the Opinion; AG Wathelet in Case C-115/15 *NA*, EU:C:2016:259, point 125 of the Opinion; and AG Szpunar in Case C-165/14 *Rendón Marín* and Case C-304/14 *CS*, EU:C:2016:75, points 119–22 of the Joint Opinion, and in Case C-133/15 *Chavez-Vilchez*, EU:C:2016:659, points 95–96 of the Opinion. See generally, Hanneke van Eijken and Pauline Phoa, 'The Scope of Article 20 TFEU Clarified in *Chavez-Vilchez*: Are the Fundamental Rights of Minor EU Citizens Coming of Age? (Case Comment)' (2018) 43 EL Rev 949.

[17] Compare Case C-333/13 *Dano*, EU:C:2014:2358, paras 85–92, on the one hand (discussed by Michael Dougan, 'Judicial Review of Member State Action under the General Principles and the Charter: Defining the "Scope of Union Law"' (2015) 52 CML Rev 1201, 1225), with Case C-709/20 *CG*, EU:C:2021:602, paras 84–92, on the other (discussed by Maria Haag, 'The *Coup de Grâce* to the Union Citizen's Right to Equal Treatment: *CG v The Department for Communities in Northern Ireland*' (2022) 59 CML Rev 1081, 1101–02).

[18] Compare *Martínez Sala* (n 8), paras 49 and 61–63 and Case C-456/02 *Trojani*, EU:C:2004:488, paras 35–44, on the one hand, with *CG* (n 17), paras 65–81. See generally, Haag (ibid); and Charlotte O'Brien, 'The Great EU Citizenship Illusion Exposed: Equal Treatment Rights Evaporate for the Vulnerable (*CG v The Department for Communities in Northern Ireland*) (Case Comment)' (2021) 46 EL Rev 801.

[19] Compare Case C-413/99 *Baumbast and R*, EU:C:2002:493, paras 89–93 and *Brey* (n 6), paras 63–79, on the one hand, with Case C-67/14 *Alimanovic*, EU:C:2015:597, paras 59–62.

[20] *Dano* (n 17). This case law is among the most commented on in EU citizenship law; from a very extensive literature, see eg Michelle Blauberger, Anita Heindlmaier, Dion Kramer, Dorte Sindbjerg Martinsen, Jessica Sampson Thierry, Angelica Schenk, and Benjamin Werner, 'ECJ Judges Read the Morning Papers: Explaining the Turnaround of European Citizenship Jurisprudence' (2018) 25 Journal of European Public Policy 1422; Anastasia Iliopoulou-Penot 'Deconstructing the Former Edifice of Union Citizenship? The *Alimanovic* Judgment' (2016) 53 CML Rev 1007; Moritz Jesse and Daniel W Carter, 'The "*Dano* Evolution": Assessing Legal Integration and Access to Social Benefits for EU Citizens' (2018) 3 *European Papers* 1186; Niamh Nic Shuibhne, 'Limits Rising, Duties

Finally, I categorize as the use of *indicative* language instances where a previous ruling *is* referenced (contra silence) but its findings are developed in a way that is *not* reasonably expected or logical (contra directness). The Court uses two key language formulations in its indicative referencing: 'see, to that effect' and 'see, by analogy'. In one sense, that wording does already suggest that *some* case law change might be under way. Yet notwithstanding their prevalence, it is perhaps surprising that 'see, to that effect' and 'see, by analogy' are not closely studied. In the next part of the chapter, their use in EU citizenship case law is therefore further unpacked, with the aim of better understanding and appropriately assessing the Court's communicative reasoning. Moreover, since these formulations appear right across the Court's case law generally, wider lessons can be drawn.

3. Analogies and Effects: What Do These Indicative Terms Mean when the Court Uses Them to Refer to Its Previous Case Law?

Analysis of the Court's citizenship case law[21] suggests that 'see, by analogy' is probably the more straightforward of the two indicative methods highlighted in Section 2 above.[22] It is normally applied *to widen the scope of a finding established in previous case law to new circumstances* and examples include:

- raising arguments based on freedom of movement against a Union citizen's home State in leaver as well as returner situations;[23]

Ascending: The Changing Legal Shape of Union Citizenship' (2015) 52 CML Rev 889; Urska Šadl and Suvi Sankari, 'Why Did the Citizenship Jurisprudence Change?' in Daniel Thym (ed), *Questioning EU Citizenship: Judges and Limits of Free Movement and Solidarity in the EU* (Hart Publishing 2017) 89; Daniel Thym, 'When Union Citizens Turn Into Illegal Migrants: The *Dano* Case' (2015) 40 EL Rev 249; and Herwig Verschueren, 'Free Movement of EU Citizens: Including for the Poor?' (2015) 22 Maastricht Journal of European and Comparative Law 10.

[21] To clarify my own methodology, all Union citizenship judgments using 'see, by analogy' and 'see, to that effect' up to 28 February 2025 were examined, with key examples rather than full data offered here given the limitations of space. AG Opinions were not included in this part of the research.

[22] Note that the Court also uses 'by analogy' language even when *not* referring to previous case law: for example, applying the provisions of Directive 2004/38 'by analogy' even when that measure does not apply directly given the facts of the case (see eg *Chavez-Vilchez* (n 16), para 55 and see generally, Case C-673/16 *Coman*, EU:C:2018:385 and *O and B* (n 6)).

[23] Eg Case C-249/11 *Byankov*, EU:C:2012:608, para 30; applying Case C-33/07 *Jipa*, EU:C:2008:396, para 17. See also, on the severity of the limitation in question, *Byankov*, para 79; applying Case C-348/96 *Calfa*, EU:C:1999:6, para 18.

- more specifically, extending case law on obstacles to freedom of movement produced by a host State to obstacles produced by the citizen's home State;[24]
- affirming that residence conditions constitute indirect discrimination in citizenship situations, drawing from economic free movement and especially the free movement of workers;[25]
- pointing out that neither Directive 2004/38 nor the legislation it replaced had addressed the question under discussion (for example, entitlement to social security benefits in a host State);[26]
- explaining Article 8 ECHR as a 'minimum threshold of protection' for Article 7 CFR in the specific context of Union citizenship;[27]
- applying principles developed for third-country nationals in EU citizenship cases;[28] and
- transposing procedural approaches between different areas of EU citizenship law.[29]

In many cases, it is not clear why the references to previous case law merit analogy language at all since the findings are essentially the same. Why not just 'see'?

However, in other cases, the analogy indicated is not so straightforward. For example, in *Brey*, the Court held that placing conditions on the right of Union citizens to reside in another Member State reflects the statement in recital 10 of Directive 2004/38 that '[p]ersons exercising their right of residence should not, however, become an unreasonable burden on the social assistance system of the host Member State during an initial period of residence'; which is, according to the Court, based on the idea that 'the exercise of the right of residence for citizens of the Union can be subordinated to the legitimate interests of the Member States—in the present case, the protection of their public

[24] Eg Case C-224/02 *Pusa*, EU:C:2004:273, para 19; applying Case C-224/98 *D'Hoop*, EU:C:2002:432, para 31. See similarly, on the principles that determine an abuse of EU rights, *McCarthy II* (n 4), para 53, applying Case C-336/94 *Dafeki*, EU:C:1997:579, paras 19 and 21. See also, on the significance of the right to family life, Case C-165/16 *Lounes*, EU:C:2017:862, para 52; applying *Metock and Others* (n 3), para 62.

[25] Eg. Case C-73/08 *Bressol and Others*, EU:C:2010:181, para 45; applying Case C-337/97 *Meeusen*, EU:C:1999:284, paras 23–24 and Case C-212/05 *Hartmann*, EU:C:2007:437, para 31.

[26] Eg *Brey* (n 6), para 65 (Directive 2004/38); applying *Grzelczyk* (n 9), para 39 (Directive 93/96).

[27] Eg Case C-4/23 *Mirin*, EU:C:2024:845, para 63; applying (from outside EU citizenship law) Case C-202/24 *Alchaster*, EU:C:2024:649, para 93.

[28] Eg *Brey* (n 6), para 68; applying Case C-578/08 *Chakroun*, EU:C:2010:117, para 48.

[29] Eg Case C-459/20 *X v Staatssecretaris van Justitie en Veiligheid*, para 52 (decisions preventing genuine enjoyment of the substance of Union citizenship rights); applying Joined Cases C-316/16 and C-424/16 *B and Vomero*, EU:C:2018:256, para 94 (decisions on personal conduct for purposes of determining a threat to public policy or public security).

finances'.[30] To support that interpretation, the Court referred 'by analogy' to *Baumbast*, *Zhu and Chen*, and *Commission v Belgium*.

Do the paragraphs expressly pointed to by the Court combine to construct that analogy? Not quite: in fact, they refer—only *fairly* comparably, I would argue—to 'subordinat[ion] to the legitimate interests of the Member State' and, thus, that 'beneficiaries of the right of residence must not become an "unreasonable" burden on the public finances of the host Member State'.[31] Thus, the use of analogy language here could be seen as masking a more significant case law development than that indicated. In other cases, the analogy is even more of a stretch—or, being generous, a highly 'creative' transposition of previous findings to different circumstances. An example relates to the significance placed on returning to work or finding another job 'within a reasonable period' for the purposes of retaining the status of worker (and thus, lawful residence and consequential entitlement to equal treatment) in a host State developed in the context of imprisonment and applied subsequently to maternity leave.[32] Nevertheless, there is some analogy at the heart of the reasoning: in this example, the inability to participate in the host State labour market because of 'confinement'—even if both experiences of confinement are so fundamentally different.

The deployment of 'see, by analogy' language seems sound overall, then. One might agree or disagree, normatively or substantively, with the *nature* or the *scale* of the legal evolution produced when this formulation is used. However, when the case law cross-references provided are traced, there is—usually at least—an extension of logic from one pocket of the Court's case law to another. Some examples where it is harder to defend that conclusion, where the extension is considerable, have been highlighted; but looking across the citizenship case law as a whole, they are genuinely small in number.

The 'see, to that effect' method is, however, more complicated: when this formulation is used, there is more divergence in terms of what function it performs. For this chapter, I have grouped relevant cases under five categories:

a. **Unnecessarily using** 'see, to that effect' where the findings in both the case in question and the previous case law referred to are essentially the same.

30 *Brey* (n 6), para 55.

31 *Baumbast* (n 19), para 90; Case C-200/02 *Zhu and Chen*, EU:C:2004:639, para 32; Case C-408/03 *Commission v Belgium*, EU:C:2006:192, paras 37 and 41.

32 Case C-507/12 *Saint Prix*, EU:C:2014:2007, para 41; applying Joined Cases C-482/01 and C-493/01 *Orfanopoulos and Oliveri*, EU:C:2004:262, para 50.

Using 'see, to that effect' is redundant, I think, where it represents a straightforward cross-reference to and application of a finding already made.[33] Again, why not just use 'see'? Sometimes findings are similar but more compressed—understandably, though: the law is more succinctly expressed in later cases when it has been established and explained already; when it becomes precedent rather than innovation.[34]

Occasionally, though, there is a greater degree of adjustment—slight at first sight, perhaps; yet more meaningful if itself then entrenched or further developed in later case law. For example, in paragraph 44 of *Grzelczyk*, the Court held that

> [w]hilst Article 4 of Directive 93/96 does indeed provide that the right of residence is to exist for as long as beneficiaries of that right fulfil the conditions laid down in Article 1, the sixth recital in the directive's preamble envisages that beneficiaries of the right of residence must not become an 'unreasonable' burden on the public finances of the host Member State. Directive 93/96, *like Directives 90/364 and 90/365, thus accepts a certain degree of financial solidarity between nationals of a host Member State and nationals of other Member States*, particularly if the difficulties which a beneficiary of the right of residence encounters are temporary (emphasis added).

However, in *Commission v Austria*, the 'effect' of that paragraph was reframed as follows: 'EU law relating to the free movement of persons *and, in particular,*

[33] Most of these instances are very straightforward: for example, the statement in paragraph 31 of *Grzelczyk* that 'Union citizenship is destined to be the fundamental status of nationals of the Member States' is often reproduced word-for-word in subsequent judgments yet with 'see, to that effect' added. See similarly, Case C-277/23 *Ministarstvo financija (Bourse Erasmus+)*, EU:C:2025:18, paras 57–58; applying cross-referring straightforwardly to Case C-562/22 *JD v OB*, EU:C:2024:55, paras 37–38. Other examples entail slightly more piecing together: see eg *Baumbast and R* (n 19), para 70 ('just like the status of migrant worker itself, the rights enjoyed by members of a Community worker's family under Regulation No 1612/68 can, in certain circumstances, continue to exist even after the employment relationship has ended'), referring to Case 389/87 *Echternach and Moritz*, EU:C:1989:130, para 21 ('[w]hen, after his father's return to the Member State of origin, the child of such a worker cannot continue his studies there because there is no coordination of school diplomas and has no choice but to return to the country where he attended school in order to continue studying, he retains the right to rely on the provisions of Community law as a child "of a national of a Member State who is or has been employed in the territory of another Member State" within the meaning of Article 12 [of Regulation 1612/68]'), and *Martínez Sala* (n 8), para 32 ('Once the employment relationship has ended, the person concerned as a rule loses his status of worker, although that status may produce certain effects after the relationship has ended, and a person who is genuinely seeking work must also be classified as a worker', with previous case law cited). See also eg *Lounes* (n 24), para 50 referring to Case C-541/15 *Freitag*, EU:C:2017:432, para 34 (link to EU law in situations involving dual nationals); Case C-221/17 *Tjebbes*, EU:C:2019:189, para 40, referring to Case C-135/08 *Rottmann*, EU:C:2010:104, paras 55–56 (implications of loss of Member State nationality for the family members of the Union citizen).

[34] Compare eg *Byankov* (n 23), para 63 with *Baumbast* (n 19), paras 84–86.

students, allows for a certain degree of financial solidarity as amongst nationals of the host Member State and nationals of other Member States' (emphasis added).[35]

These two paragraphs do *not* amount to the same thing, and one wonders if a *Grzelczyk*-type claim for equal treatment might thus still succeed now—*Dano* and *Alimanovic* notwithstanding—on the basis that students are legally distinctive; that they are legally special. Here, then, we see that a word changed here or an emphasis added there might make a significant substantive difference, that the 'effect' might not be redundant at all.

b. **Generalizing and/or explaining** in further detail a proposition already established in previous case law.[36]

In reality, how 'see, to that effect' is used in these examples is not so different from how 'see, by analogy' is used.[37] Indeed, in several judgments, both 'see, by analogy' and 'see, to that effect' are used. Sometimes the distinction between both formulations is patently meaningful,[38] but in other cases they seem to be used interchangeably and it is not clear what their respective use is actually meant to indicate.[39] These examples suggest that there can be a certain methodological looseness in the drafting of the Court's judgments, a factor of more administrative than substantive nature.

[35] Case C-75/11 *Commission v Austria*, EU:C:2012:605, para 60 (emphasis added).

[36] Eg the Court held in paras 30–31 of *D'Hoop* (n 24) that 'the opportunities offered by the Treaty in relation to freedom of movement . . . could not be fully effective if a national of a Member State could be deterred from availing himself of them by obstacles raised on his return to his country of origin by legislation penalising the fact that he has used them (see, to that effect, Case C-370/90 *Singh* [EU:C:1992:296], paragraph 23)'. In *Singh*, the Court held that '[the rights granted by Articles 45 and 49 TFEU] cannot be fully effective if such a person may be deterred from exercising them by obstacles raised in his or her country of origin to the entry and residence of his or her spouse. Accordingly, when a Community national who has availed himself or herself of those rights returns to his or her country of origin, his or her spouse must enjoy at least the same rights of entry and residence as would be granted to him or her under Community law if his or her spouse chose to enter and reside in another Member State. Nevertheless, Articles [45 and 49] of the Treaty do not prevent Member States from applying to foreign spouses of their own nationals rules on entry and residence more favour- able than those provided for by Community law.' See also eg *Zhu and Chen* (n 31), para 19, referring to Case C-148/02 *Garcia Avello*, EU:C:2003:539, paras 13 and 27.

[37] For example, we saw above that the Court has used 'see, by analogy' to apply similar principles to similar provisions of different legislation and it has used 'see, to that effect' in the same way. For example, on the scope of Directive 200438, see *Iida* (n 16), para 64, referring with respect to 'similar provisions of the instruments of European Union law prior to Directive 2004/38' to Case C-291/05 *Eind*, EU:C:2007:771, para 24; see similarly, applying the same approach to Directives 2004/38 and 90/364 respectively, Case C-86/12 *Alokpa and Moudoulou*, EU:C:2013:645, para 29, referring to *Zhu and Chen* (n 31), paras 46–47.

[38] Eg in *Saint Prix* (n 32), 'see, to that effect' is used five times whereas 'see, by analogy' is used just once (in connection with the extension of previous case law as also outlined in n 32 above).

[39] Eg *Lounes* (n 24) (four 'see, by analogy' and six 'see, to that effect'); *Brey* (n 6), (seven 'see, by analogy' and ten 'see, to that effect').

c. **Embedding or normalizing** a novel finding from previous case law.

For example, in paragraph 25 of *Onuekwere*,[40] the Court referred to paragraphs 59, 63, and 65 of its judgment in *Dias*[41] to affirm that permanent residence rights could be lost in circumstances *other than* those provided for expressly in Directive 2004/38—a controversial proposition given that expressly providing for limitations on freedom of movement and residence had been emphasized in earlier case law.[42] Thus, the sense that emerges from this category is that 'see, to that effect' can be used to mask the degree to which a judgment represents a significant legal evolution compared to previous case law. This category therefore entails cases where either the good or the damage (depending on your perspective) is *already done*, with the main purpose of the subsequent reference being to attribute a certain respectability to the earlier finding, embedding or normalizing its 'effect'.

d. **Translating** findings established in other fields of previous case law to the field of Union citizenship.[43]

It can be recalled from the discussion above that 'see, by analogy' is often used for this same purpose. One of the most controversial 'see, to that effect' translations of this kind concerns review of national rules on the loss and acquisition of Member State nationality (and thus of Union citizenship) for compliance with EU law. In EU citizenship law specifically, this line of case law began with *Rottmann*,[44] the limits of that idea under consideration (at the time of writing) in *Commission v Malta*.[45]

[40] Case C-378/12 *Onuekwere*, EU:C:2014:13.

[41] Case C-325/09 *Dias*, EU:C:2011:498.

[42] Eg *Grzelczyk* (n 9), para 31. See similarly eg *Coman* (n 22), para 24, affirming the criteria of family life 'created or strengthened in the host Member State' conceived previously in *O and B* (n 5), para 54.

[43] Eg Case C-300/04 *Eman and Sevinger*, EU:C:2006:545, para 68, referring generally to Case 199/82 *San Giorgio*, 1983:318 (compliance of rules laid down in national (electoral) law with the principles of effectiveness and equivalence). In *Bressol and Others* (n 25), there are several 'to that effect' references to the discrimination, justification, and proportionality framework applied in free movement law generally (see paras 40, 41, 48, 62, 64, 71, and 79). In Case C-490/20 *VMA v Stolichna obshtina, rayon 'Pancharevo'*, EU:C:2021:1008, para 63, case law on the free movement of goods (Case C-244/06 *Dynamic Medien*, EU:C:2008:85, para 39) and the return of illegally staying third-country nationals (Case C-112/20 *État belge (Return of the parent of a minor)*, EU:C:2021:197, para 37) is referred to 'to that effect' to signal the obligation 'to take due account' of the Convention on the Rights of the Child.

[44] *Rottmann* (n 33), paras 41–42.

[45] Case C-181/23 *Commission v Malta* (judgment was delivered on 29 April 2025, EU:C:2025:283).

e. **Misleadingly** using 'see, to that effect' because the 'effect' that is apparent to the Court is not really apparent at all when the case law references are followed.

This is the most problematic 'see, to that effect' category. In *Metock*, for example, it was acknowledged that

> the Court held in paragraphs 50 and 51 of *Akrich* that, in order to benefit from the rights provided for in Article 10 of Regulation No 1612/68, the national of a non-member country who is the spouse of a Union citizen must be lawfully resident in a Member State when he moves to another Member State to which the citizen of the Union is migrating or has migrated. However, that conclusion must be reconsidered. The benefit of such rights cannot depend on the prior lawful residence of such a spouse in another Member State (see, to that effect, *MRAX*, paragraph 59, and . . . *Commission v Spain*, paragraph 28).[46]

But when the references are followed, neither paragraph 59 of *MRAX*[47] nor paragraph 28 of *Commission of Spain*[48] communicates such an 'effect'—*at all*.

Providing a second example, *Ruiz Zambrano* represents a notorious invocation of the 'see, to that effect' method. In paragraph 42 of its judgment, the Court held that 'Article 20 TFEU precludes national measures which have the effect of depriving citizens of the Union of the genuine enjoyment of the substance of the rights conferred by virtue of their status as citizens of the Union (see, to that effect, *Rottmann*, paragraph 42)'—a profoundly under-explained leap from the earlier ruling, paragraph 42 of which had established (in a case that had nothing at all to do with rights of family reunification and, conversely, remembering that *Ruiz Zambrano* had nothing at all to do with the loss of Member State nationality and thus of Union citizenship) that

[46] *Metock* (n 3), para 58; referring to Case C-459/99 *MRAX*, EU:C:2002:461 and Case C-157/03 *Commission v Spain*, EU:C:2005:225.

[47] '[W]hile, as the Commission correctly points out, the right of a third country national married to a Member State national to enter the territory of the Member States derives under Community law from the family ties alone, the fact remains that, according to the very wording of Article 3(2) of Directive 68/360 and Article 3(2) of Directive 73/148, exercise of that right may be conditional on possession of a visa. Indeed, Article 5 of Regulation No 2317/95 defines a visa as an authorisation given or a decision taken by a Member State which is required "for entry" into its territory.'

[48] 'Article 1 of Directives 68/360, 73/148 and 90/365 extend the application of Community law concerning entry and residence on the territory of Member States to the spouses of the nationals of those States falling within those provisions, irrespective of their nationality.'

> the situation of a citizen of the Union who, like the applicant in the main proceedings, is faced with a decision withdrawing his naturalisation, adopted by the authorities of one Member State, and placing him, after he has lost the nationality of another Member State that he originally possessed, in a position capable of causing him to lose the status conferred by Article [20 TFEU] and the rights attaching thereto falls, by reason of its nature and its consequences, within the ambit of European Union law.

Indeed, in later cases, there is widespread use of 'see, to that effect' to explain what the Court had really intended in *Ruiz Zambrano*, its logic revealed over time on a 'stone by stone' basis.[49]

Brey constructs a case law story that provides an important third example given the *Dano* and *Alimanovic* case law shift that *Brey* was engaged to rationalize shortly afterwards. In paragraph 44 of *Brey*, the Court suggested that it had 'consistently held that there is nothing to prevent, in principle, the granting of social security benefits to Union citizens who are not economically active *being made conditional upon those citizens meeting the necessary requirements for obtaining a legal right of residence in the host Member State*' (emphasis added), referring, 'to that effect', to paragraphs 61–63 of *Martínez Sala* (which address equal treatment as a consequence of lawful residence in the host State and not the conditions determining the lawfulness of that residence);[50] paragraphs 32–33 of *Grzelczyk* (which confirm *Martínez Sala* and do not discuss how a 'right to legal residence in the host State' is achieved);[51] paragraphs 42–43 of *Trojani* (which, in fact, widened the scope of equal treatment to situations

[49] Eg *Chavez-Vilchez* (n 16), paras 60–69; Case C-82/16 *KA and Others*, EU:C:2018:308, paras 50–57. Koen Lenaerts, 'EU Citizenship and the European Court of Justice's "Stone-by-Stone" Approach' (2015) 1 International Comparative Jurisprudence 1.

[50] '61. As a national of a Member State lawfully residing in the territory of another Member State, the appellant in the main proceedings comes within the scope *ratione personae* of the provisions of the Treaty on European citizenship. 62. Article 8(2) of the Treaty attaches to the status of citizen of the Union the rights and duties laid down by the Treaty, including the right, laid down in Article [18 TFEU], not to suffer discrimination on grounds of nationality within the scope of application *ratione materiae* of the Treaty. 63. It follows that a citizen of the European Union, such as the appellant in the main proceedings, lawfully resident in the territory of the host Member State, can rely on Article [18] in all situations which fall within the scope *ratione materiae* of Community law, including the situation where that Member State delays or refuses to grant to that claimant a benefit that is provided to all persons lawfully resident in the territory of that State on the ground that the claimant is not in possession of a document which nationals of that same State are not required to have and the issue of which may be delayed or refused by the authorities of that State.'

[51] '32. As the Court held in paragraph 63 of its judgment in *Martínez Sala*, ... a citizen of the European Union, lawfully resident in the territory of a host Member State, can rely on Article 6 of the Treaty in all situations which fall within the scope *ratione materiae* of Community law. 33. Those situations include those involving the exercise of the fundamental freedoms guaranteed by the Treaty and those involving the exercise of the right to move and reside freely in another Member State, as conferred by Article 8a of the Treaty.'

where a residence permit (granted in accordance with national, not EU, law) is held);[52] paragraph 37 of *Bidar* (which confirms the wider perspective held in *Trojani*);[53] and paragraph 39 of *Förster* (which confirms only *Bidar*).[54]

In *Brey*, the Court therefore took a significant step on from the case law that it cited 'to that effect', and none of the paragraphs referred to in support had clearly established or pointed to it. Moreover, paragraph 44 of *Brey* was called on soon afterwards to underpin the findings in *Dano*.[55]

4. How Robust Are the Court's Case Law Referencing Methods? Navigating Sincerity and Silence

The case law presented in Sections 2 and 3 above does suggest that overall—and irrespective of whether referencing is carried out with more direct or more indicative language—the Court either follows its own previous case law or progresses it in ways that are reasonable: and crucially for present purposes, in ways that are *explained*. Conversely, the scale of reasoning gaps with respect to previous case law is small. The analysis therefore suggests, and I say this subjectively, a certain *sincerity* on the part of the Court: where previous case law exists, it is followed; and where previous case law is close to but not quite directly on the point of a subsequent case, it is transposed and progressed in ways that are logical and reasonable. Most of the cases *are* therefore both well and transparently reasoned. The health of EU citizenship case law more normatively and substantively is not, in other words, related *primarily* to the methods

[52] '42. First, as the Court has held, a social assistance benefit such as the minimex falls within the scope of the Treaty (see [*Grzelczyk*] in particular paragraph 46). 43. Second, with regard to such benefits, a citizen of the Union who is not economically active may rely on Article 12 EC where he has been lawfully resident in the host Member State for a certain time or possesses a residence permit.'

[53] 'With regard to social assistance benefits, the Court held in [*Trojani*, paragraph 43] that a citizen of the Union who is not economically active may rely on the first paragraph of Article [18 TFEU] where he has been lawfully resident in the host Member State for a certain time or possesses a residence permit.'

[54] 'With regard to social assistance benefits, the Court has held that a citizen of the Union who is not economically active may rely on the first paragraph of Article 12 EC where he or she has been lawfully resident in the host Member State for a certain time (*Bidar*, paragraph 37)' (Case C-158/07 *Förster*, EU:C:2008:630). Davies takes a different view on whether *Dano* overruled previous case law, but he focuses on *Grzelczyk* without considering *Trojani* (see Gareth Davies, 'How the Court's Path Dependence Affects Its Role as a Relational Actor' (2023) 2 European Law Open 271 at 278).

[55] 'The benefits at issue in the main proceedings, which constitute "special non-contributory cash benefits" within the meaning of Article 70(2) of the regulation, are, under Article 70(4), to be provided exclusively in the Member State in which the persons concerned reside, in accordance with its legislation. It follows that there is nothing to prevent the grant of such benefits to Union citizens who are not economically active *from being made subject to the requirement that those citizens fulfil the conditions for obtaining a right of residence under Directive 2004/38* in the host Member State (see, to this effect, [*Brey*, paragraph 44)' (para 83 of *Dano* (n 17), emphasis added). See also, *Dano*, paras 68–69.

applied in the explaining of it. Most of the time, references to previous case law are straightforward. They affirm—often verbatim—findings from previous judgments, or they extend findings established in another field of EU law to EU citizenship law.

Interestingly, then, there is no straightforward correlation between the most criticized cases and the least well-reasoned cases, at least as regards the specific question of how the Court manages its own previous case law. For example, the rulings in *Dano*, *CG*, and *Ruiz Zambrano* are both criticized and poorly reasoned; but *Rottmann* and *Alimanovic* are better reasoned yet also heavily criticized. There is also no straightforward correlation between 'better' previous case law reasoning and expansive outcomes. It is true that the Court's referencing of previous case law was more straightforward in the earlier rulings that created new streams of citizenship rights—such as *Collins* and *Bidar*—and it is also true that certain rights-narrowing cases have been less well reasoned, such as *Dano*. But there are examples of the opposite too: *Ruiz Zambrano* significantly expanded citizenship rights but was poorly reasoned from the communicative reasoning perspective in that the judgment did not explain the link made to *Rottmann*.

In most cases, then, the methods of the Court with respect to its own previous case law are both solid and effective. Yes, there is room for refinement of the 'see, by analogy' and 'see, to that effect' formulations, which are used both interchangeably and distinctively without clear rationale. So, how can we know whether their respective use is intended to be meaningful, rather than a style point from the rapporteur or drafter, or a side-effect of copy/paste?[56]

At the same time, the examples highlighted in this chapter underline that it is essential for legal researchers always to go back to the source references when the Court uses these formulations, because what the previous case(s) actually held can be rather removed from the 'analogy' but especially the 'effect' of the relevant previous case law compared to what the Court is later saying 'the law is' per the case at hand. It is essential, in other words, to take on the role of 'citation detective' and, in that way, to try and (de-)construct the reasoning of the Court on the basis of the case law breadcrumbs that have been laid.

[56] Karen McAuliffe's work has taken us behind the curtain of case law-making to some extent: see eg 'Behind the Scenes at the European Court of Justice: Drafting EU Law Stories' in Fernanda Nicola and Bill Davies (eds), *EU Law Stories: Contextual and Critical Histories of European Jurisprudence* (CUP 2017) 3; 'Hidden Translators: The Invisibility of Translators and the Influence of Lawyer-Linguists on the Case Law of the Court of Justice of the European Union' (2016) 3 *Language and Law/Linguagem e Direito* 5; and 'Precedent at the Court of Justice of the European Union: The Linguistic Aspect' in Michael Freeman and Fiona Smith (eds), *Law and Language: Current Legal Issues* (OUP 2013) 483.

Sometimes, that work is not insignificant. We can acknowledge that reasonable disagreement is an inevitable part of any case law-rich area of legal development: that there will, in other words, be reasonable disagreement over the extent to which an 'effect' or an 'analogy' attributed to a previous decision is obvious or logical or well-explained. Nevertheless, better communicative reasoning from the Court itself—in the judgments themselves—is a reasonable ask. The responsibility to communicate why a case has been decided in the way that it was lies *solely* with the Court and the better the communication of that explanation—of that reasoning—the stronger the claim to justification and, ultimately, acceptance.

A first problem highlighted in this chapter concerns the signals that previous case law references sometimes emit, especially those subduing the urge to investigate further. For how many of us really do—not just dutifully but habitually—trace each and every sequence of case references presented to us in a judgment, the inclusion of which suggests on its own terms that previous case law does already lead in this direction and therefore to this outcome? I have alluded in this chapter to the veneer of precedent and embeddedness that language such as 'analogy' and 'to that effect' implies and instates. Yet there are, as shown, examples where the paragraphs cited from previous case law simply do not reflect what the Court later suggests was already established. There is some evidence of selective use of previous case law in that respect. For Šadl, courts 'make new law by following old law'—yet she also shows how what she calls the 'potential of repetition' exemplified by 'settled' case law can be 'destabilising' and 'transformative' too.[57]

A second problem concerns judicial silence—where there is a clear departure from previous case law but no acknowledgement of it. Daniel Sarmiento shows how the judgments in *Dano* and *CG* can be classified as 'implicit revocatory rulings' and advocates instead, in the interests of greater transparency and enhanced legal certainty, that the Court adopt explicit 'explanatory' language in such situations.[58] Indeed, given how replete the judgments of the Court of Justice usually are with references to analogies and effects, the silence of no reference at all is truly deafening—and deeply damaging.

[57] Urska Šadl, 'Old Is New: The Transformative Effect of References to Settled Case Law in the Decisions of the European Court of Justice' (2021) 58 CML Rev 1761.

[58] Daniel Sarmiento, 'The "Overruling" Technique at the Court of Justice of the European Union' (2023) 15 European Journal of Legal Studies 107.

5. Conclusion

In his classic essay on judicial lawmaking, Martin Shapiro characterized courts as 'a distinctive subset of political institutions: one that must always deny that they are wielding political authority when they in fact *do* wield political authority' and continued:

> One may call this justificatory history, but I call it lying. Courts and judges always lie. Lying is the nature of the judicial activity. One must get over the moral *angst* about that and quarrel instead about what law judges make, when, and how fast. Worrying about whether judges ought or ought not to lie is foolhardy. Judges necessarily lie because that is the nature of the activity they engage in.[59]

A central question explored in this volume is whether the 'law judges make' can be—*should* be—disconnected from questions not only about how they make it but also, how they communicate and explain (how they make) it. In his newer classic essay on the making of EU citizenship law, Koen Lenaerts has rightly underlined that 'in order to fully apprehend the approach of the ECJ in an area of EU law, a critical observer should not limit him- or herself to studying the "groundbreaking" case, but he or she should also read the relevant case law predating as well as postdating that case'.[60] However, the research presented in this chapter shows that, in certain cases, doing so will only take the researcher so far. No matter how many cases one reads, what is missing sometimes is an articulation of the reasoning pathway that either brought the Court from finding A in a previous case to a quite different finding B in a later case. In some situations, finding B simply exceeds the language of analogy or effect. In other cases, the Court departs from finding A to such an extent that it could not even be mentioned in the expressing of finding B. That presents for the Court, in its own words, a 'serious inconvenience'.[61] One that should be addressed, not ignored.

This chapter acknowledges that instances of problematic communicative reasoning as regards previous case law are, in fact, rare. But their scarcity does not cancel out their impact. The judgments discussed underscore that legal

[59] Martin Shapiro, 'Judges as Liars' (1994) Harvard Journal of Law and Public Policy 155, 156 (emphasis in original).

[60] Lenaerts (n 49) 1.

[61] Eg *McCarthy* (n 4), para 51; *Mirin* (n 27), para 55.

researchers should always be curious when their attention is drawn to analogies and effects regarding previous case law: that these terms reveal nothing about the *scale* of the progression of the law on their own terms. For the Court, reflecting further on the use of these formulations would be welcome: what do they mean, respectively; when are they used; and why? Above all, when previous case law is departed from, silence is not the answer.

Whether a decision of the Court is normatively or substantively 'right' is inherently contestable. Whether it is political as much as legal, as Shapiro called attention to, will be debated. But how a decision is communicated lends itself to more objective appeals for methodological robustness. Fundamentally, processes *matter*—and perhaps never more than before, as the world constructed by law is under severe threat now all around us.

References

Blauberger M, Heindlmaier A, Kramer D, Sindbjerg Martinsen D, Sampson Thierry J, Schenk A, and Werner B, 'ECJ Judges Read the Morning Papers: Explaining the Turnaround of European Citizenship Jurisprudence' (2018) 25 Journal of European Public Policy 1422

Davies G, 'How the Court's Path Dependence Affects Its Role as a Relational Actor' (2023) 2 European Law Open 271

Dougan M, 'Judicial Review of Member State Action under the General Principles and the Charter: Defining The "Scope Of Union Law"' (2015) 52 CML Rev 1201

Haag M, 'The *Coup De Grâce* to the Union Citizen's Right to Equal Treatment: *CG v The Department for Communities in Northern Ireland*' (2022) 59 CML Rev 1081

Iliopoulou-Penot A, 'Deconstructing the Former Edifice of Union Citizenship? The *Alimanovic* Judgment' (2016) 53 CML Rev 1007

Jesse M and Carter DW, 'The "*Dano* Evolution": Assessing Legal Integration and access to Social Benefits for EU Citizens' (2018) 3 European Papers 1186

Lenaerts K, 'EU Citizenship and the European Court of Justice's "Stone-By-Stone" Approach' (2015) 1 International Comparative Jurisprudence 1

McAuliffe K, 'Precedent at the Court of Justice of the European Union: The Linguistic Aspect' in Michael Freeman and Fiona Smith (eds) *Law and Language: Current Legal Issues* (OUP 2013)

McAuliffe K, 'Hidden translators: the invisibility of translators and the influence of lawyer-linguists on the case law of the Court of Justice of the European Union' (2016) 3 Language and Law/Linguagem e Direito 5

McAuliffe K, 'Behind the Scenes at the European Court of Justice: Drafting EU Law Stories' in Fernanda Nicola and Bill Davies (eds), *EU Law Stories: Contextual and Critical Histories of European Jurisprudence* (CUP 2017)

Nic Shuibhne N, 'Limits Rising, Duties Ascending: The Changing Legal Shape of Union Citizenship' (2015) 52 CML Rev 889

O'Brien C, 'The Great EU Citizenship Illusion Exposed: Equal Treatment Rights Evaporate for the Vulnerable (*CG v The Department for Communities in Northern Ireland*) (Case Comment)' (2021) 46 EL Rev 801

Šadl U and Panagis I, 'The Force of EU Case Law: An Empirical Study of Precedential Constraint', iCourts Working Paper Series, No. 68, 2016, available at https://papers.ssrn.com/sol3/papers.cfm?abstract_id=2787119

Šadl U and Sankari S, 'Why Did The Citizenship Jurisprudence Change?' in D Thym (ed), *Questioning EU Citizenship: Judges and Limits of Free Movement and Solidarity in the EU* (Hart Publishing 2017)

Šadl U, 'Old Is New: The Transformative Effect of References to Settled Case Law in the Decisions of the European Court of Justice' (2021) 58 CML Rev 1761

Sarmiento D, 'The "Overruling" Technique at the Court of Justice of the European Union' (2023) 15 *European Journal of Legal Studies* 107

Shapiro M, 'Judges as Liars' (1994) Harvard Journal of Law and Public Policy 155

Thym D, 'When Union Citizens turn into Illegal Migrants: The *Dano* Case' (2015) 40 EL Rev 249

van Eijken H and Phoa P, 'The Scope of Article 20 TFEU Clarified in *Chavez-Vilchez*: Are the Fundamental Rights of Minor EU Citizens Coming of Age? (Case Comment)' (2018) 43 EL Rev 949

Verschueren H, 'Free Movement of EU Citizens: Including for the Poor?' (2015) 22 Maastricht Journal of European and Comparative Law 10

13

The Omnipotent Legislature in the Interpretation of Primary Law by the Court of Justice in the Fields of EU Citizenship and Direct Taxation

Alexandros Politis

1. Introductory Remarks

An important element of the reasoning of the Court of Justice in its judgments is often the relationship between the different sources of EU law. Luke Dimitrios Spieker, in his own contribution to the present book, elaborated on the Court's possible recognition of an internal hierarchy between primary law sources. Emily Hancox examined, more generally, the possible resolution of normative conflicts between primary law rules or between secondary law rules as such. While these two contributions thus addressed the interplay between rules of equal rank, this chapter focuses instead on the relationship between rules that are formally situated in a hierarchical order, namely between primary and secondary law sources. A number of authors have already argued that this relationship is not as straightforward and linear as it might appear to be. In fact, the Court acknowledges that the EU legislature is not subservient to the dictates of primary law, but it enjoys a shared responsibility for the interpretation of the latter. This has been particularly observed with regard to the wide discretion the Court affords the EU legislature when implementing the Treaty's internal market provisions.[1] This discretion essentially entails the

[1] See, among others, Eadaoin Ní Chaoimh, *The Legislative Priority Rule and the EU Internal Market for Goods* (OUP 2022); Luke Dimitrios Spieker, 'Was Grimm Wrong? Putting the Over-Constitutionalization of EU Law to the Test' (2025) 26(3) GLJ 416; Robert Schütze, '"Integration-through-Law": Grand Theory, Revisionist History' (2025) 4(2) ELO 162; Martijn van den Brink, Mark Dawson, and Jan Zglinski, 'Revisiting the Asymmetry Thesis: Negative and Positive Integration in the EU' (2025) 1 JEPP 209.

Alexandros Politis, *The Omnipotent Legislature in the Interpretation of Primary Law by the Court of Justice in the Fields of EU Citizenship and Direct Taxation* In: *The Reasoning of the Court of Justice of the EU*.
Edited by: Alezini Loxa and Luigi Lonardo, Oxford University Press.
DOI: 10.1093/9780198983002.003.0017

Court's reluctance to annul EU legislation or interpret it in light of those Treaty provisions. Martijn van den Brink recently advanced the normative argument that the Court should display deference to the choices of the EU legislature in every field of EU law, regardless of the primary law provisions at stake.[2] This is principally warranted due to the EU legislature's demo(*i*)cratic legitimacy and its institutional capacity.[3]

This chapter focuses on a particular dimension of the 'primary–secondary law' relationship. The Court may not only acknowledge the EU legislature's broad discretion in implementing the Treaties but also adapt its interpretation to the legislature's choices, even going so far as to reverse its own case law. In doing so, the Court appears to invert the formal hierarchy between primary and secondary law, thereby recognizing a 'normative inversion' within the EU legal order and attributing a form of omnipotence to the EU legislature. This phenomenon has already been detected in certain judgments by Phil Syrpis.[4] The added value of this chapter is to demonstrate that there are two particular fields where the EU legislature's (partial or general) omnipotence constitutes their inherent characteristic: EU citizens' rights and direct taxation. Although the case law in these fields has already been the subject of comparative analyses,[5] their common feature of the 'omnipotent EU legislature' has yet to be discussed. As will be argued in this chapter, this feature can be explained and justified by the special status these two fields hold within the Treaty framework itself.

2. The Partial Omnipotence of the Citizens' Rights Directive

2.1 The (in principle) expansive interpretation of the citizens' rights legislation

The role of the EU legislature in relation to the interpretation of primary law in the field of EU citizens' rights commenced after the explicit introduction of these rights in the Treaty of Maastricht. According to Article 8a(1) of that Treaty (now Article 21(1) TFEU), EU citizens enjoy the right to move and

[2] Martijn van den Brink, *Legislative Authority and Interpretation in the European Union* (OUP 2024).
[3] ibid 22–73.
[4] Phil Syrpis, 'The Relationship between Primary and Secondary Law in the EU' (2015) 2 CML Rev 461.
[5] Rita Szudoczky, 'The Influence of Primary Law on the Interpretation of Secondary Law in the field of EU Citizenship and Direct Taxation: "Whatever Works" . . .' in Dennis Weber (ed), *Traditional and Alternative Routes to European Tax Integration* (IBFD 2010) 191.

reside freely within the territory of the Member States, but 'subject to the limitations and conditions laid down in this Treaty *and by the measures adopted to give it effect*'. This wording initially gave the impression that the EU citizens' primary law rights of movement and residence shall yield to the conditions set by the EU legislature, thus inserting into the Treaties themselves a 'normative inversion' and raising 'difficult questions about the presumed hierarchy of EU legal sources'.[6] The citizens' rights enshrined in Article 21(1) TFEU are particularly relevant for economically *inactive* EU citizens, as the rights of economically active citizens are governed by the more specific Treaty provisions on the fundamental freedoms.[7] The relevant EU legislation at the time of the entry into force of the Treaty of Maastricht consisted of the general Residence Directive 90/364, the Pensioners' Residence Directive 90/365, and the Students' Residence Directive 93/96.

The Court, however, appeared to shift the normative inversion of Article 21 TFEU into the proper hierarchical superiority of primary *versus* secondary law. It did so by overlooking the conditions and limitations set by the 1990s directives, opting for interpretative solutions which often dismissed the letter of that legislation or, more generally, the will of the EU legislature.[8] Notable examples of this approach are the Court's judgments in *Grzelczyk* and in *Baumbast and R.*,[9] where 'the principle of proportionality [was] used [by the Court] to rewrite the rules laid down in secondary Community law'.[10] It is recalled that in both the cases of Mr Grzelczyk and Mr Baumbast the letter of the 1990s directives concerning the conditions for residence in another Member State was clear. According to their Article 1, EU citizens should first have 'sufficient resources' and second be covered by 'sickness insurance in respect of all risks in the host State'. Since Mr Grzelczyk did not have *any* resources whatsoever and Mr Baumbast lacked sickness insurance covering *all* risks in the host State, they both constituted a 'burden' for the host State under the express wording of Article 1 and were therefore unable to invoke an EU law right of residence. Nonetheless, the Court attached a proportionality test to the residence

[6] Niamh Nic Shuibhne, 'The Third Age of EU Citizenship', in Phil Syrpis (ed.), *The Judiciary, the Legislature and the EU Internal Market* (CUP 2012) 331, 336–37, 352, and 358.

[7] Case C-488/21, *Chief Appeals Officer and Others* ECLI:EU:C:2023:1013, para 46.

[8] Kay Hailbronner, 'Union Citizenship and Access to Social Benefits' (2005) 5 CML Rev 1245, 1264; Ferdinand Wollenschläger, 'The Judiciary, the Legislature and the Evolution of Union Citizenship', in Phil Syrpis (n 6) 327.

[9] Case C-184/99, *Grzelczyk* ECLI:EU:C:2001:458; Case C-413/99, *Baumbast and R* ECLI:EU:C:2002:493.

[10] Kay Hailbronner (n 8) 1251; Gareth Davies, 'Legislative Control of the European Court of Justice' (2014) 6 CML Rev 1579, 1601, according to whom the 'clear wording of the Directive is contradicted, and, most significantly, one of the fundamental virtues of secondary legislation is undermined, that of clarity'.

conditions requiring Member States to apply it in each individual case. To that end, the Court relied heavily on a recital common to the preambles of the 1990s directives, according to which the beneficiaries of the right of residence should not become an '*unreasonable* burden' on the public finances of the host State. According to the Court, that recital revealed the EU legislature's will to accept a 'certain degree of financial solidarity' between the nationals of the Member States.[11] The Court's reliance on a mere recital to disregard the clear wording of the directives—under the guise of a purported teleological interpretation—was rightly criticized.[12] In fact, what the Court arguably did in these cases was to attribute significant normative weight to the introduction of EU citizens' rights in the Treaties, as evidenced by its references to EU citizenship as being destined to constitute the 'fundamental status' of nationals of the Member States.[13] In this sense, 'the Court made the conditions and limitations contained in secondary legislation subordinate to the *primary law* right of free movement'.[14]

Several authors have claimed that the Court has now retreated from its expansive approach to EU citizens' rights, showing greater deference to the choices made by the EU legislature in the Citizens' Rights Directive 2004/38/EC ('CRD'). They attribute this jurisprudential shift to the all-encompassing and more detailed nature of the CRD as well as to the fact that it was adopted *after* the insertion of EU citizenship in the Treaty of Maastricht, thereby making use of the explicit normative inversion contained in today's Article 21(1) TFEU.[15] However, the Court has not totally abandoned its expansive approach. There are, in fact, a number of judgments that appear to conflict with both the context and the very wording of the CRD.

[11] *Grzelczyk* (n 9) para. 31; *Baumbast and R* (n 9) para. 82.

[12] Anastasia Iliopoulou and Helen Toner, Comment on C-184/99, Grzelczyk (2002) 3 CML Rev 609, 613: '[t]his is certainly a very audacious interpretation of the Directive, not least because the key to the Court's interpretation (the unreasonableness of the burden) lies not in the wording of the Directive itself but in the preamble to it.'

[13] *Grzelczyk* (n 9) para. 44; *Baumbast and R* (n 9) para. 90.

[14] Daniel W Carter, *The European precariat: the protection of precarious workers in the European Union* (PhD thesis, Leiden University, 2023), 98 (emphasis added).

[15] Jesse Moritz and Daniel W Carter, 'Life after the "*Dano*-Trilogy": Legal Certainty, Choices and Limitations in EU Citizenship Case Law' in Nathan Cambien, Dimitry Kochenov, and Elise Muir (eds), *European Citizenship under Stress* (Brill 2020), 137, 144, 151, and 154; Stephen Coutts, 'The Court, the Legislature and the Co-Construction of a Status of Social Integration' in Nathan Cambien, Dimitry Kochenov, and Elise Muir (eds), *European Citizenship under Stress* (Brill 2020) 126–29 and 131–34; Síofra O'Leary and Sara Iglesias Sánchez, 'Free Movement of Persons and Services' in Paul Craig and Gráinne de Búrca (eds), *The Evolution of EU Law* (3rd edn, OUP 2021) 506, 522; Ségolène Barbou des Places, 'Progression and Retrogression of the ECJ Case Law on Access to Social Benefits', in Dora Kostakopoulou and Daniel Thym (eds), *Research Handbook on European Union Citizenship Law* (Elgar 2022) 263; Martijn van den Brink (n 3) 75–76.

Notably, in *Metock*[16] the Court was asked to interpret the derived right of residence in the host State of an EU citizen's family members who are third-country nationals. As the Court clarified elsewhere, this derived right of residence is equally protected by Article 21(1) TFEU.[17] However, Article 3(1) CRD limits this right by stating that 'the CRD shall apply to all Union citizens who move to or reside in a Member State other than that of which they are a national, and to their family members . . . who *accompany* or join them' (emphasis added). Pursuant to almost all the language versions of the CRD at the time of its adoption (ie 29.4.2004), the verb 'accompany [someone]' necessarily presupposes a *parallel movement* on behalf of the accompanying person.[18] Nevertheless, the Court, relying on a teleological interpretation of the CRD, found the latter to also apply to third-country nationals who were staying irregularly in the host State and only after some time they met and, subsequently, married a migrant EU citizen. According to the Court, the *telos* of the CRD to facilitate EU citizens' right of residence—and hence the derived rights of their family members—necessarily entails a non-restrictive interpretation of the term 'accompany'.[19] Similarly to *Grzelczyk* and *Baumbast and R.*, the Court arguably attributed to this finding a primary law status since it explicitly considered the EU citizens' right of residence as a 'fundamental right'.[20] Therefore, the Court appeared, once again, to 'attach no significance to a literal reading of the [CRD]' in order to expand the EU citizens' rights enshrined in Treaties.[21]

[16] Case C-127/08, *Metock and Others* ECLI:EU:C:2008:449.

[17] Case C-133/15, *Chavez-Vilchez and Others* ECLI:EU:C:2017:354, paras 52 and 62.

[18] Interestingly, AG Maduro asserted in his Opinion that the verb 'accompany' has a dual definition, meaning either 'to go with someone' or 'to be with someone'. This is true however only regarding Portuguese (the AG's own native language) and the adjacent Spanish. The broader meaning of those two languages should not, however, override all the other language versions; see Case C-344/23, *BIOR* ECLI:EU:C:2024:696, para. 45. Instead, the exclusive consideration of the condition of *parallel movement* would ensure the uniformity of all language versions of Art 3(1) CRD given that they all require, either exclusively or alternatively, the said condition.

[19] *Metock* (n 16) paras 92–93. As regards the letter of Art 3(1) CRD, the Court commented only on the right of a third-country national family member to 'join' the EU citizen. As the Court rightly noted, in para. 87, the exercise of that right does not require the EU citizen to have already founded a family at the time of moving to the host Member State. An EU citizen may also establish a family with a third-country national *after* moving to the host State. Nevertheless, the term 'join' presupposes a *movement* by the third-country national, which implies that he does not already reside in the host State when he acquires the status of family member of the EU citizen. Therefore, the verb 'join' does not confer a general right to found a family after the EU citizen's move to the host State. Yet the Court appears to adopt such an understanding when interpreting the verb 'accompany' (see paras 90–93).

[20] *Metock* (n 16) para. 89.

[21] Anastasia Iliopoulou-Penot, 'The Transnational Character of Union Citizenship' in Michael Dougan, Niamh Nic Shuibhne, and Eleanor Spaventa (eds), *Empowerment and Disempowerment of the European Citizen* (Hart 2012) 27. See also Samantha Curie, 'Accelerated Justice or a Step Too Far? Residence Rights of Non-EU Family Members and the Court's Ruling in Metock' (2009) 2 EL Rev 310, 320, claiming that the residence right of third-country nationals 'would be deprived of its effectiveness if a literal interpretation were to be applied'.

More recently, the Court appeared to neglect anew the will of the EU legislature by resorting, this time, to an overly formalistic reading of the CRD. In *Familienkasse*[22] the Court was called to decide on the equal treatment that an EU citizen can enjoy during his lawful residence in the host State of up to three months. According to Article 6(1) CRD, during such a short-term residence, the EU citizen must only hold a valid ID or passport without having to satisfy the two residence conditions of sufficient resources and comprehensive sickness insurance. For that reason, Article 24(2) CRD stipulates that the host State is not obliged to grant any 'social assistance' to this EU citizen. *Familienkasse* concerned a family benefit granted by Germany to its own nationals, which was classified in German legislation not as a 'social assistance' benefit, but as a 'social *security*' benefit within the meaning of Article 3(1)(j) of the Social Security Coordination Regulation 883/2004. That Regulation draws indeed an explicit distinction between 'social assistance' and 'social security' benefits.[23] In *Familienkasse* the Court applied a similar distinction in the context of the CRD. It thus held that while three-month residents cannot claim 'social assistance' under Article 24(2) CRD, they are still entitled to 'social security' benefits such as the family benefits at issue.[24]

However, this insistence on an alleged literal reading of the CRD appears too formalistic. In the absence of a clear distinction between the terms 'social assistance' and 'social security' in the CRD itself, their letter should offer little guidance. This is evident by the confusion these two terms have repeatedly provoked in the translation units of the Council, the Commission, and the Court, which have on several occasions translated, in the field of EU citizens' rights, 'social assistance' into 'social security' (or vice-versa) as if they mean one and the same thing.[25] In fact, a search of the documents of the legislative procedure leading to the adoption of the CRD confirms that the legislature wanted to contain in the derogation for 'social assistance' *every* type of social benefit,

[22] Case C-411/20, *Familienkasse* ECLI:EU:C:2022:602. For another example, see Case C-244/13, *Ogieriakhi*, ECLI:EU:C:2014:2068, paras 36–40.

[23] See, analytically, in Frans Pennings, *European Social Security Law* (7th edn, Intersentia 2022) 53–69.

[24] *Familienkasse* (n 22), paras 52–54.

[25] Indicatively, as regards the Council, compare the French version of Art 1 of Pensioneers' Residence Directive 90/365/EEC, which refers to '*assistance sociale*', with the English version which refers to 'social security system'. As regards the Commission, compare the French version of point 2.1, of the commentary on Art. 7 and of Recital 19 of the Explanatory Memorandum to the CRD Proposal, which respectively refers to '*assistance sociale*', '*prestations d'assistance sociale*', and '*prestations à titre d'assistance sociale*', with their English version which refers respectively to 'social security', 'social security benefits', and 'social security provision'. As regards the Court, compare the French version of judgment C-140/12, *Brey* ECLI:EU:C:2013:565 paras 44, 72, and 77, which all refer to the general term '*prestation*[*s*] *sociale*[*s*]', whereas their English version refers to 'social security benefit[s]'.

including social security benefits. When Denmark asked, in particular, the Commission what it meant by 'social assistance' in its proposal for Article 24(2) CRD, the Commission responded that 'it should be understood as covering all forms of social benefit'.[26] The same conclusion can also be drawn from a systematic and teleological interpretation of Article 24(2) CRD.[27] Like in the cases discussed above, the expansive approach of the Court in this judgment—in disregard to the will of the EU legislature—can be attributed to the Court's reliance on the 'fundamental status' of EU citizenship laid down in the Treaties, to which it explicitly referred in the beginning of its reasoning.[28]

2.2 The Court's deference to the 'legislative overrides' effected by the Citizens' Rights Directive

As demonstrated above, the Court repeatedly interpreted secondary legislation by overlooking the will of EU legislature and instead expanding the rights of EU citizens under Article 21 TFEU. Hence, in doing so, 'the Court created substantive rights at the level of primary law'.[29] Considering that the Court also disregarded, in that way, the normative inversion contained in Article 21 TFEU, these primary law rights appeared to hold a 'super-normative' status. As the above cases illustrate, this expansive approach of the Court is observed not only against the 1990s directives but, to some extent, also against the CRD.[30] Nonetheless, a notable exception to this approach is observed when the Court is faced with the legislative overrides introduced by the CRD over the prior primary law considerations made by the Court in the context of the 1990s directives. In these specific cases, the Court appears to acknowledge a 'hegemonic attribution of supremacy to secondary law'[31] and, thus, a (partial) omnipotence of the CRD.[32]

[26] Council doc. 15380/01 of 18.12.2001, p 34, note 76.

[27] Analytically in Maria Haag, 'The Muddle about the Union Citizen's Equal Access to Social Security Benefits: Familienkasse Niedersachsen-Bremen (C-411/20)', (2023) 2 EL Rev 206, 214–15.

[28] *Familienkasse* (n 22), para 28.

[29] Niamh Nic Shuibhne, 'Limits Rising, Duties Ascending: The Changing Legal Shape of Union Citizenship' (2015) 4 CML Rev 889, 891.

[30] It is noted that the Court's expansive approach against the CRD appears more limited, which can be explained by the fact that the CRD adopted several of the prior solutions of the Court in the context of the 1990s directives, notably the proportionality test of *Grzelczyk* and *Baumbast and R*; see Articles 7(1)(b) and 14(3) and recital 16.

[31] ibid 889.

[32] This does not imply that, in the absence of a legislative override, the Court will invariably adopt an expansive approach. It means only that, where such an override is present, the Court will always defer to the EU legislature, even if this requires reversing its previous case-law.

Förster[33] is the first such case. Article 3 of the Students' Residence Directive of 1993 provided that '[t]his Directive shall not establish any entitlement to the payment of maintenance grants by the host Member State on the part of students benefiting from the right of residence'. The Court first examined the effects of that provision in *Grzelczyk*.[34] Apart from the right of residence discussed above, the Court also elaborated in *Grzelczyk* on whether Article 3 of the Students' Residence Directive enabled the host State to deny to (lawfully resident) cross-border students a social assistance benefit, such as the Belgian '*minimex*' at issue. The Court responded that 'there are no provisions in the directive that preclude those to whom it applies from receiving social benefits'.[35] As becomes apparent from the literature of the time, the Court's response could be read in two different ways. On the one hand, it could mean that while the Court accepted the express limitation of Article 3 concerning specifically *maintenance aid to students*, it entitled the latter to equal treatment with regard to all other social benefits addressed *to the general population*, such as the Belgian '*minimex*'.[36] On the other hand, the Court's response could suggest, more widely, that Article 3 merely stipulated that it did not establish *itself* a right to maintenance aid to students. Hence, the Court was not prevented from entitling students to *all types* of social benefits, including maintenance aid, on the basis of other EU law provisions, and especially Articles 18 and 21 TFEU.[37] This second reading was actually confirmed by the Court in its subsequent case law.[38] Such a reading, however, evidently contradicted the will of the EU legislature as expressed in Article 3 of the Students' Residence Directive to deprive students from maintenance aid.[39]

The EU legislature attempted to curtail the Court's case law in the CRD.[40] Article 24(2) CRD states, in clear and precise terms, that host Member States are not obliged to grant maintenance aid to students before the latter acquire

[33] Case C-158/07, *Förster* ECLI:EU:C:2008:630.

[34] *Grzelczyk* (n 9).

[35] ibid 39.

[36] Anastasia Iliopoulou and Helen Toner, Comment on C-184/99, *Grzelczyk* (2002) 3 CML Rev 609, 619.

[37] Michael Dougan, 'Fees, Grants, Loans and Dole Cheques: Who Covers the Costs of Migrant Education within the EU?' (2005) 4 CML Rev 943, 962; Anne Pieter van der Mei, 'EU Law and Education: Promotion of Student Mobility versus Protection of Education Systems', in Eleanor Spaventa and Michael Dougan (eds), *Social Welfare and EU Law* (Hart 2005) 226.

[38] *Förster* (n 33) paras 41–44.

[39] See also seventh recital of the preamble to the directive. Same, Kay Hailbronner (n 8) 1253.

[40] Siofra O'Leary, 'Equal Treatment and EU Citizens: A New Chapter on Cross-border Educational Mobility and Access to Student Financial Assistance' (2009) 4 EL Rev 612, 623, who notes that 'Art. 24(2) of Directive 2004/38 was arguably at odds with the decisions of the Court in cases like *Grzelczyk* ... In addition, it cannot be forgotten that ... *Grzelczyk* [was itself] at odds with fairly clear provisions of the Students' Residence Directive.'

the right of permanent residence. Given that this right is acquired only after five years of residence in the host State, the practical effect of Article 24(2) CRD is that it *de facto* excludes cross-border students from maintenance aid. In *Förster*,[41] the Grand Chamber of the Court fully deferred to this legislative override. The factual background of the case dated before the adoption of the CRD. The judgment, however, was delivered after both the adoption of the CRD *and* the expiry of the deadline for its transposition into the national legal orders. The Court accepted that a host State's national legislation, which laid down a requirement of a continuous five-year residence for the award of student maintenance aid, both pursued a legitimate objective and was proportionate to that objective. Interestingly, the Court also referred to Article 24(2) CRD, which '*although not applicable to the facts in the main proceedings*' also provides for a five-year residence requirement.[42] The corroboration of the Court's reasoning by reference to the non-applicable *ratione temporis* Article 24(2) CRD was widely acknowledged as 'an indication of judicial deference to the EU legislator'.[43] In addition, the said reasoning appeared contradictory with the Court's previous interpretation of Articles 18 and 21 TFEU in other case law, such as *Bidar*.[44]

A similar deference by the Court to the legislative overrides of the CRD can be attributed to its judgments in *Dano*[45] and *Alimanovic*.[46] As regards *Dano*, the Court had initially ruled in *Martínez Sala*[47] that if an EU citizen did not satisfy the residence conditions of sufficient resources and sickness insurance imposed by the 1990s directives, but resided in the host State under *national* law, he could still claim equal treatment in the host State as regards social benefits on the basis of Article 18 TFEU. Nevertheless, the purpose of the 1990s directives was precisely to bring an EU citizen within the scope of EU law *only if* he met their residence conditions. Accordingly, the 1990s directives explicitly subjected the right of residence to conditions so that EU citizens 'avoid becoming *a burden on the social assistance system* of the host Member State during their period of residence'. By ordering instead, in *Martínez Sala*,

[41] C-158/07, *Förster* [2008].

[42] Para 54 (emphasis added).

[43] Koen Lenaerts, 'European Union Citizenship, National Welfare Systems and Social Solidarity' (2011) 2 Jurisprudence 397, 418; Niamh Nic Shuibhne (n 6) 350–52 and 358.

[44] Case C-209/03, *Bidar* ECLI:EU:C:2005:169. See, among many, Christopher Vajda, 'Democracy in the European Union: What Has the Court of Justice to Say?' (2015) 2 CILJ 226, 237-238. See also extrajudicial explanation of the judgment in *Bidar* by its *juge rapporteur* (and currently President of the Court) Lenaerts in his joint contribution: Koen Lenaerts and Tinne Heremans, 'Contours of a European Social Union in the Case-Law of the European Court of Justice' (2006) 2 EuConst 101, 107.

[45] Case C-333/13, *Dano* ECLI:EU:C:2014:2358.

[46] Case C-67/14, *Alimanovic* ECLI:EU:C:2015:597.

[47] Case C-85/96, *Martínez Sala* ECLI:EU:C:1998:217.

Member States to grant social protection under Article 18 TFEU to EU citizens who reside in their territory solely under national law, the Court ignored the clear will of the EU legislature.[48] A similar stance was adopted by the Court in its subsequent judgment in *Trojani*.[49] The reaction of the EU legislature was to clarify in Article 24(1) CRD that 'all Union citizens *residing on the basis of this Directive* in the territory of the host Member State shall enjoy equal treatment with the nationals of that Member State' (emphasis added).

In *Dano*, the Court recognized that Article 24(1) CRD constitutes a specification of the principle of equal treatment of Article 18 TFEU which excludes from equal treatment those EU citizens who reside in the host State solely on the basis of national law.[50] Paradoxically, though, the Court justified the strict application of Article 24(1) CRD by using arguments which should have prevented its judgments in *Martínez Sala* and *Trojani* in the first place. Specifically, it held that to accept that persons who do not have a right of residence under [the CRD] may claim entitlement to social benefits 'would run counter to an objective of the directive ... namely preventing Union citizens who are nationals of other Member States from becoming *an unreasonable burden on the social assistance system* of the host Member State'.[51] By conceding to the persisting position of the EU legislature in Article 24(1) CRD, 'the Court abandoned, with *Dano*, its case law based on primary EU law on the sole basis of provisions found in secondary law, an inferior source of law of the Treaties'.[52]

The Court's deference in *Alimanovic* equally finds origins in *Martínez Sala*. In the latter case, the Court had also ruled that an EU citizen who does not satisfy the residence conditions of the 1990s directives but 'who is genuinely seeking work must also be classified as a worker' and thus claim equal treatment with regard to the host State's social benefits under Article 7(2) of Regulation 1612/68 on free movement of workers.[53] The Court later nuanced this ruling in *Collins*[54] by holding that a jobseeker cannot actually be considered as a 'worker' but can still, under certain conditions, claim the host State's social benefits that are addressed specifically to jobseekers by virtue of

[48] Elise Muir, 'EU Citizenship, Access to "Social Benefits" and Third-Country National Family Members: Reflecting on the Relationship Between Primary and Secondary Rights in Times of Brexit' (2018) 3 European Papers 1353, 1362 in *fine* 1363.

[49] Case C-456/02, *Trojani* ECLI:EU:C:2004:488.

[50] This was confirmed in Case C-709/20, *CG v The Department for Communities in Northern Ireland* ECLI:EU:C:2021:602, paras 81–83.

[51] *Dano* (n 45) para 74 (emphasis added). See also para 79.

[52] Ségolène Barbou des Places, 'Progression and Retrogression of the ECJ Case Law on Access to Social Benefits' in Dora Kostakopoulou and Daniel Thym (n 15), 258–59.

[53] *Martínez Sala* (n 47), paras 32 and 34.

[54] Case C-138/02, *Collins* ECLI:EU:C:2004:172.

his status as EU citizen under Article 20 TFEU. This interpretation, however, disregarded the will of the legislature in a twofold manner. It was at variance not only with Article 45 TFEU and Article 7(2) of the Regulation 1612/68, which reserved explicitly social advantages only for 'workers', but also with the 1990s directives concerning EU citizens' rights of movement and residence. This is because, by grounding its solution on EU citizenship *in general*, without referring to Article 21 TFEU and the latter's subjection to secondary law, the Court escaped the express residence conditions of the 1990s directives, which aimed precisely at preventing economically inactive citizens from becoming a burden on the host States' public finances.[55]

The Court's disregard for the legislature's will was expressly addressed by Article 24(2) CRD, which allows Member States to *refuse* social assistance to jobseekers for as long as they maintain a right of residence, and which, for that reason, 'was widely understood as an attempted override'.[56] At first, the Court, sitting in five-member Chamber formations in *Ioannidis* and *Vatsouras*, did not defer to this legislative override.[57] Probably recognizing the problematic features of this case law, the Court, sitting in a Grand Chamber formation, reversed it in *Alimanovic*.[58] The Court there recognized that the host State can deny social assistance to jobseekers, including social benefits specifically addressed to the jobseekers of that State. Hence, the Grand Chamber performed one of its central roles within the EU's judicial system, which is the resolution of questions of constitutional importance which may even necessitate a reversal of the previous (wrongly adjudicated) case law.[59]

The legislative overrides effected by the CRD also affected the Court's case law on certain other, closely related, matters.[60] Other than that, as noted above,

[55] Henri de Waele and Jochen Meulman, 'Funding the Life of Brian: Jobseekers, Welfare Shopping and the Frontiers of European Citizenship' (2004) 4 Legal Issues of Economic Integration 275, 285–86; Thomas Horsley, *The Court of Justice of the European Union as an institutional Actor, Judicial Lawmaking and Its Limits* (CUP 2018) 180–82.

[56] Gareth Davies (n 10), 1600 and literature cited therein.

[57] Case C-258/04, *Ioannidis* ECLI:EU:C:2005:559; Joined Cases C-22/08 and C-23/08, *Vatsouras and Koupatantze* ECLI:EU:C:2009:344.

[58] Takis Tridimas, 'The General Principles of Law: Who Needs Them?' (2016) 1 CDE 419, 430–31; Martijn van den Brink, 'Off Track, Again? EU Citizenship and the Right to Social Assistance' (2023) 1 HYIEL 18, 27.

[59] Sacha Prechal, 'The Many Formations of the Court of Justice: 15 Years After Nice' (2016) 5 Fordham Intl LJ 1273, 1280 *in fine* 1281.

[60] In Joined Cases C-424/10 and C-425/10, *Ziolkowski and Szeja* ECLI:EU:C:2011:866, concerning the acquisition of the right of permanent residence, the Court acknowledged, in a similar fashion to *Dano*, the intrinsic link established in the CRD between the satisfaction of its residence conditions and the entitlement to equal treatment. In Case C-299/14, *García-Nieto and Others* ECLI:EU:C:2016:114, the Court held that its reasoning in *Alimanovic* also applies in relation to the host State's power to deny pure social assistance benefits to three-month residents (to be distinguished from the social security benefits examined in *Familienkasse*).

the Court has maintained its expansive interpretation of the CRD in several other cases. In that sense, the omnipotence of the CRD is only 'partial'.

3. The General Omnipotence of the Direct Tax Legislature

In the field of direct taxation is observed, in turn, a generalized deference of the Court to the EU legislature. First, the Court has on several occasions refused to question the validity of the direct tax directives.[61] Second, it has generally resisted attributing a broad interpretation to the provisions of those directives, sticking instead to their literal wording.[62] Third, and as will be explored in this chapter, the Court's interpretation of the Treaties' fundamental freedoms appears dependent (and even subject to reversals) on the position taken by the EU legislature, which, in the field of direct taxation, is essentially only the Council which decides unanimously after the Parliament's mere consultation pursuant to Articles 114(2) and 115 TFEU. In this regard, of particular interest are the lines of case law which display the following cumulative characteristics:

- In the absence of EU legislation, the Court favours, initially, a given interpretation of the fundamental freedoms in connection to a subject-matter A.
- Subsequently, the Council adopts a directive in connection with a closely related subject-matter B.
- Once the Court is called again to interpret the fundamental freedoms in connection to the subject-matter A, it reverses its previous case law, aligning it with the approach adopted by the Council in relation to the subject-matter B.

In none of all the lines of case law fulfilling those characteristics has the Court ever acknowledged explicitly its influence by the position taken by the Council. This influence, however, is revealed in the Opinions of Advocate Generals. In addition, it offers an arguable explanation for several of the Court's judgments in direct taxation that either deviate from its established case law or even

[61] Case C-58/01, *Océ van der Grinten* ECLI:EU:C:2003:495; C-247/08, *Gaz de France* ECLI:EU:C:2009:600.

[62] Indicatively, Case C-448/15, *Wereldhave* ECLI:EU:C:2017:180 and Joined Cases C-116/16 and C-117/16, *T Denmark and Y Denmark* ECLI:EU:C:2019:135, which favoured a literal interpretation of both the positive criterion of that company being 'subject to tax' and the negative criterion of not 'being exempt' from that tax enshrined in the Parent-Subsidiary Directive 2011/96.

reverse it altogether. Indicative examples are two lines of case law concerning the fiscal use of losses.

The first one relates to the question whether a Member State A (host State) is obliged to allow a branch (permanent establishment—PE) which is located in that State, but which belongs to a company established in another Member State B, to transfer its losses to another affiliated company established in the host State A, thereby lowering the taxable profits of the latter. In *Philips Electronics*[63] the host State A of a PE refused such a transfer of losses, claiming that there was a risk of those losses also being deducted in the Member State B, where the PE's company's headquarters were established. However, the Court held that 'the risk that those losses may be used both in the host Member State where the permanent establishment is situated and also in the Member State where the non-resident company has its seat has no effect on the power of the Member State where the permanent establishment is situated to impose taxes'.[64] In other words, since the host State A anyway had the power to tax the profits of the PE and the affiliated company located within its own tax jurisdiction, it was irrelevant that any occurred losses could be possibly used again in the Member State B. Therefore, the host State A could not justify the restriction entailed by its tax legislation on the freedom of establishment of the PE's company under Article 49 TFEU. *NN A/S*[65] raised a similar question. AG Campos Sánchez-Bordona noted that it was difficult based on *Philips Electronics* to justify the national legislation at issue on the need to prevent the double use of losses. He stressed, however, that 'perhaps the time has arrived to moderate those assertions made in the judgment in *Philips Electronics*, in view of the fact that the EU legislature has paid special attention to the fight against double deduction since that judgment was delivered'.[66] In particular, he referred to the non-applicable *ratione temporis* and *materiae*—in that case ATAD Directive 2016/1164, which prohibits mismatches resulting in double deduction of losses. He then added that '[n]aturally, I am not proposing that the provisions of a directive whose transposition deadline has not yet expired should be applied to this case. I do believe, however, that Directive 2016/1164 reflects a widespread concern, the strength of which was probably not evident — and, of course, was not expressly reflected in legislation — when the judgment in *Philips Electronics* was given.'[67] The Court, albeit without referring explicitly

[63] Case C-18/11, *Philips Electronics* ECLI:EU:C:2012:532.
[64] ibid para 30.
[65] Case C-28/17, *NN A/S* ECLI:EU:C:2018:526.
[66] Opinion of AG Campos Sánchez-Bordona in Case C-28/17, *NN A/S* ECLI:EU:C:2018:86, point 64.
[67] ibid point 70.

to his reasoning, essentially followed the AG's Opinion and departed from its previous case law by allowing, under certain conditions, the host Member State A to deny the use of the PE's losses when those losses may be also used in the Member State B. Therefore, *NN A/S* can be interpreted as 'the Court affording opportunity for a Treaty compliant solution to a problem handled in the [not applicable *ratione temporis*] ATAD', with which it even reversed its prior primary law jurisprudence.[68]

The second example concerns Member States' legislation subjecting natural and legal persons to exit taxation when they transfer their assets to another Member State (or when they move themselves, together with all their assets, to another Member State). Upon such an 'exit' of assets, the home State may tax the capital gains accrued on those assets (eg increase of commercial value of shares or business equipment) during the period when those assets fall within its tax jurisdiction, but which had escaped taxation because their gains had not yet been realised (ie the assets had not been sold, thereby not generating taxable income). The aim of such an exit taxation is to preserve the host State's power to tax all the gains generated within its tax jurisdiction before the assets are removed from that jurisdiction.

The Court was first called to examine the compliance of exit taxation with the fundamental freedoms in *N*,[69] which concerned the move of the tax residence of a *natural person* and the corresponding transfer of his *private assets* (ie shares) to another Member State. The Court accepted that the home State can determine the amount of the capital gains tax upon the 'exit' of the assets. However, in order to comply with the freedom of establishment under Article 49 TFEU, it must defer the collection of the tax until their disposal (ie realization of the gains through sale) in the host State. In that way, the home State ensures equal treatment between the cross-border and the domestic situations given that assets which are not transferred from the host State's tax jurisdiction are also taxed on their capital gains only upon disposal. In addition, before collecting the tax, the home State is obliged to consider any decrease in value which occurred after the 'exit' of the assets (eg falling of the shares' value in between their 'exit' and their disposal) unless the host State does so under its own tax legislation.[70] Finally, the home State is prevented from asking for

[68] Jesper Johansson, 'Is NN A/S (C-28/17) a Potential Trendsetter?' (2021) 11 Intertax 948, 954. See also Georg Kofler, 'Cross-Border Loss Relief', in TERRA/WATTEL, *European Tax Law* (Vol. 1, Kluwer 2023), 364–66; Adam Zalasiński, 'Sharing and Shifting of Corporate Losses—The New Profit Shifting' (2023) (107a) Cahiers de Droit Fiscal International 75, 80–81.

[69] Case C-470/04, *N v Inspecteur* ECLI:EU:C:2006:525.

[70] The host State may do that if it 'steps up', ie if it considers as taxable value of the assets, at the time of their entry into its own tax jurisdiction, their commercial value (and not their original book value).

guarantees to secure the future recovery of the tax since there is sufficient EU legislation enabling the home State to seek any necessary assistance from the host State.[71]

Two years after the Court's judgment in *N*, the Council adopted a Resolution which concerned the exit taxation, not of private individuals, but of *undertakings*.[72] The Council took a diametrically opposite approach than the Court's judgment in *N*. According to the Resolution, the host State should be the only responsible to consider reductions in value incurred after the exit, thereby relieving the home State from considering them upon the collection of the exit tax. As regards the time of collection, the Resolution remained silent on whether an undertaking should have the right to defer the payment of the exit tax until the disposal of the underlying assets. The valid impression was thus given that the Council saw home Member States as enjoying the discretion to immediately both determine the tax and recover it.[73]

The Court was soon confronted with the exit taxation of *undertakings* in *National Grid Indus*.[74] Contrary to what it had decided in *N* regarding private individuals, the Court interpreted the freedom of establishment as always relieving the home State of the obligation to take account of subsequent decreases in value. To that end, the Court drew a general distinction between *natural persons* and *companies*. According to the Court, the assets of a company are assigned directly to economic activities that are intended to produce a profit. In addition, the taxable profits of a company are partly influenced by the depreciation of its assets in the balance sheet.[75] Nevertheless, such considerations are only relevant for the *non-financial* assets held by a company (machinery equipment, IP rights, etc) and not for its *financial* assets (shares, loan claims, etc). Non-financial assets are instrumental in the generation of corporate profits through the production of goods and the provision of services. This generation of profits normally continues after the exit, thereby *giving rise to taxable profits in the host State*. In addition, non-financial assets are, at the same time, depreciable, in the sense that their value is decreased with the passage of time. Companies can thus deduct from their taxable profits part of their value each year. In the case of operating assets, such as machinery equipment,

[71] *N* (n 69) paras 51–54.
[72] Council Resolution of 2.12.2008 on coordinating exit taxation (2008/C 323/01).
[73] Henk van Arendonk, 'Citizens and Taxation in the EU: Fifty Years after the Neumark Report' (2012) 3 EC Tax Review 144, 150. See also publicly expressed concerns of the Commissioner for Taxation and Customs Union in László Kovács, 'European Commission Policy on Exit Taxation' (2009) 1 STE, 3.
[74] Case C-371/10, *National Grid Indus* ECLI:EU:C:2011:785.
[75] ibid para 57.

that is due to wear and tear, while in the case of IP rights it is due to their limited protection period.[76] After those assets move to the host State, they will continue losing their value. This means that the taxable profits in the host State will be, to some extent, decreased. However, it also means that if the home State is required to consider subsequent decreases in the value of these assets, it will most likely be deprived of its right to tax any capital gains since the latter will effectively disappear. Therefore, as regards non-financial assets, it makes sense for the Court to distinguish between private individuals—as in *N*—and companies.

As said, however, all these considerations are relevant only to *non-financial assets*. While it is true that, unlike individuals, companies are usually subject to exit taxation not only on financial but also on non-financial assets, this does not justify a uniform tax treatment of all company assets, regardless of their nature. In fact, the Dutch company in *National Grid Indus* held only one financial asset, namely a debt claim. It is therefore unreasonable to subject such an asset to a tax treatment, whose justification is pertinent exclusively to non-financial assets. Accordingly, the absolute distinction drawn by the Court between private individuals and companies—instead of between financial and non-financial assets—in order to absolve the home State from considering subsequent decreases in value is over-simplistic and, thus, unconvincing.[77]

The same can be said regarding the Court's answer on the right of a company to defer the payment of the exit tax until the disposal of the underlying asset. While the Court attempted to display consistency with its previous judgment in *N*, by extending the right for a deferred payment also to companies, it stripped that right of all meaning. First, contrary to *N*, the Court held that the home State can actually ask a company for guarantees with the excuse that the risk of non-recovery of the tax increases with the passage of time. Second, the home State can subject the exercise of the company's right of deferral to the payment of interest.[78] Third, pursuant to subsequent case law, the home State does not have to defer the recovery until the disposal of the assets but can ask instead for a payment in five annual instalments, starting in the year of the exit. According to the Court, this is once more due to the 'risk of non-recovery

[76] See László Kovács (n 73); Otto Marres, 'Exit Taxes on Companies' in Ana Paula Dourado (ed), *Movement of Persons and Tax Mobility in the EU: Changing Winds* (IBFD 2013), 184.

[77] See, among many, Reinout Kok, 'Exit Taxes for Companies in the European Union after National Grid Indus' (2012) 4 EC Tax Review 200, 205; Daniël Smit, 'The National Grid Indus Case: A Pyrrhic Victory?' (2012) 1 STE, 20 and 22; Peter J Wattel, 'Exit Taxation in the EU/EEA Before and After National Grid Indus' (2012) 1 TNI 371, 372.

[78] *National Grid Indus* (n 74) paras 73–74.

[which] increases with the passing of time'.[79] As the Court explained at length in *National Grid Indus*, the asset situation of a company may be particularly complex and thus undermine the home State's effort to recover the exit tax upon the disposal of the underlying assets. Nevertheless, this is again an over-generalized statement. In AG Kokott's words, 'there can obviously be private individuals whose asset situation is just as complex as that of an undertaking', while there can be also undertakings with a very simple asset situation. That was exactly the case with the company in *National Grid Indus*, which, as said, had only one asset.

In light of this unconvincing reasoning of the Court, its judgment may be better explained by its willingness to align with the choices made by the Council in the Resolution of 2008.[80] The Court apparently drew a contradictory distinction between natural persons and companies in order to defer to the soft-law instrument adopted by the EU direct tax legislature in relation to undertakings.

The exit tax rules established by the Council Resolution and the Court's judgment in *National Grid Indus* regarding companies were consolidated in Article 5 of ATAD Directive 2016/1164. Six months after the adoption of the directive, the Court delivered its judgment in *Commission v Portugal*.[81] In that case, the Commission had deliberately contested the Portuguese legislation concerning the exit taxation of shareholders—regardless of their status—in order to get confirmation from the Court that the *N* case law was still valid for natural persons.[82] However, this time the Court found that there is no objective reason for distinguishing between taxpayers, and held that the *National Grid Indus* case law regarding the home State's power to disregard the subsequent decreases in value as well as request guarantees and interest payments, apply irrespective of the taxpayer's status.[83] In doing so, the Court reversed its prior interpretation of fundamental freedoms in its *N* judgment on private

[79] Case C-164/12, *DMC* ECLI:EU:C:2014:20, para 62; Case C-657/13, *Verder LabTec* ECLI:EU:C:2015:331, paras 50–52.

[80] For a similar view, see Servaas van Thiel, 'The European Court and Tax Sovereignty of the Member States', in Georg Kofler, Michael Lang, and others (eds), *CJEU Recent Developments in Direct Taxation 2022* (Linde 2024), 245.

[81] Case C-503/14, *Commission v Portugal* ECLI:EU:C:2016:979.

[82] Wim Roels, 'The Removal of Tax Obstacles to Living, Working, Investing, Retiring and Dying in Another Member State', in European Commission, *70 Years of EU Law: A Union for Its Citizens*, 2022, 218–19.

[83] *Commission v Portugal* (n 81) paras 55–59 and 87. Interestingly, the reversal of *N* by *Commission v Portugal* did not cover the issue of payment in instalments since the Court did not make any reference to it. That was confirmed in Case C-581/17, *Wächtler* ECLI:EU:C:2019:138, paras 66–68 where the Court acknowledged the home State's power to ask private individuals for guarantees where there is a risk of non-recovery, but not for a staggered payment of the tax.

individuals.[84] In the absence of any other explanation offered by the Court, it can arguably be inferred that the Court aligned its fundamental freedoms case law on private individuals to the dictates of the non-applicable *ratione personae* ATAD (which only applied to companies).

An analogous influence of the Court by non-applicable directives for the purposes of interpreting the Treaties' fundamental freedoms in the field of direct taxation can be observed in several other cases, which due to length constraints, cannot be analysed in this chapter.[85] What can briefly be observed, nonetheless, is that the Court probably considered in these cases that the position adopted by the Council, namely the EU direct tax legislature, in the non-applicable directives reflected its intended will on the solution to be given in the matter pending before the Court. Such a will can be readily observed in directives that are not applicable merely *ratione temporis*. A similar consideration can also be made, however, for directives that are not applicable *ratione personae*. EU legislation in substantive issues of direct taxation is focused on the taxation of companies, such as the ATAD examined in the above cases. This is explained by the fact that companies are the primary actors in cross-border economic activities, both in terms of frequency and scale. As a result, the tax disadvantages they may face—such as double taxation—or the aggressive tax planning in which they may engage have far more significant ramifications for the internal market and/or the interests of Member States than comparable activities undertaken by individuals. Accordingly, the EU direct tax legislature's abstention from harmonizing the tax treatment of individuals is likely attributable to the Member States' mere preference to concentrate their efforts on

[84] Johanna Hey, 'Taxation of Business in the EU: Special Problems of Crossborder Losses and Exit Taxation', in Christiana HJI Panayi, Werner Haslehner, and Edoardo Traversa (eds), *Research Handbook on European Union Taxation Law* (Edward Elgar 2020), 215; Andreas Musil, 'Steuerrecht: Wegzugsbesteuerung der Wertzuwächse aus einem Tausch von Gesellschaftsanteilen bei natürlichen Personen' (2017) (7) EuZW 2017, 187; Florian Haase, 'Ist der EuGH noch zu retten?' (2023) 1 Ubg 4.

[85] Indicatively, see inconsistency of judgment C-446/04, *Test Claimants in the FII Group Litigation* ECLI:EU:C:2006:774 with the traditional free movement case law, which can be attributed to the influence by the non-applicable *ratione materiae* Parent-Subsidiary Directive; see Otto Marres, 'The Parent-Subsidiary Directive', in TERRA/WATTEL (n 68) 540–41. Also compare judgment C-324/00, *Lankhorst-Hohorst* ECLI:EU:C:2002:749 with judgment C-524/04, *Test Claimants in the Thin Cap Group Litigation* ECLI:EU:C:2007:161 considering the non-applicable *ratione materiae* in the latter case Article 4(2) of the Interest & Royalty Directive 2003/49/EC; also compare judgment C-321/05, *Kofoed* ECLI:EU:C:2007:408 with judgments in Joined Cases C-116/16 and C-117/16, *T Denmark and Y Denmark* ECLI:EU:C:2019:135 and Joined Cases C-115/16, C-118/16, C-119/16 and C-299/16, *N Luxembourg 1 and others* ECLI:EU:C:2019:134, considering the non-applicable *ratione temporis* in the latter cases Article 6 of ATAD Directive; also compare judgment C-269/09, *Commission v Spain* ECLI:EU:C:2012:439 with judgment C-707/20, *Gallaher* ECLI:EU:C:2023:101 considering the non-applicable ratione *personae* and *materiae* in the latter case Art. 5(4a) of ATAD Directive. It is noted that the non-applicable *ratione materiae* directives in the above cases regulated a matter closely linked with the matter addressed before the Court.

achieving the required unanimity within the Council in relation to the more pressing issues concerning companies. The positions, however, that they take on the allocation of taxing powers in certain matters concerning companies may well reflect the positions they would adopt if those same matters were ever to be regulated with respect to individuals.

4. The Special Status of the Fields of EU Citizens' Rights and Direct Taxation within the Treaty Framework

By way of conclusion, some arguments of normative nature are in order. The Court's deference towards the EU legislature in the fields of EU citizenship rights and direct taxation can be explained—and indeed justified—by the status these two fields hold within the Treaty framework.

As regards EU citizens' rights, several authors have claimed that the Court's deference to the CRD provisions in *Dano* and *Alimanovic*—decided in 2014 and 2015 respectively—reveal an alleged alignment of the Court with the political environment of the time. They basically claim that the rise of Euroscepticism—fuelled by the financial and immigration crises and epitomized by the 2016 Brexit referendum—led the Court to retreat from its expansive approach to EU citizens' rights.[86] Accordingly, it has been argued that '[j]udgments like *Dano* and *Alimanovic* present a marked shift towards doctrinal conservatism.'[87] Nevertheless, such a political narrative fails to account for a number of restrictive judgments on EU citizens' rights delivered prior to 2014, such as *Förster*, as well as for certain recent expansive judgments, such as *Familienkasse.*

Against this background, the delicate nature of the dialogue between the Court and the EU legislature regarding EU citizens' rights can be better explained by to the diametrical opposing effects generated by Article 21(1) TFEU. On the one hand, the Court has overlooked in certain cases the legislative choices to accommodate the added value inherent in the Treaty concept of

[86] Among others, Anastasia Iliopoulou-Penot, 'Deconstructing the Former Edifice of Union Citizenship? The *Alimanovic* Judgment' (2016) 4 CML Rev 1007, 1007–08, 1012 and 1030–35; Michael Blaumberger et al., 'ECJ Judges Read the Morning Papers: Explaining the Turn-around of European Citizenship Jurisprudence' (2018) 10 JEPP 1422, 1430–37; Daniel Thym, 'The Evolution of Citizens' Rights in Light of the EU's Constitutional Development' in Dora Kostakopoulou and Daniel Thym (n 15) 58, 62–63 and 66–67.

[87] Dora Kostakopoulou and Daniel Thym, 'Conclusion: The Non-Simultaneous Evolution of Citizens' Rights', in D. Thym (ed), *The Deconstruction of EU Citizenship* (Hart 2017) 310, 316. See also Eleanor Spaventa, 'Earned Citizenship—Understanding Union Citizenship through Its Scope' in D. Kochenov (ed), *EU Citizenship and Federalism: The Role of Rights* (CUP 2017) 204, 209.

'citizenship'—a concept which similarly carries a constitutional weight within the national legal orders.[88] Once, however, the EU legislature overrides the Court's expansive case law, the Court defers, even if that necessitates the reversal of its previous primary law holdings. In doing so, it adheres to the normative inversion of Article 21(1) TFEU. This does not mean that in the absence of a legislative override the Court always favours an expansive approach, nor that it defers only when such an override is present. Rather, it indicates that without an override the Court may still interpret EU legislation expansively, whereas in its presence it will probably not do so. Such an explanation indeed reflects the 'double-faced' mandate of Article 21(1) TFEU.[89]

An argument based on the Treaty framework itself can also explain—as well as endorse—the special influence exerted on the Court by the EU legislature in the field of direct taxation. The Treaties are entirely silent as regards direct taxation, not even providing for the adoption of cooperative measures in that field as they do, for example, for social security in Article 48 TFEU. That said, the EU legislature can adopt direct tax legislation on the basis of the Union's general internal market competence. Nonetheless, given that Article 114(2) TFEU expressly excludes the harmonization of fiscal provisions under Article 114(1), all EU direct tax legislation has thus far been adopted under Article 115 TFEU, which requires a unanimous decision within the Council. This is likely because the Member States have been unwilling to incorporate matters of direct tax sovereignty into the Treaty framework, given their politically sensitive nature.[90] Once, therefore, the Member States decide to collectively exercise their sovereignty in direct tax matters within the Council, the Court understandably pays particular attention to their will—even to the point of revisiting its previous interpretations of primary law provisions.

Therefore, the Court's acknowledgment of the (partial or general) omnipotence of the EU legislature in the fields of EU citizens' rights of movement and direct taxation may be readily explained—and indeed justified—by reference

[88] Analytically, Opinion of AG Cosmas in Case C-378/97, *Wijsenbeek* ECLI:EU:C:1999:144, points 79-87; Siofra O'Leary, 'Developing an Ever Closer Union between the Peoples of Europe? A Reappraisal of the Case Law of the Court of Justice on the Free Movement of Persons and EU Citizenship' (2008) 1 YEL 167, 176–77; Niamh Nic Shuibhne, 'The Outer Limits of EU Citizenship: Displacing Economic Free Movement Rights?' in Catherine Barnard and Okeoghene Odudu (eds), *The Outer Limits of European Union Law* (Hart 2009) 167, p 181.

[89] An argument in favour of a similar approach can be made for other primary law provisions, which although laying down rights of traditional constitutional weight are nevertheless to be further developed 'in accordance with Union law and national law and practices', such as the freedom to conduct a business under Article 16 of the Charter.

[90] See Suzanne Kingston, 'The Boundaries of Sovereignty: The ECJ's Controversial Role Applying Internal Market Law to Direct Tax Measures' (2007) 9 CYELS 287, 289, and 311.

to the Treaty framework itself. This omnipotence may still be exceptionally circumscribed. This is the case where the choices made by the (otherwise omnipotent) legislature are set aside, on rare occasions, in order to preserve the protection of fundamental rights. So far, this has occurred only once in each of the two fields.[91]

In addition, the question may arise as to whether the Court may, by invoking fundamental rights, *a priori* foreclose the possibility for the EU legislature to override its primary law interpretations. This question has arisen with particular force after the Court's recent case law on Member States' duty to recognize same-sex marriages of mobile EU citizens. In *Coman*,[92] the Court had initially grounded that duty in a literal and systematic interpretation of the neutral term 'spouse' in Article 2(2) of the CRD.[93] It could therefore be argued that the EU legislature retained the power to amend either the wording or the context of the CRD in order to adopt a different solution, should it so wish. However, in its more recent judgment in *Wojewoda Mazowiecki*,[94] the Court reinforced its findings in *Coman* by grounding them, this time, in Articles 7 and 21(1) of the Charter. These lines of case law suggest that some uncertainty remains as to the limits of the EU legislature's omnipotence.

References

Barbou des Places S, 'Progression and Retrogression of the ECJ Case Law on Access to Social Benefits' in Dora Kostakopoulou and Daniel Thym (eds), *Research Handbook on European Union Citizenship Law* (Elgar 2022)

Blaumberger M et al., 'ECJ Judges Read the Morning Papers: Explaining the Turn-around of European Citizenship Jurisprudence' (2018) 10 JEPP 1422

Carter DW, *The European Precariat: The Protection of Precarious Workers in the European Union* (PhD thesis, Leiden University, 2023)

[91] As regards the field of EU citizens' rights, see Case C-709/20, *CG v The Department for Communities in Northern Ireland* ECLI:EU:C:2021:602 and comment in Maria Haag, 'The Coup de Grâce to the Union Citizen's Right to Equal Treatment: *CG v. The Department for Communities in Northern Ireland* (2022) 4 CML Rev 1081, where the Court departed from its *Dano* case law due to the serious risk of violation of the applicant's rights enshrined in Articles 1, 7, and 24 of the Charter. As regards the field of direct taxation, see Case C-694/20, *Orde van Vlaamse Balies and Others* ECLI:EU:C:2022:963 and comment in Alexandros Politis, 'La CJUE élargit le concept de secret professionnel de l'avocat en droit de l'Union', 2023 (2) CFLE 265, where the Court invalidated a provision of the 'DAC 6' directive concerning the exchange of information in the field of taxation due to the breach of the legal professional privilege derived from Article 7 of the Charter.

[92] Case C-673/16, *Coman* ECLI:EU:C:2018:385.

[93] ibid, paras 33–36.

[94] Case C-713/23, *Wojewoda Mazowiecki* ECLI:EU:C:2025:917.

Coutts S, 'The Court, the Legislature and the Co-Construction of a Status of Social Integration' in Nathan Cambien, Dimitry Kochenov, and Elise Muir (eds), *European Citizenship under Stress* (Brill 2020)

Curie S, 'Accelerated Justice or a Step Too Far? Residence Rights of Non-EU Family Members and the Court's Ruling in Metock' (2009) 2 EL Rev 310

Davies G, 'Legislative Control of the European Court of Justice' (2014) 6 CML Rev 1579

de Waele H and Meulman J, 'Funding the Life of Brian: Jobseekers, Welfare Shopping and the Frontiers of European Citizenship' (2004) 4 Legal Issues of Economic Integration 275

Dougan M, 'Fees, Grants, Loans and Dole Cheques: Who Covers the Costs of Migrant Education within the EU?' (2005) 4 CML Rev 943

Haag M, 'The Coup de Grâce to the Union Citizen's Right to Equal Treatment: *CG v. The Department for Communities in Northern Ireland* (2022) 4 CML Rev 1081

Haag M, 'The Muddle about the Union Citizen's Equal Access to Social Security Benefits: Familienkasse Niedersachsen-Bremen (C-411/20)', (2023) 2 EL Rev 206

Haase F, 'Ist der EuGH noch zu retten?' (2023) 1 Ubg 4

Hailbronner K, 'Union Citizenship and Access to Social Benefits' (2005) 5 CML Rev 1245

Hey J, 'Taxation of Business in the EU: Special Problems of Crossborder Losses and Exit Taxation' in Christiana H.J.I. Panayi, Werner Haslehner, and Edoardo Traversa (eds), *Research Handbook on European Union Taxation Law* (Edward Elgar 2020)

Horsley T, *The Court of Justice of the European Union as an institutional Actor, Judicial Lawmaking and its Limits* (CUP 2018)

Iliopoulou A and Toner H, Comment on C-184/99, Grzelczyk (2002) 3 CML Rev 609

Iliopoulou-Penot A, 'The Transnational Character of Union Citizenship', in Michael Dougan, Niamh Nic Shuibhne, and Eleanor Spaventa (eds), *Empowerment and Disempowerment of the European Citizen* (Hart 2012)

Iliopoulou-Penot A, 'Deconstructing the Former Edifice of Union citizenship? The *Alimanovic* judgment' (2016) 4 CML Rev 1007

Jesse M and Carter DW, 'Life after the "*Dano*-Trilogy": Legal Certainty, Choices and Limitations in EU Citizenship Case Law' in Nathan Cambien, Dimitry Kochenov, and Elise Muir (eds), *European Citizenship under Stress* (Brill 2020)

Johansson J, 'Is NN A/S (C-28/17) a Potential Trendsetter?' (2021) 11 Intertax 948

Kingston S, 'The Boundaries of Sovereignty: The ECJ's Controversial Role Applying Internal Market Law to Direct Tax Measures' (2007) 9 CYELS 287

Kofler G, 'Cross-Border Loss Relief', in TERRA/WATTEL, *European Tax Law* (Vol. 1, Kluwer 2023)

Kok R, 'Exit Taxes for Companies in the European Union after National Grid Indus' (2012) 4 EC Tax Review 200

Kostakopoulou D and Thym D, 'Conclusion: The Non-Simultaneous Evolution of Citizens' Rights', in D. Thym (ed), *The Deconstruction of EU Citizenship* (Hart 2017)

Kovács L, 'European Commission Policy on Exit Taxation' (2009) 1 STE 3

Lenaerts K, 'European Union Citizenship, National Welfare Systems and Social Solidarity' (2011) 2 Jurisprudence 397

Lenaerts K and Heremans T, 'Contours of a European Social Union in the Case-Law of the European Court of Justice' (2006) 2 EuConst 101

Marres O, 'Exit Taxes on Companies' in Ana Paula Dourado (ed), *Movement of Persons and Tax Mobility in the EU: Changing Winds* (IBFD 2013)

Marres O, 'The Parent-Subsidiary Directive', in TERRA/WATTEL, *European Tax Law* (Vol. 1, Kluwer 2023) 269–294

Muir E, 'EU Citizenship, Access to "Social Benefits" and Third-Country National Family Members: Reflecting on the Relationship Between Primary and Secondary Rights in Times of Brexit' (2018) 3 European Papers 1353

Musil A, 'Steuerrecht: Wegzugsbesteuerung der Wertzuwächse aus einem Tausch von Gesellschaftsanteilen bei natürlichen Personen' (2017) (7) EuZW 187

Ní Chaoimh E, *The Legislative Priority Rule and the EU Internal Market for Goods* (OUP 2022)

Nic Shuibhne N, 'The Outer Limits of EU Citizenship: Displacing Economic Free Movement Rights?' in Catherine Barnard and Okeoghene Odudu (eds), *The Outer Limits of European Union Law* (Hart 2009)

Nic Shuibhne N, 'The Third Age of EU Citizenship' in Phil Syrpis (ed), *The Judiciary, the Legislature and the EU Internal Market* (CUP 2012)

Nic Shuibhne N, 'Limits Rising, Duties Ascending: The Changing Legal Shape of Union Citizenship' (2015) 4 CML Rev 889

O'Leary S, 'Developing an Ever Closer Union between the Peoples of Europe? A Reappraisal of the Case Law of the Court of Justice on the Free Movement of Persons and EU Citizenship' (2008) 1 YEL 167

O'Leary S, 'Equal Treatment and EU Citizens: A New Chapter on Cross-border Educational Mobility and Access to Student Financial Assistance' (2009) 4 EL Rev 612

O'Leary S and Iglesias Sánchez S, 'Free Movement of Persons and Services' in Paul Craig and Gráinne de Búrca (eds), *The Evolution of EU Law* (3rd edn, OUP 2021)

Pennings F, *European Social Security Law* (7th edn, Intersentia 2022)

Pieter van der Mei A, 'EU Law and Education: Promotion of Student Mobility versus Protection of Education Systems' in Eleanor Spaventa and Michael Dougan (eds), *Social Welfare and EU Law* (Hart 2005)

Politis A, 'La CJUE élargit le concept de secret professionnel de l'avocat en droit de l'Union' (2023) 2 CFLE 265

Prechal S, 'The Many Formations of the Court of Justice: 15 Years after Nice' (2016) 5 Fordham Int'l LJ 1273

Roels W, 'The Removal of Tax Obstacles to Living, Working, Investing, Retiring and Dying in Another Member State', in European Commission, *70 Years of EU Law, A Union for Its Citizens*, 2022, 218–219

Schütze R, ''Integration-through-Law': Grand Theory, Revisionist History' (2025) 4(2) ELO 162

Smit D, 'The National Grid Indus Case: A Pyrrhic Victory?' (2012) 1 STE 20

Spaventa E, 'Earned Citizenship—Understanding Union Citizenship through Its Scope' in D Kochenov (ed), *EU Citizenship and Federalism: The Role of Rights* (CUP 2017)

Spieker LS, 'Was Grimm Wrong? Putting the Over-Constitutionalization of EU Law to the Test' (2025) 26(3) GLJ 416

Syrpis P, 'The Relationship between Primary and Secondary Law in the EU' (2015) 2 CML Rev 461

Szudoczky R, 'The Influence of Primary Law on the Interpretation of Secondary Law in the Field of EU Citizenship and Direct Taxation: "Whatever works"...' in Dennis Weber (ed), *Traditional and Alternative Routes to European Tax Integration* (IBFD 2010)

Thym D, 'The Evolution of Citizens' Rights in Light of the EU's Constitutional Development' in Dora Kostakopoulou and Daniel Thym (eds), *Research Handbook on European Union Citizenship Law* (Elgar 2022)

Tridimas T, 'The General Principles of Law: Who Needs Them?' (2016) 1 CDE 419

Vajda C, 'Democracy in the European Union: What Has the Court of Justice to Say?' (2015) 2 CILJ 226

van Arendonk H, 'Citizens and Taxation in the EU: Fifty Years after the Neumark Report' (2012) 3 EC Tax Review 144

van den Brink M, 'Off Track, Again? EU Citizenship and the Right to Social Assistance' (2023) 1 HYIEL 18

van den Brink M, Dawson M, and Zglinski J, 'Revisiting the Asymmetry Thesis: Negative and Positive Integration in the EU' (2025) 1 JEPP 209

van den Brink M, *Legislative Authority and Interpretation in the European Union* (OUP 2024)

van Thiel S, 'The European Court and Tax Sovereignty of the Member States' in Georg Kofler, Michael Lang and others (eds), *CJEU Recent Developments in Direct Taxation 2022* (Linde 2024)

Wattel PJ, 'Exit Taxation in the EU/EEA before and after National Grid Indus' (2012) 1 TNI 371

Wollenschläger F, 'The Judiciary, the Legislature and the Evolution of Union Citizenship' in Phil Syrpis (ed), *The Judiciary, the Legislature and the EU Internal Market* (CUP 2012)

Zalasiński A, 'Sharing and Shifting of Corporate Losses—The New Profit Shifting' (2023) (107a) Cahiers de Droit Fiscal International 75

14

Deciding Not to Decide: Dismissal, Narrowing, and Relinquishment at the Court of Justice of the European Union

Graham Butler

1. Introduction: Deciding Not to Decide

Determining what the Court of Justice of the European Union (the Court)[1] has decided in a given case is relatively (though not always) straightforward for a lawyer. To understand what the Court 'has decided', there is a clear operative part of the ruling at its conclusion, which formally decides the case. Naturally, how this operative part is set out is dependent on the procedural context of any given case. For cases that are references for a preliminary ruling to the Court, under Article 267 TFEU, this is the part of the ruling that the national court or tribunal is to apply to the underlying case which the Court reverts to it, after proceedings at the Court have concluded. For actions for annulment, be it at the Court of Justice or the General Court, the case is either dismissed or, where an applicant is successful, the Court states what EU legal act, or which part of an EU legal act, is to be annulled. Understanding this operative part of a ruling, replicated across the entire range of procedural avenues through which cases reach the Court,[2] the natural expectation for any lawyer is that the operative

[1] In this chapter, 'the Court' refers to the Court of Justice of the European Union (CJEU) as the judicial institution, encompassing both the Court of Justice and the General Court. Where a necessary distinction between the two courts within 'the Court' is needed, they will be referred to as the 'Court of Justice' and the 'General Court'.

[2] There is no shortage of procedural avenues in which cases are heard by the Court. See, eg, Koen Lenaerts, Kathleen Gutman, and Janek Tomasz Nowak, *EU Procedural Law* (Second Edition, Oxford University Press 2023); Viktor Luszcz, *European Court Procedure. A Practical Guide* (Hart Publishing 2020); KPE Lasok, *Lasok's European Court Practice and Procedure* (Third Edition, Bloomsbury Professional 2017); René Barents, *Remedies and Procedures before the EU Courts* (Kluwer Law International 2016).

Graham Butler, *Deciding Not to Decide: Dismissal, Narrowing, and Relinquishment at the Court of Justice of the European Union* In: *The Reasoning of the Court of Justice of the EU*. Edited by: Alezini Loxa and Luigi Lonardo, Oxford University Press. © Graham Butler 2026. DOI: 10.1093/9780198983002.003.0018

part of each ruling matches its applicable procedure, and the outcome is easily understood.

With operative parts of ruling understood, however decided, the reasoning behind the Court's rulings, and how to understand the way in which the Court reached its decision, can in some situations be a much more circumspect and treacherous exercise. Legal research focusing on the legal reasoning of the Court, quite rightly, often looks at what the Court *has said*,[3] what it has used in support of what it has said, and the previous case law that it has cited (or not cited), and analyses the outcome of the Court's ruling. Typically, the Court's ruling is then probed for its consistency with prior case law, for whether it meets the logic of the underlying EU primary law and EU secondary law to which it relates; then academics, practitioners, and others comment on how the case or cases analysed contributes to a particular field of EU law. One of the critiques of the Court's reasoning—and there is no shortage of them[4]—is that the Court insufficiently explains itself in reaching the conclusions that it does. There are many arguments for why this is the case. But this (alleged) failure of the Court to sufficiently reason the route to the operative part of its ruling is usually a critique of a decision *it has made*. In other words, the critique is as a result of *what has been decided.*

More elusive, and largely uncovered, is what the Court in many cases has *decided not to decide*. And in not deciding in a case, somewhat counterintuitively, and in a figuratively complex manner, the Court in many instances has therefore actively decided not to decide something. Within the Court's rulings (and even its actions beyond its rulings, as will be demonstrated) are moves and turns that can be difficult to detect, for they are not obvious to the naked eye, but nonetheless are evident once probed and looked at through a different lens. Such a probative lens sees many situations where matters are obviously not decided. In other words, the Court does not always lay out all the arguments presented to it in the course of a given case; nor does it lay out all the arguments not presented to it, but which it nonetheless considered in arriving at a given conclusion in its rulings. Behind every ruling and every action of the Court as an EU institution are a variety of considerations, leading ultimately to

[3] See, *inter alia*, Suvi Sankari, *European Court of Justice Legal Reasoning in Context* (Europa Law Publishing 2013); Joxerramon Bengoetxea, 'Reasoning from Consequences from Luxembourg' in Henning Koch and others (eds), *Europe. The New Legal Realism: Essays in Honour of Hjalte Rasmussen* (Djøf Publishing 2010); Anthony Arnull, *The European Union and Its Court of Justice* (2nd edn, Oxford University Press 2006) 607–21; Ulrich Everling, 'Reflections on the Reasoning in the Judgments of the Court of Justice of the European Communities', *Festskrift til Ole Due: Liber Amircorum* (GEC Gads 1994); Joxerramon Bengoetxea, *The Legal Reasoning of the European Court of Justice* (Clarendon Press 1993).

[4] See Introduction and chapter by Leczykiewicz.

matters that arise before it, but that were ultimately not decided upon in given rulings.

This chapter both reveals and resultingly maps out various strategies that the Court employs, some deliberate and some inadvertent, when it does not rule in cases, and therefore decides not to decide. It also considers the reasons, as elusive as they may be, for why the Court has decided not to decide in certain scenarios. This phenomenon, at first sight, may appear instantly paradoxical, given that, by the very role placed on it by the EU Treaties—namely that it 'shall ensure that in the interpretation and application of the Treaties the law is observed'[5]—the Court must actually render a decision in all cases that it hears, in a judicial architecture in which it has historically had very little control over its own docket. But in fact, as this chapter goes to demonstrate, there are various ways in which, given the cases presented to it, the Court actually leaves many questions of EU law undecided, and leaves it open for itself to decide on another occasion.

In demonstrating that there is evidence to support the theory that the Court engages in deciding not to decide, this chapter puts forth three methods and techniques in which the Court engages in this practice. Such methods and techniques have the objective consequence that some things are left undecided. First, the chapter examines cases where the Court opts for the 'dismissal' of a case. This could involve orders of inadmissibility for premature cases, not necessarily due to procedural shortcomings, but rather as sensitive substantive issues arise in which the Court prefers to sidestep and not answer at that given moment in time. Second, the chapter proposes that the Court engages in 'narrowing'. It does this institutionally through trying to get a firmer grip on the type of cases that it hears, by limiting procedurally avenues in which it has historically taken up more of the Court's resources than the Court believes it should have, or by, in specific cases, seeking to narrow judgments in certain scenarios by ensuring that its interpretation of arising EU law is not overinterpreted by powerful state actors, particularly in cases involving the interpretation of EU primary law. Third, the chapter highlights how the Court responds to a case by ultimately resorting to 'relinquishment'. It does this by providing answers in its operative part to a referring court through the reference for a preliminary ruling procedure, but leaving the referring national court or tribunal to choose which answer in the operative part to apply, given

[5] Article 19(1) TEU: 'The Court of Justice of the European Union shall include the Court of Justice, the General Court and specialised courts. It shall ensure that in the interpretation and application of the Treaties the law is observed. Member States shall provide remedies sufficient to ensure effective legal protection in the fields covered by Union law.'

that the proportionality assessment is left to the referring national court, which the Court gives that referring body a wide breadth to apply.

Through these 'dismissal' (section 2), 'narrowing' (section 3), and 'relinquishment' (section 4) methods and techniques, it is argued that it is evident in the case law and wider institutional actions of the Court, through both subtle and less-than-overt methods, the Court avoids ruling on cases as they are presented to it through the various procedural avenues. With these methods and techniques of 'deciding not to decide' better understood, a clearer basis for understanding why the Court engages in such methods and techniques in both past and future cases will emerge.

2. Dismissal

This first method and technique where the Court evidently is deciding not to decide a case is where it opts for the dismissal of a case. It does this through two obvious ways: ruling that a case is inadmissible, and where a case is considered to be premature. When the Court rules in cases stating that a case before it is inadmissible or manifestly inadmissible, the Court is essentially removing itself from its role as an adjudicator on the substance of a case because a procedural requirement is not met. This is most evident in cases where the Court sits as the administrative court of the EU, ordinarily at first instance before the General Court and then on appeal to the Court of Justice.[6]

Admissibility is a very obvious way in which the Court engages in the dismissal of cases within the realm of EU procedural law. One of the more well-known lines of case law in this regard is the issue of *locus standi* in respect of natural and legal persons, who have a high bar to reach.[7] Unless an applying party in action for annulment cases is a privileged or semi-privileged party within the listed body of actors within Article 263 TFEU, both natural and legal persons are given a rough ride in terms of even having their case deemed admissible,[8] for they have to be both directly concerned and individually

[6] See Caroline Naômé, *Appeals before the Court of Justice of the European Union* (Oxford University Press 2018).

[7] Famously, see Case 25/62, *Plaumann v Commission*, ECLI:EU:C:1963:17.

[8] See, eg, Angela Ward, *Judicial Review and the Rights of Private Parties in EU Law* (2nd edn, Oxford University Press 2007) 258–335. Historically, see Rosa Greaves, 'Locus Standi under Article 173 EEC When Seeking Annulment of a Regulation' (1986) 11 European Law Review 119; Albertina Albors-Llorens, 'The Standing of Private Parties to Challenge Community Measures: Has the European Court Missed the Boat?' (2003) 62 The Cambridge Law Journal 72; Paul Craig, 'Standing, Rights, and the Structure of Legal Argument' (2003) 9 European Public Law 493.

concerned.[9] At a more technical level, even though legal standing criteria are met, other procedural issues such as failure of parties to set out the forms of order sought, or ill-worded applications and such, can also lead to cases running the risk of being ruled inadmissible by the Court.

Beyond just *locus standi* considerations, however, determining whether a case is admissible before the Court based on procedural requirements, particularly in direct action cases, shows that the Court adopts 'a flexible approach',[10] accounting for many relevant factors in a given application before it. Evidently, however, there are some cases where, despite procedural formalities being formally met, the Court will nonetheless rule in cases finding applications to be inadmissible.

There has been one particular set of cases that has clearly shown that the Court was determined to dismiss the pleas at all costs. This determination stemmed from the fact that the issues involved were closely tied to the Court's own position within the EU's institutional architecture, specifically its own lawful composition, as well as the actions of EU Member States that affected such lawful composition. This was the *Sharpston* litigation.

Here, a sitting member of the Court of Justice was challenging her removal from the Court of Justice by a decision of the representatives of the governments of the Member States, claiming that they had the power to remove a member of the Court under the power prescribed to them under Article 253 TFEU. The contextual backdrop was the withdrawal of the United Kingdom from the EU ('Brexit'), which occurred in early 2020. In doing so, the representatives of the governments of the Member States were seeking to appoint a new member of the Court of Justice, thereby removing a member—her—before the end of her term of office. Here, the Court was very visibly having its composition tinkered with by the Member States, beyond the legal bounds applied to the composition of the Court, which was regulated by the Statute of the CJEU, as appended to the EU Treaties.

Quite surprisingly, in the *Sharpston* litigation, in near unison,[11] the Vice-President of the Court of Justice, the General Court, and the Court of Justice

[9] This is, of course, on the assumption they are not addressed by the EU legal act; if they are, then the *locus standi* criterion is met.

[10] Lasok (n 2) 605.

[11] See Case C-423/20 P(R), *Council v Sharpston*, ECLI:EU:C:2020:700, Order of the Vice-President of the Court of Justice; Case C-424/20 P(R), *Council and Representatives of the Governments of the Member States v Sharpston*, ECLI:EU:C:2020:705, Order of the Vice-President of the Court of Justice; Case T-180/20, *Sharpston v Council of the European Union and Conference of the Representatives of the Governments of the Member States*, ECLI:EU: T:2020:473, Order of the General Court; Case T-184/20, *Sharpston v Court of Justice of the European Union*, ECLI:EU:T:2020:474, Order of the General Court; Case T-550/20, *Sharpston v Council and Representatives of the Governments of the Member States*, ECLI:EU:T:2020:475, Order of the General Court; Case C-684/20 P, *Sharpston v Council*

itself[12] went out of their way in a series of procedural rulings to avoid dealing with the substantive issue, and the difficult yet relevant questions raised in the case, of which reprisal against one particular member of the Court of Justice was linked to that of a withdrawing Member State.[13] Here the inadmissibility power of the Court was a particularly powerful tool employed because it enabled the Court to decide not to decide the underlying substantive case. In doing so, the Court, by its actions, thus avoided, perhaps intentionally, the tremendously difficult question of having to address its own lawful composition, given the presence of a potentially unlawfully appointed member of the Court of Justice between September 2020 and October 2021,[14] covering the time in which the applicant was removed as a member of the Court of Justice and the ordinary expiry of her term of office.[15] Albeit a highly unusual scenario that was avoidable by many of the parties concerned, the *Sharpston* litigation powerfully illustrated that the Court has dismissal tools at its disposal, through use of the inadmissibility device, as a way to not to decide a case at its leisure, in the context of direct action cases.

Another form of the Court deciding not to decide is when a case is considered premature. That is to say, where the Court is willing to entertain hearing the case through the given procedure presented to it, but there are other aspects of the case in which the Court has taken upon itself to dismiss

of the European Union and Conference of the Representatives of the Governments of the Member States, ECLI:EU: C:2021:486, Order of the Court; and Case C-685/20 P, *Sharpston v Council and Representatives of the Governments of the Member States*, ECLI:EU:C:2021:485, Order of the Court.

[12] The only judicial actors that came out well, publicly, of the *Sharpston* litigation were the applicant herself, Advocate General Eleanor Sharpston, and Judge Anthony M Collins (as he was then) of the General Court, the judge hearing interim measures in the General Court, in the first ruling to come from the Court. See Case T-550/20 R, *Sharpston v Council and Representatives of the Governments of the Member States*, ECLI:EU:T:2020:416, Order of the Judge Hearing Applications for Interim Measures. Happily, the Advocate General will be better remembered for her Opinions in her many years as a member of the Court of Justice, but also for her pleadings in her time appearing before it too. See Graham Butler, 'An Advocate before Advocate General: Eleanor Sharpston at the European Courts' in Catherine Barnard, Adam Łazowski, and Daniel Sarmiento (eds), *Pursuit of Legal Harmony in a Turbulent Europe: Essays in Honour of Eleanor Sharpston* (Hart Publishing 2024).

[13] For the history at the time, see Dimitry Kochenov and Graham Butler, 'The Independence and Lawful Composition of the Court of Justice of the European Union: Replacement of Advocate General Sharpston and the Battle for the Integrity of the Institution' in Joseph HH Weiler and Gráinne De Búrca (eds), *The Jean Monnet Working Paper Series, Jean Monnet Center for International and Regional Economic Law & Justice, School of Law, New York University* (2020).

[14] Advocate General Athanasios Rantos, whose term of office *should* have commenced in October 2021, on the expiry of the term of office of Advocate General Eleanor Sharpston.

[15] A reflection on the *Sharpston* affair is offered in Dimitry Kochenov and Graham Butler, 'Independence of the Court of Justice of the European Union: Unchecked Member States Power after the Sharpston Affair' (2021) 27 European Law Journal 262; Kieran Bradley, 'Appointment and Dis-Appointment at the CJEU: Part II—The Sharpston Litigation' (2022) 21 The Law & Practice of International Courts and Tribunals 178.

the case, given alleged prematurity of the case reaching the Court. The most obvious procedural avenue where this could arise is the request for an opinion on a proposed international agreement which the EU wants to conclude with a third party bilaterally, or within third parties multilaterally.

The Opinion procedure in Opinion 218(11) TFEU states that selected parties

> may obtain the opinion of the Court of Justice as to whether an agreement envisaged is compatible with the Treaties. Where the opinion of the Court is adverse, the agreement envisaged may not enter into force unless it is amended or the Treaties are revised.[16]

This Opinion procedure has been utilized on approximately twenty-five occasions, in which the Court has provided some of its most important rulings in the field of EU external relations law.[17] As a form of pre-ratification judicial review and abstract constitutional review, it is routinely used to break a deadlock in long-running institutional debates within the EU over horizontal competence in external relations when it comes to undertaking legal commitments vis-à-vis third parties through international agreements, *inter alia*.

For every Opinion of the Court delivered on foot of a request made under Article 218(11) TFEU in recent decades, the Court has assembled itself, in terms of the formation of judges hearing such cases, as a Grand Chamber[18] or a Full Court.[19] That changed, however, when the Court was presented with a request from Belgium—a privileged party entitled to make such requests under Article 218(11) TFEU[20]—on whether the 'draft modernised Energy Charter

[16] For fuller analysis of the Opinion procedure in Article 218(11) TFEU, see Graham Butler, 'Pre-Ratification Judicial Review of International Agreements to Be Concluded by the European Union' in Mattias Derlén and Johan Lindholm (eds), *The Court of Justice of the European Union: Multidisciplinary Perspectives* (Hart Publishing 2018).

[17] Nearly all the Opinion procedure cases are analysed by several authors in Graham Butler and Ramses A Wessel (eds), *EU External Relations Law: The Cases in Context* (Hart Publishing 2022). For a comprehensive study of the procedure itself, see Stanislas Adam, *La procédure d'avis devant la Court de justice de l'Union européenne* (Bruylant 2011).

[18] Recent examples include, eg, *Opinion 3/15*, ECLI:EU:C:2016:657 (*Marrakesh Treaty*); *Opinion 1/15*, ECLI:EU:C:2017:592 (*EU–Canada PNR*); and, *Opinion 1/19*, ECLI:EU:C:2021:198 (*Istanbul Convention*).

[19] Similarly, see, eg, *Opinion 2/13*, ECLI:EU:C:2014:2454 (*EU Accession to the ECHR II*); *Opinion 2/15*, ECLI:EU:C:2017:376 (*EU–Singapore FTA*); and, *Opinion 1/17*, ECLI:EU:C:2019:341 (*EU–Canada CETA*).

[20] That said, it is conceivable that non-listed parties in Article 218(11) TFEU could make such a request, such as the High Representative (HR), given their role in some international agreements. See Graham Butler, 'The High Representative as a New Actor before the Court of Justice of the European Union' in Frank Hoffmeister and Lóránt Havas (eds), *The High Representative of the Union for Foreign Affairs and Security Policy as a Legal Actor: Liber Amicorum in Honour of Stephan Marquardt* (Brill 2025) 56–58.

Treaty (ECT)' was compatible with the EU Treaties, with particular regard to both Article 19 TEU and Article 344 TFEU, in the form of *Opinion 1/20 (Modernised ECT)*,[21] relating to the ECT, and the ongoing discussions over reform of that international agreement to which the EU is a party.

The Court was essentially being asked a question that touched upon a matter in which it previously ruled on in its *Komstroy* judgment,[22] but also its ruling in *PL Holdings*,[23] which followed its initial ruling in *Achmea* three years prior to that.[24] Those judgments, and others that followed, were negatively received in some quarters of the legal community,[25] who did not believe that such intra-EU dispute settlement provisions of legacy international agreements threatened the autonomy of the EU legal order in the way that the Court viewed them to.[26]

In *Opinion 1/20 (Modernised ECT)*, the Court essentially ruled that it was not presented with 'sufficient information', and that the case appeared 'premature'.[27] The mootness argument that the Court presented here was particularly curious, given that the substance of the case concerned the issue of intra-EU application of international agreements concluded by the EU by itself, and collectively with third states. The previous judgments of *Achmea*, *PL Holdings*, and *Komstroy* had not explicitly dealt with such a matter. The alleged prematurity of the *Opinion 1/20 (Modernised ECT)* case being referred to it by Belgium was, admittedly, helpful for it dismissing the case, leaving undecided what the EU's and Member States' role vis-à-vis the ECT is for another time. Given the various stated intentions (and some formal notifications) of EU Member States to withdraw from the ECT, ultimately, the Court's answer to the questions put to it will never be heard.

[21] *Opinion 1/20*, ECLI:EU:C:2022:485 (*Modernised ECT*).

[22] Case C-741/19, *Republic of Moldova v Komstroy LLC*, ECLI:EU:C:2021:655.

[23] Case C-109/20, *Republic of Poland v PL Holdings Sàrl*, ECLI:EU:C:2021:321.

[24] Case C-284/16, *Slovak Republic v Achmea BV*, ECLI:EU:C:2018:158.

[25] See, eg, Alan Dashwood, 'Republic of Moldova v Komstroy LCC: Arbitration under Article 26 ECT Outlawed in Intra-EU Disputes by Obiter Dictum' (2022) 47 European Law Review 127; Alan Dashwood, 'Article 26 ECT and Intra-EU Disputes—the Case Against an Expansive Reading of Achmea' (2021) 46 European Law Review 415.

[26] See further, Graham Butler, 'Investment in the EU Legal Order' in Xavier Groussot, Marja-Liisa Öberg, and Graham Butler (eds), *The EU Law of Investment: Past, Present, and Future* (Hart Publishing 2025).

[27] *Opinion 1/20*, ECLI:EU:C:2022:485 (*Modernised ECT*), paras 46 and 48.

3. Narrowing

The second method and technique where the Court evidently is deciding not to decide a case is where it opts to narrow the types of cases that come before it. Analysis first is placed on the relatively recent amendments to the Statute of the Court, designed to limit the number of cases on the docket of the Court of Justice, and second where the Court is evidently trying to limit the *erga omnes* effect of a ruling.

Institutionally, the Court has undergone several reforms in the past decade or so. The Statute has undergone revision in 2016, 2020, and 2024, marking something of a pattern of reform that is likely to continue for the foreseeable future. Each reform has been significant in its own way, changing the EU judicial architecture ever so slowly, albeit not without consequence.

First, the 2016 reform transformed the EU judiciary from a three-tier system, which included a specialized court with limited jurisdiction at the lowest level,[28] back to a two-tier system of general jurisdiction, resembling its structure in 1989. Most visually, that 2016 reform saw the abolition of the EU Civil Service Tribunal (CST), and the doubling of the size of the General Court, with each Member State now given the opportunity to nominate two persons for appointment. With that extra judicial capacity, changes also came as to the types of cases that the General Court was to hear.

At a time when the Court of Justice was in receipt of more cases than it had ever had before, the Court of Justice was keen to have certain types of cases no longer heard by it, for it was of the view that some cases had been reviewed enough times that they no longer warranted another set of judicial proceedings. In other words, it was actively in favour of a more deliberate form of docket control. To do so, it sought the introduction of an appeal filtering mechanism. This was achieved through, at the Court's request,[29] the insertion of an 'Article 58a'.[30] This provided for limiting the right of appeal to the Court of Justice in a situation when a decision of the General Court had been rendered whose case

[28] See Alberto Alemanno and Laurent Pech, 'Thinking Justice outside the Docket: A Critical Assessment of the Reform of the EU's Court System' (2017) 54 Common Market Law Review 129; Graham Butler, 'An Interim Post-Mortem: Specialised Courts in the EU Judicial Architecture after the Civil Service Tribunal' (2020) 17 International Organizations Law Review 586.

[29] The Court does not, in itself, control the Statute. That is a matter for the Parliament and Council acting under the ordinary legislative procedure. Initiatives to amend the Statute must come from the Commission, or alternatively the Court itself. In other words, the Court has the possibility to initiate a proposed change to its Statute. See Article 281 TFEU, second paragraph.

[30] See Jacopo Alberti, 'The Threshold Guardians: The Future of EU Agencies' Boards of Appeal in Light of the Recent Reforms of CJEU Statute' (2024) 16 Review of European Administrative Law 67; Luca De Lucia, 'The Shifting State of Rights Protection Vis-à-Vis EU Agencies: A Look at Article 58a of the Statute of the Court of Justice of the European Union' (2019) 44 European Law Review 809.

originated against a decision of certain independent boards of appeal of EU agencies. In essence, the Court took the view that one administrative appeal and one judicial appeal were satisfactory to ensure access to justice, and to ensure that 'the law is observed'.[31] By way of exception, the Court of Justice could allow an appeal against a decision of the General Court to proceed if, 'wholly or in part, [the case] raises an issue that is significant with respect to the unity, consistency or development of Union law'.[32]

In the years since this insertion of Article 58a into the Statute of the Court, the Court actively made use of the appeal filtering mechanism to deny cases from proceeding, thereby letting judgments of the General Court stand, and making it the *de facto* court of final instance in cases that started within EU agencies.[33] In other words, the Court of Justice was deciding not to decide on certain cases any longer. This change, after all, was made at the Court's initiation, with the EU legislature approval.

Under this 'Article 58a' appeal filtering mechanism, only exceptionally have cases been allowed to proceed.[34] In fact, the Court of Justice so much enjoyed this 2020 reform—which greatly limited the number of intellectual property cases that it heard—that during a subsequent reform adopted in 2024,[35] Article 58a was extended to cover a far greater number of boards of appeal of EU agencies. Rather than being confined to appeals emanating from the boards of appeal of the European Union Intellectual Property Office (EUIPO), the Community Plant Variety Office (CPVO), the European Chemicals Agency (ECHA), and the European Union Aviation Safety Agency (EASA), the list was extended to include the European Union Agency for the Cooperation of Energy Regulators (ACER), the Single Resolution Board (SRB), the European Banking Authority (EBA), the European Securities and Markets Authority (ESMA), the European Insurance and Occupational Pensions Authority

[31] Article 19(1) TEU, first paragraph.

[32] Article 58a, third paragraph, Protocol (No 3) on the Statute of the Court of Justice of the European Union, annexed to the EU Treaties.

[33] For criticism, see Luca De Lucia, 'The Boards of Appeal as Hybrid Adjudicators: On Some Shortcomings of Article 58a of the Statute of the Court of Justice of the European Union' in Merijn Chamon, Annalisa Volpato, and Mariolina Eliantonio (eds), *Boards of Appeal of EU Agencies: Towards Judicialization of Administrative Review?* (Oxford University Press 2022).

[34] The first such case was Case C-382/21 P, *EUIPO v The KaiKai Company Jaeger Wichmann*, ECLI:EU:C:2024:172. See Łukasz Żelechowski, 'No Direct Effect of the Paris Convention and Limited Cross-Priority Rights in EU Design Law: Question Marks after KaiKai' (2025) 62 Common Market Law Review 623.

[35] For a full account, see Sara Iglesias Sánchez, 'The 2024 Reform of the Statute of the Court of Justice of the EU and the Transformation of the EU Judicial System: Preliminary Rulings before the General Court of the EU' in Alejandro Saiz Arnaiz and Joan Solanes Mullor (eds), *The European Judiciary: A Community of Law and a Community of Judges* (Hart Publishing 2025).

(EIOPA), and the European Union Agency for Railways (ERA).[36] It also—in a very concealed manner, and curiously—added in cases brought before the General Court through the arbitration clause contained in Article 272 TFEU.[37] This was despite the fact that such proceedings under the arbitration clause are not subject to any prior administrative or judicial review, thus meaning that arbitration clause cases, post-2024, are ordinarily heard at just one instance, with the General Court being the *de facto* court of first and final instance.[38]

More importantly, however, the 2024 reform also saw, for the first time, the Court of Justice willingly let go of certain cases under the reference for a preliminary ruling procedure under Article 267 TFEU. Operationally, from 2024 therefore, under Article 50b of the Statute of the Court, cases referred to the Court of Justice under the reference for a preliminary ruling procedure from national courts and tribunals under Article 267 TFEU relating to certain confined areas of EU law—value-added tax, excise duties, the customs code, tariff classifications, passenger transport compensation, and greenhouse gas emissions trading—would be heard by the General Court.[39] In 2025, the General Court rendered its judgments in cases referred by national courts and tribunals under this newfound novelty.[40] And while it is still the case that the Court does not ultimately control the cases which it receives under the reference for a preliminary ruling procedure and decides, it is now the reality that the apex court, the Court of Justice, has now arranged the Statute in an active manner so that it passes cases on certain issues downwards within the EU judicial architecture to the General Court.

In other words, the Court of Justice succeeded in convincing the EU legislature that it should again further narrow the cases it hears. What is particularly

[36] For the particularities that arise in respect of various boards of appeal, which are wildly different from each other, see the various contributions in Merijn Chamon, Annalisa Volpato, and Mariolina Eliantonio (eds), *Boards of Appeal of EU Agencies: Towards Judicialization of Administrative Review?* (Oxford University Press 2022).

[37] Over time, various EU institutions, bodies, offices, and agencies, and even Common Security and Defence Policy (CSDP) missions under the Common Foreign and Security Policy (CFSP), have made increasing use of the arbitration clause, which confers explicit jurisdiction on the EU judiciary. See Graham Butler, 'The EU's Contractual Relations and the Arbitration Clause: Disputes at the Court of Justice of the European Union' (2021) 46 European Law Review 345.

[38] It should be noted that the Court, *post facto*, might have realized this oversight. Thus far, in the only request to allow an appeal to proceed in an arbitration clause case, it has allowed the appeal to proceed. See Case C-881/24 P, *SC v Eulex Kosovo*, ECLI:EU:C:2025:313.

[39] See, on the 2024 reform, Michal Bobek, 'Preliminary Rulings before the General Court: What Judicial Architecture for the European Union?' (2023) 60 Common Market Law Review 1515.

[40] At the time of writing (4 August 2025), fifty-one cases were pending before the General Court. The first judgment of the General Court in this regard was Case T-534/24, *Gotek*, ECLI:EU:T:2025:682, relating to excise duties. Pending cases include Case T-558/24, *Studieförbundet Vuxenskolan Riksorganisationen*, pending, relating to value-added tax (VAT); Case T-575/24, *Digipolis*, pending, relating to VAT; Case T-589/24, *A-GmbH*, pending, relating to the customs code; *inter alia*.

curious about this way of narrowing is that it does not actively involve judicial reasoning of the Court of Justice. Rather, it is about the Court exercising its position within the EU institutional architecture, to convince the EU legislature of the need to relieve itself of certain types of cases. In essence, the Court is deciding to engage in a change to its Statute, in order to not decide certain types of cases.

Another form of narrowing is when the Court tries to limit the *erga omnes* effect of its rulings. When the Court delivers its judgments, they produce *erga omnes* effect, in that they contribute to the understanding of EU law through the Court's binding interpretation. Whether it be through a range of different procedures, it is immaterial. Through the reference for a preliminary ruling procedure, the interpretation of EU law provided on any given week is not only to be dispatched back to the referring national court that made the reference, but also contributes to the wider body of case law. However, there are evidently cases where the Court is attempting to limit the *erga omnes* effect of its rulings by tightly narrowing the relevance of the ruling beyond the specific case before it which has a unique set of factual circumstances. The reasons why the Court does so may only be speculated upon after assessing the context-specific situation of each underlying dispute has been referred to it.

An illustrative example of this was the *Hanner* case,[41] referred to it by a national court in a relatively new EU Member State at the time. In essence, the Court was being asked to determine the lawfulness of a state monopoly in respect of retail sale pharmacies with EU law. The referring court was uncertain as to what provisions of EU law were actually applicable here: the general provisions on the free movement of goods (Articles 34–36 TFEU), the special provision on the free movement of goods and state monopolies of a commercial character (Article 37 TFEU),[42] or the freedom of establishment (Article 49 TFEU). Confusion lay for the referring national court, in part, because of the Court's prior judgment in a case concerning a state monopoly in respect of the retail sale of alcohol in the same Member State, *Franzén*,[43] that had been delivered some years previous.[44]

[41] Case C-438/02, *Criminal proceedings against Krister Hanner*, ECLI:EU:C:2005:332.

[42] See further, Graham Butler, 'State Monopolies and the Free Movement of Goods in EU Law: Getting Beyond Obscure Clarity' (2021) 48 *Legal Issues of Economic Integration* 285; and Graham Butler, 'State Monopolies and the Internal Market,' in *Oxford Principles of European Union Law: Volume II: The Internal Market*, eds. Robert Schütze and Takis Tridimas (Oxford: Oxford University Press, 2026).

[43] Case C-189/95, *Criminal proceedings against Harry Franzén*, ECLI:EU:C:1997:504.

[44] The *Franzén* judgment has been labelled as a 'well-known example of a poorly reasoned, and incoherent judgment'. Graham Butler, 'Sweden and the Free Movement of Alcoholic Goods in the EU Internal Market' (2023) 29 European Public Law 75, 90–91.

In *Hanner*, the Court ultimately decided to rule in the case on the basis of the special provision on the free movement of goods and state monopolies (Article 37 TFEU) alone.[45] That said, given the Opinion of the Advocate General in the case,[46] who had raised some creditable points with which the Court chose not to deal, the Court very evidently attempted to limit the *erga omnes* effect of the operative part of its ruling. It therefore tried to reduce the responsibility upon it of adjudicating on this provision of the EU Treaties for *all* state monopolies in EU Member States and tied its ruling solely to the state monopoly at hand. It stated that Article 37 TFEU 'precludes a sales regime which grants an exclusive retail right and is arranged *in the same way as the sales regime at issue in the main proceedings*'.[47]

While 'at issue in the main proceedings' is a term of use that is regularly employed in the way of stating the underlying factual issues of a case, it is much less often found in the *operative part* of rulings that the referring national court is to apply upon cases' return to national judicial proceedings. The question obviously arises as to why the Court would try to limit the *erga omnes* effect of certain rulings, such as in *Hanner*, when it would ordinarily not do so in the vast majority of its rulings.

The effects of the Court engaging in such a technique of ruling, by attempting to significantly limit the precedential value of its judgments, are not easily explainable. At face value, the Court is deciding not to decide any more than it has to. But looking beyond the *Hanner* ruling may tell more of the story. In a string of cases referred to the Court on related issues of state monopolies thereafter such as *Rosengren*,[48] *ANETT*,[49] and *Visnapuu*,[50] all the cases were effectively referred to the Court because both the *Franzén* and *Hanner* judgments were of little use beyond their context-specific circumstances. In each of these three cases, the Court shied away from utilizing both the *Franzén* and *Hanner* judgments as precedent that would help resolve the legal issues before the Court. In fact, the judgment in *Hanner*, now more than twenty years old, turned out to be the last case that the Court decided on the basis of Article 37 TFEU.[51]

[45] Case C-438/02, *Criminal proceedings against Krister Hanner*, ECLI:EU:C:2005:332, para 49.
[46] Opinion of Advocate General Léger, Case C-438/02, *Criminal proceedings against Krister Hanner*, ECLI:EU:C:2004:317.
[47] Case C-438/02, *Criminal proceedings against Krister Hanner*, ECLI:EU:C:2005:332, operative part.
[48] Case C-170/04, *Klas Rosengren and Others v Riksåklagaren*, ECLI:EU:C:2007:313.
[49] Case C-456/10, *Asociación Nacional de Expendedores de Tabaco y Timbre (ANETT) v Administración del Estado*, ECLI:EU:C:2012:241.
[50] Case C-198/14, *Valev Visnapuu v Kihlakunnansyyttäjä (Helsinki) and Suomen valtio—Tullihallitus*, ECLI:EU:C:2015:751.
[51] Instead, the Court has adopted a different approach, deciding such related cases on the general provisions on the free movement of goods (Articles 34–36 TFEU).

This attempt to limit the *erga omnes* effect of certain rulings is a form of narrowing because, by doing so, the Court is tightly circumscribing the effect of that particular case to the facts of that case alone, thus reducing the applicability of the interpreted EU law to other factual circumstances. This can be seen as a form of judicial minimalism, whereby the Court wants national courts—in future cases—to continue to send further references for a preliminary ruling to it. In the case of *Hanner*, the Court was clearly hesitant to let Article 37 TFEU be used as a justification for allowing state monopolies of a commercial character to perpetuate in Member States, and thus, parties seeking to rely on the judgment as a form of precedent would come up against that obstacle. The most credible explanation therefore lies in the fact that this case involved the interpretation of EU primary law, and not easily modifiable EU secondary law. Thus, *Hanner* was a clear demonstration of the Court deciding not to decide in other state monopolies' cases.

4. Relinquishment

The third category of cases where the Court evidently is deciding not to a decide a case is where it has opted to relinquish a case, and essentially lets the referring national court decide the case. In cases coming to the Court that are references for a preliminary ruling under Article 267 TFEU,[52] the Court is not deciding the ultimate fate of a case. Technically, it is just providing an interpretation of a provision of EU law that is being sought by the referring national court or tribunal, and the case then returns to that national court or tribunal for them to ultimately apply the interpretation of the Court. Moreover, given that the reference for a preliminary ruling procedure is open to all courts of law, from first instance bodies and other lower instance national courts all the way to higher instance national courts against 'whose decisions there is no judicial remedy',[53] the fact that lower instance national courts apply judgments of the Court can still mean that cases are appealed upwards in a national legal order.

Therefore, when the Court is rendering a judgment under the reference for a preliminary ruling procedure, it must be conscious that it has to provide that referring court or tribunal with an answer to its question, or, in the event of numerous questions of EU law, enough answers necessary to assist the referring

[52] For the most comprehensive study, see Morten Broberg and Niels Fenger, *Broberg and Fenger on Preliminary References to the European Court of Justice* (3rd edn, Oxford University Press 2021).
[53] Article 267 TFEU, third paragraph.

national court with applying the interpretation of EU law provided. This, thus far, may seem obvious. However, there have been instances whereby, for reasons not readily apparent, the Court finds itself in a position that, on close inspection, is actually leaving the national court or tribunal with quite wide discretion on whether to apply the interpretation of EU law given. In other words, it is giving a referring national court more than one answer to a given question. By doing so, the Court is ultimately leaving the national court with a decision to make, on the basis of two answers, either of which are acceptable to the Court.

A prominent example of this, which is seen in many 'classic' free movement and internal market cases,[54] is a judgment that the Court rendered in a free movement of goods case, *B S and C A (Cannabidiol (CBD))*.[55] Here, the Court was faced with the movement of a good lawfully marketed or distributed in one Member State, but not in another: a hemp oil electronic cigarette. The exact question was whether cannabidiol extracted from a cannabis sativa plant (the extracts of a plant) could benefit from the free movement of goods under Article 34 TFEU,[56] and further, whether the Member State could rely on the potential ground of exception of public health contained in Article 36 TFEU to justify the restriction on the movement of the extracts.[57]

In its judgment, the Court confirmed the existence of the restriction that lacked conformity with Article 34 TFEU,[58] and also confirmed Article 36 TFEU as grounds for potential exception upon which Member States can rely on the grounds of public health considerations.[59] All straightforward thus far, considering the extensive case law that the Court has rendered over many decades,[60] albeit infrequently so in recent times.[61] From there, however, came the

[54] See, eg, Takis Tridimas, 'The General Principles of Law: Who Needs Them?' 52 Cahiers de droit européen 419.
[55] Case C-663/18, *B S and C A*, ECLI:EU:C:2020:383 (*Cannabidiol (CBD)*).
[56] Article 34 TFEU: 'Quantitative restrictions on imports and all measures having equivalent effect shall be prohibited between Member States.'
[57] Article 36 TFEU: 'The provisions of Articles 34 . . . shall not preclude prohibitions or restrictions on imports, exports or goods in transit justified on grounds of . . . the protection of health and life of humans, . . . Such prohibitions or restrictions shall not, however, constitute a means of arbitrary discrimination or a disguised restriction on trade between Member States.'
[58] Case C-663/18, *B S and C A*, ECLI:EU:C:2020:383 (*Cannabidiol (CBD)*), paras 78–82.
[59] Case C-663/18, *B S and C A*, ECLI:EU:C:2020:383 (*Cannabidiol (CBD)*), paras 83–87.
[60] See Peter Oliver (ed), *Oliver on Free Movement of Goods in the European Union* (Hart Publishing 2010); Laurence W Gormley, *EU Law of Free Movement of Goods and Customs Union* (Oxford University Press 2009).
[61] See the insightful work here of Jan Zglinski, 'The End of Negative Market Integration: 60 Years of Free Movement of Goods Litigation in the EU (1961–2020)' (2024) 31 Journal of European Public Policy 633.

consideration about the proportionality of the national measures—in other words, what the case was actually be decided upon. The Court stated:

> *it is for the referring court* to determine whether the prohibition on marketing CBD lawfully produced in another Member State—when it is extracted from the Cannabis sativa plant in its entirety and not solely from its fibre and seeds—is appropriate for securing the attainment of the objective of protecting public health and does not go beyond what is necessary for that purpose.[62]

And in citing facts heard during the proceedings, the Court further stated:

> [t]he fact remains that *it is for the referring court* to assess the scientific data available and produced before it in order to make sure . . . that the real risk to public health alleged does not appear to be based on purely hypothetical considerations.'[63]

If the referring national court knew that it was going to have to simply make the entire assessment itself, it might not have referred the case at all, as it can hardly be said that the judgment of the Court provided the referring court much guidance at all. This is especially so when the operative part of the judgment essentially gave it two conflicting answers.

First, the Court stated that 'Articles 34 and 36 TFEU must be interpreted as precluding' the national measures.[64] In other words, the national measures *were* in conflict with the negative freedom of the free movement of goods. But second, that was, 'unless [the national measure] is appropriate for securing the attainment of the objective of protecting public health and does not go beyond what is necessary for that purpose'.[65] In other words, the national measures *were not* in conflict with the same provisions, if they were to be found proportionate. Such a proportionality analysis, without little guidance, was for the national court to undertake.

The referring national court was thus given the allowance to rule either way: that the national measures were justified on the grounds of public health, or that they were not justified on grounds of public health. That is the very reason why the referring national court actually made a reference for a

[62] Case C-663/18, *B S and C A*, ECLI:EU:C:2020:383 (*Cannabidiol (CBD)*), para 93, emphasis added.
[63] Case C-663/18, *B S and C A*, ECLI:EU:C:2020:383 (*Cannabidiol (CBD)*), para 95, emphasis added.
[64] Case C-663/18, *B S and C A*, ECLI:EU:C:2020:383 (*Cannabidiol (CBD)*), para 96.
[65] Case C-663/18, *B S and C A*, ECLI:EU:C:2020:383 (*Cannabidiol (CBD)*), para 96.

preliminary ruling in the first place. Thus, the judgment can be read as a very deliberate form of relinquishment of the Court's adjudication responsibility, given the absence of a relevant judgment from the national court with which to work.

5. Conclusion: Deciding Not to Decide

The Court has various strategies to avoid making definitive rulings in certain cases, a phenomenon that can at first sight be seen as paradoxical, given its mandate to ensure the application and interpretation of EU law.[66] This chapter has set out three methods and techniques through which the Court engages in this practice: dismissal,[67] narrowing,[68] and relinquishment.[69]

First, the Court's use of dismissal is evident in cases where it rules that a case is inadmissible or premature. This approach allows the Court to sidestep sensitive substantive issues by focusing on procedural shortcomings. Examples are plentiful, but this chapter highlighted the *Sharpston* litigation, as it served as a poignant example where the Court avoided addressing the complex issue of its own composition by ruling the case inadmissible. This method highlights the Court's ability to use procedural tools to avoid making substantive decisions that could have significant implications for it as an institution of the Union, sensitive to its own role. This method and technique of the Court may also be used to explore other reasons, in the future, in given substantive cases.

Second, the Court engages in narrowing by first constraining the types of cases it hears, and second also limiting the scope of its rulings. Institutional reforms, such as the introduction of an appeal filtering mechanism and the reassignment of certain reference for preliminary ruling cases to the General Court, demonstrate the Court's efforts to control its docket. Additionally, the Court's attempt to limit the *ergo omnes* effect of its rulings, by way of illustration as seen in the *Hanner* case, in the operative part of the judgments illustrates a technique that the Court can employ to confine the applicability of its judgments to specific factual circumstances. This form of judicial minimalism ensures, counterintuitively to the technique of docket control above, that national courts and tribunals continue to refer cases to the CJEU that are of interest when it concerns the interpretation of EU primary law (as *Hanner*

[66] Article 19(1) TEU, first paragraph.
[67] See section 2.
[68] See section 3.
[69] See section 4.

did), maintaining the Court's role at the apex of the EU legal order, while avoiding broader implications of its rulings that could be misconstrued in other contexts.

Third, the Court's practice of relinquishment involves providing referring national courts with more than one answer to a given question or questions, thereby leaving the ultimate decision to the national court itself. The *B S and C A (Cannabidiol (CBD))* case exemplifies this approach, where the Court provided answers back to the referring national courts—when the referring national court was likely hoping for a single answer to each of its questions—regarding the compatibility of national measures with EU law. By doing so, the Court effectively relinquished its adjudication responsibility, allowing the referring national court to decide based on its assessment of the proportionality of the measures.

These methods and techniques of deciding not to decide reveal the Court's nuanced approach to its judicial role. While the Court is mandated to ensure the application and interpretation of EU law—a role that the Court itself sees as being critically important—it does strategically avoid making definitive rulings in certain cases and certain scenarios to manage its docket, maintain its institutional integrity, and allow national courts to play a significant role in the application of EU law. Understanding these strategies provides a clearer basis for comprehending the Court's actions in both past and future cases, highlighting the complexity of the place where the Court sits as the judicial institution of the Union, in which it has multiple judicial hats, depending on the procedural context.

The Court's practice—through its methods and techniques—of deciding not to decide is a deliberate and multifaceted strategy that serves various purposes. It allows the Court to manage its workload, avoid contentious issues, stay involved in the big issues of EU primary law, and maintain its position within the EU institutional architecture. By employing dismissal, narrowing, and relinquishment, the Court navigates the various challenges brought upon it by its judicial mandate, while simultaneously ensuring that the interpretation and application of EU law remain dynamic and responsive to the evolving needs of the EU legal order.

This phenomenon of deciding not to decide could be seen as a matter of procedural convenience. But it is more than that. It also reflects deeper institutional and strategic considerations that the Court has in fact thought about as a matter of judicial policy. The Court's decisions (or lack thereof) contribute to the evolving interpretation of EU law, allowing for flexibility and adaptability in response to changing landscapes. These methods and techniques underscore the dynamic nature of the EU legal order. Deciding not to decide is, evidently, a sophisticated judicial strategy, and one that deserves further attention.

References

Adam S, *La procédure d'avis devant la Court de justice de l'Union européenne* (Bruylant 2011)

Alberti J, 'The Threshold Guardians: The Future of EU Agencies' Boards of Appeal in Light of the Recent Reforms of CJEU Statute' (2024) 16 Review of European Administrative Law 67

Albors-Llorens A, 'The Standing of Private Parties to Challenge Community Measures: Has the European Court Missed the Boat?' (2003) 62 The Cambridge Law Journal 72

Alemanno A and Pech L, 'Thinking Justice Outside the Docket: A Critical Assessment of the Reform of the EU's Court System' (2017) 54 Common Market Law Review 129

Arnull A, *The European Union and Its Court of Justice* (2nd Edition, Oxford University Press 2006)

Barents R, *Remedies and Procedures before the EU Courts* (Kluwer Law International 2016)

Bengoetxea J, *The Legal Reasoning of the European Court of Justice* (Clarendon Press 1993)

Bengoetxea J, 'Reasoning from Consequences from Luxembourg' in Henning Koch and others (eds), *Europe. The New Legal Realism: Essays in Honour of Hjalte Rasmussen* (Djøf Publishing 2010)

Bobek M, 'Preliminary Rulings before the General Court: What Judicial Architecture for the European Union?' (2023) 60 Common Market Law Review 1515

Bradley K, 'Appointment and Dis-Appointment at the CJEU: Part II—The Sharpston Litigation' (2022) 21 The Law & Practice of International Courts and Tribunals 178

Broberg M and Fenger N, *Broberg and Fenger on Preliminary References to the European Court of Justice* (3rd edition, Oxford University Press 2021)

Butler G, 'Pre-Ratification Judicial Review of International Agreements to Be Concluded by the European Union' in Mattias Derlén and Johan Lindholm (eds), *The Court of Justice of the European Union: Multidisciplinary Perspectives* (Hart Publishing 2018)

Butler G, 'State Monopolies and the Free Movement of Goods in EU Law: Getting Beyond Obscure Clarity' (2021) 48 *Legal Issues of Economic Integration* 285

Butler G, 'State Monopolies and the Internal Market.' In *Oxford Principles of European Union Law: Volume II: The Internal Market*, edited by Robert Schütze and Takis Tridimas, Oxford University Press, 2026

Butler G, 'An Interim Post-Mortem: Specialised Courts in the EU Judicial Architecture after the Civil Service Tribunal' (2020) 17 International Organizations Law Review 586

Butler G, 'Sweden and the Free Movement of Alcoholic Goods in the EU Internal Market.' European Public Law 29 (2023): 75

Butler G, 'The EU's Contractual Relations and the Arbitration Clause: Disputes at the Court of Justice of the European Union' (2021) 46 European Law Review 345

Butler G, 'An Advocate before Advocate General: Eleanor Sharpston at the European Courts' in Catherine Barnard, Adam Łazowski, and Daniel Sarmiento (eds), *Pursuit of Legal Harmony in a Turbulent Europe: Essays in Honour of Eleanor Sharpston* (Hart Publishing 2024)

Butler G, 'Investment in the EU Legal Order' in Xavier Groussot, Marja-Liisa Öberg, and Graham Butler (eds), *The EU Law of Investment: Past, Present, and Future* (Hart Publishing 2025)

Butler G, 'The High Representative as a New Actor before the Court of Justice of the European Union' in Frank Hoffmeister and Lóránt Havas (eds), *The High Representative of the Union for Foreign Affairs and Security Policy as a Legal Actor: Liber Amicorum in Honour of Stephan Marquardt* (Brill 2025)

Butler G and Wessel RA (eds), *EU External Relations Law: The Cases in Context* (Hart Publishing 2022)

Chamon M, Volpato A, and Eliantonio M (eds), *Boards of Appeal of EU Agencies: Towards Judicialization of Administrative Review?* (Oxford University Press 2022)

Craig P, 'Standing, Rights, and the Structure of Legal Argument' (2003) 9 European Public Law 493

Dashwood A, 'Article 26 ECT and Intra-EU Disputes—the Case Against an Expansive Reading of Achmea' (2021) 46 European Law Review 415

Dashwood A, 'Republic of Moldova v Komstroy LCC: Arbitration under Article 26 ECT Outlawed in Intra-EU Disputes by Obiter Dictum' (2022) 47 European Law Review 127

De Lucia L, 'The Shifting State of Rights Protection vis-à-vis EU Agencies: A Look at Article 58a of the Statute of the Court of Justice of the European Union' (2019) 44 European Law Review 809

De Lucia L, 'The Boards of Appeal as Hybrid Adjudicators: On Some Shortcomings of Article 58a of the Statute of the Court of Justice of the European Union' in Merijn Chamon, Annalisa Volpato, and Mariolina Eliantonio (eds), *Boards of Appeal of EU Agencies: Towards Judicialization of Administrative Review?* (Oxford University Press 2022)

Everling U, 'Reflections on the Reasoning in the Judgments of the Court of Justice of the European Communities', *Festskrift til Ole Due: Liber Amircorum* (GEC Gads 1994)

Gormley LW, *EU Law of Free Movement of Goods and Customs Union* (Oxford University Press 2009)

Greaves R, 'Locus Standi under Article 173 EEC when Seeking Annulment of a Regulation' (1986) 11 European Law Review 119

Iglesias Sánchez S, 'The 2024 Reform of the Statute of the Court of Justice of the EU and the Transformation of the EU Judicial System: Preliminary Rulings before the General Court of the EU' in Alejandro Saiz Arnaiz and Joan Solanes Mullor (eds), *The European Judiciary: A Community of Law and a Community of Judges* (Hart Publishing 2025)

Kochenov D and Butler G, 'The Independence and Lawful Composition of the Court of Justice of the European Union: Replacement of Advocate General Sharpston and the Battle for the Integrity of the Institution' in Joseph HH Weiler and Gráinne De Búrca (eds), *The Jean Monnet Working Paper Series, Jean Monnet Center for International and Regional Economic Law & Justice, School of Law, New York University* (2020)

Kochenov D and Butler G, 'Independence of the Court of Justice of the European Union: Unchecked Member States Power after the Sharpston Affair' (2021) 27 European Law Journal 262

Lasok KPE, *Lasok's European Court Practice and Procedure* (3rd edn, Bloomsbury Professional 2017)

Lenaerts K, Gutman K and Nowak JT, *EU Procedural Law* (2nd edn, Oxford University Press 2023)

Luszcz V, *European Court Procedure. A Practical Guide* (Hart Publishing 2020)

Naômé C, *Appeals before the Court of Justice of the European Union* (Oxford University Press 2018)

Oliver P (ed), *Oliver on Free Movement of Goods in the European Union* (Hart Publishing 2010)

Sankari S, *European Court of Justice Legal Reasoning in Context* (Europa Law Publishing 2013)

Tridimas T, 'The General Principles of Law: Who Needs Them?' 52 Cahiers de droit européen 419

Ward A, *Judicial Review and the Rights of Private Parties in EU Law* (Second Edition, Oxford University Press 2007)

Żelechowski Ł, 'No Direct Effect of the Paris Convention and Limited Cross-Priority Rights in EU Design Law: Question Marks after KaiKai' (2025) 62 Common Market Law Review 623

Zglinski J, 'The End of Negative Market Integration: 60 Years of Free Movement of Goods Litigation in the EU (1961–2020)' (2024) 31 Journal of European Public Policy 633

15

The Different Institutional Roles of the General Court and the Court of Justice and their Impact on the CJEU's Reasoning in the Field of EU Competition Law

*Nathan Cambien**

1. Introduction

The case law of the Court of Justice of the European Union (CJEU) has been and continues to be extensively studied. Whereas traditionally academic scholarship was broadly supportive of CJEU case law,[1] an increasing number of scholars at present point out (perceived) flaws and inconsistencies in the Court's reasoning. There are a multitude of potential reasons that may explain why the CJEU's reasoning can come across as imprecise, unconvincing, or inconsistent with earlier case law. One could consider a host of issues and different angles in this context, including the selection process and career structure of judges and their référendaires,[2] issues pertaining to the working language of the CJEU,[3] or gender balance.[4]

* All views expressed are strictly personal and do not necessarily reflect the official opinion of the Institution of which the author is a member.

[1] See also the discussion in Gerard Conway, *The Limits of Legal Reasoning and the European Court of Justice*. (CUP, 2012) 52–85; Bruno De Witte, 'European Union Law: A Unified Academic Discipline?' (2008) *EUI RSCAS* <https://hdl.handle.net/1814/10028>; Harm Schepel and Rein Wesseling, 'The Legal Community: Judges, Lawyers, Officials and Clerks in the Writing of Europe' (1997) 3 European Law Journal 165–88.

[2] Angela Huyue Zhang, 'The Faceless Court' (2016) 38 University of Pennsylvania Journal of International Law 71.

[3] Eg Anthony Arnull, 'The Working Language of the CJEU: Time for a Change?' (2018) 6 EL Rev 904.

[4] Eg Jessica Guth, 'The Court of Justice of the European Union, Gender, and Leadership', in Henriette Müller and Ingeborg Tömmel (eds), *Women and Leadership in the European Union* (OUP 2022).

Nathan Cambien, *The Different Institutional Roles of the General Court and the Court of Justice and their Impact on the CJEU's Reasoning in the Field of EU Competition Law* In: *The Reasoning of the Court of Justice of the EU*. Edited by: Alezini Loxa and Luigi Lonardo, Oxford University Press.
DOI: 10.1093/9780198983002.003.0019

The present chapter proposes to analyse the reasoning of the CJEU from an 'institutional' perspective, by focusing on the specific roles fulfilled by the two jurisdictions that make up the CJEU, the General Court (GC) and Court of Justice (ECJ).[5] The judicial impact of these different institutional roles, which are often not articulated, has not been extensively studied in academic literature[6] and merits further reflection. The contention in the chapter is that the different institutional roles of the GC and ECJ may help to explain the diverging reasoning and outcomes reached by both jurisdictions in a particular case.

The present chapter will use recent case law in the field of EU competition law as a case study to examine these issues and as a starting point to address the larger issue of institutional factors influencing the CJEU's reasoning. This field is particularly well suited to compare the outcomes of both jurisdictions, given the high percentage of GC judgments that are appealed.[7] In what comes next, I will explain what I mean by institutional roles and analyse how they play a role in explaining case law in relation to jurisdictional issues, issues of standing, and issues relating to the intensity of judicial review. I will end with concluding remarks.

2. The Different Institutional Roles of the General Court and the Court of Justice

It appears from the Council decision establishing the GC (or 'Court of First Instance', as it was then called) that its purpose was (i) to improve the judicial protection of individual interests, in respect of actions requiring close examination of complex facts and (ii) to maintain the quality and effectiveness of judicial review by enabling the ECJ to concentrate its activities on its fundamental task of ensuring uniform interpretation of EU law.[8] In line with this purpose, the GC was given jurisdiction in direct actions, whereas the ECJ kept its core competence regarding the preliminary ruling procedure, besides other

[5] While the elements mentioned in the previous paragraph, such as the working language of the CJEU or the selection process of judge and référendaires, may in turn influence how the GC and the ECJ view their institutional role, they do not as such pertain to their institutional role.

[6] That is not to say that academic literature on these issues is non-existent. See eg (focusing mainly on other issues than the present chapter does) Christoph Krenn, *The Procedural and Organisational Law of the European Court of Justice: An Incomplete Transformation* (CUP 2022).

[7] It appears from the GC's statistics that judgments in the field of competition law (including state aids) are far more likely to be appealed than those in other fields: <https://curia.europa.eu/jcms/upload/docs/application/pdf/2025-03/ra_en_statistiques_24_-tribunal_2025-03-21_11-09-14_231.pdf>.

[8] On the genesis of the GC and the purposes it was intended to serve, see the insightful analysis in Lola Avril, 'The Genesis of the Institution within the Institution: Studying the Mobilization for the Creation of the Court of First Instance' in Mikael Rask Madsen, Fernanda Nicola, and Antoine Vauchez (eds), *Researching the European Court of Justice: Methodological Shifts and Law's Embeddedness* (CUP 2022).

competences including appeals and infringement actions. The different competences of the ECJ and the GC were incorporated in the relevant provisions of EU primary law.[9]

In my view, it is clear from this division of competences that the GC's role is akin to that of an administrative court reviewing the legality of acts of the administration. By contrast, the ECJ's primary task of interpreting EU law, including the Treaties and the Charter of Fundamental Rights, is akin to that of a constitutional court or a supreme court. These different institutional roles of the GC and ECJ have been frequently analysed and acknowledged by commentators.[10] For instance, the Council of Bars and Law Societies of Europe (CCBE), on the occasion of the GC's reform, has commented as follows: 'The CCBE understands that the ECJ wishes the GC to be [...] considered to be the EU Administrative Law Court. This would allow the ECJ to be the EU Constitutional and Supreme Court with the ultimate role of ensuring the uniform interpretation of EU law.'[11]

Admittedly, the neat distinction between the competences of both jurisdictions was shaken up in September 2024 by the transfer to the GC of the competence to issue preliminary rulings in a number of fields.[12] At the moment of writing this chapter, it is too early to assess the impact of this fundamental change, and it will consequently not be taken into account for the purposes of my analysis. Yet, it appears from the regulation governing the transfer of competences that it does not fundamentally change the institutional role of both jurisdictions, but rather confirms it.[13] In fact, it is explicitly recognized

[9] See, in particular, Article 256 TFEU, which states that the GC has jurisdiction in relation to actions for annulment (Article 263 TFEU), actions for failure to act (Article 265 TFEU), actions for damages (Article 268 TFEU), staff cases (Article 270 TFEU), and pursuant to an arbitration clause (Article 272 TFEU).

[10] See already Andreas M Donner, 'The Constitutional Powers of the Court of Justice of the European Communities' (1974) 11 CML Rev 127. For more recent examples, see Lukas Bauer, 'The European Court of Justice as a Constitutional Court' (2009) 3(4) ICL Journal 268; Pierre-Emmanuel Pignarre, *La Cour de Justice de l'Union européenne, juridiction constitutionnelle* (Larcier Intersentia 2021); Alicia Hinarejos, *Judicial Control in the European Union: Reforming Jurisdiction in the Intergovernmental Pillars* (OUP 2009), Chapter 1: 'Introduction: The ECJ as a Federal Constitutional Court'. Some other commentators appear to disagree with this characterization: eg András Jakab, 'Judicial Reasoning in Constitutional Courts: A European Perspective', (2013) 14(8) German Law Journal 1215–75.

[11] Council of Bars and Law Societies of Europe, 'CCBE comments on the functioning of the General Court', <https://www.ccbe.eu/fileadmin/speciality_distribution/public/documents/PD_LUX/PDL_Position_papers/EN_PDL_20200904_CCBE-comments-on-the-functioning-of-the-General-Court.pdf>.

[12] See Regulation 2024/2019 of the European Parliament and of the Council of 11 April 2024 amending Protocol No 3 on the Statute of the Court of Justice of the European Union [2024] OJ L2024.

[13] See also Daniel Sarmiento, 'Editorial Note: On the Road to a Constitutional Court of the European Union: The Court of Justice after the Transfer of the Preliminary Reference Jurisdiction to the General Court' (2023) 19 Croatian Yearbook of European Law & Policy VII–XVII; Davor Petrić, 'The Preliminary Ruling Procedure 2.0' (2023) 8(1) European Papers 25. See also, for a critical voice, Michal Bobek, 'Preliminary Rulings before the General Court: What Judicial Architecture for the European Union?' (2023) 60 CML Rev 1515.

for the first time by the EU legislator that the ECJ has competences of a constitutional nature.[14] Moreover, the reform extends the scope of the 'filtering mechanism', which will further reduce the number of appeals before the ECJ, thereby increasing the relative importance of preliminary ruling cases in the ECJ's *contentieux*.[15]

It follows that the GC and ECJ have different institutional roles, and that there is a tendency to further solidify these roles. Yet, it is important to stress that these predominant roles are not exclusive. While the GC does typically act as an administrative court and the large majority of its judgments deal with issues of a rather technical nature (the largest category of case being intellectual property cases[16]), it also has the competence to rule on issues of a constitutional nature, such as fundamental rights.[17] Conversely, while the ECJ adjudicates on issues of a constitutional nature, it also deals with technical issues devoid of constitutional significance.[18]

However, even in cases involving issues of a technical nature—including many cases in the field of competition law—the predominant institutional role informs the judges and influences the outcome. In that regard it needs to be stressed that institutional roles are not just procedural in nature; they have a strong normative dimension too. Indeed, they are intrinsically linked to the constitutional mandate and (self-perceived) role of the ECJ and GC and can significantly influence how these courts view their roles and perform their duties, in particular in cases presenting a novel dimension. Interestingly, it is confirmed by extrajudicial writings and speeches of a number of (former) members of the GC[19] and

[14] See Regulation 2024/2019, recital 4 ('In this context, and as the Court of Justice is increasingly required, in preliminary ruling cases, to rule on matters of a constitutional nature'). See also Sara Iglesias and Daniel Sarmiento, 'A New Model for the EU Judiciary: Decentralising Preliminary Rulings as a Paradoxical Move towards the Constitutionalisation of the Court of Justice' (2024) *EU Law Live*, <https://eulawlive.com/insight-a-new-model-for-the-eu-judiciary-decentralising-preliminary-rulings-as-a-paradoxical-move-towards-the-constitutionalisation-of-the-court-of-justice-by-sara-iglesias-a/>.

[15] See Regulation 2024/2019, Article 6, modifying Article 58a of the Statute of the Court of Justice of the European Union. See also Kieran Bradley, 'The Court of Justice Appeal Filter Mechanism and Effective Judicial Protection: Throwing Out the Baby with the Bathwater?' (2024) EU Law Live, <https://eulawlive.com/the-court-of-justice-appeal-filter-mechanism-and-effective-judicial-protection-throwing-out-the-baby-with-the-bathwater/>.

[16] According to the statistics accompanying the latest annual report (Annual Report 2023 Statistics concerning the judicial activity of the General Court, <https://curia.europa.eu/jcms/upload/docs/application/pdf/2024-04/en_ra_2023_tribunal_stats_web_bat_22042024.pdf>), out of 922 total completed cases, the largest categories of cases by subject matter were intellectual property (276 cases), economic and monetary policy (104 cases), and restrictive measures (88 cases).

[17] See eg Case T-791/19 *Sped-Pro S.A. v Commission* EU:T:2022:67.

[18] Eg cases relating to the tariff classification of goods under the Combined Nomenclature.

[19] See eg Marc van der Woude, 'The Place of the General Court in the Institutional Framework of the Union' (2021) 81 EU Law Live, https://eulawlive.com/weekend-edition/weekend-edition-no81/; Ulf

ECJ[20] that they view the institutional role of both jurisdictions in line with the aforementioned distinction. It is my contention that this view influences the reasoning and rulings of the GC and ECJ and may help to explain why they sometimes arrive at different conclusions when interpreting the same legal provisions in the same case.

3. The Example of EU Competition Law

3.1 Sports cases as a gateway to issues of jurisdictional nature

The recent *International Skating Union* case provides a good illustration of how the reasoning of the GC and the ECJ can significantly diverge and lead to opposite outcomes. The case revolved around a Commission decision which found that a number of rules adopted by the International Skating Union (ISU)[21] infringed EU competition law.[22] First, according to the rules of the ISU, the organization of international competitions required its prior approval ('rule on prior authorization'). Second, athletes who took part in a competition that had not been authorized by the ISU were liable to be excluded from all competitions for a specific period or for life ('rule on eligibility'). Lastly, authorization refusals and sanctions for breach of the eligibility rules could be challenged only before the Court of Arbitration for Sport (the 'CAS'), established in Switzerland ('arbitration rule'). Awards of the CAS are subject to judicial review by the Tribunal fédéral (Swiss Federal Supreme Court).

By judgment of 16 December 2020,[23] the GC dismissed the action brought by the ISU against the Commission decision in so far as it concerned the rules governing prior authorization and eligibility. By contrast, the GC held that the

Öberg: 'A "General" Court in Name Only? (2024) 3 Concurrences 2; Nina Półtorak, 'General Court of the European Union as an Administrative Court' (Speech) (20 January 2018), Krakow University.

[20] See eg Koen Lenaerts, Kathleen Gutman, and Janek Tomasz Nowak, *EU Procedural Law* (2nd edn, OUP 2023) 27, 34; Vassilios Skouris, 'Der Europäische Gerichtshof als Verfassungsgericht?' in Detlef Merten (ed), *Verfassungsgerichtsbarkeit in Deutschland und Österreich* (Duncker and Humblot 2008) 43; Eleanor Sharpston and Geert De Baere, 'The Court of Justice as a Constitutional Adjudicator' in Anthony Arnull, Catherine Barnard, Michael Dougan, and Eleanor Spaventa (eds), *A Constitutional Order of States? Essays in EU Law in Honour of Alan Dashwood* (Hart 2011) 123.

[21] The ISU is an association headquartered in Switzerland which describes itself as the only international sports federation recognized by the International Olympic Committee in the field of figure skating and speed skating.

[22] Decision C(2017) 8230 final relating to proceedings under Article 101 [TFEU] and Article 53 of the EEA Agreement (Case AT. 40208—International Skating Union's Eligibility rules).

[23] Case T-93/18 *International Skating Union v Commission* EU:T:2020:610.

Commission was wrong to call into question the arbitration rule. The GC ruled that the arbitration rule could be justified by legitimate interests linked to the specific nature of the sport, consisting of enabling a single, specialized court to rule, in a quick, economic, and uniform manner, on a multiplicity of disputes, often having an international dimension, to which the exercise of high-level professional sporting activity may give rise.[24] Furthermore, the GC stressed that athletes and undertakings negatively affected by the prior authorization or eligibility rules could bring actions for damages before the national courts and also lodge complaints with the Commission and the national competition authorities (NCAs) for breach of the competition rules.[25]

By its judgment,[26] the ECJ dismissed the appeal lodged by the ISU against the judgment of the GC and thereby confirmed that the rules on prior authorization and eligibility were unlawful. By contrast, the ECJ accepted the cross-appeal lodged by two ice-skaters and the European Elite Athletes Association and directed against the GC's findings in relation to the arbitration rule. On the one hand, the ECJ ruled that the GC was wrong to find, in an undifferentiated and abstract manner, that the arbitration rule 'may be justified by legitimate interests linked to the specific nature of the sport'. Referring to the *Eco-Swiss* judgment,[27] the ECJ held that the GC should have verified whether the Swiss Federal Supreme Court was entitled, or, as the case may be, required, to refer questions to the ECJ on matters of EU law in order to allow for an effective review of compliance with EU competition law.[28] On the other hand, the ECJ ruled that damages actions cannot compensate for the lack of a remedy to challenge directly the rules in question, which is particularly the case given that the career of sporting professionals may be especially short. Moreover, the possibility of lodging a complaint with the Commission or an NCA could not justify the lack of such remedy either, given *inter alia* the discretion of the authorities to open a case.[29]

The reasoning followed by the GC and the ECJ, as far as the arbitration rule is concerned, stands in sharp contrast. The interesting question that needs answering is what explains this difference. One reason that enabled this divergence was that the legal norms at issue (such as the requirement of 'effective judicial review') are couched in general terms and that different interpretations

[24] Ibid, para 156.
[25] Ibid, paras 157 to 161.
[26] Case C-124/21P *International Skating Union v Commission* EU:C:2023:101.
[27] Case C-126/97 *Eco Swiss* EU:C:1999:269.
[28] Case C-124/21P *International Skating Union v Commission* EU:C:2023:101, paras 198–99.
[29] Case C-124/21P *International Skating Union v Commission* EU:C:2023:101, paras 200–03.

are therefore inherently a possibility. In this case, however, there was case law interpreting these norms which was not mentioned by the GC. This is true, in particular, for the *Eco-Swiss* judgment, which was expressly relied on by the Commission in the contested decision and formed a key precedent in the ECJ's reasoning on the compatibility of the arbitration rule with EU law. Similarly, the ECJ's case law on damages (starting with *Courage and Crehan*[30]) is well established and it does not follow from it that the possibility to obtain damages constitutes a sufficient remedy in itself, as duly noted by the ECJ.[31] Lastly, there is ample case law confirming the discretionary power of the EU Commission in relation to complaints.[32]

Arguably, therefore, the explanation for the diverging reasoning of GC and ECJ lies elsewhere. To my mind, the institutional role of both jurisdictions plays a significant role here. It is no coincidence that both jurisdictions came to the same conclusion with regard to the competitive analysis of the restrictions relating to sporting competitions (authorization rules and eligibility rules), but not with regard to the validity of arrangements giving other institutions jurisdiction over these. The latter issue has a strong constitutional dimension, as it relates to the relationship between the EU, on the one hand, and other international organizations and third countries and their judicial institutions, on the other hand. The GC has limited experience with such issues, which fall outside its natural role in competition cases, that is, reviewing whether the Commission's competitive analysis is in line with EU law, a role akin to that of an administrative court. Indeed, the arbitration rule is not an issue of competitive assessment, but rather an issue of the compatibility of the judicial structure of another international organization or third country with EU law. There is, understandably, a reluctance on behalf of the GC to 'interfere' with international relations, in particular in the absence of clear ECJ guidance on the matter. The ECJ, by contrast, has dealt with such issues in a considerable number of cases. It has consistently guarded the autonomy of the EU legal order, and has already in the past struck down rules that would lead to an external judicial body having the final say over an interpretation of EU law binding on EU institutions without the possibility to submit potential issues of EU law to the ECJ. That is true, *inter alia*, in cases concerning the jurisdiction

[30] Case C-453/99 *Courage Ltd v Bernard Crehan and Bernard Crehan v Courage Ltd and Others* EU:C:2001:465.

[31] Case C-124/21P *International Skating Union v Commission* EU:C:2023:101, para 198.

[32] See to that effect Case C-56/12 P *EFIM v Commission* EU:C:2013:575, para 57 and the case law cited. See also explicitly the Commission's complaints notice (Commission Notice on the handling of complaints by the Commission under Articles 81 and 82 of the EC Treaty, [2004] OJ C101/65).

of the European Court of Human Rights,[33] arbitral tribunals,[34] and the United Nations Convention on the Law of the Sea dispute settlement system.[35] The same logic underpins the ECJ's *ISU* judgment.[36]

The same reluctance on behalf of the GC can be seen in other cases involving relations with third countries or international organizations. For instance, in *Kadi* the GC rejected the plea relating to the breach of the right to be heard and the right to effective judicial review and showed deference to the UN legal order and its institutional setup, ruling *inter alia* that 'it is not for the Court to review indirectly whether the Security Council's resolutions in question are themselves compatible with fundamental rights as protected by the Community legal order'.[37] The ECJ, by contrast, held that both rights had been infringed and that the fact that the contested Union measures were intended to give effect to a resolution adopted by the Security Council did not mean that they could escape all judicial review by the EU courts.[38] The ECJ's bold stance may have been motivated by a desire to protect the autonomy of EU law and its values.[39]

Another example is the *Bolivarian Republic of Venezuela case.* The GC held that the Republic of Venezuela did not have standing to challenge the restrictive measures at stake before the EU courts because it was not directly concerned by them, as they did not impose obligations directly on Venezuela itself.[40] The ECJ Grand Chamber reversed that judgment and held that third States such as Venezuela have standing in such actions. The direct concern condition was satisfied, since the measures at stake prevented the Bolivarian Republic of Venezuela from obtaining numerous goods and services.[41] Again,

[33] Opinion 2/13, EU:C:2014:2454. See Bruno De Witte and Šejla Imamović, 'Opinion 2/13 on Accession to the ECHR: Defending the EU Legal Order against a Foreign Human Rights Court' (2015) 40 EL Rev 683–705.

[34] Case C-284/16 *Slowakische Republik v Achmea BV* EU:C:2018:158. See Anastasios Gourgourinis, 'After Achmea: Maintaining the EU Law Compatibility of Intra-EU BITs Through Treaty Interpretation' (2018) 3 European Investment Law and Arbitration Review 282–315.

[35] Case C-459/03 *Commission v Ireland* EU:C:2006:345. See Nikolaos Lavranos, 'The Scope of the Exclusive Jurisdiction of the Court of Justice' (2007) 32 EL Rev 83–94.

[36] See also Paschalis Paschalidis, 'ISU v Commission: Arbitration as a Reinforcement of Infringements of EU Competition Law' (2024) *Kluwer Competition Law Blog*, <https://competitionlawblog.kluwercompetitionlaw.com/2024/01/09/isu-v-commission-arbitration-as-a-reinforcement-of-infringements-of-eu-competition-law/>.

[37] Case T-315/01 *Yassin Abdullah Kadi* EU:T:2005:332, para. 283.

[38] Case C-402/05 *Yassin Abdullah Kadi and Al Barakaat International Foundation* EU:C:2008:461, para. 343.

[39] See the discussion in Giuseppe Martinico, 'The Autonomy of EU Law: A Joint Celebration of Kadi II and Van Gend en Loos' in Matej Avbelj, Filippo Fontanelli, and Giuseppe Martinico (eds), *Kadi on Trial: A Multifaceted Analysis of the Kadi Trial* (Routledge 2014) 157–71.

[40] Case T-65/18 *Venezuela v Council (Whether a third State is affected)* EU:T:2019:649.

[41] Case C-872/19P *Venezuela v Council (Whether a third State is affected)* EU:C:2021:507. See the discussion in Anthony Arnull, 'Non-Member States and Access to the Union Courts' (2022) 2 EL Rev 264.

it is plausible that the GC's 'highly artificial and unduly formalistic'[42] reasoning can be explained by its reluctance to allow standing to third states in view of the significant implications this could have on the relations between the EU and its Member States, on the one hand, and third countries, on the other hand. The ECJ, by contrast, was prepared to allow access to Union Courts for third countries, even in the absence of any reciprocal rights for EU Member States in those countries.[43] In doing so, the ECJ did not relinquish its mission to protect the autonomy of the EU legal order. In fact, as Lonardo and Ruiz Cairó have pointed out, the ECJ's judgment can be seen as a 'positive' statement of autonomy.[44] Indeed, while the ECJ accepted challenges by third states to EU legal acts, its interpretative monopoly or other essential characteristics of the EU were not affected by the ruling.

In sum, it appears from the case law discussed that the GC takes a more cautious approach to questions relating to the autonomy of the EU legal order in relation to third countries or international organizations, and leaves it to the ECJ to move the needle on such issues. The ECJ's 'constitutional' mandate to protect the autonomy and uniformity of the EU legal order makes it the natural jurisdiction for such issues.[45] This role is particularly relevant in the context of international sporting competitions which can be subject to different national and international bodies and jurisdictions, with a potential for conflicting rules and interpretations, as is also clear from a pending preliminary ruling in a dispute regarding agents' fees.[46]

3.2 State aid cases as a fertile ground for issues of standing

The different institutional roles of the GC and ECJ also help to explain their sometimes diverging interpretation of the standing requirements laid down in article 263, fourth paragraph, TFEU. While the case law does not consistently show the same pattern, in a number of cases the GC has shown readiness

[42] Case C-872/19P *Venezuela v Council (Whether a third State is affected)* EU:C:2021:37, Opinion of AG Hogan, para 109.

[43] Case C-872/19P *Venezuela v Council (Whether a third State is affected)* EU:C:2021:507, para. 52.

[44] Luigi Lonardo and Elisabet Ruiz Cairó, 'The European Court of Justice Allows Third Countries to Challenge EU Restrictive Measures: Case C-872/19 P, Venezuela v Council' (2022) 18(1) European Constitutional Law Review 120.

[45] See the analysis in Damjan Kukovec, 'Autonomy: The Central Idea of the Reasoning of the Court of Justice', (2023) 8(3) European Papers 1403.

[46] Case C-209/23 *RRC Sports*: Request for a preliminary ruling from the Landgericht Mainz (Germany) lodged on 31 March 2023. For the potential wider consequences for sports arbitration, see Antoine Duval, 'The *International Skating Union* Ruling of the CJEU and the Future of CAS Arbitration in Transnational Sports Governance' (2023) 23 Int Sports Law 467–74.

to depart from traditional case law and adopt a less restrictive interpretation of the standing requirements, while the ECJ has more firmly stuck to its traditional, rather restrictive interpretation.[47]

Recent case law in the field of state aid provides a good illustration of this phenomenon. Issues of standing have, notably, played an important role in the context of challenges brought against decisions by which the Commission decides to approve an aid measure without opening the formal investigation procedure under Article 108(2) TFEU. According to settled case law, such decisions can be challenged by any 'interested party' within the meaning of Article 1(h) of Regulation 2015/1589,[48] that is, 'any Member State and any person, undertaking or association of undertakings whose interests might be affected by the granting of aid, in particular the beneficiary of the aid, competing undertakings and trade associations'.[49] The case law has recognized that not only direct but also indirect competitors of the state aid beneficiary can qualify as interested parties. To that purpose, the indirect competitor has to demonstrate that its interests could be adversely affected by the grant of the aid.[50]

In two more recent cases the GC has given the notion of 'interested parties' an even wider interpretation, but this was not followed by the ECJ. In *Deutsche Lufthansa*,[51] the Commission had approved, without opening a formal investigation procedure, the operating aid granted by the German authorities to Frankfurt-Hahn airport. Deutsche Lufthansa (DLH) challenged this decision, considering that the operating aid made it possible for Frankfurt-Hahn airport to remain operational, and for Ryanair, the main airline operating from that airport, to compete with DLH in the Frankfurt region. The GC ruled that DLH had standing. In particular, even though DLH was not a direct competitor to the state aid beneficiary (the airport), its competitive position was affected by the aid which would indirectly support one of its main competitors in the region, namely Ryanair.[52] The GC concluded that DLH was an interested party.[53] The ECJ, on appeal, did not follow the lenient interpretation of the

[47] See also Tamara Perišin and Nathan Cambien, 'The Single Market, the Rule of Law, and Access to EU Courts: Vigilance of Individuals before the EU Courts', in Jeremias Adams-Prassl and others (eds), *The Internal Market Ideal: Essays in Honour of Stephen Weatherill* (OUP 2024) 365–86.

[48] Council Regulation (EU) 2015/1589 of 13 July 2015 laying down detailed rules for the application of Article 108 TFEU [2015] OJ L248/9.

[49] On the notion of 'interested party', see also Dimitris Vallindas, 'The Concept of "Interested Parties" in Recent Case-Law' (2022) 4 Concurrences 24–27.

[50] See, to that effect, Case C-83/09 P *Commission v Kronoply and Kronotex* EU:C:2011:341, paras 63–65; Case C-647/19 P, *Ja zum Nürburgring v Commission* EU:C:2021:666, para. 58. See also the discussion in Perišin and Cambien (n 47).

[51] Case T-218/18 *Deutsche Lufthansa v Commission* EU:T:2021:282.

[52] Case T-218/18 *Deutsche Lufthansa v Commission* EU:T:2021:282, paras 39–55.

[53] Case T-218/18 *Deutsche Lufthansa v Commission* EU:T:2021:282, para 56.

standing requirements proposed by the GC, but annulled the GC's judgment essentially on procedural grounds[54] without engaging with the merits of the argument that DLH could be qualified as an interested party.[55] The ECJ held, *inter alia*, that the GC had failed to comply with the requirements relating to the burden of proof and its duty to state reasons when holding that DLH could be qualified as an 'interested party'.[56] Moreover, the GC had wrongly considered that DLH had alleged an infringement of its procedural rights.[57]

The second case, *Braesch,* shows an even starker contrast between the GC and the ECJ. The applicants were holders of subordinated debt in a bank, BMPS, that received restructuring aid from the Italian government. The restructuring plan provided, *inter alia*, for burden-sharing measures, whereby subordinated debt would contribute to compensating for any losses incurred by BMPS before State aid was granted to it. The applicants, who claimed that they suffered severe financial losses as a consequence of this, challenged the Commission decision approving the Italian aid before the GC. The GC dismissed the plea of inadmissibility raised by the Commission.[58] It found, in particular, that the applicants were interested parties within the meaning of Article 1(h) of Regulation 2015/1589. According to the GC, the applicants had demonstrated that they suffered severe financial losses as a consequence of the burden-sharing measures. It was irrelevant that the applicants did not challenge the compatibility per se of the aid measures with the internal market. The commitments of the Italian authorities relating to the restructuring plan and burden-sharing formed an integral part of the aid measures notified, so that the Commission approval decision concerned those measures and those commitments taken as a whole.[59] The ECJ, on appeal from the Commission, overturned the judgment of the GC and held that the action was inadmissible.[60] It held that the applicants were not 'interested parties', since the losses they had invoked resulted from the Italian burden-sharing measures and not

[54] For a critical analysis of the ECJ's judgment, see Roberto Caranta, 'Procedural Overkill, or how Lufthansa (Nearly) Fell Down Again at the Threshold of Standing (Rheinland-Pfalz v Lufthansa, C-466/21 P)' EU Law Live, <https://eulawlive.com/op-ed-procedural-overkill-or-how-lufthansa-nearly-fell-down-again-at-the-threshold-of-standing-rheinland-pfalz-v-lufthansa-c-466-21-p-by-roberto-caranta/>.

[55] In contrast to the AG who, besides pointing out several procedural flaws in the GC's judgment, also analysed the GC's reasoning relating to the question whether the state aid measure at issue affected DLH's position (Case C-466/21P *Land Rheinland-Pfalz v Deutsche Lufthansa* EU:C:2023:195, AG Pikamäe, paras 79–91).

[56] Case C-466/21P *Land Rheinland-Pfalz v Deutsche Lufthansa* EU:C:2023:666, paras 84–97.

[57] Case C-466/21P *Land Rheinland-Pfalz v Deutsche Lufthansa* EU:C:2023:666, paras 98–108.

[58] Case T-161/18 *Anthony Braesch and Others v Commission* EU:T:2021:102.

[59] Case T-161/18 *Anthony Braesch and Others v Commission* EU:T:2021:102, paras 39–40.

[60] Case C-284/21 *Commission v Anthony Braesch and Others* EU:C:2023:58.

from the aid measure at issue.[61] The ECJ emphasized that the contested approval decision merely took account of the burden-sharing commitments 'voluntarily' proposed by the Italian government, but did not impose any such commitments.[62]

The judgment in *Braesch* is a good illustration of the ECJ's reluctance to follow a wider interpretation of the standing requirements, even where this is proposed by both the GC and the AG.[63] The ECJ's ruling has rightly been criticized as seeming somewhat artificial.[64] Indeed, while it is correct that the contested decision did not strictly speaking *impose* any burden-sharing requirements, these commitments were intrinsically linked to the aid measure and formed part of the package approved by the Commission. As the ECJ itself noted, a failure to comply with these requirements would give rise to misuse of the aid at issue and could require the Italian government to recover the aid.[65] Moreover, while it is also true that the Italian government was not obliged to offer burden-sharing requirements, not doing so would run a significant risk that the aid would not be approved. That is all the more the case since the Commission's Banking Communication, while not strictly speaking imposing burden-sharing measures, gives a strong indication that such measures may be required.[66] In particular, in situations of urgency such as the one at hand in *Braesch*, the possibility to not include such measures appears to be merely a theoretical one in view of the significant risk that the aid measure would not be approved as a consequence.

A similar pattern can be seen in a number of cases in other fields, in which the GC has been willing to depart from the traditional restrictive interpretation of the standing requirements in favour of a wider interpretation. A case in point is the well-known *Ville de Paris* case, which concerns an action brought by the cities of Paris, Brussels, and Madrid against the new emissions standards introduced by Regulation 2016/646.[67] While the GC found the action to be

[61] Ibid para 77.

[62] Ibid para 75.

[63] The AG agreed with the GC and proposed to dismiss the appeal introduced by the Commission (Case C-284/21 *Commission v Anthony Braesch and Others* EU:C:2022:490, Opinion of AG Rantos).

[64] Philippe Werner and Théodore Plat, 'Case C-284/21 P Commission v Braesch and Others 23(1) [2024] *European State Aid Law Quarterly* 62–68. See also Phedon Nicolaides, 'The European Commission is not Responsible for the Bail-in of Investors in Banks' (14 Feburary 2023) State Aid Uncovered <https://www.lexxion.eu/stateaidpost/the-european-commission-in-not-responsible-for-the-bail-in-of-investors-in-banks/>.

[65] Case C-284/21 *Commission v Anthony Braesch and Others* EU:C:2023:58, paras 84–87.

[66] Communication from the Commission on the application, from 1 August 2013, of State aid rules to support measures in favour of banks in the context of the financial crisis [2013] OJ C216/1.

[67] Commission Regulation (EU) 2016/646 of 20 April 2016 amending Regulation (EC) No 692/2008 as regards emissions from light passenger and commercial vehicles (Euro 6) [2016] OJ L109/1.

admissible, the ECJ disagreed, judging that the applicants did not satisfy the direct concern criterion.[68] More particularly, the ECJ found that the contested provision in the regulation did not limit the exercise of the powers of the applicant cities in relation to the protection of air quality, meaning that they were not directly concerned by it.[69]

The different interpretations of the standing requirements can, arguably, at least in part be explained by reference to what I have called the different institutional roles of the GC and the ECJ. The GC has traditionally been the jurisdiction responsible for (first instance) direct actions by individuals and undertakings. This may explain the GC's tendency in some cases to broaden the interpretation of the standing requirements and thereby increase its own impact,[70] in particular in cases with significant impact on citizens (eg environmental cases such as the *Ville de Paris* case) or undertakings (eg cases on state aids such as the ones discussed above). Interestingly, a number of former GC judges writing or speaking in an extrajudicial capacity have criticized the ECJ's interpretation of the standing requirements as being too restrictive.[71] The ECJ, on the other hand, has as its primary role its constitutional mandate to guarantee the uniformity of EU law through the preliminary ruling procedure. By not enlarging the interpretation of the standing criteria, the ECJ clearly puts the emphasis on its 'core business', being the cooperation with national courts in the context of the preliminary ruling procedures. Accordingly, in *Braesch*, the ECJ ruled that the GC was wrong to hold that the applicants could defend their interests only by seeking the annulment of the decision at issue before the EU judicature, since the national referring court had jurisdiction to rule

[68] See, respectively, Joined Cases T-339/16, T-352/16 and T-391/16 *Ville de Paris, Ville de Bruxelles and Ayuntamiento de Madrid v Commission* EU:T:2018:927 and Joined Cases C-177/19 P to C-179/19 P *Germany and Hungary v Commission and Commission v Ville de Paris and Others* EU:C:2022:10.

[69] Joined Cases C-177/19 P to C-179/19 P *Germany and Hungary v Commission and Commission v Ville de Paris and Others* EU:C:2022:10, para 94.

[70] There is abundant literature on the CJEU's perceived activism and the alleged self-interested character of its rulings, the discussion of which is outside the scope of this contribution. However, as a number of authors have argued, these elements cannot convincingly and fully explain the CJEU's case law (see already Walter Mattli and Anne-Marie Slaughter, 'Revisiting the European Court of Justice' (1998) 52(1) International Organization 177–209. See also Vlad Perju, 'Reason and Authority in the European Court of Justice' (2009) 49(2) Virginia Journal of International Law 307–78; Fabien Terpan and Sabine Saurugger, 'The Politics of the Court of Justice of the European Union' in Paul James Cardwell and Marie-Pierre Granger (eds) *Research Handbook on the Politics of EU Law* (Edward Elgar Publishing 2020) 31–49).

[71] See eg Anthony M. Collins, 'A Modest Proposal to Improve Judicial Protection in Challenges to the Validity of Union Acts' in Claude Blumann and Fabrice Picod, *Annuaire de droit de l'Union européenne* 2022 (Éditions Panthéon-Assas 2024) 3 (implicitly criticising the ECJ's judgment in *Braesch*); Marc van der Woude, Sacha Prechal, and Sybe de Vries, 'In gesprek met Réné Barents' (2022) 9 Sociaal Economische Wetgeving, 388; Natalie McNelis, 'State-Aid Challengers are "Good Guys" and Should Have Right to Appeal, EU Judge Urges' (2020) <https://mlexmarketinsight.com/news/insight/state-aid-challengers-are-good-guys-should-have-right-to-appeal-eu-judge-urges>.

on the lawfulness of that measure, possibly following a reference for a preliminary ruling under Article 267 TFEU.[72] Similarly, in the field of environmental protection, while not enlarging the standing criteria in direct actions, recent ECJ case law may have the effect of enlarging the standing of private applicants before national courts.[73] According to the ECJ, the existence of a right of access to national courts is consistent with the right to effective judicial protection without there being a need to relax the standing requirements for direct actions before the EU courts.[74]

3.3 Merger control and the meandering scope of judicial review

Another fundamental issue that has given rise to strongly diverging GC and ECJ judgments in recent years concerns the scope and intensity of the judicial review of Commission decisions in competition cases, in particular in the field of merger control. Actions challenging Commission decisions approving or blocking a proposed merger allow the GC to carry out a core aspect of its administrative jurisdiction in an area in which it has longstanding experience. Indeed, the GC (or 'Court of First Instance' as it was known back then) first issued a number of high-profile judgments in the beginning of the 2000s, quashing Commission merger decisions[75] and showing itself as prepared to subject such decisions to more intense scrutiny. The GC's increased scrutiny is often considered to be a response to growing criticism regarding a lack of sufficient judicial oversight of the Commission in the area of merger control.[76]

While GC judgments quashing a Commission merger decision are sometimes upheld by the ECJ[77] and can inspire the latter to change its case law,

[72] Case C-284/21 *Commission v Anthony Braesch and Others* EU:C:2023:58, paras 108 and 109.

[73] See eg Case C-873/19 *Deutsche Umwelthilfe eV v Bundesrepublik Deutschland* EU:C:2022:857. See the discussion in Maxime Tecqmenne, 'Turning "Public Interest Litigation" into a Positive Obligation Deriving from Article 47 of the Charter: Deutsche Umwelthilfe' (2023) 60 CML Rev 1745.

[74] Another institutional factor that may explain the difference in interpretation of the standing requirements is capacity-related. While the GC's number of judges has almost doubled in recent years, the ECJ is under increasing capacity constraints, as the number of cases has increased while the number of judges has remained almost the same (decreasing by one as a consequence of Brexit). This may also explain why the GC is more open to relaxing the standing requirements while the ECJ is not in favour of that.

[75] Case T-342/99 *Airtours plc v Commission* EU:T:2002:146; Case T-310/01, *Schneider Electric SA v Commission*, T-310/01 EU:T:2002:254 and T-5/02 *Tetra Laval BV v Commission* EU:T:2002:264.

[76] See eg Richard Whish and David Bailey, *Competition Law* (10th edn, OUP 2021) 939.

[77] As happened in one of the few other cases in which the GC annulled a Commission merger decision: Case T-194/13 *United Parcel Service, Inc. v Commission* EU:T:2017:144 (for a discussion: see Éric Barbier de La Serre, '*UPS/TNT*: Taking the Right to be Heard Seriously' (2017) 8(8) *Journal of European Competition Law & Practice* 502), upheld by the ECJ on appeal (Case C-265/17P *Commission v United Parcel Service, Inc.* EU:C:2019:23).

GC judgments pushing a stricter standard of review can also lead to strong rebuke from the ECJ. This happened, for instance, in the *Impala* case: the GC[78] annulled the Commission decision clearing the merger, but the ECJ[79] overturned this judgment. The ECJ ruled that the requirements imposed on the Commission by the GC's ruling were excessive, holding *inter alia* that the GC had erred in law by requiring 'that the Commission apply particularly demanding requirements as regards the probative character of the evidence and arguments put forward by the notifying parties in reply to the statement of objections'.[80]

Another illustration of this dynamic is provided by the more recent judgments in *CK Telecoms*. The case concerns the proposed acquisition of Telefónica Europe by CK Telecoms, a subsidiary of CK Hutchison Holding. The merger was blocked by the EU Commission,[81] in essence, because it would likely result in reduced competition in the form of non-coordinated effects on an oligopolistic market. CK Telecoms brought an action before the GC, which upheld the action and set the Commission decision aside.[82] The GC ruled, *inter alia*, that the Commission was required to produce sufficient evidence to demonstrate *with a strong probability* the existence of significant impediments following the concentration. The standard of proof applicable was therefore stricter than that under which a significant impediment to effective competition is 'more likely than not', on the basis of a 'balance of probabilities'.[83]

The Commission successfully challenged the judgment before the ECJ,[84] which accepted most pleas put forward by the Commission, including the first plea by which the Commission argued that the GC had applied a stricter standard of proof than that resulting from the case law. The ECJ essentially ruled that the GC had misinterpreted the EU Merger Regulation[85] by applying

[78] Case T-464/04 *Independant Music Publishers and Labels Association (Impala) v Commission* EU:T:2006:216.

[79] Case C-413/06 P *Bertelsmann AG and Sony Corporation of America v Independent Music Publishers and Labels Association (Impala)* EU:C:2008:392. See the discussion in Jane Golding, 'The Impala Case: A Quiet Conclusion but a Lasting Legacy' (2010) 31 *European Competition Law Review* 1.

[80] Case C-413/06 P *Bertelsmann AG and Sony Corporation of America v Independent Music Publishers and Labels Association (Impala)* EU:C:2008:392, para. 95.

[81] Commission Decision C(2016) 2796 final of 11 May 2016 declaring a concentration incompatible with the internal market (Case COMP/M.7612 – Hutchison 3G UK/Telefónica UK) [2016] OJ C357/15 (summary publication).

[82] Case T-399/16 *CK Telecoms UK Investments Ltd v Commission* EU:T:2020:217.

[83] Case T-399/16 *CK Telecoms UK Investments Ltd v Commission* EU:T:2020:217, para 118.

[84] Case C-376/20P, *Commission v CK Telecoms UK Investments Ltd* EU:C:2023:561.

[85] Council Regulation No 139/2004 of 20 January 2004 on the control of concentrations between undertakings, [2004] OJ L24/1.

a particularly demanding standard of proof which did not follow from it. According to the ECJ, it was sufficient for the Commission to demonstrate, by means of a sufficiently cogent and consistent body of evidence, that it was more likely than not that the concentration concerned would or would not significantly impede effective competition in the internal market or in a substantial part of it.[86] The ECJ decided to send the case back to the GC for a new analysis of the pleas put forward.[87]

The *CK Telecoms* case provides a clear illustration of the GC's willingness to impose higher standards of proof, paving the way for more intense judicial scrutiny of Commission decisions,[88] even if that constitutes a departure from earlier case law[89] and, one might add, from the test laid down by the legislature. The GC's extended formation, including the GC's President, provided an ideal platform for that rather radical move. The GC judgment also shows the GC's willingness to have a real impact on the debate, even at the risk of being overturned by the ECJ. The ECJ's judgment, on the other hand, preserves the consistency with earlier case law and avoids radical changes. It is striking how the ECJ rather forcefully rejects the GC's reading by referring to the wording of the EU Merger Regulation and its earlier *Impala* judgment. It appears that the ECJ considered that the standard of proof required had already been clearly established and that the GC's departure from earlier case law was unwarranted and wrong. This remarkably strong language is also used in the press release (which is approved by the reporting judge), which states: 'Having regard to the breadth, nature and scope of the errors made by the General Court, which affect the General Court's reasoning as a whole, the Court of Justice sets aside the judgment under appeal.'[90] At the same time, the ECJ is more comfortable with leaving the Commission a rather large margin of discretion, by stressing the

[86] Case C-376/20P, *Commission v CK Telecoms UK Investments Ltd* EU:C:2023:561, para. 87. The ECJ confirmed this in Case C-581/22 *thyssenkrupp AG v Commission* EU:C:2024:821, para. 127.

[87] Case C-376/20P, *Commission v CK Telecoms UK Investments Ltd* EU:C:2023:561, para. 340.

[88] Justin Lindeboom and Yasmine Bouzoraa, 'CK Telecoms and the Assessment of Horizontal Mergers in Oligopolistic Markets: Does the More Economic Approach Entail Stricter Judicial Review?' (2021) 5 Eur Competition and Reg L Rev 423.

[89] In that regard it is striking that the GC, in support of the strict standard of proof it put forward, only referred to AG Opinions, in particular AG Tizzano (Case C-12/03 *Commission* v *Tetra Laval* EU:C:2004:318P, Opinion of AG Tizzano, paras 74 and 76) and not to any ECJ judgments (GC, para 118). However, as AG Kokott pointed out, AG Tizzano's proposed test had not been followed by the ECJ (Case C-376/20P, *Commission v CK Telecoms UK Investments Ltd* EU:C:2022:817, Opinion of AG Kokott, para 47).

[90] Court of Justice Press Release No 120/23 'The General Court must rule once more on the lawfulness of the Commission's prohibition of the acquisition of Telefónica Europe ('O2') by Hutchison 3G UK ('Three')', <https://curia.europa.eu/jcms/upload/docs/application/pdf/2023-07/cp230120en.pdf>.

inherent uncertainties in the prospective analysis required under the merger control system.[91]

Similar developments can be seen in the *Illumina/Grail* case, which revolved around the question whether NCAs could refer to the Commission a concentration which did not reach the national merger control turnover thresholds.[92] The GC[93] ruled that this was possible and upheld the contested Commission decisions accepting a referral from a number of NCAs.[94] The ECJ[95] quashed the GC's judgment and ruled that the Commission had no jurisdiction to accept the referral requests at issue and to examine the concentration at stake.

At first sight, it may seem that the judgments in the *Illumina/Grail* case do not follow, and even contradict, the pattern outlined above, since the GC adopted a more lenient approach towards the Commission whereas the ECJ censored the Commission's approach. On a closer look, however, the case does fit the said pattern. Indeed, in *Illumina/Grail*, the GC adopted a wide interpretation of the competence of the Commission to accept upward referrals, thereby enlarging the categories of mergers potentially subject to Commission merger review and therefore also the scope of the GC's review in that field. That is consistent with the pattern identified, namely the GC's willingness to increase the judicial review of Commission merger decisions. Moreover, it is important to stress that the judgments are limited to the issue of the scope of the Commission's competence and do not involve an analysis of any substantive merger-related assessment. The scope of the Commission's competence is essentially of a 'constitutional' nature, and it is not surprising, therefore that the GC adopted a more deferential stance towards the Commission's interpretation of Article 22 of the EU Merger Regulation, whereas the ECJ's was less willing to endorse the Commission's claimed competence. That is fully in line with the different institutional roles as defined under section II. It can be expected that the scope of the Commission's powers in relation to upward referral requests will be further fleshed out in future case law, in particular in cases

[91] As Monti points out, 'The Grand Chamber is more trustful of the Commission [than the GC], going so far as generally ratifying the approach that the Commission developed in its guidelines' (Giorgio Monti, 'EU Merger Control after The Grand Chamber's Judgment In Commission v CK Telecoms Investments' (2024) 47(1) World Competition 11).

[92] Such 'upward' referral is provided for in Article 22 of the EU Merger Regulation.

[93] Case T-227/21, *Illumina, Inc. v Commission* EU:T:2022:447.

[94] Commission Decision C(2021) 2847 final of 19 April 2021, accepting the request of the Autorité de la concurrence française (French Competition Authority) to examine the concentration relating to the acquisition by Illumina, Inc. of sole control over Grail, Inc. (Case COMP/M.10188—Illumina/Grail) and Commission Decisions C(2021) 2848 final, C(2021) 2849 final, C(2021) 2851 final, C(2021) 2854 final and C(2021) 2855 final of 19 April 2021, accepting the requests of the Greek, Belgian, Norwegian, Icelandic, and Dutch competition authorities to join that referral request.

[95] Cases C-611/22P and C-625/22P, *Illumina and Grail v Commission* EU:C:2024:677.

stemming from Member States lacking a national merger control system[96] or having a merger control system with so-called call-in provisions.[97]

In sum, the assertiveness of the GC and its willingness to change the status quo creates fertile ground for dialogue and continuous development of the legal framework surrounding merger control, which is needed in light of the oft-heard criticism regarding lack of sufficient judicial oversight. The large number of commentaries generated[98] by the judgments discussed, as well as the mixed reception—with some commentators lauding the GC's approach in cases such as *CK Telecoms* and others rejecting it—appear to confirm its importance.

4. Concluding Remarks

When studying the reasoning of the CJEU, it is enriching not only to analyse the case law of the ECJ, but to also give due attention to the case law of the GC. The GC, while sometimes overlooked in legal literature, deserves to be fully studied in its own right, since it adjudicates on cases in fields of great importance both to citizens and to undertakings and, moreover, it increasingly acts as last instance court.[99] Furthermore, studying both GC and ECJ case law lays bare often notable differences in approach and outcomes which can give rise to interesting insights both with regard to the solution to a particular case and with regard to the role of courts in general.

As explained in this chapter, the GC and the ECJ have different institutional roles: the GC's predominant role is that of an administrative court reviewing the legality of acts of the administration, whereas the ECJ primarily acts a

[96] See case T-289/24, *Brasserie Nationale and Munhowen v Commission* EU:T:2025:655 (appeal pending before the ECJ).

[97] See eg Alan McCarthy, 'The New Irish Merger Control "Call-in" Power of the Competition and Consumer Protection Commission to Require Notification of Sub-Threshold Transactions' (2024) Journal of European Competition Law & Practice. See also pending case T-15/25, *Nvidia v Commission* (in relation to call-in powers of the Italian NCA).

[98] See, eg, Joséphine Thorson, '"Balance of harms" after CK Telecoms', (2024) 15(6) Journal of European Competition Law & Practice 379–385; Monti (n 91); Lindeboom and Bouzoraa (n 88); See, eg, on *Illumina/Grail*, Justin Lindeboom, '*Illumina/Grail*: Flawed Originalism and the Judicial Hunch' (2025) 13(1) Journal of Antitrust Enforcement 223–32, Wolf Sauter and Jotte Mulder, 'Merger Jurisdiction in EU Competition Law after Illumina/Grail: What's Next?' (2025) 13(1) Journal of Antitrust Enforcement, 215–22; Sebastian Reiter, 'Illumina/Grail: Killer Acquisition Detection Tool Fails Trial', (2024) EU Law Live <https://eulawlive.com/competition-corner/illumina-grail-killer-acquisition-detection-tool-fails-trial-by-sebastian-reiter>.

[99] That is true in several types of cases, and notably for judgments in direct actions which are not appealed and in most direct actions which are subject to the filtering mechanism. It will also be the case when the GC renders judgments pursuant to the preliminary ruling procedure, which has been possible since September 2024.

constitutional court or a supreme court. These different institutional roles influence the reasoning of each jurisdiction and judicial outcome, something that can become abundantly clear when the GC and ECJ issue diverging rulings in the same case. This chapter has analysed this influence in the field of EU competition law, and more in particular in relation to jurisdictional issues, standing issues, and issues pertaining to the scope and intensity of judicial review. The analysis has made clear that the GC tends to take a more deferential approach than the ECJ when it comes to issues having a constitutional dimension, such as the involvement in international relations. The GC, by contrast, has shown willingness to be more 'avant-garde' than the ECJ in several other matters, including a tendency towards accepting wider standing for private applicants and more intense scrutiny of Commission decisions in the field of merger control. As I have demonstrated, these patterns are not limited to the field of EU competition law, but apply in other fields of EU law as well.

These institutional factors are not typically articulated by the Union Courts, but implicitly underlie the reasoning of both jurisdictions. Expressing them more explicitly could result in more forceful reasoning and more open and fruitful dialogue between the two Union Courts, and, at the end of the day, increase the legitimacy of the CJEU.

References

Zhang AH, 'The Faceless Court' (2016) 38 University of Pennsylvania Journal of International Law 71

Arnull A, 'The Working Language of the CJEU: Time for a Change?' (2018) 6 EL Rev 904

Avril L, 'The Genesis of the Institution within the Institution: Studying the Mobilization for the Creation of the Court of First Instance' in Mikael Rask Madsen, Fernanda Nicola, and Antoine Vauchez (eds), *Researching the European Court of Justice: Methodological Shifts and Law's Embeddedness* (CUP 2022)

Barbier de La Serre É, '*UPS/TNT*: Taking the Right to be Heard Seriously' (2017) 8(8) Journal of European Competition Law & Practice 502

Bauer L, 'The European Court of Justice as a Constitutional Court' (2009) 3(4) ICL Journal 268

Bobek M, 'Preliminary Rulings before the General Court: What Judicial Architecture for the European Union?' (2023) 60 CML Rev 1515

Bradley K, 'The Court of Justice Appeal Filter Mechanism and Effective Judicial Protection: Throwing Out the Baby with the Bathwater?' (2024) *EU Law Live*, <https://eulawlive.com/the-court-of-justice-appeal-filter-mechanism-and-effective-judicial-protection-throwing-out-the-baby-with-the-bathwater/> (Accessed 18 September 2025)

Caranta R, 'Procedural Overkill, or How Lufthansa (Nearly) Fell Down Again at the Threshold of Standing (Rheinland-Pfalz v Lufthansa, C-466/21 P) *EU Law Live*, https://eulawlive.com/op-ed-procedural-overkill-or-how-lufthansa-nearly-fell-down-again-at-the-threshold-of-standing-rheinland-pfalz-v-lufthansa-c-466-21-p-by-roberto-caranta/ (Accessed 18 September 2025)

Collins AM, 'A Modest Proposal to Improve Judicial Protection in Challenges to the Validity of Union Acts', in Claude Blumann and Fabrice Picod, *Annuaire de droit de l'Union européenne* 2022 (Éditions Panthéon-Assas, 2024) 3

Conway G, *The Limits of Legal Reasoning and the European Court of Justice* (CUP 2012)

De Witte B and Imamović Š, 'Opinion 2/13 on Accession to the ECHR: Defending the EU Legal Order against a Foreign Human Rights Court' (2015) 40 EL Rev 683

De Witte B, 'European Union Law: A Unified Academic Discipline?' (2008) *EUI RSCAS* https://hdl.handle.net/1814/10028 (Accessed 18 September 2025)

Donner AM, 'The Constitutional Powers of the Court of Justice of the European Communities' (1974) 11 CML Rev 127

Duval A, 'The International Skating Union Ruling of the CJEU and the Future of CAS Arbitration in Transnational Sports Governance' (2023) 23 Int Sports Law 467.

Golding J, 'The Impala Case: A Quiet Conclusion But a Lasting Legacy' (2010) 31 European Competition Law Review 1

Gourgourinis A, 'After Achmea: Maintaining the EU Law Compatibility of Intra-EU BITs Through Treaty Interpretation' (2018) 3 European Investment Law and Arbitration Review 282

Guth J, 'The Court of Justice of the European Union, Gender, and Leadership' in Henriette Müller and Ingeborg Tömmel (eds), *Women and Leadership in the European Union* (OUP 2022)

Hinarejos A, *Judicial Control in the European Union: Reforming Jurisdiction in the Intergovernmental Pillars* (OUP 2009)

Iglesias Sánchez S and Sarmiento D, 'A New Model for the EU Judiciary: Decentralising Preliminary Rulings as a Paradoxical Move towards the Constitutionalisation of the Court of Justice' (2024) *EU Law Live*, <https://eulawlive.com/insight-a-new-model-for-the-eu-judiciary-decentralising-preliminary-rulings-as-a-paradoxical-move-towards-the-constitutionalisation-of-the-court-of-justice-by-sara-iglesias-a/>

Jakab A, 'Judicial Reasoning in Constitutional Courts: A European Perspective' (2013) 14(8) German Law Journal 1215

Krenn C, *The Procedural and Organisational Law of the European Court of Justice: An Incomplete Transformation* (CUP 2022)

Kukovec D, 'Autonomy: The Central Idea of the Reasoning of the Court of Justice' (2023) 8(3) European Papers 1403

Lavranos N, 'The Scope of the Exclusive Jurisdiction of the Court of Justice' (2007) 32 EL Rev 83

Lenaerts K, Gutman K, and Nowak JT, *EU Procedural Law* (2nd edn., OUP 2023)

Lindeboom J and Bouzoraa Y, 'CK Telecoms and the Assessment of Horizontal Mergers in Oligopolistic Markets: Does the More Economic Approach Entail Stricter Judicial Review?' (2021) 5 Eur Competition and Reg L Rev 423

Lindeboom J, '*Illumina/Grail*: Flawed Originalism and the Judicial Hunch' (2025) 13(1) Journal of Antitrust Enforcement 223

Lonardo L and Ruiz Cairó E, 'The European Court of Justice Allows Third Countries to Challenge EU Restrictive Measures: Case C-872/19 P, Venezuela v Council' (2022) 18(1) European Constitutional Law Review 120

Martinico G, 'The Autonomy of EU Law: A Joint Celebration of Kadi II and Van Gend en Loos' in Matej Avbelj, Filippo Fontanelli, and Giuseppe Martinico (eds), *Kadi on Trial: A Multifaceted Analysis of the Kadi Trial* (Routledge 2014)

Mattli W and Slaughter AM, 'Revisiting the European Court of Justice' (1998) 52(1) International Organization 177

McCarthy A, 'The New Irish Merger Control "Call-in" Power of the Competition and Consumer Protection Commission to Require Notification of Sub-Threshold Transactions' (2024) 15(7) Journal of European Competition Law & Practice 477

McNelis N, 'State-Aid Challengers Are "Good Guys" and Should Have Right to Appeal, EU Judge Urges' (2020) <https://mlexmarketinsight.com/news/insight/state-aid-challengers-are-good-guys-should-have-right-to-appeal-eu-judge-urges>

Monti G, 'EU Merger Control after the Grand Chamber's Judgment in Commission v. CK Telecoms Investments' (2024) 47(1) World Competition 11

Nicolaides P, 'The European Commission Is Not Responsible for the Bail-in of Investors in Banks' (14 Feburary 2023) State Aid Uncovered <https://www.lexxion.eu/stateaidpost/the-european-commission-in-not-responsible-for-the-bail-in-of-investors-in-banks/>

Öberg O, 'A "General" Court in Name Only?' (2024) 3 Concurrences 2

Paschalidis P, 'ISU v Commission: Arbitration as a Reinforcement of Infringements of EU Competition Law' (2024) *Kluwer Competition Law Blog*, <https://competitionlawblog.kluwercompetitionlaw.com/2024/01/09/isu-v-commission-arbitration-as-a-reinforcement-of-infringements-of-eu-competition-law/>

Perišin T and Cambien N, 'The Single Market, the Rule of Law, and Access to EU Courts: Vigilance of Individuals before the EU Courts' in Jeremias Adams-Prassl and others (eds), *The Internal Market Ideal: Essays in Honour of Stephen Weatherill* (OUP 2024)

Perju V, 'Reason and Authority in the European Court of Justice' (2009) 49(2) Virginia Journal of International Law 307

Petrić D, 'The Preliminary Ruling Procedure 2.0' (2023) 8(1) European Papers 25

Pignarre PE, *La Cour de Justice de l'Union européenne, juridiction constitutionnelle* (Larcier Intersentia 2021)

Półtorak N, 'General Court of the European Union as an Administrative Court' (Speech) (January 20, 2018), Krakow University

Reiter S, 'Illumina/Grail: Killer Acquisition Detection Tool Fails Trial' (2024) *EU Law Live* <https://eulawlive.com/competition-corner/illumina-grail-killer-acquisition-detection-tool-fails-trial-by-sebastian-reiter>

Sarmiento D, 'Editorial Note: On the Road to a Constitutional Court of the European Union: The Court of Justice After the Transfer of the Preliminary Reference Jurisdiction to the General Court' (2023) 19 Croatian Yearbook of European Law & Policy VII–XVII

Sauter W and Mulder J, 'Merger Jurisdiction in EU Competition Law after Illumina/Grail: What's Next?' (2025) 13(1) Journal of Antitrust Enforcement 215

Schepel H and Wesseling R, 'The Legal Community: Judges, Lawyers, Officials and Clerks in the Writing of Europe' (1997) 3 European Law Journal 165

Sharpston E and De Baere G, 'The Court of Justice as a Constitutional Adjudicator', in Anthony Arnull, Catherine Barnard, Michael Dougan, and Eleanor Spaventa (eds), *A Constitutional Order of States? Essays in EU Law in Honour of Alan Dashwood* (Hart 2011)

Skouris V, 'Der Europäische Gerichtshof als Verfassungsgericht?' in Detlef Merten (ed), *Verfassungsgerichtsbarkeit in Deutschland und Österreich* (Duncker and Humblot 2008)

Tecqmenne M, 'Turning "Public Interest Litigation" into a Positive Obligation Deriving from Article 47 of the Charter: Deutsche Umwelthilfe' (2023) *60 CML Rev* 1745

Terpan F and Saurugger S, 'The Politics of the Court of Justice of the European Union' in Paul James Cardwell and Marie-Pierre Granger (eds), *Research Handbook on the Politics of EU Law* (Edward Elgar Publishing 2020)

Thorson J, '"Balance of Harms" after CK Telecoms' (2024) 15(6) Journal of European Competition Law & Practice 379

Vallindas D, 'The Concept of "Interested Parties" in Recent Case-law' (2022) 4 Concurrences 24–27

van der Woude M, 'The Place of the General Court in the Institutional Framework of the Union' (2021) 81 *EU Law Live*, <https://eulawlive.com/weekend-edition/weekend-edition-no81/>

van der Woude M, Prechal S, and de Vries S, 'In gesprek met Réné Barents' (2022) 9 Sociaal Economische Wetgeving 388

Werner P and Plat T, 'Case C-284/21 P Commission v Braesch and Others' (2024) 23(1) European State Aid Law Quarterly 62

Whish R and Bailey D, *Competition Law* (10th edn, OUP 2021)

16

Conclusion: On the Horizon of Possibilities for Normative Assessments

Alezini Loxa

1. Introduction

This book took as a starting point the significance of the Court's judgments both for the development of EU law, and for the EU epistemic community in general, in order to ask: Does the Court reason *well* or *poorly*? Who can and who should establish that? And on what grounds can one offer a solid and constructive criticism of the Court's reasoning?

In the attempt to sketch possible answers to these questions, which has been the source of various great works of legal theory,[1] this work started from the assumption that we are never neutral and objective observers, an assumption which is echoed by various authors in this book.[2] Hence, the important preliminary step to any assessment of the Court lies in acknowledging one's assumptions and being transparent on the set of criteria one uses when assessing the Court's work. We hope that, by going through this volume, any reader interested in assessing the Court's reasoning will find useful considerations on how to do so. All the contributions exemplify ways of studying the Court with a focus on various aspects of legal reasoning and informed by different theoretical frameworks.

[1] See the chapter by Bengoetxea and Lonardo for a more detailed presentation of key legal theory works on judicial decision making and interpretation.
[2] See chapters by Bengoetxea and Lonardo, Nic Shuibhne, Hancox.

Alezini Loxa, *Conclusion: On the Horizon of Possibilities for Normative Assessments* In: *The Reasoning of the Court of Justice of the EU*. Edited by: Alezini Loxa and Luigi Lonardo, Oxford University Press. © Alezini Loxa 2026.
DOI: 10.1093/9780198983002.003.0020

In this concluding chapter, a brief overview of the contents of the book is provided (Section 2). Reading through the contributions will have revealed the richness and diversity of perspectives found in this book, which make the (apparently) neat structure we outlined in the introductory chapter far more complex. In this section, the initial taxonomy we offered in the introduction is revisited and complicated in an attempt to suggest a more abstract framework that could serve as a basis for future assessments.

Section 3 turns to two recurring demands running through all contributions: coherence and sincerity. By examining how these demands surface in different chapters and how they have been treated in legal theory, the main takeaways of this volume for the Court's future practice become clear.

Finally, in Section 4, future avenues of research and alternative ways of assessing the Court are presented, with emphasis on the latter's institutional responsibility to provide the academic community with the material necessary to study and understand it without prejudice to the demands of secrecy of deliberations and the effective functioning of the institution.

2. Shared Assumptions and Taxonomy

There is no shortage of ways in which one can offer an assessment or criticism of the reasoning and decision-making of the Court. And indeed, any attempt to systematize such assessments is bound to prove complicated and incomplete, as we realized in our repeated rearrangement of the contributions as means to provide the reader with ideal types.

However, to offer a normative assessment, which is not merely a subjective or critical one, one should take into account the distinct characteristics of EU law, one should be transparent about their assumptions on what EU law is and how it functions, and finally one should at least have some minimal theoretical grounding. Under this proposition, the introduction to the book offered an initial outline of our shared assumptions as well as a taxonomy of possible assessments of the Court based on different criteria. Ensuring the conceptual unity of the contributions, all of the authors in the volume could agree that the reasoning of the Court appears in the process of justification, no matter how the outcome of a decision is reached. Moreover, they all agreed that ascertaining whether a decision of the Court is good or bad is not an abstract exercise, but rather one that should take into account the distinct characteristics of

EU law. Below we will revisit the contributions as structured in the four parts of this book, before complicating our initial taxonomy.

2.1 A question of paradigm?

The first part of the book opened with contributions by Bengoetxea and Lonardo and Leczykiewicz representative of different frameworks that can inform and theoretically ground alternative assessments of the Court.

In their chapter, Bengoetxea and Lonardo in part set out a number of descriptive propositions that operate as the starting basis for the assessments undertaken in this book and in part laid out the key tenets of an internal paradigm as a basis for assessments. Understanding any good assessment of the Court as a system-specific exercise, the authors reminded us of key factors that affect the reasoning of the Court. These were structured around the importance of the internal procedures of the Court (formation of chambers, role of judge-rapporteur, lack of dissenting opinions, role of AG), the relation of the Court to other actors (the Court is seized by the parties rather than deciding its own cases and in this regard, key is its relation to national courts), the importance of legal reasons (such as interpretation, precedent, selection and application of the relevant rule, and at the same time the impossibility to seek one single textual interpretation due to the multilingual nature of EU law), and finally observance of the effectiveness of the autonomous EU legal system. The EU legal system cannot be criticized from a national mindset, as Bengoetxea and Lonardo remind us; rather, it should always be approached with a *communautaire* ethos.

However, criticism of the Court need not be confined to the internal paradigm. Rather, and perhaps more explicitly, criticisms of legal reasoning have been developed under an external perspective that challenges a strictly positivist conception of the law. In this regard, Leczykiewicz proposed a new theoretical framework to better account for the Court's reasoning. She openly challenged 'interpretation', describing it as an activity that cannot fully capture the working of the Court and the category of sources that the Court takes into account. According to Leczykiewicz, the proposition of a substantive account of the Court's reasoning can push us to acknowledge a more nuanced picture of the Court's adjudicatory activity and can enhance both judicial propriety and supranational legitimacy.

2.2 Normative indeterminacy and justificatory premises

Proceeding to assessments of legal reasons, the second part of the book—with contributions by Hancox, Spieker, Petrić, and Lonardo—suggested possible ways of rationalizing normative indeterminacy.

Hancox began by focusing on procedural principles that could be used to address the overlap of norms. She argued for the use of the *lex specialis* principle by the Court as the best way to address situations of normative overlap of provisions with the same formal rank in both primary and secondary law. She suggested that such an approach would lead to coherence with EU constitutional values such as democracy and rule of law, while it would also increase legal certainty.

Turning to substantive issues, Spieker argued for more coherence in the Courts' adjudication by the introduction of hierarchies in primary law. He suggested that the Court should proceed in a rearrangement of the Treaties through interpretation and that, similarly to a national constitutional court, it should protect the interests of Article 2 TEU as the constitutional core of this legal order. His argument built on the basis of the implied importance of the values expressed in Article 2 TEU such as democracy, fundamental rights, and effective judicial protection for the EU legal order.

Petrić on the other hand started from the importance of contestation and negotiation in EU law. Similarly to Bengoetxea and Lonardo, he suggested that the substance of the values expressed in Article 2 TEU have very different meanings across Member States, but also within the EU institutions. A way to explain and assess the case law from a *communautaire* ethos would be, according to him, understanding it through the lens of Article 1 TEU. While the demand for an ever closer union expressed in this article is equally elusive and indeterminate, according to Petrić, it calls for more open decisions and requires explicit engagement by the Court with the arguments put forward by other actors.

Lonardo concluded the analysis in this part with a focus on the CFSP. He proceeded to attempt a rational reconstruction of the case law on the jurisdiction of the Court in this area under Articles 275 TFEU and 40 TEU. Lonardo suggested that, without being explicit, the Court has actually been reasoning by implied hierarchy, invoking principles such as the rule of law and effective judicial protection to guide its interpretation of the Treaty provisions on jurisdiction in the CFSP. While such a rational reconstruction could help us make sense of the case law, which Lonardo assessed as positive for the parties, he suggested that the Court appears to do so without saying it and without sufficiently justifying it.

2.3 Formal logic and consistency

The third part of the book evaluated legal reasoning, this time from the perspective of formal logic and consistency. Bratanova von Harten, Loxa, Engel, and Markakis examined case law in specific EU law areas and offered an assessment of its internal inconsistencies as well as its effects for both the parties and the development of the EU legal order.

Bratanova von Harten focused on the application of the Charter of Fundamental Rights under Article 51(1) of the Charter. After identifying the criteria which guide the Court in its delineation of the scope of EU law for the purposes of application of the Charter (criteria which are not explicitly acknowledged by the Court), Bratanova von Harten looked at the inconsistent application of these criteria in cases relating to migrants and refugees. She suggested that there is a need for clarity in the construction of the scope of application of the Charter by the Court, and for more transparency. Otherwise, there is a risk that the effectiveness of EU secondary law, which is ensured by the avoidance of judicial review under the Charter, is perceived as more worthy of protection than the values of human rights in highly harmonized contexts.

Loxa turned to case law on the rights to family reunification of EU and non-EU citizens. Loxa's analysis suggested that the Court has ruled on the comparability of EU and non-EU citizens for the purposes of interpretation of secondary law on migration, while at the same time it has also found a lack of comparability when it comes to problematic aspects of secondary law on free movement. Similarly to Bratanova von Harten, Loxa suggested that the Court seems to prioritize the effectiveness of EU law (and the hierarchical superiority of the Citizens' Rights Directive, which is also confirmed in Politis' contribution) over the human rights of both EU and non-EU citizens.

Engel continued this section by tracing the inconsistencies of the case law of the Court in the area of legal basis litigation. She identified an increasing proceduralism as a result of the inconsistencies in the case law development of the centre of gravity theory and she suggested that more focus on substantive issues related to the choice of legal basis could enhance both democracy and legal certainty.

Markakis concluded this part by focusing on the case law of the Court in the Economic and Monetary Union and examined how it has developed over different generations of case law. His investigation identified various inconsistencies in different case law lines. Despite this, he suggested that the key jurisprudential developments in the area can be considered justified not as stemming from a single line of case law, but through mutually supporting structures developed over the years in different cases with the goal of bringing about coherence.

2.4 Procedural fairness and internal processes

The fourth and final part of the book included contributions on procedural fairness and the importance of internal processes by Nic Shuibhne, Polits, Butler, and Cambien.

Nic Shuibhne's contribution traced the sincerity of the Court in the way in which previous decisions were referenced in the case law on EU citizenship. She identified different referencing techniques and proceeded in a positive assessment of the Court's case law. However, she did point out that references to previous decisions under the formulas 'see, to that effect' and 'see, by analogy' did not always reveal how the Court has used its previous case law. Importantly, she suggested that the choice of acting like a 'citation detective' could lead to methodological robustness and enhance the objectivity of critique.

Politis continued by examining the phenomenon of normative inversion, whereby the Court seems to attribute hierarchical priority and constitutional importance to secondary law over primary law in specific areas. Looking at EU citizenship and tax law, Politis unpacked how this phenomenon takes place and its implications for the Court's adjudicative practice.

Butler instead focused on the silences of the Court, to which he attributed intent, and offered an attempt of systematization. In what appears to be a hypothetical exercise of looking into the black box of a judicial decision, Butler proposed three different ways in which the Court decides when it has 'decided not to decide' a case: dismissal, narrowing, and relinquishment. By identifying various factors which affect the Court's activity, such as maintaining institutional integrity, managing its docket, and providing more space to national courts, Butler's account understands the Court's reasoning as an iteration of judicial policy which reflects institutional and strategic considerations and is not limited to deciding what the meaning of the law is.

The book concludes with a chapter by Cambien, who examined how competition law cases are decided by the General Court and by the European Court of Justice. Identifying inconsistencies in the reasoning of the two Courts, Cambien suggested that they could be explained under a more cautious approach of the General Court, which is perceived as an administrative court, and a more ambitious approach by the ECJ, in line with its perception as a constitutional court. This explanation, while implicit in the judgments, should become more explicit, according to Cambien, in order to increase the institution's legitimacy.

2.5 Alternative classifications

In the introduction to this book, we suggested that various normative theories can guide an investigation of what a well or poorly justified decision is.[3] The various chapters in this volume were presented as exemplifying normative assessments that differ based on the object of critique and on the benchmarks of assessment.

We also suggested that a question prior to any assessment would be whether an author shares the same assumptions about the process of adjudication in general (and of the EU legal order in particular) as the Court itself does, or rejects them in part or entirely. As we also suggested in the introduction, going through the contributions of the book, it appears that most authors fully aligned with the idea of law and interpretation that the Court espouses while still being able to identify gaps in the reasoning and to propose different solutions for the evolution of its case law. At the same time, fewer authors followed an external point of view—without, however, seeking to undermine the Court's role, but rather pushing us to explore a different picture of EU law, as well as a different potential for case law development that might be missed if one were to fully align with the Court's perception of the EU legal system.

As to the first taxonomy on the object of critique, we suggested that different assessments could be offered based on what 'phase' of a judgment one focuses on: process, 'in-between', and outcome. Within these phases, one may single out one or more of the factors as influencing the Court's decision-making activity. Cambien was a clear example of focus on process, while most of the other authors would fit an assessment of the 'in-between' phase discussing the Court's use of legal reasons in its justification. Nearly all chapters touched upon

[3] See Introduction, section 3.

this 'in-between' in one way or another. An assessment of the outcome phase was implicit in all the chapters to the extent that they discussed whether the Court is persuasive for the public. We could also suggest that such outcome-focused assessments could be found in the contributions by Petrić and by Bengoetxea and Lonardo on the relation of the Court to national courts and in the contributions by Politis and Engel on the relation of the Court to the legislator. Explicitly, the chapters by Loxa, Bratanova von Harten, and Lonardo were also focused on the outcome in so far as they discussed the (positive and negative) consequences that the judgments have for the parties to the dispute.

As to the second taxonomy on benchmarks of assessment, we suggested that the assessements varied and could be focused on the standards of rational argumentation (logic, including the logic of consequences), procedural fairness, and efficiency standards. In the breakdown of the book in the introductory chapter, we suggested that Hancox, Spieker, Petrić, and Lonardo look at legal reasons in relation to normative indeterminacy; that Bratanova von Harten, Loxa, Engel, and Markakis look at inconsistencies in legal reasoning; that Nic Shuibhne, Politis, and Butler look at procedural fairness aspects; and finally, that Cambien looks at internal procedures. This representation would be an oversimplification of the various contributions to this volume. We have chosen it because we believe it leads to a representative presentation of the main approach followed by the different authors, but as with everything in life, the true picture of the contributions is more complicated and nuanced, and so is the horizon of possibilities of normative assessments.

An accurate picture of the contributions would look like Figure 16.1, with all authors simultaneously fitting one or more objects of critique and benchmarks of assessment. What was initially presented as a clear-cut table in reality looks like a tree, with authors fitting many branches of the various assessment possibilities.

At the same time, further types of normative assessment could be imagined which were not part of the contributions in the book. Internal benchmarks—such as standards of rational argumentation, procedural fairness, and efficiency—dominated the assessments collected in this volume, in contrast to external evaluations focused on outcomes. This emphasis is unsurprising given the legal background of most of the contributors, whose disciplinary training privileges the evaluation of interpretative methods over outcome-oriented or policy-based critiques. Such a focus reflects not only the methodological commitments of legal scholarship, but also an understanding that the Court's legitimacy rests as much on *how* the Court decides as on *what* it decides.

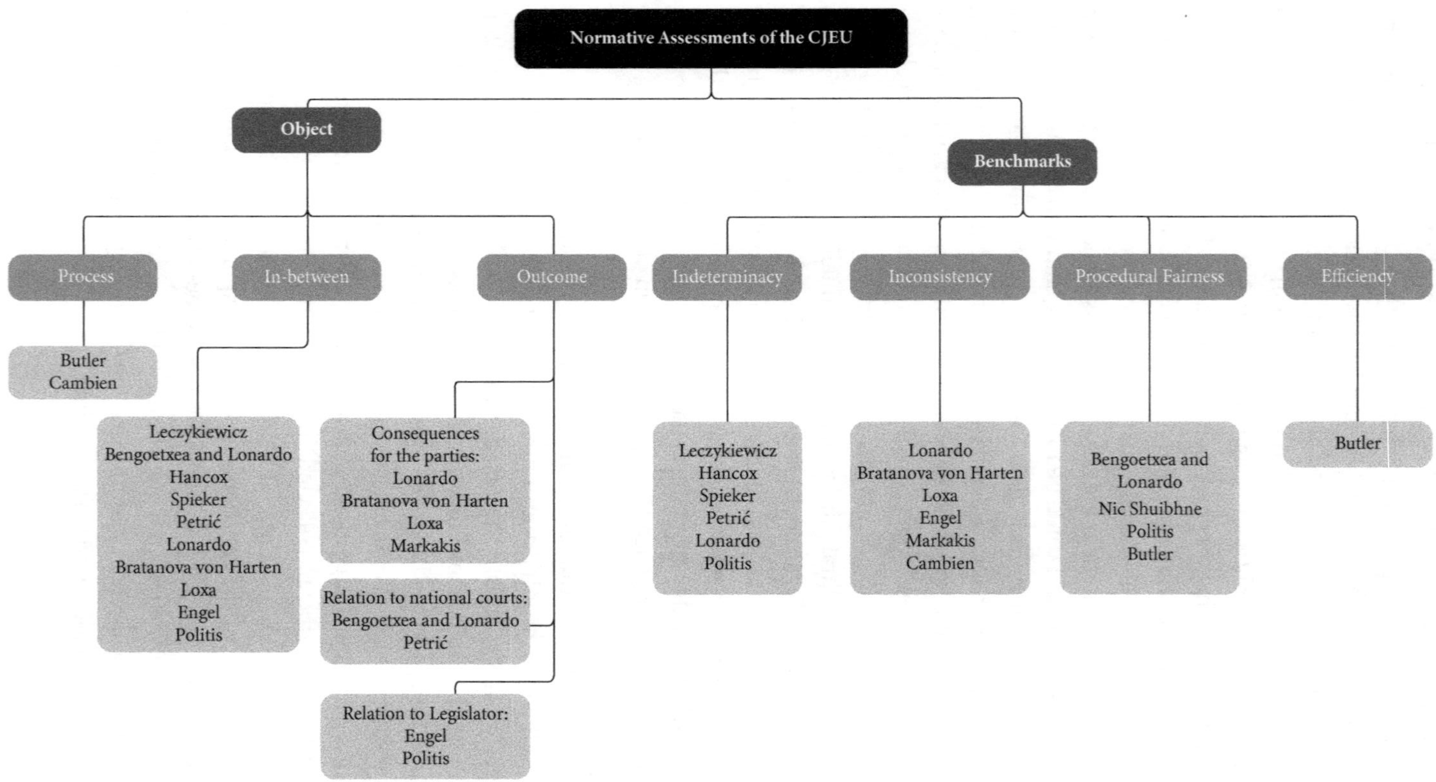

Figure 16.1 Diagram of Normative Assessments

Nevertheless, external benchmarks offer an indispensable complement to internal assessments. They situate the Court's work within its broader political, social, and economic context. External benchmarks could be thought of as 'outcome performance criteria',[4] and could include the achievement of some 'good' outcome, clarification of the law, and settlement of the dispute—that is, compliance with the judgment, the willingness of the parties to resubmit a dispute to the same court, or social and political effects produced by the decision. One can conjecture that compliance with a judgment is helped by the quality of its reasoning, but there is no conclusive evidence of the truth of this causal mechanism.[5] These assessments of the *reasoning* should distinguish between intended and unintended outcomes, and ideally refer to the intended, foreseen, or at least foreseeable consequences by the Court.[6]

In conclusion, the classifications offered in the introduction and the conclusion should not be seen as ends in themselves. Rather, what matters is where the assessment comes from (its theoretical underpinning and descriptive and normative assumptions) and what we intend to do with the assessment (do we think the Court should change something?). On the former, we invite academics to be open about their assumptions rather than being guided 'automatically' by them. On the latter, we hope that the calls for coherence and sincerity which are developed below offer a constructive way of enhancing the dialogue between the Court and its stakeholders.

3. Common Themes

What makes for a good ground for a judgment, we asked at the beginning of the volume, while accepting that such an answer can by no means be uniform or singular. After all, the notion of a good justification has historically set the basis of debates in legal theory and for the proposition of different standards of rational argumentation among various theorists.[7]

[4] Theresa Squatrito and others (eds), *The Performance of International Courts and Tribunals* (1st edn, Cambridge University Press 2018) 14.

[5] Yuval Shany, *Assessing the Effectiveness of International Courts* (Oxford University Press 2014).

[6] Neil MacCormick, 'On Legal Decisions and Their Consequences: From Dewey to Dworkin' (1983) 58 New York University Law Review 239.

[7] Robert Alexy, *A Theory of Legal Argumentation: The Theory of Rational Discourse as Theory of Legal Justification* (Oxford University Press 2010); Aleksander Peczenik, *On Law and Reason*, vol 8 (Springer Netherlands 2009); Jerzy Wróblewski, 'Paradigms of Justifying Legal Decisions' in Aleksander Peczenik, Lars Lindahl, and Bert Van Roermund (eds), *Theory of Legal Science: Proceedings of the Conference on Legal Theory and Philosopy of Science Lund, Sweden, December 11–14, 1983* (Springer Netherlands 1984).

If the reactions of the relevant interpretative community matter for the correctness of an interpretation,[8] then coherence and sincerity appear to be key demands for the reasoning of the Court. Of course the contributors to this volume cannot express themselves on behalf of the EU law scholarly community *in toto*, but their different areas of expertise, their diverse national and gender backgrounds, and the marks they (or the most senior among them) have left on the discipline of EU law and the practice of the Court, suggests that their demands should be taken seriously and should be understood as encouragement to the Court to articulate its reasoning more clearly and more consistently.

3.1 Coherence

Various contributors to the volume call for more coherence in the Court's reasoning. This should be understood in a double way, both as meaning the absence of self-contradiction in the reasoning of a specific decision and as the unity of principle proposed by MacCormick or the integrity principle of Dworkin, the idea of law speaking with one voice.[9]

In the first meaning, coherence as consistency demands the lack of contradiction and it operates as an important benchmark of rational argumentation in each decision and across decisions.[10] Inconsistency across cases may related to the selection of a source of law, as the difficulties in the identification and application of general principles show, according to Leczykiewicz. There would be incoherence also if the Court found that the Charter applies and does not apply in two similar cases as was discussed by Bratanova von Harten. The question becomes one of justifying the differences in factual or legal circumstances (distinguishing, or overruling precedent). This is also an exercise that requires a rational argumentation, absent which the justification is defective, as the chapter by Loxa on EU and non-EU migrants suggested.

In the second meaning, the demand for coherence as a unity of principle can mean different things. For MacCormick, judicial and legislative decisions in a

[8] Saul A Kripke, *Wittgenstein on Rules and Private Language: An Elementary Exposition* (Blackwell 1982).

[9] Ronald Dworkin, *Law's Empire* (10th edn, Belknap Press of Harvard Univ Press 1997) Chapter 6; MacCormick (n 6).

[10] See also Introduction.

system should make sense as being rationally related as a set to the realization of some common values or to the fulfilment of some common principles.[11] The question that naturally arises is what the difference of values and principles is. To MacCormick there is an extensional equivalence between the two. For any value understood as the pursued state of affairs which are conceived to be legitimate and desirable for the pursuit of standing aims, goals and ends, there is a principle according to which the value ought to be.[12] Observance of the principles is an intrinsic means of realizing values.[13]

In legal theories of coherence, the issue that also appears as relevant is how to identify the principles and values of a jurisdiction at a preliminary stage, and then bring coherence considerations at a later stage to hold that courts ought to adopt the outcome of the case which is favoured by the most coherent set of propositions. Different theorists have proposed different principles and values that should guide coherence in legal systems.[14] In EU law, various accounts have been proposed on what guides coherence in the reasoning of the Court,[15] and authors in this volume add to the field by proposing their own competing accounts on the values that could or ought to be understood as guiding coherence in the case law. The integrationist *telos* is an obvious candidate. But opinions diverge as to what exactly that encompasses. For example, Spieker suggested that the values of Article 2 TEU should be understood as sitting at the top of the EU legal order and that the Court ought to proceed in a reinterpretation of EU law by introducing hierarchies (and thus restoring coherence) based on these values. Such a rearrangement of primary law would introduce a new type of coherence to judicial interpretation. Petrić on the other hand suggested that we have been focusing on the values of Article 2 TEU as an emerging account of coherence, while, in reality, what has been driving the case law of the Court is the value expressed in Article 1 TEU of 'an ever closer union' that should be built in respect of unity and diversity. If we were to understand Article 1 TEU as the value guiding coherence we would be able to better

[11] Neil MacCormick, 'Coherence in Legal Justification' in Aleksander Peczenik, Lars Lindahl and Bert Van Roermund (eds), *Theory of Legal Science: Proceedings of the Conference on Legal Theory and Philosophy of Science Lund, Sweden, December 11–14, 1983* (Springer Netherlands 1984).

[12] ibid 237.

[13] ibid 237–38.

[14] See for example Dworkin (n 9) on justice, fairness, and due process; Jürgen Habermas, *Between Facts and Norms: Contributions to a Discourse Theory of Law and Democracy* (William Rehg tr, 4th edn, MIT Press 2001) on freedom, truth, normative correctness, and sincerity.

[15] Damjan Kukovec, 'Autonomy: The Central Idea of the Reasoning of the Court of Justice' (2023) 8(3) European Papers—A Journal on Law and Integration 1403; Gareth Davies, 'Internal Market Adjudication and the Quality of Life in Europe' (2015) 21 The Columbia Journal of European Law 289; Sacha Prechal and others (eds), *The Coherence of EU Law: The Search for Unity in Divergent Concepts* (Oxford University Press 2008).

explain what on first sight appears as incoherence. As the EU evolves and different challenges of global nature emerge, one could imagine the evolution of reasons grounding coherence in the future.[16]

If we do somehow opt for any of the proposed goals, we then encounter an indeterminacy problem: we 'have to assess institutions in light of their tendency to promote the chosen conception of goodness. To do so, we need a causal theory . . . Social scientists have produced a number of such theories, and it is not clear how we can choose among them.'[17] Certain theorists would also argue that the development of grand theories by courts guiding their judicial philosophy is problematic because the choice of a single theory might require social reforms which courts cannot implement, and which they arguably shouldn't in light of the absence of democratic pedigree.[18] What is more, in a legal system such as the EU one, which needs to accommodate the interests of Member States with diverse legal traditions and EU institutions with different conceptions of the good, it would be extremely hard to decide on a clear set of determinate values guiding the Court. Unlike national legal systems, EU law cannot appeal to some pre-existing morality.[19]

Hence while some authors suggest that a single grand theory could guide the interpretation of the Court, as editors we acknowledge the value of incompletely theorized agreements for constitutional pluralism and social conflict. Such types of agreements allow judges to agree on the outcome of a case while disagreeing on the rules justification and they have a particular value when it comes to multimember institutions on the basis of four distinct benefits identified by Sunstein.[20] First, they reduce the costs of legal losses and ensure compliance. According to Sunstein: 'When the authoritative rationale for

[16] Although not in the field of legal reasoning in case law, see Ioannis Kampourakis, 'A Post-Neoliberal European Order? Public Purpose and Private Accumulation in Green Industrial Policy' (2025) 88 The Modern Law Review 769, who suggests that law making in the EU is moving away from the prioritization of market competitiveness to green growth.

[17] Jon Elster, *Securities against Misrule: Juries, Assemblies, Elections* (Cambridge University Press 2013) 3.

[18] Cass R Sunstein, *Legal Reasoning and Political Conflict* (2nd edn, Oxford University Press 2018) 45–46.

[19] See Joseph Weiler, 'Deciphering the Political and Legal DNA of European Integration: An Exploratory Essay' in Julie Dickson and Pavlos Eleftheriadis, *Philosophical Foundations of European Union Law* (Oxford University Press 2012) 145; JHH Weiler, 'The Transformation of Europe Revisited: The Things that Do Not Transform' in Marlene Wind and Miguel Poiares Maduro (eds), *The Transformation of Europe: Twenty-Five Years On* (Cambridge University Press 2017) 344ff who identifies European integration as a messianic venture; see also Armin von Bogdandy, *The Emergence of European Society through Public Law: A Hegelian and Anti-Schmittian Approach* (Oxford University Press 2024), who suggests that a European society has been created on the basis of the constitutional values expressed in Article 2 TEU.

[20] Sunstein (n 18) 41ff.

the result is disconnected from abstract theories of the good or the right, the losers can submit to legal obligations, even if reluctantly, without being forced to renounce their largest ideals.'[21] Second, they allow the accommodation of changes in facts or value over time, thereby ensuring the function of legal cultures that have not attained a theoretical end state.[22] Third, there is an efficiency aspect, as they allow the resolution of disputes within limited time and capacities.[23] Fourth, they are well fitted for a system such as the EU one that has to take into account previous decisions when resolving disputes. According to Sunstein the 'use of such agreements has large advantages over more ambitious approaches, since ambitious thinkers, in order to reach horizontal and vertical coherence, will probably be forced to repudiate or disregard many decided cases'.[24] We would add that the benefits of incompletely theorized agreements are even more pronounced due to the judicial process in EU law which is based on dialogue and cooperation with national courts. The legitimacy of the Court is thus dependent on it not encroaching on the political powers of the other EU institutions and on respecting the sphere of power of national courts.[25]

Still, however, a legal system fully pervaded by incomplete theorized agreements would produce incoherence and some type of theorization would be necessary in order to avoid inconsistency, bias, or self-interest.[26] Indeed, the avoidance of incoherence and at least some theorization of agreements in the Court's case law is existential for the preservation of the autonomy of EU law as a legal order with an internal claim to validity.[27] It is for this reason that the focus on coherence does provide fruitful entry points for normative assessments of the Court. In this regard, Hancox tried to establish what is the most appropriate procedural principle to decide a case at hand, rather than offering an account of the substantive values that should guide the legal system. She proposed the principle of *lex specialis* as a necessary principle to restore coherence in the interpretation of the case law when it comes to overlaps of norms with the same legal value.

[21] ibid 41.
[22] ibid 42.
[23] ibid.
[24] ibid 43.
[25] Koen Lenaerts, 'The Court's Outer and Inner Selves: Exploring the External and Internal Legitimacy of the European Court of Justice' in Justice Maurice Adams and others (eds), *Judging Europe's Judges: The Legitimacy of the Case Law of the European Court of Justice* (Hart Publishing 2013) 14.
[26] Sunstein (n 18) 43.
[27] See Niamh Nic Shuibhne, *The Coherence of EU Free Movement Law: Constitutional Responsibility and the Court of Justice* (Oxford University Press 2013); see also Peter Van Elsuwege, 'Judicial Review and the Common Foreign and Security Policy: Limits to the Gap-Filling Role of the Court of Justice' (2021) 58 Common Market Law Review 1173 on the avoidance of normative gaps as a prerequisite for the autonomy of the EU legal order with analysis specifically focused on the CFSP.

To MacCormick, coherence imposes a negative constraint on judges: 'unless, by the coherence test, some ruling or decision is at least "weakly derivable" from existing law, it is not permissible for judges in their judicial capacity to make such a ruling or decision, however desirable on other grounds it may be.'[28] Lonardo suggests that the desirable outcomes of CFSP decisions on the Court's jurisdiction could actually be understood as coherent if the Court were to acknowledge the principle of reasoning by implied hierarchy which it appears to be using in its decision-making. It is not the lack of coherence that is the problem in the case law but rather the lack of explicit acknowledgement of the principle guiding the Court's adjudication that brings us to the second main theme of the contributions: sincerity.

3.2 Sincerity

A second common theme running through most of the contributions relates to the Court's sincerity, or transparency in its argumentation. In the communicative practice that constitutes legal reasoning, how open and transparent should the Court be when deciding a case? A minimalist would suggest that silence is golden,[29] but that does not seem to be a commonly held belief among the contributors. While some colleagues understand their role as EU law scholars to be that of deciphering the Court's silences, and this could be said to be the case for Lonardo and Cambien, this is by no means a shared understanding among all the contributors to this volume, or in the scholarly community in general, and a lot more emphasis is put on the role of legal scholarship for the critical pursuit of truth and knowledge.[30]

In relation to this demand, it should be recalled once again that the institutional restraints of the Court, and specifically the principle of collegiality that leads to the presentation of judgments as deriving from consensus decision-making, point to the existence of incompletely theorized agreements in the case law.[31] The CJEU judges can agree on the outcome of individual cases without necessarily agreeing on the general theory or principle which best accounts for these outcomes. While indeed incompletely theorized agreements serve important functions analysed in the previous section, the many and diverse

[28] MacCormick (n 11) 244.

[29] Sunstein (n 18) xii.

[30] Joseph HH Weiler, 'Epilogue: Judging the Judges—Apology and Critique' in Justice Maurice Adams and others (eds), *Judging Europe's Judges: The Legitimacy of the Case Law of the European Court of Justice* (Hart Publishing 2013); Jan Komárek, 'Freedom and Power of European Constitutional Scholarship' (2021) 17 European Constitutional Law Review 422.

[31] Lenaerts (n 25) 46.

examples of case law opaqueness precented in this book suggest the need for more transparent reasoning. Bengoetxea and Lonardo suggest, in their contribution, that the quality of the Court's reasoning in terms of transparency has significantly improved over time but there is still a lot to be done. There might be cases where silence is constructively used to help minimize conflict,[32] but there are also cases where the Court's arguments can be plausibly theorized and explained as in the analyses by Lonardo and Cambien. In such cases, if judges have indeed agreed on an abstract theory that guides them, as the contributors suggest, they should be transparent to allow a broader discussion on their motivations for outcomes.[33]

However, there are also cases where the opaqueness raises more questions than answers. Such is the case for Bratanova von Harten, who identifies differences in the construction of the scope of application of EU law for the purposes of the application of the Charter that cannot be reasonably theorized. Moreover, Nic Shuibhne traces the references of the Court in citizenship case law to examine what they reveal about the Court's reasoning with previous decisions. She suggests that 'when previous case law is departed from, silence is not the answer' and that 'better communicative reasoning from the Court itself—in the judgments themselves—is a reasonable ask'. This reflects a demand subtly running through various contributions. In the lack of clear explanation in judicial decisions, Butler goes as far as to try to systematize the silences of the Court in an attempt to offer an explanatory typology of cases in which the Court does not reach a decision. Butler interprets some silences as a choice by the Court *not* to say certain things, *not* to decide some issues raised before it.

It becomes clear that, occasionally, the Court's case law is based on reasoning that might appear cryptic, obscure, or contestable, and this is taken up by academic commentators who suggest that more transparency is needed in the legal reasoning. This demand is tied often explicitly and often implicitly to the duty to give reasons under Article 296 TFEU, Article 47 of the Charter and respect for the Rule of Law.[34] Indeed, these treaty-based rules reflect an understanding of the importance of motivation in order to avoid arbitrariness, to respect the separation of powers, to increase legal certainty, and ultimately to ensure the legitimacy of the Court and the strength of persuasion over coercion.[35]

[32] Sunstein (n 18) 39 on the value of silences.
[33] ibid 43–44.
[34] See chapters by Lonardo and Hancox.
[35] See Introduction; chapter by Bengoetxea and Lonardo; see also Jeremy Waldron, 'The Rule of Law and the Importance of Procedure' (2011) 50 Nomos 3.

Having said this, we should also acknowledge that positive evolutions have recently marked a turn in the Court's operation towards more open and transparent procedures.[36] The reform of the Statute that allows the publication of the arguments of the parties and the references of the referring national courts along with the live streaming of (many) significant hearings of the Court provides the legal scholar new insight into previously inaccessible material.[37] Before that, apart from direct actions, we could only assume the arguments of the parties in AG Opinions or in brief mentions in the Court's decision, and (usually) only to the extent that the Court or the AG agreed with the party. The earlier practice of producing summary reports of the hearings had been abandoned, leaving scholars wondering what arguments were or were not raised by the parties. In the future, an academic closely following a case from submission to resolution should normally have the tools to decipher what alternative arguments were heard, dismissed, or embraced by the Court. At the same time, this would mean that future silences of the Court on those issues would be deafening.

Overall, the repeated appearance of coherence and sincerity across the different contributions should be understood as a call to enhance the Court's legitimacy not only in relation to national courts and the parties in the dispute, but also in relation to the public, part of which is the EU law academic community. This is not a critique that relates to how *good* or *bad* the decisions of the CJEU are. The focus is not on the outcome of the various cases, but rather on the legal reasons used to support it. As Sunstein has suggested: 'The best judges do not merely make good decisions: they are also good at explaining why their decisions are good.'[38]

4. Limitations and Avenues for Future Research

This book has focused on the context of justification, with limited attention to the context of discovery.[39] What is more, as editors we made a conscious

[36] In line with Article 15 TFEU, which requires that all EU institutions shall conduct their work as openly as possible.

[37] Article 80 a on broadcasting and 95(3) on publication of written submissions, Rules of Procedure of the Court of Justice [2012] OJ L 265/1 as amended by Amendments to the Rules of Procedure of the Court of Justice [2024] OJ L 2094/1. See also Ilaria Fevola and Stefano Montaldo, 'Access to Written Submissions in Preliminary Reference Proceedings: An Evaluation of the CJEU Statute Reform and Its Contribution to Open Justice' (2025) 10(2) European Papers—A Journal on Law and Integration 357.

[38] Sunstein (n 18) 159.

[39] The context of discovery was only hinted at in the chapter by Butler.

choice to limit our method and approach to the legal discipline. As suggested by Bengoetxea and Lonardo, future research on the reasoning of the Court of Justice of the EU could incorporate findings from social sciences in order to unpack the context of discovery.

To an extent, interdisciplinary attempts to do this have taken place by tracing arguments and ideas in diverse empirical sources in order to hypothesize about how different doctrines found their way in EU law.[40] Any such attempt offers plausible hypotheses rather than definitive conclusions, as it is impossible to know what actually took place during the decision-making activity of the Court.[41] Moreover, legal studies have attempted to indirectly capture the context of discovery by focusing on Advocates General, the only members of the Court expressing individual opinions, and by tracing their influence in different lines of case law based on whether their Opinion was followed or not.[42] Still, as the former AG Bobek has suggested, such hypotheses run up against two problems.[43] First, one would need to consult documentation on the arguments of the parties to know what the AG is reacting to when writing their opinion. Second, the assessment of the effect of the AG Opinion based on whether it was referred to or not in the operative part of the judgment does not capture the full impact of an Opinion on the final decision.

Eventually, any attempt to fully capture and assess the context of discovery would only be possible by access to the notes of deliberation of individual cases which form part of the so-called *dossiers de procédure*, the files of each case held by the Court.[44] However, such access would go against the demand for secrecy of deliberations. This demand is expressed in the Statute of the Court, and it is

[40] Such studies usually trace key ideas in extra-judicial writings of members of the Court or other key actors, in interviews with practising lawyers and members of the EU institutions, in personal and European archives, and so on. See eg Vera Fritz, 'Judge Biographies as a Methodology to Grasp the Dynamics inside the CJEU and Its Relationship with EU Member States' in Antoine Vauchez, Fernanda Nicola, and Mikael Rask Madsen (eds), *Researching the European Court of Justice: Methodological Shifts and Law's Embeddedness* (Cambridge University Press 2022); Antoine Vauchez, *Brokering Europe: Euro-Lawyers and the Making of a Transnational Polity* (Cambridge University Press 2015); Michel Erpelding, 'Juristes internationalistes, juristes mixtes, Euro-Lawyers: l'apport de l'expérience semi-coloniale à l'émergence d'un droit supranational' (2022) 22 Clio @ Themis; Daniele Gallo and others (eds), *The Italian Influence on European Law: Judges and Advocates General (1952–2000)* (Hart 2024).

[41] Michal Bobek, 'Judicial Biographies and Judicial Decision-Making: A Fish Reflects on the Work of Marine Biologists' in Daniele Gallo and others (eds), *The Italian Influence on European Law: Judges and Advocates General (1952–2000)* (Hart 2024).

[42] See for example, Noreen Burrows and Rosa Greaves, *The Advocate General and EC Law* (Oxford University Press 2007).

[43] Bobek (n 41).

[44] Even then one could question to what extent a written note on deliberation fully reflects the nuances of the discussions that took place in the room. It is not uncommon for texts or protocols of different collective decision-making bodies to remain cryptic.

binding on all its members, who undertake an oath at the beginning of their term to preserve the secrecy of the deliberations of the Court.[45] And secrecy is key for the preservation of judicial independence.[46] Such goals are legitimate and their protection would overcome the interest of academics in unravelling the internal workings of the Court. That is so as regards contemporary cases.

But what about cases decided fifty or seventy years ago? Regulation 2015/496 on the deposition of archival documents by the EU institutions at the Historical Archives of the EU was adopted in order to, among others, promote access to EU archival documents thirty years after their creation and to stimulate research in the field of EU integration.[47] According to this regulation, the Court of Justice had discretion on whether it would depose its archives.[48] Indeed, taking its responsibility regarding transparency seriously, the Court first deposited its archives at the Historical Archives of the EU in 2015.[49] According to the President of the Court, this would add to the legitimacy of the institution, and it would promote knowledge by fostering legal research.[50]

At that stage it was assumed that researchers would finally be able to open the black box of discovery. Indeed, social scientists and legal researchers alike awaited with great anticipation diving into the *dossiers de procédure* of various landmark rulings and being able to engage not only with the arguments of the parties, but also with the notes of deliberation and the *rapport préalable* prepared by the judge-rapporteur.[51] This could have provided them with the opportunity to finally 'peek behind the curtain into a world that does everything in its might to remain hidden from view', and to understand why the Court decided as it did in specific cases, which actors pushed in such a direction, and how.[52]

[45] Article 35 and 53(1) Statute of the Court of Justice. On the oath see Article 4(1) Rules of Procedure of the Court of Justice [2012] OJ L 265/1.

[46] Josef Azizi, 'Unveiling the EU Courts' Internal Decision-Making Process: A Case for Dissenting Opinions?' (2011) 12 Era Forum 49, 45–47 on the importance of secrecy also in relation to the absence of dissenting opinions.

[47] Recital, 7 Council Regulation (EU) 2015/496 of 17 March 2015 amending Regulation (EEC, Euratom) No 354/83 as regards the deposit of the historical archives of the institutions at the European University Institute in Florence.

[48] Regulation (EEC, Euratom) No 354/83, Article 8(3) as amended by 2015/496.

[49] Decision of the Court of Justice of the European Union of 10 June 2014 concerning the deposit of the historical archives of the Court of Justice of the European Union at the Historical Archives of the European Union (European University Institute) OJ C 406, 7.12.2015, pp 2–3.

[50] He also mentioned the opening as a moral obligation to the future. Opening of the historical archives of the European Court of Justice, 18 December 2015, News Archive, EUI <https://www.eui.eu/Research/HistoricalArchivesOfEU/News/2015/12-17-Official-opening-of-the-European-Court-of-Justices-papers>.

[51] Bill Davies and Fernanda Nicola, 'Introduction to EU Law Stories: Contextual and Critical Histories in European Jurisprudence' in Bill Davies and Fernanda Nicola (eds), *EU Law Stories: Contextual and Critical Histories of European Jurisprudence* (Cambridge University Press 2017).

[52] Bobek (n 41) 271.

As soon as the first *dossiers de procédure* were finally accessed, it became clear that the possibilities of such research were limited.[53] Because of reasons related to the protection of privacy, commercial interests, and the secrecy of the deliberations, certain documents are redacted from the final archive accessible to the public. Most crucially for the kind of analyses undertaken in this book, the notes of the deliberation and the *rapport préalable* drafted by the judge-rapporteur are missing.[54] Such redaction significantly hampers the possibility of understanding and assessing the context of discovery. At the same time, this means that anyone interested in getting glimpses of the judicial black box would have to be informed by the working methods of historians and resort to various private, national, and European archives to make up for the absences in the CJEU archives.[55] While some researchers may be fortunate enough to access personal notes on the Court's deliberations held in the private archives of former members, such opportunities are likely to be exceptional.[56] For most scholars, access to these materials will remain limited, highlighting the challenges of studying the context of discovery of CJEU decisions.

While of course the secrecy of deliberations should be protected, one is left wondering to what extent the opening of the files of deliberation of cases decided fifty or even seventy years ago goes against the Court's autonomy and role.[57] The arguments relating to judicial independence and avoidance of external pressure are surely of relevance, but they cannot be of eternal relevance. As the Editors of the *European Constitutional Law Review* wrote before the archives had opened, 'of the arguments proposed in favour of the secrecy of the deliberations, only two are possibly of any avail: that of the authority of the

[53] Fernanda Nicola, 'Waiting for the Barbarians: Inside the Archives of the European Court of Justice' in Claire Kilpatrick and Joanne Scott (eds), *New Legal Approaches to Studying the Court of Justice: Revisiting Law in Context* (Oxford University Press 2020) 71.

[54] Art 4(2), Decision of the Court of Justice of the European Union of 10 June 2014. See also Article 4(2) Regulation (EC) 1049/2001 of the European Parliament and of the Council of 30 May 2001 regarding public access to European Parliament, Council and Commission documents. One should also add that the Court does not release the French translations of the documents submitted by the parties, which can create problems depending on one's linguistic knowledge. Moreover, the Court does not release the comparative research notes that were used in the process of deciding the case, and which were drafted by its Research and Documentation Department. For a more complete analysis of what is and is not included in a dossier de procedure accessible to the public, see Nicola (n 53).

[55] Morten Rasmussen, 'Law Meets History: Interpreting the Van Gend En Loos Judgment' in Bill Davies and Fernanda Nicola (eds), *EU Law Stories: Contextual and Critical Histories of European Jurisprudence* (Cambridge University Press 2017) 103.

[56] Rasmussen (n 55); Morten Rasmussen, 'Revolutionizing European Law: A History of the Van Gend En Loos Judgment' (2014) 12 International Journal of Constitutional Law 136 based on personal note made by Trabucchi in relation to the deliberation of the case.

[57] See also chapter by Bengoetxea and Lonardo. They deal with the separate but related issue of judges expressing themselves on case law and ask if details of the case could be revealed many years later. As they put it: 'Why should there be anything to conceal or to be too sensitive to disclose and hide from the actual motivation and public discussion of the judgments?'

Court and of its judgments. But then, what is there to hide?'[58] When it comes to decisions decided in the early years of the Court's operation the facts of the cases, the individuals involved in it, the discussions that took place have already become parts of the realm of history.[59] It would thus be an overstatement to suggest that the Court's autonomy and institutional role preclude access to the deliberations of rulings decided more than fifty years ago.

In closing this book, we would thus like to restate that future research that takes up the task of opening the black box of a judicial decision could take place without posing existential risks to the autonomy of the Court.[60] However, the pursuit of such groundbreaking research that seeks truth and knowledge and does not restrain itself to hypotheticals and assumptions is dependent on the Court's institutional responsibility to provide the epistemic community with the material necessary to study it. This can and should take place with full respect to the delicate balance between the demands of secrecy of deliberations and transparency.

References

Alexy R, *A Theory of Legal Argumentation: The Theory of Rational Discourse as Theory of Legal Justification* (Oxford University Press 2010)

Azizi J, 'Unveiling the EU Courts' Internal Decision-Making Process: A Case for Dissenting Opinions?' (2011) 12 Era Forum 49

Bobek M, 'Judicial Biographies and Judicial Decision-Making: A Fish Reflects on the Work of Marine Biologists' in Daniele Gallo and others (eds), *The Italian Influence on European Law: Judges and Advocates General (1952–2000)* (Hart 2024)

Burrows N and Greaves R, *The Advocate General and EC Law* (Oxford University Press 2007)

Davies B and Nicola F, 'Introduction to EU Law Stories: Contextual and Critical Histories in European Jurisprudence' in Bill Davies and Fernanda Nicola (eds), *EU Law Stories: Contextual and Critical Histories of European Jurisprudence* (Cambridge University Press 2017)

Davies G, 'Internal Market Adjudication and the Quality of Life in Europe' (2015) 21 The Columbia Journal of European Law 289

Dworkin R, *Law's Empire* (10th edn, Belknap Press of Harvard Univ Press 1997)

Editorial, 'For History's Sake: On Costa v. ENEL, André Donner and the Eternal Secret of the Court of Justice's Deliberations' (2014) 10 European Constitutional Law Review 191

[58] Editorial, 'For History's Sake: On Costa v. ENEL, André Donner and the Eternal Secret of the Court of Justice's Deliberations' (2014) 10 European Constitutional Law Review 191.

[59] ibid 198.

[60] Nicola (n 53) 91, who suggests that academics should keep pushing for access.

Elster J, *Securities against Misrule: Juries, Assemblies, Elections* (Cambridge University Press 2013)

Erpelding E, 'Juristes internationalistes, juristes mixtes, Euro-Lawyers: l'apport de l'expérience semi-coloniale à l'émergence d'un droit supranational' (2022) 22 Clio @ Themis

Fevola I and Montaldo S, 'Access to Written Submissions in Preliminary Reference Proceedings: An Evaluation of the CJEU Statute Reform and Its Contribution to Open Justice' (2025) 10(2) European Papers—A Journal on Law and Integration 357

Fritz V, 'Judge Biographies as a Methodology to Grasp the Dynamics inside the CJEU and Its Relationship with EU Member States' in Antoine Vauchez, Fernanda Nicola, and Mikael Rask Madsen (eds), *Researching the European Court of Justice: Methodological Shifts and Law's Embeddedness* (Cambridge University Press 2022)

Gallo D and others (eds), *The Italian Influence on European Law: Judges and Advocates General (1952–2000)* (Hart 2024)

Habermas J, *Between Facts and Norms: Contributions to a Discourse Theory of Law and Democracy* (William Rehg tr, 4th edn, MIT Press 2001)

Kampourakis I, 'A Post-Neoliberal European Order? Public Purpose and Private Accumulation in Green Industrial Policy' (2025) 88 The Modern Law Review 769

Komárek J, 'Freedom and Power of European Constitutional Scholarship' (2021) 17 European Constitutional Law Review 422

Kripke SA, *Wittgenstein on Rules and Private Language: An Elementary Exposition* (Blackwell 1982)

Kukovec D, 'Autonomy: The Central Idea of the Reasoning of the Court of Justice' (2023) 8(3) European Papers 1403

Lenaerts K, 'The Court's Outer and Inner Selves: Exploring the External and Internal Legitimacy of the European Court of Justice' in Justice Maurice Adams and others (eds), *Judging Europe's Judges: The Legitimacy of the Case Law of the European Court of Justice* (Hart Publishing 2013)

MacCormick N, 'On Legal Decisions and Their Consequences: From Dewey to Dworkin' (1983) 58 New York University Law Review 239

MacCormick N, 'Coherence in Legal Justification' in Aleksander Peczenik, Lars Lindahl, and Bert Van Roermund (eds), *Theory of Legal Science: Proceedings of the Conference on Legal Theory and Philosophy of Science Lund, Sweden, December 11–14, 1983* (Springer Netherlands 1984)

Nic Shuibhne N, *The Coherence of EU Free Movement Law: Constitutional Responsibility and the Court of Justice* (Oxford University Press 2013)

Nicola F, 'Waiting for the Barbarians: Inside the Archives of the European Court of Justice' in Claire Kilpatrick and Joanne Scott (eds), *New Legal Approaches to Studying the Court of Justice: Revisiting Law in Context* (Oxford University Press 2020)

Peczenik A, *On Law and Reason*, vol 8 (Springer Netherlands 2009)

Prechal S and others (eds), *The Coherence of EU Law: The Search for Unity in Divergent Concepts* (Oxford University Press 2008)

Rasmussen M, 'Revolutionizing European Law: A History of the Van Gend En Loos Judgment' (2014) 12 International Journal of Constitutional Law 136

Rasmussen M, 'Law Meets History: Interpreting the Van Gend En Loos Judgment' in Bill Davies and Fernanda Nicola (eds), *EU Law Stories: Contextual and Critical Histories of European Jurisprudence* (Cambridge University Press 2017)

Shany Y, *Assessing the Effectiveness of International Courts* (Oxford University Press 2014)

Squatrito T and others (eds), *The Performance of International Courts and Tribunals* (1st edn, Cambridge University Press 2018)

Sunstein CR, *Legal Reasoning and Political Conflict* (2nd edn, Oxford University Press 2018)

Van Elsuwege P, 'Judicial Review and the Common Foreign and Security Policy: Limits to the Gap-Filling Role of the Court of Justice' (2021) 58 Common Market Law Review 1173

Vauchez A, *Brokering Europe: Euro-Lawyers and the Making of a Transnational Polity* (Cambridge University Press 2015)

von Bogdandy A, *The Emergence of European Society through Public Law: A Hegelian and Anti-Schmittian Approach* (Oxford University Press 2024)

Waldron J, 'The Rule of Law and the Importance of Procedure' (2011) 50 Nomos 3

Weiler JHH, 'Deciphering the Political and Legal DNA of European Integration, An Exploratory Essay' in Julie Dickson and Pavlos Eleftheriadis, *Philosophical Foundations of European Union Law* (Oxford University Press 2012)

Weiler JHH, 'Epilogue: Judging the Judges—Apology and Critique' in Justice Maurice Adams and others (eds), *Judging Europe's Judges: The Legitimacy of the Case Law of the European Court of Justice* (Hart Publishing 2013)

Weiler JHH, 'The Transformation of Europe Revisited: The Things that Do Not Transform' in Marlene Wind and Miguel Poiares Maduro (eds), *The Transformation of Europe: Twenty-Five Years On* (Cambridge University Press 2017)

Wróblewski J, 'Paradigms of Justifying Legal Decisions' in Aleksander Peczenik, Lars Lindahl, and Bert Van Roermund (eds), *Theory of Legal Science: Proceedings of the Conference on Legal Theory and Philosopy of Science Lund, Sweden, December 11–14, 1983* (Springer Netherlands 1984)

Index

For the benefit of digital users, indexed terms that span two pages (e.g., 52–53) may, on occasion, appear on only one of those pages.